Governmental Accounting

The Willard J. Graham Series in Accounting

Consulting Editor ROBERT N. ANTHONY Harvard University

Governmental Accounting

LEON E. HAY, Ph.D., C.P.A.
Professor of Accounting
Indiana University

R. M. MIKESELL, C.P.A.
Late Professor Emeritus of Accounting
Indiana University

Fifth Edition • 1974

RICHARD D. IRWIN, INC. Homewood. Illinois 60430

IRWIN-DORSEY, LIMITED Georgetown, Ontario L7G 4B3

Fifth Edition

First Printing, May 1974
Second Printing, November 1974
Third Printing, May 1975
Fourth Printing, October 1975
Fifth Printing, January 1976
Sixth Printing, May 1976
Seventh Printing, September 1976

ISBN 0-256-01543-0
Library of Congress Catalog Card No. 73-91789

Printed in the United States of America

Preface

The late R. M. Mikesell once wrote:

> Even when developed to the ultimate stage of perfection, governmental accounting cannot become a guaranty of good government. At best, it can never be more than a valuable tool for promotion of sound financial management. It does not offer a panacea for all the ills that beset representative government; nor will it fully overcome the influence of disinterested, uninformed citizens. It cannot be substituted for honesty and moral integrity on the part of public officials; it can help in resisting but cannot eliminate the demands of selfish interests, whether in the form of individual citizens, corporations, or the pressure groups which always abound to influence government at all levels.

Professor Mikesell's words bear thoughtful rereading from time to time by teachers and students of all fields, not just governmental accounting. It is difficult to strike a balance between the pursuit of perfection in a given field in isolation and the effort to improve the total system within which we live (which often seems to involve settling for less than perfection in the elements of the system). The material in this fifth edition of *Governmental Accounting* has been extensively rewritten in an effort to reflect the thought of authoritative organizations interested in the pursuit of perfection in governmental and nonprofit accounting, but within the framework of the role of accounting in the wise management of resources entrusted to governmental and nonprofit entities. New questions, exercises, and problems have been added to support this approach.

Although omitted from the fourth edition, earlier editions of this text included coverage of governmental auditing and a chapter on college and university accounting. Developments in each field led to preparation of new chapters on each subject for inclusion in this edition. Similarly, the impact of Federal grants and contracts upon accounting, reporting, and cost determination by state and local governmental units suggested the coverage, in the chapter on Trust and Agency Funds, of Federal general revenue sharing accounting and reporting requirements, and the replacement of a former chapter on cost accounting by a new chapter on Cost Determination for Nonprofit Entities.

The author is greatly indebted to the Municipal Finance Officers Association of the United States and Canada for permission to draw on materials issued under its own name and that of the National Committee on Governmental Accounting. Another valuable source of help has been provided by the American Institute of Certified Public Accountants which has allowed use of questions and problems from the certified public accountant examinations and which permitted quotations from its publications, particularly in the audit guide series. The Hospital Financial Management Association generously permitted the use of problems from its fellowship examinations. Chapter 19 on accounting for hospitals draws extensively upon the excellent manual published by the American Hospital Association. Many valuable illustrations and suggestions for problems were obtained from published financial reports supplied by officials of the governmental units represented.

Chapters on accounting for Federal agencies and accounting for public school systems were added to the preceding edition. The author appreciates the help given by many persons in the employ of the Federal government in making available materials, in critically reviewing the original chapters, and in providing guidance for the present revisions of the chapters. Dr. Leo Herbert of the United States General Accounting Office was particularly helpful in enlisting the assistance of his colleagues in the GAO and other Federal agencies. Dr. Charles T. Roberts of the United States Office of Education graciously provided materials so that the chapter on public school accounting in this edition would reflect the most recent authoritative pronouncements.

The author is also indebted to numerous colleagues in the teaching profession who have used the book in their classrooms and who, along with interested students, have been the source of many constructive suggestions for improvement of its contents. I invite continuation of this helpful exchange of ideas.

April 1974 LEON E. HAY

Contents

1

Governmental and Nonprofit Entities— Accounting and Reporting

Federal taxes and Federal spending receive so much publicity in the United States that almost every person who reads or listens to news reports and commentary has some comprehension of the dimensions of the problem of supporting the activities of the Federal government. Even though few people have a detailed knowledge of the sources of revenue utilized by the Federal government, or the amounts which are appropriated for each of the programs of Federal agencies, many are aware of the impact upon their own paychecks of Federal withholding and social security taxes.

Each resident of the United States is also a resident of a state (or territory), and in most instances of a county, a township, a city, a school district, a library district, and a number of other overlapping jurisdictions with taxing powers. For example, a recent annual report of Murray City Corporation, Utah, notes that its residents pay property taxes to seven layers of government. The confusion this leads to is brought out in the following quotation from the Murray City report:

> Taxpayers of Murray are sometimes confused by the amount of their assessments. A frequently heard question is: "If Murray is reducing the tax levy, why aren't my taxes going down?"
>
> Part of the answer to that question is possibly an increased valuation on the taxable property. Another part, more appropriate to most tax payers, is that the levy set by 1) *Murray City* is only one of several involved in the total taxation. Others include the 2) *State Uniform School Fund,* 3) *Murray City School District,* 4) *Salt Lake County,* 5) *South Salt Lake Mosquito Abatement District,* 6) *Central Utah Water District* and 7) *Cottonwood Sanitary District.*

> Hence it is possible for Murray City to reduce its tax levy, but for one or more of the other taxing units to increase theirs, resulting in higher taxes for some citizens.[1] (Emphasis added)

The budgetary problems of states and subordinate governmental units and agencies are generally well publicized within the areas concerned. To the extent that a resident feels the burden of state and local income taxes, sales taxes, excise taxes, and property taxes he may be concerned with the "cost of government." To the extent that he fails to receive governmental services he feels he should receive he may be motivated to try to exert some influence on the use of governmental resources.

In order to understand the nature of governmental resources and to be able to evaluate the financial management of the resources, one must be able to read governmental budgets and financial reports intelligently. Governmental budgets and financial statements differ in many respects from those of profit-seeking entities. It is assumed that the reader of this text is familiar with principles of accounting for business entities, and therefore the text is focused upon the differences between governmental accounting and business accounting rather than the many similarities.[2]

Texts in governmental accounting have traditionally begun by presenting the subject in terms of municipalities rather than states or Federal government. There are several good reasons for not breaking with this tradition: (1) The operations of a typical municipality are much easier for most persons to comprehend than are the far more complex operations of a state government or the almost unbelievably complex operations of the Federal government. Readers tend to find it easier to relate municipal accounting to municipal operations than to relate the accounting and the operations of more complex units. (2) There are over 78,000 municipalities (cities, towns, counties, townships, school districts, irrigation districts, and all other units subordinate to a state) versus 50 states and one Federal government. The accountants of some municipalities do an outstanding job of providing information needed for effective financial management, and the accountants of hundreds of others do an adequate job. In thousands of municipalities, however, persons performing the accounting and financial management functions have neither sufficient education nor experience to do an effective job. Impetus for significant improvement in accounting and financial reporting for

[1] Murray City Corporation (Utah), *Annual Report and Condensed Financial Statement*, Fiscal Year 1971–72, p. 11.

[2] Readers who are not familiar with basic accounting should study any contemporary Introductory Accounting text (several are available in programmed learning format) before attempting to understand the more technical portions of Chapters 2–20. Particular attention should be given to the discussion in the introductory text of financial statements and to the explanation of double entry methodology (often called "the accounting cycle").

municipalities is expected to be provided by the accounting, reporting and auditing requirements of the State and Local Fiscal Assistance Act of 1972. (3) Authoritative professional organizations have an established body of literature relating to municipal budgeting and accounting, whereas there is little consensus on recommended accounting for the 50 states. Federal accounting recommendations seem most easily understood by persons familiar with both municipal accounting and business accounting.

A sound knowledge of municipal accounting principles is also needed in order to understand the financial reports of nonprofit entities such as hospitals, nursing homes, charitable and health organizations, and colleges and universities, since accounting principles followed by nonprofit entities are similar to those followed by municipalities. It is the purpose of this text to present the views of authoritative professional organizations as to desirable standards to be attained by governmental and nonprofit entities in their accounting and reporting.

Contributions of Professional Organizations

Among the more important professional organizations which have contributed to the advancement and improvement of governmental accounting, budgeting and reporting is the Municipal Finance Officers Association of the United States and Canada. The association membership includes representatives from municipalities in both countries and from state and provincial units and agencies. The MFOA publishes a semimonthly *Municipal Finance News Letter;* a quarterly magazine, *Governmental Finance;* occasional *Special Bulletins* on topics of current particular interest to financial managers; and research reports and books on technical subjects.

The National Committee on Governmental Accounting, sponsored by the MFOA, is comprised of representatives from almost all of the professional accounting and public administration organizations in the United States and Canada. The National Committee reviews the work of consultants periodically engaged by the MFOA to write manuals setting forth desirable accounting and reporting practices for governmental units. The chapters of this text that are concerned primarily with municipalities, 3 through 14, are based largely on the NCGA's publication, *Governmental Accounting, Auditing, and Financial Reporting*. The recommendations of the NCGA have been supplemented, and to some extent modified, by the American Institute of Certified Public Accountants' Committee on Governmental Accounting and Auditing in order to relate them more closely to generally accepted accounting principles considered binding upon certified public accountants.[3]

[3] *Audits of State and Local Governmental Units* (New York: American Institute of Certified Public Accountants, 1974).

The Federal Government Accountants Association, whose members are employed by many of the civilian and defense agencies of the executive branch and of the legislative branch of the United States government, but who are not official representatives of those agencies, publishes a quarterly magazine, *The Federal Accountant.* Articles in that magazine, and meetings of the association, assist in the development of Federal accounting. The official responsibility for the establishment of principles, standards and related requirements for Federal agencies rests with the Comptroller General of the United States. The Secretary of the Treasury, the Director of the Office of Management and Budget, the Administrator of General Services and the Chairman of the Civil Service Commission cooperate with the Comptroller General in the Joint Financial Management Improvement Program. Chapter 16 is based on the official pronouncements of these officials and their representatives.

The United States Office of Education has published two volumes concerned with accounting and reporting for public school systems. The discussion of public school accounting in Chapter 17 is based on the USOE volumes and other references listed at the end of Chapter 17. College and university accounting, the subject of Chapter 18, is based largely on the writings of the American Council on Education.

The American Hospital Association's manuals set forth accounting and reporting practices which are widely accepted as authoritative in the hospital field, and are, therefore, explained in Chapter 19 of this text.

Other organizations, such as the American Accounting Association, the National Association of Accountants, and the Financial Executives Institute serve an important function in the development and improvement of accounting and reporting of governmental and nonprofit entities through committees of persons interested in the practical and theoretical aspects of financial management outside the profit-seeking sector. These organizations publish periodicals and occasionally devote portions of their meeting programs to accounting and reporting problems of governmental and nonprofit entities.

Accounting Reports of Governmental Units

> The end toward which all governmental accounting is directed is the production of timely, accurate, pertinent, and fairly-presented financial statements and reports for use by management, legislative officials, the general public, and others having need for public financial information.[4]

[4] National Committee on Governmental Accounting, *Governmental Accounting, Auditing, and Financial Reporting* (Chicago: Municipal Finance Officers Association, 1968), p. 14.

The technical accounting aspects of financial statements for the various municipal funds, Federal government, and certain categories of nonprofit entities are illustrated and discussed in following chapters to the extent relevant to the purposes of those chapters. Management uses of financial data are also discussed in the appropriate context. In this introductory chapter, the discussion is focused upon published financial reports as a means of communicating with interested parties outside the administrative structure.

Governmental units and governmental enterprises in a number of jurisdictions are required by law to publish financial reports in newspapers as paid advertising. All too frequently the only sort of report required by law is a listing of cash receipts and a listing of cash disbursements; often there is no classification of disbursements as to function or nature, merely a listing of payees and amounts of each voucher.

The widespread recognition that lists of receipts and disbursements are totally inadequate to meet the needs of any interested parties for information has led to the consideration by many professional groups of the problems of reporting, and to the establishment of standards of "public financial reporting" by the Municipal Finance Officers Association and the National Committee on Governmental Accounting.

The Fund Structure

Illustration 1–1 emphasizes one of the most distinctive characteristics of governmental accounting: the grouping of accounts by *funds.* The word *fund* has a special, technical, meaning in governmental accounting: *A fund is defined as an independent fiscal and accounting entity with a self-balancing set of accounts recording cash and/or other resources together with all related liabilities, obligations, reserves, and equities which are segregated for the purpose of carrying on specific activities or attaining certain objectives in accordance with special regulations, restrictions, or limitations.*[5]

The dual meaning of "fund" should be noted. A fund is an accounting entity; it is also a fiscal entity created, in most instances, by operation of law. It is important to understand that any governmental unit is created by law. The pattern of governmental organization established by the Constitution of the United States—the division of functions and powers among the legislative, judicial, and executive branches—is commonly found at all levels of government within the United States. The legislative branch of the Federal government, and of state governments, authorizes the sources of revenues to be collected by the executive branch of that government, and authorizes the expenditure of those collections by the

[5] Appendix 1 of this text is a glossary of municipal accounting terminology. Definitions of terms of particular importance are given in the text at the time the term is first used. The definition of fund quoted here is taken from *Governmental Accounting, Auditing, and Financial Reporting*, pp. 6–7.

Illustration 1–1

NAME OF GOVERNMENTAL UNIT
Combined Balance Sheet–All Funds
December 31, 19x2

	General Fund	*Special Revenue Funds*	*Debt Service Funds*
Assets and Other Debits			
Cash	$258,500	$101,385	$ 43,834
Cash with fiscal agents	–	–	102,000
Investments (net)	65,000	37,200	160,990
Interest receivable on investments	50	25	1,557
Interest receivable–special assessments	–	–	–
Accounts receivable (net)	8,300	3,300	–
Unbilled accounts receivable	–	–	–
Notes receivable (net)	–	–	–
Loans receivable	–	–	–
Taxes receivable–delinquent (net)	40,500	2,500	2,843
Interest and penalties receivable on taxes (net)	3,000	–	227
Tax liens receivable (net)	14,800	–	759
Taxes receivable for other units	–	–	–
Special assessments receivable	–	–	–
Special assessment liens receivable	–	–	–
Advances to other funds	65,000	–	–
Due from other funds	2,000	–	–
Due from other governments	30,000	75,260	–
Inventories	7,200	5,190	–
Prepaid expenses	–	–	–
Restricted assets–enterprise fund:			
Cash	–	–	–
Investments (net)	–	–	–
Interest receivable on investments	–	–	–
Land	–	–	–
Buildings (net)	–	–	–
Improvements other than buildings	–	–	–
Machinery and equipment	–	–	–
Construction work in progress	–	–	–
Amount available for retirement of term bonds	–	–	–
Amount to be provided for retirement of term bonds	–	–	–
Amount available for retirement of serial bonds	–	–	–
Amount to be provided for retirement of serial bonds	–	–	–
Total Assets and Other Debits	$494,350	$224,860	$312,210
Liabilities			
Vouchers payable	$107,861	$ 33,850	$ –
Accounts payable	10,400	–	–
Contracts payable	57,600	18,300	–
Judgments payable	–	2,000	–
Due to other funds	24,189	2,000	–
Due to fiscal agent	–	–	–
Taxes collected in advance	15,000	–	–
Customer deposits	–	–	–
Accrued liabilities	–	–	–
Advance from general fund	–	–	–
Advance from municipality–general obligation bonds	–	–	–
Matured bonds payable	–	–	–
Matured interest payable	–	–	–
General obligation bonds payable–term	–	–	–
General obligation bonds payable–serial	–	–	–
Revenue bonds payable	–	–	–
Special assessment bonds payable	–	–	–
Total Liabilities	$215,050	$ 56,150	$102,000
Reserves and Fund Balances/Retained Earnings			
Reserve for encumbrances	38,000	52,355	–
Reserve for inventory of supplies	7,200	5,190	–
Reserve for advance to central garage fund	65,000	–	–
Reserve for revenue bond debt service	–	–	–
Reserve for revenue bond retirement	–	–	–
Reserve for revenue bond contingency	–	–	–
Reserves–employees retirement system	–	–	–
Contribution from:			
Customers	–	–	–
Subdividers	–	–	–
Municipality	–	–	–
General Fund	–	–	–
Investment in general fixed assets	–	–	–
Fund balance	169,100	111,165	210,210
Retained earnings	–	–	–
Total Liabilities, Reserves, and Fund Balances/Retained Earnings	$494,350	$224,860	$312,210

Illustration 1–1 (*Continued*)

Capital Projects Funds	*Enterprise Funds*	*Intra-governmental Service Fund*	*Trust and Agency Funds*	*Special Assessment Funds*	*General Fixed Assets*	*General Long-term Debt*
$ 431,600	$ 257,636	$ 29,700	$ 216,701	$232,185	$ –	$ –
–	–	–	–	–	–	–
–	–	–	1,239,260	–	–	–
–	–	–	2,666	–	–	–
–	–	–	–	350	–	–
100	21,980	–	–	–	–	–
–	7,150	–	–	–	–	–
–	2.350	–	–	–	–	–
–	–	–	35,000	–	–	–
–	–	–	–	–	–	–
–	–	–	–	–	–	–
–	–	–	–	–	–	–
–	–	–	580,000	–	–	–
–	–	–	–	644,100	–	–
–	–	–	–	1,935	–	–
–	–	–	–	–	–	–
15,000	2,000	12,000	11,189	–	–	–
625,000	–	–	–	–	–	–
–	23,030	40,000	–	–	–	–
–	1,200	–	–	–	–	–
–	113,559	–	–	–	–	–
–	176,800	–	–	–	–	–
–	650	–	–	–	–	–
–	211,100	20,000	–	–	1,259,500	–
–	356,982	55,500	–	–	2,855,500	–
–	3,538,957	12,000	–	–	1,036,750	–
–	1,640,007	15,600	–	–	452,500	–
–	22,713	–	–	–	1,722,250	–
–	–	–	–	–	–	198,205
–	–	–	–	–	–	201,795
–	–	–	–	–	–	14,005
–	–	–	–	–	–	2,385,995
$1,071,700	$6,375,514	$184,800	$2,084,816	$878,570	$7,326,500	$2,800,000
$ 29,000	$ 131,071	$ 15,000	$ –	$ 20,600	$ –	$ –
–	–	–	–	–	–	–
69,000	26,107	–	–	50,000	–	–
19,600	–	–	–	11,200	–	–
4,000	–	–	–	–	–	–
–	139	–	–	–	–	–
–	–	–	–	–	–	–
–	63,000	–	–	–	–	–
–	49,175	–	4,700	10,700	–	–
–	–	65,000	–	–	–	–
–	700,000	–	–	–	–	–
100,000	–	–	–	–	–	–
2,000	–	–	–	–	–	–
–	–	–	–	–	–	400,000
–	–	–	–	–	–	2,400,000
–	1,846,000	–	–	–	–	–
–	–	–	–	555,000	–	–
$ 121,600	$2,815,492	$ 80,000	$ 4,700	$647,500	$	$2,800,000
943,500	–	–	–	185,000	–	–
–	–	–	–	–	–	–
–	–	–	–	–	–	–
–	5,000	–	–	–	–	–
–	109,822	–	–	–	–	–
–	14,333	–	–	–	–	–
–	–	–	1,426,201	–	–	–
–	72,000	–	–	–	–	–
–	870,666	–	–	–	–	–
–	450,000	–	–	–	–	–
–	–	95,000	–	–	–	–
–	–	–	–	–	7,326,500	–
6,600	–	–	653,915	46,070	–	–
–	2,038,201	9,800	–	–	–	–
$1,071,700	$6,375,514	$184,800	$2,084,816	$878,570	$7,326,500	$2,800,000

Source: *Governmental Accounting, Auditing and Financial Reporting* (Chicago: Municipal Finance Officers Association, 1968), pp. 108–9.

executive branch for specified purposes. Further, each municipality is the creature of the state in which it is located.

Municipalities have only the resources allowed by laws of the superior jurisdiction; the legislative branch of a municipality may choose not to utilize a resource authorized by state law, but it may *not* choose to utilize an unauthorized resource. Municipalities may incur expenditures only for purposes, and in amounts, approved by the legislative branch of the municipality in accord with procedures detailed in state laws. Whether the officials of a given municipality agree that the constraints imposed by superior jurisdictions promote wise management of resources, or feel that wise management is hindered, is beside the point. The constraints are binding, the municipal official has no choice but to operate within them; the accounting system must enable the officials to comply with the legal constraints. The need to demonstrate compliance with legal requirements led to the development of the fund accounting concept, which is so basic that the term "fund accounting" is often used to denote the kind of accounting recommended for governmental and nonprofit entities.

The column headings shown in Illustration 1–1 are the names of the eight types of funds and two account groups recommended by the National Committee on Governmental Accounting. A brief explanation of each type follows:

1. General Funds. In this category are funds established to account for resources devoted to financing the general services which the governmental unit performs for its citizens. These include general administration, protection of life and property, sanitation and similar broad services. The general fund is sometimes described as the one used to account for all financial transactions not properly accounted for in another fund. Some activities, such as governmentally supported libraries, are often of sufficient importance and magnitude to have a special fund; when this is not true they become a function and responsibility of the general fund. Accounting and reporting for general funds is discussed in Chapters 3, 4, and 5 of this text.

2. Special Revenue, or Special, Funds. Funds of this class are created and operated to account for revenue designated by law for a particular purpose. For the specific purpose or function to which it is devoted, a special revenue fund is much in the nature of a general fund. Some of the governmental services for which special funds are frequently established are education, libraries, streets and bridges, welfare, etc. Accounting and reporting for special funds follows the principles and practices set forth in Chapters 3, 4, and 5.

3. Capital Projects Funds. The receipt and disbursement of all moneys used for the acquisition of capital facilities other than those financed by special assessment and enterprise funds is accounted for by capital projects funds. Capital projects funds are discussed in Chapter 6.

4. Debt Service Funds. A debt service fund is created to account for the resources devoted to the payment of interest and principal on long-term general obligation debt other than that payable from special assessments and that serviced by governmental enterprises. Chapter 7 is devoted to debt service funds.

5. Trust and Agency Funds. Trust funds and agency funds are used to account for transactions related to assets held by a governmental unit as a trustee or agent. In most cases the governmental unit does not have absolute title to the assets held; and in the remainder, they are owned with specific restrictions upon their use. Trust and agency funds are discussed in Chapter 8.

6. Intragovernmental Service Funds. Intragovernmental service funds are established by governmental units as a means of providing services to other funds or departments of the same unit in a manner that is more efficient or economical, or both, than is possible in any other way. Funds of this nature are discussed in Chapter 9.

7. *Special Assessment Funds.* Special assessment funds are designed to account for the construction, or purchase through contract, of public improvements—streets, sidewalks, and sewer systems, for example—which are financed by special levies against property owners adjudged to receive benefits from the improvements materially in excess of benefits received by the general body of taxpayers, and for the maintenance and upkeep of such assets. Chapter 10 presents the fundamentals of special assessment fund accounting.

8. Enterprise Funds. Intragovernmental service funds are established to provide services within a given governmental unit, but enterprise funds are operated to provide electric, water, gas, or other services to the general public. Except for ownership, they bear a close resemblance to investor-owned utility or other service enterprises. Chapter 11 presents accounting and reporting standards for enterprise funds.

In addition to the eight generally recognized types of funds, the NCGA recommends that governmental units employ two self-balancing groups of accounts which are accounting entities, but which are not fiscal entities and, therefore, are not funds. These groups are called the "general fixed assets group" and the "general long-term debt group." General fixed assets are those not used exclusively by any one fund, and general long-term debt is that long-term debt which is presently a liability of the municipality as a whole and not of individual funds. Chapter 12 is concerned with general fixed asset accounting; accounting for general long-term debt is discussed in Chapter 13. Interrelationships among the various funds and account groups are explained in Chapter 14.

Although funds are employed extensively and effectively to promote the use of governmental resources for their intended purposes, the practice can be carried to extremes. In the opinion of many, accounting and reporting are facilitated through use of the minimum number of funds consistent with legal and operating requirements.[6]

Integration of Budgetary Accounts

A second distinctive characteristic of governmental accounting resulting from the need to demonstrate compliance with laws governing the sources of revenues available to governmental units, and laws governing the utilization of those revenues, is the formal recording of the legally approved budget in the accounts of funds operated on an annual basis. The nature and operation of budgetary accounts are explained in appropriate detail in following chapters. Briefly: Budgetary accounts are opened as of the beginning of each fiscal year and closed as of the end of each fiscal year; therefore they have no balances at year end and are not shown in Illustration 1–1. During the year, however, the budgetary accounts of a fund are integrated with its proprietary accounts. Proprietary accounts, in the governmental sense, include accounts similar to the real and the nominal groups found in accounting for profit-seeking entities—that is, asset, liability, net worth, revenue, and expense accounts. Asset, liability, and fund balance accounts recommended by the NCGA are shown in Illustration 1–1; the nature and use of proprietary accounts are explained in following chapters.

The Basis of Accounting

In accounting for businesses, determination of the amount of net income, and the detailed causes thereof, is of foremost importance. In governmental accounting, only three types of funds—trust, intragovernmental service, and enterprise—make use of so-called "profit and loss" accounting procedures. Funds of other types record revenues and expenditures principally for control and as a basis for demonstrating compliance with their budgets; determination of net gain or net loss is not a primary consideration. Even for those funds which do attempt to determine net income, only certain trust funds have major interest in the largest possible amount of gain. Intragovernmental service and enterprise funds are operated primarily for service; they make use of revenue and expense accounts

[6] The eight funds and two account groups described are those recommended by the National Committee on Governmental Accounting in *Governmental Accounting, Auditing, and Financial Reporting*, published in the spring of 1968. The 1968 publication differs to some extent in terminology and other respects from the recommendations of the NCGA which stood from 1951 until 1968. Inasmuch as accounting reports and records of many municipalities continue to reflect the earlier recommendations, the discussion in this text of each fund and account group includes not only current NCGA recommendations, but also mention of prior recommendations likely to be encountered in practice.

to promote efficiency of operation and to guard against impairment of ability to render the services desired. For these reasons, operating statements of governmental funds are called statements of revenue and expenditures, rather than income statements.

Use of the accrual basis of accounting is considered appropriate for governmental units as well as for profit-seeking businesses. Accrual accounting means (1) that revenues should be recorded in the period in which the service is given, although payment is received in a prior or subsequent period, and (2) that expenditures should be recorded in the period in which the benefit is received, although payment is made in a prior or subsequent period. In business for profit, the accrual basis is employed to obtain a matching of costs against the revenue flowing from those costs, thereby producing a more useful statement of gain or loss. In government, use of the accrual basis enables a better comparison between actual expenditures and revenues and the amounts authorized in the budget approved by the legislative body, as well as enabling computation of the cost of rendering services.

The National Committee on Governmental Accounting recommends that the accrual basis be used in accounting for enterprise, trust, capital projects, special assessment, and intragovernmental service funds. In accounting for general, special revenue, and debt service funds, the NCGA recommends the use of the "modified accrual" basis. The modified accrual basis is defined as:

> . . . that method of accounting in which expenditures other than accrued interest on general long-term debt are recorded at the time liabilities are incurred and revenues are recorded when received in cash, except for material or available revenues which should be accrued to reflect properly the taxes levied and the revenues earned.[7]

The modified accrual basis for general, special revenue, and debt service funds is accepted by the American Institute of Certified Public Accountants as being consistent with generally accepted accounting principles.[8] The AICPA recognizes that it is not practicable to account on an accrual basis for revenues generated on a self-assessed basis, such as income taxes, gross receipts taxes, and sales taxes. For such taxes, and for other categories of revenue discussed in detail in following chapters, determination of the amount of revenue collectible is ordinarily made at the time of collection, thus placing the fund partially on the cash basis. Although the weight of authority is certainly upon accrual basis recognition of material or available revenues, the laws of a number of jurisdictions still require cash basis recognition for all revenues. Municipalities in such

[7] *Governmental Accounting, Auditing, and Financial Reporting*, p. 11.

[8] *Audits of State and Local Governmental Units*, American Institute of Certified Public Accountants, 1974.

jurisdictions must comply with the law; however, the AICPA takes the position that the primary financial statements of each governmental unit should be prepared in accord with generally accepted accounting principles and "supplemental schedules" should be prepared to disclose legal compliance.[9]

SELECTED REFERENCES

AMERICAN INSTITUTE OF CERTIFIED PUBLIC ACCOUNTANTS. *Audits of State and Local Governmental Units.* New York, 1974.

COMMITTEE FOR ECONOMIC DEVELOPMENT. *Modernizing State Government.* New York, 1967.

———. *Modernizing Local Government.* New York, 1966.

COMMITTEE ON INTERGOVERNMENTAL FISCAL RELATIONS. *Analysis: Federal Revenue Sharing.* Chicago: Municipal Finance Officers Association, 1972.

THE CONFERENCE BOARD. *Financing Local Government.* New York, 1967.

NATIONAL COMMITTEE ON GOVERNMENTAL ACCOUNTING. *Governmental Accounting, Auditing, and Financial Reporting.* Chicago: Municipal Finance Officers Association, 1968.

QUESTIONS

1–1. Anyone wishing to determine appropriate accounting principles and standards for a given municipality need consult only state laws. Comment.

1–2. The combined balance sheet for the City of Noname shows the following column headings: General Fund, Street and Bridge Fund, Capital Projects Funds, General Asset and Liability Fund, Special Assessment Fund, and Utility Fund. In what respects does the City of Noname appear to follow recommended fund usage, and in what respects does it appear to differ?

1–3. "In governmental accounting the term 'fund' is used in the same sense that it is in financial accounting for profit seeking entities." Do you agree? Why or why not?

1–4. "Fund accounting is used only by municipalities, and should be studied only by accounting majors who expect to work as municipal accountants." Comment.

1–5. Would you expect all entities which use fund accounting to have a general fund? Why or why not?

1–6. "Because budgetary accounts are used by municipalities their financial statements can never be said to be in accord with generally accepted accounting principles." Comment.

1–7. " 'Budgetary accounts' is a technical name for fixed asset accounts of a municipality because fixed assets can only be purchased if authorized by the budget." Discuss.

[9] Ibid., p. 13.

1–8. "Accrual accounting is recommended for use by enterprise, trust, capital projects, special, and intragovernmental service funds." True or False? Why?

1–9. Why is accounting for nonprofit entities discussed along with accounting for governmental units, rather than with accounting for profit-seeking enterprises? Name some categories of nonprofit entities of wide importance in the United States economy.

1–10. Even though a governmental unit may have a good system of accounting and reporting, evaluating the performance of its administrators is said to be more difficult than for a commercial enterprise of comparable size. Why might this be true?

EXERCISES

1–1. Obtain a copy of a recent annual report, and, if possible, the related budget of a municipality.* Follow the instructions below:

a) Familiarize yourself with the organization of the annual report; read the letter of transmittal or any narrative that accompanies the financial statements. Does this material discuss the financial condition of the municipality at balance sheet date? Does it discuss the most significant changes in financial condition which occurred during the year? Does it alert the reader to forthcoming changes in financial condition which are not as yet reflected in the financial statements? Does it explain the basis of accounting used by the municipality? (If so, does the municipality follow recommendations discussed in Chapter 1 of the text?) Does it explain what activities are accounted for by each of the funds included in the report? Does it mention any municipal activities which are not covered by the report; are these covered by other reports available to the public? Does it explain any terminology or reporting practices which may not agree with NCGA or AICPA recommendations because of local custom or state law?

b) List the funds and account groups whose statements are included in the report. Compare your list with the funds and groups recommended by the NCGA; note all differences. (As you study the chapters which explain each recommended fund and group refer back to your notes and determine if the differences are only in terminology or if the municipality deviates from recommendations in significant respects. Note and evaulate the deviations in accord with suggestions given in the exercises of following chapters.)

* These may be obtained from the chief financial officer of the municipality. If you do not know the exact title and address you should write "Director of Finance, City of ________," and address it to the City Hall in the city and state of your choice. Because some municipalities may not have any report available to send at the time of your request, it may be necessary to write a second or even a third city. The instructor may wish to obtain the reports and budgets before the term starts, or at least approve the selection of municipalities, so that every member of the class has a different report.

c) Are the financial statements in the report audited? By an independent CPA? By federal or state auditors? By an auditor employed by the municipality being audited? Does the auditor express an opinion that the statements are (1) "in accord with generally accepted accounting principles," (2) "in accord with generally accepted accounting principles applicable to governmental entities," (3) "in accord with state laws," or (4) is the opinion qualified in some manner or disclaimed?

CONTINUOUS PROBLEMS

NOTE: Chapters 2 through 14 of the text deal with specific knowledge needed to understand the accounting for the funds recommended for use by municipalities, and with specific aspects of financial management. In order to help the student keep the entire municipal accounting and financial management area in perspective, two series of related problems are presented. The first series covers representative activities of the City of Bingham; the problems in this series relate to all funds and account groups; they are designated 1–L, 2–L, 3–L, etc. The second series covers activities of the City of Smithville relating to only the general, capital projects, and debt service funds, the Federal General Revenue Sharing Trust Fund, and the general fixed asset and general long-term debt groups; the problems in this series are designated 1–S, 2–S, 3–S, etc.

1–L. 1. The City of Bingham has the following funds in addition to its General Fund; you are required to classify each in accordance with the types discussed on pages 8 and 9 of the text:

City Hall Annex Construction Fund. This fund was created to account for the proceeds of the sale of serial bonds issued for the construction and equipping of an annex to the city hall.

City Hall Annex Bond Debt Service Fund. Nonactuarially determined contributions and earnings thereon, for the purpose of the payment of interest on and redemption of serial bonds issued by the City Hall Annex Construction Fund, are accounted for by this fund.

Employees' Retirement Fund. This fund was established to account for actuarially determined retirement contributions and earnings thereon, and for the payment of retirement annuities.

Stores and Services Fund. This fund was established to account for centralized purchasing and management of inventories used by a number of departments of the municipal government.

Irwinville Special Assessment Fund. Property owners in an unincorporated area, called Irwinville, agreed to bear the cost of the extension of water mains into their area by the City of Bingham water utility.

Water Utility Fund. The water utility serving the City of Bingham was originally constructed and operated by a private corporation. It was subsequently sold to the city, but it is still operated on a self-supporting basis under the regulations of the State Public Service Commission.

2. In addition to the funds described above, what groups of accounts should be established for the City of Bingham? Why are these called "groups of accounts" rather than "funds"?

3. For each of its funds and account groups, the City of Bingham maintains separate, manually kept books of original entry and ledgers.

   You are required to:

   a) Open a general journal for the General Fund. Allow 7 pages of 8½ by 11-inch looseleaf journal paper, or its equivalent. (Do not open general journals for other funds until instructed to do so in subsequent "L" problems.) The form you use must allow for entry of subsidiary ledger accounts as well as general ledger accounts, and for entry of adequate explanations for each journal entry. You will use the journal as your only posting medium; it should be complete.

   b) Open a *general ledger* for the General Fund. Allow 5 lines, unless otherwise indicated below, for each of the following accounts:

Cash	20 lines
Petty Cash	
Taxes Receivable–Current	8 lines
Estimated Uncollectible Current Taxes	
Taxes Receivable–Delinquent	8 lines
Estimated Uncollectible Delinquent Taxes	
Interest and Penalties Receivable on Taxes	
Estimated Uncollectible Interest and Penalties	
Due from Other Funds	8 lines
Advance to Stores and Services Fund	
Estimated Revenues	
Revenues	8 lines
Vouchers Payable	12 lines
Tax Anticipation Notes Payable	
Due to Federal Government	12 lines
Due to Other Funds	8 lines
Appropriations	
Expenditures	20 lines
Expenditures–Prior Year	
Encumbrances	8 lines
Reserve for Encumbrances	8 lines
Reserve for Encumbrances–Prior Year	
Reserve for Advance to Stores and Services Fund	
Fund Balance	12 lines

   NOTE: If desired, a numerical classification system may be devised for the general ledger accounts to facilitate journalizing and posting transactions. The classification system should provide for subsidiary ledger accounts supporting Estimated Revenues, Revenues, Appropriations, Expenditures, and Encumbrances. *Do not open subsidiary ledgers until instructed to do so in subsequent "L" problems.*

c) The balance sheet of the general fund of the City of Bingham as of the first day of the year with which the "L" problems are concerned is shown below. Enter the balance sheet amounts directly in the appropriate general fund general ledger accounts.

CITY OF BINGHAM
General Fund Balance Sheet
as of July 1, 19–

Assets			*Liabilities, Reserves, and Fund Balance*	
Cash		$ 60,000	Vouchers payable	$187,000
Taxes receivable—delinquent	$244,000		Due to other funds	22,000
Less estimated uncollectible delinquent taxes	24,400	219,600	Total liabilities	$209,000
Interest and penalties receivable on taxes	$ 13,376		Reserve for encumbrances—prior year	14,000
Less estimated uncollectible interest and penalties	662	12,714	Fund balance	69,314
Total Assets		$292,314	Total Liabilities, Reserves, and Fund Balance	$292,314

1–S. 1. The City of Smithville maintains separate, manually kept books of original entry and ledgers for each of its funds and account groups. You are required to:

a) Open a general journal for the General Fund. Allow 5 pages of 8½ by 11-inch looseleaf journal paper, or its equivalent. (Do not open general journals for other funds until instructed to do so in subsequent "S" problems.) The form you use must allow for entry of subsidiary ledger accounts as well as general ledger accounts, and for entry of adequate explanations for each journal entry. You will use the journal as your only posting medium; it should be complete.

b) Open a general ledger for the General Fund. Allow 6 lines for each of the following accounts:

Cash
Taxes Receivable—Current
Estimated Uncollectible Current Taxes
Taxes Receivable—Delinquent
Estimated Uncollectible Delinquent Taxes
Interest and Penalties Receivable on Taxes
Estimated Uncollectible Interest and Penalties
Due from Other Funds
Due from State Government
Estimated Revenues
Revenues
Vouchers Payable

Tax Anticipation Notes Payable
Due to Other Funds
Due to Federal Government
Due to State Government
Appropriations
Expenditures
Encumbrances
Reserve for Encumbrances
Reserve for Encumbrances–Prior Year
Fund Balance

NOTE: If desired, a numerical classification system may be devised for the general ledger accounts to facilitate journalizing and posting transactions. The classification system should provide for subsidiary ledger accounts supporting Estimated Revenues, Revenues, Appropriations, Expenditures, and Encumbrances. Do *not* open subsidiary ledgers until instructed to do so in subsequent "S" problems.

c) The balance sheet of the general fund of the City of Smithville as of December 31, 197A, is shown below. Enter the balance sheet amounts directly in the proper general ledger accounts; date each "1/1/7B."

CITY OF SMITHVILLE
General Fund Balance Sheet as of December 31, 197A

Assets			*Liabilities and Fund Balance*	
Cash		$ 67,080	Vouchers payable	$330,499
Taxes receivable–delinquent	$255,544		Tax anticipation notes payable	200,000
Less estimated uncollectible delinquent taxes	62,861	192,683	Due to other funds	8,788
Interest and penalties receivable on taxes	32,238		Total liabilities	$539,287
Less estimated uncollectible interest and penalties	12,201	20,037	Fund balance	210,442
Due from other funds		21,215		
Due from state government		448,714		
Total Assets		$749,729	Total Liabilities and Fund Balance	$749,729

2

Budgets for Operations and Capital Improvements

Budgets for Resource Management

The word "budget" has unpleasant connotations to most individuals. If the word were not fixed in technical language by statute and tradition the term "operating plan" could be substituted, for in governmental bodies as well as private businesses a budget is now conceived of as a device to aid management to operate an organization more effectively. An older view of the nature of a budget still is implicit in statutes, and probably for that reason, the National Committee on Governmental Accounting still defines a budget as, "A plan of financial operation embodying an estimate of proposed expenditures for a given period of time and the proposed means of financing them."[1]

The evolution of the concept of a budget from "an estimate of proposed expenditures and the proposed means of financing them" to an "operating plan" was a natural accompaniment to the development of the concept of professional management. In public administration, as in business administration, the concept of professionalism demanded that administrators, or managers, attempt to put the scarce resources of qualified personnel and money to the best possible uses. The legal requirement that administrators of governmental units and agencies submit appropriation requests to the legislative bodies in budget format provided a basis for adapting required budgetary estimates of proposed expenditures to broader management use. The legislative appropriation process has traditionally required administrators to justify budget requests. A logical

[1] National Committee on Governmental Accounting, *Governmental Accounting, Auditing, and Financial Reporting*, p. 5.

justification of proposed expenditures is to relate the proposed expenditures of each governmental subdivision to the programs and activities to be accomplished by that subdivision during the budget period. *The type of budgeting in which input of resources is related to output of services is sometimes known as performance budgeting.*

Program budgeting is another term which is sometimes used synonymously with performance budgeting, although it has been suggested by the Municipal Finance Officers Association[2] that the term program budgeting be applied to a budget format which discloses the full cost of a function without regard to the number of organizational units that might be involved in performing the various aspects of the function, whereas a performance budget format would relate the input and output of each unit individually.

The use of performance budgeting in governmental units received significant impetus from the work of the first Hoover Commission for the Federal government. The report of this commission, presented to the Congress in 1949, led to the adoption in the Federal government of budgets then known as "cost-based budgets" or "cost budgets." The use of these designations suggests that a governmental unit desiring to use performance budgeting must have an accrual accounting system, rather than a cash accounting system, in order to ascertain routinely the costs of programs and activities. The recommendations of the second Hoover Commission led to the statutory requirement of both accrual accounting and cost-based budgeting for agencies of the executive branch of the Federal government. Federal statutes also require the synchronization of budgetary and accounting classifications, and the coordination of these with the organizational structure of the agencies. Subsequently it was realized that the planning and programming functions of Federal agencies were not performed by the same organizational segments that performed the budgeting and accounting functions, and that plans and programs were thus often not properly related to appropriation requests.

The integration of planning, programming, budgeting, and accounting has considerable appeal to persons concerned with public administration because an integrated system should, logically, provide legislators and administrators with much better information for the management of governmental resources than has been provided by separate systems. In the late 1960s there was a concentrated effort to introduce a planning-programming-budgeting system, called PPBS, throughout the executive branch of the Federal government. Considerable publicity has been given to PPBS in the Federal context and also to efforts to adapt the PPBS

[2] Lennox L. Moak and Kathryn W. Killian, *A Manual of Techniques for the Preparation, Consideration, Adoption, and Administration of Operating Budgets* (Chicago: Municipal Finance Officers Association, 1963). This manual is commonly referred to as the *MFOA Operating Budget Manual.*

concept to state and local governmental bodies. Although there are enormous differences between PPBS as it exists in a small municipality and as it exists in a Federal agency with a budget ten thousand times as large, it is reasonable to generalize that a PPB system represents an extension of the program budgeting concept to include:

1. identification of the fundamental objectives of the governmental unit,
2. explicit consideration of future year implications of any present possible decision, and
3. systematic analysis of alternative ways of meeting the governmental unit's objectives.[3]

Systematic analysis, sometimes called "systems analysis," "cost/benefit analysis," of "cost-effectiveness analysis," may, of course, be used separately from PPBS. The terms are not synonomous but are closely enough related to be so treated for present purposes. Quantitative techniques such as model building and simulation studies may be utilized as aids in evaluating alternative allocations of governmental resources just as they may for evaluating business alternatives. However simple or however sophisticated the methods used to develop information to aid in the resource allocation process, any method can produce useful output only if the data input are sufficiently reliable. This chapter and subsequent chapters are intended to provide the reader with the background needed to understand data produced by currently recommended budgeting and accounting systems. Changes in currently recommended municipal accounting that would facilitate implementation of PPBS are discussed in Chapter 14.

Program Budget Example

Illustration 2–1 presents a summary of the expenditure budget requests for the eight categories of programs of governmental services offered by a medium-sized city in the Mountain states. In addition to the total amount requested, the summary provides a brief description of each program. Detail supporting the total requested for each program is presented in the city's budget document. Illustration 2–2 presents the detail supporting Program V, Health, Safety, and General Well-Being; it shows that although Health, Safety, and General Well-Being is a program category, it is not a single program but an umbrella for programs, activities, and functions of a number of departments of the municipality. The same is true for each of the other program categories shown in Illustration 2–1.

---

[3] Harry P. Hatry, "Criteria for Evaluation in Planning State and Local Programs." This article is most easily available in Harley H. Hinrichs and Graeme M. Taylor, *Program Budgeting and Benefit-Cost Analysis* (Pacific Palisades, Calif.: Goodyear Publishing Co., Inc., 1969), p. 95.

Illustration 2–1
1974 Budget by Programs

I.	DEVELOPMENT OF HUMAN RESOURCES . . . . To provide materials and programs to enable the educational development and improvement of all citizens and to attempt to motivate maximum utilization of their opportunities.	$ 317,281
II.	TRANSPORTATION. . . . . To enable the movement of persons and goods within the City in an efficient, safe, and environmentally acceptable manner.	2,706,519
III.	PHYSICAL ENVIRONMENT AND ECONOMIC BASE . . . . To achieve the best possible physical environment throughout the community, to stabilize and preserve property values, and to establish and maintain a sound economic base.	1,329,831
IV.	HOUSING . . . . To assure that those desiring to live in this town, regardless of race, creed, or socio-economic standing, will find available housing which meets minimum safety and health standards and that they will have some choice of housing types and location within the community.	15,657
V.	HEALTH, SAFETY, AND GENERAL WELL-BEING . . . . To conserve the mental and physical health of and to insure the safety of all citizens, to eliminate unjust discrimination of all kinds, and to stimulate and facilitate maximum citizen participation in government.	630,024
VI.	CULTURE AND RECREATIONAL. To provide opportunities for citizens to relax, to enjoy nature; to exercise; to socialize; to learn or practice artistic, social, or athletic skills; and to witness or participate in cultural events.	1,174,937
VII.	SERVICES TO PROPERTY . . . . To make available the services essential for the operation and use of real property and to prevent damage to or the destruction or loss of real property.	5,691,504
VIII.	GENERAL MANAGEMENT AND SUPPORT . . . . To provide all management and support activities necessary to achieve to the City's objectives.	1,055,093
	Total All Programs.	12,920,846
	Less: Inter-fund transfer Included In Program Structure	(183,413)
	Total Budget by Programs	12,737,433

Whatever theory of management is followed, responsibility for the performance of activities must be clearly fixed. In order to accomplish this, personnel, equipment, and facilities are assigned to organizational subentities. For management purposes, therefore, a budget must be prepared for each organizational subentity and related to the program budget. The four-digit number in the left margin of Illustration 2–2 is a program element number which cross references the detailed budget of the program category to the budgets for the organizational subentities; Illustration 2–3 shows the budget for the municipal fire department. The left-hand portion of Illustration 2–3 shows the proposed budget for the forthcoming year for personal services, non personal expense, and capital outlay, each compared with the approved budget for the year in progress at the time the proposed budget is prepared, and with the actual expendi-

Illustration 2–2

Detail Budget of Program V

Code	Item	Detail	Total
	V. Health, Safety, and General Well-Being		$630,024
	A. Conservation of Health		180,565
5110	1. Public Health	$ 64,640	
5120	2. Hospital Treatment	30,000	
	3. Animal Control	44,211	
5131	A′. Dog Control	33,596	
5132	B′. Other Animals	1,992	
5133	C′. Records + Court	7,390	
5134	D′. Support	1,233	
	4. Resuscitator + Rescue Calls	41,714	
5141	A′. Volunteer Groups	1,800	
5142	B′. Public Safety–Calls	19,426	
5143	C′. Public Safety–Assemblies	5,806	
5144	D′. Public Safety–Training	12,082	
5145	E′. Ambulance	2,600	
	B. Crime Prevention		268,051
	1. Patrol	99,429	
5211	A′. Mobile	61,174	
5212	B′. Foot	2,142	
5213	C′. On-Site Arrests	0	
5214	D′. Dispatch	14,410	
5215	E′. Support	21,703	
	2. Investigation + Apprehension	119,175	
5221	A′. Intelligence Gathering	17,191	
5222	B′. Crime Investigation	35,711	
5223	C′. Records + Identification	9,309	
5224	D′. Laboratory	8,719	
5225	E′. Missing Persons	9,769	
5226	F′. Support	38,476	
5230	3. Support	4,418	
	4. Prosecution	29,626	
5241	A′. Fine Collection	469	
5242	B′. Court Cases	27,307	
5243	C′. Detention	1,850	
5250	5. Public Assemblies + Parades	5,627	
	6. Support	9,776	
5261	A′. Training	8,730	
5262	B′. Facilities + Equipment	226	
5263	C′. Other	820	
	C. Building Code Enforcement		70,474
	1. Plans Review	14,874	
5311	A′. Single-Family	3,149	
5312	B′. Multi-Family	4,449	
5313	C′. Commercial + Industrial	5,206	
5314	D′. Miscellaneous Projects	2,070	
	2. Field Inspections	37,589	
5321	A′. Single-Family	15,339	
5322	B′. Multi-Family	12,060	
5323	C′. Commercial + Industrial	6,560	
5324	D′. Miscellaneous Projects	3,630	
5330	3. Public Information	5,005	
5340	4. Administration + Support	13,006	
	D. Housing Code		28,448
5410	1. Complaints + Related Inspections	5,590	
5420	2. Programmed Inspections	7,778	
5430	3, Data + Surveys	5,980	
5440	4. Public Information	3,823	
5450	5. Administration + Support	5,277	
5500	E. Aid to Needy		75
	F. Emergency Preparation + Relief		41,203
	1. Emergency Preparedness	32,648	
5611	A′. Fallout Shelters	11,333	
5612	B′. Emergency Planning	8,910	
5613	C′. Training + Organization	9,376	
5614	D′. Warning	2,136	
5615	E′. Support	893	
	2. Disaster Operations + Relief	8,555	
5621	A′. Wind Damage	0	
5622	B′. Flooding	0	
5623	C′. Other	8,555	
	G. Inter-Group Relations		15,449
5710	1. Discrimination Cases	2,801	
5720	2. Education Programs	7,125	
5730	3. Support	5,523	
5740	4. Transient Youth Program	0	
	H. Citizen Participation		25,759
5810	1. Voter Registration	0	
5820	2. Elections	7,071	
5830	3. Public Information	13,030	
5840	4. Financial Reporting	884	
5850	5. Legal Notice Administration	2,796	
5860	6. Special Citizen Committees	1,978	
	VI. CULTURAL AND RECREATIONAL		1,174,937
	A. City Parks		442,691
6110	1. Master Planning	2,931	
6120	2. Land Acquisition	46,505	
6130	3. Construction–Design	8,344	

Illustration 2–3
Fire Department Budget

Summary				
Activity 15 *Fire*	*Division*	*Department* *Fire*	*Fund* *General Operating*	
Classification		*Actual Expenditures 1972*	*Current Budget 1973*	*Proposed Budget 1974*
Personal Services		$467,897	$543,126	$613,066
Non Personal Expense		55,681	61,715	69,299
Capital Outlay		2,751	4,680	7,809
Total		$526,329	$609,521	$690,174

Function. The Fire Department has three major functions: First, to prevent fires; second, when fires occur, to prevent loss of life and to minimize property damage; third, in response to emergency calls, to dispatch a resuscitator or other appropriate equipment for rescue operations.

Budget Comments. Most of the increase in the Fire Department budget results from Personal Services. The increase in this area reflects the 1974 general pay increases of $45,727 and the addition of three new firefighters at a cost of $24,213. These latter will complete the implementation of the three-year program of reducing the work week from 67½ hours to 56 hours. In Non Personal Expense, the increase is accounted for by uncontrollable increases in rentals and insurance, along with $2,500 for overhauling the motor and pump on Engine #11. The Capital Outlay expense consists of the following items: heart-lung resuscitator ($1,800); camera for fire investigation ($140); dictation equipment ($565); miscellaneous equipment ($986); miscellaneous construction items ($968); underwater rescue equipment ($350); and replacement of fire hose and nozzles ($3,000). The last item is a recurring expense in accordance with a programmed replacement of fire nozzles.

Budget by Programs		*Personal Services*	*Non-personal Expense*	*Capital*	*Total*
5141	Volunteer Groups	$ 00	$ 750	$ 00	$ 750
5142	Public Safety–Calls	11,721	988	2,150	14,859
5143	Public Safety–Assemblies	5,806	00	00	5,806
5144	Public Safety–Training	11,642	50	00	11,692
7111	Evacuation Planning and Civilian Training	335	55	00	390
7112	Education–School Children	9,380	50	00	9,430
7113	Lectures and Demonstrations	6,330	221	00	6,551
7114	Public Assemblies	5,915	00	00	5,915
7121	Inspections (Construction)	7,248	00	00	7,248
7122	Adjudication (Construction)	335	00	00	335
7131	Inspections (Complaints)	40,937	3,538	00	44,475
7132	Adjudication (Complaints)	335	00	00	335
7140	Investigation of Fires	1,880	1,175	140	3,195
7151	Classroom (Training)	71,333	333	00	71,666
7152	Field (Training)	31,479	1,638	00	33,117
7153	Special Schools	13,775	1,550	00	15,325
7155	Facilities–Maintenance	00	125	00	125
7161	Surveys	11,818	00	00	11,818
7162	Plan Preparation and Instruction	14,307	00	00	14,307
7171	Answering Alarms	68,233	6,063	00	74,296
7172	Dispatching	27,128	00	00	27,128
7173	Equipment Acquisition and Maintenance	25,570	7,606	3,986	37,162
7174	Equipment Testing and Operation	12,505	1,966	00	14,471
7175	Building Construction and Modification	5,580	1,580	968	8,128
7176	Building Operation and Maintenance	41,630	8,955	00	50,585
7178	Standby (Firefighting)	121,686	00	00	121,686
7182	Hydrant Testing and Records	16,447	00	00	16,447
7184	Hydrant Rental	00	29,813	00	29,813
7190	Support	49,711	2,843	565	53,119
Program Total		$613,066	$69,299	$7,809	$690,174

tures for the most recent year completed. Underneath the dollar comparisons a brief explanation of the major functions served by the department is presented along with comments intended to answer questions administrators expect city council members and interested residents to raise.

The right-hand portion of Illustration 2–3 indicates the amounts of the Fire Department budget that relate to each program element in which the Department is involved. Note, for example, that the first four lines, 5141, 5142, 5143, and 5144, list programs that are included in section A 4 of Illustration 2–2. Only in the case of the "Public Safety—Assemblies" program, 5143, does the Fire Department have sole responsibility. The Police Department budget, not reproduced here, includes the amount of $4,567 for Program 5142, Public Safety—Calls, and the amount of $390 for Program 5144, Public Safety—Training; these amounts, when added to the amounts shown for those programs in Illustration 2–3, verify that the Police and Fire Departments are the only municipal departments involved in these programs. The City Council budget, not reproduced here, shows that the Council supports the Volunteer Groups program, 5141, to the extent of $1,050; thus the Council and the Fire Department share responsibility for that program.

The budgets for each organizational subentity are summarized as shown by Illustration 2–4. The total Fire Department budget, $690,174 per Illustration 2–3, is shown on the second line under the "Public Safety" caption on Illustration 2–4. The departments and activities listed on Illustration 2–4 under the "General Operating Fund" heading are largely those commonly financed by general funds, as defined in Chapter 1. The Open Space and Major Thoroughfare Fund, Library Fund, and Permanent Parks and Recreation Fund are special funds; the Public Improvement Fund is a capital projects fund; and the General Obligation Debt Retirement Fund is a debt service fund in the NCGA terminology explained in Chapter 1. The total proposed expenditures from all funds shown in Illustration 2–4 accounts for approximately two-thirds of the total proposed expenditures for all programs shown in Illustration 2–1; the remainder of the proposed expenditures for programs are found in the expenditure budgets for the Water Utility Fund and the Sewer Utility Fund, not reproduced here.

Bases for Budgeting

The *Operating Budget Manual* of the Municipal Finance Officers Association emphasizes that if a budget is to be a realistic plan of operations it must be based on the following factors:

1. The body of law governing budget format, timing, and procedure.
2. The forces of public life which utilize the budget as an instrument of public policy.

Illustration 2–4

SUMMARY GENERAL FUND EXPENDITURE BUDGET
General Government Funds
Expenditures by Activity

Funds and Activities	*1972 Actual*	*1973 Budget*	*1974 Proposed*
GENERAL OPERATING FUND			
General government:			
City council	$ 77,750	$ 49,738	$ 51,548
Municipal court	52,304	62,567	67,552
City attorney	52,210	80,855	83,332
City manager	65,724	72,946	80,746
Total General Government	247,988	266,106	283,178
Administrative services:			
Finance	196,597	226,570	255,197
Budget and research	27,688	37,162	44,994
Personnel	35,005	43,772	54,597
Data processing	15,812	15,751	59,877
Land acquisition	12,642	11,759	13,959
Total Administrative Services	287,744	335,014	428,624
Community development:			
Housing	10,350	10,072	12,436
Planning	85,489	96,776	109,335
Zoning and building inspection	97,127	110,300	125,894
Total Community Development	192,976	217,148	247,665
Public safety:			
Police	737,789	875,930	1,059,667
Fire	526,329	609,521	690,174
Civil defense	26,119	28,058	32,648
Total Public Safety	1,290,237	1,513,509	1,782,489
Public facilities:			
Administration	33,095	25,085	25,084
Engineering–design	71,294	104,407	115,182
Transportation	105,032	113,785	398,709
Street lighting	112,895	131,244	134,454
Operations:			
Administration	21,666	23,986	32,490
Operations	417,567	538,194	417,469
Flood Control	–	–	90,969
Building maintenance	84,646	94,780	107,240
Disaster relief	330,749	–	–
Airport	–	–	8,600
Total Public Facilities	1,176,944	1,031,481	1,330,197
Parks and recreation:			
Administration	36,557	42,551	47,317
Park maintenance	235,987	263,023	404,825
Recreation	125,481	151,581	186,871
Swimming pools	45,459	48,274	57,526
Reservoir	29,383	29,203	34,572
Concessions	8,698	11,950	12,552
Reservoir concessions	–	–	31,909
Total Parks and Recreation	481,565	546,582	775,572
Health and welfare:			
Human relations	–	–	15,449
Health	51,804	59,216	64,640
Animal control	24,029	38,123	39,886
Ambulance	1,999	2,600	2,600
Hospital	30,000	30,000	30,000
Noise abatement	–	–	14,818
Total Health and Welfare	107,832	129,939	167,393
Contingency:	25,794	51,864	73,000
Adjustments:	18,066	–	–
Total General Operating Fund	$3,829,146	$4,091,643	$5,088,118
OPEN SPACE AND MAJOR THOROUGHFARE FUND			
Open space	455,244	557,700	976,760
Major thoroughfares	746,126	749,600	1,300,000
Total Open Space and Major Thoroughfare Fund	1,201,370	1,307,300	2,276,760
PUBLIC IMPROVEMENT FUND	373,570	275,000	769,500
LIBRARY FUND			
Library operations	207,305	241,105	281,158
Gifts and grants	52,482	60,000	60,000
Total Library Fund	259,787	301,105	341,158
PERMANENT PARKS AND RECREATION FUND			
Projects from .9 mill	104,916	105,000	116,250
Gifts, grants, and fees	19,727	80,335	110,748
Total Permanent Parks and Recreation Fund	124,643	185,335	226,998
GENERAL OBLIGATION DEBT RETIREMENT FUND	98,761	96,514	96,358
TOTAL GENERAL GOVERNMENT FUNDS	$5,887,277	$6,256,897	$8,798,892

3. The administrative establishment within the executive branch which initiates, formulates, seeks approval of, and supervises the execution of the budget.
4. The legislative element which determines the rules within which administrative aspirations and performance are to be carried out.
5. Relationships which exist between two or more local governments which exercise overlapping, concurrent, or related interest in resources and activities; also, inducements and restraints imposed by higher levels of government to affect the scope and level of performance of functions of local governments.
6. The productive capacity of the community as modified by the extent to which this capacity may reasonably be expected to be diverted to the public sector.
7. The broad social fabric of the community which is both a basis upon which the government rests and which the government serves and from time to time modifies.
8. The historic record of inertial and dynamic forces which have brought the community and its public programs and problems to their contemporary status.
9. The forward reach to prepare operating plans for the foreseeable future and to plan the levels of revenues and expenditures needed to make the operating plans a reality.

The factors itemized above are basic. They illustrate that the budget of a governmental unit is the product of economic, political, legal, and social factors external to the unit itself, as well as internal managerial and political factors of the unit and the economic resources of the population and area within the unit. Comparable considerations exist for business enterprises. A profit-seeking business will succeed in the long run only if it serves the needs of its customers and of society in general: the financial managers of a business must budget within this framework. In business budgeting revenues and expenses of any year are interrelated; expenses are incurred in the effort to produce revenue, and the production of revenue enables the further incurring of expenses and the further production of revenue. Revenue and expense are interdependent variables in business budgeting.

Business budgeting concepts are appropriate for governmental activities run on a business basis. A similar interrelationship may be said to exist at the Federal government level in the cases of certain General Fund expenditures which are made in order to stimulate segments of the economy; the costs of increasing economic activity tend to be recouped by increased tax revenue. At the municipal level, however, except for utilities or other business enterprises, revenue and expenditure are not interdependent variables. Expenditures are made in order to render a service to the citizens, and not in order to generate revenue. Similarly, although municipal revenues may vary from month to month, the variation of revenue has little direct effect upon the incurring of expenditures.

Budgeting Municipal Expenditures

Expenditure budgets are an administration's requests for appropriations. In practice, the preparation of municipal expenditure budgets for any one year is dependent upon the administration's budget of revenues since the revenue budget is the plan of financing the proposed expenditures. If the program, or performance, budget concept is followed, expenditure budgets are prepared for each existing and continuing work program or activity of each governmental subdivision; for each program authorized or required by action of past legislative bodies, but which has not yet been made operative; and for each new program the administration intends to submit to the legislative body for approval.

In business budgeting each ongoing program should be subjected to rigorous management scrutiny at budget preparation time to make sure that there is a valid reason for continuing the program at all. If the program should be continued, then the management must decide whether the prior allocation of resources to the program is optimal, or whether changes should be made in the assignment of personnel, equipment, space, and funds. In a well-managed governmental unit the same sort of review is given to each continuing program. The mere fact that the program was authorized by a past legislative body does not mean that the administration may shirk its duty to recommend discontinuance of a program that has ceased to serve a real need. If the program should be continued, in the judgment of the administration, the appropriate level of activity and the appropriate allocation of resources must be determined; this determination takes far more political courage and management skill than the common practice of simply extrapolating the trend of historical activity and historical cost.

If the administration is convinced that a program should be continued, and that the prior allocation of resources is relatively appropriate, the preparation of the expenditure budget is delegated to the persons who are in charge of the program. In the case of a new program the administration states the objectives of the program and sets general guidelines for the operation of the program, then delegates budget preparation to individuals who are expected to be in charge of the program when legislative authorization and appropriations are secured. In order to provide a means of ensuring that administrative policies are actually used in budget preparation and that the budget calendar and other legal requirements are met, it is customary to designate someone in the central administrative office, often the municipal finance officer, as budget officer. In addition to the responsibilities enumerated, the budget officer is responsible for providing technical assistance to the operating personnel who prepare the budgets. The technical assistance provided may include clerical assistance with budget computations as well as the maintenance of files for each program containing: (1) documents citing the legal authorization and directives, (2) relevant administrative policies, (3) historical cost and work load data, (4) specific factors affecting program costs and work loads, and (5) sources of information to be used in projecting trends.

Budgets prepared by departmental administrators should be reviewed by the central administration before submission to the municipal legislative branch because the total of departmental requests frequently exceeds the total of estimated revenues, and it is necessary to trim the requests in some manner. Central review may also be necessary to make sure enough is being spent on certain programs. Good financial management of the taxpayers' dollars is a process of trying to determine the optimum dollar input to achieve the desired service output, not a process of minimizing input. Even though the expenditures budget is a legally prescribed document, the municipal administration should not lose sight of its managerial usefulness.

Budgeting Capital Expenditures

One feature of Illustration 2–3 to which the reader's attention has not been previously directed is the "Capital Outlay" line. Accounting principles for business enterprises require that the cost of assets which are expected to benefit more than one period be treated as a balance sheet item, rather than as a charge against revenues of the period. No such distinction exists in the pronouncements of the National Committee on Governmental Accounting, except for business operations of a governmental unit. As Illustration 2–3 indicates, expenditures for long-lived assets to be used in the general operations of a municipality are treated in the appropriations process in the same manner as are expenditures for salaries, wages, benefits, materials, supplies, and services to be consumed during the accounting period. Accounting control over long-lived assets used in general operations is established, however, as described in Chapter 12 of this text.

In Illustration 2–3 the "Capital Outlay" item consists of equipment, as described in the Budget Comments section. Proposed major construction or acquisition projects are included in the Public Improvements Fund budget for legislative approval.

Effective financial management requires that the plans for any one year be consistent with intermediate and long-range plans. Municipal programs, such as the construction or improvement of streets; construction of bridges and buildings; acquisition of land for recreational use, parking lots, and future building sites; and urban renewal all may require a consistent application of effort over a span of years. Consequently, municipal administrators need to present to the legislative branch and to the public a capital improvements program, as well as revenue and expenditure budgets. Illustration 2–5 shows one such presentation which combines the projection of recommended improvements for five years beyond the forthcoming budget year with the proposed means of financing them.

Budgeting Municipal Revenues

Although municipal revenues and expenditures are not interdependent variables as business revenues and expenses are, the availability of revenue is a necessary prerequisite to the incurring of expenditures. In some jurisdictions municipalities may operate at a deficit temporarily, but it is generally conceded that they may not do so indefinitely. Thus, wise financial management calls for the preparation of revenue budgets, at least in rough form, prior to the preparation of detailed operating plans and expenditure budgets.

"Revenue" is a term which has a precise meaning in governmental accounting. The National Committee on Governmental Accounting states that revenue arises from additions to assets which: (1) do not increase any liability; (2) do not represent the recovery of an expenditure; (3) do not represent the cancellation of certain liabilities without a corresponding increase in other liabilities or a decrease in assets; and (4) do not represent contributions of fund capital in Enterprise and Intragovernmental Service funds. In short, in business accounting terminology, revenue arises from transactions that increase net assets. Sources of revenue available to a given municipality are generally closely controlled by state law; state laws also establish procedures for the utilization of available sources, and may impose ceilings on the amount of revenue that a municipality may collect from certain sources. Sources generally available for financing the routine operations of a municipal government include: property taxes, sales taxes, income taxes, license fees, fines, charges for services, grants or allocations from other governmental units, and revenue from the use of municipal money or property. Chapter 4 of this text describes revenue sources and discusses revenue accounting in some detail. The present discussion is, therefore, limited to the broad aspects of municipal revenue budgeting.

Within the framework set by legal requirements, and subject to the approval of the legislative body (which, in turn, reacts to the electorate), the determination of revenue policy is a prerogative of the administration. Major considerations underlying the policy formulation are set forth in the preceding section of this chapter. After policies are established, the technical preparation of the revenue budget is ordinarily delegated to the municipal finance officer. In order to facilitate budget preparation, experienced finance officers generally keep for each revenue

Illustration 2–5

Capital Improvements Program
Fiscal Years 1971 through 1976
Highway and Street Improvements

Priority	*Project*	*S.F.**	*FY71*	*FY72*	*FY73*	*FY74*	*FY75*	*FY76*	*Total 6 Years*
1	Haw Ridge Park, Access Road, etc.	11	8,700	25,000	11,500	5,740	–	–	50,940
2	Streets, Industrial Park	11	6,600	18,600	12,000	–	–	–	37,200
3	Improve Robertsville–Bermuda Road and Others	4, 11	140,000	50,000	50,000	100,000	100,000	–	440,000
4	Repave Non-Curb and Gutter Streets	11	27,380	23,420	–	–	–	–	50,800
5	Sidewalk Robertsville and Bermuda Road	11	25,000	–	–	–	–	–	25,000
6	Repave Emory Valley Rd., Fairbanks to Melton Lake Drive	11	25,000	25,000	–	–	–	–	50,000
7	Sidewalk, Tulsa Road, Illinois to Tuskegee	11	–	7,500	–	–	–	–	7,500
8	Sidewalk, Tuskegee Drive, Benedict to Tulsa Road	11	–	3,000	–	–	–	–	3,000
9	Emory Valley Bicycle Path	11	–	12,000	–	–	–	–	12,000
10	South Tulane Extension and Sidewalk	2a	–	–	88,000	–	–	–	88,000
11	Repave Improved Residential Streets	11	–	25,600	18,880	–	–	–	44,480
12	Marina Parking Lot	11	–	7,500	–	–	–	–	7,500
13	Road Extension to Parcel 567 from Wiltshire Drive	11	–	–	27,000	–	–	–	27,000
14	Civic Center, Stage III, Access Road to Municipal Building	11	–	–	–	23,480	–	–	23,480
15	Fairbanks Road Extension	2a	–	–	–	–	100,300	–	100,300
16	Tuskegee Drive Extension Across City-owned Parcel 405	11	–	–	–	–	–	26,700	26,700
	Total		232,680	197,620	207,380	129,220	200,300	26,700	993,900
	**Source of Funds*								
	State Street Aid	11	209,690	197,620	119,380	129,220	100,000	26,700	782,610
	General Obligation Bonds	2a	–	–	88,000	–	100,300	–	188,300
	Property Owners' Assessment	4	22,990	–	–	–	–	–	22,990
	Total Funds		232,680	197,620	207,380	129,220	200,300	26,700	993,900

A major reallocation of State Street Aid funds resulted from the decision to improve Robertsville and Bermuda Roads, together with a sidewalk, primarily to serve the West Village area and the new Linden School. A part of the funds for constructing an access road into Haw Ridge Park was reallocated to begin the repaving of Emory Valley Road in FY 1971, recognizing that title to the proposed park area has not yet been transferred from TVA. Funds for construction of Industrial Park roads and for repaving other streets were also retained in FY 1971.

For later years, additional repaving and improvement of residential streets, Industrial Park development, and sidewalk construction in the central portion of the city have been programmed.

Several projects along the Oak Ridge Turnpike that are the responsibility of the State Highway Department are no longer listed; these include lowering the vertical curve at the Minit Check, and replacement of two wooden bridges at Jefferson Avenue and the Eagles Lodge.

Actual construction of a bridge and roadway extending South Tulane from Illinois Avenue to Tuskegee Drive at Tulsa has been deferred several years. Access to the lands south of Wiltshire Drive has similarly been deferred, plans for the subdivision and development of this area having been set aside for the present.

source a file containing (1) a copy of legislation authorizing the source, and any subsequent legislation pertaining to the source, (2) historical experience of the municipality relative to collections from the source, including collections as a percentage of billings, where applicable, (3) relevant administrative policies, and (4) specific factors which affect the yield from the source, including, for each factor, the historical relationship of the factor to revenue procedures to be used in projecting the trend of factors affecting yield, and factors affecting collections. Graphic presentations of these factors are also frequently included in the file.[4]

Illustration 2–6 presents a summary general fund revenue budget for the municipality whose appropriations budgets are presented in Illustrations 2–1 through 2–4. The sources of revenue shown in the illustration are typical of many municipalities. Presentation of data comparing estimates for the budget year with the budget for the current year, and the actual revenues of the immediately prior year, is also typical. If estimates differ markedly from current and recent experience, explanations are sometimes made a part of the budget presentation by footnote, sometimes by supplementary schedules, and other times are omitted from the formal presentation with the thought that the explanations may be given orally, if called for.

Property Taxes as a Revenue Source

Although a number of arguments have been raised in recent years against reliance by local governments on property taxes, very few municipalities have eliminated them entirely and many still rely on property taxes as a major source of revenue. State governments commonly place a ceiling on the rate at which a municipality may tax property, specify the kinds of property which may be taxed, and prescribe the method of determining the assessed valuation of taxable property.

For purposes of taxation, property is frequently divided into four different classes, as follows:

1. Real estate, including land and buildings, except that owned by investor-owned utilities.
2. Tangible personal property, including household goods, automobiles, machinery, equipment, inventories, livestock, etc., except such items as are owned by investor-owned utilities.

---

[4] Moak and Killian report the results of a survey of 17 cities in the United States and Canada as to practices in revenue program formulation; see Chapter 17 especially. Finance officers of large governmental units may use more sophisticated statistical and econometric methods of revenue forecasting, particularly to evaluate alternative assumptions, but the method described here is considered the most realistic to use for preparation of a legal revenue budget.

Illustration 2–6

SUMMARY GENERAL FUND REVENUE BUDGET
General Government Funds Revenues, Gifts, and Grants

General Operating Fund	*1972 Actual*	*1973 Budget*	*1974 Proposed*
Fund balance–beginning of year	$ 784,446	$ 778,960	$ 277,519
Taxes:			
Property taxes	601,369	642,700	746,968
Less property tax deferral	–	–	(40,000)
Franchise taxes:			
Gas and electric	161,879	210,000	274,000
Telephone and telegraph	108,682	115,000	170,000
Television cable	1,400	2,000	2,500
Contribution in lieu of taxes:			
Water utility	118,600	128,000	128,000
Sewer utility	19,500	25,600	25,600
Cigarette taxes	128,232	150,000	170,000
Sales and use tax	1,858,474	2,050,000	2,521,314
Public accomodations and admissions tax	–	–	187,500
Total Taxes	2,998,136	3,323,300	4,185,882
Licenses and fees:			
Bicycle licenses	590	600	600
Alcoholic beverage fees	27,304	30,900	35,000
Health department licenses	10,238	7,000	8,000
Police and protective licenses	1,612	1,600	1,600
Amusement licenses	835	900	900
Merchandising licenses	785	800	800
Occupational licenses	5,004	5,000	5,000
Dog licenses	15,288	15,500	32,500
Total Licenses	61,656	62,300	84,400
Parking meter fees	13,179	13,000	13,000
Court fines and costs	129,469	120,000	156,500
Revenues from use of money and property	155,745	120,000	120,000
Revenues from other agencies:			
Highway users tax–State	238,356	284,000	317,000
Auto registration–$1.50 special	55,472	62,000	68,000
Auto registration–$2.50 special fee, State	–	–	102,000
Road & bridge fund–County	–	–	245,000
Specific ownership tax–County	65,025	74,000	80,000
Highway aid–State	14,140	14,000	14,000
Civil defense–Federal	12,425	13,700	16,300
Civil defense–County	6,718	7,000	8,000
Dog control–County	3,120	3,000	3,000
Disaster grant–Federal	364,872	–	–
Total Other Agencies	760,128	457,700	853,300
Revenue from parks and recreation:			
Boulder reservoir	22,355	24,000	26,000
Swimming pools	36,553	39,990	46,660
Athletics	29,918	41,465	51,057
Crafts	18,290	18,823	22,971
Social activities	14,235	14,082	20,976
Concessions	10,732	13,800	14,800
Boulder reservoir concessions	–	–	22,200
Miscellaneous revenue	883	–	–
Total Revenue from Parks and Recreation	132,966	152,160	204,664
Other revenues:			
Annexation fees	417	3,500	3,500
Sale of city property	4,671	4,000	4,000
Building inspection revenues	64,348	75,000	80,000
Street department revenues	12,101	13,000	13,000
Engineering department revenues	6,516	6,000	6,000
Miscellaneous receipts and services	16,148	10,000	10,000
Airport revenues	–	–	10,500
Total Other Revenues	104,201	111,500	127,000
General Operating Fund Revenue	4,355,480	4,359,960	5,744,746
Less: Appropriations to other general government funds	(531,820)	(400,209)	(925,838)
Total General Operating Fund Revenue	3,823,660	3,959,751	4,818,908
Amount Available	$4,608,106	$4,738,711	$5,096,427

3. Intangible property such as securities, notes and accounts receivable, bank deposits, etc.
4. Property of investor-owned utilities.

From an accounting standpoint, classification of taxable property is significant for three reasons:

1. The mechanics of inventory and valuation—that is, assessment—of property may vary according to its classification.
2. The rate of taxation may vary according to the class of property represented, for example, tangible or intangible.
3. The methods of levying and collecting taxes are likely to vary with the classification of property.

Although classification, assessment, fixing of rates, spreading (recording) the levy, and collection of taxes seem to be outside the field of accounting, municipal finance officers and accountants should possess a clear understanding of the basic procedures underlying the budgeting, collection, and expenditures of taxes for which they must do the accounting.

Assessment of Property

Methods to be used in the assessment of taxable property tend to vary with the class of property. For example, the following practices are used in one state:

1. Land and buildings, except that owned by utilities, is subject to a general reassessment every four years or upon order of the state board of tax commissioners or the state general assembly. Reassessment is conducted more or less by schedule and formula, presumably based on actual cash value. Improvements added or removed between general assessments are reported to and recorded by local assessors. Land and building assessment values are filed in the county auditor's office.

2. Tangible personal property of specified kinds is assessed annually. Household goods are exempt from taxation and mobile homes are assessed according to a special plan. Individual taxpayers report their taxable tangible property on forms prescribed by a state agency. Assessment sheets originated by property owners are systematically arranged and filed in the county assessor's office, where they are open to public inspection. The valuation of tangible personal property for taxation is legally supposed to be one-third of actual cash value.

3. Taxation of intangible personal property is based upon self-assessment by the property owner. Each property owner lists his taxable intangibles on his state income tax return and shows their value at the end of the year for which taxes are payable. The total value arrived at is subject to taxation at the rate of 0.25 percent of value.

4. Property of investor-owned utilities is assessed by the state board of tax commissioners. The state board reports to each county assessor the final valuations for utilities in his county.

Taxation of real estate and most tangible personal property is as of a certain date each year. Whoever owns those classes of property on that day—March 1 in the state used as an example above—is the owner of record for tax purposes. (Incidence of taxes on intangibles and at least one kind of tangible property—mobile homes—is based upon detailed provisions of special laws applying to them.)

Determining Property Tax Revenue

Two widely different procedures of determining property tax revenue are commonly encountered in practice: (1) the municipality simply multiplies the assessed valuation of property in its jurisdiction by a flat rate—either the maximum rate allowable under state law or a rate determined by local policy or law—or (2) the property tax is treated as a residual source of revenue as shown in Illustration 2–7.

Illustration 2–7

CITY OF VANDALIA
Statement of Amount to Be Raised by Property Taxes for 1975
July 31, 1974

Requirements:		
Estimated expenditures, August 1–December 31, 1974		$1,401,000
Proposed appropriation for 1975		2,822,000
Estimated working balance required for beginning of 1976		173,000
Estimated total requirements		$4,396,000
Resources other than tax levy for 1975:		
Actual balance, July 31, 1974	$ 218,000	
Amount to be received from second installment of 1974 taxes	811,000	
Miscellaneous receipts expected during balance of 1974	652,000	
Revenue expected from sources other than property taxes during 1975	1,136,000	
Estimated total resources other than property tax levy		2,817,000
Amount required from property taxes in 1975		$1,579,000

In order for the municipality to raise a given amount from property taxes ($1,579,000 in Illustration 2–7), it must determine the tax rate which, when applied to the assessed valuation of property within its jurisdiction, will yield the desired amount. Although this procedure sounds simple, there are at least two complicating factors of concern to a municipal finance officer: the fact that not all taxes levied for a certain year will be actually collected during that year, and the fact that various classes of property may be totally exempt from local property tax and other classes may be partially exempt. For example, property acquired by governmental units prior to the assessment date is excluded from total assessed valuation but government property acquired since the assessment date and property owned by religious, charitable, and fraternal organizations and used for non-business purposes may be included in the assessment but exempt from taxation. Partial exemptions commonly found include:

1. Homestead Exemptions. Under this form of relief a home owner is granted an exemption of a given amount which is applied against the assessed valuation of his home, the excess of the latter over the former being the net assessed valuation subject to taxes.

2. Mortgage Exemptions. This form of exemption is intended to give some tax relief to property owners paying interest on indebtedness against the property being taxed. In one state with a mortgage exemption law, a given owner of real estate is entitled to one mortgage exemption of $1,000, or one-half the assessed valuation of property, whichever is less. Although applicable to all kinds of real estate, the exemption was intended to provide a limited measure of homestead relief.

3. Military Service Exemptions. The terms of this form of exemption are variable. The factors determining eligibility and the amount of relief available may be the period of service, the degree of disability, and the nature of the property owned.

4. Blind Person Exemptions. The nature of this form of exemption is manifest from the title, but legal eligibility of a given person may depend upon the nature of the property owned and the general economic status of the individual.

5. Exemption Based on Age and Economic Status. This form of exemption is based upon the relationship of three variables: age, assessed value of taxable property owned, and annual income as defined by the applicable law.

To illustrate the effect of exemptions on the property tax rate of a municipality, assume that the following is true for the City of Vandalia:

Total property subject to taxes		$121,230,110*
Exemptions:		
Mortgage	$6,979,360	
Veterans	1,054,700	
Old age	711,415	
Religious, charitable, and similar organizations	3,826,750	
Total exemptions		12,572,225
Net assessed valuation		$108,657,885

*** This figure excludes possibly $200,000,000 or more of property serviced by the county, city and township governments. This is mostly state-owned property but includes property owned by the Federal government, labor unions, lodges, veterans' organizations, fraternities, sororities, local schools, etc.**

Assume further that historical data and economic forecasts for the City indicate that only 96 percent of the 1975 levy will be collected in 1975. Thus, if the net levy is to be $1,579,000 (per Illustration 2–7), the gross levy must be $1,579,000 ÷ .96, or $1,644,792. The tax rate must be, therefore, the gross levy of $1,644,792 divided by the net assessed valuation of $108,657,885, or .015137. In some areas the rate may be expressed in terms of "mills" or thousandths of a dollar; in others, in terms of dollars and cents per hundred dollars of assessed valuation; and in still others, in terms of dollars and cents per thousand dollars of assessed valuation. Thus the rate for property taxes payable in 1975 for the City of Vandalia may be said to be 15.14 mills per dollar, $1.52 per $100, or $15.14 per $1,000—rounding in each case to two places to the right of the decimal, as is customary.[5]

Property located in a city or town is also, in most states, located within a township, an independent school district, various special districts, and a county—all of which also levy taxes on the property within their boundaries. In many states a single bill is sent to the owner of each parcel of property for the total of all the property taxes levied against the parcel. Illustration 2–8 shows the composition of the total tax rate for taxable property located in Monroe County, Indiana.

Intergovernmental Revenue

There is some tendency to think that the most important source of intergovernmental revenue must be payments each municipality receives from the Federal government under the State and Local Fiscal Assistance Act of 1972—commonly called "general revenue sharing." Federal payments under that act totaled $5.3 billion for the first year, however, compared with $12.3 billion provided for that year under other Federal legislation for transfer to state and local governments as "special revenue sharing" for purposes such as crime reduction, education, manpower training, transportation, and urban and rural community development. Other types of direct assistance by the Federal government are grants-in-aid for specific programs, such as urban renewal, community affairs, and community planning; and loans.

Municipalities receive significant amounts of revenue from state governments also. Often the payments from the states are the municipality's statutory share of taxes levied and collected by the state such as gasoline taxes, motor vehicle excise taxes and license fees, and alcoholic beverage taxes. Additionally municipalities receive payments from state governments under state appropriations of general revenues.

For each source of intergovernmental revenue a given municipality expects to receive there are problems in foreseeing with reasonable ac-

[5] Note that if exemptions had not been allowed, the tax rates would have been determined by dividing the gross levy by the total assessed valuation, $121,230,110, so that the rate would have been 13.57 mills, $1.36 per $100, or $13.57 per $1,000. The effect of allowing exemptions from property taxes to favored classes of property owners simply shifts the burden to property owners not in favored classes.

Illustration 2–8
Composition of Total Property Tax Rate
Monroe County, Indiana

LEGAL NOTICE **LEGAL NOTICE** **LEGAL NOTICE** **LEGAL NOTICE** **LEGAL NOTICE**

NOTICE TO TAXPAYERS OF MONROE COUNTY OF TAX LEVIES AND RATES

Notice is hereby given that the Tax Duplicates for the several taxing units in Monroe County for the year 1972 payable in 1973 are now in the hands of the County Treasurer who is ready to receive the taxes charged thereon. The following table shows the tax levies and rates on each one hundred dollars ($100) of net assessed valuation of taxable real estate and personal property in each taxing unit.

Due January 1, 1973—First installment delinquent after the 10th day in May—Second Installment delinquent after the 10th day in November.

LOUISE L. GOODMAN, Monroe County Treasurer

TAX RATES CHARGED FOR YEAR 1972 PAYABLE IN THE YEAR 1973		TOWNSHIPS											CITIES AND TOWNS					
	NAME OF FUND	BEAN BLOSSOM	BENTON	BLOOMINGTON	CLEAR CREEK	INDIAN CREEK	PERRY	POLK	RICHLAND	SALT CREEK	VAN BUREN	WASHINGTON	BLOOMINGTON-BLGTN. CITY	BLOOMINGTON-PERRY CITY	VAN-BUREN CITY	RICHLAND CITY	ELLETTSVILLE	STINESVILLE
STATE RATES	State Fair Board	.0035	.0035	.0035	.0035	.0035	.0035	.0035	.0035	.0035	.0035	.0035	.0035	.0035	.0035	.0035	.0035	.0035
	State Forestry	.0065	.0065	.0065	.0065	.0065	.0065	.0065	.0065	.0065	.0065	.0065	.0065	.0065	.0065	.0065	.0065	.0065
	TOTAL STATE	.01	.01	.01	.01	.01	.01	.01	.01	.01	.01	.01	.01	.01	.01	.01	.01	.01
COUNTY RATES	County General	.75	.75	.75	.75	.75	.75	.75	.75	.75	.75	.75	.75	.75	.75	.75	.75	.75
	County Welfare	.19	.19	.19	.19	.19	.19	.19	.19	.19	.19	.19	.19	.19	.19	.19	.19	.19
	County Health Dept.	.03	.03	.03	.03	.03	.03	.03	.03	.03	.03	.03	.03	.03	.03	.03	.03	.03
	Aviation	.02	.02	.02	.02	.02	.02	.02	.02	.02	.02	.02	.02	.02	.02	.02	.02	.02
	Aviation Bond Fund	.08	.08	.08	.08	.08	.08	.08	.08	.08	.08	.08	.08	.08	.08	.08	.08	.08
	Courthouse Annex Bond	.005	.005	.005	.005	.005	.005	.005	.005	.005	.005	.005	.005	.005	.005	.005	.005	.005
	Cumulative Courthouse	.02	.02	.02	.02	.02	.02	.02	.02	.02	.02	.02	.02	.02	.02	.02	.02	.02
	Cumulative Bridge	.10	.10	.10	.10	.10	.10	.10	.10	.10	.10	.10	.10	.10	.10	.10	.10	.10
	Re-Assessment	.055	.055	.055	.055	.055	.055	.055	.055	.055	.055	.055	.055	.055	.055	.055	.055	.055
	County Fair	.01	.01	.01	.01	.01	.01	.01	.01	.01	.01	.01	.01	.01	.01	.01	.01	.01
	TOTAL COUNTY	1.26	1.26	1.26	1.26	1.26	1.26	1.26	1.26	1.26	1.26	1.26	1.26	1.26	1.26	1.26	1.26	1.26
LIBRARY RATES	County Library	.25	.25	.25	.25	.25	.25	.25	.25	.25	.25	.25	.25	.25	.25	.25	.25	.25
	Library Bond	.10	.10	.10	.10	.10	.10	.10	.10	.10	.10	.10	.10	.10	.10	.10	.10	.10
	TOTAL LIBRARY	.35	.35	.35	.35	.35	.35	.35	.35	.35	.35	.35	.35	.35	.35	.35	.35	.35
CIVIL TOWNSHIP RATES	Township	.10	.09	.03	.07	.12	—	.54	—	.18	.04	.05	.03	—	.04	—	—	.10
	Poor Relief	—	.02	.06	.05	.05	.01	.20	.02	.10	.04	.08	.06	.01	.04	.02	.02	—
	Fire Protection	.11	.27	.30	.20	—	.34	—	.20	.20	.35	—	—	—	—	—	—	—
	Civil Township Bond			.11														
	TOTAL TOWNSHIP	.21	.38	.50	.32	.17	.35	.74	.22	.48	.43	.13	.09	.01	.08	.02	.02	.10
SCHOOL RATES	General Fund (School)	4.26	4.60	4.60	4.60	4.60	4.60	4.60	4.26	4.60	4.60	4.60	4.60	4.60	4.60	4.26	4.26	4.26
	Debt Service Fund	1.04	.82	.82	.82	.82	.82	.82	1.04	.82	.82	.82	.82	.82	.82	1.04	1.04	1.04
	Cumulative Building	—	.43	.43	.43	.43	.43	.43	—	.43	.43	.43	.43	.43	.43	—	—	—
	TOTAL SCHOOL	5.30	5.85	5.85	5.85	5.85	5.85	5.85	5.30	5.85	5.85	5.85	5.85	5.85	5.85	5.30	5.30	5.30
CORPORATION RATES	Corporation												3.015	3.015	3.015	3.015	1.10	2.00
	Street												—	—	—		1.24	—
	Park & Recreation												.42	.42	.42	.42	.08	—
	Cemetery												—	—	—	—	—	—
	Police Pension												.192	.192	.192	.192	—	—
	Firemen's Pension												.108	.108	.108	.108	—	—
	Corporation Bond												.075	.075	.075	.075	—	—
	Cumulative Bldg. & Equip.												—	—	—		.10	—
	Park Dist. Bond												.05	.05	.05	.05	—	—
	TOTAL CORPORATION RATES												3.86	3.86	3.86	3.86	2.52	2.00
TOTAL PROPERTY TAX RATES	**TOTAL RATES**	7.13	7.85	7.97	7.79	7.64	7.82	8.21	7.14	7.95	7.90	7.60	11.42	11.34	11.41	10.80	9.46	9.02

State of Indiana, Monroe County, SS: I, John Davis, Auditor of Monroe County, hereby certify that the above is a correct copy of all tax levies and rates of taxes collectible in Monroe County in the year 1973.
Signed: JOHN W. DAVIS, Auditor, Monroe County, Indiana

28—7—14

curacy the amount which should be included in the annual revenue budget, because the municipality can control neither the basis of the distribution nor the timing of the distribution by the state or Federal agency. Generally, however, the distributing agencies provide information to municipalities as to probable amounts of distributions from continuing sources during a budget period. Similarly, a municipality can usually determine from the appropriate state or Federal agency whether grants for which the municipality has applied are likely to be approved (and the extent to which payments are likely to be made on approved grants).

Grants for specific programs may give rise to municipal general fund revenue if the terms of the grant do not require the creation of a special revenue fund, capital projects fund, or trust fund. Federal general revenue sharing payments must be accounted for in a separate fund according to the language of the Federal statute. The State and Local Fiscal Assistance Act requires that both the planned use of the general revenue sharing payments (the budget) and a statement of actual expenditures be published by the local government in a newspaper of general circulation within the geographic area; both the budget and the statement of expenditures must also be submitted to the Secretary of the Treasury. State taxes which are shared with municipalities are also frequently subject to special budgeting, accounting, and reporting restrictions.

The Budget Calendar

The date by which the budget must be submitted by the municipal administration to the legislative body is set by law in many states. Customarily, state statutes also establish the fiscal year for municipalities within the state, require publication of the proposed budget a certain number of times by certain dates, and set a date for adoption of the budget by the legislative body. A procedure for changing elements of the budget after it has been legally adopted is also usually provided by the statute.

In order to provide an orderly procedure within the administrative offices for preparation and review of the budget before submission to the legislative body a more complete timetable, or calendar, needs to be established than that set by statute. As a guide, a manual published by the Municipal Finance Officers Association suggests the following time allotments for medium-sized and large cities for major phases in the budget process:

For preparation of departmental estimates	30 days
For central budget agency and executive review and action	45 days
For preparation of budget document	20 days
For legislative and public consideration	60 days
For executive approval, veto, and preparation for budget execution	30 days
Total elapsed time from the distribution of budget request forms to the beginning of the fiscal year	185 days[6]

For smaller municipalities, the manual suggests, the time margins may be trimmed by 20 to 25 days; but reported experience indicates that any total allocation of less than 160 days is likely to prove unsatisfactory.

Budget Administration

Acceptance and adoption of the budget is evidenced by the signing of the certificate of validation by members or representatives of the legislative body and by the chief executive or a representative of the executive department. However, the budget may not yet have the force of law.

[6] Moak and Killian, p. 67.

For example, in one state, budgets of each local unit must be explained and justified by a representative of the unit before a county tax adjustment board in a duly advertised public hearing during which interested taxpayers may state objections to or support for the detail of each budget. The county tax adjustment board is empowered to reduce but not to increase appropriations. After action by the county tax adjustment board, the budgets must be submitted to the state tax board which, after a hearing, may increase, decrease, or approve the budget without change. Thereupon, the budget becomes legally binding during the year to come.

After final certification of a budget, legal advertisement must be made of tax levies for the coming year (Illustration 2–8) and tax bills are prepared for each parcel of real property and for each owner of taxable personal property, in order that tenders of payments may be accepted without delay. If revenue collections normally lag in each year, arrangements for short-term financing may be necessary; if so, arrangements as required by law should be made in advance.

On the expenditure side of the budget, it may be desired to regulate the use of appropriations so that only specified amounts may be used from month to month or from quarter to quarter. The purpose of such control is to prevent expenditure of all or most of the authorized amount early in the year, without providing reserves for unexpected requirements arising later in the year. A common device for regulating expenditures is the use of allotments. An allotment may be described as an internal allocation of funds on a periodic basis usually agreed upon by the department and the chief executive or his representative. While variable in form, allotment schedules are essentially period allocations of the amount appropriated for specific purposes.

Recording the Budget

Numerous details of accounting for transactions closely related to the budget are set forth in subsequent chapters, particularly those on general fund revenues and expenditures and general fund operations; general journal entries to record adoption of the budget are illustrated in this chapter. Two basic requirements must be accomplished by the accounting entry or entries recording the budget's provisions:

1. The total amount of expenditures authorized by the legislative body must be recorded by a credit to Appropriations.

2. The resources provided or contemplated by the legislative body for financing the authorized expenditures must be recorded by a debit to Estimated Revenues.

Estimated Revenues and Appropriations are controlling accounts; each is supported by subsidiary ledger detail, as described in Chapters 4 and 5. At the time that Estimated Revenues is debited to recognize the addition to the resources of the municipality, an offsetting credit may be made to Fund Balance, an account which serves the function of the net worth accounts in accounting for profit-seeking entities. Thus if a revenue budget totaling $3,706,000 for the general fund of a municipality is adopted by the legislative body, the following general journal entry might be made to enable proper recording of the facts in general ledger and subsidiary ledger accounts.

Estimated Revenues	$3,706,000	
Fund Balance		$3,706,000
To record the revenue budget approved for the year 1975:		

Revenue ledger:	Debit
Taxes:	
Taxes on property	$ 931,250
Sales taxes	860,000
Licenses and permits:	
Building and trade permits	$ 225,000
Business licenses	35,000
Intergovernmental revenues	1,654,750

Similarly, at the time that Appropriations is credited to recognize the allocation of municipal resources by the legislative process, Fund Balance should be debited. Assuming the municipal general fund appropriations enacted by the legislative branch totaled $3,680,000, the following entry might be made to enable proper recording of the facts in the general ledger and subsidiary ledger accounts.

Fund Balance	$3,680,000	
Appropriations		$3,680,000
To record the expenditure budget approved for the year 1975:		

Appropriations expenditures ledger:	Credit
General government:	
Council	$ 44,319
Various others (itemized)	205,000
Public safety:	
Police Department:	
Supervision	119,443
Various others (itemized)	1,119,310
Fire Department:	
Supervision	55,830
Various others (itemized)	751,203
Various others (itemized)	1,384,895

It would, of course, be perfectly satisfactory to prepare a combined entry to record Estimated Revenues and Appropriations and the net effect upon Fund Balance; this is often done in practice.

Budget Control Reports and Budget Amendments

During a fiscal year the collections of revenues need to be compared periodically with the budgeted collections in order to evaluate both actual performance and budgeting techniques. Similarly, the actual expenditures need to be compared with the appropriations to facilitate financial management and control over operations, and because the administration is subject to legal penalties for overspending appropriations. Illustration 2–9 shows a useful form of periodic control report.

Budget control reports may disclose circumstances that make it desirable to amend a budget during the period it covers. Reduction of amounts originally appropriated may be necessary because of revenue curtailment. Generally, the procedure for budget amendment is specified by law. Assuming legally required procedures have been followed, the entry to reflect a change in both Estimated Revenues and Appropriations would be as follows, using an assumed amount:

Appropriations	24,000	
Estimated Revenues		24,000

Subsidiary ledger debits and credits would need to be made in order to support each of the above controlling accounts. Any difference between the two kinds of reductions would require a debit or credit to Fund Balance.

Appropriations may need to be increased to cover requirements unforeseen when the budget was enacted or to authorize additional expenditures for purposes not adequately provided for in the first place. The increase may be financed out of the fund balance or out of anticipated revenues in excess of the amount originally estimated. To record an increase of appropriations out of the fund balance an entry such as the following might be made, using an assumed amount:

Fund Balance	50,000	
Appropriations		50,000

The credit to Appropriations would be supported by credits to subsidiary accounts representing the purposes covered by the action. If the additional appropriation were based on an expectation of more revenue than originally anticipated, Estimated Revenues would be substituted for Fund Balance in the foregoing entry.

A third type of interim change in a budget consists of transferring amounts of authorizations from one purpose to another. Thus, if it is discovered that an amount appropriated for one purpose apparently is in excess of requirements for the year, whereas that appropriated for another is inadequate, the legislative body may act to effect a transfer from the former to the latter. The transfer having been approved according to law, an entry such as the following might be made:

Appropriations	4,000	
Appropriations		4,000

Appropriations expenditure ledger:	*Debit*	*Credit*
Police Department—traffic control	4,000	
Fire department—fire prevention		4,000

Illustration 2–9

CITY OF OAK SPRINGS
Monthly Budget Report
Revenues

Submitted by: J. H. Myers, Treas.
Date: November 30, 1974

		November			Year to Date			
Items	*Estimate for Year*	*Budget Estimate*	*Actual Revenue*	*Over (or Under*) Estimate*	*Budget Estimate*	*Actual Revenue*	*Over (or Under*) Estimate*	*Balance Not Yet Realized*
General fund:								
Taxes	$1,376,400	$13,000	$12,800	$ 200*	$1,270,200	$1,271,800	$ 1,600	$104,600
Licenses and permits	211,300	10,900	9,950	950*	202,400	192,100	10,300*	19,200
Fines and forfeits	95,900	8,600	9,010	410	86,200	87,350	1,150	8,550
Intergovernmental revenue	405,000	31,000	33,400	2,400	328,600	322,700	5,900*	982,300
Totals	$2,088,600	$63,500	$65,160	$1,660	$1,887,400	$1,873,950	$13,450*	$214,650
Library fund:								
Taxes	$ 378,300	$ 3,600	$ 2,570	$1,030*	$ 376,700	$ 376,900	$ 200	$ 1,400
Intergovernmental revenue	214,050				107,025	107,025		107,025
Charges for services	52,600	6,300	7,050	750	46,730	45,810	920*	6,790
Totals	$ 644,950	$ 9,900	$ 9,620	$ 280*	$ 530,455	$ 529,735	$ 720*	$115,215

Obviously, the net effect of the above entry is reflected in the subsidiary account changes. In order to provide control over the entries made in subsidiary ledgers and to provide a proper audit trail, however, systems should require formal data input as illustrated and should not allow informal adjustment of subsidiary ledger accounts.

Accounting for Allotments

In the event a governmental unit desires close control over expenditures by periods, allotments may be formally recorded in ledger accounts. This procedure might begin with the budgetary entry, in which Unallotted Appropriations would replace Appropriations, as follows:

Estimated Revenues	1,000,000	
Unallotted Appropriations		990,000
Fund Balance		10,000

If it is assumed that $300,000 is the amount formally allotted to departments or divisions for the first period, the following entry could be made:

Unallotted Appropriations	300,000	
Allotments		300,000

Expenditures can be recorded periodically as reports are received from using departments or divisions. Under this procedure, closing entries transfer Expenditures balances into Allotments, and Allotments balances into Unallotted Appropriations.

Budgets for Other Funds

The foregoing discussion of budgets applies principally to those of general funds. Other types of funds operate under budgets of varying forms, some similar, some widely different from general fund budgets.

Most similar to general fund budgets are those of special revenue funds, which are analogous to general funds for the activities they represent. Regulations governing control of special revenue fund budgets frequently differ from those applying to general fund budgets, since special revenue funds are often managed by special boards or commissions, and their relationship to the general government is likely to affect budgeting procedure. However, this influence lies principally in the mechanics of budget preparation and subsequent handling; so, from an accounting standpoint, general fund and special revenue fund budgets are much alike, differing mostly in size and complexity.

Opinions and practices vary widely with respect to budgeting for the six other types of funds. Ordinarily budgets are not necessary for nonexpendable trust funds or agency funds. Budgets may not be required by law for enterprise funds, intragovernmental service funds, or expendable trust funds. Since these kinds of funds are ordinarily operated on a business basis the fund manager should prepare operating plans and financial plans, but need not record the budget in the fund accounts, except in those few jurisdictions which mandate budgetary accounts for all funds. Debt service funds generally require formal annual budgets because the funds must handle the payment of interest on all outstanding issues of general obligation debt other than that payable from special assessment and enterprise funds, as well as the redemption of debt maturing during the year, as is discussed in Chapter 7.

Capital projects funds and special assessment funds are two types of funds employed to account for resources devoted to construction or other means of acquiring fixed assets. The formal authorizations for these two kinds of funds are equivalent to project budgets in that they authorize expenditures up to a given amount. Project budgets may be supplemented by annual budgets which afford closer control by the legislative body, by dividing the total authorization into segments each of which receives final approval in the light of progress and developments to date. Annual or other short-term budgets are necessary for a capital projects fund created to finance a number of related projects.

SELECTED REFERENCES

FRY, CARROLL J. *A Practical Approach to Performance-Program Budgeting for a Small City*. Municipal Finance Officers Association Special Bulletin 1971G. Chicago, 1971.

HINRICHS, HARLEY H., and TAYLOR, GRAEME M. *Program Budgeting and Benefit-Cost Analysis*. Pacific Palisades, California: Goodyear Publishing Co., Inc., 1969.

LAWRENCE, CHARLES. "A Study of a Program Budget for a Small City," *The Journal of Accountancy*, vol. 134, no. 5 (November 1972), pp. 52–57.

MOAK, LENNOX L., and KILLIAN, KATHRYN W. *A Manual of Techniques for the Preparation, Consideration, Adoption, and Administration of Operating Budgets*. Chicago: Municipal Finance Officers Association, 1963.

———. *A Manual of Suggested Practice for the Preparation and Adoption of Capital Programs and Capital Budgets by Local Governments*. Chicago: Municipal Finance Officers Association, 1964.

MORRISON, WILLIAM G., JR. and TORNELLO, Robert J. "An Automated Line-Item Budgeting System for Local Government," *Management Controls*, vol. 19, no. 11 (November 1972), pp. 270–73.

ODELL, ROBERT M., JR. *Budgeting Grants-In-Aid*. Municipal Finance Officers Association Special Bulletin 1972F. Chicago, 1972.

REILLY, PAUL R. "An Activity Costing Approach to Budgeting," *Accounting and Management Concepts and the Budgetary Process*. Municipal Finance Officers Association Special Bulletin 1972A. Chicago, 1972; pp. 1–7.

WHITE, CARL L. *Revenue Forecasting Techniques*. Municipal Finance Officers Association Special Bulletin 1972G. Chicago, 1972.

QUESTIONS

2–1. Why is the National Committee on Governmental Accounting's definition of a budget (quoted on the first page of this chapter) incomplete? What is the modern concept of budgeting?

2–2. Differentiate between program budgets and performance budgets. What extensions of the program budgeting concept are included in a PPB system?

2–3. Assuming that the typical municipal budget is a collection of departmental budgets, each of which shows only the department's requested appropriation for personal services, materials and supplies, and capital outlays; specify the advantages and disadvantages each of the following groups would find if a municipality were to convert to a program budget:

a) the municipality's central administration
b) the municipality's departmental administrators
c) the municipality's legislative body
d) the municipality's taxpayers

2–4. Describe concisely the interrelationship of municipal revenue and expenditure budgets. Compare this with the interrelationship that exists in business budgeting.

2–5. Why is the preparation of revenue budgets ordinarily centralized in the municipal finance office, and the preparation of expenditure budgets decentralized throughout the administration?

2–6. Can you see any reason why budgets for capital expenditures should be prepared for several years beyond the operating budget year, even though the total amount is not to be appropriated for the operating budget year?

2–7. What are some of the factors to be taken into account in preparing revenue estimates for inclusion in a budget?

2–8. Generally accepted principles of accounting do not require the recording of budgets in the accounts. Why are budgetary accounts recommended for general and special revenue funds? What two budgetary accounts are usually found in a general fund?

2–9. Why should municipal finance officers and accountants be concerned with property tax assessment procedures?

2–10. What two ways of viewing property tax revenue are commonly encountered in practice?

2–11. "Federal general revenue sharing, and other types of intergovernmental revenue, simplify the municipal budgeting, accounting, and reporting practices." Do you agree? Why, or why not?

2–12. "It is reasonable to start preparing departmental budget estimates about 30 days before the beginning of the budget year." Do you agree? Why, or why not?

2–13. What is meant by "budget control report"? What information should be presented in such a report? Why?

2–14. Explain the purpose of replacing an Appropriation account with an Unallotted Appropriations account.

2–15. How should budgeting for an enterprise fund differ from budgeting for a general fund?

EXERCISES AND PROBLEMS

2–1. Obtain a copy of a recent municipal budget.* Follow the instructions below.

a) Familiarize yourself with the organization of the budget document; read the letter of transmittal or any narrative that accompanies the budgets.

Does this material discuss the major changes in sources of revenue and amounts of revenue which are expected to occur during the budget year?

Does the narrative material discuss the major changes in nature (or purpose) and amounts of budgeted expenditures?

Does the narrative discuss the objectives of the municipality and the plans the administration proposes beyond the budget year?

Do charts, graphs or tables accompany the narrative? If so, what purpose are they intended to serve?

b) Does the revenue budget disclose clearly the source of revenue for each fund? List the principal sources for each fund.

If comparative information is given, is the extent of reliance on each source changing? How?

Is estimated revenue for the budget year compared with the budget for the current year and with actual revenue for the preceding year?

To what exent does the municipality rely on property taxes?

Are property taxes levied each year at the same rate, at a decreasing rate, or at an increasing rate?

Are comparative figures shown over time for changes in population and/or assessed valuation?

Is the tax rate computation shown?

Is budgeted revenue under the State and Local Fiscal Assistance Act of 1972 shown as a resource of the general fund? a special revenue fund? a trust fund?

In addition to Federal general revenue sharing, what other sources of intergovernmental revenue are budgeted for the coming year? Which of these are related to specific programs? Do these require matching funds from local sources?

c) Is the expenditure budget structured in the program format, the performance format, or neither?

If program budgeting is used, is the crosswalk to the budget for each organizational unit shown?

---

* See Exercise 1–1 footnote on how to obtain one, if you do not already have one.

For each organizational unit, does the expenditure budget show detail justifying the requests for personal services, contractual services, materials and supplies, capital outlays, or whatever other expenditure categories are used?
For the budget year does the document show departmental requests, amounts approved by the administration, and/or amounts approved by the municipal legislative branch?

d) Are capital outlays budgeted for the coming year related to a capital expenditure program extending over three, five, or more years?
Are budgeted general fund capital outlays related to budgeted outlays of capital projects funds and other funds?
Are the means of financing capital outlays for the budget year, and for forthcoming years, disclosed?

e) Does the budget document clearly disclose budgeted issues and/or redemption of long-term debt? Is the effect of budgeted changes in long-term debt upon legal debt margin shown?

f) Are budgets for enterprise funds, libraries, and schools included in the budget document? If not, does the budget document refer to separately issued budgets for these or other activities?

2–2. Comment on the computation of "Amount Required from Property Tax Levy" shown below. Disregard amounts. What items may have been erroneously omitted? What items have been erroneously included? Are any items misclassified?

Requirements:		
Estimated total expenditures, September 1, 1974–February 28, 1975		$ 403,000
Proposed appropriation for fiscal 1976		964,000
Actual balance in fund, September 1, 1974 (deficit)	$ (11,000)	
Less: Estimated miscellaneous receipts, September 1, 1974–February 28, 1975	23,000	12,000
Estimated additional appropriation required for remainder of fiscal 1975		51,000
Liquidation of loan from street fund		20,000
Total requirements		$1,426,000
Resources other than the property tax levy for fiscal 1976:		
Advance from water fund	$ 25,000	
Estimated revenue from property taxes, balance of fiscal 1975	431,000	
Estimated miscellaneous revenue, fiscal 1976	81,000	
Prepayment of fiscal 1977 taxes in fiscal 1976	32,000	
Total resources other than property tax levy		569,000
Amount required from Property Tax Levy, Fiscal 1976		$ 857,000

2–3. The City of Carter general fund has budgeted the following general fund revenues and expenditures:

Estimated revenues:	
Taxes	$1,400,000
Licenses and permits	300,000
Fines and forfeits	200,000
Intergovernmental revenues	800,000
Appropriations:	
General administration	$120,000
Police	760,000
Fire	740,000
Health and welfare	560,000
Public works	500,000
Insurance	30,000

a) Assuming a reasonably responsible level of financial management, what is the minimum figure the administration of the City of Carter expects to have as the General Fund Balance at the conclusion of the current year? Explain.

b) Show in general journal form the entry which would be necessary to record the budget, assuming it is legally approved, at the beginning of the budget year.

2–4. *a*) If the mayor and council of the City of Carter agree that the budget for the year following the one for which the budget is shown in Exercise 2–3 should reflect the PPBS concept, to what are they committing themselves?

b) Assume that the budget of the City of Carter is legally amended to reflect an increase in the estimated revenue from fines and forfeits of $50,000 and an increase in appropriations for Health and Welfare of $40,000. Show in general journal form the entry to record the budget amendment.

2–5. The common council of Forest City adopted for the city general fund a budget which is shown below in summary form:

Appropriations:	
Personal services	$206,400
Contractual services	48,200
Commodities	104,700
Other charges	66,500
Estimated revenues:	
Taxes	$211,800
Licenses and permits	25,800
Fines and forfeits	36,900
Intergovernmental revenue	149,100
Charges for services	6,600

a) Assume that Forest City employs a system of quarterly allotments to enhance expenditure control. Record the complete budget as of January 1.

b) Assume that allotments for the first quarter were as follows, and make the appropriation entry as January 1.

Personal services	$50,400
Contractual services	26,100
Commodities	19,600
Other charges	15,700

Show subsidiary ledger accounts for both unallotted appropriations and allotments.

c) Assume that during the fourth quarter permission was received from the legislative body to transfer $6,500 already allotted for commodities to personal services.

d) Assume that total allotments for the year were $418,700 (appropriation total same as in (a) above) and that expenditures reported by departments totaled $417,630. Make the required closing entries, omitting all reference to subsidiary ledger accounts. For a balancing account, if one is needed, use Fund Balance.

2–6. From the information given below, you are required to prepare a work program for certain operations for the City of Trenton for 1975. Monthly figures need be shown for January and February only.

Estimated volume and unit costs for 1974 are as follows:

Operation	*Units*	*Unit Cost*
A.	60,000	$1.00
B.	48,000	$2.00

Percentages of estimated annual volume for January and February, 1975 are as follows:

Operation	*January*	*February*
A.	10 percent	15 percent
B.	5 percent	5 percent

Composition of unit costs by percentages for the three operations for 1974 is estimated as follows:

Item	*Operations* *A*	*B*
Labor.	80%	60%
Materials	16	30
Supervision	4	5
Machine rental	. . .	. . .
Operation and maintenance of equipment.	. . .	5

The following changes are expected to affect the costs of the products in 1975:

1. Cost of labor per hour will increase 20 percent.
2. Time required per unit will increase 15 percent.
3. Cost of materials will increase 30 percent.
4. Due to improved engineering processes, quantity of materials is expected to decrease on an average of 10 percent per unit.
5. The cost of supervision per unit will increase 5 percent.
6. Operation and maintenance of equipment will increase 25 percent.
7. For operation A, it is proposed to substitute machine work for one half the labor, at a cost of $0.30 per unit for machine rental.

Volume changes for 1975 are estimated as follows:

Operation	*Percentage Change*
A.	+10
B.	+15

For each cost element (labor, material, etc.) of each product, compute unit cost to the nearest tenth of one cent, and report estimated unit costs for 1975 as the totals of all elements.

2–7. Below is a collection of information of the major kinds needed in determining the amount of revenue required to be raised by property taxes and for calculation of a tax rate for the City of Liberty general fund.

Amount of expenditures budget approved by city council for 1975 operations	$ 1,913,000
Estimated expenditures July 31 to December 31, 1974 . . .	872,000
Estimated amount to be received by city general fund in the December, 1974, tax distribution by the county treasurer	971,000
Actual balance of general fund at July 31, 1974	340,000
Estimated working balance required at December 31, 1975, based upon projected expenditures for 1976	793,000
Assessed value of real and tangible personal property compiled by county assessor's office as of March 1, 1974 . . .	37,866,290
Estimated miscellaneous revenue:	
July 31–December 31, 1974.	74,000
All of 1975	160,000
Total of mortgage, military service and other exemptions on file for 1975 taxes	4,739,840
Estimated amount of state and federal aid to be received for general fund use in 1975.	850,000

You are required to do the following things:

a) Determine the amount of property tax levy required for the City of Liberty general fund for 1975.

b) Compute the tax rate, in dollars and cents, per $100 of net assessed value, required to be levied for the City of Liberty general fund to raise the amount of revenue needed according to your statement for (*a*).

c) Using the amount of cash required from the property tax levy as shown in the solution to (*a*), determine the amount of levy necessary if it is estimated that 3 percent of the levy will not be collected and that, of the bills paid, 20 percent will earn a 2 percent discount.

2–8. The records of a municipality revealed a total of approximately $54,000,000 of assessable property located within its jurisdiction; but $2,500,000 of this valuation claimed mortgage exemptions, and $800,000 claimed military service and other exemptions.

a) What percentage of tax levy would be required to raise $1,260,000 of taxes, assuming 100 percent collection? Carry decimals to ten thousandths, which will give percentages in hundredths.

b) What rate, in terms of dollars and cents per $100 of valuation, is represented by the percentage rate in (*a*)?

c) What percentage of tax levy would be required to raise $1,260,000 if there were no exemptions in the situation described above?

d) How much extra tax will have to be paid on each $10,000 assessed value of nonexempt property to cover the amount lost by the exemptions?

CONTINUOUS PROBLEMS

2–L. The following budget for the general fund of the City of Bingham (see Problem 1–L) was legally adopted.

Estimated revenues:	
Property taxes	$2,635,000
Interest and penalties on taxes	7,000
Licenses and permits	443,000
Fines and forfeits	236,000
Intergovernmental revenue	831,000
Charges for services	101,000
Miscellaneous revenue	50,000
Total estimated revenues	$4,303,000
Appropriations:	
General government:	
City council and clerk	$ 62,000
Central administration	177,500
Municipal court and attorney	113,700
Finance	214,800
Personnel	94,000
Public safety:	
Police	710,200
Fire	716,100
Building safety	91,400
Animal pound	18,500
Traffic engineering	93,800
Public works	708,000
Health	200,000
Public welfare	256,000
Recreation	385,000
Contributions	373,000
Miscellaneous	46,000
Total appropriations	$4,260,000

1. You are required to:

a) Record the budget in the general journal. Include general ledger accounts, subsidiary ledger accounts, and adequate explanations for each entry (and for all journal entries in all "L" problems).

b) Post the entries to *general* ledger accounts. Do not open subsidiary ledger accounts until instructed to do so in subsequent "L" problems.

2. You are required to:

   a) Compute the general fund tax rate in dollars and cents (to the nearest cent) per $100 assessed valuation for the City of Bingham. A noted macroeconomist, R. C. Burner, computed the "gross Bingham product" as $1 billion. The "true cash value" of the real and taxable personal property within the city limits of Bingham, as of the last assessment date, was estimated to be $600,000,000 by the local newspaper editor, who maintains that everybody (except the newspaper) must have been underassessed, because the total assessed valuation of real and taxable personal property on that date amounted to only $160,000,000. It is estimated that two percent of the gross levy will be uncollectible.

   b) A resident of the City of Bingham is required to pay property tax levies of the state, county, township, and metropolitan school district, as well as the city general fund. If the rates per $100 assessed valuation are for the state, $0.01; county, $1.51; township, $.30, and school district, $3.50—what total amount of taxes would a Bingham taxpayer have to pay if his real property assessment amounted to $6,000? He had no taxable personal property.

   c) Assume that the state in which the City of Bingham is located has a mortgage exemption law. This law provides that each property owner whose home is subject to a duly recorded mortgage may claim an exemption from taxation of $1,000 assessed valuation of real property, or the face of the mortgage, whichever is less. If mortgage exemptions granted total $6,000,000, compute the total property tax the taxpayer in part (*b*) would have to pay if:

      1. He had filed for and received a mortgage exemption of $1,000.
      2. He had not filed for or received any mortgage exemption.

2–S. 1. The following budget for the general fund of the City of Smithville (see Problem 1–S) was legally adopted for the calendar year 197B.

Estimated revenues:	
Taxes	
Real property	$ 980,000
Sales	820,000
Interest and penalties on taxes	10,000
Licenses and permits	306,000
Fines and forfeits	184,000
Intergovernmental revenue	302,000
Charges for services	58,000
Miscellaneous revenue	20,000
Total estimated revenues	$2,680,000

Appropriations:	
General government	$ 276,000
Public safety:	
Police	524,200
Fire	509,800
Building safety	57,600
Public works	491,400
Health and welfare	343,500
Parks and recreation	260,000
Contributions	248,000
Miscellaneous	49,500
Total appropriations	$2,760,000

You are required to:

a) Record the budget in the general journal. Include general ledger accounts, subsidiary ledger accounts, and adequate explanations for each entry (and for all journal entries in all "S" problems).

b) Post the entries to the *general* ledger accounts. Do not open subsidiary ledger accounts until instructed to do so in subsequent "S" problems.

2. The City of Smithville's Director of Finance wishes to develop a program budget for internal management purposes. The following program categories and subcategories are to be used:

1000 Transportation
- 1100 Planning
- 1200 Street Construction and Maintenance
- 1300 Parking
- 1400 Sidewalks
- 1500 Traffic Control

2000 Physical Environment and Economic Base
- 2100 Planning and Design
- 2200 Landscaping
- 2300 Noise Abatement

3000 Health, Safety and General Well Being
- 3100 Public Health
- 3200 Animal Control
- 3300 Crime Prevention
- 3400 Building and Housing Inspection
- 3500 Ambulance Service and Rescue Calls
- 3600 Aid to Individuals and Groups

4000 Cultural and Recreational
- 4100 Parks Maintenance
- 4200 Swimming Pools
- 4300 Tennis
- 4400 Baseball
- 4500 Other Group Programs

5000 Services to Property
- 5100 Fire Protection
- 5200 Theft and Vandalism Protection
- 5300 Water Supply and Treatment
- 5400 Water Distribution
- 5500 Sanitary Sewer Collection and Treatment
- 5600 Solid Waste Collection and Disposal

6000 General Management and Support
- 6100 Legislative and Legal
- 6200 Administration
- 6300 Accounting and Budget
- 6400 Personnel
- 6500 Data Processing
- 6600 Purchasing

Analysis of departmental budgets, and consultations with department heads, indicate that the departmental appropriations budgets (shown in 2–S–1) should be charged to program subcategories as shown below. Before distributing any departmental budget to program subcategories, distribute the Contributions appropriation to the departments in the following percentages:

Department	*Percentage*
General government	15
Public safety–Police	32
Public safety–Fire	29
Public safety–Building safety	3
Public works	16
Health and welfare	3
Parks and recreation	2

Distribution of departmental budgets to program subcategories:

General government

Program	*Percentage*
1100	5
2100	5
2300	3
6100	15
6200	30
6300	18
6400	9
6500	10
6600	5

Public safety–police

Program	*Percentage*
1300	2
1500	43
3300	25
5100	3
5200	27

Public safety–fire

Program	*Percentage*
3500	5
5100	95

Public safety–building safety

Program	*Percentage*
3400	100

Public works

Program	*Percentage*
1100	1
1200	70
1300	1
1400	2
2100	1
2200	15
5600	10

Parks and recreation

Program	*Percentage*
2200	5
4100	40
4200	15
4300	5
4400	5
4500	30

Health and welfare

Program	*Percentage*
3100	30
3200	10
3500	10
3600	50

Miscellaneous

Program	*Percentage*
1100	10
2100	10
2300	10
5600	10
6100	10
6200	50

You are required to determine the budget for the Transportation program; show the budget for each of the subcategories within that program. (NOTE: The program budget will not be used as a basis for journal entries in this problem or in subsequent "S" problems.)

3

General Funds and Special Revenue Funds: General Operation

The general fund of a municipality is the entity which accounts for all the assets and resources used for financing the general administration of the municipality and the traditional services provided to the citizens. General funds are sometimes known as operating funds or current funds; the purpose, not the name, is the true test of identity. The typical municipality now engages in many activities which for legal and historical reasons are financed by sources other than those available to the general fund. Whenever a tax or other revenue source is authorized by a legislative body to be used for a specified purpose only, a municipality availing itself of that source is expected to create a *special revenue fund* in order to be able to demonstrate that all revenue from that source was used for the specified purpose only. A common example of a special revenue fund is one used to account for state gasoline tax money distributed to the municipality; in many states the use of this money is restricted to the construction and maintenance of streets, highways, and bridges. The accounting treatment recommended for special revenue funds by the National Committee on Governmental Accounting is identical with that recommended for general funds. In order to avoid excessive repetition of the phrase "general funds and special revenue funds" the term "general fund" is used in the latter portion of this chapter and in following chapters to include both categories of funds. General funds and special revenue funds are also referred to generically as *revenue* funds.

The Liquidity Viewpoint

Municipal corporations have unlimited life, just as business corporations do. However, the going concern concept typical of accounting for business enterprises is subject to some modification in the case of accounting for municipalities. Not only are the operations of a municipality accounted for in a series of *funds,* which are themselves legal entities, but the functioning of the revenue funds, and certain other funds as explained in other chapters, is dependent upon regular periodic legislative authorizations. In government, fiscal periods of one year predominate; biennial periods are found in some states. Revenue fund accounting may be said to be based on a liquidity viewpoint. Revenue funds account only for liquid assets which are available for appropriation for fund purposes and only for liabilities which will be liquidated by use of those assets. Liquid assets include cash and all other assets which may be expected to be converted into cash in normal fund operations. (Inventories of supplies which will be used by revenue fund departments may properly be accounted for by revenue funds, although, as discussed in Chapter 9, there is good reason for establishing an intragovernmental service fund to account for sizable inventories.) Land, buildings, and equipment utilized in revenue fund operations are not accounted for by revenue funds because they are not normally converted into cash.

The arithmetic difference between the total of assets available for appropriation and the total of current liabilities of the fund is the "Fund Balance." Citizens of the municipality have no legal claim on any excess of liquid assets over current liabilities; therefore, the Fund Balance is not analogous to the capital accounts of an investor-owned entity. It is, of course, true that an excess of liquid assets over current liabilities represents assets available to extinguish liabilities incurred in future operations, and thus reduces the amount of revenues to be raised in future periods. The converse is true, also; an excess of current liabilities over liquid assets indicates that revenues in excess of expected future liabilities will have to be raised.

The Modified Accrual Basis

The proprietary accounts of a revenue fund include Revenue and Expenditure accounts in addition to the asset, liability, and Fund Balance accounts. *Revenue,* in municipal accounting terminology, is similar in meaning to the same term in accounting for profit-seeking entities: an addition to the assets which is not offset by a decrease in assets or an increase in liabilities of the fund. In short, an increase in Fund Balance. The National Committee on Governmental Accounting and the American Institute of Certified Public Accountants recommend that revenue of general funds and special revenue funds be recognized on the *modified accrual* basis. Under the modified accrual basis those items of revenue for which a valid receivable can be recorded in advance of their due date, such as property taxes, should be recognized on the accrual basis; all other revenue items are recognized on the cash basis because the time of collection generally coincides with the determination of the amount.

Expenditure is a municipal accounting term which replaces both the terms "costs" and "expenses" used in accounting for profit-seeking entities. Expenditures are decreases in Fund Balance. Under the modified accrual basis, as well as the full accrual basis, an expenditure is recognized when a liability to be met from fund assets is incurred. Legally, an expenditure and the accompanying liability should be recognized only for those items and in those amounts for which available legal appropriations exist. It is important to note that an appropriation is considered to be expended in the amount of a liability incurred whether the liability is for salaries, supplies, or a long-lived capital asset. (The acquisition of capital assets is recorded in the general fixed asset group of accounts, not in the revenue fund which financed their acquisition.)

The Revenue account is a general ledger control account which is related to the Estimated Revenues general ledger control account introduced in Chapter 2. For each control account subsidiary accounts must be kept to correspond with each item shown in the revenue budget. During the fiscal year periodic comparisons of estimated and actual revenues should be made, as illustrated in Chapter 4. Normally, during a fiscal year the total amount of budgeted revenues, shown by the debit balance of the Estimated Revenues account, will exceed the amount of revenue recognized to date, shown by the credit balance of the Revenues account; the excess of Estimated Revenues over Revenues, therefore, represents a *resource* of the municipality—legally budgeted revenues which are expected to be recognized as assets before the end of the fiscal year.

Similarly, Expenditures is a general ledger control account which is related to the Appropriations control account introduced in Chapter 2. Subsidiary accounts must be kept for each legally approved appropriation. During the fiscal year periodic comparisons of appropriations and expenditures should be made, as illustrated in Chapter 5. In interim financial statements the debit balance of Expenditures is shown as a deduction from the credit balance of Appropriations to indicate the portion of appropriations available for expenditure at the date of the interim statement. As of that date, however, a portion of unexpended appropriations may have been *encumbered,* that is, goods or services chargeable against the appropriations may have been ordered. Encumbrance accounting, described below, comprises one element of the modified accrual basis of accounting.

Encumbrance Accounting

Recall that an expenditure is recognized when a liability is incurred; hiring employees, issuing purchase orders, or signing contracts give rise to contingent liabilities which will become actual liabilities in the normal course of events when services and goods are received.

Because stiff penalties may be imposed on an administrator who incurs liabilities for any amount in excess of that appropriated, or for any purpose not covered by an appropriation, or who incurs liabilities after the authority to do so has expired, prudence dictates that each purchase order and each contract be reviewed before it is signed to determine that a valid and sufficient appropriation exists to which the expenditure can be charged when goods or services are received. In order to keep track of purchase orders and contracts outstanding it is recommended that the Encumbrance control account (and a subsidiary account as illustrated in Chapter 5) be charged, and the Reserve for Encumbrances account credited, for the amount of each purchase order or contract issued. When goods or services are received, two entries are necessary: (1) Reserve for Encumbrances is debited and Encumbrances (and the proper subsidiary account) is credited for the appropriate amount; and (2) Expenditures is debited and a liability account is credited for the amount to be paid the creditor.

Although salaries and wages of municipal employees must be chargeable against valid and sufficient appropriations in order to give rise to legal expenditures, many municipalities do not find it necessary to encumber the departmental personal services appropriations for estimated payrolls of recurring, relatively constant amounts. Departments having payrolls that fluctuate greatly from one season to another may follow the encumbrance procedure to make sure that the personal service appropriation is not overexpended.

ILLUSTRATIVE CASE

The previous sections of this chapter present in brief some of the major differences of revenue fund accounting from accounting for profit-seeking entities. The significance of these differences is best understood in the context of an extended illustration. In this section common transactions and events in the operation of a revenue fund are discussed and the necessary accounting entries are illustrated. Resulting financial statements are presented in final sections of this chapter.

Assume that as of the end of the fiscal year, 197A, the Town of Merrill's general fund had the following balances in its accounts:

	Debit	*Credit*
Cash	$ 90,000	
Taxes receivable–delinquent	230,000	
Estimated uncollectible delinquent taxes		$ 11,500
Interest and penalties receivable on taxes	4,469	
Estimated uncollectible interest and penalties		1,327
Vouchers payable		160,000
Due to federal government		13,623
Reserve for encumbrances–prior year		27,450
Fund balance		110,569
	$324,469	$324,469

Recording the Budget

At the beginning of the following fiscal year, 197B, it is necessary to record the budget (assuming that all legal requirements have been complied with). If the total of the estimated revenue budget for 197B is $2,628,000, and the total of the appropriations budget for 197B is $2,700,000, the necessary entry to record the budget (assuming the detail of each budget is as shown in the entry) would be:

1. Estimated Revenues	2,628,000	
Fund Balance	72,000	
Appropriations		2,700,000
Revenue ledger:	*Debit*	
Property taxes	1,300,000	
Interest and penalties on delinquent taxes	2,500	
Sales taxes	480,000	
Licenses and permits	220,000	
Fines and forfeits	308,000	
Intergovernmental revenue	280,000	
Charges for services	35,000	
Miscellaneous	2,500	
Appropriation Expenditures ledger:		*Credit*
General government		330,000
Public safety		1,040,000
Public works		610,000
Health and welfare		460,000
Parks and recreation		115,000
Contributions		135,000
Miscellaneous		10,000

Tax Anticipation Notes Payable

In the trial balance shown for the Town of Merrill there are two items, Vouchers Payable and Due to Federal Government, which are current liabilities. Assuming that the town Treasurer wishes to pay these in full within 30 days after the date of the trial balance, he is forced to do some cash forecasting because the balance of Cash is not large enough to pay the $173,623 debt. In addition to this immediate problem, he, and most other municipal treasurers, is faced with the problem that cash disbursements during a fiscal year tend to be approximately level month-by-month, whereas cash receipts from major revenue sources are concentrated in just a few months. For example, property tax collections are concentrated in two separate months, such as May and November, when the installments are due; collections by the municipality from the state or Federal governments of revenues collected by the superior jurisdictions for distribution to municipalities are also usually concentrated in one or two months of the year. Therefore, the Treasurer of the Town of Merrill may forecast that he will need to disburse approximately one-fourth of the budgeted appropriations before major items of revenue are received; one-fourth of $2,700,000 is $675,000. This amount plus current liabilities at the beginning of the year, $173,623, equals $848,623, or, roughly, $850,000 expected cash disbursements in the period for which the forecast is made. Experience may indicate that a conservative forecast of collections of delinquent taxes and interest and penalties thereon during the forecast period will amount to $200,000. Further, assume that the Treasurer's review of the items in the Estimated Revenues budget indicates that at least $60,000 will be collected in the forecast period. Therefore, total cash available to meet the $850,000 disbursements is $350,000 ($90,000 cash as of the beginning of the period, plus the $200,000 and $60,000 items just described), leaving a deficiency to be met by borrowing of $500,000. The taxing power of the municipality is ample security for short-term debt; local banks customarily meet the working capital needs of a municipality by accepting a "tax anticipation note" from the municipal officers. If the amount of $500,000 is borrowed at this time the necessary entry is:

		Debit	Credit
2.	Cash	500,000	
	Tax Anticipation Notes Payable		500,000

Encumbrance Entry

Purchase orders for materials and supplies chargeable to the following appropriations were issued in the total amount of $306,000:

General government	$ 28,000
Public safety	72,000
Public works	160,000
Parks and recreation	36,000
Health and welfare	10,000

The entry to record the encumbrance for the purchase orders is:

3.	Encumbrances	306,000	
	Reserve for Encumbrances		306,000
	Appropriation expenditures ledger:	*Debit*	
	General government	28,000	
	Public safety	72,000	
	Public works	160,000	
	Parks and recreation	36,000	
	Health and welfare	10,000	

Payment of Liabilities as Recorded

Checks were drawn to pay the vouchers payable and the amount due to the Federal government as of the end of 197A:

4.	Vouchers Payable	160,000	
	Due to Federal Government	13,623	
	Cash		173,623

Notice that it is not necessary in the above entry to know what appropriations were affected at the time that goods and services giving rise to the liabilities were received, because, under the accrual concept, the appropriations were considered as expended in 197A when the goods and services were received.

Payrolls and Payroll Taxes

The gross pay of employees of general fund departments amounted to $420,000. The Town of Merrill does not use the encumbrance procedure for payrolls. Deductions from gross pay for the period amount to $24,570 for employees' share of FICA tax; $50,400, employees' Federal withholding tax; and $6,240 employees' state withholding tax—the first two will, of course, have to be remitted by the town to the Federal government, and the last item will have to be remitted to the state government. The gross pay is chargeable to the appropriations as indicated by the Appropriations Expenditures ledger debits. Assuming the liability for net pay is vouchered, the entry is:

5a.	Expenditures	420,000	
	Vouchers Payable		338,790
	Due to Federal Government		74,970
	Due to State Government		6,240

Appropriations expenditures ledger:	*Debit*
General government	58,800
Public safety	260,400
Public works	67,200
Health and welfare	12,600
Parks and recreation	21,000

Payment of the vouchers for the net pay results in the following entry:

5b.	Vouchers Payable	338,790	
	Cash		338,790

Inasmuch as the Town is liable for the employer's share of FICA taxes, $24,570, and for contributions to additional retirement funds established by state law, assumed to amount to $12,250 for the pay period ended, it is necessary that the Town's liabilities for its contributions be recorded. These obligations were provided for in the Appropriations budget under the caption "Contributions," which is short for "Contributions to Retirement Funds."

6.	Expenditures	36,820	
	Due to Federal Government		24,570
	Due to State Government		12,250
	Appropriation expenditures ledger:	*Debit*	
	Contributions	36,820	

Encumbrances of Prior Year

In the trial balance as of the end of 197A the item "Reserve for Encumbrances—Prior Year" indicates that purchase orders or contracts issued during 197A were open at the end of the year—that is, the goods or services had not yet been received. When the goods or services are received in 197B their cost is properly chargeable against the appropriations of 197A, not against the appropriations of 197B. The Appropriations account for 197A was closed at the end of that year, and the open balance of the Reserve for Encumbrances account was transferred to Reserve for Encumbrances—Prior Year so that the contingent liability would show properly in the general fund balance sheet as of the end of 197A. When the goods or services are received in 197B an Expenditures—Prior Year account is created as shown in the entry below, which assumes that the invoices for goods and services ordered in 197A and received in 197B were approved for payment in the amount of $27,555:

7.	Expenditures—Prior Year	27,555	
	Vouchers Payable		27,555

If all the 197A purchase orders and contracts have now been filled, there will be no further need for the Expenditures—Prior Year account or for the Reserve for Encumbrances—Prior Year account. The two may be closed at this time, or at the end of 197B, whichever is more convenient. Since the two are not equal in amount the difference is charged (or credited, if the actual liability is less than the amount encumbered) to Fund Balance. The closing entry is:

8.	Reserve for Encumbrances—Prior Year	27,450	
	Fund Balance	105	
	Expenditures—Prior Year		27,555

Recording Property Tax Levy

The property tax levy for 197B was determined as described in Chapter 2. In brief, the budgeted revenue from property taxes for 197B is $1,300,000 (see entry 1 in this series); if the estimated loss from uncollectible property taxes is 5%, the gross levy must be $1,300,000 ÷ .95, or $1,368,421. At the time property tax bills, totaling $1,368,421, are prepared, the following entry is necessary if the modified accrual basis is used.

		Debit	Credit
9.	Taxes Receivable—Current	1,368,421	
	Estimated Uncollectible Current Taxes		68,421
	Revenues		1,300,000

Revenue ledger:	Credit
Property taxes	1,300,000

As the above entry indicates, "Revenues" is a control account in the general fund general ledger. It is supported by a subsidiary ledger in the manner illustrated in Chapter 4. "Taxes Receivable—Current" is also a control account, just as is the "Accounts Receivable" account of a business entity; each is supported by a subsidiary ledger which shows how much is owed by each taxpayer, or customer. Ordinarily, the subsidiary ledger supporting the real property taxes receivable control is organized by parcels of property according to their legal descriptions, since unpaid taxes are liens against the property regardless of changes in ownership. Because of its conceptual similarity to accounting for business receivables, taxes receivable subsidiary ledger accounting is not illustrated in this text.

Recognition of Expenditures for Encumbered Items

Some of the materials and supplies ordered (see entry 3) were received. Invoices for the items received totaled $269,000; related purchase orders totaled $269,325. After inspection of the goods and supplies and preaudit of the invoices they were approved for payment; vouchers were issued. Since the purchase orders had been recorded as encumbrances against the appropriations it is necessary to reverse the encumbered amount and record the expenditure in the amount of the actual liability. (The appropriations assumed to be affected are as shown in the subsidiary ledger entries):

		Debit	Credit
10.	Reserve for Encumbrances	269,325	
	Expenditures	269,000	
	Encumbrances		269,325
	Vouchers Payable		269,000

Appropriation expenditures ledger:	*Expenditures* Debit	*Encumbrances* Credit
General government	12,300	12,250
Public safety	72,000	72,000
Public works	150,600	150,900
Parks and recreation	30,000	30,000
Health and welfare	4,100	4,175

Revenue Recognized on Cash Basis

Revenue from licenses and permits, fines and forfeits, and other sources not susceptible to accrual is recognized on the cash basis. Collections to date in 197B are assumed to be as shown in entry 11:

11.	Cash	27,400	
	Revenues		27,400

Revenues ledger:	Credit
Licenses and permits	13,200
Fines and forfeits	10,800
Charges for services	3,000
Miscellaneous	400

Collection of Delinquent Taxes

Delinquent taxes are subject to interest and penalties which must be paid at the time the tax bill is paid. It is possible for a municipality to record the amount of the penalties at the time that the taxes become delinquent. Interest may be computed and recorded periodically to keep the account on the accrual basis; it must also be computed and recorded for the period from the date of last recording to the date when a taxpayer pays his delinquent taxes. Assume that taxpayers of the Town of Merrill have paid delinquent taxes totaling $150,000, on which interest and penalties of $1,500 had been recorded as receivable at the end of 197A; further assume that $300 additional interest was paid for the period from the first day of 197B to the dates on which the delinquent taxes were paid. Since it is common for the cashier receiving the collections to be able to make entries only in a cash receipts journal which provides columns for credit to Taxes Receivable—Current, Taxes Receivable—Delinquent, and Interest and Penalties Receivable on Taxes, or to originate computer source documents which have the same effect, it is necessary to record the $300 interest earned in 197B in a separate entry such as the following:

12a	Interest and Penalties Receivable on Taxes	300	
	Revenues		300

Revenues ledger:	Credit
Interest and penalties on delinquent taxes	300

The collection of all amounts may, therefore, be recorded by:

12b.	Cash	151,800	
	Taxes Receivable—Delinquent		150,000
	Interest and Penalties Receivable on Taxes		1,800

Correction of Errors

No problems arise in the collection of current taxes if they are collected as billed; the collections are debited to Cash and credited to Taxes Receivable—Current. Sometimes, even in a well-designed and well-operated system, errors occur and must be corrected. If, for example, the assessed valuation of a parcel of property were legally reduced, but the tax bill erroneously issued at the higher valuation, the following correcting entry would be made when the error was discovered, assuming the corrected bill to be $364 smaller than the original bill. (The error also caused a slight overstatement of the credit to Estimated Uncollectible

Current Taxes in entry 9, but the error in that account is not considered material enough to correct.)

13.	Revenues	364	
	Taxes Receivable—Current		364
	Revenues ledger:	*Debit*	
	Property taxes	364	

Postaudit may disclose errors in the recording of expenditures during the current year, or during a prior year. If the error occurred during the current year, the Expenditures account and the proper Appropriations Expenditures subsidiary account can be debited or credited as needed to correct it. If the error occurred in a prior year, however, the Expenditure account in error has been closed to Fund Balance, so theoretically the correcting entry should be made to the Fund Balance account. The "all-inclusive income statement" practice that is considered appropriate for profit-seeking entities does not have equal acceptance in governmental accounting because of the greater importance of legal constraints on governmental actions. For example, if a municipality collects from a supplier an amount which was erroneously paid in a preceding year, the appropriation for the year of the collection is not increased by the amount collected; it remains as originally budgeted. As a practical matter, collections from suppliers of prior years' overpayments may be budgeted as Miscellaneous Revenues, and credited to the Revenues account.

Interim Financial Statements

Periodically during a year it is desirable to prepare financial statements for the information of administrators and members of the legislative branch of the municipality. Illustration 3–1 shows how a balance sheet would look for the Town of Merrill if it were prepared in 197B after the entries numbered 1 through 13 above were made.

The interim balance sheet, Illustration 3–1, reflects the balances of both proprietary and budgetary accounts. Instead of "Assets," which those familiar with accounting for profit-seeking entities would expect, the caption must be "Assets and Resources," because the excess of Estimated Revenues over Revenues is not an asset as of balance sheet date, but does indicate the amount which will be added to assets when legally budgeted revenues are recognized on the modified accrual basis. Similarly, the caption is not "Equities," or "Liabilities and Capital," or other title commonly found in financial reports of profit-seeking entities, but "Liabilities, Appropriations, Reserves, and Fund Balance." The liabilities section is consistent with that of profit-seeking entities, but the next three sections are all subdivisions of the taxpayers' equity. The first of the three discloses the amount appropriated for the year, less the amount of appropriations which have been expended during the year to date, and less the amount

Illustration 3–1

Interim Balance Sheet
TOWN OF MERRILL
General Fund
Balance Sheet as of Month, Day, 197B

Assets and Resources

Cash			$ 256,787
Taxes receivable–current		$1,368,057	
Less: estimated uncollectible current taxes		68,421	1,299,636
Taxes receivable–delinquent		80,000	
Less: estimated uncollectible delinquent taxes		11,500	68,500
Interest and penalties receivable on taxes		2,969	
Less: estimated uncollectible interest and penalties		1,327	1,642
Estimated revenues		2,628,000	
Less: Revenues		1,327,336	1,300,664
Total Assets and Resources			$2,927,229

Liabilities, Appropriations, Reserves, and Fund Balance

Vouchers payable			$ 296,555
Due to Federal government			99,540
Due to State government			18,490
Tax anticipation notes payable			500,000
Total Liabilities			$ 914,585
Appropriations		$2,700,000	
Less: Expenditures	$725,820		
Encumbrances	36,675	762,495	
Available appropriations			1,937,505
Reserve for encumbrances			36,675
Fund balance			38,464
Total Liabilities, Appropriations, Reserves, and Fund Balance			$2,927,229

of appropriations which have been encumbered by purchase orders and contracts outstanding at balance sheet date; the net is the amount which legally may be expended or encumbered during the remainder of the budget year. In Illustration 3–1 only one item, Reserve for Encumbrances, is shown in the Reserve section, which discloses the portion of net assets and resources which is not available for appropriation because contingent liabilities exist (or because, as discussed later in the Town of Merrill example, certain assets will not be converted into cash in the normal operations of the fund). The remaining section, Fund Balance, discloses that portion of the taxpayers' equity which is available for appropriation. Fund Balance, it should be emphasized, is the excess of the sum of actual assets and budgeted resources over the sum of actual liabilities, available appropriations, and reserves for assets not available for appropriation; in short, it has both proprietary and budgetary aspects.

Interim statements and schedules should be prepared to accompany the interim balance sheet to disclose other information needed by administrators and members of the legislative body; statements comparing the detail of budgeted and actual revenues are illustrated in Chapter 4, and statements comparing appropriations, expenditures, and encumbrances in detail are shown in Chapter 5. Interim statements of Revenue and Expenditures, or changes in Fund Balance, are similar to the end-of-the-year statements illustrated at the end of this chapter.

Illustration of Events Subsequent to Date of Interim Statements

Transactions and events such as the collection of revenue and receivables, and the encumbering and expenditure of appropriations, would obviously occur frequently in a municipality of any appreciable size. Since entries for the recurring events would be similar to the entries illustrated above, it seems unnecessary to present entries for these events in the portion of 197B subsequent to the date of the interim balance sheet shown as Illustration 3–1. Entries for common general fund transactions and events not previously illustrated are shown in the following sections.

Revision of the Budget

Comparisons of budgeted and actual revenues, by sources, and comparisons of departmental or program appropriations with expenditures and encumbrances, as well as interpretation of information which was not available at the time the budgets were originally adopted, may indicate the desirability or necessity of legally amending the budget during the fiscal year. For example, assume that the revenue budget of the Town of Merrill was legally increased by $10,000 in the Charges for Services category, and by $25,000 in the Miscellaneous category, in order to finance the major portion of a legal increase in Appropriations for Health and Welfare in the amount of $40,000. The remainder of the increase in that appropriation was financed by a $5,000 transfer from the Public Works appropriation. The following entry records these amendments:

14.	Estimated Revenues	35,000	
	Appropriations		35,000
	Revenues ledger:	*Debit*	
	Charges for services	10,000	
	Miscellaneous	25,000	
	Appropriation expenditures ledger:	*Debit*	*Credit*
	Public works	5,000	
	Health and welfare		40,000

Collection of Current Taxes

Collections of the first installment of property taxes levied by the Town of Merrill amount to $820,834. Since the revenue was recognized at the time the levy was recorded (see entry 9) the following entry suffices at this time:

15.	Cash	820,834	
	Taxes Receivable—Current		820,834

Repayment of Tax Anticipation Notes

As tax collections begin to exceed current disbursements it becomes possible for the Town of Merrill to repay the local bank for the money borrowed on tax anticipation notes. Just as borrowing the money did not involve the recognition of revenue, the repayment of the principal is merely the extinguishment of debt of the general fund and not an expenditure. Payment of interest, however, must be recognized as the expenditure of an appropriation, because it requires a reduction in the net assets of the fund. Assuming the interest to be $6,250, and that the amount is properly chargeable to the Miscellaneous appropriation, the entry is:

16.	Tax Anticipation Notes Payable	500,000	
	Expenditures	6,250	
	Cash		506,250
	Appropriation expenditures ledger:	*Debit*	
	Miscellaneous	6,250	

Procedures of some municipalities would require the interest expense to have been recorded as an encumbrance against the Miscellaneous appropriation at the time the notes were issued, and the liability for the principal and interest to have been vouchered before payment. Even if these procedures were followed by the Town of Merrill, the net result of all entries is achieved by entry 16.

Interfund Transactions

Water utilities ordinarily provide fire hydrants and water service for fire protection at a flat annual charge. A municipally owned water utility is accounted for by an enterprise fund and should be expected to support the cost of its operations by user charges. Fire protection is logically budgeted for as an activity of the fire department, a general fund department. Assuming that the amount charged by the water utility to the general fund for hydrants and water service is $30,000, and that the fire department budget is a part of the Public Safety category in the Town of Merrill example, the general fund should record its liability as:

17a.	Expenditures	30,000	
	Due to Water Utility Fund		30,000
	Appropriation expenditures ledger:	*Debit*	
	Public safety	30,000	

Municipal utility property is not assessed for property tax purposes, but a number of municipal utilities make an annual contribution to the general fund of the municipality in recognition of the fact that the utility does receive police and fire protection, and other municipal services. If the water utility of the Town of Merrill agrees to contribute $25,000 to the general fund in lieu of taxes, the general fund entry is:

17b.	Due from Water Utility Fund	25,000	
	Revenues		25,000

Revenue ledger:		*Credit*
Miscellaneous		25,000

Adjusting Entries

Physical Inventories. If a municipality is large enough to have sizable inventories of supplies which are used by a number of departments and funds it is generally recommended that the purchasing function be centralized and the supply activity be accounted for by an intragovernmental service fund. For one reason or another some municipalities have not created the appropriate intragovernmental service fund and account for the supply activity as a part of the general fund. In either case accountants would feel that better control was provided if perpetual inventory accounts were kept; this procedure is illustrated in Chapter 9. Many smaller municipalities, such as the Town of Merrill, not only account for supply activity in the general fund, but do so only on the basis of periodic physical inventories. (If only minor amounts are involved, no accounting records at all may be kept.) Materials and supplies purchased by the Town of Merrill during 197B were charged to Expenditures when the invoices were approved for payment. If, at the end of the year, physical inventories show that materials and supplies costing $10,000 are on hand in general fund departments in the Public Works category, and materials and supplies costing $2,300 in Public Safety departments, the entry to record inventories would be:

18a.	Inventory of Supplies	12,300	
	Expenditures		12,300

Appropriation Expenditures ledger:		*Credit*
Public safety		2,300
Public works		10,000

Since the inventory will not be converted into cash in the normal operations of the general fund it is not a liquid asset whose carrying cost should be reflected in Fund Balance (which would be the result of closing the Expenditures account to Fund Balance at year end). It is an asset, however, which will be used in future operations of the fund, and which will relieve future periods of the necessity for incurring expenditures; therefore the cost of the inventory may be reflected as a "Reserve for Inventory of Supplies." This reserve account is classified for balance sheet purposes in the same manner as discussed for Reserve for Encumbrances in regard to the interim balance sheet. The following entry accomplishes the necessary classification:

		Debit	Credit
18b.	Fund Balance	12,300	
	Reserve for Inventory of Supplies		12,300

Write-off of Uncollectible Delinquent Taxes. Just as officers of profit-seeking entities should review aged trial balances of receivables periodically in order to determine the adequacy of allowance accounts, and authorize the write-off of items judged to be uncollectible, so should officers of a municipality review aged trial balances of taxes receivable, and other receivables. Although the levy of property taxes creates a lien against the underlying property in the amount of the tax, accumulated taxes may exceed the market value of the property, or, in the case of personal property, the property may have been removed from the jurisdiction of the municipality. When delinquent taxes are deemed to be uncollectible, the related interest and penalties must also be written off. If the Treasurer of the Town of Merrill receives approval to write off delinquent taxes totaling $4,630, and related interest and penalties of $480, the entry would be:

		Debit	Credit
19.	Estimated Uncollectible Delinquent Taxes	4,630	
	Estimated Uncollectible Interest and Penalties	480	
	Taxes Receivable—Delinquent		4,630
	Interest and Penalties Receivable on Taxes		480

When delinquent taxes are written off, the tax bills are retained in the files, although no longer subject to general ledger control, because changes in conditions may make it possible to collect the amounts in the future. If collections of written-off taxes are made it is highly desirable to return the tax bills to general ledger control by making an entry which is the reverse of the write-off entry, so that the procedures described in connection with entries 12a and 12b may be followed.

Reclassification of Current Taxes. Assuming that all property taxes levied by the Town of Merrill in 197B were to have been paid before the end of the year, any balance of taxes receivable at year-end is properly classified as "delinquent," rather than "current." The related allowance for estimated uncollectible taxes should also be transferred to the "delinquent" classification. An entry to accomplish this, using amounts assumed to exist in the accounts at year-end, is:

		Debit	Credit
20.	Taxes Receivable—Delinquent	273,000	
	Estimated Uncollectible Current Taxes	68,421	
	Taxes Receivable—Current		273,000
	Estimated Uncollectible Delinquent Taxes		68,421

Accrual of Interest and Penalties. Delinquent taxes are subject to interest and penalties, as discussed previously. If the amount of interest and penalties earned in 197B by the general fund of the Town of Merrill and not yet recognized is $3,030, but it is expected that only $2,300 of that can be collected, the following entry is necessary:

21.	Interest and Penalties Receivable on Taxes	3,030	
	Estimated Uncollectible Interest and Penalties		730
	Revenues		2,300

Revenues ledger:	*Credit*
Interest and penalties on delinquent taxes	2,300

Reclassification of Reserve for Encumbrances. Inasmuch as appropriations for 197B may no longer be encumbered after the end of that year, the Reserve for Encumbrances is redesignated Reserve for Encumbrances—Prior Year. If the balance is $72,540 at the end of 197B, the entry is:

22.	Reserve for Encumbrances	72,540	
	Reserve for Encumbrances—Prior Year		72,540

Pre-Closing Trial Balance

Assuming that the illustrated entries for the transactions and events pertaining to the year 197B for the Town of Merrill have been made and posted, and that a number of other entries which are not illustrated because they pertain to similar transactions and events have been made and posted, the trial balance below shows the general fund general ledger accounts before closing entries:

	Debit	*Credit*
Cash	$ 60,664	
Taxes receivable–delinquent	303,000	
Estimated uncollectible delinquent taxes		$ 75,291
Interest and penalties receivable on taxes	5,519	
Estimated uncollectible interest and penalties		1,577
Due from water utility fund	25,000	
Inventory of supplies	12,300	
Estimated revenues	2,663,000	
Revenues		2,667,000
Vouchers payable		88,444
Due to federal government		74,263
Due to state government		19,605
Due to water utility fund		30,000
Appropriations		2,735,000
Expenditures	2,660,161	
Encumbrances	72,540	
Reserve for encumbrances–prior year		72,540
Reserve for inventory of supplies		12,300
Fund balance		26,164
	$5,802,184	$5,802,184

Closing Entries

The essence of the closing process for a municipal revenue fı the transfer of the balances of the nominal proprietary account the balances of the budgetary accounts for the year to the Fund Balance account. Individual accountants have preferences as to the sequence in which this is done, and as to the combinations of accounts in each closing entry. Any sequence and any combination, however, should yield the same result that closing entries for a profit-seeking entity do: all financial events in the history of the organization are summarized in the balance sheet accounts. This effect is achieved by entry 23:

		Debit	Credit
23.	Revenues	2,667,000	
	Appropriations	2,735,000	
	Estimated Revenues		2,663,000
	Expenditures		2,660,161
	Encumbrances		72,540
	Fund Balance		6,299

Although entry 23 affects five general fund general ledger control accounts, it is not considered necessary to make closing entries in their subsidiary ledger accounts because separate subsidiary ledgers are kept for each budget year.

It is important to notice that the closing entry has the effect of reversing the entry made to record the budget (1) and the entry made to amend the budget (14). Therefore, after the closing entry is posted, the Fund Balance account is purely a proprietary account and not one in which historical and expected effects are mixed, as is true during a year. That is, it again represents the net amount of liquid assets available for appropriation for fund purposes.

Year-End Financial Statements

The balance sheet for the general fund of the Town of Merrill as of the end of 197B is shown as Illustration 3–2. Since only proprietary accounts are open, the captions "Assets" and "Liabilities, Reserves and Fund Balance" are used instead of the captions used in the interim balance sheet, Illustration 3–1. The amount due from the water utility fund is offset against the amount due to the same fund and only the net liability is shown in the balance sheet, in accord with the recommendation in the AICPA's *Audits of State and Local Government Units.*

A second statement of value in the administration of general funds is an analysis of changes in fund balance, comparable to the statement of changes in retained earnings used in management of corporations for profit. Statements of this kind may be in either summary or detailed form. The summary form, which is favored by the National Committee on Governmental Accounting, is based upon the fact that the net change in fund balance during a fiscal period is the result of one or more of four common causes of a proprietary nature, which may be itemized in the statement. The detailed form, considered by some accountants to be more informative, presents a comparative summary of both budgetary and proprietary changes. The essential difference between the two

Illustration 3–2

Year-end Balance Sheet
TOWN OF MERRILL
General Fund Balance Sheet as of
December 31, 197B

Assets

Cash		$ 60,664
Taxes receivable–delinquent	$303,000	
Less: Estimated uncollectible delinquent taxes	75,291	227,709
Interest and penalties receivable on taxes	5,519	
Less: Estimated uncollectible interest and penalties	1,577	3,942
Inventory of supplies		12,300
Total Assets		$304,615

Liabilities, Reserves, and Fund Balance

Vouchers payable	$ 88,444
Due to federal government	74,263
Due to state government	19,605
Due to water fund	5,000
Total Liabilities	$187,312
Reserve for encumbrances–prior year	72,540
Reserve for inventory of supplies	12,300
Fund balance	32,463
Total Liabilities, Reserves, and Fund Balance	$304,615

forms of statement derives from the fact that budgetary entries have only a temporary effect upon Fund Balance.

The four changes most likely to appear in the summary form of Fund Balance statement (see Illustration 3–3) are as follows:

1. The difference between actual revenues and actual expenditures during the period.
2. Encumbrances recorded but not converted to firm liabilities during the period, and debited to Fund Balance as a reservation of fund balance.
3. Increases or decreases of reserves established in a prior period or periods.
4. Direct debits or credits to Fund Balance to record correction or prior period transactions.

Schedules supporting balance sheet items such as cash, temporary investments (if any), and taxes receivable are often presented in municipal annual reports to disclose the names of banks in which municipal accounts are kept, the nature of the investments, and the ages of the receivables. Similarly, statements showing the sources of revenues and the purposes of the expenditures accompany the Analysis of Changes in Fund Balance. Statements of revenues and expenditures are illustrated in Chapters 4 and 5, respectively.

Illustration 3–3

TOWN OF MERRILL
General Fund
Analysis of Changes in Fund Balance
For the Fiscal Year Ended December 31, 197B

Fund Balance, January 1, 197B		$110,569
Add: Excess of revenues over expenditures:		
Revenues	$2,667,000	
Expenditures	2,660,161	6,839
Total balance and additions		$117,408
Deduct:		
Reserve for encumbrances, December 31, 197B	72,540	
Reserve for inventory of supplies	12,300	
Expenditures of 197A in excess of reserve for encumbrances, December 31, 197A	105	84,945
Fund Balance, December 31, 197B		$ 32,463

SELECTED REFERENCES

AMERICAN INSTITUTE OF CERTIFIED PUBLIC ACCOUNTANTS. *Audits of State and Local Governmental Units.* New York, 1974.

KENTUCKY MUNICIPAL ACCOUNTING MANUAL. Frankfort, Ky.: State Local Finance Office, Kentucky Department of Finance, 1971.

LOUISIANA MUNICIPAL AUDIT & ACCOUNTING GUIDE. New Orleans: Society of Louisiana Certified Public Accountants and Louisiana Municipal Association, 1972.

NATIONAL COMMITTEE ON GOVERNMENTAL ACCOUNTING. *Governmental Accounting, Auditing, and Financial Reporting*, chaps. 2 and 3, Chicago, 1968.

Uniform System of Accounts for Cities. Albany, NY: State of New York Department of Audit and Control Division of Municipal Affairs, 1966 with revisions through 1972. Also *Uniform System of Accounts for Towns*, 1971; *Uniform System of Accounts for Counties*, 1968; *Uniform System of Accounts for Villages*, 1973.

QUESTIONS

3–1. What municipal activities are commonly accounted for in a general fund? In a special revenue fund?

3–2. Is the "going concern" concept used in accounting for profit-seeking entities equally applicable to accounting for revenue funds? Explain.

3–3. In the balance sheet of a profit-seeking entity it is important to classify assets and liabilities as current or long-term. Is this true for the balance sheet of a governmental unit general fund? Explain.

3–4. In your opinion, is the balance sheet of a municipal general fund a reliable indicator of the municipality's financial condition? Explain.

3–5. Briefly explain what is meant by the "modified accrual" basis of accounting.

3–6. Distinguish between:

a) Expenditure and Encumbrance.
b) Revenues and Estimated Revenues.
c) Reserve for Encumbrances and Encumbrances
d) Reserve for Encumbrances and Fund Balance.
e) Appropriations and Expenditures.

3–7. Is there any general basis for determining how large a general fund Fund Balance should be carried from one year to the next in a prudently managed municipality? Explain.

3–8. The name formerly recommended by the NCGA for the account now called "Estimated Uncollectible Taxes" was "Reserve for Uncollectible Taxes." Do you think some similar change should be made in Reserve for Encumbrances? Defend you answer.

3–9. What is the meaning of the term "Resource" in the caption of an interim balance sheet for a revenue fund? Why is the term not used in a year-end balance sheet for a revenue fund?

3–10. Compare the significance of the Fund Balance during a fiscal year with its significance in a year-end balance sheet.

EXERCISES AND PROBLEMS

3–1. Utilizing the municipal annual report obtained for Exercises 1–1, follow the instructions below.

a) What title is given the fund which functions as a general fund (as described in Chapter 3)?
Does the report state the basis of accounting which is used for the general fund? If so, is the financial statement presentation consistent with the stated basis (i.e., some reports claim that the modified accrual basis was used, but show no receivables in the balance sheet or any other evidence that material and available revenues are accrued)?
If the basis of accounting is not stated analyze the statements to determine which basis is used—full accrual, modified accrual, or cash basis.
Is the same basis used for both revenues and expenditures?
Is the basis used consistent with NCGA and AICPA recommendations, as set forth in this text?

b) What statements and schedules pertaining to the general fund are presented? In what respects (headings, arrangement, items included, etc.) do they seem similar to statements illustrated or described in the text? In what respects do they differ?
What purpose is each statement and schedule intended to serve? How well, in your reasoned opinion, does each statement and schedule accomplish its intended purpose? (You, after reading the first three chapters of this text carefully, have a much greater understanding of the purposes of general fund accounting and

reporting than most other citizens, and even than most non-accountants in elective or appointive municipal governmental positions.)

Are any noncurrent or nonliquid assets included in the general fund balance sheet? If so, are they offset by accounts in the "Reserve" section? Are any noncurrent liabilities included in the general fund balance sheet?

c) What special revenue funds are included in the report? Are they described as special revenue funds, or only by a title such as "Library Fund," "School Fund," "Street Fund," etc.?

Does the report specify why each special revenue fund was created (cite state statute, municipal ordinance or other legislative or administrative action)?

What are the sources of revenue for each fund?

Is the basis of accounting for these funds stated, or must it be determined by analysis of the statements?

Is the same basis used for all special revenue funds? Is it the same basis as used for the general fund? If not, does the report explain why each basis is used?

Is the basis of accounting for special revenue funds consistent with NCGA and AICPA recommendations?

d) What statements and schedules pertaining to the special revenue funds are presented? In what respects (headings, arrangement, items included, etc.) do they seem similar to statements illustrated or described in the text? In what respects do they differ?

What purpose is each statement and schedule intended to serve? How well, in your reasoned opinion, does each statement and schedule accomplish its intended purpose?

Are any noncurrent or nonliquid assets included in the special revenue fund balance sheet? If so, are they offset by accounts in the "Reserve" section? Are any noncurrent liabilities included in the special revenue fund balance sheet?

3–2. In an analysis of changes in fund balance the following differences between actual compared with estimated revenue occurred during the year:

Revenues	$ 4,000 deficiency
Expenditures	10,000 deficiency
Reserve for encumbrances	6,000 deficiency
Reserve for supplies inventory	3,000 excess

What was the excess or deficiency of actual fund balance compared with estimated or expected fund balance at the end of the year?

3–3. A governmental unit maintains an inventory of materials and supplies, with an average balance of $20,000. It is expected that the inventory will be about normal at December 31, 1974. Estimated usage of materials and supplies during 1975 is $139,000. How much should be appropriated for materials and supplies purchases in the 1975 budget? Explain.

3–4. At the end of a fiscal period certain accounts of a general fund had the following balances: Appropriations, $526,000; Estimated Revenues, $523,000; Expenditures, $514,000; Revenues, $521,000. Appropriations included an authorization for an $8,400 expenditure which could not be consummated until the following year and no purchase order had been issued on it. Make what you think to be an appropriate closing entry or closing entries for the above information, including all accounts.

3–5. The City of Walden fiscal year ends on September 30. Near the end of September, a purchase order for $2,200 was issued. Delivery was received on October 11 of the same calendar year. Demonstrate by illustrative journal entries the accounting which should have been made for the purchase, assuming the invoice approved for payment amounted to $2,200.

3–6. A special revenue fund of the Village of Olton had the following account balances as of the end of a recent fiscal year: Cash, $2,340; Inventory of Supplies, $660; Machinery and Equipment, $15,390; Accounts Payable, $1,098; Ten-year Notes Payable, $10,654; Reserve for Encumbrances—Prior Year, $539; Fund Balance, $6,099; Revenues Collected, $64,732; Appropriations, $64,732; Expenditures, $64,193; and Encumbrances, $539.

a) What basis of accounting is apparently used? Why?
b) From the information given, list the account balances which would be eliminated, or adjusted, in order to bring the fund accounts into agreement with NCGA and AICPA recommendations.
c) What additional information is needed in order to bring the fund accounts into agreement with NCGA and AICPA recommendations?

3–7. The following is a list of the ledger accounts of the general fund of the City of Garfunkle, as of September 30 of the current year. (*a*) Determine the amount of Fund Balance as of that date without preparing a balance sheet. *Show computations.* (*b*) Prepare *in good form* an interim balance sheet.

Accounts payable	$ 10,700
Appropriations	551,600
Cash	111,400
Due to other funds	5,900
Encumbrances	12,000
Estimated revenues	556,200
Estimated uncollectible current taxes	22,000
Expenditures	129,000
Petty cash	500
Reserve for encumbrances	12,000
Revenue	457,300
Tax anticipation notes payable	120,000
Taxes receivable–current	383,000
Fund balance	?

3–8. At September 30, 197A, the Fund Balance account of Town of Minnie Creek general fund showed a credit balance of $31,000 after closing entries. The entry made October 1, 197A to record the fiscal year 197B budget was:

Estimated Revenues	789,400	
Appropriations		771,600
Fund Balance		17,800
To record budget for fiscal year ending September 30, 197B.		

There were no amendments of the budget during fiscal 197B. The September 30, 197B closing entry was as follows:

Revenues	791,900	
Appropriations	771,600	
Fund Balance	13,500	
Expenditures		769,500
Estimated Revenues		789,400
Encumbrances		18,100
To close temporary accounts for fiscal 197B, and transfer their net balance to Fund Balance account.		

During fiscal 197B the fund received $45 cash as a refund on an expenditure of a prior year. The amount was credited to Fund Balance.

a) You are required to prepare a detailed analysis of changes in Town of Minnie Creek general fund balance during the fiscal year 197B, using the information detailed above.

b) What difference would it make in the statement if a Reserve for Inventory of Supplies had been established from Fund Balance, in in the amount of $8,000? In which section of your statement would the $8,000 be shown and what would be the amount of Fund Balance at September 30, 197B?

3–9. At the beginning of a certain year the accounts of a small city had the balances listed below:

	Debit	*Credit*
Cash on hand and in bank	$ 6,230	
Due from school corporation	1,980	
Taxes receivable	31,756	
Estimated uncollectible taxes		$12,607
Interest and penalties receivable	1,884	
Estimated uncollectible interest and penalties		739
Due to water fund		108
Vouchers payable		3,615
Accrued expenses		433
Fund balance		24,348
	$41,850	$41,850

During the year the following transactions, stated in summary form, took place:

1. The city council, county board of review, and state tax board approved a budget which provided for revenues of $713,000 and expenditures of $716,000.
2. The revenue budget included an estimate of $100,500 from miscellaneous revenue. The remainder of estimated revenue was to be provided by a property tax levy that, with shrinkage of 2 percent because of uncollectibles, would yield the required amount. The required amount was levied.
3. Total encumbrances for commodities and services, except personal services, amounted to $652,300.
4. Additional interest and penalties charged on past due taxes during the year totaled $3,864, of which one-third was deemed uncollectible.
5. Personal services of $59,040 were paid during the year.
6. Supplies which had cost $1,419 were transferred to the school corporation during the year.
7. Collections during the year were as follows:

Taxes	$618,100
Interest and penalties	2,017
Due from school corporation	2,320
Miscellaneous revenues (not accrued)	101,200

8. Taxes receivable of $13,600 and interest and penalties of $811 were written off as uncollectible.
9. $2,801 of this year's tax levy was canceled because of duplications.
10. Invoices totaling a net amount $641,100, applying to purchases and contracts which had been encumbered at $639,070, were received during the year and vouchered, with which was included the accrued expense at the beginning of the year and the amount due to the water fund.
11. Vouchers payable totaling $643,840 were paid.
12. Expenses incurred but not yet recorded at the close of business at the end of the year totaled $516.

Required:

a) Make T accounts and record the balances as of the beginning of the year.
b) Record the transactions directly in the T accounts.
c) Record directly in the T accounts the closing entry or closing entries.
d) Prepare a balance sheet as of the end of the year.
e) Prepare a detailed analysis of changes in Fund Balance.

3–10. A new bookkeeper employed by the Town of Bentonville began his duties on January 20, 197B, following departure of his predecessor. Records of the town appeared to be in general disorder, as well as mostly fragmentary. He began by selecting the general fund for immediate attention and discovered what appeared to be fairly dependable records of three items as follows, correct for December 31, 197A.

Cash (confirmed from bank statements)	$40,000
Inventory of supplies	10,000
Accounts payable	35,000

Further investigation over a period of time revealed the following additional information about Bentonville's general fund, on or before the end of 197A:

1. After diligent search and extensive use of adding machines the new bookkeeper arrived at $45,000 as the amount of prior years' taxes uncollected at January 1, 197A, and at $175,000 as the probable amount of the levy for that year.
2. From adding machine tapes, deposit slips, copies of tax receipts, and other similar evidence he recorded as the apparent amounts which had been collected during 197A: $20,000 on prior years' levies and $140,000 on the levy for 197A.
3. Recognizing that some taxes might have been paid without a careful record having been made, the bookkeeper set up liberal estimates for uncollectible taxes, for December 31, 197A. He provided $15,000 for prior years' taxes and $10,000 for the 197A levy.
4. Statements from the central stores fund showed $5,000 due to that fund and other evidence showed $2,000 due from the street fund. Both of these amounts were confirmed by the affected funds.
5. Shortly after the new bookkeeper's arrival an invoice for $180 was received for services rendered for the city in 197A.
6. A quantity of supplies with an invoice for $418 was received during January, 197B, shortly before the new bookkeeper's arrival. No formal encumbrance for the purchase order, dated November 30, 197A, had been made. No other similar bills were found.
7. When the bookkeeper showed the town board his preliminary adjusted figures for December 31, 197A, members of the board recognized a number of prior years' tax bills which they considered uncollectible and instructed him to write off an amount that totaled $2,000 before setting up his records for the beginning of 197B.

Required:

Assuming that new journals and ledgers are to be opened, effective January 1, 197B, show in general journal form the entry, or entries, necessary to record the opening balances in the new general ledger accounts for the general fund of the Town of Bentonville.

3–11. The Town of New Madison current fund had the following after-closing trial balance at April 30, 197C, the end of its fiscal year "197C":

	Debit	Credit
Cash		$ 1,860
Taxes receivable–delinquent	$57,400	
Estimated uncollectible delinquent taxes		18,300
Interest and penalties receivable	2,469	
Estimated uncollectible interest and penalties		1,327
Inventory of supplies	15,480	
Vouchers payable		3,440
Due to federal government		5,887
Reserve for inventory of supplies		15,480
Fund balance		29,055
	$75,349	$75,349

During the six months ended October 31, 197C, the first six months of fiscal year 197D, the following transactions, in summary form, occurred:

1. The budget for fiscal 197D, which detailed estimated property tax revenues of $182,000, estimated revenues from other sources of $97,000, and appropriations of $270,000, was recorded.
2. The town board authorized a temporary loan of $30,000 in the form of a 120-day note payable and the loan was obtained at a discount of 6 percent per annum. (Debit Expenditures for discount.)
3. The property tax levy for fiscal 197D was recorded. Net assessed valuation of taxable property for the year was $3,800,000 and the tax rate was $5.10 per hundred. It was estimated that 4 percent of the levy would be uncollectible. Classify this tax levy as current.
4. Purchase orders, contracts, etc., in the amount of $93,150 were issued to vendors and others.
5. $93,700 of current taxes, $24,100 of delinquent taxes, and interest and penalties of $1,016 were collected. Due to delinquencies in payment of the first installment of taxes, additional penalties of $1,413 were levied.
6. Total payroll during the first six months was $46,209. Of that amount, $2,703 was withheld for employees' FICA tax liability, $6,331 for employees' federal income tax liability, and $1,942 for state taxes; the balance was paid in cash.
7. The employer's FICA tax liability of $2,703 was recorded.
8. Revenues from sources other than taxes were collected in the amount of $31,050.
9. Amounts due the federal government as of April 30, and amounts due for FICA taxes and state and federal withholding taxes during the first six months of fiscal 197D, were vouchered.
10. Purchase orders and contracts encumbered in the amount of $86,070 were filled at a net cost of $86,491, which was vouchered.
11. $97,146 cash was paid on vouchers payable and credit for cash discount earned was $803. (Credit Expenditures.)
12. By direction of the town board, the town's depository charged the temporary loan to the town's bank balance.

Required:

a) Journalize transactions for the six months ended October 31. You need not record subsidiary ledger debits and credits.

b) Prepare an interim balance sheet as of October 31, 197C.

3–12. This problem continues problem 3–11. During the second six months of fiscal 197D the following transactions which affected the current fund of the Town of New Madison occurred:

1. Due to a change in a state law, effective July 1, it appeared the town would receive $10,000 less state revenue than was estimated. An entry was made to correct the revenue estimate but no reduction of appropriations was made.
2. Purchase orders and other commitment documents in the amount of $95,404 were issued during the latter six months.
3. Property taxes of $530 and interest and penalties receivable of $109, which had been written off in prior years, were collected. Twenty-one dollars of additional interest which had accrued since the write-off was collected at the same time.
4. Personnel costs, excluding the employer's share of the FICA tax, totaled $31,817 for the second six months. Withholdings amounted to $5,090 for FICA and federal withholding tax, and $1,273 for state withholding tax; the balance was paid in cash.
5. The employer's FICA tax of $1,862 was recorded as a liability.
6. The county board of review discovered unassessed properties of a total taxable value of $51,000 located within the town boundaries. The owners of these properties were charged with taxes at the town rate of $2.00 per hundred dollars assessed value.
7. Current taxes of $71,310, delinquent taxes of $9,201, interest and penalties of $1,032, and miscellaneous revenue of $54,212 were collected. No part of any of these amounts was included in any other transaction.
8. Accrued interest and penalties, estimated to be 30 percent uncollectible, was recorded in the amount of $2,100.
9. All unpaid current year's taxes having become delinquent after the first Monday in November were transferred to that classification.
10. All amounts due to the federal government and state government were vouchered.
11. Invoices and bills for goods and services which had been encumbered at $96,218 were received in the amount of $95,413 and were vouchered.
12. Personal property taxes of $3,994 and interest and penalties of $418 were written off because of inability to locate the property owners.
13. A physical inventory of materials and supplies at April 30, 197D, showed a total of $17,321.
14. Payments made on vouchers during the second half-year totaled $99,842.

Required:

a) Journalize transactions for the second half of fiscal 197D.
b) Journalize closing entries.
c) Prepare a balance sheet as of April 30, 197D.
d) Prepare an analysis of changes in Fund Balance for the fiscal year ended April 30, 197D.

CONTINUOUS PROBLEMS

3–L. Presented below are a number of transactions of the general fund of the City of Bingham which occurred during the first six months of the year for which the budget given in Problem 2–L was prepared. You are required to:

a) Record in the general journal the transactions given below. Make any computations to the nearest dollar. For each entry affecting budgetary accounts show subsidiary account titles and amounts as well as general ledger control account titles and amounts.

1. A general tax levy in the amount of $2,688,776 was made. It is estimated that 2 percent of the tax will be uncollectible.
2. Tax anticipation notes in the amount of $250,000 were issued.
3. Purchase orders, contracts, and other commitment documents were issued against appropriations in the following amounts:

	Amount
General government:	
Central administration	$ 67,000
Finance	18,600
Personnel	10,400
Public safety:	
Police	48,750
Fire	109,250
Public works	342,000
Health	112,000
Public welfare	103,000
Recreation	138,000
Miscellaneous	16,000
Total	$965,000

4. The general fund collected the following in cash: delinquent taxes, $212,000; interest and penalties receivable on taxes, $10,720; licenses and permits $188,000; fines and forfeits, $103,000; charges for services, $24,500; and miscellaneous, $27,000.
5. A petty cash fund was established for general operating purposes in the amount of $6,000.
6. General fund payrolls totaled $983,000. Of that amount $124,950 was withheld for employees' income taxes, and $57,505 was withheld for employees' FICA tax liability; the

balance was paid in cash. The encumbrances system is not used for payrolls. The payrolls were for the following departments:

General government:	
City council and clerk	$ 31,110
Central administration	54,346
Municipal court and attorney	57,450
Finance	80,015
Personnel	38,312
Public safety:	
Police	200,403
Fire	180,728
Building safety	35,190
Animal pound	10,250
Traffic engineering	41,200
Public works	111,732
Health	22,066
Public welfare	28,653
Recreation	91,545
Total	$983,000

7. The liability for the city's share of FICA taxes, $57,505, was recorded. The amount was budgeted as a part of the Contributions appropriation.
8. Invoices for some of the services and supplies ordered in transaction (3) were received and approved for payment; departments affected are shown below:

	Actual	*Estimated*
General government:		
Central administration	$ 58,900	$ 60,500
Finance	20,100	18,600
Personnel	10,300	10,000
Public safety:		
Police	40,000	38,350
Fire	104,375	100,150
Public works	300,000	298,500
Health	111,700	112,000
Public welfare	98,100	97,800
Recreation	122,125	125,000
Miscellaneous	12,400	12,000
Totals	$878,000	$872,900

9. Delinquent taxes receivable in the amount of $11,683 were written off as uncollectible. Interest and penalties accrued on these taxes amounted to $584; this was also written off.
10. Invoices for all items encumbered in the prior year were received and approved for payment in the amount of $14,180. (In addition to recording the transaction, also close the Expenditures—Prior Year account and the Reserve for Encumbrances—Prior Year to Fund Balance at this time.)
11. Collections of the first installment of current year's taxes totaled $1,380,000.
12. Payments on general fund vouchers amounted to $1,070,000.
13. Collections on delinquent taxes written off in a prior year

amounted to $438. Interest and penalties collected on these taxes was $44 additional ($30 of this had been accrued at the time the accounts were written off).

14. The general fund vouchered its required contributions to the Employees' Pension Fund, $58,980; its liability for employees' income taxes withheld; the total amount of FICA tax liability; and the amount due other funds on July 1. Checks were drawn for all these vouchers.

15. In view of current information, the city council revised the budget for the current year as shown below:

General Fund	*Budget Adjustments Inc. (Dec.)*
Estimated revenues:	
Taxes	–
Licenses and permits	$ 3,000
Fines and forfeits	4,000
Intergovernmental revenue	(21,000)
Charges for services	–
Miscellaneous revenue	5,000
Appropriations:	
General government:	
City council and clerk	$ 2,500
Central administration	64,200
Municipal court and attorney	4,800
Finance	(3,750)
Personnel	1,750
Public Safety:	
Police	$ (4,000)
Fire	(4,000)
Building safety	1,500
Animal pound	2,800
Traffic engineering	(8,800)
Public works	–
Health	–
Public welfare	$ 14,000
Recreation	–
Contributions	(68,000)
Miscellaneous	(3,000)

b) Post each entry to the general ledger accounts. Do not open subsidiary ledger accounts until instructed to do so in a subsequent "L" problem.

c) Prepare a trial balance of the general fund general ledger as of December 31, 19__, the end of the first six months of the fiscal year.

d) Prepare in good form an interim balance sheet for the general fund as of December 31, 19__.

3–S. Presented below are a number of transactions of the general fund of the City of Smithville which occurred during the year for which the budget given in Problem 2–S was prepared, the calendar year 197B.

a) Record in the general journal the transactions given below. Make any computations to the nearest dollar. For each entry affecting budgetary accounts show subsidiary account titles and amounts as well as general ledger control account titles and amounts.

1. The real property tax levy for the year was made to yield the budgeted amount, assuming that 98 percent of the levy would be collectible.
2. Encumbrances in the following amounts were recorded against the appropriations indicated:

General government	$ 55,200
Public safety–Police	52,420
Public safety–Fire	50,980
Public safety–Building safety	5,760
Public works	147,420
Health and welfare	103,050
Parks and recreation	78,000
Miscellaneous	24,750
	$517,580

3. Cash collections during the year totaled: current property taxes, $735,000; delinquent property taxes, $180,000; interest and penalties receivable on taxes, $25,088—of which $19,643 had been accrued as of the first of the year, and $5,445 was revenue of the current year (make the entry to record this revenue); the amounts due from other funds and from the state government at the beginning of the year; licenses and permits, $303,500; fines and forfeits, $186,000; intergovernmental revenue, $150,000; charges for services, $43,000; miscellaneous revenue, $18,463; and sales taxes, $836,000.
4. General fund payrolls for the year totaled $2,004,542. Of that amount $220,454 was withheld for employees' federal income taxes; $110,265 for employees' share of FICA taxes; $44,908 for employees' state income taxes; and the balance was paid in cash. The payrolls were chargeable against the following departmental appropriations:

General government	$226,320
Public safety–Police	487,506
Public safety–Fire	463,918
Public safety–Building safety	46,080
Public works	353,808
Health and welfare	226,710
Parks and recreation	182,000
Miscellaneous	18,200

5. The municipality's share of FICA taxes, $110,265, and the municipality's contribution to other retirement funds administered by the state government, $149,350, were recorded as liabilities.
6. Invoices for some of the services and supplies recorded as encumbrances in transaction (2) were received and approved

for payment as listed below. Related encumbrances were canceled in the amounts listed below:

	Expenditure	*Encumbrance*
General government	$ 54,656	$ 55,200
Public safety–Police	53,240	52,420
Public safety–Fire	44,364	45,000
Public safety–Building safety	5,760	5,760
Public works.	113,490	113,400
Health and welfare	105,000	103,050
Parks and recreation	72,000	75,000
Miscellaneous	24,700	24,750
	$473,210	$474,580

7. Checks were drawn in payment of vouchers totaling $700,000; in payment of the tax anticipation notes and the amount due other funds as of December 31, 197A; in payment of $6,000 interest on the notes; $400,584 of the amount due the federal government for withholding taxes and FICA taxes; and $40,306 of the amount due to the state government for state withholding tax and contributions to the state retirement funds. Interest expense is budgeted in the Miscellaneous appropriation.
8. The appropriations budget was legally amended as follows:

	Increases	*Decreases*
General government	$ 5,000	
Public safety–Police	16,600	
Public safety–Fire	4,500	
Public safety–Building safety		$ 5,700
Public works.	10,000	
Health and welfare		11,700
Parks and recreation		3,000
Contributions	11,615	
Miscellaneous		600
	$47,715	$21,000

9. The City of Smithville received notification that the state government would remit $150,000 to it early in the next fiscal year; this amount had been included in the budget for the current year as "Intergovernmental revenue."
10. Interest and penalties receivable on delinquent taxes was increased by $11,987; $4,685 of this was estimated as uncollectible.
11. Current taxes receivable uncollected at year end, and the related estimated uncollectible current taxes account, were both transferred to the delinquent category.
12. Delinquent taxes receivable in the amount of $16,247 were written off as uncollectible. Interest and penalties already recorded as receivable on these taxes, amounting to $14,302, was also written off. Additional interest on these taxes which had legally accrued was not recorded since it was deemed uncollectible in its entirety.
13. Postaudit disclosed that $9,760 which had been recorded during the year as an encumbrance and, later, as an expenditure in

the same amount, of the general government appropriation of the general fund should have been charged to the Sewage Utility Fund. An interfund invoice was prepared for $9,760 by the general fund.

14. Services received by the general government departments of the general fund from other funds amounted to $8,990; the liability was recorded by the general fund.

b) Post each entry to the general ledger accounts. Do not open subsidiary ledger accounts until instructed to do so in subsequent "S" problems. Prepare a trial balance of the general ledger.

c) Prepare and post the necessary general fund general ledger closing entries, as of December 31, 197B

d) Prepare in good form a balance sheet for the general fund, as of December 31, 197B

e) Prepare in good form an Analysis of Changes in Fund Balance for the year ended December 31, 197B

4

General Funds and Special Revenue Funds: Revenue Accounting

Revenue, in governmental accounting, is defined in general terms as an increase in Fund Balance. General funds and special revenue funds operated in accord with recommendations of the National Committee on Governmental Accounting recognize "material and available" revenues on the accrual basis; all other revenues are recognized on the cash basis. Chapter 2 discusses some of the problems of budgeting revenues. Chapter 3 discusses general ledger accounting for revenues. In each chapter reference is made to the discussion of detailed revenue accounting in this chapter.

Functions of Revenue Accounting

The primary functions of general fund and special revenue fund detailed revenue accounting are as follows:

1. To provide means for determining whether all revenue which should have been received has, in fact, been received.
2. To furnish information for preparing various kinds of financial statements.
3. To implement budgeting and planning for the future by giving necessary information about sources of revenue which have been utilized and the amount obtained from each source. Revenue information is greatly enhanced in value if it conforms to standards and practices followed generally in the field of governmental accounting. Of special importance is adherence to prevailing classifications, such as those recommended by the National Committee on Governmental Accounting.

Three major influences prevent a complete standardization of revenue classification. One of these is honest difference of opinion; the nature of some revenue transactions is such that they might easily fit into two or more classifications. A second influence is lack of information; it is not possible to describe all revenue subclasses with such clarity that their meaning will be unquestionably clear to all readers. The third influence is difference in variety and volume of revenue transactions; variations of those kinds lead to many different selections and combinations of titles, each designed best to fit requirements of the governmental unit for which it was established. Development of informative and dependable revenue classifications is promoted in the main by two factors. One of these is the existence of well-prepared classification manuals, and the other is free and continuing exchange of information between governmental accountants.

The primary classification of governmental revenue is by fund and source. However, within a given primary classification, two or more secondary classes may be desirable for better and more significant description of the revenue. Thus, under the primary classification Intergovernmental Revenue, it may be necessary to have a secondary class for Federal Grants and another for State Grants, each of which in turn may have subclasses.

The most authoritative classification of governmental revenue is that approved by the National Committee on Governmental Accounting for a large municipality. However, with deletions and additions it is adaptable to smaller units of governments and states. The classification provides principally for revenues of general, special revenue, capital projects, and debt service funds. The six *source* classes recommended by the committee are:

Taxes
Licenses and permits
Intergovernmental revenue
Charges for services
Fines and forfeits
Miscellaneous revenue

The classification does not provide for revenue transactions of utility or other enterprise funds; these are expected to be consistent with the classifications used by investor-owned utilities or other enterprises.

The sixfold classification applies to revenues of *funds*, rather than of *governmental units*. Some transactions represent revenue for a fund but not for the governmental unit; others represent revenue for a governmental unit but not for a fund. A capital projects fund sells bonds but does not pay them at maturity. The proceeds are revenue to the capital projects fund but not to the governmental unit, because another of its funds will have to pay the liability. The student should recall that each fund is not only an accounting entity but also a fiscal entity, created, usually, because of the requirements of law. A governmental unit, therefore, is not a "unit" in the absolute sense of the word; it is a collection of related fiscal and accounting entities. These concepts will become clearer with the study of Chapters 5 through 14.

Referring again to the sixfold classification, it is probable that many revenue funds require all six of the source classes. Some may require more, some fewer. Each municipality must be guided in its classifications by relevant state law, and by the terms of grants.

Taxes

Taxes are of particular importance because (1) they provide a very large portion of the revenue of governmental units on all levels, and (2) they are compulsory contributions to the cost of government, whether the affected taxpayer approves or disapproves of the levy.

Ad valorem (based on value) property taxes are a mainstay of financing for many units of local government, but are omitted from the financial plans of most states and the Federal government. Some property taxes are levied on a basis other than property *values*, one illustration being the tax on some kinds of financial institutions in relation to the deposits at a specified date. Some other kinds of taxes are sales taxes, net income taxes, gross receipts taxes, death and gift taxes, and interest and penalties on delinquent taxes.

Ad valorem taxes lend themselves to use of the accrual basis of accounting. This is true because both values and rates must be determined in advance of the period in which the resulting taxes are to be collected. For that reason, the liability of each individual taxpayer is ascertainable at the beginning of each collection period. This permits accrual of charges against the taxpayer, as discussed in preceding chapters.

Even though taxes become liens upon the underlying property, collections in a given period sometimes fall substantially short of the amount levied. If expenditure commitments are based upon the amount levied but actual collections fall short of anticipations, the result may be a condition of financial stringency for the taxing unit. Accordingly, *laws of some states require municipalities to record all revenue*, including tax revenue, *on the cash basis*. If the cash basis is applied strictly, the receivable from billed taxes cannot be recorded as an asset even though by all accounting criteria it should be. A procedure which permits placing the receivable under accounting control but defers recognition of the revenue until it is collected is illustrated below:

	Debit	Credit
Taxes Receivable—Current	1,000,000	
Estimated Uncollectible Current Taxes		20,000
Reserve for Uncollected Taxes		980,000

The entry above records the levy of property taxes, assumed to be in the amount of $1,000,000 with two percent estimated as uncollectible. The debit and the first credit agree with those of entry 9 of the illustrative case in Chapter 3. The second credit, however, is to Reserve for Uncollected Taxes, instead of Revenues. The nature of Reserve for Uncollected Taxes is consistent, under cash basis theory, with that of other reserves discussed in Chapter 3. The balance of the Reserve for Uncollected Taxes would be deducted from the net Taxes Receivable on the balance sheet, so that the net noncash item does not add to the asset total.

When some of the taxes are collected, the following two entries are necessary:

Cash	365,000	
Taxes Receivable—Current		365,000
Reserve for Uncollected Taxes	365,000	
Revenues		365,000

Revenues ledger:	*Credit*
Property taxes	365,000

The two entries are illustrated because the first one summarizes entries that would be made from source documents originated by the cashier each time taxes are collected. The second entry shows that, periodically, the accounts must be adjusted to reflect the collection of the Uncollected Taxes and the cash basis recognition of revenue.

Discounts on Taxes. Some governmental units utilize a cash discount system to encourage early payment of property taxes. Although a small amount of revenue is lost from discounts taken, the practice minimizes the use of short-term borrowing or, another alternative, carrying over a sizable available cash balance from the preceding period. If not prohibited by law, discounts are best accounted for as reductions of the amount of revenue to be derived from a given tax levy. Thus, if a tax levy totals $200,000 and the estimated discounts that will be taken amount to $1,800, the latter figure may be subtracted from the amount of the levy, along with the estimated loss from uncollectible taxes, to give the net estimated revenue. Assuming an estimated loss from uncollectible taxes of $3,100, the $200,000 levy, with discount provision, would be recorded as follows:

Taxes Receivable—Current	200,000	
Estimated Uncollectible Current Taxes		3,100
Estimated Discounts on Taxes		1,800
Revenues		195,100

Revenues ledger:	*Credit*
Property Taxes	195,100

Payment of taxes within the discount period requires a debit to the Estimated Discounts on Taxes account of the amount earned, in the following manner, using assumed amounts:

Cash	197	
Estimated Discounts on Taxes	3	
Taxes Receivable—Current		200

If discounts are taken in excess of the amount of allowance created, the excess will be debited to Revenues—Property Taxes. Any balance remaining in the allowance after the close of the discount period should be transferred to Revenues—Property Taxes by a credit to that account and a debit to the Estimated Discounts on Taxes account.

As a device for closer control against unwarranted granting of discounts, it may be required that discounts on taxes be covered by an appropriation. Under this method the allowance for discounts is not established when the tax levy is recorded. Discounts granted are debited to Expenditures in the following manner, assuming an entry for one month's collection of taxes:

Cash	23,640	
Expenditures—Discount on Taxes	360	
Taxes Receivable—Current		24,000

Most kinds of nonproperty taxes do not lend themselves to use of the accrual basis. They are sometimes described as self-assessing, which means that primary responsibility for determination and reporting of the tax liability lies with the taxpayer. The governmental unit has no effective way of determining in advance the amounts of business earnings, sales of goods or services, or net income subject to taxation, so no advance charges may be made. The nature of nonproperty taxes does not preclude the making of estimates, but charges to individuals based on such income are not feasible even though applicable rates are known well in advance of the tax period. Budgeting and accounting for nonproperty taxes is discussed in Chapters 2 and 3, respectively.

Licenses and Permits

Licenses and Permits include those revenues collected by a governmental unit from individuals or business concerns for various rights or privileges granted by the government. Some licenses and permits are primarily regulatory in nature, with minor consideration to revenue derived; whereas others are not only regulatory but provide large amounts of revenue as well, and some are almost exclusively revenue producers. Licenses and permits may relate to the privilege of carrying on business for a stipulated period, the right to do a certain thing which may affect the public welfare, or the right to use certain public property. Vehicle and alcoholic beverage licenses are found extensively on the state level and serve both regulatory and revenue functions. States make widespread use of professional and occupational taxes for purposes of control. Municipalities make extensive use of licenses and permits to control the activities of their citizens; and from some they derive substantial amounts of revenue. Commonly found among municipal licenses and permits are building permits, vehicle licenses, amusement licenses, business and occupational licenses, animal licenses, and street and curb permits. Revenue from parking meters, formerly included in this class, has been transferred to Charges for Services in the latest pronouncement of the National Committee on Governmental Accounting.

Regardless of the governmental level or the purpose of a license or permit, the revenue it produces must be accounted for on a cash basis. Applicable rates or schedules of charges for a future period may be established well in advance, and fairly reliable information may be available as to the number of licenses or permits to be issued; but the probable degree of fluctuation in the latter factor is so great as to prevent satisfactory use of the accrual basis. Uncertainty as to volume of licenses or permits likewise creates a problem in determining whether all revenue paid in for rights or privileges has been accounted for by those employees making collections. Comparisons with records of previous years, survey or inspection to locate and identify persons or businesses subject to the license, and the use of prenumbered standard license or permit forms are control practices which minimize failure to collect or to account for amounts collected. All collections from licenses and permits should be reported on a standard form with complete information to facilitate entry in the Cash Receipts record, of whatever nature, and to assure that a proper audit may be made at any time in the future.

Intergovernmental Revenue

Each main category of Intergovernmental Revenue—federal, state, and local—has three subdivisions: grants, shared revenues, and payments in lieu of taxes. Briefly described, the three classes have the following meanings:

1. A grant is a receipt of money not related to any specific revenue of the grantor. Welfare grants illustrate this class.
2. Shared revenue is a receipt of money related to specific revenue collected by the grantor. At the federal level there are currently two kinds of shared revenue: *general* and *special*, as discussed in Chapter 2.
3. Payments in lieu of taxes are receipts of money from another governmental unit which, while not subject to taxes by the recipient unit, nevertheless agrees to make a contribution for taxes it would have had to pay as a private individual, either real or corporate. An example is a payment by a city in lieu of taxes it would have had to pay on property located outside the city limits.

Some kinds of intergovernmental revenues can well be accounted for on the accrual basis while other kinds cannot. Of the first category an example is grants by state and federal agencies. Ordinarily the amounts of such grants are announced somewhat in advance of their actual distribution, which makes it possible to record the revenue with a debit to Due from State Government or some such title, even to the extent of designating the agency or department from which the grant is forthcoming. Distributions of shared revenues, stating amounts, are frequently announced in advance of the actual disbursements and are obviously adapted to accrual. In its *Audits of State and Local Governmental Units,* the AICPA suggests that the terms of each grant be reviewed for guidance as to whether revenues from the grant should be recognized on the cash or the accrual basis.

Charges for Services

Charges for Services includes revenue from charges for all activities of a governmental unit, except the operations of utilities, airports, public housing, and other similar semicommercial enterprises. A few of the many revenue items included in this category are: court costs; special police service; refuse collection charges; street, sidewalk, and curb repairs; receipts from parking meters; library use fees (not fines); and tuition.

Chapter 5 presents a classification of general fund expenditures by function. The grouping of Charges for Services revenue is correlated with the functional classification of expenditures. For example, one functional group of expenditures is named General Government, another Public Safety, and so on. A governmental unit, in connection with providing general government service, collects some revenue such as court cost charges, fees for recording legal documents, zoning and subdivision fees, and others. Thus Charges for Services is divided into functions. Subclasses are provided for the different kinds of revenue related to each function. The National Committee on Governmental Accounting recommends the following scheme for identifying revenue from the Highways and Streets service:

343 Highways and Streets
- 343.1 Street, sidewalk and curb repairs
- 343.2 Parking meters
- 343.3 Street lighting charges
- 343.4 Bridge and tunnel tolls
- 343.5 – 343.9 Others

It should be borne in mind that Highways and Streets is primarily an expenditure classification. The scheme described for classifying service charges seeks to correlate revenue from given kinds of service with costs incurred in providing the service.

Few kinds of charges for services lend themselves to accounting on the accrual basis.

Fines and Forfeits

Revenue from Fines and Forfeits includes fines and penalties for commission of statutory offenses and for neglect of official duty; forfeitures of amounts held as security against loss or damage, or collections from bonds or sureties placed with the government for the same purpose; and penalties of any sort, except those levied on delinquent taxes. Library fines are included in this category. If desired, Fines and Forfeits may be the titles of two accounts within this revenue class; or they may be subgroup headings for more detailed breakdowns.

Revenues of this classification are generally accounted for on the cash basis. In direct contrast with general property taxes, neither rates nor base or volume may be predetermined with any reasonable degree of accuracy for this type of revenue. Because of these uncertainties, it is often difficult to determine whether all amounts paid by transgressors have been accounted for. However, money collected and reported is accounted for as illustrated in Chapter 3 for revenue on a cash basis.

Miscellaneous Revenue[1]

Although the word "miscellaneous" is not informative and should be used sparingly, its use as the title of a revenue category is necessary. It (1) substitutes for other possible source classes which might have rather slight and infrequent usage and (2) minimizes the need for forcing some kinds of revenue into source classifications in which they do not generically belong. While Miscellaneous Revenue in itself represents a compromise, its existence aids in sharpening the meanings of other source classes. The heterogeneous nature of items served by the title is indicated by the following listing: interest earnings (other than on delinquent taxes); rents and royalties; sales of, and compensation for loss of, fixed assets; contributions from public enterprises (utilities, airports, etc.); escheats (taking of property in default of legally qualified claimants); contributions and donations from private sources; balances from discontinued funds; and "other."

Some items of Miscellaneous Revenue, such as interest earnings on investments, might well be accrued but mostly they are accounted for on the cash basis.

Other Classifications

The reader is reminded that the source classes discussed in preceding sections of this chapter are those recommended by the NCGA for use by general, special revenue, debt service, and capital projects funds. Even though classification of revenue by source classes and subdivisions of classes is of predominant importance, other groupings may be required by law, or may better fit the needs of a given municipality. As an example of the latter, in addition to showing classes and subdivisions a governmental unit may desire to identify and group its general fund revenues

[1] Some governmental units are required by law to include in revenue amounts received from other funds for payment of specific liabilities. An example is money received from another fund for payment of maturing bonds payable. This is not revenue in the true sense.

by the organizational units (street department, city court, city engineer's office, etc.) which collected the revenue. Organizational identification is useful in connection with accounting control (establishing individual responsibility) and for auditing purposes. Organizational classification is accomplished, basically, by recording on each revenue ledger sheet the department responsible for collection of the revenue recorded thereon. It is merely an addition to the system of identifying by source and subclass.

Revenue Ledger

The discussions in Chapters 2 and 3 of the Revenue control account and the Estimated Revenues control account refer briefly to the functions of the subsidiary ledger that supports each. This section presents the essential considerations of revenue subsidiary ledger accounting.

There is no standard prescribed form for revenue ledger accounts. The widespread use of electronic data processing for municipal accounting purposes enables many municipalities to produce subsidiary records, as well as general ledgers, as computer print-outs. Smaller municipalities use mechanical or manual methods of record-keeping. Whatever the data processing system, certain general requirements prevail. The revenue subsidiary account form should provide for showing at least the following information:

1. Complete heading, including account code.
2. Dates of entries.
3. Explanation or reference.
4. Folio or posting reference column.
5. Items affecting the Estimated Revenues control account.
6. Items affecting the Revenues control account.
7. Balance, or Estimated Revenue Not Yet Realized.

A simple arrangement of the basic information is shown in Illustration 4–1.

Illustration 4–1 shows the subsidiary ledger account for estimated and actual revenues arising from licenses and permits in the hypothetical small city referred to in the Chapter 3 illustrative case. A similar subsidiary ledger account would be kept for each other item of revenue shown in the budget. The heading of Illustration 4–1 indicates that in an actual municipality it is useful to keep subsidiary records in much more detail than that illustrated in the Town of Merrill example. The amount of detail actually kept is suggested by the discussion of each of the sources of revenue in the early sections of this chapter. Thus, in the Licenses and Permits source class subsidiary records should be kept for each kind of license or permit available to the municipality; such as business licenses for restaurants, bars, grocery stores, theaters;

Illustration 4–1

Revenue Ledger
TOWN OF MERRILL
General Fund

Class: Licenses and Permits — Number: 351.1
Subclass: — Title:

Date		Reference	*Estimated Revenues*	*Revenues*	*Balance*
197B					
January 1	Budget estimate	J 79	$220,000		$220,000
31	Collections	CR 32		$13,200	206,800

permits for building construction, motor vehicle operation; marriage licenses, burial permits, dog licenses, etc.

As a technical note: since the single subsidiary ledger supports two general ledger control accounts, Estimated Revenues and Revenues, it is essential that all tranactions affecting the budget, whether increases or decreases, be posted to affect Estimated Revenues, whereas all transactions involving the recognition of revenue be posted to affect Revenues. Using Illustration 4–1 as an example, since Estimated Revenues, the control account, is debited for the amount of budgeted revenue, amounts posted in the column provided in the subsidiary ledger for Estimated Revenues would normally be debits; in the event that the budget is reduced, the reduction would be credited to the Estimated Revenues control account and, to keep the subsidiary in agreement with the control, the reduction would have to be shown as a negative item in the appropriate subsidiary ledger column headed "Estimated Revenues." Similarly, recognition of revenue is reflected in the general ledger account Revenues by a credit; therefore, the Revenues column in the subsidiary ledger is normally for credits. In the event that it is necessary to show a decrease in the amount of revenue recognized, the amount must be posted as a negative item in the Revenues column of the subsidiary ledger in order that the Revenues column of the subsidiary ledger support the Revenues control account in the general ledger.

Statements of Actual and Estimated Revenues

Financial statements should do at least two things for administrators and managers: (1) give information in the form of figures and comparisons, and (2) raise questions. The main questions raised should be:

1. What caused this condition or change?
2. Is the condition or change favorable or unfavorable?
3. If favorable, what can be done to retain it or accelerate it?
4. If unfavorable, what can be done in the way of correction?

In general, financial statements containing information in comparative form are more useful than those confined to a single set of data.

Interim Comparisons of Actual and Estimated Revenue. Probably the most important statement of general fund revenue is one detailing by sources and classes the amounts estimated by the governmental unit's legislative body for a given period, the amount of revenue actually received (or accrued, if the accrual basis is used), and the excess or deficiency of estimated revenues as compared with actual revenues. Illustration 4–2 is taken from *Governmental Accounting, Auditing, and Financial Reporting*, the National Committee on Governmental Accounting's most recent publication, to show a recommended form of statement comparing actual and estimated revenue at a point in time during a fiscal year. The format illustrated assumes that the revenues budget was prepared on a monthly basis, which, as discussed in Chapter 2, provides the most meaningful managerial information. If the budget officer of a given municipality has not yet achieved the preparation of monthly revenue budgets, the interim statement of actual and estimated revenue should compare budgeted revenue for the year, in as much detail as is shown in the revenue ledger, with revenue realized for the portion of the fiscal year elapsed to the date of the statement. The comparison, in the latter case, is not as helpful as Illustration 4–2 is for determining whether the budget is realistic and whether the actual revenue billing or collection procedures are operating as planned; but the fact that most sources of revenue are not billed or received evenly throughout a fiscal year makes it unreasonable to prepare a comparison on the assumption that in each month one-twelfth of the amount budgeted for the year should have been recognized.

Comparisons of actual and estimated revenues serve a twofold purpose in the administration of general fund financial operations. For one thing, they provide fund management with a comprehensive and detailed comparison between the revenue anticipated and that actually realized. Excesses of actual over estimated revenue will be of interest, but primary attention should be focused on substantial deficiencies of the actual figures as compared with the estimated ones. Such differences may be accounted for in one or more of three ways, as follows:

1. Change in conditions, including laws, ordinances, or other regulations, between the time of estimating and the time of collecting.
2. Failure to collect revenue or loss of revenue after collection through misappropriation or other illegal activity.
3. Intentional overestimation of revenue to support appropriations beyond the amount of revenue which could honestly be expected.

In the second place, revenue statements are indispensable aids to successful planning for the future. They reveal what sources have been drawn upon in the past and the amounts obtained from each source. Ordinarily,

Illustration 4–2

NAME OF GOVERNMENTAL UNIT
General Fund Statement of Actual and Estimated Revenue
For the Month of September, 19x2, and Nine Months Ended September 30, 19x2

Source of Revenue	Total Estimated 19x2	Month of September, 19x2 Estimated	Month of September, 19x2 Actual	Month of September, 19x2 Actual Over (Under) Estimate	Nine Months Ended September 30, 19x2 Estimated	Nine Months Ended September 30, 19x2 Actual	Nine Months Ended September 30, 19x2 Actual Over (Under) Estimate	Balance to Be Collected
Taxes:								
General property taxes–current	$ 880,000	$ –	$ –	$ –	$ 860,000	$ 865,000	$ 5,000	$ 15,000
Penalties and Interest on delinquent taxes–general property	2,500	–	–	–	2,200	2,100	(100)	400
Total Taxes	882,500	–	–	–	862,200	867,100	4,900	15,400
Licenses and permits:								
Business licenses and permits	105,500	9,000	8,600	(400)	89,500	72,500	(17,000)	33,000
Nonbusiness licenses and permits	20,000	1,800	1,900	100	17,000	18,000	1,000	2,000
Total Licenses and Permits	125,500	10,800	10,500	(300)	106,500	90,500	(16,000)	35,000
Intergovernmental revenue:								
Federal grants	55,000	–	–	–	55,000	55,000	–	–
State grants	145,000	45,000	45,000	–	130,000	130,000	–	15,000
Total Intergovernmental Revenue	200,000	45,000	45,000	–	185,000	185,000	–	15,000
Charges for services:								
General government	40,000	3,200	3,100	(100)	28,000	27,000	(1,000)	13,000
Public safety	10,000	900	800	(100)	8,200	8,100	(100)	1,900
Highways and streets	8,000	700	750	50	6,200	6,275	75	1,725
Sanitation	12,000	1,000	1,100	100	9,000	9,200	200	2,800
Culture-recreation	20,000	1,650	1,400	(250)	14,100	11,900	(2,200)	8,100
Total Charges for Services	90,000	7,450	7,150	(300)	65,500	62,475	(3,025)	27,525
Fines and forfeits:								
Fines	27,500	2,065	2,110	45	22,100	22,050	(50)	5,450
Forfeits	5,000	420	480	60	3,800	3,850	50	1,150
Total Fines and Forfeits	32,500	2,485	2,590	105	25,900	25,900	–	6,600
Miscellaneous revenue:								
Interest Earnings	1,500	100	90	(10)	1,000	980	(20)	520
Rents and Royalties	18,000	1,600	1,650	50	13,500	14,000	500	4,000
Total Miscellaneous Revenue	19,500	1,700	1,740	40	14,500	14,980	480	4,520
TOTAL REVENUE	$1,350,000	$67,435	$66,980	$(455)	$1,259,600	$1,245,955	$(13,645)	$104,045

most of these may be relied upon in the future; but changes may have eliminated some, whereas others promise either substantially more or substantially less contributions in subsequent periods. Furthermore, comparisons between revenue statements of one general fund and those of other similar general funds may suggest potential sources not previously drawn upon.

Year-end Comparisons of Actual and Estimated Revenues. Year-end comparisons of actual and estimated revenues for each budgetary fund are often included in municipal published reports. Significant differences between actual and estimated revenues from individual sources are usually discussed in the narrative comments accompanying the statements and schedules. Illustration 4–3 presents a comparison of the estimated and

Illustration 4–3

TOWN OF MERRILL
General Fund
Statement of Actual and Estimated Revenues
For the Year Ended December 31, 197B

			Actual Over (Under) Estimate	
Sources of Revenue	*Estimate*	*Actual*	*Amount*	*Percent*
Taxes:				
Property taxes	$1,300,000	$1,299,636	$ (364)	(0.03)
Interest and penalties on taxes	2,500	2,600	100	4.00
Sales taxes	480,000	485,000	5,000	1.04
Total Taxes	$1,782,500	$1,787,236	$ 4,736	0.27
Licenses and permits	220,000	213,200	(6,800)	(3.09)
Intergovernmental revenue	280,000	284,100	4,100	1.46
Charges for services	45,000	43,264	(1,736)	(3.86)
Fines and forfeits	308,000	310,800	2,800	0.91
Miscellaneous	27,500	28,400	900	3.27
Total General Fund Revenue	$2,663,000	$2,667,000	$ 4,000	0.15

actual revenues of the Town of Merrill. Data presented in the statement are those introduced in the illustrative case in Chapter 3, with the addition of data as to collections, by sources, shown only in total in that chapter.

Illustration 4–3 is presented in the same detail as to revenue source classes, as included in the Chapter 3 illustrative case. An actual municipality might present the statement in the same detail as shown in the revenue ledger, or it might use a summarized form, with schedules supporting each major revenue class considered to be of interest to the legislators, creditors, taxpayers, or other groups.

SELECTED REFERENCES

AMERICAN INSTITUTE OF CERTIFIED PUBLIC ACCOUNTANTS. *Audits of State and Local Governmental Units.* New York, 1974.

MUNICIPAL FINANCE OFFICERS ASSOCIATION OF THE UNITED STATES AND CANADA. *Municipal Finance,* vol. 37, no. 3 (May 1965). Entire issue is about municipal revenues. The magazine is now titled *Governmental Finance.*

NATIONAL COMMITTEE ON GOVERNMENTAL ACCOUNTING. *Governmental Accounting, Auditing, and Financial Reporting,* chap. 2 and pp. 188–90. Chicago, 1968.

WHITE, CARL L. *Revenue Forecasting Techniques.* Municipal Finance Officers Association Special Bulletin 1972G. Chicago, 1972.

QUESTIONS

4–1. What is the distinction between the full accrual basis of recognition of revenues and the modified accrual basis recommended by the National Committee on Governmental Accounting? In your answer bring out the significance of the distinction for a citizen's interpretation of municipal revenue statements.

4–2. What are the primary functions of detailed revenue accounting by a general fund or a special revenue fund?

4–3. If state law requires a municipality to follow the cash basis of accounting for revenues, yet the municipal finance officer feels that taxes receivable should be placed under accounting control, suggest a procedure to accomplish both objectives.

4–4. Below is a list of revenue titles taken from various governmental reports. You are required to state in which of the National Committee on Governmental Accounting's six source classes each item should be recorded.

a) Engineering service fees.
b) Sales taxes levied by the governmental unit.
c) Receipts from county in payment for rural library service.
d) Transfers from discontinued funds.
e) Dog licenses.
f) Traffic violation penalties.
g) Forfeiture, by owners, of property confiscated for taxes.
h) Royalties from oil wells on city property.
i) Charges for waste collection and disposal.
j) Contributions to "conscience" fund.
k) Plumbers' registration fees.
l) City's share of state severance tax.
m) Charges for pumping basements.
n) Federal grant for airport improvements.
o) Sale of unused land.

p) Peddlers' license fees.
q) Real estate taxes—current year.
r) Rentals from restricted parking areas for home owners and others.

4–5. In the Town of Rockville's accounting system is a stipulation that all revenue shall be accounted for on the modified accrual basis. Below is shown a list of Rockville general fund transactions of a revenue or semirevenue nature. State which ones should be recognized as revenue in the year of occurrence.

a) Collection of prior years' taxes.
b) Increase in materials and supplies inventory compared with amount at end of prior year.
c) Collection of taxes applicable to prior year which, due to an assessor's error, had not been recorded in that year.
d) Refund on current year's expenditures.
e) Collection of accounts receivable for charges for services.
f) Collection of current-year property taxes.
g) Charge to a special revenue fund for supplies transferred to it.
h) Receipt of refund on prior year's expenditures.
i) Collection of taxes which had been written off in prior year.
j) Receipt of money from issue of tax anticipation notes.
k) Collection of money for vendors' license fees.
l) Recording of property tax levy.
m) Recording charges to outlying districts for fire protection service.
n) Receipt of money in prepayment of a property owner's next-year taxes.

4–6. If the data found in a revenue ledger depends on the perceived needs of municipal administrators, state laws, and the ideas of the systems designer, are there any general requirements which apply? Explain.

4–7. The revenue statement of a small municipality included the following revenue classes: state and federal payments; judiciary; city taxes; licenses; city government operations. To which one of the six standard sources classes does each of the five classes most closely correspond?

4–8. Compare and contrast the purposes for preparing interim comparisons of actual and estimated revenues with the purposes for preparing year-end comparisons of actual and estimated revenues. Indicate in each case what data you feel should be presented in the comparison, and why.

EXERCISES AND PROBLEMS

4–1. Utilizing the municipal annual report obtained for Exercise 1–1, follow the instructions below:

a) Does the report contain a general fund statement of actual and estimated revenues for the year, a statement of actual revenues only, or a statement of revenues and expenditures?
What system of classification of revenues is used in the statements? Do the major classes used agree with the source classes listed in

Chapter 4? If there are differences, are they minor differences of terminology, or major differences in system of classification?
If differences between actual and estimated revenues are shown, are percentage differences presented, or only differences in dollars?
Do the statements show the original revenue budget and all budget adjustments during the year, only the amended budget, or is the item identified only as "Budget" or "Estimate"?
Based on the information presented as to actual revenues, list the three most important sources of general fund revenue.
Is the municipality dependent upon any single source for as much as one-third of its general fund revenue?
What proportion of revenues is derived from property taxes?
Is the property tax collection experience disclosed?
Are charts, graphs, or tables included which show the changes over time in reliance on each revenue source?

b) Does the report contain detailed statements of revenues for each of the special revenue funds or for special revenue funds as a class? For each of the special revenue fund revenue statements presented answer the questions listed in Part *a*) of this exercise.

4–2. Show the general journal entry which properly records each of the following events. If you feel no entry is needed explain why none is needed (subsidiary ledger accounts should be indicated).

a) The Mayor of the City of Bloomington approved the following budget: Taxes, $2,900,000; Licenses and Permits, $250,000; Fines and Forfeits, $50,000; Intergovernmental Revenue, $460,000.

b) A tax levy of $2,890,000 was recorded; it is estimated that 1 percent of the levy will be uncollectible.

c) During the year, the city's revenue budget was legally reduced by $100,000 to reflect a change in the apportionment of state gasoline taxes to the city.

d) During the year it was found that one property owner had been billed for $485 taxes on property which he had sold to another person who also was billed for taxes on the property. The charge against the previous owner was cancelled.

e) Total collections during the year amounted to: Taxes, $2,800,000; Licenses and Permits, $275,000; Fines and Forfeits, $44,000; and Intergovernmental Revenue, $357,000.

4–3. In a general fund balance sheet there appeared the following information: Taxes Receivable, $96,050; Reserve for Uncollected Taxes, $84,300; Estimated Uncollectible Taxes, $11,750. How did the procedure for accounting for revenue, as indicated by the three items, affect the fund balance, as compared with the modified accrual basis used in accounting for tax revenue? State the amount and nature (increase or decrease) of the difference. Show the section or sections of a general fund balance sheet in which the three items should be found, and the arrangement of the items within the section or sections.

4–4. A revenue statement found in the annual report of the Village of Oak Park, Illinois, is illustrated below.

a) If you were an interested resident of Oak Park, would the statement serve your revenue information needs? Why or why not? What additional revenue data, if any, would you find interesting?

VILLAGE OF OAK PARK, ILLINOIS
General and Special Revenue Funds
Combined Statement of General Governmental Revenue
(and Comparison with Estimated Revenue)
Year ended December 31, 1971

Source and Fund	*Estimated Revenue*	*Actual Revenue*	*Actual Over (Under) Estimated*
Taxes:			
Property:			
General	$1,412,582	$1,411,788	(794)
Special revenue	1,038,266	1,037,670	(596)
Total property taxes	2,450,848	2,449,458	(1,390)
Other–general	2,748,000	2,876,557	128,557
Total taxes	5,198,848	5,326,015	127,167
Licenses and permits–general	458,000	471,995	13,995
Intergovernmental revenue:			
General	56,450	38,997	(17,453)
Special revenue	294,812	745,056	450,244
Total intergovernmental revenue	351,262	784,053	432,791
Charges for services:			
General	32,350	31,226	(1,124)
Special revenue	190,144	155,738	(34,406)
Total charges for services	222,494	186,964	(35,530)
Fines and forfeits–general	300,000	290,150	(9,850)
Interest on investments:			
General	2,500	2,376	(124)
Special revenue	–	22,224	22,224
Total interest on investments.	2,500	24,600	22,100
Miscellaneous revenue:			
General.	103,064	105,528	2,464
Special revenue	68,629	14,914	(53,715)
Total miscellaneous revenue	171,693	120,442	(51,251)
Total revenue.	$6,704,797	$7,204,219	499,422

b) If you were a newly-elected member of the village board of trustees (legislative branch), would the statement serve your revenue information needs? Why or why not? What additional revenue information would you request the Village Manager to provide?

4–5. Below is a listing of budgeted and actual revenue of the City of Clermont general fund for the fiscal year ended September 30, 19—. Prepare a comparative statement of estimated and actual revenue, with items grouped according to the six conventional source classes of revenue (taxes, licenses and permits, etc.). Under column heading of "Excess-Deficiency* of Actual Compared with Estimated" show the amount and percentage of change. Carry percentages to nearest tenth of one percent.

Item	*Estimated*	*Actual*
Vehicle code fines	$ 250,000	$ 252,215
Loading permits	500	630
Property taxes	4,242,508	4,265,752
Oil well royalties	132,000	125,037
Interest on temporary investments	3,500	4,212
Welfare apportionment from county	346,219	328,012
Penalties and interest–delinquent taxes	12,000	11,872
Court costs–fees and charges	48,000	58,996
Business licenses	280,000	344,888
State-collected motor vehicle license fees	481,510	524,620
Confiscation of contract performance deposits	10,000	8,700
Littering violation penalties	1,000	1,350
Federal Aid to Dependent Children	12,000	12,279
Amusement taxes	22,000	20,147
Special police service revenue	15,000	17,300

4–6. The following accounts were found in the Revenues ledger of the general fund of the City of Cochran.

Property Taxes

	Reference	*Estimated Revenues*	*Revenues*	*Balance*
1/1/7C	GJ1	$2,400,000	$	$2,400,000
2/28/7C	GJ6	(200,000)	2,200,000	0

Licenses and Permits

	Reference	*Estimated Revenues*	*Revenues*	*Balance*
1/1/7C	GJ1	$ 400,000	$	$ 400,000
1/31/7C	CRJ4		160,000	240,000
2/28/7C	CRJ7		50,000	190,000

4–6 (*Continued*)

Intergovernmental Revenue

	Reference	Estimated Revenues	Revenues	Balance
1/1/7C	GJ1	$ 600,000	$	$ 600,000

Charges for Services

	Reference	Estimated Revenues	Revenues	Balance
1/1/7C	GJ1	$ 150,000	$	$ 150,000
2/28/7C	CRJ7		45,000	105,000

Assuming the above accounts are correct, and that there are no other general fund revenue classifications, you are to answer the following questions. *Show all necessary computations in good form.*

a) What should be the balance of the Estimated Revenues control account?

b) What was the original approved budget for Estimated Revenues for 197C?

c) 1. Was the 197C Estimated Revenues budget adjusted during the year?
   2. If so, when?
   3. If so, how much?
   4. If so, was the original budget increased or decreased?

d) What should be the balance of the Revenues control account?

e) Compute, if you can, the amount of revenue received in cash in the first two months of 197C. If you cannot compute this figure, explain what data are lacking.

4–7. Among the records and statements delivered to a senior accountant directing the audit of a municipality was the one depicted below. During the course of their investigation the auditors obtained the following supplementary information, and made the following decisions:

1. The amount described as a franchise tax was, in fact, an amount received as a lump-sum payment for rental of town property occupied by a private utility.
2. The amount reported as engineering fees was not a licensing charge but the total, both estimated and actual, of charges to private citizens for engineering services provided by the town's work force.
3. Penalties on delinquent taxes and interest on delinquent taxes pertain to the items reported under general property taxes.

4–7 (*Continued*)

TOWN OF WOLCOTT
General Fund
Financial Statement, April 30, 197D

	Estimated	*Actual*
Taxes:		
General property taxes:		
Current year's taxes	$ 699,840	$ 701,310
Prior years' taxes	66,900	64,200
Total general property taxes	$ 766,740	$ 765,510
Other taxes:		
Franchise taxes	$ 1,500	$ 1,500
Amusement taxes	21,000	19,600
Distribution of state intangible taxes	11,000	12,400
Total other taxes	$ 33,500	$ 33,500
Total taxes	$ 800,240	$ 799,010
Licenses and permits:		
Parking meter receipts	$ 37,600	$ 29,400
Engineering fees	17,040	21,660
Burial permits	1,300	970
Building permits	21,630	19,407
Total licenses and permits	$ 77,570	$ 71,437
Fines, forfeitures, and penalties:		
City court fines	$ 6,000	$ 6,840
Deposits forfeited	2,000	2,140
Penalties on delinquent taxes	1,800	1,630
Total fines, forfeitures, and penalties	$ 9,800	$ 10,610
Rents and royalties:		
Petroleum royalties	$ 150,000	$ 201,600
Auditorium rentals	12,000	12,800
Discounts on purchases	440	420
Interest on delinquent taxes	660	710
Swimming pool revenue	11,000	13,600
Total rents and royalties	$ 174,100	$ 229,130
Revenue from other agencies and persons:		
Distribution of state gasoline taxes	$ 91,440	$ 89,660
Insurance settlement for fire loss	12,000	15,770
"Conscience" money—tax evasion	500	690
Money received from bond retirement fund	30,000	30,000
County contribution for airport expansion	9,000	9,000
Total revenue from other agencies and persons	$ 142,940	$ 145,120
Charges for services:		
Pumping water from basements	$ 200	$ 520
Mowing weeds on vacant lots	1,000	1,100
Proceeds from sale of property	2,000	12,650
Waste collection and disposal charges	12,000	13,380
Total charges for services	$ 15,200	$ 27,650
Grand Totals	$1,219,850	$1,282,957

4. Discounts on purchases should be considered as reductions of cost.
5. Distributions of state gasoline taxes should be received directly by and accounted for by the town's street fund.
6. Town of Wolcott general fund consistently records cash received from a special bond retirement fund, for payment of bonds, as immediately creating a liability which it captions Matured Bonds Payable. The town has not, to date, established a bona fide debt service fund but retires bonds through its general fund.
7. The town's auditorium is managed by the general fund but a special revenue fund administers the swimming pool and is entitled to revenue from the operation.

You are required to do the following things:

a) The revenue statement received by the auditors does not use the current source classes of revenue, and it includes items which are not actually revenue to the general fund. Prepare a revenue statement with a correct heading using the sixfold classification of revenue now recommended for general fund operations.

b) Do you think there are any striking variances between estimated and actual revenue in Town of Wolcott's statement? If so, what do you think might be a plausible explanation?

c) State arguments for and against inclusion of $12,000 from settlement of a fire loss in the general fund revenue budget.

4–8. Many years ago the Town of Shelburn, which accounted for revenue on the accrual basis, incurred serious financial difficulty because collections of property taxes fell far short of the amount of revenue shown when the tax levy was recorded. Soon thereafter the use of the accrual basis for revenue was officially prohibited, but recording of the tax levy as charges against property owners was approved.

At June 30, the end of a fiscal year, Shelburn's general fund ledger showed the following names and balances of accounts related to property taxes:

Estimated uncollectible taxes–current year	$ 29,000
Estimated uncollectible taxes–prior year	78,000
Estimated revenues–current year's taxes.	835,000
Estimated revenues–prior years' taxes	58,000
Reserve for uncollected taxes–current year	56,000
Reserve for uncollected taxes–prior year	31,000
Revenue–current year's taxes.	811,000
Revenue–prior years' taxes	65,000
Taxes receivable–current year.	66,000
Taxes receivable–prior years	107,000

It is the practice to transfer at the end of each month the amount collected during the month from Reserve for Uncollected Taxes to

Revenue. This had not yet been done at the end of June, as evidenced by the fact that the sum of reserve for uncollected taxes and estimated uncollectible taxes for both this and prior years exceeded the balances of the related taxes receivable accounts.

For the forthcoming fiscal year the town board had ordained a tax rate which would produce a total levy of approximately $830,000, of which four percent was expected to be uncollectible.

You are required to do the following things:

a) Make all entries required at June 30. Use Fund Balance as the balancing account for the estimated revenue and revenue accounts. Accounts related to the current year's taxes receivable may be transferred to prior-years classification at this time.

b) Record the tax levy for the new fiscal year.

CONTINUOUS PROBLEMS

4–L. This problem continues the "L" problems concerning the City of Bingham.

Required:

a) Open all necessary Revenue subsidiary ledger accounts (see Problem 2–L) for the general fund. An appropriate form is illustrated in Chapter 4.

b) Post to the Revenue subsidiary ledger appropriate general journal entries made in Problems 2–L and 3–L.

c) Prepare in good form a statement comparing the adjusted general fund revenue budget with the actual revenues for the first six months. [Make sure that the total estimated revenues and total revenues shown on this statement agree with the amounts of the same items shown on the balance sheet for December 31 prepared for Problem 3–L, requirement (*d*).]

d) Classify the revenue items below under the captions used by the City of Bingham:

1. Interest on bank deposits
2. Aircraft landing fees
3. Sale of scrap
4. Sale of land and buildings
5. Group life insurance dividend
6. Vehicle code fines
7. Parking meter collections
8. State gasoline tax apportioned to the city
9. Federal grant for mass transportation
10. City sales tax

4–S. This problem continues the "S" problems concerning the City of Smithville.

Required:

a) Open all necessary Revenue ledger accounts (see Problem 2–S) for the general fund. An appropriate ledger form is illustrated in Chapter 4.

b) Post to the Revenue ledger appropriate amounts as shown in general fund general journal entries prepared from the information given in problems 2–S and 3–S.

c) Prepare a statement of actual and estimated revenue for the general fund of the City of Smithville for the year. (Make sure that the total actual and estimated revenues on this statement agree with the ending balances of the Revenues and Estimated Revenues control accounts respectively, in the Smithville general fund general ledger.)

5

General Funds and Special Revenue Funds: Expenditure Accounting

Under the modified accrual basis recommended by the National Committee on Governmental Accounting for general, special revenue, and debt service funds, and the full accrual basis recommended for all other types of funds in which budgetary accounts are recorded, expenditures of appropriations are recognized at the time actual liabilities authorized by the appropriations are incurred. Expenditures result in decreases in Fund Balance. The term includes all charges for services, supplies, and capital outlays, and for provision for payment of debt not already recorded as a fund liability.[1]

The basis of all expenditure accounting is classification, "classification" being principally a systematic device for assisting in the description of the transactions classified. Adequate control is impossible without precise description. *The primary classification of governmental expenditures is by funds.* Thus, by indicating the fund to which a given expenditure pertains, a certain degree of classification or description is provided. This is true because of the more or less standardized nature of the funds commonly used. To illustrate, the mere fact that a given expenditure applies to an intragovernmental service fund serves to identify it immediately as being related to service rendered by a governmental department or office which specializes in serving other departments or offices.

The classification of budgeted expenditures by programs and by organizational unit is discussed and illustrated in Chapter 2. Other classifica-

[1] Under NCGA recommendations, concurred in by the AICPA, interest on general long-term debt is recognized as an expenditure on the cash basis, rather than on the accrual basis, by funds utilizing the modified accrual basis. This exception is discussed in Chapter 7 concerning debt service funds.

tions are possible, and may be useful for planning and control purposes. Classifications by character, object, function, and activity are discussed briefly in following paragraphs.

Classification by Character

Classification by character, as defined by the NCGA, is based on the fiscal period that benefits from a particular expenditure. A common classification of expenditures by character recognizes three groups:

Current expenses
Capital outlays
Debt service

Debt service includes both payments of principal and interest on bonds and contributions to debt service funds. Current expenses include those expenditures made for day-to-day operation, administration, and maintenance, most of the benefit of which is current in nature. Capital outlays are, as the name implies, those that create values to be realized over a longer period of time, in the nature of land, structures, and improvements.

Little correlation or integration exists between classification by character and the other bases of classification. Character classifications cut irregularly across the other systems of classification and bear no logical or consistent relationship to any of them.

Character classification of expenditures is potentially of great significance to taxpayers and other citizens. Properly used, it could give them valuable information for appraising the cost of government during a given period. Generally speaking, expenditures for debt retirement relate to actions incurred by previous administrations. Capital outlays are current expenditures which are expected to provide benefits in future periods; under conventional fund accounting "principles," no costs will be recorded in the periods which receive the benefits. It appears, however, that expenditures in the first character class, "current expenses," are the most influential on the public mind, strongly influencing popular attitudes toward responsible officials.

Classification by Object

The *object* of an expenditure is the thing for which the expenditure was made. The NCGA scheme of object classification recommended for use by small and medium-sized units includes the following major classes:

Personal service	Other services and charges
Supplies	Capital outlays

Many other object classifications are encountered in practice, generally more detailed than that listed above. Greater detail can, of course, be achieved by the utilization of subclasses under the four NCGA major titles. Thus, personal service may be subdivided on the basis of permanence and regularity of employment of the persons represented; and each of these subclasses may be further subdivided to show whether the services performed were regular, overtime, or extra. Employee benefits may be recorded in as much detail as desired as subclasses of the personal services class. "Other services and charges," obviously must be subdivided if the class is to provide any useful budgeting and control information. Professional services, Communication, Transportation, Advertising, Printing and binding, Insurance, Public utility services, Repairs and maintenance, Rentals, Aid to other governments, and Miscellaneous are subdivisions suggested by the NCGA.

Capital outlays, which is listed as a title under both the character and object classifications, should be subdivided in order to provide information needed in accounting by the general fixed assets group for the assets acquired.[2] Titles such as Land, Buildings, Improvements other than buildings, and Machinery and equipment are useful subclasses of the Capital outlays class.

Classification by Function and Activity

Functions, in NCGA terminology, are the broad purposes for which expenditures are made. *Activities* are the specific types of work performed to accomplish each broad purpose. Functions of municipalities which are general governmental units include:

General government	Conservation and development
Public safety	Debt service
Public works	Intergovernmental expenditures
Health and welfare	Miscellaneous
Culture and recreation	

Activities within the general government function include:

Legislative	Elections
Judicial	Financial administration
Executive	Other

A further subdivision of each activity class may be useful to bring this expenditure classification scheme into agreement with the organizational

[2] Under an object classification literally followed, the cost of construction of fixed assets by employees of a municipal fund would be dispersed among the personal services, supplies and other services and charges classes. That is, the cost of salaries, wages, and benefits would be charged to *personal services;* the cost of materials used, to *supplies;* the cost of transportation of materials, construction equipment rentals, etc., to *other services and charges*. From this the reader concludes that the object classification would be avoided by any knowledgeable accountant. Nevertheless, it is frequently used by profit-seeking businesses as well as municipalities with primitive systems.

structure of the municipality. For instance, the Legislative activity class may be subdivided into: Municipal council or commission, Legislative committees and special bodies, Ordinances and proceedings, and Clerk of council. Similarly, the Police activity within the Public safety function may be subdivided into: Police administration, Crime control and investigation, Traffic control, Police training, Support services, Special detail services, and Police stations and buildings. Each of the subdivisions may be further subdivided so that costs can be accumulated by responsibility centers, and so that costs of related subactivities can be reaggregated as program elements in a program budgeting and accounting system.

Appropriations Expenditures Ledgers

The discussions in Chapters 2 and 3 of Appropriations, Expenditures, and Encumbrances refer briefly to the subsidiary ledger that supports all three of the general ledger control accounts. The procedures used by a given municipality in accounting for the encumbrance and expenditure of individual appropriations depend, of course, largely upon the legal, accounting, and reporting requirements under which the fund is being operated, and the data processing equipment available. Minimum requirements include provision for the following information:

1. Complete identification of the account as to such of the following items as are pertinent:

   a) Fund.
   b) Organizational unit.
   c) Function.
   d) Activity.
   e) Object class.
   f) Character.

   This information may be given in both verbal and code form.
2. Amount of appropriation for the purpose represented by the account.
3. Expenditures chargeable to the amount appropriated.
4. Encumbrances on account of orders, contracts, or other forms of commitment which have not reached the ascertained liability stage.

From the minimum requirements described in items 2, 3, and 4 above, the form may be expanded to provide any other information needed for planning and control purposes. A simple form of appropriation ledger account is shown in Illustration 5–1. The data in the illustration are from the illustrative case in Chapter 3 and pertain to the appropriation for the general government function. (In order to minimize repetitive detail, the data are not shown in that case for the activity appropriations in the functional classifications. In an actual municipality subsidiary accounts must be kept in at least as much detail as is presented in the appropriation

Illustration 5–1

TOWN OF MERRILL
Appropriation and Expenditure Ledger

Code No.: 0605-03
Fund: General
Function: General Government
Department:
Activity:
Object Class:
Character:

Year: 197B

Month and Day	Reference	Encumbrances			Expenditures		Appropriations	
		Debit	Credit	Open	Debit	Total	Credit	Available Balance
Jan 2	Budget						$330,000	$330,000
	Purchase orders issued	$28,000		$28,000				302,000
	Payrolls				$58,800	$ 58,800		243,200
	Invoices approved for payment		$12,250	15,750	12,300	71,100		243,150
Dec 31	Totals	$66,410	$56,960	$ 9,450		$320,251		$ 299

ordinance, and may be kept in greater detail if needed for management purposes.)

In the subsidiary ledger form illustrated, columns are provided for both debits and credits to Encumbrances, since the Encumbrances control account is routinely debited when commitment documents are issued and credited when goods or services are received. An "open" column is provided in the Encumbrance section in which the running balance of encumbrances issued and not yet cancelled is shown, as a convenience in determining outstanding encumbrances, and to facilitate preparation of interim statements.

As explained in Chapter 3, the Expenditures control account is debited when expenditures are recorded; it is credited only if an expenditure of the year is recovered during the year. Provision of only one column in the Expenditures section of the subsidiary ledger to record individual expenditures is usually adequate; credits for recovered expenditures, or for corrections of erroneous subsidiary ledger postings, can be shown as negative items in that column. Entry of the running total of expenditures to date in the "Total" column facilitates preparation of interim statements.

The original appropriation is entered in the Appropriations Credit column, and in the Available Balance column. Any legally approved increases (or decreases) in the appropriation are posted to the Credit column as additions (or subtractions). The Available Balance is reduced by the amount of encumbrances recorded, by the excess of expenditures over encumbrances, and by reductions in the appropriation. Available Balance is increased in the event that expenditures are less than the amount of encumbrance cancelled, and in the event that the appropriation is legally increased.

In order to provide an audit trail, the purchase order number, contract number, voucher number, appropriation ordinance reference, or other identification should be entered in the Reference column to correspond with each entry in the Encumbrance, Expenditure, or Appropriation sections.

Interim Comparisons of Actual and Estimated Expenditures

The reasons for systematically providing periodic administrative review of the budgeted and actual expenditures for each appropriation are even more compelling than the reasons for periodic review of budgeted and actual revenues: in addition to obvious reasons relating to good financial management, municipal administrators are liable to legal penalties for overspending appropriations, or creating liabilities for purposes not authorized by appropriations. Illustration 5–2, taken from *Governmental Accounting, Auditing, and Financial Reporting*, shows a recommended form of interim statement of actual and estimated ex-

Illustration 5–2

NAME OF GOVERNMENTAL UNIT
General Fund
Statement of Actual and Estimated Expenditures
For the Month of September, 19x2, and Nine Months Ended September 30, 19x2

		Expenditures–September, 19x2			*Expenditures–Jan.–Sept., 19x2*					
Function/Activity/Object	*19x2 Appro-priation (Revised)*	*Estimated*	*Actual*	*Actual Under (Over) Estimated*	*Estimated*	*Actual*	*Actual Under (Over) Estimated*	*Unex-pended Balance*	*Encum-brances*	*Unencum-bered Balance*
General government:										
Legislative:										
Personal services	$ 15,000	$ 1,000	$ 1,000	$ –	$ 12,000	$ 12,000	$ –	$ 3,000	$ –	$ 3,000
Supplies	1,000	800	700	100	800	775	25	225	25	200
Other services and charges	3,000	300	350	(50)	2,200	1,725	475	1,275	475	800
Capital outlays	1,000	–	–	–	–	–	–	1,000	–	1,000
Total Legislative	20,000	2,100	2,050	50	15,000	14,500	500	5,500	500	5,000
Judicial (itemize by object)	17,000	1,200	1,075	125	10,800	10,575	225	6,425	225	6,200
Executive (itemize by activity and object)	92,000	6,975	6,575	400	66,000	64,175	1,825	27,825	1,550	26,275
Total General Government	129,000	10,275	9,700	575	91,800	89,250	2,550	39,750	2,275	37,475
Public safety[1]	277,300	22,140	22,465	(325)	205,000	204,800	200	72,500	500	72,000
Highways and streets[1]	94,500	7,800	7,700	100	69,000	68,000	1,000	26,500	800	25,700
Sanitation[1]	50,000	4,175	4,025	150	37,400	37,100	300	12,900	250	12,650
Health[1]	47,750	3,730	3,455	275	31,850	31,350	500	16,400	475	15,925
Welfare[1]	51,000	4,600	4,575	25	40,800	39,590	1,210	11,410	800	10,610
Culture-recreation[1]	59,000	4,350	4,250	100	48,900	47,575	1,325	11,425	1,025	10,400
Education[1]	591,450	49,300	48,200	1,100	449,600	443,150	6,450	148,300	1,500	146,800
Total	$1,300,000	$106,370	$104,370	$2,000	$974,350	$960,815	$13,535	$339,185	$7,625	$331,560

[1] For illustrative purposes only, functional totals are shown here. In actual practice, each function should include detailed breakdowns on the basis of subfunctions (if any), activity, and object of expenditure.

Source: National Committee on Governmental Accounting, *Governmental Accounting, Auditing, and Financial Reporting*, p. 27.

penditures. "Estimated expenditures" is the appropriation approved in the original budget, and revised by any subsequent appropriation ordinances for which all legally required actions have been successfully taken.

The statement shown as Illustration 5–2 can be prepared in that detail only if the budgeted expenditures were prepared on a month-by-month basis. Although expenditures of a number of appropriations are made on a reasonably level basis throughout the year, it is not generally useful to prepare a comparative statement on the assumption that the estimated expenditure for each month should be one-twelfth of the appropriation. Accordingly, if monthly expenditure budgets are not available the interim statement may be prepared on a year-to-date basis. Whatever format is used for the presentation of interim comparisons of actual and estimated expenditures, the statements should serve the primary purposes of showing whether the fund is apparently being operated within its budget allowances, whether curtailments appear to be necessary in the future, or whether transfers or additional appropriations should be sought. A secondary purpose of interim expenditure statements is to aid in the preparation of the following year's budget. This is true because a budget for a given year is likely to be prepared some months before the year begins; and to determine new revenue requirements for the following year, it is necessary to know how much balance (or possibly deficit) will be carried over from the current year. Such a determination has a greater degree of accuracy if it is based upon a formal statement of operations for the year to date.

Year-End Comparisons of Actual and Estimated Expenditures

Year-end comparisons of actual and estimated expenditures serve three major purposes:

1. They show in detail the manner in which the governmental unit administration has conformed or endeavored to conform to the authorizations granted it by the legislative body.
2. They form the basis for judging the efficiency and wisdom with which taxes and other revenues have been used by organizational units and for various purposes such as functions, activities, objects, etc.
3. They are indispensable in the preparation of future years' budgets.

As with interim statements, terminal expenditures statements are found in many different forms, reflecting differences in what governmental administrators wish to show and to some extent differences in laws under which governmental reporting is done. Illustration 5–3 presents a year-end comparison of actual and estimated expenditures for the Town of Merrill. Data presented in the statement are those shown in the illustrative case in Chapter 3, with the addition of expenditure and encumbrance data

Illustration 5–3

TOWN OF MERRILL
General Fund
Statement of Actual and Estimated Expenditures
For the Year Ended December 31, 197B

Function	*Appropriations*	*Expenditures*	*Encumbrances*	*Unencumbered Balance*
General government	$ 330,000	$ 320,251	$ 9,450	$ 299
Public safety.	1,040,000	1,024,531	15,365	104
Public works.	605,000	575,034	29,400	566
Health and welfare	500,000	491,035	8,325	640
Parks and recreation	115,000	104,640	10,000	360
Contributions	135,000	134,820		180
Miscellaneous	10,000	9,850		150
Total.	$2,735,000	$2,660,161	$72,540	$2,299

by appropriation. Illustration 5–3 shows appropriation, expenditure, and encumbrance data only at the function level, consistent with the illustrative case. Published annual reports of actual municipalities ordinarily present the comparison for activity appropriations, and many also show the comparison at the object level of classification.

In the Chapter 3 illustrative case, and typically in actual municipalities, expenditures are made during a fiscal year which result from commitments made during a prior year. Under the method illustrated in Chapter 3, expenditures of prior years are charged to an account of that title which is closed, along with the related Reserve for Encumbrances—Prior Years account, to Fund Balance. Since such expenditures do not relate to the 197B appropriations they are omitted from the statement shown as Illustration 5–3; only the difference between the actual expenditure and the amount provided in the Reserve for Encumbrances—Prior Year is shown as a deduction in the Analysis of Changes in Fund Balance (Illustration 3–3), and therefore the amount of the expenditure is not disclosed in any of the statements illustrated. Disclosure of expenditures pertaining to prior years can be made by a separate statement, or by the addition of three columns (Reserve for Encumbrances, 197A; Expenditures, 197A; and Charge to Fund Balance) in the statement of actual and estimated expenditures.

Other Treatments of Encumbrances Outstanding at Year-End

In addition to the method of accounting for encumbrances outstanding at the end of a fiscal year illustrated in Chapter 3 and assumed to this point, other methods exist in practice. In at least one state the law requires that outstanding encumbrances be added to the appropriations budgeted for the following year. In this case the Reserve for Encumbrances account, as well as the Encumbrances account, may be closed at year-end, because, in essence, the encumbered amount is reappropriated for the following year and is not carried forward as a reservation of Fund Balance. Thus at the beginning of the following year it is necessary to debit Encumbrances and credit Reserve for Encumbrances for the amount of purchase orders, contracts, or other commitment documents carried over from the prior year. From that point on no distinction need be made in the accounting records between expenditures arising from encumbrances of the prior year and those arising from encumbrances of the current year.

If it is not necessary to reappropriate amounts of encumbrances outstanding at year end, and the Reserve for Encumbrances account is carried forward as illustrated in preceding sections, some municipalities prefer to debit the expenditures, when they occur in the following year, directly to the Reserve for Encumbrance account rather than to an Expenditures—Prior Year account. Others use Expenditures accounts with slightly different titles from that illustrated, such as "Expenditures Chargeable to Reserve for Encumbrances," or "Expenditures Chargeable to Prior Years Appropriations." In any of these cases, if the amount expended differs from the amount encumbered the difference must be debited or credited to Fund Balance.

SELECTED REFERENCES

American Institute of Certified Public Accountants. *Audits of State and Local Governmental Units.* New York, 1974.

National Committee on Governmental Accounting. *Governmental Accounting, Auditing, and Financial Reporting,* pp. 15, 18, 25, 27, 191–201. Chicago, 1968.

QUESTIONS

5–1. Distinguish between *expenditure* and *disbursement* as the terms are used in governmental accounting.

5–2. In some jurisdictions, municipalities are required to publish in local newspapers chronological lists of disbursements, showing amount and name of payee for each disbursement. Compare and contrast the utility of this information to the interested citizen versus the utility of a statement of expenditures classified by object, and versus one classified by function and activity.

5–3. In a certain governmental agency, purchase orders and other commitment documents were charged against the unencumbered, unexpended balance of the proper appropriation before the documents were approved and signed by the chief fiscal officer. Is this a reasonable procedure? Explain.

5–4. A computer expert, with no governmental experience, proposed a system for a city which, in effect, provided three separate subsidiary files supporting Appropriations, Expenditures, and Encumbrances, respectively. Comment on the advantages and disadvantages of the proposed system. Do the advantages seem to outweigh the disadvantages, or vice versa?

5–5. It is illegal for governmental units to spend money for any purpose unless a valid appropriation for that purpose exists.

a) Does this legal rule assure good financial management for each governmental unit? Why or why not?

b) Illustrate the form of Appropriation Expenditure subsidiary ledger account that would be most useful under present generally recommended procedures to make sure the legal rule is complied with.

5–6. Assuming a municipality wishes to prepare program budgets, yet also prepare budgets useful for management control, suggest the expenditure classification system you feel should be used. Defend your answer.

5–7. Is there any necessity for a municipality to use the same expenditure classification system in its general fund accounting system as in its budget? Why or why not?

5–8. Is it true that expenditure of more in a given year than has been appropriated for that year will result in a cash overdraft? Explain.

5–9. For a certain governmental unit an expenditures statement prepared on the cash basis showed $580,650 for personal services. A similar statement prepared on the accrual basis showed $591,110. Explain the probable cause or causes of difference between the two amounts.

5–10. What basis of expenditure classification would best reveal purchases of unusual amounts of certain items? Unusual amounts of expenditures by certain departments?

EXERCISES AND PROBLEMS

5–1. Utilizing the municipal annual report obtained for Exercise 1-1, follow the instructions below:

a) Does the report contain a general fund statement of actual and estimated expenditures for the year, a statement of actual expenditures only, or a statement of revenues and expenditures?
What system of classification of expenditures is used in the statements? If the system of classification is not one discussed in Chapter 5, does it appear to be more or less informative than any of those discussed in the chapter?
If differences between actual and estimated expenditures are shown, are percentage differences shown, or only differences in dollars?

Do the statements show the original expenditure budget and all budget adjustments during the year, only the amended budget, or is the item identified only as "Budget" or "Estimate"?
Does the total of encumbrances and actual expenditures exceed the appropriation in any case? If so, do notes to the statements furnish any explanation?
Do the statements disclose expenditures made during the year which were authorized by appropriations of a preceding year (perhaps identified as "Charged to Reserve for Encumbrances—Prior Year") If so, how? How are encumbrances outstanding at the end of the fiscal year reported in the balance sheet and supporting statements?
Based on the information presented as to actual expenditures, list the five categories which cause the largest expenditures.
Does the report contain, perhaps in the narrative section, any information which would enable the reader to determine what results were achieved for the expenditures?
Are charts, tables, or graphs presented to show the trend of general fund expenditures, by category, for a period of ten years? Or is expenditure data related to population of the municipality, square miles within the municipality, or work-load statistics (such as tons of solid waste removed, number of miles of street constructed, etc.)?

b) Does the report contain statements for expenditures for each of the special revenue funds, or for special revenue funds as a class? For each of the special revenue fund expenditure statements presented answer the questions listed in part *a* of this exercise.

5–2. Show the entry in general journal form that properly records each of the following related events. Subsidiary ledger accounts as well as general ledger accounts should be indicated. If you feel no entry is needed explain why none is needed.

a) The appropriation budget of Queen Anne County was legally adopted. It provided for General Administration, $180,000; Highways, $200,000; Welfare, $95,000; and Public Safety, $500,000.

b) Purchase orders were issued for road graders, $40,000; two desks for the Welfare department, $400; and three automobiles for the use of sheriff's deputies, $7,800.

c) Invoices were received for the three automobiles in the amount of $7,875 (ordered in part *b* of this problem). The invoices were approved for payment.

d) Bonds issued by the county in the amount of $600,000 to finance the construction of highways thirty years ago matured. The holders requested payment.

e) The road grader manufacturer notified the purchasing agent that the road graders (ordered in part *b*) could not be shipped until August. The county's fiscal year ends July 31. Show the entry to close the accounts that pertain to this matter.

5–3. The appropriation expenditures account for Office Supplies of the City of X for a certain year is reproduced below:

CITY OF X
Appropriation Expenditures
Office Supplies

Purchase No.	*Explanation*	*Appropriations*	*Encumbrances Debit*	*Encumbrances Credit*	*Expenditures*	*Unencumbered Unexpended Balance*
	Budget	$2,200				$2,000
350	Purchase order-towels		$ 60			1,940
356	Purchase order-stationery		130			1,810
	Refund of prior year expenditure	30				1,840
370	Purchase order-filing supplies		80			1,760
350	Invoice			$ 60	$ 65	1,755
378	Purchase order-typewriter		160			1,595
380	Contract for washing office windows		200			1,395
356	Invoice			140	140	1,255
	Transfer of stationery to library fund	33				1,288
	Refund on P.O. 350	2				1,290
370	Invoice			80	70	1,300
380	Invoice			200	200	1,100
385	Purchase order-furniture		800			300
	Transfer to personal services account	400*				700

* **Debit**

The general fund manual of accounts described Office Supplies as "tangible items of relatively short life to be used in a business office."

Determine each of the following (show all computations in intelligible form):

a) Amount of net appropriation for office supplies for the year.
b) The valid amount of encumbrances outstanding against this appropriation at the end of the year.
c) The net amount of expenditures made during the year which were properly chargeable to this appropriation.
d) The unencumbered unexpended balance of this appropriation at the end of the year.

5–4. An expenditure statement found in the annual report of the Village of Oak Park, Illinois, is illustrated on page 125.

a) If you were an interested resident of Oak Park, would the statement present sufficient information to meet your needs? Why or why not? What additional appropriation and expenditure data, if any, would you find useful?

5–4 (*Continued*)

VILLAGE OF OAK PARK, ILLINOIS
General and Special Revenue Funds
Combined Statement of General Governmental Expenditures
(and Comparison with Appropriations)
Year Ended December 31, 1971

Function and Fund	*Appropriations*	*Actual Expenditures*	*Actual Over (Under) Appropriations*
General government:			
Corporate	$ 996,785	$ 952,990	(43,795)
Public liability insurance	18,894	20,464	1,570
Municipal audit	15,559	17,000	1,441
Public benefit	889	126	(763)
	1,032,127	990,580	(41,547)
Public Safety:			
Corporate	2,745,810	2,592,102	(153,708)
Civil defense	213,505	88,813	(124,692)
	2,959,315	2,680,915	(278,400)
Highways and streets:			
Corporate	237,811	233,693	(4,118)
Street and bridge	233,713	217,652	(16,061)
Vehicle tax	248,673	231,393	(17,280)
Motor fuel tax	–	553,077	553,077
	720,197	1,235,815	515,618
Sanitation:			
Corporate	325,000	367,232	42,232
Garbage	221,876	218,474	(3,402)
Total sanitation	546,876	585,706	38,830
Health–corporate	179,913	186,487	6,574
Culture and recreation:			
Recreation	431,566	421,765	(9,801)
Library	744,700	424,341	(320,359)
	1,176,266	846,106	(330,160)
Employee retirement–Illinois Municipal Retirement	311,191	343,750	32,559
Total General Government Expenditures	$6,925,885	$6,869,359	(56,526)

b) If you were a newly-elected member of the village legislative branch, would the statement serve your information needs? Why or why not? What additional appropriation and expenditure information would you request the Village Manager to provide?

5–5. The City of Mt. Vernon routes all transactions for buying of commodities and services through three departments: purchasing, accounting, and finance. Several events in the history of a purchase transaction are shown below. Some of them require no formal accounting entry, but others do. You are required to make journal entries for those transactions which require it. Omit explanations but show the *date* and number for each entry journalized.

1. On January 12, 197E, bids were requested on a piece of equipment to be purchased for the street fund. Availability of an unencumbered unexpended appropriation for the purchase previously had been ascertained.
2. After consideration of bids received it was decided to accept that of the Andover Manufacturing Co., at a price of $4,315. A purchase order was prepared and sent to the accounting department on January 27. Availability of funds was again ascertained; the purchase order was approved on February 1 and returned to the purchasing department, which mailed the order the next day.
3. A shipping notice was received from Andover on February 12 and the goods were received on the 18th.
4. Copies of the invoice were received by the accounting department on February 17, followed on February 20 by copies of the receiving report for the equipment. All details of the purchase having been found to be in order, the invoice was approved for payment on February 24 and sent to the finance department on the same day.
5. A "paid" copy of the invoice was received from the finance department on February 27.

5–6. The Town of Dubois employs a system of quarterly allotments to aid in control of its general fund expenditures. (Accounting for allotments is illustrated in Chapter 2.)

For a given year estimated expenditures of $380,000 were provided for in the appropriations ordinance. For the first quarter, departments financed by the general fund received total allotments of $86,000. By the end of the quarter, expenditures totaling $81,000 had been reported. (You may omit entries in Encumbrances and Vouchers Payable.) Toward the end of the year it became apparent that additional appropriations would be required. A supplemental appropriation of $3,000 was legally approved. Total allotments for the last three quarters amounted to $297,000. Also for the last three quarters departments reported expenditures totaling $302,000. You are required to prepare general journal entries to:

a) Record the legislative body's budget action.
b) Record the first quarter allotment.
c) Record the first quarter expenditures.
d) Record the additional appropriation.
e) Record the allotment for the last three quarters.
f) Record expenditures reported for the last three quarters.
g) Make entries to close the budgetary and nominal accounts used in entries *a* through *f*.

5–7. The following data were taken from the accounts of the Town of Ridgedale after the books had been closed for the fiscal year ending June 30, 19x3:

	Balances 6-30-x2	19x3 Changes Debits	Credits	Balances 6-30-x3
Cash	$180,000	$ 955,000	$ 880,000	$255,000
Taxes receivable	20,000	809,000	781,000	48,000
	$200,000			$303,000
Estimated uncollectible taxes	4,000	6,000	9,000	7,000
Vouchers payable	44,000	880,000	889,000	53,000
Due to intragovernmental service fund	2,000	7,000	10,000	5,000
Due to debt service fund	10,000	60,000	100,000	50,000
Reserve for encumbrances	40,000	40,000	47,000	47,000
Fund balance	100,000	20,000	61,000	141,000
	$200,000	$2,777,000	$2,777,000	$303,000

The following additional data are available:

1. The budget for the year provided for estimated revenues of $1,000,000 and appropriations of $965,000.
2. Expenditures totaling $895,000, in addition to those chargeable against Reserve for Encumbrances, were made.
3. The actual expenditure chargeable against Reserve for Encumbrances was $37,000.

Required:

Prepare a worksheet to compare estimated revenues with actual revenues and encumbrances and expenditures with appropriations and other authorizations. The worksheet should have the following column headings:

Column Number	*Heading*
5	Balance Sheet, 6/30/x2
6 & 7	19x3 Transactions (Debit & Credit)
8	Estimated Revenues
9	Actual Revenues
10	Encumbrances and Expenditures
11	Appropriations and Other Authorizations
12	Balance Sheet, 6/30/x3

Formal journal entries are not required.

(AICPA, adapted)

5–8. The following information pertains to the operations of the general fund of K County. Functions of this county government include operating the county jail and caring for the county courts.

Funds to finance the operations are provided from a levy of county tax against the towns of the county; from the state distribution of unincorporated business taxes; from board of jail prisoners assessed against the towns and against the state; and from interest on savings accounts.

The balances of the asset accounts of the fund after closing at the end of the prior fiscal year were as shown below. There were no liabilities.

Cash on hand	$ 320
Cash in checking accounts	41,380
Cash in savings accounts	60,650
Inventory of jail supplies	3,070
Due from towns and state for board of prisoners	3,550

The budget for the current year as adopted by the county commissioners provided for the following items of revenue and expenditures:

1. Town and county taxes	$20,000
2. Jail operating costs	55,000
3. Court operating costs	7,500
4. Unincorporated business taxes	18,000
5. Board of prisoners (revenue)	5,000
6. Commissioners' salaries and expenses	8,000
7. Interest on savings (credited to savings account)	1,000
8. Miscellaneous expenses	1,000

The following memoranda represent all the transactions that were debited to expenditures or credited to revenues during the year, with all expenditure bills vouchered and paid by the end of the year.

Item (1) was transacted exactly as budgeted.	
Item (2) cash disbursements amounted to	$55,230
Item (3) amounted to	7,110
Item (4) amounted to	18,070
Item (5) billings amounted to	4,550
Item (6) amounted to	6,670
Item (7) amounted to (added to savings)	1,050
Item (8) amounted to	2,310

During the year, $25,000 was transferred from savings accounts to checking accounts. At year-end, the jail supply inventory amounted to $5,120; cash (prisoners' board money) of $380 was on hand; and $1,325 of prisoners' board bills were unpaid. You are required to do the following things:

a) On columnar paper list account titles and balances to make a complete trial balance as of the beginning of the year.

b) Determine total estimated revenues and total appropriations and make an entry in the second pair of money columns (Transactions for current year) to record the budget. Record general ledger accounts only.

c) Record all the transactions stated above. Since all expense bills have been vouchered and paid by year-end, Vouchers Payable may be omitted and all expenditures recorded as cash transactions. All expenditures and all revenues may be recorded in totals. Revenue collections may be debited to Cash on Hand.

d) Make entries for other transactions not specifically stated but required to produce the balances stated in the problem.
e) In the third pair of money columns include a trial balance of the fund before closing at the end of the current year.

(AICPA, adapted)

5–9. The Town of Abrams general fund proprietary accounts had the following balances as of the beginning of a certain fiscal year:

	Debit	*Credit*
Cash	$ 30,000	
Taxes receivable–delinquent	160,000	
Estimated uncollectible delinquent taxes		$ 18,000
Inventory of supplies	14,000	
Vouchers payable		90,000
Taxes collected in advance		1,770
Due to other funds		10,530
Reserve for inventory of supplies		14,000
Reserve for encumbrances–prior year		13,300
Fund balance		56,400
	$204,000	$204,000

1. The budget, with estimated revenue summarized by source classes and appropriations by functions, was as follows:

Estimated revenues:		
Taxes	$876,000	
Licenses and permits	72,000	
Intergovernmental revenue	190,000	
Other sources	83,000	
Total		$1,221,000
Appropriations:		
General government	$120,000	
Public safety	440,000	
Public works	250,000	
Health and welfare	230,000	
Other functions	70,000	
Total		1,110,000
		$ 111,000

2. Encumbrances issued against the various functional appropriations during the year were as follows:

General government	$ 12,000
Public safety	80,000
Public works	160,000
Health and welfare	65,000
Other functions	59,000
Total	$376,000

3. A current-year tax levy of $895,000 was recorded, with uncollectibles estimated at $20,000.
4. Tax collections were $120,000 on prior years' levies and $644,000 on the current year's levy.
5. Personnel costs, for which no encumbrances had been recorded,

were credited to Vouchers Payable during the year in the amount of $718,500 distributed as follows:

General government	$104,000
Public safety	351,000
Public works	90,300
Health and welfare	163,300
Other functions	9,900

6. Invoices for all items encumbered during the prior year were received and approved for payment in the amount of $13,100. (Charge Expenditures—Prior Year. Close this account and Reserve for Encumbrances—Prior Year to Fund Balance.)
7. Invoices were received and approved for payment for items ordered in documents recorded as encumbrances in transaction 2 of this problem. The following appropriations were affected:

	Actual Expenditure	*Encumbrances Cancelled*
General government	$ 11,200	$ 11,400
Public safety	77,500	77,300
Public works	150,350	150,100
Health and safety	64,750	65,000
Other functions	59,500	59,000
	$363,300	$362,800

8. Revenue other than taxes collected during the year consisted of $71,000 licenses and permits; $185,000 intergovernmental revenue; and $66,000 from other sources.
9. $10,500 of prior years' taxes were written off and $2,200 of current year's taxes were abated (cancelled) to correct errors. (Latter not charged to estimated uncollectible account.)
10. Payments on vouchers payable totaled $1,088,600.
11. A physical inventory of materials and supplies as of year-end showed a total of $27,400. The supplies inventory was adjusted accordingly, as was the Reserve for Inventory of Supplies. The entire inventory is for the Public Works department.
12. The taxes collected in advance in the prior year were recorded as revenue of the current year. Cash totaling $1,700 was received in prepayment of next year's taxes. (Record as two separate transactions.)

Required:

a) Enter the beginning balances in T-accounts representing the general ledger of the Town of Abrams general fund.

b) Journalize transactions (1) through (12), showing subsidiary ledger detail as well as general ledger accounts.

c) Open a revenue ledger and an appropriations expenditure ledger. Post journal entries to all general ledger and subsidiary ledger accounts affected.

d) Prepare a general ledger trial balance. Prove that the subsidiary ledger totals agree with the general ledger controls for Estimated Revenues, Revenues, Appropriations, Expenditures, and Encumbrances.

e) Prepare entries to close general ledger budgetary and nominal accounts, to reclassify current taxes and related estimated uncollectible account as delinquent, and to designate Reserve for Encumbrances as "Prior year."

f) Prepare a Balance Sheet as of the end of the year, and an Analysis of Changes in Fund Balance, a Statement of Actual and Estimated Revenues, and a Statement of Actual and Estimated Expenditures, for the year for which data are given.

CONTINUOUS PROBLEMS

5–L. This problem continues the series of "L" problems concerning the City of Bingham. You are required to:

a) Open and post, in as much detail as possible, Appropriation Expenditures subsidiary ledger accounts for the general fund. Use the pertinent information from Problems 2–L and 3–L. An appropriate form is illustrated in Chapter 5.

b) Prepare in good form a statement comparing the adjusted Appropriations budget with the expenditures and encumbrances for the first six months of the year. (Make sure that the total appropriations, total expenditures, and total encumbrances as shown by this statement agree with the amounts of the same items shown on the December 31 balance sheet prepared for Problem 3–L.)

c) Below are described transactions of the second six months of the year. Record each transaction in the general journal.

1. Purchase orders, contracts, and other commitment documents totaling $823,000 were issued against the following appropriations:

General government:	
Central administration	$ 48,190
Finance	18,000
Personnel	2,300
Public safety:	
Police	211,800
Fire	182,900
Building safety	16,000
Animal pound	2,000
Traffic engineering	3,300
Public works	120,710
Health	40,000
Public welfare	104,800
Recreation	52,000
Miscellaneous	21,000

2. Invoices for services and supplies were received and approved for payment: Actual, $908,500; Estimated, $903,000.

	Expenditure	*Encumbrance*
General government:		
Central administration	$ 56,690	$ 54,690
Finance	18,000	18,000
Personnel	2,700	2,700
Public safety:		
Police	224,000	222,000
Fire	186,000	186,000
Building safety	16,000	16,000
Animal pound	2,000	2,000
Traffic engineering	3,300	3,300
Public works	161,810	160,310
Health	40,000	40,000
Public welfare	110,000	110,000
Recreation	63,000	63,000
Miscellaneous	25,000	25,000

3. Payrolls were computed, liabilities for withholdings were recorded, and the net paid in cash, as follows: General Fund—Gross Pay, $1,138,700; Income Tax Withheld, $141,300; FICA Tax Withheld, $63,700. Payrolls are not encumbered. The distribution was:

General government:	
City council and clerk	$ 33,000
Central administration	62,000
Municipal court and attorney	61,000
Finance	92,800
Personnel	44,000
Public safety:	
Police	241,400
Fire	219,600
Building safety	40,800
Animal pound	8,900
Traffic engineering	40,000
Public works	130,000
Health	26,000
Public welfare	33,200
Recreation	106,000

4. The city's liability for FICA tax, $63,700, was recorded as an expenditure of the Contributions appropriation.
5. Collections of the second installment of current year's taxes were $1,149,000.
6. The general fund collected the following revenue in cash: Licenses and Permits, $259,000; Fines and Forfeits, $135,000; Intergovernmental Revenue, $807,000; Charges for Services, $78,000; and Miscellaneous, $28,000.
7. A taxpayer who had been classified as delinquent proved that he had paid general taxes of $237 when due. Audit disclosed that a former employee had embezzled $237—through oversight of the Treasurer, the employee had not been bonded. The audit also disclosed that tax bills totaling $2,586 on several pieces of property had been sent to both the present and the prior owner, and no tax bills at all had been prepared for several pieces of property—general taxes of $2,250 should

have been charged. (Correct all accounts affected; do not adjust the Estimated Uncollectible Taxes account.)

8. Tax anticipation notes issued by the general fund were paid at maturity at face amount plus interest of $5,000. (Charge Miscellaneous for the expenditure.)
9. The petty cash fund was reimbursed for $4,810. (Charge central administration for the entire expenditure.)
10. The general fund vouchered and paid its liability for employees' income taxes withheld, the total liability for FICA taxes, and the required contribution to the employees' pension funds, $124,500.
11. The general fund recorded its liabilities to other funds for services received during the year, $20,000. ($15,300 should be charged to the Fire departmental appropriation and $4,700 to central administration.
12. The general fund paid vouchers in the amount of $880,000.
13. The general fund made a long-term advance of $30,000 cash to the stores and services fund.
14. Current taxes receivable and related estimated uncollectibles were transferred to the delinquent category. Interest and penalties accrued on delinquent taxes amounted to $11,240; of this amount it is estimated that $4,880 is uncollectible.

d) Post to the general ledger and prepare a trial balance before adjustment of the accounts of the general fund. Post to the subsidiary ledgers and make sure the totals of the subsidiary ledger columns agree with the balances of their respective control accounts.

e) Prepare and post the necessary closing entries for the general fund.

f) Prepare in good form a balance sheet as of the end of the fiscal year, June 30, 19__.

g) Prepare in good form an analysis of changes in Fund Balance for the year.

h) Prepare a statement of actual and estimated revenues, and a statement of actual and estimated expenditures for the year.

5–S. This problem continues the series of "S" problems concerning the City of Smithville.

Required:

a) Open and post, in as much detail as possible, Appropriation Expenditures subsidiary ledger accounts for the general fund. Use your general journal as the source of the entries. An appropriate ledger form is illustrated in Chapter 5.

b) Prepare in good form a statement of actual and estimated expenditures for the year. Make sure that the total appropriations, total expenditures, and total encumbrances as shown by this statement agree with the general ledger control account balances before closing.

6

Capital Projects Funds

The receipt and disbursement of moneys for the construction or acquisition of capital facilities is accounted for by capital projects funds.[1] Receipts for such purposes arise from the sale of bonds, grants from other governmental units, transfers from other funds, or gifts from citizens.

The reason for creating a fund to account for each capital project is the same as the reason for creating special revenue funds: to provide a formal mechanism to enable administrators to ensure that revenues dedicated to a certain purpose are used for that purpose and no other, and to enable administrators to report to creditors, and other grantors of capital projects fund revenue, that their requirements regarding the use of the revenue were met.

Capital projects funds differ from general and special revenue funds in that the latter categories have a year-to-year life, whereas each capital projects fund exists only for the duration of the project. A fund is created when a capital project or a series of related projects is legally authorized; it is closed when the project or series is completed. Budgetary accounts need not be used because the legal authorization to engage in the project is in itself an appropriation of the total amount which may be obligated for the construction or acquisition of the capital asset specified in the project authorization. Estimated revenues need not be recorded because few contractors will start work on a project until financing is ensured

[1] Prior to 1968 "Bond Funds" rather than capital projects funds, were recommended by the NCGA; they served much the same purposes but did not record revenues from grants or any sources other than bond issues. Municipalities in several states still use Bond Funds rather than Capital Projects Funds.

through sale of bonds or receipt of grants or gifts. To provide control over the issuance of contracts and purchase orders, which may be numerous and which may be outstanding for several years in construction projects, it is recommended that the encumbrance procedure described in Chapter 3 be used. Since the purpose of the capital project fund is to account for the acquisition and disposition of revenues for a specific purpose, it (as is true for general and special revenue funds) contains proprietary accounts for only liquid assets and for the liabilities to be liquidated by those assets. Neither the capital assets acquired nor any long-term debt incurred for the acquisition is accounted for by a capital projects fund; the General Fixed Assets group and the General Long-Term Debt group account for these items, in the manner presented in Chapters 12 and 13.

As discussed in preceding chapters, the acquisition of capital assets from current revenues of a general or special revenue fund is budgeted and accounted for by that fund; no capital projects fund would be involved in accounting for these more or less routine acquisitions involving relatively modest amounts.

Legal Requirements

Since a governmental unit's power to issue bonds constitutes an ever-present hazard to the welfare of its property owners in particular[2] and its taxpayers in general, the authority is ordinarily closely regulated by legislation. The purpose of legislative regulation is to obtain a prudent balance between public welfare and the rights of individual citizens. In some jurisdictions most bond issues must be approved by referendum, in others by petition of a specified percentage of taxpayers. Not only must bond issues be approved according to law but other provisions, such as method and timing of payments from the proceeds, and determination of validity of claims for payment, must be complied with. A knowledge of all details related to a bond issue is prerequisite to the avoidance of difficulties and complications which might otherwise occur.

Participation of state and federal agencies in financing capital acquisitions by local government adds further complications to the process. Strict control of how such grants are used is imperative for assuring wise use of the funds. This necessitates more or less dictation of accounting and reporting procedures to provide information necessary for proving or disproving compliance with terms of the grants. Details of the fund structure and operation should provide for producing all the required information when it is needed.

[2] An issue of general bonds is virtually a mortgage upon all taxable property within a governmental unit's jurisdiction. Responsibility for payments of principal and interest on general bonded debt provides for no consideration of a property owner's financial condition, his ability or inability to pay.

Accomplishment of a capital acquisition project may be brought about in one or more of three different ways:

1. Outright purchase from fund cash.
2. By construction, utilizing the governmental unit's own working force.
3. By construction, utilizing the services of a private contractor.

General Outline of Capital Projects Fund Accounting

A capital budget being a 3-year, 5-year, 10-year (etc.) plan of capital asset acquisitions, the segment representing a given year becomes activated by incorporating it, with any desired revisions, into the annual comprehensive budget for that year. For the specific project or projects planned for initiation in the budget year, this consists of authorizing the necessary expenditures for consummation of the project or projects and approving the setting in motion of measures designed for financing them. This will consist of one or more of: (1) authorizing a bond issue, (2) collection of contributions from other funds, or (3) receiving previously arranged grants from state and/or federal agencies.

The National Committee on Governmental Accounting recommends that the full accrual basis of accounting be used for capital projects funds, rather than the modified accrual basis used for revenue funds. Even though the full accrual basis is recommended, it is further recommended that revenue from a bond issue be recorded at the time the issue is sold, rather than the time it is authorized, because authorization of an issue does not guarantee its sale.

In the following illustration of accounting for representative transactions of a capital projects fund it is assumed that the town council of Merrill authorized an issue of $150,000 of 5 percent bonds as partial financing of a fire station expected to cost approximately $210,000, with the estimated $60,000 additional to be contributed in equal parts by three townships. The project, to utilize land already owned by the town, was done partly by a private contractor and partly by the town's own working force. Completion of the project was expected within the current year. Transactions and entries were as shown below. For economy of time and space vouchering of liabilities will be omitted.

The $150,000 bond issue, which had received referendum approval by taxpayers, was officially approved by the town council:

No formal entry is required by current recommendations of the NCGA. A memorandum entry may be made.

The sum of $2,000 was borrowed from the National Bank for defraying engineering and other preliminary expenses.

		Debit	Credit
1.	Cash	2,000	
	Bond Anticipation Notes Payable		2,000

The claim for contributions by the three townships was recorded.

		Debit	Credit
2.	Due from Other Governmental Units	60,000	
	Revenues		60,000

(Consistent with the NCGA recommendation of full accrual accounting, the receivable is recorded.)

Total purchase orders and other commitment documents issued for supplies, materials, items of minor equipment and labor required for the project amounted to $73,200.

		Debit	Credit
3.	Encumbrances	73,200	
	Reserve for Encumbrances		73,200

A contract was made for certain work to be done by a private contractor in the amount of $135,000.

		Debit	Credit
4.	Encumbrances	135,000	
	Reserve for Encumbrances		135,000

Special engineering and miscellaneous costs which had not been encumbered were paid in the amount of $1,400.

		Debit	Credit
5.	Expenditures	1,400	
	Cash		1,400

When the project was approximately half finished the contractor submitted billing for a payment of $65,000.

		Debit	Credit
6.	Reserve for Encumbrances	65,000	
	Encumbrances		65,000
	Expenditures	65,000	
	Contracts Payable		65,000

(This entry records conversion of a contingent liability to a firm liability, eligible for payment upon proper authentication. Contracts Payable records the status of a claim under a contract between the time of presentation and verification for vouchering or payment.)

Payments of $15,000 each were received from the three townships.

		Debit	Credit
7.	Cash	45,000	
	Due from Other Governmental Units		45,000

The National Bank Loan was repaid.

		Debit	Credit
8.	Bond Anticipation Notes Payable	2,000	
	Cash		2,000

The bond issue was sold locally, without brokerage costs, at par.

		Debit	Credit
9.	Cash	150,000	
	Revenues		150,000

(If a formal entry for authorization of the bonds had been made, this entry would credit Bonds Authorized—Unissued.)

The contractor's initial claim was fully verified and paid.

10.	Contracts Payable	65,000	
	Cash		65,000

Balances due from other governmental units were collected.

11.	Cash	15,000	
	Due from Other Governmental Units		15,000

Total disbursements for all costs encumbered in Transaction 3 amounted to $70,900.

12.	Reserve for Encumbrances	73,200	
	Encumbrances		73,200
	Expenditures	70,900	
	Cash		70,900

Billing for the balance on his contract was received from the contractor.

13.	Reserve for Encumbrances	70,000	
	Encumbrances		70,000
	Expenditures	70,000	
	Contracts Payable		70,000

Inspection revealed only minor imperfections in the contractor's performance and upon correction of these his bill was paid.

14.	Contracts Payable	70,000	
	Cash		70,000

All requirements and obligations related to the project having been fulfilled, the nominal accounts were closed.

15.	Revenues	210,000	
	Expenditures		207,300
	Fund Balance		2,700

The project having been completed for $2,700 less than the amount of revenue raised, the capital projects fund is closed. The remaining cash is transferred to a debt service fund which will pay interest on the bonds sold for this project, and redeem that bond issue at maturity.

16.	Fund Balance	2,700	
	Cash		2,700

Summary of Capital Projects Fund Accounting

The foregoing highly simplified illustration demonstrates most of the conventional transactions of a capital projects fund, although numerous variations in sequence may occur. The kinds of transactions may be characterized as follows:

1. Recording, informally or formally, the project authorization: direction to construct or acquire by purchase a specified capital asset and grant of permission to employ specified resources in doing so.

2. Providing preliminary financing through a short-term loan, if necessary.
3. Initiating activity by ordering materials and services and letting a contract.
4. Recording expenditures for materials and services and for progress in performance of the contract.
5. Liquidating liabilities for the costs mentioned in (4), also for the temporary loan.
6. Disposing of residual assets, or obtaining money to finance a deficit, in accordance with ordinances, laws, or other restrictions applicable to the situation at hand.
7. Closing all accounts not closed as a result of recording the foregoing operations.

Bond Premium, Discount, and Accrued Interest on Bonds Sold

In the preceding illustration, the Town of Merrill sold its bonds at par and spent all the proceeds. This simplified the related accounting but does not represent prevailing experience; sale at a premium is more common. Using assumed amounts and observing currently authoritative practice, sale of $500,000 par value of bonds at a premium of $9,000 might be recorded as follows:

Cash	509,000	
Revenues		500,000
Premium on Bonds		9,000

Accounting for the premium as a separate item implies that the amount is not available for use in consummating the purpose of the fund but must be transferred to another fund: one for paying principal and interest on the debt or any other fund designated by proper authority. If net proceeds of the bond sale are, in fact, available for expenditure by the capital projects fund the amount of premium might be added to the Revenues credit.

State statutes commonly prohibit the sale of municipal bonds at a discount. Even in states in which bonds may be sold at a discount it seems to be usual for municipalities to negotiate with bond buyers an interest rate sufficiently high for the issue to sell at par or above; if this is not possible sale of the issue is usually delayed until changes in market conditions, or changes in the financial position of the municipality, make possible sale at par or above. In the event that bonds are sold at a discount an appropriate entry might be, using the same amounts as assumed in the entry above:

Cash	491,000	
Discount on Bonds	9,000	
Revenues		500,000

Crediting Revenues for $500,000 carries the implication that if necessary the discount is expected to be counterbalanced at a future date by receipt of money from another source. In the absence of a $9,000 subsidy by another fund the discount would normally be written off against Revenues. When it is known in advance that the discount will not be made up by transfers from other sources, a debit to Cash and a credit to Revenues, each for par value less discount, would suffice.

Profit-seeking entities amortize bond premium and accumulate bond discount in order to state bond interest expense at its "true" amount (as defined in generally accepted accounting principles). Capital projects funds are concerned with accounting for the receipt and expenditure of revenues designated for the construction or acquisition of capital facilities; they are not concerned with income determination. Accordingly, bond premium is not amortized and bond discount is not accumulated by capital project funds. Other funds and account groups affected by the bond sale and debt service are discussed in following chapters; none of these funds or groups record amortization of bond premium or accumulation of bond discount.

Should a bond sale occur between interest dates, with the result that an amount of accrued interest is included in the total selling price, the amount of accrual may be managed and accounted for in either of two ways:

1. The amount of accrued interest collected may not be recorded in the capital projects fund at all but in the debt service fund or whatever other fund will pay the interest.
2. The amount of accrual collected may be recorded in the capital projects fund, with a credit to Due to_____, and subsequently transferred to the creditor fund.

Circumstances permitting, the former is favored on account of its simplicity.

Sale of bonds to finance a capital project is sometimes avoided, in whole or in part, through an agreement by the contractor to accept bonds in full or part payment for his services. This arrangement, though recommended by its simplicity, does not have widespread usage. It forces the financing upon the contractor. Not being a specialist in finance, his costs are likely to be above those of an expert, thus increasing the amount which he must bid on the project. However, the practice has some satisfied users.

Retained Percentages

It is practically universal to require contractors on large-scale contracts to give performance bonds, providing for indemnity to the governmental unit for any failure on the contractor's part to comply with terms and specifications of the agreement. Before final inspection of a project can be completed the contractor may have moved his working force and equipment to another location, thus making it difficult for him to remedy possible objections to his performance. Also, the shortcoming alleged by the governmental unit may be of a controversial nature, with the contractor unwilling to accede to the demands of the governmental unit; and results of legal action in such disagreements are not predictable with certainty.

To provide more prompt adjustment on shortcomings not large or convincing enough to justify legal action, and not recoverable under the contractor's bond, as well as those which the contractor may admit but not be in a position to rectify, it is common practice to withhold a portion of the contractor's remuneration until final inspection and acceptance have come about. The withheld portion is normally a contractual percentage of the amount due on each segment of the contract.

In the Town of Merrill illustration the contractor submitted a bill for $65,000 which, upon preliminary approval, was recorded as follows:

Expenditures	65,000	
Contracts Payable		65,000

Assuming the contract provided for retention of 5 percent, current settlement on the billing would be recorded as follows:

Contracts Payable	65,000	
Cash		61,750
Contracts Payable—Retained Percentage		3,250

Upon final acceptance of the project, the retained percentage is liquidated by a payment of cash. In the event that the governmental unit which made the retention finds it necessary to spend money on correction of deficiencies in the contractor's performance, the payment is charged to Contracts Payable—Retained Percentage.

Judgments Payable, Bond Anticipation Notes Payable, and the Problem of Interest Expense

In the process of constructing (and occasionally only purchasing) long-term assets, governmental units may be subjected to claims for damages alleged to have been caused to persons or property. Some claims are clearly not valid, some are clearly valid, and others must be litigated. Judgments Payable is the title of a liability account recording a claim based upon a court decision. Recording a judgment payable requires the following entry, amount assumed:

Expenditures	5,000	
Judgments Payable		5,000

Theoretically, all judgment claims likely to arise in the process of acquiring a capital asset should be foreseen and provided for in the project authorization. Any judgment amount not so provided for usually requires an additional authorization to be financed by additional bonds, or grants from other funds or governmental units. A given judgment liability technically cannot be encumbered or recorded as a liability until an appropriation sufficient to cover it has been made by the governmental unit's legislative body. If a sufficient appropriation exists to cover a certain claim in litigation, an encumbrance may be recorded, if legislatively approved, on the basis of an assumed adverse decision.

Bond Anticipation Notes Payable is a liability resulting from the borrowing of money for temporary financing before issuance of bonds. Delay in perfecting all details connected with issuance of bonds and postponement of the sale until a large portion of the proceeds is needed are the prevailing reasons for preliminary financing by use of bond anticipation notes. The "bond anticipation" description of the debt signifies an obligation to retire the notes from proceeds of a proposed bond issue. The account is increased and decreased for the same reasons and in the same manner employed for Tax Anticipation Notes Payable discussed in Chapter 3.

Interest must almost always be paid on Bond Anticipation Notes Payable, and frequently on Judgments Payable. Both practical and theoretical problems are involved in the payment of interest on liabilities. Practically, payment of interest by the capital projects fund reduces the amount available for construction or acquisition of the assets, so the administrators of the capital projects funds would wish to pass the burden of interest payment to another fund. Logically, the debt service fund set up for the bond issue should bear the burden of interest on bond anticipation notes, and possibly on judgments, but at the time this interest must be paid the debt service fund may have no assets. It would also appeal to the capital projects funds administrators that interest on the bond anticipation notes and judgments should be paid by the general fund (or any other fund with available cash). If such interest payments had been included in the appropriations budget by the general fund (or other fund) the payment would be legal; if not, then the capital projects fund might be able to arrange for the other fund to pay the interest and agree to repay the amount later.

If the capital projects fund bears the interest expense on bond anticipation notes, judgments, or other short-term debt, either initially or ultimately, it must, if it follows the chart of accounts recommended by the National Committee on Governmental Accounting, charge the interest expense to Expenditures. Charges to a capital projects fund expenditure account serve as a basis for recording the cost of capital assets by the general fixed assets group. Interest during the period of construction is considered by the NCGA as an element which should be included in the cost of capital assets carried in the general fixed asset group of accounts[3]—a practice which is followed in the public utility field, as discussed in Chapter 11. The NCGA recognizes, however, that payment of interest by one fund and payment of other construction costs by another fund make it difficult to ensure that an appropriate amount of interest is capitalized; therefore the procedure is not mandatory.[4] If a municipality chooses to exclude interest from the cost of capital assets, interest on short-term debt of a capital projects fund could be charged to an Interest Expense account rather than to Expenditures; the expense account would be closed to Fund Balance at the end of the fiscal period.

If interest on short-term debt of a capital projects fund is borne by a debt service fund, or any fund other than the capital projects fund, the municipal accountant must make sure that the interest expense is added to the total expenditures of the capital projects fund, if the capital assets are to be stated at "cost" as defined by the NCGA. Or he must make sure that interest is *not* added if "cost" is defined locally as excluding interest. Since debt service funds routinely pay interest on long-term debt incurred for capital projects, the interest on long-term debt during the period of construction presents the same problem as interest on short-term debt.

Depreciation on general fixed assets is not recorded by municipalities, and there is no determination of municipal net income for reporting or for federal income tax purposes; therefore, the inclusion or exclusion of interest as an element of asset cost is largely a matter of theoretical concern at this time.

Investments

Interest rates payable by governmental units on general obligation long-term debt have been significantly under interest rates which the governmental units can earn on temporary investments of high quality such as United States Treasury bills and notes, bank certificates of deposit, and government bonds with short maturities. Consequently, there is considerable attraction to the practice of selling bonds as soon as possible after a capital project is legally authorized, and investing the proceeds to earn a net interest income. (This practice also avoids the problems and costs involved in financing by Bond Anticipation Notes Payable, described in the preceding section.)

Interest earned on temporary investments is available for use by the capital projects fund in some jurisdictions; in others laws or local practices

[3] *Governmental Accounting, Auditing, and Financial Reporting*, (Chicago: Municipal Finance Officers Association, 1968), p. 94.

[4] Ibid., p. 44.

require that the interest income be transferred to the debt service fund, or to the general fund. If interest income is available to the capital projects fund, it should be recognized on the accrual basis as a credit to Revenues. If it will be collected by the capital projects fund but must be transferred, the credit for the income earned should be to Due to Other Funds; if the interest will be collected by the debt service fund, or other fund which will recognize it as revenue, no entry by the capital projects fund is necessary.

Multiple-Period and Multiple-Project Bond Funds

Thus far, discussion of capital projects fund accounting has proceeded on the tacit assumption that initiation and completion of projects occur in the same fiscal year. Many projects large enough to require a capital projects fund are started in one year and ended in another. Furthermore, a single comprehensive authorization may legalize two or more acquisition or construction projects as segments of a master plan of improvements. Both multiple-period and multiple-project activities require some deviations from the accounting activities which suffice for one-period, one-project accounting.

First manifestation of the difference will appear in the budgeting procedure. Whereas for a one-period operation a single authorization might adequately cover the project from beginning to end, annual budgets, in one form or another, may be desirable or even required for those extending into two or more periods. This practice is resorted to as a means of keeping the project under the legislative body's control and preventing unacceptable deviations which might result from lump-sum approval, in advance, of a long-term project. Likewise, a large bond issue, to be supplemented by grants from outside sources, may be authorized to cover a number of projects extending over a period of time but not planned in detail before initiation of the first project. Such an arrangement requires the fund administration to maintain control by giving final approval to the budget for each project only as it comes up for action.

For a multiple-projects fund, it is necessary to identify encumbrances and expenditures in a way that will indicate the project to which each encumbrance and expenditure applies, in order to check for compliance with the project budget. This can be accomplished by adding the project name or other designation (City Hall, or Project No. 75) to the encumbrance and expenditure account titles. This device is almost imperative for proper identification in the recording of transactions, and facilitates preparation of cash and expenditure statements for multiproject operations.

In accounting for encumbrances for multiperiod projects there is some difference of opinion as to desirable procedure to be followed in relation to encumbrances outstanding at the end of a period. In the management of revenue funds, for example, operations in terms of amounts of revenues and expenditures during a specified standard period of time (quarter, half year, etc.) provide measures of accomplishment. Because capital projects are rarely of the same size and may be started and ended at any time of year, periodic comparisons are of slight significance. Furthermore, although the personnel of a legislative body may change at the beginning of a year during which a capital project is in progress, the change is unlikely to affect materially the project's progress. Although the operations of a capital projects fund are project-completion oriented, with slight reference to time, the NCGA recommends that Encumbrances, Expenditures, and Revenues accounts be closed to Fund Balance at year-end in order to facilitate preparation of capital projects fund financial statements for inclusion in the municipality's annual report on a basis consistent with year-end statements of other funds.

The procedure recommended by the National Committee on Governmental Accounting does produce year-end capital projects fund balance sheets which appear similar to those of revenue funds illustrated in preceding chapters. The similarity of appearance and terminology may be misleading, however. The Fund Balance account of a general or special revenue fund represents net liquid assets available for appropriation whereas the Fund Balance account of a multiple-period capital projects fund represents net assets which have already been set aside for the acquisition of specified capital facilities. The Fund Balance of a multiple-period capital projects fund is comparable to the unexpended unencumbered appropriation item on an interim balance sheet of a revenue fund; it is *not* comparable to the Fund Balance of a revenue fund.

Re-Establishment of Encumbrances

The year-end closing procedure recommended by the National Committee on Governmental Accounting for use by capital projects funds artificially chops the Expenditures pertaining to each continuing project into fiscal-year segments, rather than allowing the total cost of each project to be accumulated in a single Expenditures account. Similarly, closing the Encumbrance account of each project into Fund Balance at year-end creates some procedural problems in accounting in the subsequent year. The procedure illustrated for revenue funds (designation of the Reserve for Encumbrances account as Reserve for Encumbrances–Prior Year, and charging the Expenditures–Prior Year when goods and services are received, rather than charging the Expenditures account) could be followed. The procedure illustrated for revenue funds is logical in that case because each appropriation expires at year-end, and yearly Expenditure and Encumbrance accounts are needed to match with the yearly Appropriation account. The authorization (appropriation) for a capital project, however, does not expire at the end of a fiscal year, but continues for the life of the project. Accordingly, if the procedure illustrated for revenue funds is followed, the expenditures for goods and services ordered in one year and received in a subsequent year would not be charged to Expenditures, even though they applied to the continuing appropriation. For that reason, if NCGA recommendations are followed as to closing nominal accounts, it appears necessary to reestablish the Encumbrance account at the beginning of each year as shown by the following entry (amount assumed):

Encumbrances	210,000	
Fund Balance		210,000

If the Encumbrance account is re-established, subsequent receipt of goods or services entered as encumbrances in a prior year may be accounted for in the same manner as if they had been ordered in the current year:

Reserve for Encumbrances	210,000	
Expenditures	210,000	
Vouchers Payable		210,000
Encumbrances		210,000

Financial Statements for Capital Projects Funds

To give protection against unintended uses of their grants for capital improvements, it is common practice for state and federal governmental agencies to require reports of how their money is being used. Required reports may be conventional financial statements, or reports in a form specified by the grantor. Some grantors require the statements or reports to be accompanied by the opinion of an independent certified public accountant, or by the report of auditors employed by a state audit agency. In other instances the statements or reports need not be accompanied by an auditor's opinion, but are merely subject to audit by the grantor agency or its designated auditors.

Illustration 6–1 presents four statements of one capital projects fund of a municipality. It should be noted that although the statements are year-end statements in terms of the fiscal year of the city, they are interim statements in terms of the life of the capital project.

The four statements illustrated, Balance Sheet, Analysis of Changes in Fund Balance, Statement of Actual and Estimated Revenues, and Statement of Actual and Estimated Expenditures and Encumbrances, present adequate detail for published reports. For internal management purposes, and for external review of project management, additional information is needed as to whether the work accomplished to statement date is commensurate with expenditures to date, and whether the remaining work can be accomplished with the available assets and resources.

Illustration 6–1

CITY OF ENCANTO
Streets and Highways Fund

Balance Sheet
June 30, 1974

Exhibit 15

Assets

Cash in treasury	$4,705,493
Investments (cost)	3,909,844
Accounts receivable	236,870
Due from other agencies	697,147
Accrued interest on investments purchased	1,285
Total Assets	$9,550,639

Liabilities, Reserves and Fund Balance

Reserve for encumbrances (Schedule 15-C)	$4,914,483
Fund balance (Schedule 15-A)	4,636,156
Total Liabilities, Reserves and Fund Balance	$9,550,639

Analysis of Changes in Fund Balance
Year Ended June 30, 1974

Schedule 15-A

Fund balance at July 1, 1973		$10,741,945
Add revenues (Schedule 15-B)		8,256,082
Total		$18,998,027
Deduct:		
Expenditures (Schedule 15-C)	$9,447,388	
Encumbrances (Schedule 15-C)	4,914,483	
Total Deductions		14,361,871
Fund Balance at June 30, 1974 (Exhibit 15)		$ 4,636,156

Statement of Actual and Estimated Revenue
Year Ended June 30, 1974

Schedule 15-B

	Budget Estimate	*Revenue*	*Revenue Over or (Under) Estimate*
Motor vehicle fuel taxes:			
Section 2107 S & H Code	$3,086,700	$3,313,004	$ 226,304
Section 2107.5 S & H Code	20,000	20,000	–
Section 2106 S & H Code	3,055,300	3,234,252	178,952
Total Motor Vehicle Fuel Taxes	$6,162,000	$6,567,256	$ 405,256
Federal grants	2,596,000	1,145,167	(1,450,833)
Sale of real property	–	22,935	22,935
Rental income	–	20,551	20,551
Interest on Investments	600,000	481,764	(118,236)
Reimbursement of Prior Year Expenditures	214,000	18,409	(195,591)
Total Revenue (Schedule 15-A)	$9,572,000	$8,256,082	$(1,315,918)

Statement of Estimated and Actual Expenditures and Encumbrances
Year Ended June 30, 1974

Schedule 15-C

Streets and Highways	*Budget Estimate*	*Expenditures*	*Encumbrances*
Construction and rights-of-way	$11,550,807	$6,636,324	$4,914,483
Transfer to general fund (maintenance)	2,682,197	2,682,197	–
Transfer to other funds	128,867	128,867	–
Total (Schedule 15-A)	$14,361,871	$9,447,388	$4,914,483

Illustration 6–2

CITY OF DAVIDSON
Capital Projects Funds
Combined Balance Sheet
as of June 30, 1974

Assets	Library Bonds of 1964	Open Space Land Bonds of 1964	Bridge Bonds of 1966	Park Bonds of 1966	Hospital Improvement Bonds of 1967	Park Improvement Bonds of 1973
Cash	$ 9,495	$ 17	$ –	$ 44,328	$ 32,335	$ 64,607
Investments, at cost	–	–	–	200,000	–	200,000
Due from U.S. Government	–	244,020	–	81,060	–	211,536
Total Assets	$ 9,495	$ 244,037	$ –	$ 325,388	$ 32,335	$476,143
Liabilities, Reserves and Fund Balances						
Accounts payable	$ 517	$ $ –	$ –	$ –	$ –	$ 15,603
Due to other funds	–	–	–	–	–	420
Reserve for encumbrances	8,398	244,020	–	–	–	25,059
Fund balance	580	17	–	325,388	32,335	435,061
Total Liabilities, Reserves and Fund Balances	$ 9,495	$ 244,037	$ –	$ 325,388	$ 32,335	$476,143

Analysis of Changes in Fund Balances
for the year ended June 30, 1974

	Library Bonds of 1964	Open Space Land Bonds of 1964	Bridge Bonds of 1966	Park Bonds of 1966	Hospital Improvement Bonds of 1967	Park Improvement Bonds of 1973
Bond or amount authorized	$2,350,000	$1,000,000	$1,500,000	$3,250,000	$350,000	$400,000
Expenditures and encumbrances of prior years, less revenue	2,334,653	755,963	1,493,166	3,003,825	317,665	384,664
Balance, July 1, 1973	$ 15,347	$ 244,037	$ 6,834	$ 246,175	$ 32,335	$ 15,336
Reserve for encumbrances, July 1, 1973	–	–	–	–	–	60,141
Cancellation of encumbrance	–	–	–	2,000	–	–
Revenue during the year	–	–	–	81,060	–	469,219
Less expenditures and encumbrances during the year	14,767	244,020	6,834	3,847	–	109,635
Balance, June 30, 1974	$ 580	$ 17	$ –	$ 325,388	$ 32,335	$435,061

Combined Financial Statements

If, as is common, several capital projects funds are in existence during a given year, columnar statements may be prepared to combine the presentation of similar information. Illustration 6–2 shows a combined balance sheet and an analysis of changes in the respective fund balances. Statements of revenues and expenditures should accompany the statements in Illustration 6–2 but are not shown here because of their similarity to those previously illustrated.

SELECTED REFERENCES

MARTIN, T. LEROY. "Accounting for Debt Service and Capital Projects Funds," *Municipal Finance*, vol. 40, no. 3 (February 1968), pp. 121–27.

NATIONAL COMMITTEE ON GOVERNMENTAL ACCOUNTING. *Governmental Accounting, Auditing and Financial Reporting*, pp. 47–49. Chicago, 1968.

QUESTIONS

6–1. Why are capital projects funds recommended for use by municipalities?

6–2. How does a "capital project" differ from a "capital outlay" of a revenue fund? Give examples of capital projects and of capital outlays.

6–3. What sources of revenue are generally available for capital project fund usage?

6–4. Why is encumbrance accounting recommended for capital projects funds even though it is not considered necessary to record estimated revenues or appropriations?

6–5. "Since full accrual accounting is recommended for use by capital projects funds, the categories of assets and liabilities of such funds are the same as those found in balance sheets of profit-seeking entities." Do you agree? Why or why not?

6–6. If bonds sold to finance a capital project are sold at a premium, what legal question arises? Discuss the accounting treatment appropriate to two of the common answers to the legal question.

6–7. A public improvement project was accomplished by a combination of using the municipality's own working force and contracting with a private contractor. Before completion of a project a quantity of materials was salvaged and sold for cash. To what account should the sale be credited?

6–8. Should the Expenditures account of a capital projects fund be charged with depreciation of heavy equipment used on the project, assuming all work is done by the governmental unit's own working force? Explain the logic of your answer.

6–9. Does the method or timing of financing the construction or acquisition of general fixed assets have an effect upon their recorded cost? Explain your answer.

6–10. The successful bidder on a capital projects fund-financed improvement contract began work on the project but was unable to complete it, whereupon his bonding company assumed its responsibility and let a contract to another bidder at a price below the originally contracted amount. What changes were required in the governmental unit's accounting records because of the circumstances described above?

EXERCISES AND PROBLEMS

6–1. Utilizing the municipal annual report obtained for Exercise 1–1, follow the instructions below:

a) What title is given the funds which function as capital projects funds, as described in Chapter 6? ("Bond Funds" and Capital Improvement Funds are common titles.)
Does the report state the basis of accounting used for capital projects funds? If so, is the financial statement presentation consistent with the stated basis? (i.e. the report may state that the accrual basis was used, but no receivables are shown, or there is a "Reserve for Receivables," or the report refers to "disbursements," rather than "expenditures.")
If the basis of accounting is not stated, analyze the statements to determine which basis is used—full accrual, modified accrual, or cash basis.
Is the same basis used for both revenues and expenditures?
Is the basis used consistent with the NCGA and AICPA recommendations discussed in Chapter 6?

b) What statements and schedules pertaining to capital projects funds are presented?
Are there separate statements for each project, or are combined statements used?
In what respects (headings, arrangement, items included, etc.) do they seem similar to statements illustrated or described in the text? In what respects do they differ? Are any differences merely a matter of terminology or arrangement, or do they represent material deviations from recommended accounting and reporting for capital projects funds?

c) What are the sources of revenue for the capital projects funds? If general obligation bonds are a source, have any been sold at a premium? At a discount? Did bond premium or discount affect the Fund Balances of the capital projects funds?

d) How much detail is given concerning capital projects fund expenditures? Is the detail sufficient to meet the information needs of administrators? Legislators? Creditors? Grantors? Interested residents?

6–2. The proceeds of the sale of general obligation bonds issued to finance the acquisition of capital facilities was $1,032,500. The face amount of the bond issue was $1,000,000; $12,500 of the proceeds represented interest accrued on the bonds to date of sale.

a) From the viewpoint of the municipality as a whole, how much revenue is realized from the bond sale? Why?
b) If $1,020,000 of the proceeds is available to a capital projects fund, how much revenue should be recognized by that fund? Why?
c) Over what time period should premium on bonds sold be amortized? Explain your answer.
d) If several months are expected to elapse between receipt of bond proceeds and payment for the capital assets being acquired, what action should be taken by the municipal finance officer?
e) What are the accounting and financial implications of the course of action you recommended in part (d)?

6–3. A municipality, having presently idle money on hand in a capital projects fund, invested $60,000 of it in United States Treasury Notes. When the notes were sold $595 was received for accrued interest but the market value had declined $50. Make appropriate entries for purchase and sale of the notes.

6–4. The amount of $125,000 had been withheld from amounts owing to a contractor. Certain deficiencies were discovered in work done by the contractor, who was not in a position to make the necessary corrections. The latter work was done by a second contractor, who charged $7,500 for his work. Record the adjustment transaction and also final settlement with the main contractor.

6–5. At December 31, 19x3 the City of Newark's fire station construction fund had a balance of $680,000, after closing entries had been journalized and posted.

The project was authorized during 19x3 in the total amount of $2,300,000, to be financed $750,000 by the Federal government, $250,000 by the state government, and the remainder by a bond issue. Most of the work was to be done by various private contractors.

Cash from both grants was received in full during 19x3. None of the bonds had been sold as of December 31, 19x3. Cash not disbursed during 19x3 was invested on December 31, 19x3.

a) Assuming NCGA accounting recommendations are followed,

1. How much revenue was recognized by the fund in 19x3? From what sources?
2. How much did 19x3 expenditures total?

During 19x4 the following events occurred:

1. Expenditures of the fund totaled $1,230,000 on construction contracts and $40,000 for other fund purposes.

2. Contract encumbrances outstanding at year end totaled $701,000.
3. Interest on temporary investments totaled $1,400.

b) Prepare an analysis of changes in fund balance for 19x4.
c) Comment on the significance of the negative fund balance as of December 31, 19x4.

6–6. Assuming that all the following possibilities are legal, compare and contrast the desirability of each from the viewpoint of (1) the person in charge of administering capital projects funds, and (2) taxpayers residing in the municipality.

a) $1,000,000 face value of 20-year general obligation bonds can be sold at 99 with semi-annual interest coupons bearing the nominal annual rate of 4.0%. The discount would be borne by the debt service fund.
b) Same as *a*, except the discount would be borne by the capital projects fund.
c) The same bond issue can be sold at 102 with interest coupons bearing the nominal rate of 4.25%; the premium would be transferred to the debt service fund.
d) Same as *c*, except the premium would be retained by the capital projects fund.

6–7. The town council of the Town of Crothersville decided to embark upon the construction of a recreation center to be financed partly by revenue bonds and partly by a grant from an agency of the Federal government. Due to uncertainty as to the exact amount of aid to be received from Federal tax money and, therefore, the total amount of bond financing required, it was decided to defer the bond sale until better information was available. Constructing and equipping the center is expected to cost a total of $2,500,000.

1. Preliminary planning and engineering expenses were incurred in the amount of $11,500. No money was immediately available for paying these costs (credit Vouchers Payable).
2. Supplies to be used by the city's own working force in connection with the project were ordered in the amount of $7,050.
3. A contract was let under competitive bids for a major segment of the project in the amount of $2,170,000.
4. Sale of buildings presently occupying the site of the future recreation center, which site was donated by a philantropist, brought $3,100 cash to the recreation center fund.
5. All the supplies referred to in (2) were received at a net cost of $6,090.
6. A bill (not encumbered) was received from the street fund for work done on the project in the amount of $2,080. The bill is approved for payment.

7. A bill for $200,000 was received from a contractor for a portion of work which had been completed under the general contract.
8. The bond issue not yet having been prepared for marketing, it was decided to provide temporary financing by borrowing on bond anticipation notes payable in the amount of $250,000. They were discounted at 2 percent for the time till maturity.
9. The contractor's bill, less a 5 percent retention was vouchered for payment.
10. All vouchers payable, except $970 about which there was some controversy, were paid.
11. Fiscal year-end closing entries are prepared.

Required:

a) Prepare journal entries to record the above information.
b) Prepare a fund balance sheet, using "December 31, 19__" as the date.
c) Prepare a statement of estimated and actual expenditures and encumbrances for the period ended December 31, 19__.

6–8. In 19x5 the City of Vincennes began the work of expanding its sewer system, to be financed by a bond issue supplemented by state and Federal grants. Estimated total cost of the project was $1,600,000; $800,000 was to come from the bond issue, $600,000 from a Federal grant, and the balance from a state grant. The capital projects fund to account for the project was designated as the Sewer System Expansion Fund.

The following transactions occurred in 19x5.

1. A $25,000 loan was supplied by the general fund.
2. The amounts to be supplied by the other governmental units (state and Federal) were recorded as due. (Record amounts due in separate accounts.)
3. A contract was let to Reynolds Construction Company for the major part of the project on a bid of $1,450,000.
4. A bill was received from the city's stores and services fund for supplies provided to this fund in the amount of $20,000.
5. A voucher payable was recorded for a $1,680 billing from the local telephone company for the cost of moving some of its underground properties necessitated by the sewer project.
6. A billing of $480,000, was received from Reynolds for billable progress to date on the project.
7. Preliminary planning and engineering costs of $19,500 were paid to the Midwest Engineering Company. There had been no encumbrance for this cost.
8. Revenue collected during 19x5 was as follows:

From Federal government	$300,000
From state government	100,000
From sale of bonds at par	800,000

9. The amount due to the general fund and the amount billed by the contractor, less 5 percent retainage, were paid.
10. Temporary investments were purchased at a cost of $675,000, of which $1,500 was for accrued interest purchased (debit Revenues for the accrued interest purchased).
11. Closing entries were prepared as of December 31, 19x5.

Required:

a) Prepare journal entries to record the above information.
b) Prepare a balance sheet as of December 31, 19x5.
c) Prepare an analysis of changes in fund balance for the period, assuming the date of authorization was July 1, 19x5.

6–9. This problem presents the transactions of the City of Vincennes Sewer System Expansion fund (see Problem 6–8) for 19x6:

1. Encumbrances in effect on December 31, 19x5, were reestablished on January 1, 19x6.
2. The city board of works decided upon a further extension of the sewer and, after necessary legal actions, awarded the addition to the original contractor at $450,000. Additional bonds were authorized in that amount.
3. An additional billing submitted by the contractor in the amount of $900,000 was recorded as a liability.
4. Investments were disposed of for cash totaling $677,600, which included $4,100 accrued interest (all of which is revenue of this fund).
5. Bonds authorized this year were sold at 101, but the premium was paid directly to the sewer system expansion debt service fund.
6. The contractor's second billing, less 5 percent retention, was paid.
7. The contractor reported the project completed, including the work authorized in 19x6, subject to final inspection and approval by the supervising engineers, and submitted his bill for the balance of the contract. The final bill was recorded as a liability.
8. Balances due from the state and Federal government were received.
9. The amount due on the contractor's last billing, less 5 percent retained was paid.
10. The vouchers payable and the amount due to the stores and services fund were paid.
11. Upon final inspection a defect was discovered and reported to the contractor. Having moved his working force and equipment to another job, he authorized correction of the defect at a cost not to exceed $20,000. The correction was made at a cost of $19,700, which was paid from the project cash account.
12. The balance due to the contractor was paid to him.
13. All nominal accounts were closed.

14. The balance of cash was transferred to the sewer system expansion debt service fund (debit Fund Balance) on November 17, 19x6.

Required:

a) Prepare journal entries to record the above information.
b) Prepare a statement of revenues and expenditures for the entire life of the fund.

6–10. The common council of the Town of Warrensburg approved a $2,000,000 issue of 5 percent bonds to help finance a general improvement program estimated to cost a total of $2,700,000. Action of the council was approved by vote of property owners in the municipality. Based on estimated cost of the two projects, the town council formally allocated $600,000 to the office building and the remainder to the hospital addition. A Federal grant of $700,000, to be used for the hospital addition, was applied for.

For control purposes, encumbrances, reserve for encumbrances, and expenditures are to be identified as to whether they relate to the central office building or to the hospital project, by use of the following account titles:

Encumbrances—Hospital Addition
Reserve for Encumbrances—Hospital Addition
Expenditures—Hospital Addition
Encumbrances—Office Building
Reserve for Encumbrances—Office Building
Expenditures—Office Building

The following transactions occurred:

1. An advance of $10,000 was received from the general fund.
2. $800 was paid, without prior encumbrance, for preliminary expenses related to the office building.
3. Half of the bonds were sold for 102 plus accrued interest from January 1 to March 31, date of the sale; money from premium and accrued interest was transferred to the debt service fund for these bonds.
4. Materials for work to be done on the office building by the city work force were ordered in the amount of $43,200.
5. A contract was let for a major portion of the office building construction at a total price of $480,000.
6. All materials ordered for the office building were received at a total cost of $43,400 (credit Vouchers Payable).
7. Prior to completion of the office building, changes in plans and specifications were requested by the city. By agreement of the two parties involved, the changes were incorporated in the contract at an additional cost of $15,000.
8. The advance from the general fund was repaid.
9. Payrolls for work done by the city working force on the office

building totaled $54,100 (do not voucher) and were paid, as were the bills for materials.

10. The remainder of the bonds were sold on September 30. They yielded 102 and accrued interest from July 1; premium and accrued interest were recorded as a liability to the debt service fund.
11. A bill was received from the construction company for the amount of the office building contract as revised.
12. The amount of contribution expected from the Federal government was recorded as a receivable.
13. Premium and accrued interest on the second bond sale were transferred to a debt service fund.
14. The claim of the office building contractor was paid less a retained percentage amounting to $24,750.
15. A contract was let for construction of a hospital addition at an estimated cost of $1,450,000.
16. $200,000 of the amount due from the Federal government was received.
17. The office building project having been found acceptable, the balance due the contractor was paid.
18. Various general expenses incurred on the hospital addition were paid at a cost of $77,600.
19. Land made necessary by the hospital addition was acquired at a cost of $119,000, paid in cash.
20. A bill based upon 30 percent of the hospital construction contract was received; the liability was recorded.

The period ended at this stage of the project and you are required to do the following things:

a) Journalize the foregoing transactions and post them to T accounts or post directly from transactions to T accounts.

b) Prepare a trial balance, assuming a date of December 31, 197E.

c) Prepare an analysis of changes in fund balance, observing the following requirements:

1. Include a Total, an Office Building, and a Hospital Addition column.
2. Report authorizations for the two classes according to information in the beginning instructions.

CONTINUOUS PROBLEMS

6–L. The voters of the City of Bingham approved the issuance of general obligation bonds in the face amount of $3,000,000 for the construction and equipping of an annex to the city hall. City engineers were to work on the plans. Architects were also to be retained. It is anticipated that the excavation, grading, and paving of parking lots will be accomplished by the city Department of Public Works, but that all other construction will be handled by contractors.

You are required to:

a) Open a general journal for the City Hall Annex Construction Fund. Record the transactions below, as necessary. Use account titles listed under requirement (*c*).

1. On the first day of the year the total face amount of bonds bearing an interest rate of 5 percent were sold at $60,000 premium. The bonds are to mature in blocks of $150,000 each year over a 20-year period. The premium was transferred by the City Hall Annex Construction Fund to the City Hall Annex Bond Debt Service Fund.
2. The City Hall Annex Construction Fund purchased land needed for the site for the annex for $185,000; this amount was paid.
3. Legal and other costs of the bond issue were paid in the amount of $10,000.
4. Architects were engaged at a fee of 6 percent of the bid of the contractors. It is estimated that the architect's fee will be $150,000.
5. Preliminary plans were received and the architects were paid $20,000.
6. The detailed plans and specifications were received and a liability in the amount of $100,000 to the architects was recorded.
7. Advertisements soliciting bids on the construction were run at a cost of $125. This amount was paid.
8. Excavation and grading was started by the city Department of Public Works. The City Hall Annex Construction Fund was to reimburse the General Fund for the actual cost of payroll and fringe benefits of laborers who worked on this project, and was to pay an agreed-upon rental for the equipment used. Paving materials were to be purchased by the City Hall Annex Construction Fund (to be encumbered as ordered). It was estimated that the cost to the City Hall Annex Construction Fund would be $95,000 for work done by the Department of Public Works.
9. Construction bids were opened and analyzed. A bid of $2,300,000 was accepted and the contract let.
10. Excavation and rough grading were finished. The General Fund presented the City Hall Annex Construction Fund with an invoice for $20,000 payroll cost, $6,000 fringe benefit costs, and $18,000 equipment rentals. The payroll and equipment charges were approved for payment, but the amount of the fringe benefits was disputed and no liability was recorded for the $6,000.

11. The contractor requested a partial payment of $1,400,000. This amount was approved for payment.
12. Vouchers payable to the contractor and the General Fund were paid. One-half of the amount due the architects was paid.
13. Paving materials were ordered at an estimated total cost of $30,000.
14. Furniture and equipment for the annex were ordered at an estimated total cost of $230,000.
15. The contractor completed the construction and requested payment of the balance due on the contract. After inspection of the work the amount was vouchered and paid.
16. Paving materials were received. The invoices, totaling $30,460, were approved for payment.
17. The Department of Public Works did the finish grading and paved the parking lots. The payroll totaled $24,000; fringe benefits, $7,200; and equipment rental, $20,000. The Construction Fund approved payment of $44,000 to the General Fund.
18. Furniture and equipment was received at a total actual installed cost of $231,500. Invoices were approved for payment.
19. Both amounts billed by the General Fund for fringe benefits were settled for a total of $10,600. The liability for this amount was recorded.
20. The remainder of the architect's fee was approved for payment. The City Hall Annex Construction Fund paid all outstanding liabilities.

b) Record in the general fund general journal all entries which should be made for the transactions above.

c) Open a general ledger for the City Hall Annex Construction Fund. Use the account titles shown below. Allow 5 lines unless otherwise indicated. Post the entries to the City Hall Annex Construction Fund general ledger.

Cash—12 lines
Revenues
Premium on Bonds
Vouchers Payable—12 lines
Due to Other Funds—8 lines
Expenditures—15 lines
Encumbrances—18 lines
Reserve for Encumbrances—18 lines
Fund Balance

d) Prepare a City Hall Annex Construction Fund trial balance.

e) The City Hall Annex Construction Fund was closed. Remaining assets were transferred to the City Hall Annex Bond Debt Service Fund. Record the proper journal entries in the City Hall Annex Construction Fund and post to its general ledger.

6–S. Early in 197B the voters of the City of Smithville authorized general obligation bond issues totaling $4,000,000 as partial financing for a series of projects to construct or reconstruct streets, curbs, sidewalks, bridges, culverts, and storm sewers in various parts of the city. The estimated total cost of the series of projects was $7,000,000. In addition to the proceeds of the bonds, $600,000 was to be transferred from the Federal General Revenue Sharing Trust Fund during 197B and $600,000 a year during each of the four following years to the Street Improvement Fund.

Required:

a) Open a general journal for the Street Improvement Fund. Record the transactions below, as necessary. Use account titles listed under requirement (*c*).

1. Plans and specifications for the first project, to be known as "Stombaugh Street Project," were prepared by the city engineer's office (a general fund department). The General Fund sent the Street Improvement Fund an interfund invoice for $18,000; the Street Improvement Fund recorded the liability.
2. The Federal General Revenue Sharing Trust Fund transferred to the Street Improvement Fund United States Treasury Notes with a face value of $300,000. The remaining $300,000 due from the Trust Fund in 197B was recorded as a current receivable; the $2,400,000 due in future years was recorded as a deferred receivable. Interest of $4,000 was accrued on the Treasury Notes at date of transfer; when the interest is received it must be paid to the Trust Fund.
3. Advertisements soliciting bids for the first project were published at a cost of $200; this amount was paid from General Fund cash. The Street Improvement Fund is to repay the General Fund.
4. Bonds in the amount of $1,000,000 were sold at $1,019,880, $4,880 of which was interest accrued from the date of the bonds to date of sale. Cash in the amount of the premium and accrued interest was transferred by the Street Improvement Fund to the Street Improvement Bond Debt Service Fund. $500,000 of the bond proceeds was invested in 60-day 6% certificates of deposit.
5. Construction bids were opened and analyzed. A bid of $1,200,000 was accepted and the contract let. The contract called for a 5% retention from each progress payment, and from the final payment, until final inspection and acceptance by the city engineers.
6. The contractor requested a progress payment of $400,000. This amount was paid, less the agreed-upon 5% retention.
7. The total amount due the General Fund was paid.
8. Two property owners along Stombaugh Street claimed that

the new sidewalk was not where they had given easements. A resurvey proved that the sidewalk was laid erroneously, but the city did not feel the property owners were entitled to damages. The property owners brought suit and were awarded a total of $6,000, which was recorded as a liability. The amount will be borne by the Street Improvement Fund; it will not be recoverable from the contractor.

9. Interest of $9,000 on the Treasury Notes was collected; the $4,000 due the Federal General Revenue Sharing Trust Fund was paid. The remainder was retained for use by the Street Improvement Fund.
10. Plans and specifications for the second street improvement project, to be known as the "Hatchett Street Project," were prepared by the city engineer's office. An interfund invoice in the amount of $16,500 was received from the General Fund and approved for payment.
11. Advertisements soliciting bids for the second project were published at a cost of $225. The amount was paid by the Street Improvement Fund.
12. The contractor for the first project requested a progress payment of $600,000. This amount was recorded as a liability.
13. Construction bids for the second project were opened and analyzed. A bid in the amount of $980,000 was accepted and the contract, bearing a 5% retention clause, was let.
14. The certificates of deposit matured; the face amount plus interest was collected. The interest is considered to be revenue of the Street Improvement Fund.
15. The amount due the contractor (see Transaction 12) was paid, as was the amount due the General Fund. The judgments, including interest of $300, were paid. The interest is to be borne from the Street Improvement Fund.
16. Cash in the amount of $300,000 was received from the Federal General Revenue Sharing Trust Fund. The amount was invested in United States Treasury Notes at par; no interest was accrued on the notes at date of purchase.
17. $6,000 interest was accrued on Treasury Notes at year end. The accrual and all year-end closing entries were recorded.

b) Record in the general fund general journal all entries which should be made for the transactions above.

c) Open a general ledger for the Street Improvement Fund. Use the account titles shown below. Allow 12 lines for cash and 6 lines for each other account. Post the entries made in (*a*) to the general ledger.

Cash
Investments
Due from Other Funds—Current
Due from Other Funds—Deferred

Accrued Interest on Investments Acquired
Interest Receivable on Investments
Premium and Accrued Interest on Bonds Sold
Contracts Payable
Contracts Payable—Retained Percentage
Judgments Payable
Due to Other Funds
Encumbrances—Stombaugh Street Project
Encumbrances—Hatchett Street Project
Reserve for Encumbrances—Stombaugh Street Project
Reserve for Encumbrances—Hatchett Street Project
Expenditures—Stombaugh Street Project
Expenditures—Hatchett Street Project
Revenues
Fund Balance

d) Prepare a balance sheet for the Street Improvement Fund as of December 31, 197B.

e) Prepare an analysis of changes in fund balance for the year then ended showing the detail of revenues recognized during the year, and the detail of expenditures and reserves for encumbrances for the two projects.

7

Debt Service Funds

General obligation long-term debt incurred to provide money to pay for the construction or acquisition of capital facilities, or for any other purposes, can be repaid only from revenue raised in subsequent years to service the debt. Therefore, it must be evident to the reader who has followed the logic of the discussion of revenue funds and of capital projects funds, that the recommended municipal accounting information system includes a fund to account for revenue which is raised to service long-term debt. Earlier in this century municipal issues of long-term debt commonly matured in total on a given date. In that era bond indentures often required the establishment of a "sinking fund," sometimes operated on an actuarial basis. Some sinking fund term bond issues are still outstanding, but they are dwarfed in number and amount by *serial* bond issues, in which the principal matures in installments. Whether contributions to debt service funds are required by the bond indenture to be approximately equal year-by-year, or not, good politics and good financial management suggest that the burden on the taxpayers be spread reasonably evenly rather than lumped in the years that issues or installments happen to mature. Unless the revenues for payment of interest and principal on general obligation long-term debt are to be raised directly by the debt service fund they must be included in the revenues budget of the fund which will raise the revenue (often the general fund) and also in that fund's appropriations budget as transfers to the debt service fund. Since the debt service fund is a budgeting and accounting entity, it should prepare a revenues budget which includes revenues to be transferred from other funds as well as revenues which it will raise directly or which will be earned on its investments. The appropriations budget of a debt service fund should include amounts which will be required during the budget period to pay interest on outstanding long-term debt and to repay any maturing issues or installments.

The National Committee on Governmental Accounting recommends that debt service fund accounting be on the *modified accrual* basis, which is the basis recommended for use by revenue funds. One peculiarity of the modified accrual basis (which is not discussed in Chapter 3 because it relates only to debt service funds) is that interest on long-term debt is accounted for on the cash basis. For example, if the fiscal year of a municipality ends on December 31, 19x5, and the interest coupons on its bonds are payable on January 1 and July 1 of each year, the amount payable on January 1, 19x6, would not be considered as a liability in the balance sheet of the debt service fund prepared as of December 31, 19x5. The rationale for this recommendation is that the interest is not legally due until January 1, 19x6, consequently its payment is ordinarily included in the appropriations budget for 19x6, so the interest cannot be considered as relating in any manner to 19x5. The same reasoning applies to principal amounts which mature on the first day of a fiscal year; they are not liabilities to be recognized in statements prepared as of the day before. The American Institute of Certified Public Accountants' audit guide, *Audits of State and Local Governmental Units,* indicates that in the event 19x5 appropriations include January 1, 19x6, interest and/or principal payment, the appropriation expenditures (and resulting liabilities) should be recognized in 19x5.[1]

In addition to term bonds and serial bonds, debt service funds may be required to service debt arising from the use of notes or warrants having a maturity more than one year after date of issue. Although each issue of long-term or intermediate-term debt is a separate obligation and may have legal restrictions and servicing requirements which differ from other issues, the NCGA recommends that, if legally permissible, all general obligation debt to be serviced from general property tax revenues be accounted for by a single Debt Service Fund. Subsidiary records of that fund can provide needed assurance that restrictions and requirements relating to each issue are properly budgeted and accounted for. The NCGA further recommends that as few additional debt service funds as is consistent with applicable laws be created to account for debt service revenue sources other than general taxes. (Debt service funds, in the sense in which the term is used in this chapter, are *not* created for debt serviced by special assessment funds or enterprise funds, which account for their own debt service activities as described in Chapters 10 and 11.)

In some jurisdictions the general obligation debt service function is

[1] P. 82.

performed within the accounting and budgeting framework of the general fund rather than by a separate debt service fund. In such cases the accounting principles and procedures discussed in this chapter should be followed for the debt service activities of the general fund to the extent consistent with local law.

Debt Service Accounting for Regular Serial Bonds

Accounts recommended for use by debt service funds created to account for revenues to be used for the payment of interest and principal of serial bond issues are similar to those recommended for use by general and special revenue funds, but not exactly the same. Serial bond debt service funds should record the budget in Estimated Revenues and Appropriations control accounts and subsidiary accounts, just as revenue funds should, but their operations do not involve the use of purchase orders and contracts for goods and services, so the Encumbrance account is not needed. Proprietary accounts of a serial bond debt service fund include Revenues and Expenditures control and subsidiary accounts; and liquid asset, current liability, and Fund Balance accounts. Liquid assets of a serial bond debt service fund are held for the purpose of paying interest on outstanding bonds and retiring the principal installments as they fall due; for the convenience of bondholders the payment of interest and the redemption of matured bonds is ordinarily handled through the banking system. Usually the municipality designates a bank as "Fiscal Agent" to handle interest and principal payments for each issue. The assets of a debt service fund may, therefore, include "Cash with Fiscal Agent," and the appropriations, expenditures, and liabilities may include amounts for the service charges of fiscal agents. Investment management may be performed by municipal employees or by banks, brokers, or others who charge for the service; investment management fees are a legitimate charge against investment revenues.

There are four types of serial bonds: regular, deferred, annuity, and irregular. If the total principal of an issue is repayable in a specified number of equal annual installments over the life of the issue, it is a *regular* serial bond issue. If the first installment is delayed for a period of more than one year after the date of the issue, but thereafter installments fall due on a regular basis, the bonds are known as *deferred* serial bonds. If the amount of annual principal repayments is scheduled to increase each year by approximately the same amount that interest payments decrease (interest decreases, of course, because the amount of outstanding bonds decreases) so that the total debt service remains reasonably level over the term of the issue, the bonds are called *annuity* serial bonds. *Irregular* serial bonds may have any pattern of repayment which does not fit the other three categories.

Accounting for debt service of regular serial bonds furnishes the simplest illustration of recommended debt service fund accounting. Assume that the Town of Alva has an issue of regular 4% serial bonds amounting to $800,000 face value outstanding at the end of a year designated as 19y0. Bonds with a face value of $50,000 are to mature on January 1 of the following year, 19y1. Interest for the year will amount to $31,000—$16,000 on January 1 (2% × $800,000) and $15,000 on July 1 (2% × $750,000). The budget for 19y1 must provide $81,000 in revenues and $81,000 in appropriations. The source of the revenues is assumed to be transfers from the general fund.

If all bonds which have matured previously and all interest coupons have been presented and paid on the date due, the fund need have no assets or liabilities as of December 31, 19y0; thus all accounts are in balance at the start of 19y1. The first entry necessary in 19y1 is the entry to record the budget:

Estimated Revenues	81,000	
Appropriations		81,000

If the general fund transferred to the debt service fund the entire amount due on January 1, the debt service fund entry is:

Cash	81,000	
Revenues		81,000

The liability for bonds and interest payable on January 1 is recorded as:

Expenditures	66,000	
Bonds Payable		50,000
Interest Payable		16,000

When the bonds and interest are paid, the following entry is needed:

Bonds Payable	50,000	
Interest Payable	16,000	
Cash		66,000

Similarly when the second interest payment is legally due, July 1, the following entry is made:

Expenditures	15,000	
Interest Payable		15,000

When the liability is paid:

Interest Payable	15,000	
Cash		15,000

At year end the budgetary and nominal accounts are closed in the manner shown below:

Revenues	81,000	
Appropriations	81,000	
Expenditures		81,000
Estimated Revenues		81,000

Since all cash received was disbursed, the debt service fund would have no need to present a balance sheet, and would present only a simple statement of revenues and expenditures to show that it properly discharged its function relating to the regular serial bond issue.

Debt Service Accounting for Deferred Serial Bonds

If a municipality issues bonds other than regular serial bonds, debt service fund accounting is somewhat more complex than that illustrated above. In the entries below it is assumed that the Town of Alva has outstanding a deferred serial bond issue in the total amount of $2,000,000. Each installment is in the amount of $200,000; the first installment matures 10 years after date of issue, and the final installment 20 years after date of issue. Interest coupons are payable on January 1 and July 1 of each year at the nominal annual rate of 4%. Debt service is financed from taxes levied by the general fund and transferred to the debt service fund, and from net earnings on debt service fund investments. The general fund budgets its contributions to the debt service fund in an amount equal to interest to be paid during the budget year, plus a level contribution of $80,000 to be invested by the debt service fund and used for principal repayment when the installments fall due. Half of the level contribution is paid by the general fund to the debt service fund each six months. Illustration 7–1 shows the debt service fund balance sheet at the end of the tenth year (19y0) following the date of the serial bond issue:

Illustration 7–1

TOWN OF ALVA
Deferred Serial Bond Debt Service Fund
Balance Sheet as of December 31, 19y0

Assets		*Liabilities and Fund Balance*	
Cash with fiscal agent	$ 2,200	Interest payable	$ 2,200
Investments	1,130,625	Fund balance	1,157,375
Interest receivable on investments	26,750		
Total Assets	$1,159,575	Total Liabilities and Fund Balance	$1,159,575

The Cash with Fiscal Agent and Interest Payable items shown in Illustration 7–1 are offsetting. Matured interest coupons have not yet been presented to the fiscal agent for payment. This is common since bondholders may live in many different locations so the coupons take a number of days to work their way through banking channels to the fiscal agent even if they are paid on the due date by banks where the bondholders reside. On any given interest payment date some bondholders may not find it convenient to clip their coupons, or may forget about it. Eventually, most of the coupons will be presented to the fiscal agent. The fiscal agent has sufficient cash on hand to pay the coupons when presented.

Although interest of $40,000 and a principal payment of $200,000 are due the day after the date of the balance sheet illustration above, neither are shown as liabilities under the modified accrual basis recommended for use by debt service funds. Both items are properly included in the 19y1 budget, as would be the interest payment due July 1, 19y1, of $36,000 (2% of $1,800,000, the principal amount of bonds not yet matured. Even if some of the bonds due January 1, 19y1, are not presented for payment on that date they cease to bear interest on that date.) It is assumed that the fiscal agent charges no fee in consideration of the fact that it has interest-free use of the municipality's cash on deposit with it. It is also assumed that investments are managed by municipal employees and no management fee is charged. The appropriation budget for 19y1 totals, therefore, $276,000. The revenues budget consists of the general fund contribution of $76,000 for interest and $80,000 (the level contribution for principal repayment), and assumed estimated earnings on investments of $49,500. The entry to record the 19y1 budget is:

		Debit	Credit
1.	Estimated Revenues	205,500	
	Fund Balance	70,500	
	Appropriations		276,000

Subsidiary records, as needed, would be kept in the manner illustrated in Chapters 3, 4, and 5. Since the records, and their use, is the same, they are omitted from this chapter.

The receivable from the general fund is recorded since revenues are to be recognized on the modified accrual basis:

		Debit	Credit
2.	Due from Other Funds	156,000	
	Revenues		156,000

The amount needed for the January 1 interest payment ($40,000) and half of the $80,000 level contribution from the general fund (another $40,000) are received in cash on the first day of the year, January 1, 19y1:

		Debit	Credit
3.	Cash	80,000	
	Due from Other Funds		80,000

Both the bond payment due January 1 and the interest payable on January 1 are recorded as expenditures of the appropriation. (Under the modified accrual basis the expenditure is recorded when the liability becomes actual rather than when the bondholders are paid.) Thus the entry is:

		Debit	Credit
4.	Expenditures	240,000	
	Interest Payable		40,000
	Bonds Payable		200,000

Since $80,000 cash has been received from the general fund it is necessary to convert only $160,000 of investments to cash in order to make the proper remittance to the fiscal agent. The conversion of investments to cash, and the transfer of cash to the fiscal agent for the January 1 payments, are recorded in the following entries:

		Debit	Credit
5.	Cash	160,000	
	Investments		160,000
6.	Cash with Fiscal Agent	240,000	
	Cash		240,000

When interest receivable as of December 31, 19y0 is collected and invested, the entries are:

		Debit	Credit
7.	Cash	26,750	
	Interest Receivable on Investments		26,750
8.	Investments	26,750	
	Cash		26,750

Assuming that only $190,000 face value of bonds, and interest coupons amounting to $39,300, were presented for redemption by the date of the fiscal agent's report, the following entry is necessary:

		Debit	Credit
9.	Bonds Payable	190,000	
	Interest Payable	39,300	
	Cash with Fiscal Agent		229,300

Prior to July 1, the date the second semi-annual interest coupons for the year fall due, the debt service fund collects the remainder of its revenue from the general fund:

		Debit	Credit
10.	Cash	76,000	
	Due from Other Funds		76,000

Interest payable July 1 is recorded as an expenditure and cash is transferred to the fiscal agent in the amount of coupons payable July 1:

		Debit	Credit
11.	Expenditures	36,000	
	Interest Payable		36,000
12.	Cash with Fiscal Agent	36,000	
	Cash		36,000

Interest on investments is received in cash in the amount of $24,250. This amount and the balance of cash received from the general fund is invested:

		Debit	Credit
13.	Cash	24,250	
	Revenues		24,250
14.	Investments	64,250	
	Cash		64,250

Notice is received from the fiscal agent that it had paid coupons totaling $35,100:

15.	Interest Payable	35,100	
	Cash with Fiscal Agent		35,100

Interest receivable on investments accrued at year-end is computed as $24,750; this accrual is recorded:

16.	Interest Receivable on Investments	24,750	
	Revenues		24,750

Budgetary and nominal accounts for 19y1 are closed:

17.	Appropriations	276,000	
	Revenues	205,000	
	Fund Balance	500	
	Estimated Revenues		205,500
	Expenditures		276,000

After recording the entries for 19y1, the Town of Alva serial bond debt service fund balance sheet would be as presented in Illustration 7–2.

Illustration 7–2

TOWN OF ALVA
Deferred Serial Bond Debt Service Fund
Balance Sheet as of December 31, 19y1

Assets		*Liabilities and Fund Balance*	
Cash with fiscal agent	$ 13,800	Interest payable	$ 3,800
Investments	1,061,625	Bonds payable	10,000
Interest receivable on investments	24,750	Total Liabilities	$ 13,800
		Fund balance	1,086,375
Total Assets	$1,100,175	Total Liabilities and Fund Balance	$1,100,175

Note that for the first time the balance sheet of the serial bond debt service fund reflects a portion of the bonded debt—the face value of bonds which have matured and become payable from assets of the debt service fund, but which have not yet been presented by the bondholders to the fiscal agent for payment. The remaining bonds which have not yet matured are reflected in the balance sheet of the General Long-Term Debt group, as illustrated in Chapter 13.

In addition to the balance sheet, the revenues, expenditures, and changes in fund balance during the fiscal period should be reported for each debt service fund. Typically, there are relatively few categories of revenue, expenditures, and other fund balance changes to report, so that they may all be included in a single statement. Illustration 7–3 presents a Statement of Revenues, Expenditures, and Fund Balances for the

Illustration 7–3

TOWN OF ALVA
Deferred Serial Bond Debt Service Fund
Statement of Revenues, Expenditures, and Fund Balances
For the Year Ended December 31, 19y1

Revenues:		
Transfers from general fund	$156,000	
Interest on investments	49,000	
Total Revenues		$ 205,000
Expenditures:		
Redemption of serial bonds	$200,000	
Interest on bonds	76,000	
Total Expenditures		276,000
(Deficit) to fund balance		$ (71,000)
Fund balance, January 1, 19y1		1,157,375
Fund balance, December 31, 19y1		$1,086,375

Town of Alva Deferred Serial Bond Debt Service Fund for the year ended December 31, 19y1.

Any information in addition to statements illustrated above which would be helpful to municipal administrators, members of the municipal legislative branch, interested residents, and creditors should, of course, be presented. In the Town of Alva serial bond debt service fund example, for instance, over one million dollars of investments have been accumulated for use in bond principal payment. It is probable that everyone concerned with evaluating the financial management of this fund would want the balance sheet to be accompanied by a schedule presenting a list of the securities held, their cost, and their market value as of balance sheet date. The net amount of realized gains or losses on investments sold during the year would be presented in the Statement of Revenues, Expenditures, and Fund Balances; if the detail would be meaningful in the evaluation of investment management, the detail should be presented in supporting schedules.

Debt Service Accounting for Term Bonds

Term bond issues mature in their entirety on a given date, in contrast to serial bonds which mature in installments. Required revenues of term bond debt service funds may be determined on an "actuarial" basis or on less sophisticated bases designed to produce approximately level contributions during the life of the issue. If an actuarial basis is not used, accounting procedures and statements illustrated for the deferred serial bond issue of the Town of Alva are appropriate for use by term bond debt service funds. In order to illustrate the differences that exist when an actuarial basis is used, the following example is based on the assumption that the Town of Alva has a term bond issue amounting to $1,500,000 with a 20-year life. The term bonds bear semiannual interest coupons with a nominal annual rate of 4.25%, payable on January 1 and July 1. Revenues of the debt service fund are transfers from the general fund and earnings on investments of the debt service fund. Transfers from the general fund are computed in accord with annuity tables on the assumption that contributions for principal repayment will be invested and will earn 4% per year compounded semiannually. Annuity tables are illustrated in Appendix 3. Table D in Appendix 3 shows that an annuity of $1 invested at the end of each period will amount to $60.4019832 at the end of forty periods, if the periodic compound interest is 2% (as is specified in the Town of Alva example). Since the amount needed for bond repayment at the end of forty six-month periods is $1,500,000, the general fund contribution for bond principal repayment must be $1,500,000 ÷ 60.4019832, or $24,834 at the end of each six-month period throughout the life of the bonds. Contributions for each bond interest payment must be $31,875 ($1,500,000, the face of the bonds, X 4.25%, the annual nominal interest rate X ½ year).

For every year after the year of issue, the budget for the term bond debt service fund of the Town of Alva, reflecting the conditions described in the preceding paragraph, will include required contributions from the general fund of two contributions of $24,834 each for investment for eventual principal repayment, and two contributions of $31,875 each for interest payment. The budget will also include earnings on debt service fund investments computed in accord with actuarial requirements. Assuming that this is the second year of the term bond debt service fund's operation and that the actuarial assumption is that the fund will earn 4% per year compounded semiannually, the required earnings for the year amount to $2,523. The entry to record the revenues budget is shown below; the titles given to the accounts debited are as recommended by the National Committee on Governmental Accounting.

Required Additions	113,418	
Required Earnings	2,523	
Fund Balance		115,941

If the debt service fund is to accumulate the amount needed to retire the term bond issue at maturity, both additions and earnings must be received, and invested, in accord with the actuarial assumptions. Therefore it is important for the fund accounts to facilitate the preparation of statements which will disclose whether actual additions and actual earnings have been in accord with the budget. The recommended chart of accounts for term bond debt service funds uses Revenues to record the actual additions and Interest Earnings to record the actual earnings. Both additions and earnings are recorded on the modified accrual basis.

At year-end Revenues, Interest Earnings, and the related budgetary accounts are closed to Fund Balance.

Term bond debt service fund entries for appropriations and expenditures, the establishment and collection of receivables, the payment of liabilities, and the transfer of cash to fiscal agents are the same as illustrated for serial bond debt service funds. In the serial bond debt service fund illustration, however, consistent with discussions in regard to revenue funds and capital projects funds, the recommended accounting assumes that investments are to be held only for relatively short periods of time and, consequently, premium or discount on investments purchased is neither separately recorded nor amortized. With respect to term bond debt service funds, the NCGA recommendations recognize that investments may be held until maturity (at which time par would be received) so that separate disclosure of premium and discount on investments is appropriate, and amortization of premium and accumulation of discount is necessary. For example, if the term bond debt service fund purchases investments with a face value of $24,000 at 102, and $300 accrued interest, the entry to record the purchase would be:

Investments	24,000	
Unamortized Premium on Investments	480	
Interest Earnings	300	
Cash		24,780

Assuming $600 interest on the investments is received, the entry is:

Cash	600	
Interest Earnings		600

Either at the time interest is received, or at year-end as a part of the adjusting and closing process, the amortization of the premium should be computed and recorded. Intermediate financial accounting textbooks discuss the amortization computation in the context of profit-seeking entities; the discussion is equally applicable to non-profit-seeking entities. Assuming that the amount of amortization of premium on the investments of the term bond debt service fund of the Town of Alva for the period under consideration is $18, the entry is:

Interest Earnings	18	
Unamortized Premium on Investments		18

Amortization of premium and discount on investments, discussed here in the context of term bond debt service fund accounting, should also be a part of the accounting plan for a serial bond debt service fund which expects to hold investments until maturity.

Combined Statements for Debt Service Funds

Statements and schedules for term bond debt service funds are similar to those illustrated for serial bond debt service funds (see Illustrations

7–2 and 7–3, for example). If a municipality has several debt service funds their statements and schedules may be combined. Combined statements and schedules presented in *Governmental Accounting, Auditing, and Financial Reporting* are reproduced here as Illustrations 7–4, 7–5, 7–6, and 7–7.

Illustration 7–4

NAME OF GOVERNMENTAL UNIT
Debt Service Funds
Balance Sheet
December 31, 19x2

Assets	*Total*	*19u3 School Building*	*19v3 Public Health Center*	*19w2 Street, Bridge, Drainage*	*19w8 Parks and Playground*	*19x2 Civic Center*
Cash	$ 43,834	$ 26,304	$	$10,755	$ 4,275	$2,500
Cash with fiscal agents	102,000	–	102,000	–	–	–
Taxes receivable–delinquent (net) (Illus. 7-6)	2,843	1,693	–	750	400	–
Interest and penalties receivable on taxes (net)	227	227	–	–	–	–
Tax liens receivable (net)	759	759	–	–	–	–
Investments (Illustration 7-7)	159,200	115,700	–	–	43,500	–
Unamortized premiums	2,515	2,140	–	–	375	–
Less: Unamortized discounts	(725)	(630)	–	–	(95)	–
Total investments	160,990	117,210	–	–	43,780	–
Interest receivable on investments	1,557	1,157	–	–	400	–
Total Assets	$312,210	$147,350	$102,000	$11,505	$48,855	$2,500
Liabilities and Fund Balances						
Bonds payable	$100,000	–	100,000	–	–	–
Interest payable	2,000	–	2,000	–	–	–
Fund balance (Illustration 7-5)	210,210	147,350[1]	–	11,505	48,855[2]	2,500
Total Liabilities and Fund Balance	$312,210	$147,350	$102,000	$11,505	$48,855	$2,500

[1] Actuarial requirement, $143,700.
[2] Actuarial requirement, $48,670.
Source: National Committee on Governmental Accounting, *Governmental Accounting, Auditing, and Financial Reporting*, p. 40.

Illustrations 7–4, 7–5, and 7–6 not only show combined statements, but illustrate that debt service funds which levy taxes directly account for taxes receivable in the same manner as is discussed in Chapter 3. Illustration 7–6, therefore, illustrates a form of schedule which supports the Taxes Receivable-Delinquent (Net) item on the combined debt

Illustration 7–5

NAME OF GOVERNMENTAL UNIT
Debt Service Funds
Statement of Revenues, Expenditures, and Fund Balances
For the Fiscal Year Ended December 31, 19x2

	Total	*19u3 School Building*	*19w2 Street, Bridge, Drainage*	*19w8 Parks and Play-ground*	*19x2 Civic Center*
Revenues:					
General property taxes:					
Current	$ 77,800	$ 8,400	$49,000	$20,400	$ –
Delinquent	1,239	600	–	639	–
Interest and penalties	138	90	–	48	–
Total general property taxes	79,177	9,090	49,000	21,087	–
Revenue from use of money and property:					
Interest on investments	4,900	4,130	–	770	–
Amortization of discounts on investments	251	246	–	5	–
Total	5,151	4,376	–	775	–
Less: Amortization of premiums on investments	511	486	–	25	–
Net Interest on Investments	4,640	3,890	–	750	–
Revenue from other agencies:					
Shared State Taxes	41,500	–	41,500	–	–
Other Revenues:					
Premiums on Bonds Sold	2,500	–	–	–	2,500
TOTAL REVENUES	127,817	12,980	90,500	21,837	2,500
Expenditures:					
Redemption of serial bonds	60,000	–	60,000	–	–
Interest on bonds	40,300	4,500	25,800	10,000	–
Fiscal agents fees	120	50	–	70	–
TOTAL EXPENDITURES	100,420	4,550	85,800	10,070	–
Excess (Deficit) to Fund Balance	27,397	8,430[1]	4,700	11,767[2]	2,500
Fund Balances, January 1, 19x2	182,813	138,920	6,805	37,088	–
Fund Balances, December 31, 19x2	$210,210	$147,350	$11,505	$48,855	$2,500

[1] Actuarial requirement for the year was $8,250.
[2] Actuarial requirement for the year was $11,500.
Source: National Committee on Governmental Accounting, *Governmental Accounting, Auditing, and Financial Reporting,* p. 41.

service funds balance sheet (Illustration 7–4), and, additionally, supports the similar item in general fund and special revenue funds not illustrated here. Similarly, Illustration 7–7 presents a form of schedule which supports the Investments item in the combined balance sheet of the debt service funds, and, also, the Investments item in the balance sheets of all other funds of that municipality as of the given date. The statements

Illustration 7–6

NAME OF GOVERNMENTAL UNIT
Combined Schedule of Delinquent Taxes Receivable by Funds
December 31, 19x2

		Funds		
Delinquent Taxes by Year	*Total*	*General*	*Special Revenue*	*Debt Service*
Delinquent Taxes:				
19x1	$49,360	$44,300	$2,100	$2,960
19x0	4,203	3,200	600	403
19w9	2,220	1,800	300	120
Total Delinquent Taxes	55,783	49,300	3,000	3,483
Less: Estimated uncollectible delinquent taxes	9,940	8,800	500	640
Net Delinquent Taxes Receivable	$45,843	$40,500	$2,500	$2,843
(Illustrations)		–	–	7–4

Source: National Committee on Governmental Accounting, *Governmental Accounting, Auditing, and Financial Reporting*, p. 116.

illustrated do not assume that the investments themselves are *pooled* for purposes of investment management. Accounting for pooled investments is discussed in Chapter 19 with respect to hospital endownment funds, and in Appendix 3 with respect to investments in general.

Accounting for Debt Refunding

If debt service fund assets accumulated for debt repayment are not sufficient to repay creditors when the debt matures, or if the interest rate on the debt is appreciably higher than the municipality would have to pay on a new bond issue, or if the covenants of the existing bonds are excessively burdensome, the municipality may issue refunding bonds. The proceeds of a refunding issue are accounted for as revenue of the debt service fund which is to repay the existing debt. The appropriation for debt repayment is accounted for as illustrated in the Town of Alva serial bond debt service fund example (see entries 1, 4, 6, and 9).

If a municipality has accumulated no assets at all for debt repayment, it is probable that no debt service fund exists. In such a case a debt service fund should be created to account for the revenue from the refunding bond issue and the repayment of the old debt. When the debt is completely repaid, the debt service fund relating to the liquidated issue should be closed and a debt service fund for the refunding issue should be created and accounted for as described in this chapter.

Illustration 7–7

NAME OF GOVERNMENTAL UNIT
Combined Schedule of Investments—All Funds
December 31, 19x2

Description	*Bond Certificate Numbers*	*Interest Rates (%)*	*Maturity Dates*	*Par Value*	*Unamortized Premiums*	*Unamortized Discount*	*Total Book Value*
General Fund:							
Certificate of Deposit—X National Bank	4366	4	–	$ 65,000	–	–	$ 65,000
Special Revenue Funds:							
Certificates of Deposit—Y National Bank	1870	3.5	–	25,200	–	–	25,200
U.S. Treasury Notes	32494–501	4	5-15-73	12,000	–	–	12,000
Total Special Revenue Funds				37,200			37,200
Debt Service Funds:							
City of D Bonds—1962	3610–3642	3	1-1-80	33,000	$ 375	–	33,375
City of D Bonds—1962	3742–3751	3	1-1-82	10,000	–	$ 95	9,905
City of FW Bonds—1968	1440–1529	4	7-1-85	80,000	2,140	–	82,140
City of FW Bonds—1968	1570–1599	4	7-1-88	30,000	–	630	29,370
Time Deposit—Z State Bank	–	4	–	6,200	–	–	6,200
Total Debt Service Funds (Illustration 7–4)				159,200	2,515	725	160,990
Trust and Agency Funds:							
U.S. Treasury Bonds—1975	B7–63110*	3	6-15-75	200,000	–	–	200,000
U.S. Treasury Bonds—1978	B12–63402*	4	9-15-78	350,000	–	–	350,000
U.S. Treasury Bonds—1980	B14–10631*	4	10-1-80	250,000	–	–	250,000
City of H Bonds	140–239	3.5	1-1-81	100,000	3,600	–	103,600
City of A Bonds	265–293	3.5	7-1-78	29,000	–	1,450	27,550
City of SA Bonds	1440–1589	3	1-1-90	150,000	560	–	150,560
W Independent School District Bonds	462–511	3.5	7-1-84	50,000	–	100	49,900
State of T Highway Bonds	2120–2199	4	9-1-90	80,000	–	–	80,000
KW Power Authority Bonds	640–659	3	3-1-72	20,000	–	–	20,000
Time Deposit—Q National Bank	–	3.5	–	7,650	–	–	7,650
Total Trust and Agency Funds				1,236,650	4,160	1,550	1,239,260
Enterprise Fund—Water and Sewer:							
Certificate of Deposit—X National Bank	3640	4	–	101,000	–	–	101,000
Certificate of Deposit—Y National Bank	1982	3.5	–	75,800	–	–	75,800
Total Enterprise Funds				176,800	–	–	176,800
Total—All Funds				$1,674,850	$6,675	$2,275	$1,679,250

*Trust Receipts—Bonds held by G Trust Company, New York City, N.Y.

SELECTED REFERENCES

AMERICAN INSTITUTE OF CERTIFIED PUBLIC ACCOUNTANTS. *Audits of State and Local Governmental Units*. New York, 1974.

NATIONAL COMMITTEE ON GOVERNMENTAL ACCOUNTING. *Governmental Accounting, Auditing, and Financial Reporting*, chap. 4, "Debt Service Funds." Chicago, 1968.

THOMPSON, F. CORINE AND NORGAARD, RICHARD L. *Sinking Funds and Their Use and Value*. New York: Financial Executives Research Foundation, Inc., 1967.

QUESTIONS

7–1. Bonds to be retired by a debt service fund are recorded in the fund when they mature or are called. Why are they not recorded in the fund throughout their life?

7–2. It is conceivable that a debt service fund for an issue of regular serial bonds might be financially nonexistent at the ends of some fiscal periods during its total life, i.e., have no assets or liabilities and, necessarily, no fund balance. If this is true why should the fund be created at all?

7–3. What asset and liability accounts would you expect to find in the statements for a deferred serial bond debt service fund? Why would you expect deferred serial bonds to create a more complex accounting situation than regular serial bonds?

7–4. What sources of revenue are commonly utilized for general obligation debt service by municipalities?

7–5. How would the liability section of a balance sheet of a debt service fund kept on the recommended modified accrual basis differ from one for a debt service fund kept on a full accrual basis?

7–6. This chapter makes no mention of comparison of periodic statements for debt service funds. Does this appear to be an organic omission or is there a positive reason for it?

7–7. One argument advanced in favor of financing with term bonds secured by some sort of a sinking fund is that earnings on investments held by the debt fund will reduce the amount of support required from other sources. What is your opinion of the validity of this argument?

7–8. "If a certain municipality has eight general obligation bond issues outstanding, it should also operate eight separate debt service funds." Do you agree? Why or why not?

7–9. A southern city operates a large-scale actuarial-type debt service fund which is financed largely by vending machine licenses, various kinds of fees, and a variable amount from the general fund. Why does the general fund contribution need to be variable?

7–10. "The debt service function for revenue bonds issued by a municipal enterprise should be accounted for as described in Chapter 7." Do you agree? Why or why not?

EXERCISES AND PROBLEMS

7–1. Utilizing the municipal annual report obtained for Exercise 1–1, follow the instructions below:

a) How is the general obligation debt service function handled—by the general fund, by a special revenue fund, or by one or more debt service funds? If there is more than one separate debt service fund, what kinds of bond issues or other debt instruments are serviced by each fund? Is debt service for bonds to be retired from enterprise revenues, and for bonds to be retired from special assessments, accounted for by enterprise funds and special assessment funds respectively?

Does the report state the basis of accounting used for debt service funds? If so, is the financial statement presentation consistent with the stated basis? If the basis of accounting is not stated, analyze the statements to determine which basis is used—full accrual, modified accrual, or cash basis. Is the basis used consistent with the recommendations of the NCGA and AICPA discussed in Chapter 7?

b) Have the debt service funds accumulated investments? Does the report contain a schedule or list of investments of debt service funds? Does the report disclose gains and losses on investments realized during the year? Does the report disclose net earnings on investments during the year? What percentage of the revenue of each debt service fund is derived from earnings on investments? What percentage of the revenue of each debt service fund is derived from taxes levied directly for the debt service fund? What percentage is derived from transfers from other funds? List any other sources of debt service revenue and indicate the relative importance of each of these sources.

Are revenues for term bond debt service budgeted on an actuarial basis? If so, are additions and earnings received as required by the actuarial computations?

Compare the balances of the debt service funds with the amount of long-term debt outstanding. Considering the debt maturity dates as well as the amount of debt, and the apparent quality of debt service fund investments, does the debt service activity appear properly managed?

c) Are fiscal agents employed? Are investments managed by municipal employees or by outsiders? If fiscal agents are employed, does the balance sheet disclose the amount of cash in their possession? If so, does this amount appear reasonable in relation to interest payable and matured bonds payable? Do the statements, schedules, or narratives disclose for how long a period of time debt service funds carry a liability for interest on matured but unpresented coupons, and for matured but unpresented bonds?

If fiscal agents are employed, do they charge fees? If so, is the basis of the fee disclosed? What percentage of interest and principal payments is the fiscal agent's fee? Are fees accounted for as expenditures of debt service fund appropriations? If not, how are they accounted for, and by which fund?

If outside investment managers are employed, is the basis of their fees disclosed? Are the fees accounted for as additions to the cost of investments, or as expenditures?

d) In addition to statements or schedules mentioned in Parts *a*, *b*, and *c* of this Exercise, what statements and schedules pertaining to debt service funds are presented? Are there separate statements for each bond issue, or are combined statements used? In what respects (headings, arrangement, items included, etc.) do they seem similar to statements illustrated or described in the text? In what respects do they differ? Are any differences merely a matter of terminology or arrangement, or do they represent material deviations from recommended accounting and reporting for debt service funds?

7–2. The debt service fund balance sheet found in an annual report of the City of Mobile, Alabama, is reproduced on the following page. Study the balance sheet and list (a) the items which appear to be in accord with recommended debt service fund accounting, and (b) the items which appear to differ from recommended debt service fund accounting.

7–3. The only information about debt service funds of the City of Mobile in addition to the balance sheet (Exercise 7–2) is the "Statement of Sources, Applications and Changes in Fund Balance" reproduced on a following page. Study this statement and comment on the extent to which the City of Mobile appears to adhere to recommended debt service fund accounting and reporting.

7–4. The debt service fund statements in an annual report of the City of Mobile are reproduced on following pages.

a) If you were considering the purchase of several of the 1970 Capital Improvements bonds of the City of Mobile, would the statements serve your information needs? Why or why not? What additional information, if any, would you want before you made your final decision on the bond purchase?

b) If you were a resident of the City of Mobile interested in evaluating the manner in which the city administration performs the debt service function, would the statements serve your information needs? Why or why not? What additional information, if any, would you want?

7–5. Your examination of the accounts of your new client, the City of Delmas, as of June 30, 1971 revealed the following (Items 1, 2, and 3 intentionally omitted):

4. On June 30, 1971, the City issued $200,000 in special assessment bonds at par to finance a street improvement project estimated to cost

CITY OF MOBILE
Debt Service Funds
Balance Sheet–September 30, 1971

Assets	*Total*	*1961 Auditorium and Hospital*	*1963 Capital Improvements*	*1964 Capital Improvements*	*1969 Capital Improvements*	*1970 Capital Improvements*	*1971 Capital Improvements*
Cash	$ 13,136	$ 5,065	$ 1,740	$ 163	$ 2,306	$ 1,977	$ 1,885
Investments	1,388,559	716,646	207,449	138,302	202,606	84,008	39,548
Accrued interest receivable on improvements	2,936	1,688	636	449	163	–	–
Total Assets	$1,404,631	$723,399	$209,825	$138,914	$205,075	$85,985	$41,433
Liabilities and Fund Balance							
Accrued interest payable	$ 296,069	$ 38,687	$ 22,979	$ 38,705	$104,140	$50,125	$41,433
Fund balance	1,108,562	684,712	186,846	100,209	100,935	35,860	–
Total Liabilities and Fund Balance	$1,404,631	$723,399	$209,825	$138,914	$205,075	$85,985	$41,433

CITY OF MOBILE
Debt Service Funds
Statement of Sources, Applications, and Changes in Fund Balances
Fiscal Year Ended September 30, 1971

	Total	*1961 Auditorium and Hospital*	*1963 Capital Improvements*	*1964 Capital Improvements*	*1969 Capital Improvements*	*1970 Capital Improvements*	*1971 Capital Improvements*	*1972 General Refunding*
Sources:								
Interest on investments	$ 73,072	$ 47,442	$ 6,502	$ 3,897	$ 11,613	$ 3,445	$ –	$ 173
Transfers from capital improvements fund	2,413,706	390,500	365,000	271,000	965,300	388,506	33,400	–
Transfers from auditorium and hospital fund	94,000	–	–	–	60,000	34,000	–	–
Total	2,580,778	437,942	371,502	274,897	1,036,913	425,951	33,400	173
Applications:								
Redemption of serial bonds	1,255,000	240,000	345,000	205,000	365,000	100,000	–	–
Interest on bonds	1,375,796	241,125	58,739	86,857	648,258	307,417	33,400	–
Transfer to general fund	27,181	–	–	–	–	–	–	27,181
Transfers to capital improvements warrants	94,000	94,000	–	–	–	–	–	–
Total	2,751,977	575,125	403,739	291,857	1,013,258	407,417	33,400	27,181
Excess [Deficiency]	[171,199]	[137,183]	[32,237]	[16,960]	23,655	18,534	–	[27,008]
Fund balance at beginning of year	1,279,761	821,895	219,083	117,169	77,280	17,326	–	27,008
Fund balance at end of year	$1,108,562	$684,712	$186,846	$100,209	$ 100,935	$ 35,860	$ –	$ –

$225,000. The project is to be paid by a $15,000 levy against the City (payable in fiscal year 1971–72) and $210,000 against property owners (payable in five equal annual installments beginning October 1, 1971). The levy was made on June 30. A $215,000 contract was let for the project on July 2, 1971, but work has not begun.

5. On July 1, 1969, the City issued $400,000 in 30-year, 6% general obligation term bonds of the same date at par to finance the construction of a public health center. Construction was completed and the contractors fully paid a total of $397,500 in fiscal year 1970–71.
6. For the health center bonds the City sets aside General Fund revenues sufficient to cover interest (payable seminannually on July 1 and January 1 of each year) and $5,060 to provide for the retirement of bond principal, the latter transfer being made at the end of each fiscal year and invested at the beginning of the next. Your investigation reveals that such investments earned $304 during fiscal year 1970–71, the exact amount budgeted. This $304 was received in cash and will be invested at the beginning of the next year.

Required:

Prepare journal entries to establish a debt service fund for the City of Delmas and to record the events for the period given. Also prepare any necessary adjusting and closing entries as of June 30, 1971, the end of the fiscal year.

(AICPA, adapted)

7–6. A municipality plans to provide for retirement of $3,000,000 of term bonds by annual additions to an accumulation fund. There will be 20 years in which to accomplish the plan and it is estimated that a net of 5 percent per annum, compounded annually, can be realized. Contributions to the fund will be made at the end of each period.

a) Compute the necessary periodic contribution for debt repayment using the annuity tables in Appendix 3.

b) What information would you need, in addition to the results of your computation in part (*a*), in order to be able to prepare the revenue budget for debt service for the proposed term bond issue?

7–7. The Town of Alva serial bond debt service fund balance sheet as of December 31, 19x9, is presented below:

TOWN OF ALVA
Serial Bond Debt Service Fund
Balance Sheet, as of December 31, 19x9

Assets		*Liabilities and Fund Balance*	
Cash with fiscal agent.	$ 800	Interest payable	$ 800
Investments	1,000,000	Fund balance	1,025,000
Interest receivable on investments	25,000		
Total Assets. . .	$1,025,800	Total Liabilities and Fund Balance	$1,025,800

Required:

a) Prepare entries in general journal form to reflect, as necessary, the following information:

1. The revenues budget for the serial bond debt service for 19y0 consists of estimated revenues to be transferred from the general fund of $160,000, and estimated revenues of $52,250 from earnings on investments. The appropriations budget consists of bond interest to be paid by the fiscal agent on January 1, $40,000, and bond interest to be paid by the fiscal agent on July 1, $40,000.
2. The receivable from the general fund is recorded.
3. Half of the transfer from the general fund is received in cash.
4. Interest payable on January 1, 19y0, is recorded as a liability.
5. Cash is transferred to the fiscal agent in the amount of the interest coupons due on January 1.
6. Interest receivable as of December 31, 19x9 is collected and invested; the remainder of cash received from the general fund is invested.
7. The fiscal agent reports that it has paid interest coupons in the amount of $39,200.
8. The remainder due from the general fund is collected.
9. Interest payable on July 1 is recorded.
10. Cash in the amount of the interest coupons due on July 1 is transferred to the fiscal agent.
11. Interest on investments is received in cash in the amount of $25,625. This amount and the balance of cash received from the general fund is invested.
12. Notice is received from the fiscal agent that it has paid interest coupons totaling $39,400.
13. Accrued interest receivable on investments at year end is computed as $26,750.
14. Budgetary and nominal accounts for 19y0 are closed.

b) Prepare a balance sheet for the Town of Alva serial bond debt service fund as of December 31, 19y0.

c) Prepare a statement of revenues, expenditures, and fund balances for the fund for the year ended December 31, 19y0.

7–8. The City of Porter had outstanding 4½% term bonds, scheduled to mature July 1, 1975, in the amount of $600,000. Early in 1975 only $100,000 had been accumulated to apply on retirement of the bonds so a proposal was made to refund the remainder with 5% serial bonds, to mature at the rate of $25,000 every year, beginning July 1, 1976. Enough bondholders accepted the proposal to make it feasible and the budget for the fiscal year ending June 30, 1976 was set up to pay all the interest due on July 1 and $100,000 to bondholders. The $100,000 represented by the fund balance was in a noninterest-bearing cash account.

a) The following transactions occurred in the *term* bonds debt service fund during the year ended June 30, 1976. Record them in general journal form.

1. The budget for the year was recorded.
2. The general fund supplied enough cash revenue to pay all interest.
3. The $100,000 of bonds were recorded as liabilities.
4. Interest for the year and the bond liability were paid. (No fiscal agent was used.)
5. All remaining open accounts were closed.

b) A serial bonds debt service fund was created to account for debt service activities related to the new issue. During the year ended June 30, 1976 the following transactions occurred. Record them in general journal form:

1. The budget for the year was recorded. Estimated revenues, to be raised from taxes levied directly for this fund, were in the amount of one year's interest payments and the first serial bond repayment. Appropriations were budgeted only for the interest legally due during the fiscal year.
2. Taxes receivable were levied to yield the amount of estimated revenues, assuming that 2% of the taxes would be uncollectible.
3. Of the taxes, 90% were collected; the remainder, and the related reserve, were classified as delinquent.
4. Interest due on January 1, 1976, was recorded as a liability.
5. Cash in the amount of the January 1, 1976, interest payment was transferred to a fiscal agent; remaining cash was invested.
6. The fiscal agent reported that all interest coupons due on January 1 had been paid.
7. Interest on investments was: collected in cash during the year, $780; accrued at year-end, $170. Interest and penalties receivable on taxes totaled $255, of which $55 is estimated as uncollectible.
8. Budgetary and nominal accounts for the year were closed.

c) Prepare a serial bond debt service fund balance sheet as of June 30, 1976.

d) Prepare a serial bond debt service fund statement of revenues, expenditures, and fund balance for the year ended December 31, 1976.

CONTINUOUS PROBLEMS

7–L. The City of Bingham created a City Hall Annex Bond Debt Service Fund to be used to retire the bonds issued to pay for the construction of the City Hall Annex (see Problem 6–L), and to pay the interest on these bonds.

You are required to:

a) Open a general journal for the City Hall Annex Bond Debt Service Fund and record the transactions below, as necessary. Use account titles illustrated in Chapter 7.

1. The budget for the year was legally adopted. The budget provided estimated revenues equal to the appropriations for one year's interest on the City Hall Annex bonds and the redemption of the first block of bonds (see Problem 6–L for data concerning the bonds). Appropriations were provided for the first semiannual interest payment.
2. Taxes were levied by the debt service fund in the amount of $250,000. Of this amount, $5,000 was expected to be uncollectible.
3. Cash equal to the premium on the bonds was received from the City Hall Annex Construction Fund (see transaction 1, Problem 6-L). The premium is not to be amortized; credit Revenues for the entire amount.
4. U.S. Treasury bills of $60,000 face value, maturing in 180 days, were purchased for $58,020 cash. Revenue was recognized at the time of purchase.
5. Taxes receivable were collected in the amount of $160,000.
6. Interest due at the end of the first six months was recorded as a liability.
7. Cash in the amount of interest due was transferred to a fiscal agent. The remainder of cash was invested in certificates of deposit.
8. Taxes receivable were collected in the amount of $80,000. The balance of taxes receivable, and the related estimated uncollectible account, were classified as delinquent.
9. The Treasury bills matured; cash was received for the face value.
10. The fiscal agent reported that interest coupons totaling $74,500 had been paid.
11. Cash to close the City Hall Annex Construction Fund was received (see Problem 6–L–e).
12. Information was received that on the last day of the year interest totaling $2,850 had been added to the certificates of deposit.
13. Interest and penalties on delinquent taxes as of year-end was computed as $500, of which $200 was expected to be uncollectible.
14. Budgetary and nominal accounts for the year were closed.

b) Prepare a balance sheet for the City Hall Annex Bond Debt Service Fund as of year-end.

c) Prepare a Statement of Revenues, Expenditures, and Fund Balance for the City Hall Annex Bond Debt Service Fund for the year.

7–S. The City of Smithville created a Street Improvement Bond Debt Service Fund to be used to retire the bonds issued for the purposes described in Problem 6–S, and to pay the interest on the bonds. The $1,000,000 worth of bonds issued during 197B were dated January 1, 197B, and were each in the denomination of $5,000, bearing coupons with the nominal annual interest rate of 4.5%. The first coupon was payable July 1, 197B; additional coupons were payable January 1 and July 1 of each following year until the maturity of the bond. Forty bonds are to mature ten years after date of issue, and forty bonds are to mature each year thereafter until all the bonds·issued in 197B have matured.

Required:

a) Open a general journal for the Street Improvement Bond Debt Service Fund. Record the transactions below as necessary. Use account titles illustrated in Chapter 7.

1. The budget for 197B was legally adopted. Since the bond issue was authorized after the general fund budget for 197B was legally adopted, the debt service fund budget provided estimated revenues equal to the appropriation for the interest payment to be made during 197B. Revenue sources were to be transfers from the Street Improvement Fund for premium and accrued interest sold, and transfers from the General Fund Miscellaneous appropriation for the remainder needed.
2. The transfer from the Street Improvement Fund (See transaction 4, Problem 6–S) was received.
3. The transfer from the General Fund was received.
4. The July 1, 197B, interest payment was made.
5. Budgetary and nominal accounts for the year were closed.

b) Prepare a statement of revenues, expenditures, and fund balance for the year ended December 31, 197B.

It is expected that additional Street Improvement Bonds in the total amount of $2,000,000 will be issued in 197C. It is expected that the additional bonds will be of the $5,000 denomination and will bear interest at the nominal annual rate of 4.5%. The additional bonds will be dated January 1, 197C.

The first interest coupon will be payable July 1, 197C; interest coupons will be payable January 1 and July 1 of each following year until maturity. Forty bonds of the 197C issue will mature 10 years after date of issue, and 40 bonds will mature each year thereafter until all bonds of the 197C issue have matured.

c) Record the following events and transactions for 197C, as necessary.

1. The budget for 197C was legally adopted. The budget provided estimated revenues to be transferred from the general fund in an amount equal to the appropriations for interest for the year on all Street Improvement Bonds expected to be outstand-

ing during the year, plus an amount of $150,000 to be invested by the debt service fund for eventual bond redemption. The budget also provided for earnings of $4,500 on debt service fund investments. No premium or accrued interest on bonds sold is included in the 197C estimated revenues; if the debt service fund does receive such items from the Street Improvement Fund they will be invested and used for eventual bond redemption.

2. On January 1 the general fund transferred $22,500 in cash to the debt service fund; the remainder due from the general fund was recorded as a receivable.
3. Bond interest coupons due January 1 were paid.
4. The fund received $43,000 from the Street Improvement Fund as premium and accrued interest on the $2,000,000 face value of bonds sold on March 1, 197C. This amount is invested in 6% United States Treasury Notes purchased at par. The notes mature March 1, 197E; interest dates are March 1 and September 1.
5. The amount due from the general fund is received on June 30.
6. Bond coupons due July 1, 197C, are paid; on July 1 all remaining cash is invested in long-term certificates of deposit at 6% per annum, compounded semiannually.
7. Semiannual interest on Treasury Notes is received on September 1.
8. Necessary adjusting and closing entries were made as of December 31, 197C.

d) Prepare a balance sheet as of December 31, 197C.

e) Prepare a statement of revenue, expenditures, and fund balance for the year ended December 31, 197C.

8

Trust and Agency Funds

Trust funds and agency funds are employed by individuals, institutions, governmental bodies, and others to assist in administration of, and accounting for, assets held under trust or agency agreements. As applied to public affairs, it may be said of trust funds that they are legal and accounting devices used by governmental units in discharging their responsibility for property of which they do not have absolute ownership but which must be utilized for a certain purpose or group of purposes. Agency funds are legal and accounting devices used by governmental units (and others) for administering assets that come into their possession incidentally in connection with the discharge of some responsibility resting upon them by virtue of law or other similar authority. In practice the legalistic distinctions between trust funds and agency funds are not of major significance. The important and perhaps the sole consideration from an accounting standpoint is: What can and what cannot be done with the fund's assets, in accordance with laws and other pertinent regulations?

The name of a particular fund is not a reliable criterion for determining the correct accounting basis for trust and agency funds. Merely calling a fund by one name or another has no influence upon the transactions in which it may engage. In fact, the words "trust" and "agency" are frequently omitted from the titles of funds in this classification. Examples are "public employees' retirement fund" and "condemnation and grading fund": the former a trust fund, the latter an agency fund, each classified according to the circumstances under which its assets are held. It is sometimes said that a practical basis for distinguishing between the two types is the length of time specific assets are held. But this is not a wholly reliable guide, since there is no generally recognized pronouncement stating the maximum time restriction for holding assets to constitute an agency fund; nor is there a minimum time to constitute a fund of the trust variety. As suggested earlier, if not explicitly so stated, the exact name or designation of a given fund is of little significance in establishing its accounting procedures and limitations; these depend upon the enactment that brought about creation of the fund, plus all other regulations under which it operates. Regulations include pertinent statutes, ordinances, wills, trust indentures, and other instruments of endowment, resolutions of the governing body, general purposes of the fund, kinds and amounts of assets held, etc. This aggregate of factors, or such as are applicable to a given fund, determines the transactions in which it may and should engage.

AGENCY FUNDS

An agency fund comes into existence because the governmental unit, in its capacity as agent for accomplishing some particular mission, becomes incidentally a custodian of assets. When this occurs, accounts are required to record not only the assets received but also the liabilities to those for whose benefit they were received. The other major transaction or transactions of the fund will be disbursement of the assets to their real owners. Although revenue and expenditure transactions are not impossible for an agency fund, they are not typical. Furthermore, an agency fund will have little or no Fund Balance; the proceeds of any fee levied for the service rendered belong to some other fund and should be shown as a liability to that fund.

The agency relationship does not always require creation of an agency fund. For example, a municipality must act as agent of the Federal and state governments in the collection of employees' withholding taxes, social security taxes, and retirement contributions. As illustrated in the chapters dealing with revenue funds, amounts withheld from employees' pay by the municipality acting as agent for higher levels of government are ordinarily credited to a revenue fund current liability account at the time the withholding is recorded, and debited to the same liability account when the amount is remitted to the state or Federal government. If required by law or administrative decision in a given jurisdiction, a separate agency fund is operated by the municipality to account for employees' taxes and contributions. If a separate agency fund is not required by law, it appears perfectly acceptable for the fund which accounts for the gross pay to account for the withholdings and contributions in the manner described in Chapter 3; this is so because the agency relationship is incidental to the primary purposes of the fund which accounts for gross pay, the amounts tend to be small in relation to total expenditures, and the agency relationship is ordinarily discharged on a rather current basis.

Agency Funds for Revenue Collection

An agency relationship which does, logically, result in the creation of an agency fund is the collection of taxes or other revenues, by one governmental body, for several of the funds it operates and for a number of other governmental units and their funds. Sales taxes, gasoline taxes, motor vehicle taxes, and many other taxes are commonly collected by a state government agency and apportioned, on the basis specified by law, to other state units and to governmental bodies within the state. At the local government level it is common for the treasurer of each county to serve as collector for all property taxes owed by persons owning property within the county. For example, Illustration 8–1 shows that a taxpayer owning property in that part of the City of Bloomington, Indiana, lying in Perry Township of Monroe County received a property tax bill from the county Treasurer for the total property tax levied for 24 separate funds of 6 different governmental bodies (State of Indiana, 2; Monroe County, 10; County Library, 2; Perry Township, 1; Monroe County Community School Corporation, 3; City of Bloomington, 6). Whereas, if the taxpayer's property lay in Perry Township outside the city limits, the tax bill included the taxes levied by only 19 separate funds of 5 different governmental bodies (State of Indiana, 2; Monroe County, 10; County Library, 2; Perry Township, 2; and Monroe County Community School Corporation, 3). Thus it is obvious that tax agency fund records must be organized in a manner facilitating proper distribution of tax collections. "Proper distribution" means that the taxes collected for each parcel of property must be distributed to each of the governmental bodies (and by it to each of its funds) in the proportion the tax levied by the body (or its funds) bears to the total levied against the parcel for that year. Thus, in the example given, taxes collected on property lying in Perry Township within the City of Bloomington should be distributed 3.86 (City tax rate)/11.34 (total tax rate) to the City Corporation, 5.85/11.34 to the School Corporation, .01/11.34 to Perry Township, etc., while taxes collected on property lying in Perry Township outside the City of Bloomington should be distributed 5.85/7.82 to the School Corporation, .35/7.82 to Perry Township, etc. The Perry Township Fire Protection Fund would receive .34/7.82 of tax collections for the year from property in the township which is outside the city and nothing for property which is inside the city limits [since property within the city receives fire protection from the city—and pays for it in the city's Corporation Fund (general fund) tax rate].

Tax agency fund accounting problems are somewhat more complex than the preceding paragraph indicates. Tax collections in any given year normally relate not only to current taxes of that year, but also to taxes

Illustration 8–1

Composition of Total Property Tax Rate
Monroe County, Indiana

LEGAL NOTICE LEGAL NOTICE LEGAL NOTICE LEGAL NOTICE LEGAL NOTICE

NOTICE TO TAXPAYERS OF MONROE COUNTY OF TAX LEVIES AND RATES

Notice is hereby given that the Tax Duplicates for the several taxing units in Monroe County for the year 1972 payable in 1973 are now in the hands of the County Treasurer who is ready to receive the taxes charged thereon. The following table shows the tax levies and rates on each one hundred dollars ($100) of net assessed valuation of taxable real estate and personal property in each taxing unit.

Due January 1, 1973—First installment delinquent after the 10th day in May—Second installment delinquent after the 10th day in November.

LOUISE L. GOODMAN, Monroe County Treasurer

TAX RATES CHARGED FOR YEAR 1972 PAYABLE IN THE YEAR 1973		TOWNSHIPS											CITIES AND TOWNS					
	NAME OF FUND	BEAN BLOSSOM	BENTON	BLOOMINGTON	CLEAR CREEK	INDIAN CREEK	PERRY	POLK	RICHLAND	SALT CREEK	VAN BUREN	WASHINGTON	BLOOMINGTON-BLGTN. CITY	BLOOMINGTON-PERRY CITY	VAN-BUREN CITY	RICHLAND CITY	ELLETTSVILLE	STINESVILLE
STATE RATES	State Fair Board	.0035	.0035	.0035	.0035	.0035	.0035	.0035	.0035	.0035	.0035	.0035	.0035	.0035	.0035	.0035	.0035	.0035
	State Forestry	.0065	.0065	.0065	.0065	.0065	.0065	.0065	.0065	.0065	.0065	.0065	.0065	.0065	.0065	.0065	.0065	.0065
	TOTAL STATE	.01	.01	.01	.01	.01	.01	.01	.01	.01	.01	.01	.01	.01	.01	.01	.01	.01
COUNTY RATES	County General	.75	.75	.75	.75	.75	.75	.75	.75	.75	.75	.75	.75	.75	.75	.75	.75	.75
	County Welfare	.19	.19	.19	.19	.19	.19	.19	.19	.19	.19	.19	.19	.19	.19	.19	.19	.19
	County Health Dept.	.03	.03	.03	.03	.03	.03	.03	.03	.03	.03	.03	.03	.03	.03	.03	.03	.03
	Aviation	.02	.02	.02	.02	.02	.02	.02	.02	.02	.02	.02	.02	.02	.02	.02	.02	.02
	Aviation Bond Fund	.08	.08	.08	.08	.08	.08	.08	.08	.08	.08	.08	.08	.08	.08	.08	.08	.00
	Courthouse Annex Bond	.005	.005	.005	.005	.005	.005	.005	.005	.005	.005	.005	.005	.005	.005	.005	.005	.005
	Cumulative Courthouse	.02	.02	.02	.02	.02	.02	.02	.02	.02	.02	.02	.02	.02	.02	.02	.02	.02
	Cumulative Bridge	.10	.10	.10	.10	.10	.10	.10	.10	.10	.10	.10	.10	.10	.10	.10	.10	.10
	Re-Assessment	.055	.055	.055	.055	.055	.055	.055	.055	.055	.055	.055	.055	.055	.055	.055	.055	.055
	County Fair	.01	.01	.01	.01	.01	.01	.01	.01	.01	.01	.01	.01	.01	.01	.01	.01	.01
	TOTAL COUNTY	1.26	1.26	1.26	1.26	1.26	1.26	1.26	1.26	1.26	1.26	1.26	1.26	1.26	1.26	1.26	1.26	1.26
LIBRARY RATES	County Library	.25	.25	.25	.25	.25	.25	.25	.25	.25	.25	.25	.25	.25	.25	.25	.25	.25
	Library Bond	.10	.10	.10	.10	.10	.10	.10	.10	.10	.10	.10	.10	.10	.10	.10	.10	.10
	TOTAL LIBRARY	.35	.35	.35	.35	.35	.35	.35	.35	.35	.35	.35	.35	.35	.35	.35	.35	.35
CIVIL TOWNSHIP RATES	Township	.10	.09	.03	.07	.12	—	.54	—	.18	.04	.05	.03	—	.04	—	—	.10
	Poor Relief	—	.02	.06	.05	.05	.01	.20	.02	.10	.04	.08	.06	.01	.04	.02	.02	—
	Fire Protection	.11	.27	.30	.20	—	.34	—	.20	.20	.35	—	—	—	—	—	—	—
	Civil Township Bond			.11														
	TOTAL TOWNSHIP	.21	.38	.50	.32	.17	.35	.74	.22	.48	.43	.13	.09	.01	.08	.02	.02	.10
SCHOOL RATES	General Fund (School)	4.26	4.60	4.60	4.60	4.60	4.60	4.60	4.26	4.60	4.60	4.60	4.60	4.60	4.60	4.26	4.26	4.26
	Debt Service Fund	1.04	.82	.82	.82	.82	.82	.82	1.04	.82	.82	.82	.82	.82	.82	1.04	1.04	1.04
	Cumulative Building	—	.43	.43	.43	.43	.43	.43	—	.43	.43	.43	.43	.43	.43	—	—	—
	TOTAL SCHOOL	5.30	5.85	5.85	5.85	5.85	5.85	5.85	5.30	5.85	5.85	5.85	5.85	5.85	5.85	5.30	5.30	5.30
CORPORATION RATES	Corporation												3.015	3.015	3.015	3.015	1.10	2.00
	Street												—	—	—		1.24	—
	Park & Recreation												.42	.42	.42	.42	.08	—
	Cemetery												—	—	—	—	—	—
	Police Pension												.192	.192	.192	.192	—	—
	Firemen's Pension												.108	.108	.108	.108	—	—
	Corporation Bond												.075	.075	.075	.075	—	—
	Cumulative Bldg. & Equip.												—	—	—		.10	—
	Park Dist. Bond												.05	.05	.05	.05	—	—
	TOTAL CORPORATION RATES												3.86	3.86	3.86	3.86	2.52	2.00
TOTAL PROPERTY TAX RATES	**TOTAL RATES**	7.13	7.85	7.97	7.79	7.64	7.82	8.21	7.14	7.95	7.90	7.60	11.42	11.34	11.41	10.80	9.46	9.02

State of Indiana, Monroe County, SS: I, John Davis, Auditor of Monroe County, hereby certify that the above is a correct copy of all tax levies and rates of taxes collectible in Monroe County in the year 1973.
Signed: JOHN W. DAVIS, Auditor, Monroe County, Indiana
28—7—14

levied in several prior years and sometimes include advance collections of taxes for the following year. In many jurisdictions not only does the total tax rate vary from year to year, but the proportion that the rate of each governmental body (and each fund) bears to the total rate also varies from year to year. Interest and penalties on delinquent taxes must also be computed at statutory rates and collected by the tax agency fund for distribution to the participating governmental bodies and funds.

Accounting for Tax Agency Funds

The method of accounting for the distribution of tax proceeds depends upon how the levy was recorded. The simplest situation involving a distribution problem exists where each fund of the governmental unit records its own tax levy, with collections handled by a central treasurer's department. This means only that if the general fund, special revenue funds (if any), debt service funds, or any others are authorized to make direct levies of property taxes, each records its levy on its own books, with collections administered by a central office. Under this plan the central collecting office periodically (daily, weekly, monthly, etc.) ascertains the share of each fund in the collections and distributes them on the determined basis.

To illustrate the procedure of accounting for collections for other units, there will be given a series of entries, beginning with the levies and extending through final settlement. To begin with, let it be assumed that for a given year a county government levies on its own account the amount of $600,000 in property taxes, from which it expects to realize $590,000. For the same year, there is certified to it the amount of $480,000 in property taxes to be collected for other units, the total levy to be billed to taxpayers in a combined amount on a composite rate. Further, let it be assumed that it is expected that $9,000 of the $480,000 will not be collectible. The county levy, which, it will be assumed, is for the general fund alone, will be recorded in the standard form for such a levy, as follows:

Taxes Receivable—Current	600,000	
Estimated Uncollectible Current Taxes		10,000
Revenues		590,000

Other units using the tax agency fund will record levies which may be summarized as follows (estimated loss figure assumed):

Taxes Receivable—Current	480,000	
Estimated Uncollectible Current Taxes		9,000
Revenues		471,000

Let it be assumed the county has established a tax agency fund, for use in administering its responsibility as an agent for collecting taxes. *The tax agency fund entry* for recording the two levies certified to it would be as follows:

1. Taxes Receivable for Other Funds and Units	1,080,000	
Tax Agency Fund Balance		1,080,000

Note that the tax agency fund assumes liability for gross levies and not merely for net amounts expected to be collected. Since "Tax Agency Fund Balance" is virtually a liability account, there could be little objection to supplanting it with "Due to Other Funds and Units," or another similar title.

Since it was assumed that taxpayers were being billed on a composite rate, collections during a given period of time must be distributed proportionately among the units represented in the total levy. Continuing on the basis of $600,000 levied for one unit and $480,000 for another or others, distributions of amounts collected on this joint levy will be shared to the extent of \$600,000/\$1,080,000 by the former and \$480,000/\$1,080,000 by the latter. A \$540,000 collection would be shared in the amount of \$600,000/\$1,080,000 times \$540,000, or \$300,000, by the county, and \$480,000/\$1,080,000 times \$540,000, or \$240,000, by the other governmental unit or units. Collection of \$540,000 by the county tax agency fund and remission to the levying funds would be recorded as follows:

Tax Agency Fund Entries

		Debit	Credit
2.	Cash	540,000	
	Taxes Receivable for Other Funds and Units		540,000
	To record collection.		
3.	Tax Agency Fund Balance	540,000	
	Due to County General Fund		300,000
	Due to Other Governmental Unit		240,000
	To record amounts to be distributed to other fund and unit.		
4.	Due to County General Fund	300,000	
	Due to Other Governmental Unit	240,000	
	Cash		540,000
	To record remittance of cash.		

The last two entries can be combined into one with elimination of the "Due to ——" accounts by supporting the remittance entry with a schedule showing distribution to the participants. However, there may be some advantage in formalizing the distribution by use of a journal entry, as done above. The method preferred in actual practice probably depends upon the number of participants, length of period between calculation of distribution and making of settlement, and possibly other attending circumstances. Receipt of collection remittances would be recorded by the participating fund and unit in the same manner as direct collections are recorded.

In recording the entry for the transfer of collections from the county tax agency fund to the other unit, it was assumed that no charges were made for the collecting service. To illustrate the effect of a service charge by the county, it will be assumed that a fee of 0.5 percent is charged by the county on all amounts collected for other units. *On the tax agency fund books* the following entry should be made:

		Debit	Credit
5.	Tax Agency Fund Balance	1,200	
	Due to County General Fund		1,200

Transfer of the amount from the agency fund will require a debit to Due to County General Fund, with a credit to Cash. This entry and the preceding one should be combined with those recording distribution and settlement. For the county general fund entry, a credit to Revenues will be required. It should be noted that only \$238,800 will pass from the tax agency fund to the other governmental unit, which will record the receipt in the following manner:

Entry by Receiving Fund

Cash	238,800	
Expenditures	1,200	
Taxes Receivable—Current		240,000

The foregoing entries summarize general procedures of tax levies and distribution. One fact should be emphasized: a vast amount of detail is ordinarily involved in making proper accounting when one fund or unit serves as collecting and distributing agent for other funds or units. Using controlling accounts for the several levies is indispensable for economy of time and for accuracy. Controls must show not only the amounts to be collected for the various funds and units, but the years to which they apply. The collecting agent should be able to correlate every amount collected with the levy to which it applies.

TRUST FUNDS

Trust funds differ from agency funds principally in degree: Frequently a trust fund is in existence over a longer period of time than an agency fund; it represents and develops vested interests to a greater extent; and it involves more complex administrative and financial problems.[1] In both trust and agency funds the governmental unit has a fiduciary relationship with the creators and beneficiaries of the trust or agency. A historically important reason for the creation of a trust fund is the acceptance by a municipality of trusteeship over assets to be invested to produce income to be used for specified purposes (generally cultural or educational). The fair market value of the assets placed in trust under such an agreement is referred to as the principal, or corpus, of the trust. Since the principal of this form of trust must be held intact in order to produce income, the trust is called *nonexpendable*. The income from the assets may be used for only the purposes specified by the trustor; therefore, the income is *expendable*. Separate funds should be established to account for expendable and nonexpendable assets.

In addition to the nonexpendable vs. expendable classification, trust funds may also be classified as *public* or *private*. Public trust funds are those whose principal or income, or both, must be used for some public purpose; the beneficiaries of private trust funds are private individuals or organizations.[2] The preceding definition should not be taken too literally, because public employee retirement funds are classified as public

[1] National Committee on Governmental Accounting, *Governmental Accounting, Auditing, and Financial Reporting*, (Chicago, Municipal Finance Offices Association, 1968) p. 75.

[2] Ibid., p. 75.

trust funds even though the beneficiaries are individuals. Funds established for the purpose of holding performance deposits of licensees under a governmental unit's regulatory activities are examples of private trust funds.

Accounting for Trust Funds—General Recommendations

The rules of law pertaining to testamentary and intervivos trusts are applicable to trusts in which a municipality acts as trustee; trust fund accounting information systems are therefore constrained by the trust laws of the several states. A primary problem is the distinction between transactions which affect the trust principal, or corpus, and transactions which relate to trust income. A case in point is the accounting treatment of depreciable assets. None of the categories of funds discussed thus far in this text accounts for capital assets; even capital projects funds account for only the receipt and disposition of current assets used for the acquisition of capital assets, not for the capital assets themselves. However, if capital assets are included in the principal of a trust fund they obviously must be accounted for. Under the general rules of trust law cash basis accounting is assumed, which means that the fund would include the fair market value of the capital assets at date of creation of the trust until the assets were disposed of; no depreciation during that time would be recognized.

In many jurisdictions it is possible for a trustor to specify that the income of the fund should be computed on the accrual basis. If that is done, depreciation would be recognized as an expense and cash retained in the nonexpendable fund to offset the decrease in book value of depreciable assets, thus maintaining the fund principal at its original dollar amount in respect to the depreciable assets. Accrual accounting, accompanied by "funding the depreciation," (as the retention of cash to offset depreciation expense is called) enables the administrators to maintain the principal intact, in the sense of maintaining the original dollar amount, which the general rules of trust law and cash basis accounting do not do. More important than maintaining fund principal at its original dollar amount is maintaining or enhancing the earning power of the assets placed in trust. Cash basis accounting offers no help in the measurement of the degree of success of trust fund administrators in maintaining or improving the earning power of the assets comprising the fund principal. Accordingly, the National Committee on Governmental Accounting recommends that trust funds be kept on the full accrual basis.[3] The recommendation assumes that an objective of trust funds is the production

[3] The AICPA reinforces this recommendation by taking the position that cash basis statements do not show financial position and financial operations in accord with generally accepted accounting principles, therefore CPAs are required to qualify any opinion they may express on such statements. (*Audits of State and Local Governmental Units*, p. 127.

of net income to be used to support the purposes for which the trust was created. If interested persons are to be able to determine how effectively trust fund administrators have managed the assets, it is obvious that trust fund annual reports should include comparative accrual-based income statements, as well as a detailed listing of trust fund investments as of the end of the fiscal year. The lists of trust fund assets should show both cost (or fair market value at date of acquisition) and market value as of the date of the statement. The transactions by the trustee during the year are of interest also; in recognition of this it is common for trust fund administrators to report purchases and sales of investments during the year, disclosing gains and losses on the sales. (It is a general rule of law that gains and losses on sales of principal assets serve to increase or decrease the principal rather than affect the income.[4] If transactions in principal invesments are made for the purpose of maximizing earnings rather than for the purpose of maintaining the safety of the principal, a good case can be made that the gains or losses should increase or decrease the income. In many jurisdictions a trustor can specify how the gains and losses are to be considered.)

Budgetary Accounts. Budgetary accounts are not generally needed for nonexpendable trust funds because transactions of the fund result in changes in the fund principal only incidentally; by definition the principal cannot be appropriated or expended. Expendable trust funds, on the other hand, may be required by law to use the appropriation procedure to ensure adequate notice to parties at interest as to the expenditure of fund assets. If the appropriation procedure is required, the use of budgetary accounts is recommended for reasons discussed at length in preceding chapters of this text.

Illustrative Entries—Trust Principal and Trust Revenue Funds

As an illustration of the nature of accounting for trust principal and trust revenue, assume that the Town of Big Springs had not been operating a public library prior to October 1, 19x5. On October 1, 19x5, James Jones died, having made a valid will which provided for the gift of his residence and various securities to the town for the establishment and operation of a free public library.[5] The gift was accepted by the

[4] William L. Cary and Craig B. Bright observe in *The Law and the Lore of Endowment Funds* (New York: Ford Foundation, 1969) that this is the position taken in the Uniform Principal and Income Acts which have been adopted by a majority of the states, but that the acts have no direct application to endowment funds of charitable corporations or of educational institutions. (p. 13). J. Peter Williamson, *Investments: New Analytic Techniques* (New York: Praeger Publishers, 1971, p. 88), states that "There are signs that the rule is breaking down."

[5] This illustration is based on a CPA examination problem prepared by the American Institute of Certified Public Accountants. The "solution" is that of the authors, not the AICPA.

town. The library funds and operation were placed under the control of trustees. The terms of the gift provided that not in excess of $5,000 of the principal of the fund could be used for the purchase of equipment, building rearrangement, and purchase of such "standard" library reference books as, in the opinion of the trustees, were needed for starting the library. Except for this $5,000, the principal of the fund is to be invested, and the income therefrom used to operate the library in accordance with appropriations made by the trustees.

In order to keep trust principal transactions clearly distinguished from trust revenue transactions, the town treasurer decides to establish two funds: a Public Library Endowment Principal Fund, and a Library Endowment Revenue Fund. The latter fund is to be accounted for in the same manner as any other municipal revenue fund (see Chapters 3, 4, and 5).

The property received from the estate by the trustees was as follows:

Description	*Face or Par*	*Appraised Value*
Residence of James Jones:		
Land	–	$ 2,500
Building (25-year estimated life)	–	20,000
Bonds:		
AB Company	$34,000	32,000
C and D Company	10,000	11,200
D and G Company	20,000	20,000
Stocks:		
M Company, 6 percent preferred	12,000	12,600
S Company, 5 percent preferred	10,000	9,600
K Company, common (300 shares)	No par	12,900
GF Company (200 shares)	4,000	14,500

The receipt of the property by the trustees is properly recorded in the *Endowment Principal* fund by the following entry (note that the trustees are responsible for the appraised value, or fair market value, of the trust assets, not for their face or par value):

		Debit	Credit
1.	Land	2,500	
	Building	20,000	
	Investments	112,800	
	Endowment Principal Fund Balance		135,300

Since no cash was received from the executors, and the trustees were required by terms of the trust to use principal cash to pay for building rearrangement and the purchase of equipment and reference books, the trustees sold 100 shares of G F Company stock; proceeds were $6,875. The stock had been recorded in Endowment Principal fund accounts at $7,250, therefore there is a loss on the sale of $375. Under trust law this loss does not need to be charged against revenue of the period, but should be considered as a reduction in the principal fund balance. Therefore, the appropriate entry in the *Endowment Principal Fund* is:

2. Cash	6,875	
Endowment Principal Fund Balance	375	
Investments		7,250

As authorized by the trust, the trustees spent $1,310 for alteration of the house so that it could serve as a public library, $725 for general reference books, and $2,180 for equipment having an estimated life of 10 years. No further disbursements of principal fund cash will be made by the trustees for these purposes. The entry in the *Endowment Principal Fund* is:

3. Endowment Principal Fund Balance	4,215	
Cash		4,215

The trustees adopted the following budget for the year beginning January 1, 19x6, for the operation of the library:

Estimated revenue from investment	$5,000
Estimated revenue from fines, etc.	200
Appropriation for salaries	3,600
Appropriation for subscriptions	300
Appropriation for purchase of books	800
Appropriation for utilities, supplies, etc.	400

Since two separate funds are to be used, and the Endowment Revenue Fund is to be operated as a revenue fund, it is necessary to record the budget in the *Endowment Revenue Fund* by the following entry:

4. Estimated Revenues	5,200	
Appropriations		5,100
Endowment Revenues Fund Balance		100

The trustees sold the C and D Company bonds for $11,550, including accrued interest of $80. A portion of the proceeds were reinvested in L and M Company no-par common stock—total cost of this stock being $9,655, including commissions and taxes amounting to $42.50. The accrued interest on bonds sold is trust revenue and should be recorded in the *Endowment Revenue Fund:*

5. Cash	80	
Revenue		80

The C and D Company bonds were received by the trustees from the executors and recorded at a value of $11,200; since $11,470 was received from their sale ($11,550 less $80 accrued interest) the gain on the sale of $270 belongs to the *Endowment Principal Fund.* The entry to record the sale, therefore, is:

6. Cash	11,470	
Investments		11,200
Endowment Principal Fund Balance		270

Commissions and taxes on the purchase of stock are considered to be a part of the cost of the stock whether it is purchased by a profit-seeking entity or a governmental trust fund. The purchase of the stock, although involving a *disbursement of cash*, does not involve an *expenditure of trust assets;* it is merely a change in the form of assets held by the *Endowment Principal Fund*, and its purchase is recorded by the following entry:

7. Investments	9,655	
Cash		9,655

The trustees received a property tax bill on the land and former Jones residence, now used as a public library. The taxes were based on the 19x5 assessment made before James Jones died, therefore, they were a liability of the estate and should be paid from *Endowment Principal Fund* cash. (After the property passed into the hands of the trust, it should have been removed from the tax rolls and no more tax bills should be received by the trustees.)

8. Endowment Principal Fund Balance	200	
Cash		200

During the first six months of the first year of the operation of the public library cash was received from the following sources: interest and dividends, $3,100; fines, $20; and a gift for the purchase of books, $200. All of these clearly relate to the operation of the library. The first two sources were included in the Endowment Revenue Fund budget (see entry 4). Gifts were not anticipated at the time the budget was prepared, and therefore Estimated Revenues does not include any amount from this source. Because the amount of the gift is relatively large, it is credited directly to the *Endowment Revenues Fund* balance. (If the trustees should decide to amend the revenues budget, the procedure illustrated in Chapter 2 would be followed; in this illustration it is assumed that the trustees of the Big Springs Public Library did not wish to amend the revenues budget.)

9. Cash	3,320	
Revenues		3,120
Endowment Revenues Fund Balance		200

The $200 gift for purchase of books, mentioned above, is in addition to the amount appropriated for that purpose. In order that library clerical employees may treat all book purchases in the same manner, it is desirable to amend the *Endowment Revenues Fund* appropriations budget, as shown by the following entry:

10. Endowment Revenues Fund Balance	200	
Appropriations		200

During the first six months of the first year of the operation of the library, cash was disbursed for the following purposes: salaries, $1,500; purchase of books, $900; magazine subscriptions, $230; and supplies and other expenses, $260. All of these items had been included in the *Endowment Revenues Fund* appropriations budget. The fund bookkeeper had not recorded encumbrances for any item, and therefore the following entry is sufficient:

	Debit	Credit
11. Expenditures	2,890	
Cash		2,890

At the end of the first six months there were miscellaneous expenses unpaid, amounting to $90. Also, there were outstanding purchase orders for books in the amount of $70; encumbrances had not been recorded when the purchase orders were issued. If interim financial statements are to be prepared, the encumbrances and accrued liabilities should be recorded in the *Endowment Revenues Fund:*

	Debit	Credit
12. Expenditures	90	
Encumbrances	70	
Accounts Payable		90
Reserve for Encumbrances		70

Illustrative Financial Statements

On June 30, 19x6, the trustees have had control of the endowment principal for nine months. The library has been in operation for six months. The Endowment Principal Fund balance sheet as of June 30, 19x6, is shown in Illustration 8–2. An analysis of changes in fund balance for the period is shown in Illustration 8–3, and a statement of receipts and disbursements of principal fund cash is shown as Illustration 8–4.

Illustration 8–2

BIG SPRINGS PUBLIC LIBRARY
Endowment Principal Fund
Balance Sheet, June 30, 19x6

Assets		*Fund Balance*	
Cash	$ 4,275	Fund Balance	$130,780
Investments	104,005		
Land	2,500		
Building	20,000		
Total Assets	$130,780	Total Fund Balance	$130,780

Related statements for the Endowment Revenues Fund are shown as Illustrations 8–5, 8–6, and 8–7. Note that these statements follow the format for interim statements of revenue funds illustrated in Chapter 3.

Illustration 8–3

BIG SPRINGS PUBLIC LIBRARY
Endowment Principal Fund
Analysis of Changes in Fund Balance
October 1, 19x5–June 30, 19x6

Balance, October 1, received from executor		$135,300
Add: Gain on sale of investments		270
Total to account for		$135,570
Less: Loss on sale of investments	$ 375	
Taxes accrued before October 1, 19x5	200	
Renovation, references, and equipment	4,215	4,790
Balance, June 30, 19x6		$130,780

Illustration 8–4

BIG SPRINGS PUBLIC LIBRARY
Endowment Principal Fund
Statement of Cash Receipts and Disbursements
October 1, 19x5–June 30, 19x6

Balance, October 1, 19x5		None
Cash Receipts:		
Sales of investments		$18,345
Cash Disbursements:		
Purchase of investments	$9,655	
Renovation, references, and equipment	4,215	
Property taxes accrued before October 1, 19x5	200	
Total Cash Disbursements		14,070
Balance, June 30, 19x6		$ 4,275

Illustration 8–5

BIG SPRINGS PUBLIC LIBRARY
Endowment Revenues Fund
Balance Sheet, June 30, 19x6

Assets and Resources			
Cash			$ 510
Estimated revenues		$5,200	
Less: Revenues		3,200	2,000
Total Assets and Resources			$2,510
Liabilities, Appropriations, Reserves, and Fund Balance			
Accrued liabilities			$ 90
Appropriations		$5,300	
Less: Encumbrances	$ 70		
Expenditures	2,980	3,050	2,250
Reserve for encumbrances			70
Fund balance			100
Total Liabilities, Appropriations, Reserves, and Fund Balance			$2,510

Illustration 8–6

BIG SPRINGS PUBLIC LIBRARY
Endowment Revenues Fund
Analysis of Changes in Fund Balance
January 1–June 30, 19x6

Balance, January 1, 19x6	None
Additions:	
Estimated revenues	$5,200
Gift for purchase of books	200
Total Available	$5,400
Less: Appropriations	5,300
Balance, June 30, 19x6	$ 100

Illustration 8–7

BIG SPRINGS PUBLIC LIBRARY
Endowment Revenues Fund
Statement of Cash Receipts and Disbursements
January 1–June 30, 19x6

Balance, January 1, 19x6		None
Cash receipts:		
Interest and dividends	$3,180	
Fines	20	
Gift for purchase of books	200	$3,400
Cash disbursements:		
Salaries	$1,500	
Purchase of books	900	
Magazine subscriptions	230	
Supplies and miscellaneous	260	2,890
Balance, June 30, 19x6		$ 510

ACCOUNTING FOR PUBLIC EMPLOYEE RETIREMENT FUNDS

Billions of dollars are invested in retirement funds—New York State alone has almost $8 billion of investment assets in its retirement funds. Although many municipal employees are covered by Federal social security acts and by state-administered retirement funds, a number of municipalities operate retirement funds. These funds differ from the trust funds discussed above in that both the principal and income are expendable under conditions set forth in the enabling legislation. An increasing number of retirement funds are operated on an actuarial basis. Actuarial computations of contributions depend upon assumptions as to policies regarding retirement ages and benefits payable; as to salary levels; mortality experience; and investment experience. All those factors change over time; therefore, whether the contributions to the fund are made by use of an actuarially determined schedule or whether the municipality's share of contributions depends on legislative appropriations determined by political expediency, it is evident that a principal function of a retirement trust fund information system is to match the assets and resources of the fund with the liabilities and reserves of the fund. The liabilities and reserves include the prospective demands for benefits based on current actuarial determinations. Under those conditions the Fund Balance will disclose whether accumulated contributions, earnings, and receivables of the fund are adequate to meet the expected demands on the fund or whether there is an actuarial deficiency which will require increased future contributions. In the latter case the deficiencies may be reflected in an account named Actuarial Deficiency; this account is offset by a debit balance in Fund Balance.

Budgetary Accounts. Retirement funds may be administered as a separate unit with an independent operating budget, or they may be administered by employees of a General Fund department, such as the Finance Department. In the latter event administrative costs of the retirement fund are borne by the General Fund and need not be recorded in the Retirement Fund. If a Retirement Fund has its own administrative budget, it should record the budget in its accounts in the same manner as is recommended for a revenue fund. Present recommendations of authoritative organizations do not require retirement funds to record budgetary entries for actuarially required additions and earnings, although such a practice would be consistent with the recommendation for term bond debt service funds discussed in Chapter 7.

Subsidiary Ledgers. A retirement fund may receive contributions from employees covered by the retirement plan, as well as from the governmental unit(s) whose employees are covered, or only from the employing unit. The first kind of plan is known as *contributory*, the second as *noncontributory*. A contributory plan must keep records for each active employee to show the employee's name, birth date, sex, social security number, the date he entered employment covered by the retirement plan, optional benefits he elected, beneficiaries' names and relationships, contributions for each pay period, earnings on accumulated contributions, and whatever other data is required by the retirement plan. A noncontributory plan must keep the same information (except, obviously, for employee contributions). Either kind of plan may provide that former employees who terminated employment before becoming eligible for retirement have vested rights and benefits or that they may receive credit for prior service if they reenter employment; records must therefore be kept for former employees as well as for active employees. Records must also be kept for each employee, or beneficiary, who is receiving benefits, showing the amount of the benefit, reason for entitlement, payment options, payment dates, and other information required under the plan or that experience indicates may be needed. Retirement funds, whether contributory or noncontributory, must also keep records of contributions required from each employing unit whose employees participate in the plan, and of contributions actually received from each employing unit. In addition to subsidiary ledgers for employee data and employer data, subsidiary ledgers must be kept for all data necessary for the management and control of retirement fund investments.

Reserves. Six accounts recommended for use by public employee retirement funds differ in nature and use from accounts previously described in this text. The accounts and their descriptions are:[6]

> Reserve for Employees' Contributions. A reserve in a Trust Fund for a public employee retirement system which represents the amount of accumulated contributions made by employee members plus interest earnings credited in accordance with applicable legal provisions.
>
> Reserve for Employer Contributions. A reserve in a Trust Fund for a public employee retirement system which represents the amount of accumulated contributions paid by the governmental unit as employer plus interest earnings credited in accordance with applicable legal provisions.
>
> Actuarial Deficiency in Reserve for Employer Contributions. A reserve in a Trust Fund for a public employee retirement system which represents the amount of the actuarial deficiency in contributions made by a governmental unit as employer.
>
> Reserve for Membership Annuities. A reserve in a Trust Fund for a public employee retirement system which represents the amount set aside for payment of annuities to retired members. In a joint contributory system, this reserve is established at the time of employee retirement by transfers from accumulations in the Reserve for Employees' Contributions and Reserve for Employer Contributions accounts.
>
> Reserve for Variations in Actuarial Assumptions. An unallocated reserve in a Trust Fund for a public employee retirement system which reflects adjustments to reserves for retirement benefits in force resulting from variations in mortality, turnover, and interest experience.
>
> Reserve for Undistributed Interest Earnings. An unallocated reserve in a Trust Fund for a public employee retirement system which represents interest earnings of the system that have not been distributed to other reserves such as the Reserve for Employees' Contributions and the Reserve for Employer Contributions.

An actuarial deficiency may exist in reserves other than the Reserve for Employer Contributions: if so, appropriately named deficiency accounts should be added to, or substituted for, those described above. An Actuarial Deficiency in Reserve for Employer Contributions may exist because all employees active at the time the retirement system was created were given credit toward retirement benefits for their years of service before the plan was created. In this very common situation few employers found it possible to contribute sufficient assets to the retirement system to fund the prior service liability fully at the time

[6] *Governmental Accounting, Auditing, and Financial Reporting,* pp. 186–87.

the system was created. It is common for employers to amortize the unfunded portion of prior service liabilities by contributions over a period of years. Actuarial deficiencies in employers' contributions for current service should not occur, but do arise because of diversion of governmental resources to more immediate needs.

Illustrative Case—Public Employees Retirement Fund

Accounting and reporting for a small municipal retirement fund is illustrated by the hypothetical Town of Lyle Employees' Retirement Fund. The fund is administered by general fund employees; the retirement fund does not bear any administrative expense. Employee and employer contributions to the fund are based on actuarial computations and are changed infrequently to give effect to recommendations of actuaries who examine the fund periodically. The balance sheet of the Town of Lyle Employees' Retirement Fund as of December 31, 19x5, is shown below:

Illustration 8–8

TOWN OF LYLE
Employees' Retirement Fund
Balance Sheet
December 31, 19x5

Assets		
Cash		$ 18,360
Due from general fund		8,744
Interest receivable on investments		40,256
Investments at par	$3,100,000	
Add: Unamortized premium	3,922	3,103,922
Total Assets		$3,171,282
Liabilities, Reserves, and Fund Balance		
Annuities payable		$ 12,000
Reserves for:		
Employees' contributions		1,154,694
Employers' contributions		971,828
Actuarial deficiency in employer contributions		292,120
Membership annuities		1,020,000
Variation in actuarial assumptions		10,200
Undistributed interest earnings		2,560
Fund balance		(292,120)
Total Liabilities, Reserves, and Fund Balance		$3,171,282

Employees' contributions are collected through payroll withholding by the employer, the General Fund. The General Fund sends copies of the payrolls to the Employees' Retirement Fund as notice of employees' contributions. The employer contributions are computed as a predetermined percentage of the payrolls. Assuming that some time elapses between the date of computation and the date the General Fund remits the contributions to the Employees' Retirement Fund, and that amounts are as shown in the entry, the receivable should be recorded by the latter:

		Debit	Credit
1.	Due from General Fund	481,824	
	Contributions—Employees		237,045
	Contributions—Employer		244,779

The General Fund remits the employee contributions it has withheld and its employer contributions in accord with an agreed-upon schedule. If the total remitted in the period is $480,360, the collection of the receivable is recorded as shown in the following entry.

		Debit	Credit
2.	Cash	480,360	
	Due from General Fund		480,360

It is important that the retirement fund cash balances be held to the minimum amount needed for immediate needs, so that the remainder of cash can be invested to increase fund earnings. Assume that $340,000 cash is invested in high-quality bonds with long maturities. Face value of the bonds is $330,000; premium is $6,000, and accrued interest purchased is $4,000.

		Debit	Credit
3.	Investments	330,000	
	Unamortized Premiums on Investments	6,000	
	Accrued Interest on Investments Purchased	4,000	
	Cash		340,000

When employees retire, the portion of the contributions reserve accounts representing the expected benefits to be paid them is transferred to Reserve for Membership Annuities. The amounts shown below are assumed to apply to employees of the Town of Lyle retiring during 19x6.

		Debit	Credit
4.	Reserve for Employees' Contributions	21,279	
	Reserve for Employer Contributions	21,279	
	Reserve for Membership Annuities		42,558

When employees resign, or die before retiring, their contributions and earnings on the contributions are ordinarily returned to the employee (or his estate, if he is deceased). Since some time is required for processing the claims, the amount to be returned is ordinarily recorded as a liability; when the check is issued, the liability, of course, is liquidated. The following two examples illustrate the entries assumed to apply in this case. (If the plan requires additional benefits to be paid to beneficiaries of the deceased, Reserve for Employer Contributions must also be debited. It is assumed that the retirement plan of the Town of Lyle does not require this.)

5.	Reserve for Employees' Contributions	77,235	
	Due to Deceased Employees' Estates		16,485
	Due to Resigned Employees		60,750
6.	Due to Deceased Employees' Estates	16,485	
	Due to Resigned Employees	60,750	
	Cash		77,235

Amounts to be paid to annuitants are considered to be expenditures of Employees' Retirement Fund assets. Assuming that the amount of annuities for 19x6 is $63,000, the entry would be:

7.	Expenditures	63,000	
	Annuities Payable		63,000

The following entry would be made if annuity checks are written in the amount of $66,000 during 19x6.

8.	Annuities Payable	66,000	
	Cash		66,000

Assuming that during the year interest on investments is collected in the amount of $153,000, including interest receivable as of December 31, 19x5, and the interest on investments purchased during the year:

9.	Cash	153,000	
	Interest Receivable on Investments		40,256
	Accrued Interest on Investments Purchased		4,000
	Interest Earnings		108,744

Investments with a par value of $150,000 were purchased:

10.	Investments	150,000	
	Cash		150,000

Premiums on investments should be amortized in accord with generally accepted accounting principles. Methods of amortizing premiums are discussed in Appendix 3. Assuming that the amortization for 19x6 is computed as $496, the entry to record the amortization is:

11.	Interest Earnings	496	
	Unamortized Premiums on Investments		496

Interest earnings accrued at the end of 19x6 must be computed and recorded since the retirement fund is to be accounted for on the full accrual basis. Assuming the amount to be $68,800, the entry is:

12.	Interest Receivable on Investments	68,800	
	Interest Earnings		68,800

Contributions accounts are nominal accounts and should be closed to their related reserves:

13.	Contributions—Employees	237,045	
	Contributions—Employers	244,779	
	Reserve for Employees' Contributions		237,045
	Reserve for Employer Contributions		244,779

Expenditures, a nominal account, should be closed to Reserve for Membership Annuities:

		Dr.	Cr.
14.	Reserve for Membership Annuities	63,000	
	Expenditures		63,000

In accord with legal requirements $178,000 of interest earnings was distributed to Reserve for Employees' Contributions, Reserve for Employer Contributions, and Reserve for Membership Annuities, in the amounts of $79,000, $66,000, and $33,000 respectively.

		Dr.	Cr.
15.	Interest Earnings	178,000	
	Reserve for Employees' Contributions		79,000
	Reserve for Employer Contributions		66,000
	Reserve for Membership Annuities		33,000

The balance of Interest Earnings for the year is closed to Reserve for Undistributed Interest Earnings.

		Dr.	Cr.
16.	Reserve for Undistributed Interest Earnings	952	
	Interest Earnings		952

On the advice of the consulting actuary the Reserve for Variation in Actuarial Assumptions was adjusted to its present value at the end of 19x6.

		Dr.	Cr.
17.	Reserve for Membership Annuities	1,048	
	Reserve for Variation in Actuarial Assumptions		1,048

The actuarial deficiency in the fund at year end was determined to have been reduced by $34,750:

		Dr.	Cr.
18.	Actuarial Deficiency in Employer Contributions	34,750	
	Fund Balance		34,750

Retirement Fund Financial Statements. After giving effect to the entries for 19x6, the Town of Lyle's Employees' Retirement fund would have the balance sheet shown as Illustration 8–9.

An analysis of changes in reserves and Fund Balance is shown in Illustration 8–10.

In addition to the balance sheet and analysis of changes in reserves and fund balance, it is considered desirable for a retirement fund to present a statement of cash receipts and disbursements. Illustration 8–11 shows this statement for the illustrative case.

GENERAL REVENUE SHARING TRUST FUNDS

The State and Local Fiscal Assistance Act of 1972, the act providing for fiscal assistance by the Federal government to state and local governments under the general revenue sharing program, requires the establishment of a trust fund on the books of the Treasury of the United States

Illustration 8–9

TOWN OF LYLE
Employees' Retirement Fund
Balance Sheet
December 31, 19x6

Assets		
Cash		$ 18,485
Due from general fund		10,208
Interest receivable on investments		68,800
Investments, at par	3,580,000	
Add: Unamortized premiums on investments	9,426	3,589,426
Total Assets		$3,686,919
Liabilities, Reserves, and Fund Balance		
Annuities payable		$ 9,000
Reserves for:		
Employees' Contributions		1,372,225
Employer Contributions		1,261,328
Actuarial deficiency in employer contributions		257,370
Membership annuities		1,031,510
Variation in actuarial assumptions		11,248
Undistributed interest earnings		1,608
Fund Balance		(257,370)
Total Liabilities, Reserves, and Fund Balance		$3,686,919

"and a trust fund on the books of each unit of government receiving payments under the act." Federal trust funds are discussed in Chapter 16; the discussion in this section deals with the budgeting, accounting, and reporting requirements established for state and local governmental general revenue sharing trust funds.

Units of local government which receive payments under the Federal general revenue sharing program are required to "establish a trust fund and deposit all entitlement funds received and all interest earned thereon in the trust fund."[7] Each recipient government is required to "use, obligate, or appropriate" entitlement payments and interest thereon within 24 months from the date of each Treasury Department check, unless an extension of time is obtained from the Secretary of the Treasury. Trust fund revenues must be expended in accord with the "laws and procedures applicable to the expenditure of its own revenues."

The appropriation budgeting procedures described in Chapter 2, and the appropriation accounting procedures described in Chapters 3, 4, and 5 are illustrative of procedures applicable to general revenue sharing trust funds. The purposes for which expenditures may be made are re-

[7] Quotations in this section are taken from Public Law 92–512, the State and Local Fiscal Assistance Act of 1972, and from regulations issued by the Secretary of the Treasury under authority of the Act.

Illustration 8–10

TOWN OF LYLE
Employees' Retirement Fund
Analysis of Changes in Reserves and Fund Balance
For the Year Ending December 31, 19x6

	Reserves For						
	Employees' Contributions	*Employer Contributions*	*Actuarial Deficiency*	*Membership Annuities*	*Variation in Actuarial Assumptions*	*Undistributed Interest Earnings*	*Fund Balance*
Balance, January 1, 19x6	$1,154,694	$ 971,828	$292,120	$1,020,000	$10,200	$2,560	$(292,120)
Add:							
Employees' contributions	237,045						
Employer contributions		244,779					
Interest earnings	79,000	66,000		33,000		(952)	
Total Balance and Additions	$1,470,739	$1,282,607	$292,120	$1,053,000	$10,200	$1,608	$(292,120)
Transfers:							
Annuities awarded	(21,279)	(21,279)		42,558			
Actuarial adjustments							
Current annuities				(1,048)	1,048		
Future annuities			(34,750)				34,750
Balances after Transfers	$1,449,460	$1,261,328	$257,370	$1,094,510	$11,248	$1,608	$(257,370)
Deductions:							
Expenditures: Annuities				63,000			
Refunds: Deaths	16,485						
Refunds: Resignations	60,750						
Balances, December 31, 19x6	$1,372,225	$1,261,328	$257,370	$1,031,510	$11,248	$1,608	$(257,370)

Illustration 8–11

TOWN OF LYLE
Employees' Retirement Fund
Statement of Cash Receipts and Disbursements
For the Year Ended December 31, 19x6

Cash balance, January 1, 19x6		$ 18,360
Receipts:		
Employees' contributions	$237,045	
Employer contributions	243,315	
Interest	153,000	
Total Receipts		633,360
Total cash available		$651,720
Disbursements:		
Investments purchased at par	$480,000	
Premiums on investments purchased	6,000	
Accrued interest on investments purchased	4,000	
Refunds–resignations	60,750	
Refunds–deaths	16,485	
Annuity payments	66,000	
Total Disbursements		633,235
Cash Balance, December 31, 19x6		$ 18,485

stricted to "priority expenditures," which are defined as: (1) "ordinary and necessary maintenance and operating expenses" for public safety, environmental protection, public transportation, health, recreation, libraries, social services for the poor or aged, and financial administration; and (2) "ordinary and necessary capital expenditures authorized by law." No state government or unit of local government may use, directly or indirectly, any part of the general revenue sharing funds as a contribution for the purpose of obtaining Federal funds under any Federal law which requires the State or local government to make a contribution in order to receive Federal funds. In addition to adhering to state laws relating to publication of and hearings on appropriation budgets, each governmental unit expecting to receive funds under the State and Local Fiscal Assistance Act must file a "report of planned use" with the Secretary of the Treasury not less than 30 days in advance of each entitlement period. These reports must specify the amounts and purposes for which expected amounts will be spent, obligated, or encumbered. The Act requires that the "report of planned use" be published in a newspaper of general circulation within the geographic area of the government submitting the report. Illustration 8–12 shows a published report.

After the close of each entitlement period, each governmental unit must file a "report of actual use" with the Secretary of the Treasury. As Illustration 8–13 shows, Actual Use reports are similar to Planned Use reports, but also include a Trust Fund Report which informs the Treasury of interest earnings, expenditures, and the balance on hand.

Illustration 8–12
Report of Planned Use of Revenue Sharing Allocation

OMB FORM 48-R0503 12-31-74

THIS REPORT TO BE RETURNED TO

DEPARTMENT OF THE TREASURY
OFFICE OF REVENUE SHARING
1900 PENNSYLVANIA AVE. N.W.
WASHINGTON, D.C. 20226

THE GOVERNMENT OF

MONROE COUNTY PLANS TO USE ITS REVENUE SHARING ALLOCATION FOR THE ENTITLEMENT PERIOD JULY 1, 1973 THRU JUN 30, 1974, IN THE FOLLOWING MANNER BASED UPON AN ESTIMATED TOTAL OF $465,879

ACCOUNT NO.

15 1 053 053
MONROE COUNTY
COUNTY AUDITOR
BLOOMINGTON INDIANA 47403

(K) [x] EXECUTIVE PROPOSAL. Check this block if this plan is based on an executive proposal

(L) DEBT How will the availability of revenue sharing funds affect the borrowing requirements of your jurisdiction?

- [ ] AVOID DEBT INCREASE
- [x] NO EFFECT
- [ ] LESSEN DEBT INCREASE
- [ ] TOO SOON TO PREDICT EFFECT

(M) TAXES In which of the following manners is it expected that the availability of Revenue Sharing Funds will affect the tax levels of your jurisdiction? Check as many as apply.

- [ ] WILL ENABLE REDUCING RATE OF A MAJOR TAX.
- [ ] WILL REDUCE AMOUNT OF RATE INCREASE OF A MAJOR TAX.
- [x] WILL PREVENT INCREASE IN RATE OF A MAJOR TAX
- [x] NO EFFECT ON TAX LEVELS
- [ ] WILL PREVENT ENACTING A NEW MAJOR TAX
- [ ] TOO SOON TO PREDICT EFFECT

OPERATING/MAINTENANCE EXPENDITURES

PRIORITY EXPENDITURE CATEGORIES (A)	PLANNED EXPENDITURES (B)	PERCENT PLANNED FOR MAINTENANCE OF EXISTING SERVICES (C)	PERCENT PLANNED FOR NEW OR EXPANDED SERVICES (D)
1 PUBLIC SAFETY	$	%	%
2 ENVIRONMENTAL PROTECTION	$ 50,000	100 %	%
3 PUBLIC TRANSPORTATION	$ 254,879	100 %	%
4 HEALTH	$ 46,000	100 %	%
5 RECREATION	$	%	%
6 LIBRARIES	$	%	%
7 SOCIAL SERVICES FOR AGED & POOR	$	%	%
8 FINANCIAL ADMINISTRATION	$	%	%
9 TOTAL PLANNED OPERATING/MAINTENANCE EXPENDITURES	$ 350,879		

CAPITAL EXPENDITURES

PURPOSE (E)	PLANNED EXPENDITURES (F)	PERCENT PLANNED FOR: EQUIPMENT (G)	CONSTRUCTION (H)	LAND ACQUISITION (I)	DEBT RETIREMENT (J)
10 MULTI-PURPOSE AND GENERAL GOVT.	$ 15,000	100%	%	%	%
11 EDUCATION	$	%	%	%	%
12 HEALTH	$	%	%	%	%
13 TRANSPORTATION	$ 42,000	100%	%	%	%
14. SOCIAL DEVELOPMENT	$	%	%	%	%
15 HOUSING & COMMUNITY DEVELOPMENT	$	%	%	%	%
16 ECONOMIC DEVELOPMENT	$	%	%	%	%
17 ENVIRONMENTAL CONSERVATION	$	%	%	%	%
18 PUBLIC SAFETY	$ 18,000	100%	%	%	%
19 RECREATION + CULTURE	$ 20,000	50%	50 %	%	%
20 OTHER (Specify) County & Regional Planning & Zoning	20,000	%	100 %	%	%
21 OTHER (Specify)	$	%	%	%	%
22 OTHER (Specify)	$	%	%	%	%
23 TOTAL PLANNED CAPITAL EXPENDITURES	$ 115,000				

(N) ASSURANCES (Refer to Instruction G)

The news media have been advised that a complete copy of this report has been published in a local newspaper of general circulation. I have records documenting the contents of this report and they are open for public and news media scrutiny.

I assure the Secretary of the Treasury that the statutory provisions listed in Part G of the Instructions accompanying this report will be complied with by this recipient government with respect to the entitlement funds reported hereon.

William K. Hanna 9/19/73
SIGNATURE OF CHIEF EXECUTIVE OFFICER — DATE

Daily Herald Telephone
NAME OF NEWSPAPER

William K. Hanna - President County Commissioners
NAME & TITLE — PLEASE PRINT

9/19/73
DATE PUBLISHED

ORS FORM NO. 3229 JULY 1973

RETURN THIS REPORT TO DEPT. OF TREASURY

THIS REPORT TO BE RETURNED TO THE DEPT. OF THE TREASURY

Source: The Department of the Treasury. This form is being revised for 1974.

Illustration 8–13
Report of Actual Use of Revenue Sharing Payment

ORS FORM 3237
JULY 1973

THIS REPORT TO BE RETURNED TO

DEPARTMENT OF THE TREASURY
OFFICE OF REVENUE SHARING
1900 PENNSYLVANIA AVE. N.W.
WASHINGTON, D.C. 20226

THE GOVERNMENT OF

MONROE COUNTY

HAS USED ITS REVENUE SHARING PAYMENT FOR THE PERIOD BEGINNING

JAN 1, 1972 ENDING JUN 30, 1973

IN THE FOLLOWING MANNER BASED UPON A

TOTAL PAYMENT OF $403,408

ACCOUNT NO.
15 1 053 053

MONROE COUNTY
COUNTY AUDITOR
BLOOMINGTON INDIANA 47403

(L) DEBT How has the availability of revenue sharing funds affected the borrowing requirements of your jurisdiction?

- [ ] AVOIDED DEBT INCREASE
- [x] NO EFFECT
- [ ] LESSENED DEBT INCREASE
- [ ] TOO SOON TO PREDICT EFFECT

(M) TAXES In which of the following manners did the availability of Revenue Sharing Funds affect the tax levels of your jurisdiction? Check as many as apply.

- [ ] ENABLED REDUCING THE RATE OF A MAJOR TAX.
- [ ] REDUCED AMOUNT OF RATE INCREASE OF A MAJOR TAX.
- [x] PREVENTED INCREASE IN RATE OF A MAJOR TAX
- [x] NO EFFECT ON TAX LEVELS
- [ ] PREVENTED ENACTING A NEW MAJOR TAX
- [ ] TOO SOON TO PREDICT EFFECT

RETURN THIS REPORT TO DEPT. OF TREASURY

OPERATING/MAINTENANCE EXPENDITURES

PRIORITY EXPENDITURE CATEGORIES (A)	ACTUAL EXPENDITURES (B)	PERCENT USED FOR MAINTENANCE OF EXISTING SERVICES (C)	PERCENT USED FOR NEW OR EXPANDED SERVICES (D)
1 PUBLIC SAFETY	$	%	%
2 ENVIRONMENTAL PROTECTION	$ 47,000.00	%	100 %
3 PUBLIC TRANSPORTATION	$ 253,900.00	96 %	4 %
4 HEALTH	$	%	%
5 RECREATION	$	%	%
6 LIBRARIES	$	%	%
7 SOCIAL SERVICES FOR AGED & POOR	$	%	%
8 FINANCIAL ADMINISTRATION	$ 44.93	%	100 %
9 TOTAL ACTUAL OPERATING/MAINTENANCE EXPENDITURES	$ 300,944.93		

CAPITAL EXPENDITURES

PURPOSE (E)	ACTUAL EXPENDITURES (F)	PERCENT USED FOR: EQUIPMENT (G)	CONSTRUCTION (H)	LAND ACQUISITION (I)	DEBT RETIREMENT (J)
10 MULTI-PURPOSE AND GENERAL GOVT.	$	%	%	%	%
11 EDUCATION	$	%	%	%	%
12 HEALTH	$	%	%	%	%
13 TRANSPORTATION	$ 101,100.00	100 %	%	%	%
14 SOCIAL DEVELOPMENT	$	%	%	%	%
15 HOUSING & COMMUNITY DEVELOPMENT	$	%	%	%	%
16 ECONOMIC DEVELOPMENT	$	%	%	%	%
17 ENVIRONMENTAL CONSERVATION	$	%	%	%	%
18 PUBLIC SAFETY	$	%	%	%	%
19 RECREATION CULTURE	$	%	%	%	%
20 OTHER (Specify)	$	%	%	%	%
21 OTHER (Specify)	$	%	%	%	%
22 OTHER (Specify)	$	%	%	%	%
23 TOTAL ACTUAL CAPITAL EXPENDITURES	$ 101,100.00				

(N) CERTIFICATION (Please Read Instruction 'F').

The news media have been advised that a complete copy of this report has been published in a local newspaper of general circulation. I have records documenting the contents of this report and they are open for public and news media scrutiny.

Additionally, I certify that I am the chief executive officer and, with respect to the entitlement funds reported hereon, I **certify** that they have not been used in violation of either the priority expenditure requirement (Section 103) or the matching funds prohibition (Section 104) of the Act.

(O) TRUST FUND REPORT

Revenue Sharing Funds Received Thru June 30, 1973	$ 403,408.00
Interest Earned	$ 5,484.00
Total Funds Available	$ 408,892.00
Amount Expended	$ 402,044.93
Balance	$ 6,847.07

William K. Hanna
SIGNATURE OF CHIEF EXECUTIVE OFFICER

William K. Hanna, President, Monroe County Board of Commissioners
NAME & TITLE - PLEASE PRINT

Daily Herald Telephone Courier Tribune
NAME OF NEWSPAPER

August 24, 1973
DATE PUBLISHED

OMB FORM 48-R0506

THIS REPORT TO BE RETURNED TO THE DEPT. OF THE TREASURY

Source: The Department of the Treasury. This form is being revised for 1974.

Actual Use reports must also be published in a newspaper. At the same time these reports are published in one newspaper, notice of publication must be given to all other news media in the area, and copies of the reports given to all news media on request. Detailed data supporting Planned Use and Actual Use reports must be made available for public inspection by each governmental unit. General revenue sharing trust fund reports and records are to be audited as required by the Secretary of the Treasury. Audits of these trust funds may be conducted by the same governmental auditors, or independent public accountants, who regularly audit the receiving units' other funds. Audits must be made in accord with *Standards for the Audit of Governmental Organizations, Programs, Activities and Functions* issued by the Comptroller General of the United States.

It should be stressed that reports required under the State and Local Fiscal Assistance Act of 1972 are to be related to *entitlement periods* specified in the Act. The first three periods specified are six-month periods: January 1–June 30, 1972; July 1, 1972–December 31, 1972; January 1–June 30, 1973.[8] The next three periods specified are one-year periods, coinciding with Federal fiscal years: July 1, 1973–June 30, 1974; July 1, 1974–June 30, 1975; and July 1, 1975–June 30, 1976. The Act, as passed in 1972, established the general revenue sharing program for five calendar years; therefore the final entitlement period specified in the 1972 Act is a six-month period: July 1–December 31, 1976. Under the law each State or local government has 24 months from the date of each entitlement check to "use, obligate, or appropriate" it, unless an extension of time is obtained from the Secretary of the Treasury. (*Obligate* is a Federal term equivalent to the term *encumber* used by State and local governmental units.) Thus a State or local governmental unit could take more than two years to appropriate the funds for any entitlement period, then appropriate it for a construction project which would take several years to complete. Throughout the entitlement period itself, the length of time after the end of the entitlement period until appropriation, and the length of time after appropriation until disbursement of all the money received for that entitlement period from the U.S. Treasury and all the interest thereon, it would be necessary to maintain the accounting identity of the entitlement period. There are several ways in which this may be accomplished: a separate General Revenue Sharing Trust Fund may be used for each entitlement period, or a single General Revenue Sharing Trust Fund may be used with separately designated budgetary and

[8] The first period had expired before the act became law; checks for the first period were not issued until the second period had almost expired. Regulations under the act became effective halfway through the third period. Therefore, reporting requirements for the first three periods differed from those for succeeding periods.

nominal accounts and separately designated Fund Balance Accounts kept for each entitlement period. Budgetary and nominal accounts of a General Revenue Sharing Trust Fund present, therefore, an accounting problem similar to those of capital projects funds discussed in Chapter 6: they relate to periods which may not coincide with the fiscal year of the municipality. Accordingly, if they are closed at the end of the municipal fiscal year in order to facilitate preparation of the municipal annual report, it is desirable to reverse the closing entries for the revenue sharing budgetary and nominal accounts at the beginning of the following fiscal year in order to facilitate preparation of legally required reports for the funds of each entitlement period.

Illustrative Case—General Revenue Sharing Trust Fund

As an illustration of budgeting, accounting, and reporting appropriate for use by a General Revenue Sharing Trust Fund of a municipality, assume that the Town of Alva receives word from the United States Department of the Treasury that for the entitlement period July 1, 19x5–June 30, 19x6 it will receive a check in the amount of $500,000. Accordingly, the town prepares a revenue budget in the amount of the entitlement check, plus expected interest earnings in the amount of $10,000. The appropriation budget, adopted in accord with applicable state laws, authorized "priority expenditures" for the following: Transfers to the General Fund in the amount of $280,000 for the purchase of "ordinary and necessary" capital equipment for the Police Department ($60,000), Fire Department ($120,000), and Street Department ($100,000); transfers to General Fund in the amount of $180,000 for "ordinary and necessary" maintenance and operating expenses for the Health Department ($70,000), Recreation Department ($60,000), and Welfare Department ($50,000); and transfers to the Sewer Utility Fund in the amount of $50,000 for the purchase of a sewer cleaning machine. The general journal entry to record the budget for the entitlement period would be:

		Debit	Credit
1.	Estimated Revenues	510,000	
	Appropriations		510,000

Subsidiary ledgers to record the detail of actual and estimated revenues and the detail of appropriations, expenditures, and encumbrances (if any) should be kept as described in Chapters 4 and 5. Assuming that the entire entitlement for the period will be received in one check early in the period, it is not necessary to record a receivable from the U.S. Treasury. Receipt of the check is recorded as follows:

		Debit	Credit
2.	Cash	500,000	
	Revenues		500,000

Expenditure of the appropriations should be recorded on the accrual basis. Thus, if the amounts appropriated are recorded as liabilities, the entry is:

3.	Expenditures	510,000	
	Due to General Fund		460,000
	Due to Sewer Utility Fund		50,000

Cash in the amount appropriated by the General Revenue Sharing Trust Fund for General Fund maintenance and operating expenses is transferred to the General Fund:

4.	Due to General Fund	180,000	
	Cash		180,000

Cash appropriated for capital expenditures of the General Fund and the Sewer Utility Fund will not need to be transferred until equipment has been received and payment approved. In order to earn interest, the temporarily surplus cash is invested:

5.	Investments	320,000	
	Cash		320,000

Assuming interest is received in cash in the amount of $3,600 during the July 1, 19x5–December 31, 19x5, period, and interest accrued as of December 31, 19x5, amounts to $900 additional, the following entry summarizes these events:

6.	Cash	3,600	
	Interest Receivable on Investments	900	
	Revenues		4,500

If the fiscal year of the Town of Alva ends on December 31, 19x5, the budgetary and nominal accounts of the General Revenue Sharing Trust Fund may be closed to facilitate preparation of statements for inclusion in the town's annual report, although the entitlement period will not end until June 30, 19x6. A closing entry as of December 31, 19x5 would be:

7.	Appropriations	510,000	
	Revenues	504,500	
	Fund Balance	5,500	
	Estimated Revenues		510,000
	Expenditures		510,000

Illustration 8–14 shows the balance sheet prepared as of December 31, 19x5, for the General Revenue Sharing Trust Fund for the entitlement period July 1, 19x5–June 30, 19x6. If balances exist in any Revenue Sharing Trust Fund for a previous entitlement period, balance sheets for such funds should also be shown in the Town of Alva's report for 19x5.

The deficit in Fund Balance shown in Illustration 8–14 results from the fact that the total appropriations were regarded as expended and recorded as liabilities to other funds at the outset of the period, and

Illustration 8–14

TOWN OF ALVA
General Revenue Sharing Trust Fund
For the Entitlement Period July 1, 19x5–June 30, 19x6
Balance Sheet as of December 31, 19x5

Assets		*Liabilities and Fund Balance*	
Cash	$ 3,600	Due to general fund	$280,000
Interest receivable on investments	900	Due to sewer utility fund	50,000
Investments	320,000	Fund balance (deficit)	(5,500)
Total Assets	$324,500	Total Liabilities and Fund Balance	$324,500

from the fact that revenue from interest earnings was budgeted for the entire 12-month period but the balance sheet is prepared as of a date when investments have been earning interest for somewhat less than six months. Accordingly, it is informative to prepare a Statement of Actual and Estimated Revenues and Expenditures (Illustration 8–15) and a Statement of Cash Receipts and Disbursements (Illustration 8–16) to accompany each General Revenue Sharing Trust Fund balance sheet.

Since the fund was closed halfway through the entitlement period to enable preparation of statements for inclusion in the municipal report for the calendar year, but legally required reports must be prepared for the entitlement period, it is desirable to reverse the closing entry

Illustration 8–15

TOWN OF ALVA
General Revenue Sharing Trust Fund
For the Entitlement Period July 1, 19x5–June 30, 19x6
Statement of Actual and Estimated Revenues and Expenditures
For the Six Months Ending December 31, 19x5

	Estimated	*Actual*	*Actual Over (Under) Estimated*
Revenues:			
Transfers from U.S. Treasury	$500,000	$500,000	–
Interest on investments	10,000	4,500	($5,500)
Total Revenues	$510,000	$504,500	($5,500)
Priority expenditures:			
Maintenance and operating expenses	$180,000	$180,000	–
Health	70,000	70,000	–
Recreation	60,000	60,000	–
Social services for poor and aged	50,000	50,000	–
Capital expenditures:	$330,000	$330,000	–
Public safety (Police and Fire depts.)	180,000	180,000	–
Public transportation (Street dept.)	100,000	100,000	–
Environmental protection (Sewer Utility)	50,000	50,000	–
Total Priority Expenditures	$510,000	$510,000	–
Fund Balance (Deficit)	$ none	($ 5,500)	($5,500)

Illustration 8–16

TOWN OF ALVA
General Revenue Sharing Trust Fund
For the Entitlement Period July 1, 19x5–June 30, 19x6
Statement of Cash Receipts and Disbursements
For the Six Months Ended December 31, 19x5

Cash balance, July 1, 19x5		$ none
Receipts:		
From U.S. Treasury	$500,000	
Interest	3,600	
Total Receipts		$503,600
Disbursements:		
Transfers to general fund	$180,000	
Purchase of temporary investments	320,000	
Total Disbursements		500,000
Cash Balance, December 31, 19x5		$ 3,600

shown as no. 7 and reestablish the budgetary and nominal accounts. Entry 8 accomplishes this.

8. Estimated Revenues	510,000	
Expenditures	510,000	
Appropriations		510,000
Revenues		504,500
Fund Balance		5,500

If during the last six months of the entitlement period it was necessary to sell the investments to obtain cash to transfer to the General Fund and the Sewer Utility Fund, the following entry would be made, assuming that the investments were sold at par and that $6,400 was received for interest earned to date of sale:

9. Cash	326,400	
Investments		320,000
Interest Receivable on Investments		900
Revenues		5,500

When transfers authorized by the appropriations budget are made, they may be recorded as:

10. Due to General Fund	280,000	
Due to Sewer Utility Fund	50,000	
Cash		330,000

At the end of the entitlement period the following entry may be made to close budgetary and nominal accounts:

11. Appropriations	510,000	
Revenues	510,000	
Estimated Revenues		510,000
Expenditures		510,000

At this point the assets and liability accounts are in balance because exactly as much interest was collected as was estimated. It is unnecessary, therefore to prepare a balance sheet at the end of the entitlement period. If more had been collected, a cash balance would remain in the fund; it would be offset by Fund Balance after entitlement period-end closing entries were made. The town would have to appropriate the balance for a "priority expenditure," and disburse the remaining cash to expend the appropriation and close the fund.

Illustration 8–17 shows the Statement of Actual and Estimated Revenues and Expenditures for the entire entitlement period. Because all revenues were received in cash by period end, and all expenditures disbursed by period end, a Statement of Cash Receipts and Disbursements need not be prepared.

Illustration 8–17

TOWN OF ALVA
General Revenue Sharing Trust Fund
Statement of Actual and Estimated Revenues and Expenditures
For the Entitlement Period July 1, 19x5–June 30, 19x6

	Estimated	*Actual*	*Actual Over (Under) Estimated*
Revenues:			
Transfers from U.S. Treasury	$500,000	$500,000	$ –
Interest on investments	10,000	10,000	–
Total Revenues	$510,000	$510,000	$ –
Priority Expenditures:			
Maintenance and operating expenses:	$180,000	$180,000	$ –
Health	70,000	70,000	–
Recreation	60,000	60,000	–
Social services for poor and aged	50,000	50,000	–
Capital expenditures:	$330,000	$330,000	–
Public safety (Police and Fire depts.)	180,000	180,000	–
Public transportation (Street dept.)	100,000	100,000	–
Environmental protection (Sewer Utility)	50,000	50,000	–
Total Priority Expenditures	$510,000	$510,000	$ –
Fund Balance, June 30, 19x6	$ none	$ none	$ –

SELECTED REFERENCES

American Institute of Certified Public Accountants. *Audits of State and Local Governmental Units*. New York, 1974.

Comptroller General of The United States. *Standards for Audit of Governmental Organizations, Programs, Activities & Functions*. Washington: United States General Accounting Office, 1972.

Municipal Finance Officers Association. *Accounting and Operating Handbook for Public Employee Retirement Systems*. Chicago: Municipal Finance Officers Association, 1966.

———. *Accounting For a Public Employee Retirement System, Special Bulletin 1972B.* Chicago, 1972.

NATIONAL COMMITTEE ON GOVERNMENTAL ACCOUNTING. *Governmental Accounting, Auditing, and Financial Reporting.* Chicago: Municipal Finance Officers Association, 1968.

UNITED STATES OF AMERICA. *Public Law 92-512, State and Local Fiscal Assistance Act of 1972.*

———. *Fiscal Assistance to State and Local Governments, Federal Register* vol. 38, no. 35, Part III, February 22, 1973.

QUESTIONS

8–1. What are the general distinctions between agency funds and trust funds?

8–2. Does the existence of an agency relationship always require the creation of an agency fund? Why or why not?

8–3. It is possible for a permanent agency fund to have, in a normal manner, no financial structure (no balance sheet) at the end of a fiscal period. How?

8–4. What are the most important factors which cause tax agency fund accounting to be complex?

8–5. What is meant by "nonexpendable cash" in trust fund accounting?

8–6. If the general rules of trust law assume cash basis accounting, why is accrual basis accounting recommended for trust funds by the National Committee on Governmental Accounting?

8–7. In accounting for a testamentary trust, there is a problem of separating the items that should be charged against principal from the items that should be charged against income. As to each of the following items, you are to state whether it should be charged against principal or against income, assuming that the most general rule of law is to be followed. Give any explanation you may consider necessary in connection with your answers.

a) Federal estate taxes paid.
b) Interest paid on mortgage on real estate.
c) Depreciation of real estate.
d) Legal fees for collection of rent.
e) Special assessment tax levied on real estate for street improvement.
f) Amortization of premium on bonds which had been purchased by the testator.
g) Loss on sale of trust investments.
h) Taxes on vacant city lots.

(AICPA)

8–8. What is the most important subsidiary record of a public employees' retirement fund? Why?

8–9. What is the meaning of the term "actuarial deficiency" in public employees retirement accounting? Why is an Actuarial Deficiency in Employer Contributions Account often found in retirement fund balance sheets? Does the presence of such an account indicate fund insolvency?

8–10. Would you expect to find budgetary accounts in a general revenue sharing trust fund ledger? Why or why not?

EXERCISES AND PROBLEMS

8–1. Utilizing the municipal annual report obtained for Exercise 1–1, follow the instructions below:

a) Are trust and agency funds combined in statements shown in the annual report, or are they shown separately? Are employees' and employer's FICA tax contributions, and contributions to other retirement funds, accounted for by the general fund, by an agency fund, by a retirement trust fund, or in some other manner (describe)?

Does the report state the basis of accounting used for trust and agency funds? Are all funds in this category accounted for on the same basis? If so, is the financial statement presentation consistent with the stated basis? If the basis is not stated, analyze the statements to determine which basis is used—full accrual, modified accrual, or cash basis. Is the basis used consistent with that recommended in the text? Are non-expendable assets and expendable assets accounted for in separate funds? If not, are Fund Balance accounts for each category kept separate?

b) Does the report contain a schedule or list of investments of trust funds? Are the investments identified as belonging to specific trust funds, or merely to "trust funds"? Does the report disclose gains or losses realized on sales of investments during the year? Does the report disclose net earnings on investments during the year?

If trust funds own depreciable assets, is depreciation taken? If so, is depreciation considered as a charge against principal or against income?

Are any trust funds operated as profit-seeking businesses? If so, does the annual report contain income statements for the businesses?

c) Are the municipal employees covered by a retirement fund operated by the municipality, the State, by the Federal Social Security Administration, or by two or more of these?

If the municipality operates one or more retirement funds, are the retirement fund financial statements accompanied by a separate audit report, or are they included in the auditors' opinion accompanying the other funds? Are the retirement fund statements accompanied by an actuary's report? If not, is reference made to the actuary's report in the balance sheet, in notes to the financial statements, or in the auditors' report? Does the retirement fund have an "actuarial deficiency," or an "unfunded prior service liability"? If so, is this condition explained in the notes accompanying the statement?

d) Are separate general revenue sharing trust fund statements shown for each entitlement period, if entitlement periods do not coincide exactly with the fiscal periods of the municipality? Do the statements properly disclose the amounts which have been expended and encumbered for each "priority expenditure"? Are the revenue sharing trust fund statements accompanied by an auditors' opinion, or a certificate of an elected official, attesting to fact that the governmental unit has used the revenue sharing funds only for priority expenditures?

8–2. The Town of Deerfield reports its tax rates in terms of cents, or dollars and cents, per $100 of taxable valuation. For the three years indicated, the town's composite rates were as shown below:

Fund or unit	*19x5*	*19x6*	*19x7*
Current fund	$ 3.12	$ 3.14	$ 3.20
Police and firemen's pension fund	.44	.39	.33
Deerfield school corporation	4.95	4.98	5.01
Jackson township	.13	.12	.14
Madison county	1.71	1.73	1.72
Composite rates	$10.35	$10.36	$10.40

Taxes on property within the town limits of Deerfield are collected by the town treasurer, who then distributes them to the participating funds and units. Collections during the second half of 19x7 totaled $6,246,250, which represented collections of the following levies in the following amounts:

From 19x5 levy	$ 50,250
From 19x6 levy	470,400
From 19x7 levy	5,725,600

The county tax of $1.72 per $100 of assessed valuation for 19x7 was constituted as follows:

General fund	$ .86
Debt service fund	.53
Public assistance fund	.21
Bridge repair fund	.12
Total	$1.72

Required:

a) How much of the town treasurer's collections during the second half of 19x7 should be remitted to the county? Show computations in good form.

b) How much of the county's share of collections on the 19x7 levy should be considered as revenue of the county general fund? Show computations in good form.

8–3. By the consent of, and in compliance with, orders of proper authorities, the County of Hardin assumed, as of January 1, 197D, the responsibility of collecting all property taxes levied within its boundaries. In order to reimburse the county for estimated administrative expenses of operating the tax agency fund, the agency fund is to deduct 1 percent from the collections for the town, the school district, and the townships. The total amount deducted is to be added to the collections for the county and remitted to the county general fund.

The following events occurred in 197D:

1. Current year tax levies to be collected by the agency fund were:

County general fund	$ 320,000
Town of Moorland	1,280,000
Hardin Co. Consolidated School District	1,920,000
Various townships	960,000

2. $2,688,000 current taxes were collected during the first half of 197D.
3. Liabilities to all the funds and units as the result of the first half-year collections were recorded. (A schedule of amounts collected for each participant, showing amounts withheld for the county general fund and net amounts due the participants, is recommended for determining amounts to be recorded for this transaction.)
4. All money in the agency fund was distributed.
5. $7,100 was charged back to the Town of Moorland because of errors in the computation of that unit's current taxes.

Required:

a) Make journal entries for the tax agency fund records for those of the foregoing transactions which affected that fund.

b) Make journal entries for the county general fund for such of the foregoing transactions as affected that fund, beginning with its tax levy entry, including provision for a 4 percent possible loss.

c) Make entries for the Town of Moorland general fund for which the town's property tax levy had been made. Begin with the levy entry, providing for a 4 percent loss.

8–4. In the City of Oxford there were four trust and agency funds: metropolitan school system employees' general retirement fund, city employees' retirement fund, employees' benefit plan fund, and payroll deductions fund. Below are several paragraphs of financial information as of June 30, 19x6, about the four funds.

1. Total general cash of the four funds aggregated $702,816, distributed: $103,590 to the school system retirement fund; $476,381 to city employees' retirement fund; $91,077 to the benefit plan fund; and the balance to the payroll deduction fund. In addition to general cash, the school system fund had $307 of petty cash.
2. Fund members and disability pensioners owed a total of $131,874, distributed: general city employees, $60,104; school system, $71,009; and the balance to the benefit plan. Only the school system carried an allowance for losses that amounted to $1,202.
3. For contributions and transfers to the benefit plan fund, various other city funds owed it $92,066.
4. Ownership of United States Treasury bonds by the funds totaled $30,374,000, distributed: $18,999,000 to the city employees' retire-

ment fund; $11,075,000 to the school system; and the balance to the benefit plan fund.

5. United States Treasury Notes having a current redemption value of $5,039,654, owned by the funds, were distributed: $3,001,218 to the city employees' fund; $1,992,003 to the school system; and the remainder to the benefit plan.
6. Two of the funds owned $14,661,000 par value of City of Oxford bonds. Of this, $11,044,000 belonged to city employees' fund, and the remainder to the school system.
7. The City of Oxford bonds had been acquired at a premium. At June 30, 19x6, the unamortized balance on the $14,661,000 par value totaled $399,874, of which $198,444 was applied to bonds held by the school system fund and the balance to city employees' retirement fund.
8. Accrued interest income at June 30, 19x6, consisted of $286 for the employees' benefit plan; $47,401 for the school system; and $164,713 for the city employees.
9. The school system retirement fund had prepaid insurance of $114, and office furniture and fixtures with an unamortized cost of $6,411, while the benefit plan fund had prepaid hospital and surgical benefit premiums of $16,409.
10. Accounts payable to members and beneficiaries totaled $53,418, owed as follows: $19,003 by the benefit plan; $30,001 by the school system; and the balance by the city employees' fund. Sundry accounts payable of $20,105 were owed by the benefit plan fund, and $193 by the school system fund.
11. The school system fund owed $16 to other funds and $901 to employees, while the payroll deduction fund owed $1,816 to other funds.

You are required to do the following things:

a) Prepare a trial balance for each of the funds at June 30, 19x6. The balance of each fund will have to be derived. If desired, these may be in combined columnar form.

b) Give the probable reason or reasons why the payroll deduction fund has so few accounts compared with the other three funds.

c) Give the probable reason or reasons why the four funds had such a small amount of liabilities except to members and beneficiaries.

d) What additional information would you need in order to prepare balance sheets for the retirement funds in the recommended form?

8–5. At X College a student organization agency fund is operated by the college administration to serve as the receiving and disbursing agent for various campus organizations. Money collected by the affected organizations is presented to a college administrative office for deposit, with credit to Fund Balance, a controlling account, and to the proper subsidiary ledger account. Expenditures made by the organizations are reported to the administrative office and disbursements are made on behalf of the reporting organization, whose ledger account is charged. Money not expected to be needed soon is transferred to the college investment pool. Income on investments is transferred to a general fund which pays operating expenses of the agency fund.

At June 30, 197E, the student organization agency fund had the following trial balance:

	Debit	*Credit*
Cash	$21,490.00	
Investments	27,692.04	
Vouchers payable.		$ 8,188.02
Fund balance		40,994.02
	$49,182.04	$49,182.04

During the next six months the following transactions occurred:

1. Purchases of investments were vouchered in the amount of $19,860, which included $310 accrued interest.
2. $92,675.30 was received from student organizations for deposit.
3. Uncollectible checks totaling $297 were charged back to various student organizations.
4. During the period, the college transferred to its general fund the amount of $15.20 held in the name of an organization which had been defunct for several years (not vouchered).
5. During the period, the college trustees decided to pool the investments of all institutional funds; those belonging to the student organization agency fund, including those reported in the first transaction, were transferred at book value to the pool (debit Investments—Pool).
6. Cash received as interest on investments during the period amounted to $790, which included the amount of interest which had been purchased. The actual income was credited to Due to General Fund. All other income collected during the period (on pooled investments) was collected by the college administration and retained to cover costs of administering the fund.
7. Bills and statements presented by student organizations for payment during the period totaled $89,404, which was vouchered and charged to their accounts.
8. Payment was stopped on $180 of old outstanding checks, while other old checks amounting to $250 for which the payees could not be located were voided, and the total of $430 was credited back to the respective student organizations.
9. Toward the end of the period it became necessary for the college administration to transfer $5,000 from the agency fund's share in pooled investments to its cash account.
10. One organization disbanded and its credit of $92.80 was refunded for distribution among its members. The transaction was vouchered.
11. $7,861.00 of vouchers payable remained unpaid at the end of the period and the amount owing to the general fund had not been settled.

You are required to do the following things:

a) Open T accounts for the student organization agency fund for June 30, 197E, journalize and post the above transactions, and take a trial balance for December 31, 197E. (Appendix 3 presents a brief discussion of accounting for pooled investments.)

b) State how the balance on deposit at a given time to the credit of a given student organization would be determined.

8–6. From the ledger accounts and transactions in Problem 8–5 you are required to prepare a statement of cash receipts and disbursements for the student organization agency fund for the six months ended December 31, 197E. In determining the amounts paid for various purposes by the payment of vouchers payable, it may be assumed that both the beginning and ending unpaid balances of vouchers payable were for expenses of student organizations. All debits and credits to Cash during the period, however made, are to be included as receipts or disbursements.

8–7. At December 31, 19x8, the police and fire employees' retirement fund, City of Claremore, had the following trial balance:

	Debit	*Credit*
Cash	$ 124,533	
Due from general fund	1,550	
Investments, at par	9,693,020	
Unamortized premium on investments	129,847	
Annuities payable		$ 11,185
Reserve for employees' contributions		3,947,760
Reserve for employer contributions		3,654,321
Reserve for membership annuities		2,306,509
Fund balance		29,175
	$9,948,950	$9,948,950

Transactions during 19x9 were:

1. The contributions due from the general fund were computed as $2,346,944 in total; this amount included $1,133,462 of employees' contributions and $1,213,482 of employer contributions.
2. Contributions transferred by the general fund to the retirement fund during the year totaled $2,330,904; this amount included $1,133,462 employees' contributions and $1,197,442 employer contributions.
3. Purchases of investments during the year were as follows: United States Treasury bonds, $1,387,740; City of Claremore, $962,000 par value at a premium of $5,505. Interest accrued at the time of purchase of the bonds amounted to $9,363.
4. Transfers to Reserve for Membership Annuities for persons retiring during the year totaled $127,674; half of this amount was transferred from Reserve for Employees' Contributions, and half from Reserve for Employer Contributions.
5. The expenditure for retirement annuities for the year was $189,000.

6. Investments with par value of $200,000, on which all premium had been amortized, were redeemed during the year.
7. Payments to annuitants totaled $191,085; the total included Annuities Payable on December 31, 19x8.
8. Contributions of $61,419 were returned to resigned employees.
9. Unclaimed checks were redeposited during the year in the amount of $1,058. They were credited to Annuities Payable.
10. Cash collections of income on investments during the year totaled $260,082, which included the amount accrued on investments purchased. Income accrued at the end of 19x9 amounted to $62,077.
11. Amortization of premium for 19x9 was $6,185.

Required:

a) Record the 19x9 transactions. Use account titles given in the trial balance; if other account titles are needed, refer to the Illustrative entries in Chapter 8.

b) Prepare closing entries for December 31, 19x9. Interest Earnings is to be closed to Reserve for Employees' Contributions, Reserve for Employer Contributions, and Reserve for Membership Annuities in the following amounts: $122,947, $109,850, and $73,814.

c) Prepare a balance sheet as of December 31, 19x9.

d) Prepare a statement of cash receipts and disbursements for 19x9.

e) Prepare a detailed analysis of changes in reserves and Fund Balance.

8–8. Illustrated below is the entire portion which deals with Federal general revenue sharing in the annual report of a city in New England:

Revenue Sharing Funds Applied to City Budget

Accounts	*Itemized Use*	*Total Applied*
General Administration:		$ 26,000.00
26 voting machines @ $1000	$26,000.00	
City Hall debt:		750.00
Heating system study	750.00	
Public Works–Street Division:		114,000.00
Special street paving	81,500.00	
Northfield Street project	20,000.00	
Berlin Street sidewalk	8,000.00	
Gallison Hill bridge	4,500.00	
Public Works–Equipment Dept.:		50,000.00
Sewer cleaning machine	50,000.00	
Debt service requirements:		135,428.00
Street improvement–Bailey Ave.	20,578.00	
Fire Dept.–aerial ladder	47,390.00	
Fire Dept.–1000 gal. pumper	41,260.00	
Taylor St.–property purchase	15,600.00	
Traffic control system	10,600.00	
Parking meter debt retirement:		24,555.00
Meter Note #1–Chittenden	7,800.00	
Meter Note #2–Howard	6,255.00	
Due Gen. Fund for Meter Notes	10,500.00	
Total Revenue Sharing Funds Applied to City Budget		$350,733.00

Required:

Comment on the extent to which the above presentation evidences that the city has adhered to the budgeting, accounting, and reporting requirements relating to Federal general revenue sharing funds.

CONTINUOUS PROBLEMS

8–L. The City of Bingham (see Problems 1–L. through 7–L.) has had an Employees' Retirement Fund for many years. The fund is financed by actuarially determined contributions from the city general fund; the employees make no contribution. Administration of the retirement fund is handled by general fund employees and the retirement fund does not bear any administrative expenses.

The balance sheet of the retirement fund as of the beginning of the year with which this problem is concerned is shown below:

CITY OF BINGHAM
Employees' Retirement Fund
July 1, 19–

Assets			*Liabilities, Reserves, and Fund Balance*	
Cash		$ 6,360	Annuities payable	$ 6,0
Interest receivable on investments		15,000	Reserve for employer contributions	550,0
Investments, at par	$750,000		Reserve for membership annuities	204,6
Add: Unamortized premium	840	750,840	Reserve for variation in actuarial assumptions	3,6
			Reserve for undistributed interest earnings	2,2
			Fund balance	5,8
Total Assets		$772,200	Total Liabilities, Reserves, and Fund Balance	$772,2

a) Open a general journal for the Employees' Retirement Fund of the City of Bingham. Record the following events in the general journal.

1. The interest receivable on investments as of the beginning of the year was collected in cash.
2. A liability for annuities payable was recorded in the amount of $75,000.
3. Contributions from the general fund in the amount of $49,980 were received.
4. Interest earnings received in cash amounted to $30,000; additional interest earnings were accrued in the amount of $16,000. One-twelfth of the beginning balance of premium on investments was amortized.
5. Annuities in the amount of $78,000 were paid.
6. Contributions from the general fund in the amount of $54,500 were received.

7. Contributions revenue for the year was transferred to the appropriate reserve account.
8. Advice from the actuary resulted in a transfer of $81,000 from the Reserve for Employer Contributions to the Reserve for Membership Annuities because of retirements during the year.
9. Interest earnings of $12,800 were distributed to Reserve for Membership Annuities and interest earnings of $35,200 were distributed to Reserve for Employer Contributions; the balance of the Interest Earnings account was closed to the Reserve for Undistributed Interest Earnings.
10. Investments of $70,000 were purchased at par.
11. Make all necessary closing entries.

b) Prepare an Employees' Retirement Fund balance sheet as of year end.

c) Prepare a Statement of Cash Receipts and Disbursements of the retirement fund for the year.

d) Prepare an Analysis of Changes in Retirement Reserves and Fund Balance for the retirement fund for the year.

8–S. The balance sheet of the General Revenue Sharing Trust Fund of the City of Smithville (See Problems 1–S through 7–S) as of December 31, 197A, halfway through the entitlement period ending June 30, 197B (closing entries had been made to facilitate preparation of the city's annual report for the year ending December 31, 197A), is presented below:

CITY OF SMITHVILLE
General Revenue Sharing Trust Fund
Balance Sheet
December 31, 197A

Assets		*Liabilities*	
Cash	$ 6,000	Due to sewage utility fund	$100,000
Interest receivable on investments	5,833	Due to special welfare fund	111,000
Investments	500,000	Fund balance	300,833
Total Assets	$511,833	Total Liabilities	$511,833

a) Open a general journal for the General Revenue Sharing Trust Fund of the City of Smithville and record in it the following events which took place in 197B:

1. In order to facilitate preparation of legally required reports for the entitlement period ending June 30, 197B, the following entry was made to reverse the December 31, 197A, closing entry: debit Estimated Revenues $960,400; debit Expenditures $655,000; debit Fund Balance $833; credit Appropriations $660,400; credit Revenues $955,833.

2. The fund balance was appropriated for transfer to the Street Improvement Fund in the amount of $300,000.
3. United States Treasury Notes having a face value of $300,000 were transferred to the Street Improvement Fund, as authorized by the appropriation budget. Interest of $4,000 was accrued on the notes at date of transfer ($3,500 of this amount was accrued as of December 31, 197A); when the Street Improvement Fund collects the interest on the notes, it must pay $4,000 to the General Revenue Sharing Trust Fund.
4. The remaining investments were sold at par on the date interest of $6,000 was collected (this includes $2,333 interest receivable as of December 31, 197A).
5. $4,000 was received from the Street Improvement Fund, as agreed (see Transaction 3 above).
6. The amounts due the Sewage Utility Fund and the Special Welfare Fund were paid.
7. The General Revenue Sharing Trust Fund received an invoice from the General Fund for $5,000 to reimburse it for administrative expenses incurred for the Trust Fund. This amount did not exceed appropriations made on July 1, 197A, for that purpose. The invoice was determined to be for items allowable as "priority expenditures." It was approved and paid.
8. Budgetary and nominal accounts for the entitlement period were closed.

b) Prepare a statement of actual and estimated revenues and expenditures for the entitlement period ending June 30, 197B, showing detail of revenues by source and detail of expenditures by purpose. (Assume that estimated and actual revenues from the U.S. Treasury were $950,000. Further assume that the appropriation and expenditures for sewage utility capital expenditure were each $355,000; the appropriation and expenditures for the Special Welfare Fund were each $300,000; the appropriation for financial administration was $5,400 and the expenditure $5,000; and the appropriation and expenditure for street improvement were as given in the transactions for the period.)

c) Record in the general journal the following events which took place in the first half of the entitlement period starting July 1, 197B and ending June 30, 197C.

1. The budget for the entitlement period was legally adopted. The revenues budget provided for revenues from the U.S. Treasury of $950,000, and interest earnings of $12,000. Appropriations are: transfers to Street Improvement Fund for capital expenditures, $600,000; transfers to Sewage Utility Fund for capital expenditures, $360,000; and transfers to General Fund for administration of General Revenue Sharing Trust Fund, $2,000.
2. A check for $950,000 was received from the U.S. Treasury.

3. Liabilities to the three funds were recorded in the amounts shown in the appropriations budget.
4. Cash was transferred to the following funds in the following amounts: Street Improvement Fund, $300,000; Sewage Utility Fund, $360,000. The remainder of cash was invested.
5. Interest received in cash amounted to $4,350 during the July 1–December 31, 197B, period. Interest earnings accrued as of December 31, 197B, amounted to $1,450 additional.
6. Nominal and budgetary accounts were closed as of December 31, 197B, to facilitate preparation of General Revenue Sharing Trust Fund statements for inclusion in the City of Smithville annual report.

d) Prepare a balance sheet for the General Revenue Sharing Trust Fund as of December 31, 197B.

e) Prepare a statement of actual and estimated revenues and expenditures for the General Revenue Sharing Trust Fund for the six months period ended December 31, 197B.

f) Prepare a statement of cash receipts and disbursements for the General Revenue Sharing Trust Fund for the six months ended December 31, 197B.

9

Intragovernmental Service Funds

All of the municipal funds discussed in previous chapters (general, special revenue, capital projects, debt service, agency, and trust funds) owe their existence to legal constraints placed upon the raising of revenue and/or the use of resources for the provision of services to the public or segments thereof, and for the acquisition of facilities to aid in the provision of services. As governmental units became more complex it became apparent that efficiency should be improved if services used by the several departments or funds were combined in a single administrative unit. Purchasing is a common example, as is a motor pool. A logical name for a fiscal and accounting entity created to account for resources used for providing centralized services is Intragovernmental Service Fund. The reason for the creation of funds in this category is to improve the management of resources; however, it should be stressed, a fund is a fiscal entity as well as an accounting entity, consequently establishment of a fund is ordinarily subject to legislative approval.

Establishment and Operation

The ordinance, or other legislative action, which authorizes the establishment of an intragovernmental service fund should also specify the source, or sources, of revenues which are to be used for fund operations. The original allocation of resources to the fund may be derived from a transfer of assets of another fund, such as the General Fund or an Enterprise Fund, intended as a contribution not to be repaid, or a transfer which is in the nature of a long-term advance to be repaid by the intragovernmental service fund over a period of years. Alternatively, or additionally, the resources initially allocated to an intragovernmental service fund may be acquired from the proceeds of a bond issue. Since intragovernmental service funds are established to improve the management of resources, it is generally considered that they should be operated, and accounted for, on a business basis. Application of this general truth to a specific case can lead to conflict between managers who wish the freedom to operate the fund in accord with their professional judgment, and legislators who wish to exercise considerable control over the decisions of the intragovernmental service fund managers.

For example, assume that municipal administrators request the establishment of a fund for the purchasing, warehousing, and issuing of supplies used by a number of municipal funds and departments. At the time of the request, since no intragovernmental service fund exists, each fund or department must include in its budget its requested appropriation for supplies, its requested appropriation for salaries and wages of personnel engaged in purchasing and handling the supplies, and its requested appropriation for any operating expense or facility costs associated with the supply function. Accordingly, legislators tend to feel that through their control over budgets they are controlling the investment in supplies and the use of supplies by each fund and department. Legislators would tend to feel that if they approved the establishment of an intragovernmental service fund which had authority to generate operating revenues sufficient to perpetuate the fund without annual appropriations, the supply function would no longer be subjected to annual legislative budget review, and the legislature would "lose control" after the initial allocation of resources to the fund. Administrators would tend to feel that if an intragovernmental service fund did not have authority to generate operating revenues sufficient to perpetuate the fund, and to spend those revenues at the discretion of fund management rather than at the discretion of persons possibly more concerned with reelection than with financial management, there would be little to be gained by establishment of the service fund. The two opposing views should be somewhat balanced by the fact that the customers of an intragovernmental service fund are, by definition, other funds and departments of the governmental entity; therefore, each using fund and department must include in its appropriations budget request justification for the amount to be spent (i.e., transferred to the service fund) for supplies, so the legislative branch continues to exercise budgetary review over the amount each fund and department budgets for supplies. If the legislative branch were to set pricing policies for the service fund, and policies governing the use of current earnings, and retention of earnings, and require the submission of periodic financial statements to evidence that its policies were followed, the legislature would be able to maintain considerable control over the function performed by the service fund, yet leave the fund managers freedom to operate at their discretion within the policies set by the legislative branch.

One of the more difficult problems to resolve to the satisfaction of persons with opposing views is the establishment of a pricing policy. "Cost" is obviously an incomplete answer: historical cost of the supplies themselves, whether defined as fifo, lifo, average, or specific identification, will not provide sufficient revenue to replace supplies issued if replacement prices have risen since the last purchase, or to increase the inventory quantities if the scale of municipal operations is growing. Payroll and other cash operating expenses of the service fund must be met; and if the original capital of the service fund is to be repaid from earnings of the service fund, prices must be set at a level which will generate revenue for debt retirement. If the service fund is to be operated on a true business basis, it must also be able to finance from its operations replacement, modernization, and expansion of plant and equipment used in fund operations. Prices charged by the service fund, however, should be less than the using funds and departments would have to pay outside vendors for equivalent products and services, if the existence and continued operation of the service fund is to be justified.

Because of the considerations mentioned in preceding paragraphs, many different approaches to intragovernmental service fund operations may be found in practice. Since accounting systems should give appropriate recognition to operating policies, as well as to legal requirements, practices vary from those of profit-seeking businesses at one extreme to those discussed in this text in the chapters relating to revenue funds, at the other extreme. In the illustrations given in following sections of this chapter it is assumed that the financial objective of intragovernmental service funds is to recover from operating revenues the full cost of operations, with enough net income to allow for replacement of inventories in periods of rising prices, and enough increase in inventory quantities to meet the needs of using funds and departments whose scale of operations is increasing. Similarly, it is assumed that net income should be sufficient to allow for replacement of fixed assets used by the service fund, but that expansion of the facilities must be financed through contributions from other funds authorized in their appropriations budgets. Managers of intragovernmental service funds must prepare operating plans—budgets—as a management tool. In the illustrations it is assumed that budgets of intragovernmental service funds are submitted to the legislative body, and to the public, for information but not for legal action, and that therefore the budget is not formally recorded in service fund accounts. Similarly, managers of businesses must be kept informed of the status of outstanding purchase orders and contracts, but encumbrances need not be recorded in the accounts in order to accomplish this.

Accounting for an intragovernmental service fund concerned with the functions of purchasing, warehousing, and issuing supplies is illustrated in the following section of this chapter.

Illustrative Case—Supplies Fund

Assume that the administrators of the Town of Merrill obtain approval from the Town Council to centralize the purchasing, storing, and issuing functions as of January 1, 197C, and to administer and account for these functions in a Supplies Fund. The town's General Fund is to contribute to the new fund its December 31, 197B, inventory of supplies and $25,000 in cash to be used for working capital. The town's Water Utility Fund is to advance $100,000 to the Supplies Fund to be used for acquisition of a building and equipment needed to handle the supply function efficiently; the advance is to be repaid by the Supplies Fund in twenty equal annual installments. The receipt of the cash and supplies should be recorded by the Supplies Fund in the following manner[1]:

1.	Cash	125,000	
	Inventory of Supplies	12,300	
	Contribution from General Fund		37,300
	Advance from Water Utility Fund		100,000

Assume that a satisfactory warehouse building is purchased for $70,000; $10,000 of the purchase price is considered as a cost of the land. Necessary warehouse machinery and equipment is purchased for $20,000. Delivery equipment is purchased for $10,000. If the purchases are made for cash, the acquisition of the assets would be recorded in the books of the intragovernmental service fund as:

2.	Land	10,000	
	Building	60,000	
	Machinery and Equipment—Warehouse	20,000	
	Equipment—Delivery	10,000	
	Cash		100,000

Additional supplies would need to be ordered to maintain inventories at a level commensurate with expected usage. Encumbrances need not be recorded for purchase orders issued, and so information about the dollar value of purchase orders is omitted from this illustration. During 197C it is assumed that supplies are received and and related invoices are approved for payment in the amount of $169,800; the entry needed to record the asset and the liability is:

3.	Inventory of Supplies	169,800	
	Vouchers Payable		169,800

The General Fund of the Town of Merrill (see Chapter 3) accounted for supplies on the physical inventory basis. The Supplies Fund, however, should account for its inventories on the perpetual inventory basis since

[1] General fund entries and water utility fund entries for this transaction are illustrated in Chapters 11 and 14.

the information is needed for proper performance of its primary function. Accordingly, when supplies are issued the inventory account must be credited for the cost of the supplies issued. Since the using fund will be charged an amount in excess of the inventory carrying value, the receivable and revenue accounts must reflect the selling price. The mark-up above cost should be determined on the basis of budgeted expenses and other items to be financed from net income, in relation to expected requistitions by using funds. If the budget for the Town of Merrill's Supplies Fund indicates that a mark-up of 30% is needed, issues to General Fund departments of supplies costing $162,000 would be recorded by the following entries:

4a.	Cost of Supplies Issued	162,000	
	Inventory of Supplies		162,000
4b.	Due from General Fund	210,600	
	Billings to Departments		210,600

The account title Billings to Departments, used in journal entry 4b, is the title suggested in *Governmental Accounting, Auditing, and Financial Reporting* by the National Committee on Governmental Accounting.

During the year it is assumed that purchasing expenses totaling $18,000, warehousing expenses totaling $11,000, and delivery expenses totaling $12,000 were incurred. If all liabilities are vouchered before payment, the entry would be:

5.	Purchasing Expenses	18,000	
	Warehousing Expenses	11,000	
	Delivery Expenses	12,000	
	Vouchers Payable		41,000

If collections from the General Fund during 197C totaled $203,000, the entry should be:

6.	Cash	203,000	
	Due from General Fund		203,000

Assuming that payments on vouchers during the year totaled $198,000, the entry is made:

7.	Vouchers Payable	198,000	
	Cash		198,000

The advance from the water utility fund is to be repaid in twenty equal annual installments; repayment of one installment at the end of 197C is recorded as:

8	Advance from Water Utility Fund	5,000	
	Cash		5,000

It is assumed that the building used as a warehouse was estimated at the time of purchase to have a remaining useful life of 20 years;

the warehouse machinery and equipment was estimated to have a useful life of 10 years, and the delivery equipment to have a useful life of 5 years. If the purchasing office occupies 10 percent of the space in the warehouse building, 10 percent of the building depreciation may be considered purchasing expense; $300 of building depreciation is thus charged to purchasing expense and $2,700 to warehousing expense. The latter account is also charged $2,000 for machinery and equipment depreciation expense. Delivery expense is charged $2,000 for equipment depreciation during the year.

		Debit	Credit
9.	Purchasing Expense	300	
	Warehousing Expense	4,700	
	Delivery Expense	2,000	
	Allowance for Depreciation—Building		3,000
	Allowance for Depreciation—Machinery and Equipment—Warehouse		2,000
	Allowance for Depreciation—Equipment—Delivery		2,000

Organizations which keep perpetual inventory records must adjust the records periodically to reflect shortages, overages, or out-of-condition stock disclosed by physical inventories. Adjustments to the Inventory account are also considered to be adjustments to the operating expenses of the period. In this illustrative case it is assumed that no adjustments were found to be necessary at year-end.

Assuming that all revenues and expenses applicable to 197C have been properly recorded by the entries illustrated above, the nominal accounts should be closed as of December 31, 197C:

		Debit	Credit
10.	Billings to Departments	210,600	
	Cost of Supplies Issued		162,000
	Purchasing Expenses		18,300
	Warehousing Expenses		15,700
	Delivery Expenses		14,000
	Excess of Net Billings to Departments over Costs		600

Excess of Net Billings to Departments over Costs (or Excess of Costs over Net Billings to Departments if operations resulted in a loss) is the account title provided in the National Committee on Governmental Accounting chart of accounts, in place of Profit and Loss or Income Summary or Current Earnings—the titles commonly found in profit-seeking businesses. Whatever title is used for the account summarizing the results of operations for the period, the account should be closed at year-end. The recommended title of the account that records earnings retained in the intragovernmental service fund is the same as the title commonly used for profit-seeking businesses: Retained Earnings.

		Debit	Credit
11.	Excess of Net Billings to Departments Over Costs	600	
	Retained Earnings		600

Illustrative Statements

The balance sheet of the Supplies Fund of the Town of Merrill as of December 31, 197C, is shown by Illustration 9–1.

The results of operations of an intragovernmental service fund should be reported periodically in a Statement of Operations, which is the equivalent of an income statement for a profit-seeking entity. In order

Illustration 9–1

TOWN OF MERRILL
Supplies Fund
Balance Sheet as of December 31, 197C

Assets			
Current Assets:			
Cash			$ 25,000
Due from general fund			7,600
Inventory of supplies at average cost			20,100
Total Current Assets			$ 52,700
Fixed Assets:			
Land		$10,000	
Building	$60,000		
Less: Allowance for depreciation	3,000	57,000	
Machinery and equipment–warehouse	$20,000		
Less: Allowance for depreciation	2,000	18,000	
Equipment–delivery	$10,000		
Less: Allowance for depreciation	2,000	8,000	
Total Fixed Assets			$ 93,000
Total Assets			$145,700
Liabilities, Contributions, and Retained Earnings			
Current Liabilities:			
Vouchers payable			$ 12,800
Total Current Liabilities			$ 12,800
Long-Term Debt:			
Advance from water utility			$ 95,000
Total Liabilities			$107,800
Contributions from general fund			37,300
Retained earnings			600
Total Liabilities, Contributions, and Retained Earnings			$145,700

Illustration 9–2

TOWN OF MERRILL
Supplies Fund
Analysis of Changes in Retained Earnings
For the Year Ended December 31, 197C

Balance of Retained Earnings, January 1, 197C	$ none
Add: Excess of Net Billings to Departments over Costs, 197C	600
Balance of Retained Earnings, December 31, 197C	$ 600

to provide full disclosure of the results of all transactions and events during a period, an Analysis of Changes in Retained Earnings should accompany the balance sheet and Statement of Operations. Illustration 9–2 presents the Analysis of Changes in Retained Earnings during 197C for the Town of Merrill Supplies Fund. Illustration 9–3 presents the related Statement of Operations.

Illustration 9–3

TOWN OF MERRILL
Supplies Fund
Statement of Operations
For the Year Ended December 31, 197C

Billings to departments		$210,600
Less: Cost of supplies issued		162,000
Gross Margin		$ 48,600
Less: Purchasing expenses	$18,300	
Warehousing expenses	15,700	
Delivery expenses	14,000	
Total Operating Expenses		48,000
Excess of Net Billings to Departments over Costs		$ 600

Inasmuch as assets were provided for the Supplies fund from sources other than revenues of the period, and assets were applied to debt repayment as well as to the acquisition of assets and the payment of operating expenses, a Statement of Changes in Financial Position (Statement of Source and Application of Funds), or a Statement of Cash Receipts and Disbursements, for the year ended December 31, 197C, should also be prepared. Illustration 9–4 presents a Statement of Cash Receipts and Disbursements for the Town of Merrill Supplies Fund.

Intragovernmental Service Funds with Manufacturing Activities

The Supplies Fund of the Town of Merrill, for which journal entries and statements are illustrated in the preceding section of this chapter, is re-

Illustration 9–4

TOWN OF MERRILL
Supplies Fund
Statement of Cash Receipts and Disbursements
For the Year Ended December 31, 197C

Balance, January 1, 197C			$ none
Cash Receipts:			
Contributions from general fund		$ 25,000	
Long-term advance from water utility fund		100,000	
Collection of billings to general fund		203,000	
Total Cash Receipts			328,000
Total cash available during year			$328,000
Cash Disbursements:			
Repayment of installment due on long-term debt		$ 5,000	
Purchase of land		10,000	
Purchase of warehouse building		60,000	
Purchase of warehouse equipment		20,000	
Purchase of delivery equipment		10,000	
Cost of supplies purchased	$169,800		
Purchasing expense	18,000		
Warehousing expense	11,000		
Delivery expense	12,000		
Costs and expenses vouchered	$210,800		
Less: vouchers payable, Dec. 31, 197C	12,800		
Disbursements for costs and expenses		198,000	
Total cash disbursements			303,000
Balance, December 31, 197C			$ 25,000

sponsible for purchasing, storing, and issuing supplies used by other funds and departments of the town. Many municipalities have funds similar to that of the Town of Merrill. It is also common to find printing shops, asphalt plants, or other service units which produce a physical product to be used by municipal funds and departments, or which facilitate the operations of the other funds and units by performing maintenance or repair jobs, or which even perform a temporary financing function.

If an intragovernmental service fund performs a continuous process manufacturing operation, its accounting system should provide process cost accounts. If a service fund performs a manufacturing, maintenance, or repair operation on a job-order basis, the fund's accounting system should provide appropriate job-order cost accounts. To the extent that operations, processes, or activities are capable of being standardized, cost standards for materials, direct labor, and overhead should be established; in such cases the accounting system should provide for the routine measurement and reporting of significant variances from the standards. It is assumed that the reader of this text is familiar with cost accounting theory and practice; the subject is therefore not discussed in detail here. Chapter 20 presents a brief discussion of cost determination for nonprofit entities.

Dissolution of an Intragovernmental Service Fund

When an intragovernmental service fund has completed the mission for which it was established, or when its activitity is terminated for any other reason, dissolution must be accomplished. Liquidation may be accomplished in any one of three ways or in combinations thereof. The three ways are: (1) transfer of the fund's assets to another fund which will continue the operation as a subsidiary activity, e.g., a supply fund becoming a *department* of the general fund; (2) distribution of the fund's assets in kind to another fund or other funds; (3) conversion of all its noncash assets to cash and distribution of the cash to another fund or other funds. Dissolution of an intragovernmental service fund, as for a private enterprise, would proceed by prior payments to outside creditors, followed by repayment of long-term advances not previously amortized and, finally, liquidation of net worth. The entire process of dissolution should be conducted according to pertinent law and the discretion of the appropriate legislative body. Fund capital contributed by another fund logically would revert to the contributor fund, but law or other regulations may dictate otherwise. If fund capital has been built up out of charges in excess of costs, then liquidation will follow whatever regulations may govern the case; and if none exist, then the appropriate governing body must decide upon the recipient or recipients.

SELECTED REFERENCES

Coleman, Jack W. "Working Capital Funds: Theory and Practice," *Municipal Finance*, vol. 40, no. 3 (February 1968), pp. 130–38.

National Committee on Governmental Accounting. *Governmental Accounting, Auditing, and Financial Reporting*, chap. 7, Chicago, 1968.

QUESTIONS

9–1. Some municipalities account for the supply function in the accounting structure of the general fund, others account for the supply function by means of an intragovernmental service fund. Under what conditions would the former treatment be acceptable? Under what conditions should the latter treatment be used?

9–2. "Intragovernmental service funds have revenues, therefore they should use the modified accrual basis of accounting recommended for revenue fund." Do you agree? Why or why not?

9–3. In a recent year the stores and duplicating fund of a large city provided supplies and duplicating service to other funds in the total amount of $473,020. The fund is of the intragovernmental service type and is fully self-supporting. The same year its operating statement showed a net loss of $426. Based on those facts, was the fund, in your opinion, well managed? Defend your answer.

9–4. "Since the reason for the establishment of intragovernmental service funds is to facilitate management of resources, and not primarily to demonstrate compliance with law, they may be established at the discretion of municipal administrators." Comment.

9–5. Budgetary accounts are ordinarily not required for intragovernmental service funds by law, therefore budgets need not be prepared for the funds. Do you agree? Why or why not?

9–6. A governmental unit provided original financing for its Materials and Supplies Fund by transfer of $30,000 cash from its General Fund. The transferee fund credited the amount to Advance from General Fund. Assuming that the terminology is correct, how should the Advance account be classified in the statements of the Materials and Supplies Fund? How should the corresponding account be shown in the statements of the General Fund?

9–7. If the transfer referred to in Question 9–6 had been credited to Contribution from General Fund, how should the latter account be classified in the statements of the Material and Supplies Fund (again assuming that the account used fits the facts of the transfer)? How should the corresponding account, if any, be shown in the statements of the General Fund?

9–8. A municipal purchasing fund follows the policy of charging all departments substantially more than the sum of actual cost and normal overhead for materials and supplies bought for them. Annually an amount of cash equal to the net gain by that method is transferred to the library fund. Comment on the merits or demerits of that procedure.

9–9. Depreciation of general fixed assets is not recorded in the accounts of any of the funds or account-groups. If a building is transferred from the General Fixed Assets Group to an intragovernmental service fund because the character of its use changes, should the service fund record building depreciation expense? Explain.

9–10. What are some of the more important considerations in establishing a pricing policy for an intragovernmental service fund?

EXERCISES AND PROBLEMS

9–1. Utilizing the municipal annual report obtained for Exercise 1–1, follow the instructions below:

a) What activities of the municipality are reported as being administered by intragovernmental service funds (working capital funds, revolving funds, rotary funds, and industrial funds are other names used for funds of the type discussed in Chapter 9)? Does the report state the basis of accounting used for the intragovernmental service funds? (Are all funds in this category accounted for on the same basis?) If so, is the financial statement presentation consistent with the stated basis? If the basis of accounting is not stated, analyze the statements to determine which basis is used—full accrual, modified accrual, or cash basis. Is the basis used consistent with the recommendations discussed in Chapter 9?

b) In the balance sheet(s) of the intragovernmental service fund(s) are assets classified in accord with practices of profit-seeking businesses, or are current, fixed, and other assets not separately disclosed? If there are receivables other than from other funds, are allowances for estimated uncollectibles provided? Are allowances for depreciation deducted from related fixed asset accounts?
Are current liabilities and long-term debt properly distinguished in the balance sheet? Are long-term advances from other funds properly distinguished from capital contributions received from other funds or from bond issues? Are retained earnings (or deficits) from operations clearly distinguished from capital contributions?

c) Are budgetary accounts (Estimated Revenues, Appropriations, Encumbrances) used by the intragovernmental service funds? From what sources were revenues actually obtained by each service fund? How are costs and expenses of each fund classified: by character, object, function, or activity (see Chapter 5 for definitions of these terms)? Are noncash expenses, such as depreciation, separately disclosed? Do the revenues of each fund exceed the costs and expenses of the period? Compute the net income (or net loss) of each fund in this category as a percentage of its operating revenue for the period. Does the net income (or net loss) for any fund exceed five percent of operating revenues? If so, do the statements, or the accompanying text, explain what the excess is being used for, or how the deficiency is being financed?

d) Is a statement of application of funds presented for intragovernmental service funds? If so, how do the sources of funds shown in this statement relate to the sources of revenues shown in the Statement of Operations? How do the items shown under the "Funds Applied" caption relate to the cost and expense items shown in the Statement of Operations?

9–2. A combined statement of operations of the intragovernmental service funds of the Metropolitan Government of Nashville and Davidson County, Tennessee, for the year ended June 30, 1972, is shown below. In what respects does the statement evidence that the funds are being operated and accounted for in the manner recommended by the National Committee on Governmental Accounting and described in Chapter 9? Does the statement indicate any differences between the apparent accounting and operating policies used and those discussed in Chapter 9? Your answer should be brief, but specific.

METROPOLITAN GOVERNMENT OF NASHVILLE AND DAVIDSON COUNTY
Intragovernmental Service Funds–General Services District
Statement of Operations for the Year Ended June 30, 1972

	Combined Intragov-ernmental Service Funds	*Central Printing Fund*	*Motor Pool Fund*	*Farm and Dairy Fund*	*Highway and Street Supply Fund*	*Office Supply and Storeroom Fund*	*Schools Central Storeroom Fund*
Revenue:							
Charges to other departments	$2,226,467	$ 76,324	$861,154	$34,513	$172,304	$ 97,359	$ 984,813
Sale of livestock	15,268	–	–	15,268	–	–	–
Contribution from other funds	61,413	57,021	–	–	–	4,392	–
Miscellaneous income	20,118	–	17,807	2,311	–	–	–
Total Revenue	$2,323,266	$133,345	$878,961	$52,092	$172,304	$101,751	$ 984,813
Cost of Sales:							
Inventory, July 1, 1971	$ 639,844	$ 1,974	$ 22,890	$43,470	$ 62,105	$ 12,802	$ 496,603
Direct costs–							
Purchases	1,124,452	33,251	9,644	–	15,119	94,725	971,713
Gasoline, oil, fuel, antifreeze	268,363	–	266,957	–	1,406	–	–
Tires, tubes, batteries, lubrication	43,156	–	42,290	–	866	–	–
Feed	11,888	–	–	11,888	–	–	–
Repair parts	66,272	–	66,272	–	–	–	–
Automobile and truck repairs	49,708	–	49,708	–	–	–	–
	$2,203,683	$ 35,225	$457,761	$55,358	$ 79,496	$107,527	$1,468,316
Less inventory, June 30, 1972	608,827	2,678	23,386	36,672	27,735	13,973	504,383
Total Cost of Sales	$1,594,856	$ 32,547	$434,375	$18,686	$ 51,761	$ 93,554	$ 963,933
Gross Operating Revenue	$ 728,410	$100,798	$444,586	$33,406	$120,543	$ 8,197	$ 20,880
Operating Expenses:							
Salaries and wages	$ 507,982	$ 56,430	$295,700	$31,764	$112,928	$ 11,160	$ –
Matching funds payroll expenses	56,449	6,771	34,504	3,058	10,571	1,545	–
Printing, duplication, typing, and binding	3,097	1,078	2,019	–	–	–	–
Utility services	13,635	513	7,254	179	5,526	163	–
Equipment rental	2,887	1,350	1,489	–	–	48	–
Repairs and maintenance services	3,872	3,796	–	76	–	–	–
Travel	962	960	2	–	–	–	–
Other contractual services	24,073	389	23,684	–	–	–	–
Supplies	11,724	–	9,197	2,527	–	–	–
Materials	7,395	–	–	79	7,316	–	–
Provision for depreciation	58,402	5,168	50,582	2,652	–	–	–
Insurance	10,661	–	10,542	119	–	–	–
Total Operating Expenses	$ 701,139	$ 76,455	$434,973	$40,454	$136,341	$ 12,916	$ –
Excess (deficit) of revenue over expenses	$ 27,271	$ 24,343	$ 9,613	$ (7,048)	$ (15,798)	$ (4,719)	$ 20,880

9–3. Your examination of the accounts of your new client, the City of Delmas, as of June 30, 1971 revealed the following:

1. On December 31, 1970, the City paid $115,000 out of General Fund revenues for a central garage to service its vehicles, with $67,500 being applicable to the building which has an estimated life of 25 years, $14,500 to land and $33,000 to machinery and equipment which has an estimated life of 15 years. A $12,200 cash contribution was received by the garage from the General Fund on the same date.
2. The garage maintains no records, but a review of deposit slips and canceled checks revealed the following:

Collections for services to City departments financed from the General Fund	$30,000
Office salaries	6,000
Utilities	700
Mechanics' wages	11,000
Materials and supplies	9,000

3. The garage had uncollected billings of $2,000, accounts payable for materials and supplies of $500 and an inventory of materials and supplies of $1,500 at June 30, 1971.

Required:

Prepare journal entries which should be made to establish an intragovernmental service fund for the City of Delmas and to record the events for the period given. Also prepare any necessary adjusting and closing entries as of June 30, 1971, the end of the fiscal year.

(AICPA, adapted)

9–4. Prairie City operates an insurance fund of the intragovernmental service type. The fund manages and finances the various kinds of insurance carried by the city. It pays all premiums to the insurers, then as premiums expire, they are charged to the specific funds to which they pertain. All costs—personnel, utilities, etc.—of operating the insurance fund are borne by the general fund. At April 30, 19x6, the trial balance of the Insurance Fund was as follows:

	Debit	*Credit*
Cash with city treasurer	$ 39,863	
Prepaid insurance premiums	204,722	
Vouchers payable		$114,585
Contribution from general fund		105,000
Contribution from water fund		25,000
	$244,585	$244,585

During the year ended April 30, 19x7, the following transactions, in summary form, occurred:

1. The fund was billed by insurance companies for $141,650 premiums falling due on insurance coverage for the various funds of the city.
2. A total of $161,759 was charged to various funds on account of premiums which expired during the year.

3. A total of $9,473 was received from insurance companies as premium adjustments during the year. This was credited to the amount owed by various funds for current year's expirations.
4. $136,905 was paid on amounts owed to insurance companies, for the benefit of Prairie City funds and agencies.
5. Additional financing for the fund was received in the form of an $80,000 contribution of cash by the general fund.
6. $152,286 was collected on the amount of expirations charged to the various funds.

a) The fund described above is similar to an agency fund. State what you perceive to be its primary difference from a true agency fund.
b) State what you consider to be the justification for operation of a separate fund for accounting for insurance premium payments and expirations.
c) In the fund described above there are no transactions related to settlement of losses. State the reason why.
d) The fund does not have an account in the nature of Excess of Net Billings Over Costs, or Retained Earnings. State why not.

9–5. At December 31, 197C, the central purchasing fund, City of Hogue had the following trial balance.*

	Debit	*Credit*
Cash	$ 3,080	
Inventory of supplies	41,300	
Due from other funds	13,650	
Equipment	6,940	
Allowance for depreciation–Equipment		$ 2,130
Vouchers payable		7,010
Contribution from general fund		47,040
Reserve for encumbrances		8,600
Retained Earnings		190
	$64,970	$64,970

The following transactions occurred during 197D:

1. Reserve for Encumbrances is closed to Retained Earnings.
2. During 197D, purchase orders for supplies totaling $591,000 were issued by the fund.
3. Purchase orders totaling $588,000 were filled at an invoiced total cost of $589,600 and vouchers were prepared in that amount.
4. Purchasing expenses were vouchered in the amount of $15,875; warehousing expenses were vouchered in the amount of $12,000.
5. Supplies having a computed cost of $579,300 were issued to other funds. To this was added a five percent mark-up on cost.

* Although encumbrance accounting is not recommended for use by intragovernmental service funds by the National Committee on Governmental Accounting, applicable laws of a number of jurisdictions require encumbrance accounting to be used. In other municipalities it is used at the preference of finance officers. As will be noted in the trial balance, the City of Hogue uses encumbrance accounting; therefore your solution should be consistent with the facts.

6. $619,230 was received through cash transfers from other funds.
7. Vouchers liquidated during the year amounted to $616,800.
8. An employee was detected in the act of pilfering stores. An inventory of supplies following the incident revealed a physical inventory total $900 less than the book inventory balance. The former employee's bonding company made full restitution in cash for the $900 difference.
9. Supplies of a recorded cost of $580 were consumed in the normal operations of the fund. (Charge Warehousing Expense.) No markup was charged on supplies used by the purchasing fund.
10. Depreciation of equipment was recorded at ten percent of cost of equipment. (Charge Warehousing Expense.)
11. A physical inventory taken as of December 31, 197D, disclosed that stores costing $49,950 were on hand; the Inventory account was adjusted accordingly. (Charge Warehousing Expense.)
12. Nominal accounts were closed to Excess of Costs Over Net Billings. Encumbrances were closed to Retained Earnings.*

Required:

a) Record the transactions for 197D in general journal form, or by direct posting to T accounts (if you take the latter option, first enter the balances as of December 31, 197C).

b) Prepare a balance sheet for the Purchasing Fund as of December 31, 197D.

c) Prepare an Analysis of Changes in Retained Earnings for the year.

d) Prepare a Statement of Operations of the Purchasing Fund for the year ended December 31, 197D.

9–6. As of the beginning of a certain year, the automotive service fund of Erie City had the following balance in its real accounts:

	Debit	*Credit*
Cash on hand and in bank	$ 1,100	
Due from street fund	2,020	
Accounts receivable	340	
Service supplies inventory	7,060	
Machinery and equipment	30,000	
Allowance for depreciation–machinery and equipment		$11,000
Buildings	21,000	
Allowance for depreciation–buildings		7,000
Land	3,700	
Due to Federal government		860
Due to utility fund		80
Accounts payable		2,170
Advance from general fund		45,000
Retained earnings (deficit)	890	
	$66,110	$66,110

* This closing procedure is used by the municipality whose report served as a source for this problem.

During the fiscal year the following transactions (summarized) occurred:

1. Operating employees were paid $29,000 wages in cash, and additional wages of $3,200 were withheld for Federal taxes.
2. Salaries paid in cash during the year amounted to $9,000. An additional amount of $1,800 was withheld for Federal taxes.
3. Cash remitted to the Federal government during the year for taxes withheld amounted to $4,600.
4. Utility bills received during the year amounted to $2,350 (debit Utility Services).
5. Office expense paid in cash during the year amounted to $1,050.
6. Service supplies purchased on account during the year totaled $37,500.
7. Parts and supplies used during the year totaled $38,110 (at cost).
8. Charges to departments during the fiscal year were as follows:

General fund	$44,500
Street fund	42,000
Nongovernmental agencies	1,200

9. During the year an old account receivable of $75 was authorized to be written off because the debtor agency denied the validity of the charge.
10. Unpaid balances at year-end were as follows:

General fund	$2,100
Street fund	1,830
Nongovernmental agencies	425

11. Electric and water bills due to the utility fund at year-end totaled $210.
12. Cash payments for miscellaneous expense during the year totaled $190.
13. Accounts payable at year-end amounted to $2,750.
14. Annual depreciation is recorded at the following rates:

Machinery and equipment	10%
Buildings	3%

15. A physical inventory of parts and supplies at year-end totaled $6,675 (credit Cost of Parts and Supplies Used for the adjustment).
16. Nominal accounts for the year were closed.

Required:

Prepare a Statement of Operations for the year. Utility services are estimated to be 90% direct costs and 10% indirect costs.

9–7. From the following information concerning the City of Langdon, you are to prepare:

a) A statement of operations for the Maintenance Service Fund of the city.
b) A balance sheet for the Maintenance Service Fund.

The accounts of the General Fund as of the beginning of the period were as follows:

Cash	$1,000
Taxes receivable–delinquent	8,000
Accounts payable	7,000
Reserve for encumbrances	1,500
Retained earnings	500

The following transactions for the current year are to be considered:

1. The budget which was adopted for the year provided for taxes of $275,000, special assessments of $100,000, fees of $15,000, and license revenues of $10,000. Appropriations were $290,000 for general fund operations and $100,000 for the purpose of establishing a maintenance service fund.
2. All taxes and special assessments became receivable.
3. Cash receipts for the general fund included:

Taxes for the year	$260,000
Special assessments	100,000
Fees	16,000
Licenses	9,500
Taxes receivable–delinquent, plus interest of $500. Tax liens were obtained on the remainder of the delinquent taxes.	5,500

4. Contracts amounting to $75,000 were let by the general fund.
5. Services rendered by the maintenance service fund to other departments included: general fund, $40,000; utility fund, $20,000, of which $5,000 remained uncollected at the end of the year.
6. The following cash disbursements were made by the general fund:

Maintenance service fund	$100,000
Accounts payable of the preceding year	7,000
Outstanding orders at beginning of year were all received and paid for	2,000
Expenses of fund incurred during year	145,000
Stores purchased for central storeroom established during year	5,000
Contracts let during year	30,000
Permanent advance to newly created petty cash fund	1,000
Services performed by maintenance service fund	35,000
Salaries paid during year	30,000

7. The following cash disbursements were made by the maintenance service fund:

Purchase of equipment (estimated useful life 10 years)	$60,000
Purchase of materials and supplies, of which one fifth remained at end of year	40,000
Salaries and wages, as follows:	
Direct labor	9,000
Office salaries	2,000
Superintendent's salary	4,000
Heat, light, and power	2,000
Office expenses	500

8. All unpaid taxes become delinquent.
9. Stores inventory in general fund amounted to $2,000 at year end.

(AICPA, adapted)

9–8. At April 30, 1975, the General Fund and the Stores and Services Fund of the Town of Weston showed the following account balances:

General Fund

Advance to stores and services fund	$ 61,307
Appropriations	1,129,553
Cash	27,675
Encumbrances	184,755
Estimated revenues	1,249,062
Estimated uncollectible taxes	8,191
Expenditures	98,779
Fund balance	62,663
Investments	410,000
Reserve for advance to stores and services fund	61,307
Reserve for encumbrances	184,755
Revenues from fees, licenses, etc.	12,000
Revenues from taxes	1,003,419
Taxes receivable	465,000
Vouchers payable	34,690

Stores and Services Fund

Advance from general fund	$ 61,307
Cash	19,250
Due from general fund	17,160
Due from water fund	4,320
Retained earnings	423
Jobs in process	1,630
Overhead	30*
Inventory of materials and supplies	32,940
Vouchers payable	13,540

*Credit

It should be noted that:

a) All jobs are for the general fund.

b) The general fund does not record encumbrances for stores requisitioned from the stores and services fund, but does record encumbrances for jobs ordered.

The following transactions occurred:

1. Until this time the General Fund had followed the practice of making no formal entry for receipt of either supplies or services from the Stores and Services Fund until payment was made. Beginning now, a liability is to be recorded when the supplies or services are received. For recording the amount due to the Stores and Services Fund at May 1, it may be assumed that all service and jobs not paid for have been received in the current fiscal year. Included in the unpaid total was the cost of jobs which had been encumbered in the amount of $6,205. Liabilities to the Stores and Services Fund are to be credited to Due to Stores and Services Fund.
2. Cash received during May consisted of the following:

From fees, licenses, etc.	$ 4,387
From taxes	58,741
From sale of investments at book value	250,000

3. May purchase orders issued by the Stores and Services Fund amounted to $15,627. May purchase orders issued by the General Fund for items not obtainable through the Stores and Services Fund totaled $126,403.
4. Jobs expected to cost $22,010 were requisitioned during May, all by the General Fund.
5. Purchases received and invoices vouchered during May by the Stores and Services Fund were $12,124. The General Fund received items which had been encumbered in the amount of $294,615; vouchers for these items totaled $296,708.
6. Payrolls for May were vouchered in the following amounts:

Stores and Services Fund for jobs in process	$ 8,051
General Fund	13,636

7. Overhead costs vouchered by the Stores and Services Fund during May totaled $2,519. Overhead is absorbed by charging using funds and activities (including jobs) ten percent more than the cost of supplies issued to them.
8. Cost of supplies issued during May by the Stores and Services Fund for jobs in process was $15,490, for direct issue to the General Fund $3,090, and for issue to the Water Fund $1,420.
9. Jobs were completed and transferred to the General Fund during the month at an accumulated cost of $22,580; the estimated cost of the jobs was $21,060.
10. Additional appropriations amounted to $2,516.
11. A petty cash fund of $1,500 was established in the General Fund.
12. Checks were issued in the following amounts during May:

By the General Fund:	
On account of vouchers payable	$285,345
On account of indebtedness to Stores and Services Fund . . .	18,910
By the Stores and Services Fund:	
On account of vouchers payable	25,728
By the Water Fund:	
On account of indebtedness for stores	4,732

Required:

a) Prepare all journal entries for May which should be made by the Stores and Services Fund.

b) Prepare all journal entries for May which should be made by the General Fund.

CONTINUOUS PROBLEMS

9–L. The City of Bingham established a Stores and Services Fund to be operated as an intragovernmental service fund to improve purchasing procedures and facilitate inventory management.

You are required to:

a) Open a general journal for the Stores and Services Fund; enter the following transactions, in accord with preferred intragovernmental service fund practices. All transactions are for the first month of operations of this fund, which is the last month of the city's fiscal year for which transactions are given in preceding "L" problems.

1. The advance was received from the General Fund [see transaction 13 of part (*c*), Problems 5–L].
2. Warehouse and office space was not available in city-owned buildings; space was rented in a privately owned building for $200 a month. Six months' rent was paid in advance.
3. A cash expense budget was prepared by the City Controller for this new fund. In addition to rent, the estimated expenses were $480 a year for utilities ($120 for water, a city-owned utility; $100 for a telephone; $200 for electricity; and $60 for gas—all privately-owned utilities); $9,600 for salaries; and $260 a year for operation and maintenance of warehouse equipment. (The warehouse equipment was in the basement of City Hall; nobody was quite clear as to when it had been purchased, for what purpose, by whom, or how much it had cost. It was usable, however, and when it was cleaned and minor repairs were made by the Department of Public Works employees, the equipment was turned over to the Stores and Services Fund. The controller estimated that new equipment would have cost $6,000; the estimated remaining useful life of the existing equipment was 10 years, or, about two-thirds as long as new equipment would have been expected to last.)
4. In order to put the Stores and Services Fund on a completely self-sustaining basis it was decided to charge using departments for the stores plus a mark-up sufficient to recover expected cash expenses plus depreciation of equipment. Stores issues for one year were forecast to be $100,000, at cost. Compute the mark-up rate.
5. Invoices for stores received were approved for payment in the amount of $10,145.
6. Vouchers outstanding were paid, as was payroll totaling $800.
7. Invoices were approved for payment: $10, water; $5, gas; $8, telephone; $20, electricity; and $8,000, stores.
8. Stores costing $12,000 were issued to the General Fund; an interfund invoice in the proper amount was prepared.
9. Vouchers outstanding were paid.
10. The Stores and Services Fund used stores of its own which had cost $100.
11. Adjusting and closing entries were recorded as of the end of the first month of operations.

b) Prepare a balance sheet for this fund as of the end of the fiscal year.

c) Prepare a statement of operations of this fund for one month in this fiscal year.

9–S. The City of Smithville does not have an intragovernmental service fund.

10

Special Assessment Funds

Special assessment funds, or local improvement funds as they are sometimes called, are established and operated to provide services that are of demonstrably greater benefit to a certain group of citizens than to others. More often, these services consist of providing permanent improvements of one kind or another; but they may be of current nature, such as street lighting, maintenance of parking areas, and maintenance of drainage ditches.[1] Funds for the latter type of services are comparable to special revenue funds, with assessments payable in one or two amounts; but they are in the nature of special assessments because the amounts of the assessments tend to vary directly in proportion to the amount of benefit received. Capital improvement projects commonly financed through the medium of special assessment funds include construction of streets, sidewalks, curbs, gutters, sewer systems, drainage ditches, etc. By way of contrast with special assessment projects are those construed to be of benefit to citizens generally, such as construction of public buildings, the cost thereof to be spread among all property owners within the unit's jurisdiction. Although the greater portion of special assessment project costs are borne by a group of specially benefited owners, the project may have some value to the general public, in which case a "contribution" may be levied against the general government so that all taxpayers of the unit will share to a degree in the cost. Furthermore, as owner of property within the area in which the improvement is to

[1] Special assessments are sometimes accounted for in a general fund or special revenue fund. This practice should be employed only for small projects. Special assessment funds providing service may operate on a continuing basis, as a general fund, and have a fund balance.

be made, the governmental unit itself may be assessed in the same manner and on the same basis as private owners.

Owing to the extensive use of special assessments for obtaining local improvements, the need for protecting property owners from capricious and arbitrary levies, and the great amount of detail involved in accounting for projects of any size, most states have enacted comprehensive legislation governing the operation and record keeping of special assessment funds. Local ordinances established under authority of the state legislation set forth the detailed provision of each special assessment, so special assessment fund accounting must conform to local regulations as well as to the more general law of the state. Among the most important points to be covered by special assessment regulations, including both state and local, are these:

1. The method of organizing projects and obtaining authorization for them. Authorization refers particularly to approval by those against whose properties the assessments will be levied.
2. How projects may be financed, with special reference to financing while assessments are in the process of collection.
3. Methods of distributing the cost of projects among the benefited property owners, supplemented by procedures for considering grievances.
4. The plan of collections, including the foreclosure procedure to be followed if other methods prove unsuccessful.

In special assessment accounting procedure, it is customary practice to use the words "Special Assessment" jointly in account titles referring to assessments, e.g., Special Assessments Receivable and Special Assessment Liens. To economize on time and space in this chapter, the word "Special" will be omitted from all such titles. It should be understood that this omission in no way alters the meaning of the title in which it occurs.

Recommendations by National Committee on Governmental Accounting

Changes in state laws, local ordinances, and opinions espoused by professional accounting organizations are responsible for variations and changes in accounting practices recommended for special assessment fund accounting. Recommendations of the National Committee on Governmental Accounting are probably the most influential of all, but changes in local law generally come slowly, and recommendations made in 1968 by the NCGA have not yet been adopted by all municipalities. Accordingly, the current recommendations are compared with the preceding recommendations in the tabulation on page 255.

Transaction or Situation	NCGA Recommendation: Former[2]	NCGA Recommendation: Current[3]
Formal authorization of project.	Debit Improvements Authorized; credit Appropriations.	No entry in ledger accounts.
Levy of assessments against property owners.	Debit Special Assessments Receivable; credit Improvements Authorized.	Debit Special Assessments Receivable; credit Fund Balance.
Authorization to issue bonds.	Memorandum entry: debit Unissued Bonds; credit Bonds Eligible to be Sold.	No entry in ledger accounts.
Accounting for cash designated for different purposes (construction, bond payment, etc).	Use a separate cash account for each different purpose (Cash for Construction, etc.).	No separation of cash in ledger accounts.
Accounting for excess or deficiency of assets for various purposes (construction, bond payment, etc.).	Use a separate equity account for each purpose group (Unappropriated Surplus–Construction; Unappropriated Surplus–Bond Payment, etc.).	Combine all equity items in Fund Balance account.

General Plan of Operation

The most common tangible basis for initiating special assessment projects is a petition by persons desiring some kind of permanent improvement of a public nature. Sometimes the petitioners may contemplate the financing of the project by the general government. If the major benefits expected to be derived are largely centered in one locality, the petition should be converted to the exact form prescribed by law for special assessment projects. A highly significant event in the project's progress is the formal authorization by the appropriate legislative body, frequently called the "board of works." Unless required by law, no ledger entry is mandatory for recording the project's final approval, but if one is desired the following would be properly descriptive:

Improvements Authorized	100,000	
Appropriations		100,000

Stated in nonaccounting terms, the entry says that the legislative body approves the spending of $100,000 (Appropriations credit) on a project and establishes a resource of like amount (Improvements Authorized), in this instance collection of assessments, to finance the improvements. If the formal entry approach is employed, an identification of the project

[2] National Committee on Governmental Accounting, *Municipal Accounting and Auditing*. Chicago, 1951. pp. 54–72.

[3] National Committee on Governmental Accounting, *Governmental Accounting, Auditing, and Financial Reporting*, Chicago, 1968. Chapter IX.

should be included in the Improvements Authorized title by adding "4th Street Sewer," "Project No. 22," or some similar wording.

The second major event in the project's history is the actual levying of assessments against the body of property owners designated in the organization of the project. The substance of this action is the conversion of a general proclamation of intention to assess (Improvements Authorized) into charges of ascertained amounts against individual property owners and their properties. "Their properties" is significant for the reason that unpaid special assessments have the legal force of liens against the properties to which they pertain. If no entry was made for a formal recording of the projects authorization, the assessment might be journalized as follows:

Assessments Receivable..................................	100,000	
Fund Balance..................................		100,000

Had a preceding entry recorded the assessment authorization, the credit account to be shown above would be Improvements Authorized.

In actual practice, if assessments are payable in installments, the debit member of the above entry should be divided into two parts to indicate amounts now due and amounts on which payments may be deferred to later periods. Assessments that have become due and are not paid within a stipulated period are classified as delinquent and sometimes incur a penalty; proper accounting requires the transfer of delinquent assessments into a special controlling account ordinarily called "Assessments Receivable—Delinquent." In supplementary records, amounts due from individual property owners must be shown in detail, as explained at greater length elsewhere in this chapter.

It will be noted that the above entry for recording assessments makes no provision for estimated losses. This differs from the revenue fund entry for recording property taxes, in which the amount of the credit to Revenue is only the difference between the total levy and an estimated amount of uncollectible taxes, recorded in a valuation reduction account. Perhaps the basic reason for assuming that all assessments will be collected, by one device or another, is that they represent liens upon real property; and, if necessary, resort may be made to legal seizure and sale of the property. Special assessments for improvements are presumed to increase the valuation of the property by at least the amount of the assessment; so, in theory, there should be no loss. In practice, the right of seizure and sale has not been an absolute safeguard against losses, particularly in times of financial stringency, nor for assessments on property in areas not fully developed. Recognizing that a certain amount of loss is almost inevitable for some types of projects in spite of all precautions to the contrary, some governmental units do provide an allowance for expected losses, thereby reducing the probability of a deficit and the necessity of obtaining supplementary financing from other sources.

Assessments are collected, and for these transactions the following entry may be made:

Cash..	100,000	
Assessments Receivable........................		100,000

In practice, collections do not occur in lump-sum amounts. For a given project, they may be spread in smaller amounts over a period of several years. General ledger credits must indicate whether amounts collected apply on delinquent, current, or deferred installments; and supporting details must show the amounts to be credited to each individual property owner participating in the payments and the exact installment, or installments, to which credits are to be applied.

Another fundamental transaction of special assessment funds is expenditure of money for the purpose or purposes contemplated in the establishment of the fund. Although most expenditures of this type of fund will normally be routed through the stages of encumbrance and liability before payment, in a manner to be illustrated later, the final effect is shown in the following entry:

Fund Balance................................	100,000	
Cash..		100,000

The results of the basic special assessment fund entries, through the one immediately preceding, may be summarized as follows:

1. Omitting a formal entry for project authorization—all accounts will be in balance after all cash has been expended.
2. Making a formal entry for the authorization—after the entry for expenditure of cash, Expenditures and Appropriations, each with a $100,000 balance, will be open. They should be disposed of by a closing entry.

In the foregoing entries the accounting framework of special assessment funds has been introduced and illustrated. Actual accounting for funds of this type must deal with many intricacies and complications, probably more than for other types of funds involving equal amounts of money. In the following sections, approved practices for treating these situations will be set forth in considerable detail.

Interim Financing

Special assessments, except for current services, are rarely, if ever, collected in lump-sum amounts, as is illustrated in a preceding entry for the collection of assessments. To avoid undue hardship on property owners, assessments may be payable in installments over several years, which means that interim financing must be resorted to if accomplishment of the project is to be effected in the near future. Furthermore, on account of the uncertain cost of large-scale public improvements, it may be advantageous to defer even the levying of the assessment until more nearly exact information is available about the total cost of the project; and this postponement of the levy moves still further into the future the final collection of installments.

To provide means for immediate financing of improvements, governmental units may issue bonds. This action should have been provided for in the original plans for the project in order that authority to issue the bonds could be obtained from affected property owners when they voted upon the proposed improvement. Three possibilities exist for dealing with the bond authorization. One is to make no ledger entry for it. A second is to debit Bonds Authorized—Unissued and credit Bonds Payable. The third would debit Unissued Bonds and credit Bonds Eligible to be Issued. Following the first authorization procedure, sale of the bonds would be recorded by a Cash debit and Bonds Payable credit. Following the second, the credit would be to Bonds Authorized—Unissued, leaving Bonds Payable to record the bond liability. Following the third, the authorization entry would be canceled by reversal and Bonds Payable would be credited for the cash received. It should be noted that whichever authorization and issue procedure is followed the ultimate result is:

Cash	100,000	
Bonds Payable		100,000

It is probable that the first and second procedures would be the choices of the three. It is noteworthy that bonds issued by a special assessment fund become liabilities of the issuing fund, to be paid from assessments and collections made by it.

In the above discussion, no indication has been given as to the factor or factors determining the amount of the bond issue. It is not necessarily the total cost of the project. If assessments are levied early in the course of the project, with early maturity of some installments, the bond issue need not be for the full cost of the improvement because installment collections will provide a portion of the early financing. Another plan which may reduce the amount required to be raised from bonds is the use of an intragovernmental service fund to provide direct financing or even to perform the actual work, with reimbursement to follow completion of the project. In the meantime, one or more of the earlier installments might have been collected, thus reducing the amount to be raised through the use of bonds.

Another form of interim financing which is sometimes used precedes the issue of bonds. This is the use of short-term notes. A large-scale use of this method includes financing all or most of the cost of the project through the issuance of notes, which are subsequently retired when the required amount of the bond issue has been definitely ascertained. If the required amount of the bond issue can be determined early in the course of the project, use of short-term notes may be limited to immediate requirements for engineering, planning, and other preliminary costs. Notes of the kind referred to in this section are frequently characterized as "bond anticipation notes." If immediate financial requirements are small and the law permits, an advance from the general fund may obviate the necessity of using notes. Entries for transactions associated with financing by notes are as follows:

	Debit	Credit
Cash	25,000	
Bond Anticipation Notes Payable		25,000
Issuance of notes for estimated cash requirements pending bond issue.		
Cash	200,000	
Bonds Payable		200,000
To record the sale of bonds at par.		

If laws, ordinances, or departmental requirements require the use of special cash accounts, "Cash" in the first entry would become "Cash for Construction." In the second entry "Cash for Notes" would be debited for $25,000, and "Cash for Construction" debited for $175,000.

Features of Special Assessment Bonds

The primary security for special assessment bonds is the levy against properties for their portion of the project cost. In theory, no other security should be necessary because, in the event of continued default in payments, the governmental unit may foreclose on the benefited property. Although a public improvement may increase the physical value of the property, it may not be possible to find a buyer for it, on account of business and economic conditions or other factors tending to make the property currently unsalable for the amount of charges against it. To improve the marketability of special assessment bonds, the governmental unit may permit its full faith and credit to be pledged as security for their payment, in the event that collections from benefited properties are insufficient to pay the debt. This feature also generally qualifies the bonds for a lower interest rate since interest on general obligation bonds is exempt from Federal income tax.

If the fund bonds are secondarily secured by the full faith and credit of the governmental unit, they are commonly described as "general obligation special assessment bonds," or more briefly as "general special assessment bonds"; whereas if security is limited to the benefited properties, they are referred to as "special-special assessment bonds." Within the latter type of bonds, there are three recognized classes, the peculiar characteristics of which have significant accounting implications:

1. Least restrictive of the group are special-special assessment bonds which may be paid, without reference to individual bonds, from collections of installments on certain pieces of property.

2. In some instances, specific bonds of the issue must be paid only from collections of installments on certain pieces of property.
3. In the most extreme case, specific bonds must be paid only from collections of certain installments of assessments against certain properties.

These limitations call for the exercise of extreme care in matching installment collections with the bonds to which they may legally be applied and in the management of foreclosure proceedings when installments lapse into actionable default.

Both "general obligation special assessment bonds" and "special-special assessment bonds" must be accounted for as debt of the special assessment fund since the intent is that they be serviced from special assessment resources. The municipality is, however, contingently liable for servicing the "general obligation special assessment bonds" in case the special assessment fund does not pay interest and principal when due. The contingent liability is disclosed by a footnote to the Statement of General Long-Term Debt. A suggested form for such a footnote is:

> In addition to the long-term debt exhibited in this statement, the City of ________ has a contingent liability against its full faith and credit on $____________ of special assessment bonds recorded in the Special Assessment Fund. The general credit of the municipality is obligated only to the extent that liens foreclosed against properties involved in the special assessment district are insufficient to retire outstanding bonds.[4]

The footnote to the Statement of General Long-Term Debt should fully disclose the effect of the general obligation special assessment bonds upon the bonding power of the governmental unit. The importance of such disclosure is discussed in Chapter 13 of this text.

Accounting for Assessments

One of the early requirements in the operation of a special assessment fund is determination of what parcels of property should be included within the "benefit district," the name given to the area that will receive assessable benefits, and how the total expected cost should be allocated to the parcels of property. There is no universal formula or general rule for determining the limits of the benefit district and none for graduating assessments against the benefited properties. Assessments for operation of sewage disposal plants may be based upon usage of water, which is reasonably objective; but even so, the use of a sewage plant does not vary proportionately with the volume of water consumption. Streets may be presumed to represent greater values to owners of property adjacent thereto, but they are likely to be used by many other residents of the

[4] *Governmental Accounting, Auditing, and Financial Reporting,* p. 101.

particular neighborhood and to increase neighborhood property values. The exact definition of the benefit district and the scaling of individual assessments therein are matters of judgment to be supplemented by arbitrary rules and regulations which should strive for uniformity of treatment among property owners in similar situations.

After the limits of the benefit district have been decided upon and some method or scheme for distributing the cost has been selected, the next step is one of determining the amounts of assessments against individual properties. Compilations of individual assessments are called "assessment rolls" or "assessment ledgers," both of which are subsidiary records for showing all transactions with owners of each property in the district. Forms of assessment rolls or ledgers vary, but all must provide for showing at least the following basic facts:

1. Identification of the improvement or project.
2. Legal description of the property in terms of location.
3. Name and address of owner.
4. Amount of assessment.
5. Number of installments or detailed listing of installments with due dates.
6. Charges for interest on unpaid assessments.
7. Record of collection of all charges.

One form of assessment record consists of a multicolumnar spread sheet, on which each property is given a single line, with individual properties listed vertically on the sheet. Division of the assessment into installments, interest charges, and credits for collections is provided by a series of parallel columns. The general plan of this form is shown in Illustration 10–1. The installments section of Illustration 10–1 may be expanded to provide for the number of installments into which the assessment is divided. A modification of the roll form of record in Illustration 10–1

Illustration 10–1

CITY OF STANFORD
Special Assessment Roll
Public Improvement Project No. 73

Legal Description of Property	Name and Address of Property Owner	Amount of Assessment	Installment No. 1			Installment No. 2		
			Date Paid	*Principal*	*Interest*	*Date Paid*	*Principal*	*Interest*
Lot 10, Seminary Addition	George M. Robinson	$840	8-10-x8	$84		8-26-x9	$84	$30.24
Lot 11, Seminary Addition	John E. Baugh	900	8-23-x8	90		8-31-x9	90	32.40

consists of listing vertically the original installments for each property, with columns extended to the right for recording such information as adjustments, collections, interest, etc. This means that if the assessment is payable in 10 installments, 11 lines (one for the total of all installments) will be given to each property.

An alternative assessment record consists of a separate card, segment of magnetic tape, or other file device, for each parcel of property, referred to as a Special Assessment Ledger. One attribute of the Special Assessment Ledger is that it gives an opportunity for showing more details about each assessment, without producing a record too cumbersome for convenient handling. Whatever, form is used for the special assessment ledger, each account should contain the information shown in Illustration 10–2.

Illustration 10–2

SPECIAL ASSESSMENT LEDGER ACCOUNT

Property: Lot No. 10, Seminary Addition
Owner: George M. Robinson

Project No.: 73
Description: Sewer
Total Assessment: $840

			Collections				
Installment No.	*Due Date*	*Amount*	*Date*	*Receipt No.*	*Principal*	*Interest*	*Remarks*
1 . . .	Sept. 1, 19x8	$84	Aug. 10, 19x8	139	$84		
2 . . .	Sept. 1, 19x9	84	Aug. 26, 19x9	365	84	$30.24	

Since the assessment roll or Special Assessment Ledger is subsidiary to the general ledger assessments receivable accounts, special care in recording transactions, supplemented by frequent reconcilements, is necessary to keep the subsidiary and control records in agreement. Without going into a detailed discussion concerning the operation of the various installment accounts, it may be said that the following relationships must exist for accurate records:

1. When an assessment is levied and recorded in the general ledger, the amount debited to the Assessments Receivable account or accounts must equal the total of the assessments shown by the detailed assessment records. If one installment is now due, the amount of that installment as shown by the assessment records should be debited to Assessments Receivable—Current. The amounts of all other installments, as shown by the assessment records, should be debited to Assessments Receivable—Deferred.

2. When the period arrives for payment of an installment that has heretofore been classified as deferrred, the total amount of this installment as shown by the assessment roll or ledger should be debited to Assessments Receivable—Current and credited to Assessments Receivable—Deferred.

3. When the period for payment of an installment has passed, the unpaid balance of Assessments Receivable—Current should be transferred to Assessments Receivable—Delinquent by a credit to the former and a debit to the latter. Assuming that installment No. 2 is the one being converted to the delinquent classification, the balance transferred must equal the total of unpaid balances of installment No. 2 in the assessments records.

Forced Collections

Effective administration of special assessment collections requires definite rules for the addition of interest to delinquent installments and for the initiation and prosecution of foreclosure action when a certain stage of delinquency, frequently two years' installments, has been reached. Laxity in the application and collection of interest leads to further delinquency and tends to increase the number of assessments for which foreclosure actions are necessary. Completed foreclosure actions are of two kinds. In one case, contingent title to the property, subject to redemption within a stipulated period, is sold to a third party. In the other case, contingent title is taken by the special assessment fund itself.

Some governmental units sell installment delinquent property by requiring the purchaser to pay only costs of holding sale, accrued interest against the property, and those installments now due or past due. Thus the buyer is subrogated for the previous owner by doing two things:

1. Paying all charges and installments due and payable to date.
2. Assuming responsibility for payment of deferred installments plus interest charges thereon.

On the other hand, the buyer may be required to pay *all* installments and all other charges in order to obtain provisional title. This more drastic requirement is justified by the fact that the buyer acquires the property (provisionally) in an arm's-length transaction in which he was not compelled to participate. The previous owner had no choice, since his property was located in the benefit district. Deferral of installments was a device to lighten the burden of what may have been an involuntary debt. Explanations and illustrations in the following paragraphs will relate to total collection sales since they include all elements of the partial payment sales. For present purposes it is being assumed that the special assessment fund to which the discussion and illustrations pertain is being operated under regulations or other circumstances which do not require segregation of cash to be used for different purposes.

Special assessment laws prescribe procedures to be followed when foreclosure proceedings must be employed to collect installments. They include, among other things, legal notification to the property owner of the intention to offer his property for sale and public advertising of the intended sale. As indicated above, costs of these actions become an additional charge against the property. Assuming the total costs of holding the sale to be $200, the following entry would be made:

Cost of Holding Sale	200	
Cash		200

Below is illustrated a complete entry for sale of property, amounts assumed:

Cash	2,120	
Assessments Receivable—Delinquent		300
Assessments Receivable—Current		150
Assessments Receivable—Deferred		1,350
Interest Receivable		120
Cost of Holding Sale		200

Recovering the cost of holding the property sale eliminates the Cost of Holding Sale account, which may be characterized as a suspense account. In the above examples, it proved to be an asset, in the form of a charge that was eventually paid by the successful bidder for the property. In case the special assessment fund had taken title to the property and subsequently transferred it to the general government without compensation, Cost of Holding Sale would have terminated as an expense account, to be charged off as later illustrated.

As indicated previously, especially for properties not fully developed, third parties may not offer the full amount of charges against the property, with the result that the special assessment fund acquires the property with only provisional title. Assuming the same charges against the property as before, the following entry would be made:

Assessment Sale Certificates	2,120	
Assessments Receivable—Delinquent		300
Assessments Receivable—Current		150
Assessments Receivable—Deferred		1,350
Interest Receivable		120
Cost of Holding Sale		200

The effect of the above entry is to accumulate all values represented by the assortment of charges against the property into one asset account, Assessment Sale Certificates, which represents provisional ownership of the property. Provisional ownership may be converted into cash, for use in carrying out the improvement project, through redemption by the previous owner within the time allotted by law; or it may be sold, either to private buyers or to another unit of the government. Regardless of the transferee, the special assessment fund should receive cash to cover all charges accumulated in the Assessment Sale Certificates account. This would call for the same detailed accounting as if the amounts had been collected in due course without foreclosure. Transfer of the assessment sale certificate for cash in full would require an entry such as the following:

Cash	2,120	
Assessment Sale Certificates		2,120

Special assessment fund administrations have often found it necessary to take absolute title to property for which no buyer could be found. This experience has been most frequent in connection with special assessment projects in undeveloped areas. Since a special assessment fund is not constituted for permanent ownership of real estate, property which cannot be sold must be transferred to another fund or to the general fixed assets group of accounts. The amount accumulated in the Assessment Sale Certificates account with respect to a given property represents charges that had been set up against the property as assessments and interest receivable, which the fund management had expected to convert into cash for payment of construction, bonds, and interest costs. If the amount of the assessment sale certificate is to be extinguished by a no-charge disposal of the property, the effect is a reduction of the amounts available for the three purposes stated above.

Accounts to be used for recording the disposal depend upon whether the fund is required to maintain a separation of assets and equities (fund balance) pertaining to its construction and its debt service activities, i.e., payment of debts and interest. If such is not the case a two-member entry is sufficient.

Fund Balance	2,120	
Assessment Sales Certificates		2,120

Illustrative Transactions and Entries

As indicated in earlier parts of this chapter, the life history of a special assessment fund may be of long duration from the original authorization to the final payment on the indebtedness. However, most kinds of transactions typical of a special assessment fund are likely to occur in the early years of its existence. The majority of these typical transactions are included in the example to follow. Since foreclosures are discussed in the preceding section, they are omitted from the transactions illustrated below.

In compliance with all pertinent laws and regulations, a special assessment project for the construction of a storm sewer was authorized by the city of X at an estimated cost of $750,000. This legal action is comparable to the enactment of a budget for a revenue fund; however, present recommendations of the National Committee on Governmental

Accounting favor omission, or memorandum recording, of what might be called the budgetary entry.

To cover preliminary costs pending more extensive financing, a temporary loan was obtained from the general fund in the amount of $60,000:

	Debit	Credit
1. Cash	60,000	
Due to General Fund		60,000

Bids were opened and a contract let for the main construction project in the amount of $650,000:

	Debit	Credit
2. Encumbrances	650,000	
Reserve for Encumbrances		650,000

Based on the contract mentioned above, and taking into account other probable costs, an assessment roll was prepared in the amount of $600,000 with $120,000 additional to be contributed by the city. Assessments were to be paid in 10 equal installments, and it was anticipated that the city's share would be paid in two equal installments. The first installment and the city's share of the cost were to be used for construction, whereas collections from the remaining installments were to be used for bond retirement:

	Debit	Credit
3. Assessments Receivable—Current	60,000	
Assessments Receivable—Deferred	540,000	
Due from General Fund	120,000	
Fund Balance		720,000

(Had a budgetary entry been made to record authorization of the project, the credit above would have been replaced by a $720,000 credit to Improvements Authorized.)

Engineering and other preliminary costs related to the construction project were paid in the amount of $50,000:

	Debit	Credit
4. Expenditures	50,000	
Cash		50,000

(Although recorded as a direct cash payment, this transaction might have been routed through a voucher system and recorded in a Vouchers Payable account before actual payment. For brevity, in the examples to follow, expenditure transactions will not be recorded as vouchers payable before disbursement.)

A bond issue not to exceed $600,000, was duly authorized; bonds in the amount of $250,000 were sold at par:

	Debit	Credit
5. Cash	250,000	
Bonds Payable		250,000

(If required by law or other regulation, the bond authorization might have been formally recorded by a debit to Bonds Authorized—Unissued and a credit to Bonds Payable, in which case the sale of the bonds would have required a credit to the former account.)

In compliance with the terms of the construction contract, the contractor submitted a bill for partial payment based on the supervising engineer's certification of 40 percent completion:

		Debit	Credit
6.	Reserve for Encumbrances	260,000	
	Encumbrances		260,000
	Expenditures	260,000	
	Contracts Payable		260,000

Interest receivable accrued on assessments during the first year amounted to $12,000.

		Debit	Credit
7.	Interest Receivable	12,000	
	Interest Revenues		12,000

During the first year, one half of the city's share of the cost and 90 percent of the current assessment, with interest, were collected:

		Debit	Credit
8.	Cash	124,800	
	Due From General Fund		60,000
	Assessments Receivable—Current		54,000
	Interest Receivable		10,800

Unpaid assessments due in the current year were transferred to the delinquent classification:

		Debit	Credit
9.	Assessments Receivable—Delinquent	6,000	
	Assessments Receivable—Current		6,000

The contractor's bill, less 5 percent retained as a performance guaranty, was paid:

		Debit	Credit
10.	Contracts Payable	260,000	
	Cash		247,000
	Contracts Payable—Retained Percentage		13,000

The advance from the general fund was repaid:

		Debit	Credit
11.	Due to General Fund	60,000	
	Cash		60,000

Unpaid bond interest accumulated at the end of the year amounted to $7,500.

		Debit	Credit
12.	Interest Expense	7,500	
	Interest Payable		7,500

A trial balance of the above special assessment fund, assuming December 31, 19x8, as the date, is shown in Illustration 10–3.

Closing entries for the fund at December 31, 19x8, are:

		Debit	Credit
13.	Fund Balance	700,000	
	Expenditures		310,000
	Encumbrances		390,000
14.	Interest Revenues	12,000	
	Interest Expense		7,500
	Fund Balance		4,500

Illustration 10–3

CITY OF X
Storm Sewer Special Assessment Fund
Trial Balance, December 31, 19x8

	Debit	Credit
Cash	$ 77,800	
Assessments receivable–delinquent	6,000	
Assessments receivable–deferred	540,000	
Due from general fund	60,000	
Interest receivable	1,200	
Interest payable		$ 7,500
Contracts payable–retained percentage		13,000
Bonds payable		250,000
Reserve for encumbrances		390,000
Fund balance		720,000
Interest revenues		12,000
Expenditures	310,000	
Encumbrances	390,000	
Interest expense	7,500	
	$1,392,500	$1,392,500

Comments on Closing Entries

Closing Encumbrances in a special assessment fund at the end of a period before the project is completed is not a necessity, for the same reasons as discussed in the chapter relating to Capital Projects Funds: authorizations to spend are primarily on a project basis, possibly supplemented by memorandum allocations by periods as a means of better control over a multiperiod project. Additions to the cost of general fixed assets being constructed or acquired by special assessment funds are made (in the General Fixed Assets Group of accounts) on the basis of expenditures during a period, therefore it is desirable to summarize the special assessment fund expenditures at the end of each period. A reason for closing Encumbrances, as well as Expenditures, at year-end, is to facilitate preparation of special assessment fund financial statements on the same bases as the statements of other funds.

Similarly, as is true of Capital Projects funds, it is desirable to reestablish the Encumbrances account at the beginning of the following period by reversing the appropriate portion of the prior period's closing entry.

Illustrative Balance Sheet

A balance sheet as of December 31, 19x8, for the special assessment fund of the City of X is shown as Illustration 10–4.

Concurrently with balance sheet preparation a schedule, or schedules, should be drawn from the special assessment roll or ledger, showing delinquent and deferred assessments and interest payable by individual properties and property owners. Totals shown by these schedules must

Illustration 10–4

CITY OF X
Storm Sewer Special Assessment Fund
Balance Sheet, December 31, 19x8

Assets

Cash		$ 77,800
Assessments receivable:		
Delinquent	$ 6,000	
Deferred	$540,000	546,000
Due from general fund		60,000
Interest receivable		1,200
Total Assets		$685,000

Liabilities, Reserve, and Fund Balance

Liabilities:		
Interest payable	$ 7,500	
Contracts payable–retained percentage	13,000	
Bonds payable	250,000	
Total Liabilities		$270,500
Reserve for encumbrances		390,000
Fund balance		24,500
Total Liabilities, Reserve, and Fund Balance		$685,000

agree with the appropriate controls—delinquent assessments receivable, deferred assessments receivable, and interest receivable—in the general ledger.

Illustrative Entries for Second Year

In the following transactions and entries for the second year, it is assumed that the construction project is finished, together with the closing of accounts related to the construction, leaving mainly the collection of assessments and payment of bonds to the remaining periods.

The encumbrances closed at the end of 19x8 were reestablished in the Encumbrances account:

1. Encumbrances	390,000	
Fund Balance		390,000

The second installment became due:

2. Assessments Receivable—Current	60,000	
Assessments Receivable—Deferred		60,000

An order for additional work was issued to an Intragovernmental Service Fund, the estimated cost being $20,000.

3. Encumbrances	20,000	
Reserve for Encumbrances		20,000

Interest charged to property owners' accounts during the year amounted to $31,000:

	Account	Debit	Credit
4.	Interest Receivable	31,000	
	Interest Revenues		31,000

Collections on current assessments during the year amounted to $52,000, along with $29,000 for interest receivable and the balance of the city's share of the cost:

	Account	Debit	Credit
5.	Cash	141,000	
	Due from General Fund		60,000
	Assessments Receivable—Current		52,000
	Interest Receivable		29,000

Collections of delinquent assessments during the year totaled $3,000 with interest collections of $1,700, of which $1,200 had previously been accrued:

	Account	Debit	Credit
6.	Cash	4,700	
	Assessments Receivable—Delinquent		3,000
	Interest Receivable		1,200
	Interest Revenue		500

Of the remaining authorized bonds, $290,000 par value were sold at 101 plus accrued interest, which amounted to $2,800.

	Account	Debit	Credit
7.	Cash	295,700	
	Premium on Bonds		2,900
	Interest Expense		2,800
	Bonds Payable		290,000

The contractor presented a bill for the balance of his contract:

	Account	Debit	Credit
8.	Reserve for Encumbrances	390,000	
	Encumbrances		390,000
	Expenditures	390,000	
	Contracts Payable		390,000

Bond interest paid during the year amounted to $16,000, including the $7,500 accrued at the end of last year:

	Account	Debit	Credit
9.	Interest Payable	7,500	
	Interest Expense	8,500	
	Cash		16,000

(An entry could have been made at the beginning of this year to reverse the adjusting entry which recorded accumulated bond interest. If that had been done, the two above debits would have been joined in a single debit to Interest Expense for $16,000.)

The Intragovernmental Service Fund presented a bill for $18,000 for services performed, and the encumbrance was cancelled in full. Payment was made:

	Account	Debit	Credit
10.	Reserve for Encumbrances	20,000	
	Encumbrances		20,000
	Expenditures	18,000	
	Cash		18,000

The contractor's bill, less 5 percent retained, was paid:

		Debit	Credit
11.	Contracts Payable	390,000	
	Contracts Payable—Retained Percentage		19,500
	Cash		370,500

Bonds payable of $50,000 par value were paid; interest on these bonds amounting to $1,000 was also paid.

12.	Bonds Payable	50,000	
	Interest Expense	1,000	
	Cash		51,000

Unpaid current assessments were declared delinquent:

13.	Assessments Receivable—Delinquent	8,000	
	Assessments Receivable—Current		8,000

Interest accrued on bonds at the end of the year amounted to $15,000:

14.	Interest Expense	15,000	
	Interest Payable		15,000

A trial balance of the storm sewer special assessment fund at December 31, 19x9 would appear as shown in Illustration 10–5.

Illustration 10–5

CITY OF X
Storm Sewer Special Assessment Fund
Trial Balance, December 31, 19x9

	Debit	*Credit*
Cash	$ 63,700	
Assessments receivable–delinquent	11,000	
Assessments receivable–deferred	480,000	
Interest receivable	2,000	
Interest payable		$ 15,000
Contracts payable–retained percentage		32,500
Bonds payable		490,000
Fund balance		414,500
Interest revenues		31,500
Premium on bonds		2,900
Expenditures	408,000	
Interest expense	21,700	
	$986,400	$986,400

Appropriate closing entries for December 31, 19x9, would be as follows. (It is assumed that the bonds sold at a premium will mature in ten years; therefore 10% of the premium is amortized per year on the straight-line basis):

15a.	Premium on Bonds	290	
	Interest Expense		290
15b.	Fund Balance	397,910	
	Interest Revenues	31,500	
	Expenditures		408,000
	Interest Expense		21,410

A balance sheet of the fund at December 31, 19x9 would appear as shown in Illustration 10–6.

Illustration 10–6

CITY OF X
Storm Sewer Special Assessment Fund
Balance Sheet, December 31, 19x9

Assets		
Cash		$ 63,700
Assessments receivable:		
Delinquent	$ 11,000	
Deferred	480,000	491,000
Interest receivable		2,000
Total Assets		$556,700
Liabilities and Fund Balance		
Liabilities:		
Interest payable		$ 15,000
Contracts payable–retained percentage		32,500
Bonds payable, at par	$490,000	
Premium on bonds	2,610	492,610
Total Liabilities		$540,110
Fund balance		16,590
Total Liabilities and Fund Balance		$556,700

Two other kinds of statements of value in special assessment fund accounting and reporting are statements of cash receipts and disbursements, and analyses of changes in fund balance, shown in Illustrations 10–7 and 10–8.

Combined and Other Statements

For the purpose of reducing the bulk of municipal annual reports it is common practice to prepare columnar statements so that information relating to all special assessment funds may be *combined.* (Each special assessment fund is a legal entity, so the statements should not be *consolidated.*) In those jurisdictions in which it is necessary to keep separate cash accounts, and Fund Balance accounts, for construction, bond repayment, and interest payments, it is also common practice to prepare columnar statements to demonstrate that the fund has complied with legal requirements. Illustration 10–9 shows a Statement of Cash Receipts and Disbursements for the City of X on the assumption that three cash accounts are required; this statement should be compared with Illustration 10–7, which assumes that cash segregation is not required.

Assessment Rebates

Assessment rebates include reductions of amounts now charged to beneficiaries of the fund and refunds of amounts already collected. Trans-

Illustration 10–7

CITY OF X
Storm Sewer Special Assessment Fund
Statement of Cash Receipts and Disbursements, 19x9

Items	
Balance, December 31, 19x8	$ 77,800
Receipts:	
Collection of delinquent assessments	$ 3,000
Collection of city's share of cost—one half	60,000
Sale of bonds	290,000
Collection of 19x9 installment	52,000
Premium on sale of bonds	2,900
Collection of interest on bonds sold between interest dates	2,800
Collection of interest on installments	30,700
Total receipts	$441,400
Total beginning balance and receipts	$519,200
Disbursements:	
Payments on construction contract	$370,500
Other construction expenditure	18,000
Regular interest payment on bonds	16,000
Payment of interest on bonds at retirement	1,000
Retirement of bonds	50,000
Total disbursements	$455,500
Balance, December 31, 19x9	$ 63,700

Illustration 10–8

CITY OF X
Storm Sewer Special Assessment Fund
Analysis of Change in Fund Balance, 19x9

Project Authorization	$750,000
Fund balance, December 31, 19x8:	$ 24,500
Additions:	
Reestablishment of 19x8 encumbrances closed at December 31, 19x8	$390,000
Interest revenue earned	31,500
Total additions	$421,500
Total beginning balance and additions	$446,000
Deductions:	
Expenditures	$408,000
Interest expense incurred; Less bond premium amortized	21,410
Total deductions	429,410
Fund balance, December 31, 19x9	$ 16,590

Illustration 10–9

CITY OF X
Storm Sewer Special Assessment Fund
Statement of Cash Receipts and Disbursements, 19x9

Items	*Total*	*Construction*	*Bonds*	*Interes*
Balances, December 31, 19x8	$ 77,800	$ 67,000	None	$10,80
Receipts:				
Collection of delinquent assessments	$ 3,000	$ 3,000		
Collection of city's share of cost–one half	60,000	60,000		
Sale of bonds	290,000	290,000		
Collection of 19x9 installment	52,000		$52,000	
Premium on sale of bonds	2,900			$ 2,90
Collection of interest on bonds sold between interest dates	2,800			2,80
Collection of interest on installments	30,700			30,70
Total receipts	$441,400	$353,000	$52,000	$36,40
Total beginning balance and receipts	$519,200	$420,000	$52,000	$47,20
Disbursements:				
Payments on construction contract	$370,500	$370,500		
Other construction expenditure	18,000	18,000		
Regular interest payment on bonds	16,000			$16,00
Payment of interest on bonds at retirement	1,000			1,00
Retirement of bonds	50,000		$50,000	
Total disbursements	$455,500	$388,500	$50,000	$17,00
Balances, December 31, 19x9	$ 63,700	$ 31,500	$ 2,000	$30,20

actions of the first kind, commonly called "abatements," are more numerous than refunds. Rebates will be discussed in two groups, based upon the reason for the adjustment.

Rebates of one kind are brought about by errors in the assessment levy, the word "error" being used here in a very general sense. More specifically, rebates of this sort are based upon findings that certain individual assessments are in excess of the amount legally owed; in fact, the entire amount of some individual assessments may be canceled. More common causes of adjustments falling in this category are incorrect classification of property, arithmetical errors in calculation of assessment, errors in description of property, and exceeding the legal limit of assessment based on ratio to property value. Standard procedures are usually prescribed for presentation and consideration of claims based upon alleged overassessment. A finding in favor of the claimant calls for a rebate of the amount allowed by the reviewing body, but this allowance will not necessarily be equal to the amount claimed.

Journalizing a rebate of this kind usually calls for canceling all or part of the original assessment, this assertion being predicated upon the assumption that payments are likely to be withheld while the amount of the assessment is in dispute. Credits for the rebate will depend upon the present classification of installments, that is, their distribution as to delinquent, current, and deferred. Assuming a rebate of 25 percent on a $600 assessment, of which $60 is now current and the balance deferred, the following entry would be required:

Fund Balance[5]	150	
Assessments Receivable—Current		15
Assessments Receivable—Deferred		135

Special care should be observed in explaining the above entry and in posting to the Special Assessments Ledger, in order to guard against suspicions of irregularity in reducing the amount shown as owing. If payments of installments and interest have been made before the granting of the rebate, proportionate amounts of cash may be refunded, thus requiring modification of the credit members of the above entry.

Rebates of the second kind apply to all property owners within the benefit district and are brought about by completion of the project at a total cost which is less than the amount levied against the properties, plus any amount to be contributed by the governmental unit. Excess levies are likely to occur only when enacted before the total cost of the improvement is known. In general, an excess assessment is indicated when a project nears completion at an estimated total cost which is substantially less than the amount which apparently will be produced by the total of assessments and grants.

The existence of a construction surplus having been ascertained, it remains to decide upon when and how to dispose of the balance. From an administrative standpoint, rebates should be withheld beyond all reasonable possibility that widespread defaults on assessments and losses in foreclosure might impair the fund's ability to pay bonds as they mature. Furthermore, statutory regulations may even prohibit the rebating of assessments until the bonds are paid in full. An important factor in judging probable collectibility of unpaid installments is the ratio of assessment balances to the value of properties to which they apply, taking into account other possible liens, such as property taxes.

Even though a construction excess exists, it may not be rebated. First, it may be so small that the cost of distribution would exceed the amount to be distributed. Unless rebating is specifically required by law, a small credit in Fund Balance may, at the discretion of the special assessment fund governing body, be transferred to some other fund. If the excess is to be rebated, the amount, here assumed to be $25,000, may be closed as follows:

Fund Balance	25,000	
Reserve for Rebates		25,000

If the construction excess were in the form of cash, to be refunded to property owners, Rebates Payable might well be substituted as the

[5] If proceeds of assessments are restricted as to purposes (construction, bonds, etc.), the fund balance debit should be divided to show any difference which may be required by the restrictions.

credit member of the above entry. A contruction excess embodied partly in cash and partly in uncollected assessments should be apportioned according to law or, if no legal restrictions apply, in some manner equitable to all property owners. The division of the rebate between cash and credit having been determined, in this case \$10,000 cash and \$15,000 credit, for illustration, the following entry might be made:

Reserve for Rebates	25,000	
Rebates Payable		10,000
Assessments Receivable		15,000

The credit to Assessments Receivable should be divided between delinquent, current, and deferred assessments according to a decision by the governing body. Needless to say, the credit members of the above entry must be supported by detailed schedules by properties and owners, with Assessments Receivable details posted to the Special Assessments Ledger. Rebates Payable will be liquidated by cash disbursements, the entries for which are obvious.

Construction Deficits

A construction deficit may arise from one or both of two causes, set forth below:

1. Excess of total project cost over the total amount levied against property owners and the governmental unit, plus any supplementary contributions from other sources. This condition is most likely to arise when assessments are levied before the total cost of the project is ascertained.
2. Large-scale defaulting of installments, coupled with inability to dispose of foreclosed properties for the amount of charges standing against them.

Three general possibilities are available for elimination of construction deficits, the one to be selected depending upon such factors as the amount of the deficiency, laws and ordinances governing special assessments, and local circumstances:

1. If the deficit is of small amount, it may be covered by a transfer from other improvement funds, if permitted by law, or by a contribution from a revenue fund, general or special.
2. If sufficient help is not available from other improvement funds, even a sizable deficit might be covered by the general government in preference to levying and collecting additional amounts from owners of property located in the benefit district.
3. Deficiencies of major proportions are likely to call for additional or supplemental assessments. The nature of supplemental assessments is of such importance that the next section is devoted to the subject.

If the deficit is eliminated by direct receipt of cash from some other fund, the following simple entry (amount assumed) will suffice:

Cash	2,000	
Fund Balance		2,000

Accounting for Supplemental Assessments

Supplemental assessments are, as the name indicates, charges to property owners in addition to the original levy which was made to cover the cost of the improvement. They may be resorted to for one or the other of two purposes, as follows:

1. To finance a deficiency brought about by losses in the collection of installments, in amounts of such size that incidental aid from other funds would be inadequate.
2. To finance improvement costs materially in excess of the original estimate, as well as costs for additions to the original project.

As with other phases of special assessment activities, supplemental levies should comply with all applicable laws and ordinances, particularly with respect to the rights of affected property owners. To record a supplemental assessment of $15,000 for eliminating a construction deficit, the following entry might be made:

Assessments Receivable—Supplemental	15,000	
Fund Balance		15,000

The above entry establishes a separate control account for the extra levy, and a new subsidiary record for property owners is required. Supplemental assessments, if of considerable amount, may be payable by installments, with the same accounting procedures as used for the original levy. However, the use of a new control and new subsidiary accounts is not mandatory: the additional levy may be regarded as an expansion of the first one and prorated over the subsequent installments of the original. The increased assessment would then be debited to Assessments Receivable—Deferred and entered in the assessment ledger accounts already established. It may be that not all deficit and additional financing is supplied by property owners. If the governmental unit was charged for a part of the original estimate, it may be expected to bear part of the additional cost. To record this fact would require a debit to Due From General Fund (or other fund or unit) along with the charge to Assessments Receivable—Deferred.

Inadequacy of the original budget to cover the cost of the project is indicated if total charges to Expenditures and Encumbrances closely approach the original authorization, with a substantial part of the project estimated cost not yet recorded. Upon official action of the appropriate governing body to increase the total authorization, an assessment levy is legal and may be made when needed to help finance the fund project, which may be immediately or some weeks or months hence.

When the levy has been established, it would be recorded in the usual manner for a special assessment, debiting Assessments Receivable—Current (or Deferred) or Assessments Receivable—Supplemental, as required by the proposed manner of collection. Although discussed in connection with construction deficits, supplemental assessments may be initiated to provide funds for bond payments, also.

Termination of Special Assessment Funds

Terminating the affairs of a special assessment fund is a twofold responsibility. One, bringing to a close the transactions and records for its expenditure transactions, is relatively simple of accomplishment in both time and manner. The other, settling its financing activities, may be attended by delay and some measure of difficulty. It may be that holders of some bonds cannot be located and some assessments cannot be collected until well after the scheduled date of payment of collection.

After all legitimate costs of the project, excluding those of a financial nature, have been recorded in Expenditures this account is closed to Fund Balance. If the project has extended into two or more fiscal periods, it may be that expenditures have been closed into Fund Balance at the end of each prior period, leaving a relatively small amount to be closed at the end of the final period. Should a balance of any amount remain in Fund Balance after all construction costs have been paid, it may be rebated to property owners and a participating governmental unit, if any; or it may be disposed of in any other legal way as determined by responsible persons. Disposing of deficits has already been discussed in the section entitled "Construction Deficits."

Assuming that the project has involved the acquisition of a permanent improvement, rather than providing a current service, the question arises as to the amount to be capitalized as a fixed asset. Should it include the total cost of the project; or should property owners' contributions be excluded, since they are supposed to increase the value of private property? The prevailing opinion appears to favor capitalization of both public and private contributions, with a clear indication in accounts of the General Fixed Assets Group to show the amounts contributed by each. Entries in that group of accounts are illustrated in Chapter 12.

In summary, the financial operations of a special assessment fund include levying and collecting installments and managing payment of bonds. The financial operations are likely to continue long after the improvement has been acquired. One factor which may cause material delay in terminating the financial activities is difficulty in the collection of installments. Although the fund management is vested with power to enforce collections by foreclosure, if necessary, conditions may render such action inadvisable at the moment unless mandated by law. Delay in the installment collection process is likely to interfere with the orderly payment of bonds, it is clear, unless temporary financing can be obtained from other sources; but this is only a shifting of the liability. Even though cash is available for the payment of bonds, some delay may be encountered in paying them because of difficulty in locating bondholders, especially if the fund has been involved in financial troubles to the extent of casting serious discredit on the value of the bonds. In the event of failure to locate bondholders, the special assessment fund becomes virtually a trust fund, unless the bonds and cash for their payment can legally be transferred to a special trust fund for that purpose. The balance remaining after all liabilities have been paid or transferred—financing surplus, as it were—may be rebated or given to another fund; whereas a deficit would be disposed of as provided by law, probably through assistance from another fund.

SELECTED REFERENCES

National Committee on Governmental Accounting. *Governmental Accounting, Auditing, and Financial Reporting*, chap. 9. Chicago, 1968.

Novak, Terry L. "A Model Special Assessment Law," *Governmental Finance*, vol. I, no. 1 (February 1972), pp. 8–11.

QUESTIONS

10–1. What sorts of projects may be equitably financed by special assessment funds?

10–2. In what respects does a special assessments fund differ from a capital projects fund? From a special revenue fund?

10–3. In the balance sheet of Central City's special assessment fund there is an account entitled Estimated Uncollectible Assessments Receivable—$21,000. Since special assessments for tangible improvements are liens upon the improved property, what circumstances might justify the allowance?

10–4. Does levying a special assessment upon residential property constitute revenue for the levying fund? For the municipality as a whole?

10–5. In a certain state, the special assessment fund procedure is employed for the construction of agricultural land drainage ditches. Original financing of these projects is by term bonds. A state law specifies that if installments are paid before their due dates, interest continues to accrue until the due date. Why?

10–6. List at least five different items of information which must be provided for in the design of any form of subsidiary record of special assessments.

10–7. Some of the following accounts are recommended by the NCGA for use in special assessment funds, some are not. List each account recommended for use in special assessment fund.

1. Assessments Receivable
2. Bonds Payable
3. Cash
4. Expenditures
5. Encumbrances
6. Estimated Revenues
7. Fund Balance
8. Reserve for Inventories
9. Retained Earnings
10. Actuarial Deficiency in Contributions

10–8. What is an *abatement?* How does an abatement differ from a rebate?

10–9. "Because a special assessment fund relates primarily to activities for a project, rather than activities of a fiscal year, it is not necessary to accrue expenditures or revenues at year-end." Do you agree? Why or why not?

10–10. "Any municipality which has more than one special assessment fund should consolidate them all for annual report purposes." Do you agree? Why or why not?

EXERCISES AND PROBLEMS

10–1. Utilizing the municipal annual report obtained for Exercise 1–1, follow the instructions below:

a) Does the report state the basis of accounting which is used for special assessment funds? If so, is the financial statement presentation consistent with the stated basis? If the basis of accounting is not stated, analyze the statements to determine which basis is used—full accrual, modified accrual, or cash basis. Is the same basis used for both revenues and expenditures? Is the basis used consistent with the recommendations discussed in Chapter 10? Is an Estimated Uncollectible Assessments account used?

b) What statements and schedules pertaining to special assessment funds are presented? Are there separate statements for each project, or are combined statements used? In what respects (headings, arrangement, items included, etc.) do they seem similar to statements illustrated or described in the text? In what respects do they differ? Are any differences merely a matter of terminology or arrangement, or do they represent material deviations from recommended accounting and reporting for special assessment funds? Is a single cash account used, or are three used, for each fund? Is a single Fund Balance account used, or are three used, for each special assessment fund?

c) What are the sources of financing for the special assessment funds? If general obligation bonds are a source, have any been sold at a premium? at a discount? Is bond premium or discount being amortized over the life of the bonds, or was it all closed to Fund Balance in the year of issue? Has the municipality, or other governmental unit, contributed to the cost of the project? If so, what proportion of cost is being borne by municipal funds or governmental units? What proportion of cost is being borne by the taxpayers in the benefit district? Does the balance sheet show Assessments Receivable classified as to current, delinquent, and deferred, or only as one amount? Does the report indicate how the total cost was apportioned to the parcels of property located in the benefit district? If so, does the basis appear equitable to you? Why or why not?

d) How much detail is given concerning special assessment fund expenditures? Is the detail sufficient to meet the information needs of administrators? legislators? creditors? interested residents? For those projects which are incomplete at the date of the financial statements does the report compare the percentage of total authorization for each project expended to date with the percentage of completion? For those projects completed during the fiscal year does the report compare the total expenditures for each project with the authorization for each project. For each cost overrun, how was the overrun financed? If assessments levied exceeded the amount needed, what disposition was made of the excess?

10–2. The Combined Balance Sheet for the Special Assessment Funds of the City of San Diego, California, as of June 30, 1972, is shown below.

THE CITY OF SAN DIEGO
SPECIAL ASSESSMENT FUNDS
COMBINED BALANCE SHEET
June 30, 1973

	Total	Penasquitos Sewer District Funds	Other Special Assess-ment Funds
ASSETS			
Cash in Treasury	$ 697,067	$ 392,676	$304,391
Investments (Cost)	875,083	875,083	–
Amount to Be Provided for Payment of Serial Bonds	9,350,000	9,350,000	–
Bonds Authorized and Unissued	5,500,000	5,500,000	–
TOTAL ASSETS	$16,422,150	$16,117,759	$304,391
LIABILITIES			
Serial Bonds Payable	$ 9,350,000	$ 9,350,000	$ –
RESERVES AND FUND BALANCES			
Continuing Appropriations	$ 222,235	$ –	$222,235
Reserve for Encumbrances	27,506	–	27,506
Reserve for Matured and Unpaid Interest	29,379	29,379	–
Reserve for Authorized Expenditures	5,500,000	5,500,000	–
Fund Balances	1,293,030	1,238,380	54,650
TOTAL RESERVES AND FUND BALANCES	$ 7,072,150	$ 6,767,759	$304,391
TOTAL LIABILITIES, RESERVES, AND FUND BALANCES	$16,422,150	$16,117,759	$304,391

In the report the balance sheet is supported by a Combined Statement of Revenue and a Combined Statement of Expenditures for the year ended June 30, 1973. In what respects does the balance sheet indicate that San Diego follows the recommendations of the National Committee on Governmental Accounting discussed in Chapter 10? In what respects does San Diego apparently differ from recommendations discussed in the chapter?

10–3. Your examination of the accounts of your new client, the City of Delmas, as of June 30, 1971, revealed the following (items 1, 2, and 3 are intentionally omitted.):

4. On June 30, 1971 the City issued $200,000 in special assessment bonds at par to finance a street improvement project estimated to cost $225,000. The project is to be paid by a $15,000 levy against the City (payable in fiscal year 1971–72) and $210,000 against property owners (payable in five equal annual installments beginning October 1, 1971). The levy was made on June 30. A $215,000 contract was let for the project on July 2, 1971, but work has not begun.

Required:

Prepare journal entries to establish a special assessment fund for the City of Delmas and to record the events for the period given. Also prepare any necessary adjusting and closing entries as of June 30, 1971, the end of the fiscal year.

(AICPA, adapted)

10–4. In 197E, the Town of Chelm initiated a program of sidewalk construction and street curb improvement to be financed mainly by assessments against benefited properties. This project was designated as No. 84. Engineering and construction estimates placed the total cost of the project at $600,000, of which the city government agreed to contribute $50,000.

Assessments against property owners, payable in installments of annually increasing amounts over a perod of eight years, called for $40,000 in the first installment, for construction cash; with the remaining $510,000 to be deferred, with proceeds to be used for bond retirement. Provision for current financing of contract costs included a bond issue of $510,000 to be sold early in 197F.

During 197E the following transactions occurred in special assessment fund No. 84:

1. The governmental unit's expected contribution was recorded.
2. A construction contract was awarded in the amount of $530,000.
3. $20,000 cash was received as a short-term loan from the town general fund.
4. Engineering and other "early stage" costs were paid in the amount of $8,000.
5. All assessments were levied, with first payments due in 197F.

Required:

Assuming that three cash accounts and three fund balance accounts (construction, bond repayment, and interest payment) must be used, to the extent applicable, prepare a balance sheet for the town of Chelm Special Assessment Fund No. 84 as of December 31, 197E.

10–5. In 19x5 the citizens of the Town of Aurora took action to construct public works project No. 138 using special assessment financing, with assistance from the town general fund to the extent of $60,000. Estimated total cost of the project was $900,000. During 19x5 the following transactions occurred:

1. The governmental unit's share of cost was recorded.
2. The town's finance intragovernmental service fund advanced $30,000 cash.
3. $40,000 assessments receivable were recorded as currently due and $800,000 were recorded in the deferred category.
4. A contract in the amount of $850,000 was awarded.
5. To capitalize on a favorable bond market, $800,000 par value of bonds were sold at a net price of $812,000.
6. Cash in the amount of $734,000 was paid for temporary investments; $4,000 of that amount was for purchase of accrued interest.
7. An invoice for $150,000 received from the contractor for work done to date was recorded as a liability.
8. Noncontract costs, which had not been encumbered, were paid in the amount of $13,000.
9. Interest on temporary investments amounting to $14,600 was received in cash; $7,300 additional interest receivable was accrued at year-end.
10. Interest on bonds was paid in the amount of $24,000; interest payable accrued at year-end amounted to $8,000. Bond premium in the amount of $600 is to be amortized in 19x5.
11. Necessary closing entries for the year were made.

Required:

a) Record the transactions for 19x5 in general journal form, or directly in T accounts.
b) Prepare a balance sheet as of December 31, 19x5.
c) Prepare a statement of cash receipts and disbursements for the period ending December 31, 19x5.

10–6. Thomas McCarver's assessment on a public improvement project in his neighborhood was $2,400, payable in eight equal annual installments. The first installment was recorded as current when the levy was recorded. Thereafter, each year's installment was transferred from deferred to current at the beginning of the year. Current installments unpaid at the end of a year were transferred to the delinquent classification at that time.

Because of financial difficulties, McCarver had made no payments on his assessment by the end of the second year. Foreclosure action was begun early in the third year. Necessary legal processes were completed and the sale was held late in the first month of the fourth installment year. McCarver's share of the cost of advertising and holding the sale was $30. Interest of $70 had accrued on McCarver's assessment and had been duly recorded before the sale.

a) Record the sale assuming that the property was sold for exactly the amount of total charges against it.
b) Record the sale assuming that the property brought $2,800, of which the special assessment fund received its share and held the balance for McCarver.
c) Record the sale assuming that the purchaser was required to pay past-due and current claims against the property and to assume liability for the noncurrent indebtedness.
d) Record the facts assuming that no satisfactory bids were received and the special assessment fund took provisional title to the property.
e) Record sale of the property after the special assessment fund had taken provisional title to it, the consideration being just the total charges against it.
f) Record transfer of the property, after provisional title had been taken, as in (*d*), to the city park system, with no consideration.

10–7. In 19x6 the City of Madrid began organization of a special assessment project to finance a major improvement of streets in one area of the town. Preliminary estimates placed the approximate cost at $4,300,000. A project of that amount was legally approved by all parties concerned. At the same time, a $4,000,000 issue of term bonds was approved.

1. Early in 19x7 a contract for the major part of the job was let in the amount of $4,100,000.
2. $150,000 was borrowed from a local bank on an interest-bearing note.
3. The bond issue was sold in total at a net price of $4,020,000.
4. An invoice for $1,250,000 on the main contract was received and recorded as a liability.
5. Investments with a face value of $2,500,000 were purchased at par plus $25,000 accrued interest.
6. The contractor's invoice, less a 5 percent retention, was paid.
7. A special assessment of $4,250,000 was levied against property owners in the benefit district; $425,000 is considered current, the remainder is deferred.
8. $100,000 cash interest was collected on investments. $10,000 additional interest on investments was accrued at year-end.
9. Interest paid on bonds and notes totaled $100,000; interest unpaid, but accrued at year-end, totaled $20,000.

10. $90,000 was paid for miscellaneous construction expense which had not been encumbered.
11. Collections on the current installment of assessments totaled $400,000. The first installment did not bear interest.
12. Uncollected current assessments were reclassified as delinquent.
13. Amortization of Premium on Bonds amounted to $1,000 for the year.
14. Year-end closing entries were made.

Required:

a) Record the foregoing transactions, either by journalizing or by direct posting.
b) Prepare a balance sheet as of December 31, 19x7.
c) Prepare an analysis of changes in Fund Balance for 19x7.

10–8. This problem continues the preceding problem. The following transactions and events related to the City of Madrid's Special Assessment Fund occurred in 19x8.

1. Encumbrances as of December 31, 19x7, were reestablished, and the accruals for interest receivable and interest payable on 12/31/x7 (See Problem 10–7, entries 8 and 9) were reversed.
2. $425,000 of assessments were classified as current.
3. Miscellaneous construction expenditures of $45,000 (not encumbered) were paid in cash.
4. An invoice for $1,450,000 was received from the contractor and recorded as a liability.
5. Investments which cost $1,000,000 were sold at par plus $25,000 for interest accrued at date of sale.
6. $380,000 of current and $5,000 of delinquent assessments, plus $34,000 interest revenue, was collected.
7. The contractor's latest invoice, less a 5 percent retention, was paid.
8. The assessment fund management succeeded in buying $10,000 par value of the fund's bonds at par and $300 of accrued interest.
9. As a result of a wage settlement ending a prolonged strike, the contract was amended, as provided in the contract, to cover additional wage costs which would accrue from the settlement. It was agreed that $150,000 would be added to the contract price, and both the project authorization and the contract were increased by that amount.
10. $180,000 interest expense was paid on bonds.
11. An invoice was received from the contractor for $400,000 and recorded as a liability.
12. The note payable and $2,500 interest were paid.
13. Interest on investments collected in cash during the year amounted to $60,000.
14. Unpaid current assessments were reclassified as delinquent.

15. Accrued interest receivable on investments amounted to $6,000 at year-end. Accrued interest payable on bonds amounted to $20,000 at year-end. Bond premium to be amortized amounted to $1,000 for the year.
16. Year-end closing entries were made.

Required:

a) Record the transactions for 19x8 by journalizing or by direct posting.
b) Prepare a balance sheet as of December 31, 19x8.
c) Prepare an analysis of changes in Fund Balance for 19x8.

CONTINUOUS PROBLEMS

10–L. In order to receive water service from the City of Bingham, the residents of a large unincorporated area adjacent to the city, called Irwinville, agreed to bear the cost of extending the water mains into their area and constructing the service lines. The city water utility agreed to bear the cost of expanding its facilities as needed. In order to make it possible for the property owners to pay for the mains and service lines, the Irwinville Special Assessment Fund was established.

You are required to:

a) Open an Irwinville Special Assessment Fund general journal and enter the following transactions, as applicable, using a single Cash account and a single Fund Balance account.

1. The cost of expansion of the mains was estimated at $500,000. This amount was authorized to be spent for that purpose. The Special Assessment Fund was authorized to issue $450,000 in bonds.
2. Assessments totaling $500,000 were levied, payable in five equal installments, the first being due in 30 days from date of levy, and the other four at annual intervals thereafter. The first installment was to be used for construction, the principal of the other four for bond repayment, and interest received was to be used for interest payment. The second, third, fourth, and fifth installments bore interest at the rate of 5½ percent per year from date of assessment. Interest is accrued annually on all unpaid installments, as shown by the following example:

   Assume total assessment of a taxpayer was $5,000. He would be expected to pay the first installment, $1,000, within 30 days of the assessment. The second installment, $1,000, plus one year's interest on the second, third, fourth, and fifth installments (5½% × $4,000 = $220), would be due one year from date of assessment and payable within 30 days from due date. The third installment, $1,000, plus one year's interest on the third, fourth, and fifth installments ($5\frac{1}{2}\% \times \$3,000 = \$165$) would be due two years from date of assessment and payable within 30 days from due date, etc.

Upon completion of the project any remainder in the Special Assessment Fund was to be distributed to the persons assessed, in proportion to the amount each had paid.

3. In order to secure an operating cash balance, the fund borrowed $25,000 on its note payable to a local bank. The note was to be repaid from the proceeds of the bond issue.
4. An engineering firm charged $20,000 for drawing up the bid specifications; advertising for bids cost $120. These amounts were paid.
5. Several individuals paid their entire assessments in full, thereby avoiding any interest charges: these payments totaled $20,000.
6. The Willis Company was awarded the contract for $460,000; progress payments were to be subject to a 10 percent retention until final approval of the work.
7. In addition to the amount collected in transaction 5, collections of the first installment totaled $90,000; the remainder of the first installment was declared delinquent.
8. At the end of the first year, 4½ percent notes with a face value of $400,000 were issued at par. The legality of this transaction received advance approval of the attorney general, and the authority to issue bonds was withdrawn. The notes are not backed by the full faith and credit of any governmental unit.
9. The note due the local bank was repaid, plus $250 interest.
10. The Willis Company submitted a progress billing for $215,000. This was approved for payment and paid, subject to the retention clause in the contract.
11. The second installment of the assessment fell due and was transferred to "current." Interest for one year was accrued on *all* unpaid installments.
12. In addition to the amount collected in transaction 5, collections of the second installment totaled $88,000, and the proper amount of interest was collected from taxpayers who paid the second installment. The remainder of the second installment and the interest not collected were declared delinquent.
13. The Willis Company submitted final billing for the remainder of the contract price. The billing was approved and paid, subject to the retention clause.
14. Legal proceedings were instituted against delinquent property owners. The proceedings cost $280.

    Persons owing $4,000 on the first installment, and $6,000 on the second, paid the installments in full, plus interest to six months after the due date of the second installment. They also paid $200 penalties to reimburse the fund for legal expenses. The property against which the remaining delinquent installments had been levied was foreclosed and sold for the amount of charges against it (as of six months after the due date of the second installment); the buyer assumed the liability for installments not yet due.

15. The engineers gave final approval to the work done by the Willis Company, and the amounts retained were paid. The engineers charged $5,000 for the inspection; this amount was recorded as a liability.
16. One year's interest on the notes was paid, and notes amounting to $100,000 were redeemed.
17. The third assessment was transferred to "current." Interest for one year was accrued on all unpaid installments.
18. Closing entries for the year were made.

b) Open a general ledger for this fund and post the transactions recorded in part (*a*).
c) Prepare a balance sheet for the Irwinville Special Assessment Fund.
d) Prepare a Statement of Cash Receipts and Disbursements for the year.

10–S. The City of Smithville does not have any funds in the special assessment category at the present time, nor has it had any in the past year.

11

Enterprise Funds

Enterprise funds are used by governmental units to account for activities which render services to the general public on a user charge basis. The most common examples of governmental enterprises are public utilities, notably water and sewer utilities. Electric and gas utilities, transportation systems, airports, ports, hospitals, toll bridges, produce markets, liquor stores, and public housing projects are other examples frequently found. Services of the kinds mentioned are generally accounted for by enterprise funds because they are intended to be largely self-supporting; however, they are properly accounted for by a revenue fund by those municipalities which support the activities largely from general or special revenue sources other than user charges.

Almost every kind of enterprise operated by a municipality has its counterpart in the private sector. In order to take advantage of the work done by regulatory agencies and trade associations to develop useful accounting information systems for the investor-owned enterprises, it is recommended that municipally-owned enterprises use the accounting structures developed for investor-owned enterprises of the same nature. In general, it is recommended that enterprise funds account for plant and equipment as well as current assets, long-term debt as well as current liabilities, and that the full accrual basis of accounting be followed. Budgetary accounts should be used only if required by law. Debt service and construction activities of a municipal enterprise are accounted for within the enterprise fund, rather than by separate debt service and capital project funds. Thus, the reports of enterprise funds are self contained, and creditors, legislators, or the general public can evaluate the performance of a municipal enterprise on the same bases as they can the performance of investor-owned enterprises in the same industry.

By far the most numerous and important enterprise services rendered by municipalities are public utilities. In this chapter, therefore, the example used is that of a water utility fund.

Illustrative Water Utility Fund Statements

The balance sheet shown as Illustration 11–1 follows the format recommended by the National Association of Railroad and Utilities Commissioners and by the Federal Power Commission.[1] Many municipal utilities arrange assets and liabilities in the same sequence as other municipal enterprises—current assets before plant and current liabilities before long-term debt—so that combined statements can be prepared for all enterprise funds and for all municipal funds. Both the regulatory format illustrated and the customary format followed by profit-seeking enterprises are considered to be acceptable for use by municipally-owned utilities, in the absence of particular legal requirements.[2] An important reason for regulatory agencies' preference for listing plant before current assets and long-term debt before current liabilities is said to be that plant is customarily a much larger share of total assets, and long-term debt a much more important source of financing. In Illustration 11–1, "Utility Plant—Net" amounts to 81 percent of total assets, and long-term debt is over 84 percent of total debt.

Utility Plant—Net

In Illustration 11–1 only three items are shown in the Utility Plant—Net section: Utility Plant in Service, Construction Work in Progress, and Accumulated Depreciation. The first two items are part of a general category, Utility Plant, provided in both the NARUC (National Association of Railroad and Utilities Commissioners) and FPC (Federal Power Commission) systems of accounts, and by many state regulatory commissions. Some idea of the detail required in reports to regulatory commissions may be gained from a listing of other summary accounts in the Utility Plant category: Utility Plant Purchased or Sold, Utility Plant in Process of Reclassification, Utility Plant Leased to Others, Property Held for Future Use, and Completed Construction Not Classified. The first item in this category, *Utility Plant in Service*, is the total *original* cost of six subcategories of plant assets: intangible plant, source of supply

[1] See the Selected References at the end of this chapter.

[2] Leon E. Hay and D. J. Grinnell, *Water Utility Accounting*, Chicago and New York: Municipal Finance Officers Association and American Water Works Association, 1970. This position, is supported by *Audits of State and Local Governmental Units*, AICPA, 1974, p. 82.

plant, pumping plant, water treatment plant, transmission and distribution plant, and general plant. Each of the six subcategories is supported by appropriate subsidiary accounts. For example, intangible plant consists of the costs of organization, franchise and consents, and any other intangible costs "necessary and valuable in the conduct of utility operations." Source of supply plant consists of land and land rights; structures and improvements; collecting and impounding reservoirs; lake, river, and other intakes; wells and springs; infiltration galleries and tunnels; supply mains; and other water source plant. Each of the accounts within each subcategory is supported by necessary subsidiary records for each individual asset detailing its description, location, cost, date of acquisition, estimated useful life, salvage value, depreciation charges, and any other information needed for management planning and control, regulatory agency reports, financial statements, or special reports to creditors.

Construction Work in Progress. The second Utility Plant item shown on the balance sheet, Illustration 11–1, is Construction Work in Progress. This account represents the accumulated costs of work orders for projects which will result in items reportable as Utility Plant when completed, and is, of course, supported by the work orders for projects in progress. Each work order, in turn, is supported by documents supporting payments to contractors and to suppliers, or supporting charges for materials, labor, and overhead allocable to the project.

In addition to the Utility Plant category of accounts two other categories of accounts are required to be shown in the Utility Plant—Net section of the balance sheet: Accumulated Provision for Depreciation and Amortization of Utility Plant, and Utility Plant Adjustments. In the first of these, the following items are separately disclosed in statements furnished regulatory agencies: Accumulated Provision for Depreciation of Utility Plant in Service, Accumulated Provision for Depreciation of Utility Plant Leased to Others, Accumulated Provision for Depreciation of Property Held for Future Use, Accumulated Provision for Amortization of Utility Plant in Service, Accumulated Provision for Amortization of Utility Plant Leased to Others, and Accumulated Provision for Amortization of Property Held for Future Use. The latter three accounts are used because the costs of certain intangible assets described above are included in the Utility Plant category.

Utility Plant Adjustments, the final category to be shown in the Utility Plant—Net balance sheet section, consists of three summary accounts: Utility Plant Acquisition Adjustments, Accumulated Provision for Amortization of Utility Plant Acquisition Adjustments, and Other Utility Plant Adjustments. The first two accounts exist because the predominant rule in utility regulation and related accounting practice is that *utility plant shall be stated in the books of account at cost (less amortization) to the owner who first devoted the property to public service.* Among

Illustration 11–1

CITY AND COUNTY OF HONOLULU
Board of Water Supply
Balance Sheet—June 30, 1972

Assets

Exhibit L

Utility Plant—at original cost:		
In service	$157,474,141	
Construction work in progress	3,810,108	
Total	161,284,249	
Less accumulated depreciation	45,686,869	
Utility Plant—net		$115,597,380
Construction Funds:		
Cash and certificates of deposit (including accrued interest)		10,735,832
Refunding and Bond Retirement Trust Accounts:		
Cash and certificates of deposit (including accrued interest) (Note 1)		363,139
Special Funds:		
Cash and certificates of deposit (including accrued interest)	2,991,927	
United States Government obligations (at amortized cost, plus accrued interest)	1,126,257	
Total Special Funds . . . (Schedule 3—Illustration 11–2)		4,118,184
Current Assets:		
Cash, certificates of deposit, and United States Government obligations (at cost, including accrued interest)		
Operating fund	2,634,136	
Bond and interest redemption fund . . . (Note 2)	3,883,370	
Refunding and bond retirement trust accounts . . . (Note 1)	982,600	
Cash on hand	4,350	
Special deposits in bank	18,107	
Accounts receivable:		
Billed (less allowance for uncollectible accounts of $25,000)	962,229	
Unbilled	1,459,314	
Materials and supplies (at average cost)	1,109,198	
Prepaid Insurance	58,259	
Total Current Assets		[illegible]

Deferred Debits:		
Unamortized debt expense and premium–net	23,127	
Miscellaneous–net	149,139	
Total Deferred Debits		172,266
Total Assets		$142,098,364

Liabilities and Retained Earnings

Long-term Debt: (See Schedule 4 to Exhibit K)		
Revenue bonds	$ 25,140,000	
Revenue bonds subject to refunding program	955,000	
General obligation water bonds	13,855,000	
Total	39,950,000	
Less portion payable within one year	2,460,000	
Total Long-term Debt		$ 37,490,000
Current Liabilities:		
Accounts payable	335,372	
Accrued vacation pay	1,712,229	
Long-term debt payable within one year	2,460,000	
Matured revenue bonds not presented	1,572,000	
Accrued and matured interest payable	704,662	
Customer advances for construction (estimated portion payable within one year)	240,000	
Service installation and contract bid deposits	18,107	
Total Current Liabilities		7,042,370
Customer Advances for Construction (less estimated portion refundable within one year)		1,280,296
Contributions in Aid of Construction:		
Government	16,892,563	
Other	58,629,984	
Total Contributions in Aid of Construction		75,522,547
Retained Earnings . . . (Schedule 1–Illustration 11-3 and Note 3)		20,763,151
Total Liabilities and Retained Earnings		$142,098,364

The accompanying schedules and notes are an integral part of Exhibit L.

Illustration 11–1 (*continued*)

CITY AND COUNTY OF HONOLULU
Board of Water Supply
Notes to the Financial Statements

1. Refunding Bonds and Proceeds Held in Trust
   Pursuant to the refunding provision of the $16,000,000 Consolidated System Revenue Refunding and Improvement Bonds, Series "D," sold on June 4, 1963, substantially all of the refunding portion of the proceeds were invested in U.S. Government obligations and held in trust by the Chemical Bank of New York. These investments and their earnings, plus earnings from certificates of deposit and cash held by the Director of Finance, City and County of Honolulu, have provided sufficient funds to redeem, at various maturity and call dates, all of the Suburban Water System and Consolidated System bonds subject to the refunding program, and to meet related interest and call premium requirements.

   At June 30, 1972, the Director of Finance, City and County of Honolulu, held cash and certificates of deposit totaling $1,345,739 for the Refunding and Bond Retirement Trust account. The portion of cash and certificates of deposit to be used to redeem the balance of bonds to be called on July 15, 1972, and their related call premiums, is included in the balance sheet under current assets.
2. Bond and Interest Redemption Fund
   The restricted and unrestricted portions of the bond and interest redemption fund at June 30, 1972 were as follows:

Restricted:		
Interest applicable to:		
Bonds not matured	$ 609,782	
Bonds matured for which coupons have not been presented for payment	38,250	$ 648,032
Principal applicable to:		
Bonds not matured	1,310,626	
Bonds matured, not presented for payment	1,572,000	2,882,626
Total		3,530,658
Unrestricted		352,712
Total		$3,883,370

3. Retained Earnings
   Retained earnings at the end of June 30, 1972 and 1971 comprised the following accounts:

	1972	*1971*
Surplus at inception of respective system:		
Metropolitan, July 1, 1929	$ 1,537,824	$ 1,537,824
Suburban, January 1, 1940	597,324	597,324
Revenue bond reserve funds	3,400,375	3,855,940
Renewal and replacement reserve fund	610,254	419,673
Insurance reserve fund	107,555	107,523
Unappropriated	14,509,819	12,028,511
Total	$20,763,151	$18,546,795

4. Depreciation
   Provision for depreciation has been computed under the straight-line method. In addition to the amount shown separately in operating expenses, $98,573 was charged to clearing accounts.
5. Commitments and Contingent Liabilities
   All full-time employees of the Board are covered under the Employees' Retirement System of the State of Hawaii. The Board's share of retirement expense for the year was $569,947 which includes amortization of prior service cost over fifty years from July 1, 1964. The System's policy is to fund pension cost accrued.

   Commitments, principally for the Board's construction program approximated $3,528,009 at June 30, 1972.

utilities accountants, this has the technical name of *original cost*.[3] Any premium paid by the present owner over and above such cost less amortization is in the general nature of payments for goodwill by nonutility enterprises. But utilities enjoy monopoly privileges and are subject to corresponding restrictions. One of the restrictions is that earnings shall not exceed a fair rate of return. Since goodwill is the capitalized value of excess earnings, utilities can have no goodwill (in the accounting sense). Premium on plant purchased is therefore accounted for as Utility Plant Acquisition Adjustments. The amount of acquisition adjustment capitalized is amortized over a period of time determined by the appropriate regulatory body; accumulated amortization is disclosed in the Accumulated Provision for Amortization of Utility Plant Acquisition Adjustments account. The third account in this group, Other Utility Plant Adjustments, is used to disclose any differences between book cost and original cost not properly includible elsewhere.

In addition to the original cost concept a further difference between what is considered to be proper accounting for utility plant and what is considered to be proper accounting for plant of enterprises in other industries lies in the definition of capitalizable interest. In both utilities and nonutilities the net cost for the *period of construction* of interest on borrowed funds used for construction purposes is considered as proper element of plant cost. In utility practice, however, it is also considered proper to impute interest for the period of construction on utility funds used for construction, and to charge the imputed interest as an element of plant cost.

Other Property and Investments

Three sections shown in Illustration 11–1 below "Utility Plant—Net" are Construction Funds, Refunding and Bond Retirement Trust Accounts, and Special Funds. All three are classified as Restricted Assets and are properly shown in the Other Property and Investments balance sheet classification provided by the NARUC and FPC. Other Property is defined as property which is not being used for utility purposes or being held for future utility use. Investments includes long-term advances to other municipal funds and any other long-term investments of the utility fund. Restricted Assets, as the name indicates, are assets which may not be expended for normal operating purposes because of requirements of regulatory authorities, provisions in bond indentures or other legal agreements, or as a result of actions of the utility governing board.

The section captioned Construction Funds in Illustration 11–1 exists for the same reason that a capital projects fund would be established

[3] Federal Power Commission, *Uniform System of Accounts Prescribed for Public Utilities and Licensees* (Washington, D.C.: U.S. Government Printing Office, 1970), p. 2.

by the nonutility operations of a municipality: to segregate assets which are to be expended for construction, so that their use for that purpose can be more easily demonstrated. The title Construction Funds is consistent with the usage of utility regulatory bodies, but from the standpoint of municipalities it is an unfortunate title because utility construction funds do not meet the NCGA definition of a fund—they are not self-balancing sets of accounts. A better title, recommended in *Water Utility Accounting* published jointly by the American Water Works Association and the Municipal Finance Officers Association, is Cash and Investments Restricted for Construction.

Refunding and Bond Retirement Trust Accounts, as a long-term asset, and the related item with the identical title shown in the Current Assets section of Illustration 11–1, are explained by Note 1 accompanying the balance sheet. The Refunding and Bond Retirement Trust Accounts serves somewhat the same function that debt service funds do for nonutility operations of a municipality. As Note 2 indicates, the Bond and Interest Redemption Fund, carried in the Current Assets section, also has a debt service function. Neither the Bond and Interest Redemption Fund nor the Refunding and Bond Retirement Trust Accounts are funds in the governmental accounting sense of the word; they are not self-balancing sets of accounts.

The Special Funds classification of assets in Illustration 11–1 is presented in more detail in a schedule shown here as Illustration 11–2. The three "funds" shown in this category are, again, not funds in the governmental accounting sense of the word, but are somewhat closer to being so than Construction Funds or Refunding and Bond Retirement Trust Accounts, because the three Special Funds not only are segregated assets as shown by Illustration 11–2 but also are offset by segregated amounts of retained earnings as explained in Note 3 to the financial statements (see Illustration 11–1). The Revenue Bond Reserve Funds in this category functions as a debt service fund for water utility revenue bonds not subject to the refunding program accounted for in the manner previously discussed. The Renewal and Replacement Fund consists of cash and investments to be used for plant renewal and replacement. Similarly, the Insurance Reserve Fund consists of cash and investments the use of which is restricted to insurance purposes. Other "special funds" sometimes provided in accounting systems required by utility regulatory agencies include depreciation funds (assets set aside in the amount of accumulated provisions for depreciation), amortization funds (assets set aside in the amount of accumulated amortization), and "funds" to provide for "employee pensions, savings, relief, hospital, and other purposes not provided for elsewhere."[4]

[4] Ibid., p. 101–26.

Illustration 11–2

CITY AND COUNTY OF HONOLULU
Board of Water Supply
Special Funds–June 30, 1972

Schedule 3
to Exhibit L

Revenue Bond Reserve Funds:		
Cash and certificates of deposit (including accrued interest)	$2,284,128	
United States Government obligations (at amortized cost, plus accrued interest)	1,116,247	
Total Revenue Bond Reserve Funds		$3,400,375
Renewal and Replacement Fund:		
Cash and certificates of deposit (including accrued interest)		610,254
Insurance Reserve Fund:		
Cash	97,545	
United States Government obligations (at cost, plus accrued interest)	10,010	
Total Insurance Reserve Fund		107,555
Total Special Funds		$4,118,184

Current and Accrued Assets and Deferred Debits

The section of the balance sheet labeled Current Assets in Illustration 11–1 is called Current and Accrued Assets in the NARUC and FPC uniform systems. Certain accounts appearing in this section are related to those in preceding sections of the balance sheet, and are discussed above. The remainder of the accounts in this section are not peculiar to utilities and need not be discussed here. Similarly, accounts to be found in the Deferred Debits section are familiar to the reader who has studied intermediate accounting for profit-seeking enterprises. The title "Unamortized Debt Expense and Premium—Net" in Illustration 11–1 appears to vary from general regulatory requirements, however, which specify that unamortized debt discount and unamortized debt premium *not* be set off against each other. It is generally required that unamortized debt premium be shown in the Deferred Credits section along with Customer Advances for Construction.

The Federal Power Commission and National Association of Railroad and Utilities Commissioners provide, in their suggested systems of accounts, that undistributed balances in clearing accounts be shown in the Deferred Debits section of a utility balance sheet. Clearing accounts are suspense accounts which are used for accumulating all transactions of given kinds, pending final decision as to the exact title or titles to be debited for each entry in the clearing account. Transportation Expense Clearing, Shop Expense Clearing, and Stores Expense Clearing, are examples of clearing accounts commonly used by utilities.

Long-Term Debt

Regulatory agencies commonly require that long-term debt be shown in a utility balance sheet before current liabilities. Bonds are the customary form of long-term debt. Bonds issued by a utility are usually secured by the pledge of certain portions of the utility's revenue, the exact terms of the pledge varying with individual cases; bonds of this nature are called revenue bonds. Some utility bonds are secured not only by a pledge of a certain portion of the utility's revenues but also by an agreement on the part of the town's or city's general government to subsidize the utility in any year in which its normal revenue is inadequate for compliance with the terms of the bond indenture. Other utility bonds carry the pledge of the governmental unit's full faith and credit, although the intent is to service them from utility revenues rather than general taxes. The latter are, therefore, technically *general obligation* bonds. The National Committee on Governmental Accounting recommends that general obligation bonds intended to be serviced from utility revenues be shown as a liability by both the enterprise fund and by the general long-term debt group of accounts. The latter group of accounts may disclose the liability by footnote rather than in the body of the Statement of General Long-Term Debt, if the intention is clearly expressed in the bond ordinance, according to the American Institute of Certified Public Accountants.[5] A suggested form for such a footnote is presented on page 260 of this text.

Municipally-owned utilities may have received advances from the municipal general fund, or other funds. The portion of such advances which is to be repaid within one year from balance sheet date should be reported as a current liability; the remainder is properly reported in the long-term debt section of the utility balance sheet.

Current Liabilities

Items commonly found in the current liability section of a utility balance sheet are shown under that caption in Illustration 11–1. The first three items under that caption need no comment here. The fourth, Matured Revenue Bonds Not Presented, is self-explanatory; certain bonds have matured but have not been presented to the utility for repayment. The liability for the matured bonds is offset by the bond interest and redemption fund in the Current Asset section (see Note 2 accompanying the balance sheet in Illustration 11–1), as is the fifth item in the Current

[5] *Audits of State and Local Governmental Units,* New York: 1974, p. 79. If the bond ordinance does not provide for regular and recurring debt service from enterprise revenues, the bond proceeds should be shown as Contribution from Municipality, instead of Bonds Payable, on the books of the enterprise fund; in that event the bonds are properly included in the Statement of General Long-term Debt. See Chapter 13 of this text for discussion of general long-term debt.

Liability section, Accrued and Matured Interest Payable. From the presence of these offsetting current asset and current liability accounts it is evident that the utility fund follows the recommended practice of accounting for debt service operations for all bonds to be redeemed by the utility. No separate debt service funds or capital projects funds are used by utilities or other municipal enterprise fund structure.

Customer Advances for Construction, the sixth item in the Current Liabilities section of the balance sheet shown in Illustration 11–1, and the related item shown separately below the Current Liability section, result from the practice of utilities of requiring customers to advance to the utility a sizable portion of the estimated cost of construction projects to be undertaken by the utility at the request of the customer. If the advances are to be refunded, either wholly or in part, or applied against billings for service rendered after completion of the project, they are classified as shown in Illustration 11–1. When a customer is refunded the entire amount to which he is entitled according to the agreement or rule under which the advance was made, the balance, if any, is transferred to Contributions in Aid of Construction.

Service Installation and Contract Bid Deposits, the final item in the Current Liabilities section, is the sum of two items. The first, often called Customer Deposits, represents amounts deposited with the utility as security for the payment of bills. The second represents amounts received by the utility from contractors as bid deposits. The item "Special Deposits in Bank" in the Current Assets section of Illustration 11–1 exactly offsets the Service Installation and Contract Bid Deposits liability.

Deferred Credits

Two items generally found in the Deferred Credits section of a utility balance sheet, Unamortized Premium on Debt and Customer Advances for Construction, are related to items shown in the Deferred Debits and Current Liabilities sections of Illustration 11–1, respectively, and are discussed above under those headings. Investor-owned utilities have need for other accounts classified as deferred credits by regulatory agencies, but municipally-owned utilities ordinarily do not.

Operating Reserves

Uniform charts of accounts published by NARUC and FPC provide for an Operating Reserve balance sheet section to be shown between the Deferred Credits and the Contributions in Aid of Construction sections. Operating reserves accounts such as Property Insurance Reserve, Injuries and Damages Reserve, Pensions and Benefits Reserve, Amortization Reserve—Federal, and Miscellaneous Operating Reserves, are provided in the uniform charts of utility accounts. "Reserve," in general accounting terminology, refers to a segregation of retained earnings; accounts in this section of a utility balance sheet are segregated, as their names indicate, because of decisions to self-insure, to provide for probable liabilities for injuries or damages, or to offset assets to be used for pensions and benefits purposes, or to comply with requirements of creditors or regulatory bodies. Apparently no Operating Reserve section is required of the utility whose balance sheet is shown as Illustration 11–1, although, as shown in Illustration 11–2, the utility has a relatively minor amount of assets set aside in an Insurance Revenue Fund.

Contributions in Aid of Construction

Contributions in Aid of Construction differ from Customer Advances for Construction in that Contributions represent additions to equity which are expected to be permanent whereas advances are to be repaid as explained in the discussion under the heading of Current Liabilities above. Contributions include donations in cash, services, or property from states, municipalities, Federal agencies, individuals, and others. As indicated in Illustration 11–1, the separate accounts are customarily kept to facilitate disclosure of the sources of contributions.

Retained Earnings

Although it is generally true that municipalities own utilities in order to have the capacity to render services to residents, rather than as a device to earn revenues, it is obviously in the best interests of taxpayers that the utility be self-supporting. Operating revenues, therefore, must be set at a level expected to cover operating expenses, provide for debt service, and finance routine capital projects. For these reasons it is customary for municipally-owned utilities to accumulate retained earnings just as investor-owned utilities do—although perhaps not to the same extent. Illustration 11–3 shows the combined statement of revenues and expenses and retained earnings accompanying the balance sheet shown as Illustration 11–1. The net income for the year amounts to 14.67 percent of operating revenues, but only about 1.6 percent of total assets. Total retained earnings amount to approximately one-seventh of total assets. Note 3 to the balance sheet (see Illustration 11–1) discloses (1) the amount of retained earnings ("surplus") of predecessor utilities at the date they were brought into the present utility, (2) the amounts of retained earnings appropriated to function as Fund Balances of the Special Funds, and (3) the unappropriated balance of earnings retained since the existing utility commenced operations.

Revenue Accounts

Operating Revenues. Utility operating revenues include sales of the principal product (water in the case of the utility illustrated in this chapter) together with items such as forfeited discounts and penalties;

Illustration 11–3

CITY AND COUNTY OF HONOLULU
Board of Water Supply
Statement of Revenues and Expenses and Retained Earnings
For the Fiscal Year Ended June 30, 1972

Schedule 1
to Exhibit L

Operating Revenues		$15,107,336
Less: Operating Expenses:		
Source of supply	$ 102,285	
Pumping	1,438,621	
Water Treatment	84,216	
Transmission and distribution	1,037,096	
Customers' accounts	857,817	
Administrative and general:		
Employees' retirement	798,758	
Other	1,515,613	
Maintenance	2,780,528	
Provision for Depreciation . . . (Note 4)*	3,699,342	
Total Operating Expenses		12,314,276
Net Operating Income		2,793,060
Add: Non-operating Income:		
Interest	1,156,708	
Miscellaneous (principally from jobbing and contract work–net)	66,423	
Total Non-operating Income		1,223,131
Total Income		4,016,191
Less: Non-operating Expenses:		
Interest on long-term debt	1,915,271	
Interest charged to construction	(141,778)	
Amortization of debt premium and expense–net	7,550	
Amortization of call premium on bond redemption	15,990	
Other	2,802	
Total Non-operating Expenses		1,799,835
Net Income for Year		2,216,356
Retained Earnings, July 1. 1971. . . (Note 3)*		18,546,795
Retained Earnings, June 30, 1972 . . . (Note 3)*		$20,763,151

* See Illustration 11-1.

fees for changing, connecting, or disconnecting service; rents from property; sales of byproducts; profit or loss on incidental sales of materials and supplies; and any other revenues from operations. Sales of the principal product are accounted for and reported by customer classes for which separate rate structures exist. For example, unmetered, or flat-rate, sales to general customers are separated from metered sales to general customers. If the rate schedule so indicates, the single account Sales to General Customers should be replaced by accounts for residential sales, commercial sales, and industrial sales. Private fire protection service, public fire protection service, other sales to public authorities, sales to irrigation customers, and sales for resale are operating revenue accounts needed by many water utilities. Comparable accounts are used by electric, gas, and other utilities.

Operating Expenses. Illustration 11–3 shows a section of the income statement captioned Operating Expenses. The items under that caption, such as Source of Supply, themselves represent categories of "operation and maintenance" expense accounts. Detail provided in the NARUC suggested system of accounts indicates the information needed for the management of, and regulation of, utilities. For example, Source of Supply *operation* expense accounts include: Operation Supervision and Engineering, Operation Labor and Expenses, Purchased Water, Miscellaneous Expenses, and Rents. Source of Supply *maintenance* expense accounts include: Maintenance Supervision and Labor, Maintenance of Structures and Improvements, Maintenance of Collecting and Impounding Reservoirs, Maintenance of Lake, River, and Other Intakes, Maintenance of Wells and Springs, Maintenance of Infiltration Galleries and Tunnels, Maintenance of Supply Mains, and Maintenance of Miscellaneous Water Source Plant. Apparently the utility from whose report Illustration 11–3 was taken shows only the operation expenses for the Source of Supply, Pumping, Water Treatment, Transmission and Distribution, and Customers' Accounts categories, and classifies all maintenance expenses under the Maintenance heading; this alternative appears to provide less useful managerial information than the NARUC recommendations would.

The treatment of depreciation expense (Provision for Depreciation) in Illustration 11–3 is in agreement with the NARUC suggested system of accounts. Amortization of plant acquisition adjustments, amortization of intangible assets, and tax expenses are also to be reported as separate items according to accounting systems published by regulatory authorities. Although separate disclosure of the depreciation charges, amortization charges, and taxes for the period is clearly of interest to regulatory authorities, distribution of these expenses to responsibility centers would provide useful managerial information and should be done for statements prepared for use within a utility.

It should be noted that recommended operating expense accounts do not provide either utility management or utility regulatory bodies with a matching of the revenues and costs by classes of customers. Accordingly, there is no current measure of the adequacy or equity of rates charged each class of customers. As the need is perceived, utilities prepare cost of service studies—generally to justify a proposed increase in the schedule of rates. Discussion of cost of service studies is beyond the scope of this chapter.

Other Income and Deductions; Interest Charges. The items shown in the sections of Illustration 11–3 captioned Non-operating Income and

Non-operating Expenses are classified as Other Income and Deductions, and Interest Charges in the NARUC and FPC systems. In addition to interest and dividend income and net income from merchandising, jobbing, and contracting work, shown as the Non-operating Income in Illustration 11–3, net income from nonutility operations, net rentals of nonutility property, gain on disposition of property, and miscellaneous nonoperating income are classified as Other Income. Loss on disposition of property, miscellaneous amortization, and miscellaneous income deductions such as donations, premiums on life insurance where the utility is beneficiary, penalties or fines, and expenditures for civic, political, or related activities are classified by regulatory bodies as Other Income Deductions. Interest Charges, in the NARUC and FPC charts of accounts, includes Interest on Long-Term Debt, Amortization of Debt Discount and Expense, Amortization of Premium on Debt (a credit in this section), Interest on Debt to Associated Companies or Municipality, Other Interest Expense, and Interest Charged to Construction (a credit in this section). The manner in which Interest Charged to Construction is related to Interest on Long-Term Debt is shown in the Non-operating Expenses section of Illustration 11–3.

Statement of Changes in Financial Position

Readers of utility financial statements who are seriously attempting to understand the utility's financial activities and to evaluate its financial management often find a Statement of Changes in Financial Position of considerable value. For example, accrual-based net income is not a good measure of the amount of working capital generated from operations because a high proportion of total assets, typically, are invested in depreciable and amortizable assets, and noncash expenses are correspondingly high in relation to total expenses. A Statement of Changes in Financial Position provides good disclosure of noncash expenses and their effect upon the provision of resources. Similarly, explicit disclosure of changes in the amount of utility plant, changes in long-term debt, and changes in special funds, is also often of importance to readers of utility statements. Illustration 11–4 shows the Statement of Changes in Financial Position to accompany the statements shown as Illustrations 11–1, 11–2, and 11–3.

Illustrative Accounting for a Water Utility Fund

The discussion in preceding pages of utility fund financial statements includes by implication the essential characteristics of accounting necessary both for municipally-owned utilities and for investor-owned utilities. In this section accounting for characteristic transactions of a utility fund is illustrated in general journal entry format.

It is assumed that the Town of Merrill is located in a state which permits enterprise funds to operate without formal legal approval of their

Illustration 11–4

CITY AND COUNTY OF HONOLULU
Board of Water Supply
Statement of Changes in Financial Position
For the Fiscal Year Ended June 30, 1972

Schedule 2
to Exhibit L

Source of Funds:	
Working capital provided from operations:	
Net income	$ 2,216,356
Add expenses not requiring outlay of working capital:	
Depreciation	3,797,915
Amortization—net	23,540
Working capital provided from operations for the year	6,037,811
Contributions in aid of and customer advances for construction—net	4,225,545
Decrease in construction funds	1,313,075
Decrease in refunding and bond retirement trust accounts	397,276
Decrease in special funds	264,952
Other—net	16,188
Total	$12,254,847
Application of Funds:	
Utility plant additions	$ 8,438,093
Long-term debt paid or becoming current liability	2,460,000
Other—net	107,233
Increase in working capital	1,249,521
Total	$12,254,847
Summary of Increases (Decreases) in Components of Working Capital:	
Cash, certificates of deposit, and United States Government obligations	$ (2,802,352)
Accounts receivable	195,830
Materials and supplies	71,164
Total	(2,535,358)
Long-term debt payable within one year	(4,138,000)
Accrued and matured interest payable	(447,530)
Matured revenue bonds not presented	1,054,000
Accrued vacation pay	62,338
Accounts payable and other current accounts—net	(315,687)
Total	(3,784,879)
Increase in Working Capital	$ 1,249,521

budgets. Utility, or other enterprise, management must prepare operating budgets and capital expenditure budgets as management tools. For the illustrative case it is assumed that the budgets are submitted to the municipal administrators, to the municipal legislative body, and to the public, for information, not for legal action. Accordingly, the budget is not formally recorded in enterprise fund accounts. Similarly, utility management must be informed periodically of the status of outstanding construction contracts and purchase orders, but encumbrances need not be recorded in the accounts in order to accomplish this.

Assume that as of December 31, 197A, the accountants for the Town of Merrill Water Utility Fund prepared the following post-closing trial balance.

TOWN OF MERRILL
Water Utility Fund
Trial Balance
December 31, 197A

	Debit	*Credit*
Utility plant in service	$3,315,000	
Construction work in progress	125,000	
Accumulated provision for depreciation of utility plant		$ 463,500
Special funds	62,600	
Cash	126,000	
Customer accounts receivable	69,000	
Accumulated provision for uncollectible accounts		2,900
Materials and supplies	28,700	
Accrued utility revenues	14,800	
Unamortized debt discount and expense	5,300	
Revenue bonds payable		1,750,000
Accounts payable		33,200
Customer deposits		23,700
Customers advances for construction		21,000
Contributions from Municipality		1,000,000
Contributions from customers		252,000
Appropriated retained earnings		62,600
Unappropriated retained earnings		137,500
Totals	$3,746,400	$3,746,400

The item Accrued Utility Revenues in the trial balance represents unbilled customer accounts receivable at year end; this treatment is an accepted alternative to the one shown in Illustration 11–1. Metered service billings are based upon reports of meter readings at regular intervals and the application of rates according to the amount of service used. Utilities that meter their service make extensive use of cycle billing, which in substance consists of billing part of their customers each day, instead of billing by calendar months. Under this plan meter reading is a continuous day-by-day operation, with billings following shortly after the filing of the meter readers' reports. Individual meters are read on approximately the same day each month, or every other month, in order that each bill cover approximately the same number of days usage. Cycle billing eliminates the heavy peak load of accounting and clerical work which results from uniform billing on a calendar month basis. It does, however, result in a sizable amount of unbilled receivables on any given date, thus requiring accrual of unbilled receivables as of financial statement date in order to state assets and sales properly. When individual bills are prepared, it is not feasible to determine whether a portion of the bill has been accrued, and, if so, how much. The simplest procedure, therefore, is to reverse the accrual entry as of the start of the new fiscal year. Assuming that the entire December 31, 197A, Town of Merrill Water Utility Fund revenues accrual has been credited to Sales of Water, the following entry is appropriate as of January 1, 197B:

1.	Sales of Water	14,800	
	Accrued Utility Revenues		14,800

When utility customers are billed during the year, appropriate revenue accounts are credited. Assuming that during 197B the total bills to nonmunicipal customers amounted to $696,000, bills to the Town of Merrill General Fund amounted to $30,000, and that all revenue was from sales of water, the following entry summarizes the events:

2.	Customer Accounts Receivable	696,000	
	Due From General Fund	30,000	
	Sales of Water		726,000

If collections from nonmunicipal customers totaled $680,000 for water billings, entry no. 3 is needed:

3.	Cash	680,000	
	Customer Accounts Receivable		680,000

During 197B the Town of Merrill established a Supplies Fund and the Water Utility Fund advanced $100,000 to the Supplies Fund as a long-term loan. The entry by the Supplies Fund is illustrated in Chapter 9 (see Chapter 9 illustrative entry no. 1). The following entry should be made by the Water Utility Fund.

4.	Long-Term Advance to Supplies Fund	100,000	
	Cash		100,000

Materials and supplies in the amount of $138,000 were purchased during the year by the Water Utility Fund. The liability is recorded as:

5.	Materials and Supplies	138,000	
	Accounts Payable		138,000

Materials and supplies chargeable to the accounts itemized in the entry below were issued during the year.

6.	Source of Supply Expenses	18,000	
	Pumping Expenses	21,000	
	Water Treatment Expenses	24,000	
	Transmission and Distribution Expenses	13,000	
	Construction Work in Progress	66,000	
	Materials and Supplies		142,000

Payrolls for the year were chargeable to the accounts shown in the entry below. Tax Collections Payable is the account provided in the NARUC and FPC systems to report "the amount of taxes collected by the utility through payroll deductions or otherwise pending transmittal of such taxes to the proper taxing authority." Taxes Accrued is the account provided in the NARUC and FPC systems to report the liability for taxes which are the expense of the utility, such as the employer's share of social security taxes. In the entry below it is assumed that the employer's share of social security taxes is charged to the same accounts that the employees' gross earnings are; it is also assumed that checks have been issued for employees' net earnings.

	Account	Debit	Credit
7.	Source of Supply Expenses	8,200	
	Pumping Expenses	15,700	
	Water Treatment Expenses	17,500	
	Transmission and Distribution Expenses	76,250	
	Customer Accounts Expenses	96,550	
	Sales Expenses	17,250	
	Administrative and General Expenses	83,150	
	Construction Work in Progress	30,400	
	Taxes Accrued		13,800
	Tax Collections Payable		51,750
	Cash		279,450

Bond interest in the amount of $105,000 was paid. Amortization of debt discount and expense amounted to $530.

	Account	Debit	Credit
8.	Interest on Long-term Debt	105,000	
	Amortization of Debt Discount and Expense	530	
	Unamortized Debt Discount and Expense		530
	Cash		105,000

Interest in the amount of $12,900 was considered to be properly chargeable to contruction:

	Account	Debit	Credit
9.	Construction Work in Progress	12,900	
	Interest Charged to Construction		12,900

Construction projects on which costs totaled $220,000 were completed and the assets placed in service:

	Account	Debit	Credit
10.	Utility Plant in Service	220,000	
	Construction Work in Progress		220,000

Collection efforts were discontinued on bills totaling $3,410. The customers owing the bills had paid deposits to the water utility totaling $2,140; the deposits were applied to the bills and the unpaid remainder was charged to the accumulated provision for uncollectible accounts.

	Account	Debit	Credit
11.	Customer Deposits	2,140	
	Accumulated Provision for Uncollectible Accounts	1,270	
	Customer Accounts Receivable		3,410

Customers deposits amounting to $1,320 were refunded by check to customers discontinuing service (see entry 12a). Deposits totaling $2,525 were received from new customers (see entry 12b).

	Account	Debit	Credit
12a.	Customer Deposits	1,320	
	Cash		1,320
12b.	Cash	2,525	
	Customer Deposits		2,525

Customers advances for construction in the amount of $14,000 were applied to their water bills; in accord with the agreement with the customers the remainder of the advances were transferred to Contributions from Customers.

		Debit	Credit
13.	Customers Advances for Construction	21,000	
	Customer Accounts Receivable		14,000
	Contributions from Customers		7,000

Payments of accounts payable totaled $133,200. Payments of Taxes Accrued amounted to $13,500, and payments of Tax Collections Payable amounted to $50,000.

		Debit	Credit
14.	Accounts Payable	133,200	
	Taxes Accrued	13,500	
	Tax Collections Payable	50,000	
	Cash		196,700

The Water Utility Fund agreed to pay $25,000 to the town General Fund as a contribution in lieu of property taxes. The entry in the General Fund is illustrated in Chapter 3 (see Chapter 3, illustrative entry 17b). The following entry records the event in the books of the Water Utility Fund:

		Debit	Credit
15.	Contribution in Lieu of Taxes	25,000	
	Due to General Fund		25,000

The Supplies Fund paid its first installment of $5,000 to the Water Utility Fund as partial repayment of the long-term advance. Entry 8 in Chapter 9 illustrates the effect on the accounts of the Supplies Fund. The effect on the accounts of the Water Utility Fund is recorded by the following entry:

		Debit	Credit
16.	Cash	5,000	
	Long-Term Advance to Supplies Fund		5,000

At year-end entries to record depreciation expense, the provision for uncollectible accounts, and unbilled customers accounts receivable should be made as illustrated by entry 17. Amounts are assumed.

		Debit	Credit
17.	Depreciation Expense	102,750	
	Customer Accounts Expenses	3,980	
	Accrued Utility Revenues	15,920	
	Accumulated Provision for Depreciation of Utility Plant		102,750
	Accumulated Provision for Uncollectible Accounts		3,980
	Sales of Water		15,920

In accord with the revenue bond indenture, $100,000 was transferred from operating cash to the Special Funds Category. The transfer requires an appropriation of retained earnings of an equal amount.

		Debit	Credit
18a.	Special Funds	100,000	
	Cash		100,000
18b.	Unappropriated Retained Earnings	100,000	
	Appropriated Retained Earnings		100,000

Illustration 11–5

TOWN OF MERRILL
Water Utility Fund
Balance Sheet
December 31, 197B

Assets and Other Debits

Utility Plant:			
Utility plant in service		$3,535,000	
Construction work in progress		14,300	
Total Utility Plant		$3,549,300	
Accumulated provision for depreciation of utility plant		566,250	
Net Utility Plant			$2,983,050
Other Property and Investments:			
Long-term advance to supplies fund		$ 95,000	
Special funds		162,600	
Total			257,600
Current and Accrued Assets:			
Cash		$ 31,055	
Customer accounts receivable	$67,590		
Accumulated provision for uncollectible accounts	5,610	61,980	
Due from general fund		5,000	
Materials and supplies		24,700	
Accrued utility revenues		15,920	
Total			138,655
Deferred Debits:			
Unamortized bond discount and expense			4,770
Total Assets and Other Debits			$3,384,075

Liabilities and Other Credits

Long-term Debt:		
Revenue bonds payable		$1,750,000
Current and Accrued Liabilities:		
Accounts payable	$ 38,000	
Customer deposits	22,765	
Taxes accrued	300	
Tax collections payable	1,750	
Total		62,815
Contributions In Aid of Construction:		
Contributions from municipality	$1,000,000	
Contributions from customers	259,000	
Total		1,259,000
Retained Earnings:		
Appropriated retained earnings	$ 162,600	
Unappropriated retained earnings	149,660	312,260
Total Liabilities and Other Credits		$3,384,075

Nominal accounts for the year were closed:

19.	Sales of Water	727,120	
	Interest Charged to Construction	12,900	
	Source of Supply Expenses		26,200
	Pumping Expenses		36,700
	Water Treatment Expenses		41,500
	Transmission and Distribution Expenses		89,250
	Customer Account Expenses		100,530
	Sales Expenses		17,250
	Administrative and General Expenses		83,150
	Interest on Long-term Debt		105,000
	Amortization of Debt Discount and Expense		530
	Contribution in Lieu of Taxes		25,000
	Depreciation Expense		102,750
	Unappropriated Retained Earnings		112,160

The balance sheet for the Town of Merrill Water Utility Fund as of December 31, 197B, would appear as shown in Illustration 11–5, assuming the format recommended by National Association of Railroad and

Illustration 11–6

TOWN OF MERRILL
Water Utility Fund
Statement of Revenues and Expenses and Retained Earnings
for the Year Ended December 31, 197B

Utility Operating Revenue:		
Sales of water		$727,120
Operating Expenses:		
Source of supply expenses	$ 26,200	
Pumping expenses	36,700	
Water treatment expenses	41,500	
Transmission and distribution expenses	89,250	
Customer account expenses	100,530	
Sales expenses	17,250	
Administrative and general expenses	83,150	
Depreciation expense	102,750	
Contribution in lieu of taxes	25,000	
Total Operating Expenses		522,330
Utility Operating Income		$204,790
Interest Charges:		
Interest on Long-term Debt	$105,000	
Amortization of Debt Discount and Expense	530	
Interest Charged to Construction	(12,900)	
Total Interest Charges		92,630
Net Income		$112,160
Unappropriated Retained Earnings, January 1, 197B		137,500
Total		$249,660
Less: Appropriation of Retained Earnings		100,000
Unappropriated Retained Earnings, December 31, 197B		$149,660
Appropriated Retained Earnings, January 1, 197B		$ 62,600
Add: Appropriated During Year		100,000
Appropriated Retained Earnings, December 31, 197B		$162,600

Illustration 11–7

CITY OF LAS VEGAS, NEVADA
Enterprise Funds
Balance Sheet, June 30, 1972

	Total	Sewage Disposal Fund	Off-Street Parking Fund	Cemetery Fund
Assets				
Current assets:				
Cash	$ 490,819	$ 444,641	$ 19,206	$ 26,972
Investments, at cost (market value $539,826)	539,826	539,826		
Accounts receivable	348,688	278,235	2,691	67,762
Accrued interest receivable	8,095			8,095
Total current assets	1,387,428	1,262,702	21,897	102,829
Restricted assets:				
Debt service:				
Cash	8,200		8,200	
Investments, at cost (market value $220,000)	220,000		220,000	
Bond reserve:				
Cash	392,802		392,802	
Cemetery perpetual care:				
Cash	8,271			8,271
Investments, at cost (market value $302,724)	322,429			322,429
Accounts receivable	36,780			36,780
Total Restricted Assets	988,482		621,002	367,480
Fixed assets, at cost:				
Land	2,668,841	186,351	2,463,025	19,465
Buildings	2,374,963	59,400	2,287,640	27,923
Improvements other than buildings	19,175,708	18,940,262	85,188	150,258
Machinery and equipment	34,045	8,438	20,365	5,242
	24,253,557	19,194,451	4,856,218	202,888
Less accumulated depreciation and amortization	4,397,987	4,068,520	246,179	83,288
Total Fixed Assets	19,855,570	15,125,931	4,610,039	119,600
Total Assets	$22,231,480	$16,388,633	$5,252,938	$589,909

	Total	Sewage Disposal Fund	Off-Street Parking Fund	Cemetery Fund
Liabilities, Reserves, Contributions, and Retained Earnings				
Current liabilities (payable from current assets):				
Accounts payable	$ 37,688	$ 22,531	$ 6,904	$ 8,253
Matured and accrued interest payable	53,582	53,582		
Advance from municipality, general obligation bonds	582,000	342,000	240,000	
Due to General Fund	2,657			2,657
	675,927	418,113	246,904	10,910
Current liabilities (payable from restricted assets):				
Matured and accrued interest payable	85,636		85,636	
Total current liabilities	761,563	418,113	332,540	10,910
Other liabilities:				
Advance from municipality, general obligation bonds	7,193,000	2,958,000	4,235,000	
Reserves:				
Reserve for debt service	564,468	421,904	142,564	
Reserve for bond retirement	392,802		392,802	
Reserve for cemetery perpetual care	367,480			367,480
Total Reserves	1,324,750	421,904	535,366	367,480
Contributions:				
Municipality	4,745,607	3,356,113	1,147,430	242,064
Subdividers and individuals	6,200,668	6,200,668		
Special improvement districts	803,788	803,788		
State and federal grants	906,976	906,976		
Total Contributions	12,657,039	11,267,545	1,147,430	242,064
Retained earnings (deficit)	295,128	1,323,071	(997,398)	(30,545)
Total	$22,231,480	$16,388,633	$5,252,938	$589,909

Utilities Commissioners and Federal Power Commission is followed. Note that the amount due to the General Fund is offset against the amount due from that fund, and only the net amount of the receivable, $5,000, is shown as an asset.

Illustration 11–6 presents the Statement of Revenues and Expenses and Retained Earnings for the year ended December 31, 197B, for the Town of Merrill Water Utility Fund.

Combined Financial Statements of Enterprise Funds

In order to reduce the bulk of municipal annual reports it is common for municipalities which operate more than one enterprise fund to prepare a *combined columnar* balance sheet so that all enterprise funds may be included in a single statement. Similarly, statements of retained earnings, income, and changes in financial position are often prepared in combined columnar form. When balance sheets of utility funds are combined with balance sheets of other utilities, the customary business format is used rather than the regulatory format shown in Illustrations 11–1 and 11–5. A combined enterprise fund in columnar form is shown as Illustration 11–7.

SELECTED REFERENCES

AMERICAN INSTITUTE OF CERTIFIED PUBLIC ACCOUNTANTS. *Audits of State and Local Governmental Units.* New York, 1974.

AVERY, WILLIAM J. "Accounting and Financial Administration of a Municipal Transit System," *Muncipal Finance*, vol. 42 (May 1970), pp. 17–26.

FEDERAL POWER COMMISSION. *Uniform System of Accounts Prescribed for Public Utilities and Licensees.* Washington, D.C.: U.S. Government Printing Office, 1970.

HAY, LEON E. AND GRINNELL, D. J. *Water Utility Accounting.* Chicago and New York: Municipal Finance Officers Association and American Water Works Association, 1970.

NATIONAL ASSOCIATION OF RAILROAD AND UTILITIES COMMISSIONERS. *Uniform System of Accounts for Water Utilities.* Washington: NARUC, 1958.

NATIONAL COMMITTEE ON GOVERNMENTAL ACCOUNTING. *Governmental Accounting, Auditing, and Financial Reporting*, chap. 6. Chicago, 1968.

PIATT, RICHARD B. "Computer Applications for a Utility," *Municipal Finance*, vol. 39, no. 2. (November 1966) pp. 67–73.

SUELFLOW, JAMES E. *Public Utility Accounting: Theory and Applications.* East Lansing, Mich: Michigan State University Institute of Public Utilities, 1973.

United States Housing Assistance Administration, Department of Housing and Urban Development. *Accounting Manual—Uniform System of Accounts and Accounting Requirements for Federally Aided Low-Rent Public Housing.* Washington, D.C., 1967.

QUESTIONS

11–1. What information is needed about a fund to know whether it may be classified properly as an enterprise fund or whether it should be classified as a revenue fund? As an intragovernmental service fund?

11–2. Chapter 11 illustrates accounting for a water utility fund. If a municipality operates a hospital as an enterprise, how may a municipal administrator or an accountant find out what accounting structure is appropriate? If a municipality operates a produce market as an enterprise, how may a municipal administrator or an accountant find out what accounting structure is appropriate?

11–3. In general, how may a municipal administrator or accountant determine the appropriate basis of accounting for a nonregulated municipal enterprise? A municipal enterprise in a regulated industry?

11–4. A governmental utility sought to issue bonds to finance the cost of a major expansion program. The action was opposed by a militant organization which contended that need for the bond issue resulted from mismanagement. Spokesmen for the organization asserted that over a period of several years the utility had made large contributions to the city's general fund, which action had been highly favorable to railroads and other large corporations in that it reduced substantially their property taxes. What do you consider to be the main points or issues in this controversy?

11–5. What are the meanings of "original cost" and "adjustment account" as used in public utility accounting? (AICPA)

11–6. In his annual report, a city auditor criticized the administrative officials of a utility for using depreciation fund assets to increase the utility plant, that is, to build more lines. In the absence of other information, what is your opinion of his criticism?

11–7. Frequently it is not possible to distribute all amounts in clearing accounts before the close of the fiscal period. How should undistributed amounts be shown in the financial statements?

11–8. Why are regulated utilities generally required to present plant assets before current assets, and long-term debt before current liabilities, in balance sheets? If a municipality is located in a state in which municipal utilities are not regulated, what arguments are there for following the regulatory format illustrated in Chapter 11? For following the format illustrated in preceding chapters of this text?

11–9. Briefly describe proper enterprise fund accounting for debt service and construction activities; compare or contrast this treatment with municipal debt service and construction activities of a general nature.

11–10. If a municipality issues general obligation bonds which are to be serviced by enterprise fund revenues, what treatment should be given to the bonds in the enterprise fund balance sheet? In the Statement of General Long-term Debt?

EXERCISES AND PROBLEMS

11–1. Utilizing the municipal annual report obtained for Exercise 1–1, follow the instructions below:

a) What activities of the municipality are reported as being administered by enterprise funds? Does the municipality own and operate its water utility? Electric utility? Gas utility? Transportation system? Are combined statements presented for all enterprise funds, or are separate statements presented for each enterprise fund? Are all enterprise funds accounted for on the full accrual basis? Are all funds in this category earning revenues at least equal to costs and expenses? If not, how is the operating deficit being financed? What sources furnished the original investment in fund assets?

b) Is it possible to tell from the report whether utilities of this municipality are subject to the same regulation as investor-owned utilities in the same state? (If the utility statements follow the format of the NARUC and FPC, as illustrated in Chapter 11, there is a good chance that the municipally-owned utilities are subject to at least some supervision by a regulatory agency.) What rate of return on sales (or operating revenues) is being earned by each utility fund? What rate of return on total assets is being earned by each utility fund?

Are sales to other municipal funds separately disclosed? Are there receivables from other funds? Is there any evidence that utilities contribute amounts to the general fund in lieu of taxes to help support municipal services received by the utility?

Is depreciation taken on utility plant? Are accounting policies and accounting changes properly disclosed in accord with APB Opinions? If so, what method of depreciation is being used? Is the *original cost* basis used for plant assets—is a plant acquisition adjustment account shown? If so, over what period is the acquisition adjustment being amortized?

Does each utility account for its own debt service and construction activities in the manner described in Chapter 11? What Special Funds, or Restricted Assets, are utilized by each utility? Is Retained Earnings appropriated in an amount equal to or exceeding Special Funds, or Restricted Assets?

c) Are nonutility enterprise funds accounted for in the same manner as investor-owned enterprises in the same industries (in order to answer this you may need to refer to publications of trade associations, or to handbooks or encyclopedias of accounting systems found in business libraries)? If you cannot find information about investor-owned counterparts of the municipal nonutility enterprise funds, do the statements of the latter evidence that generally accepted accounting principles devised for profit-seeking businesses were used?

11–2. *a*) The City of St. Petersburg, Florida, Water Fund Combined Balance Sheet for the year ended September 30, 1971, is shown below. In what respects does the statement evidence that the fund is being operated and accounted for in the manner described in Chapter 11?

b) The Combined Balance Sheet is accompanied in the St. Petersburg report by a statement of changes in combined retained earnings. The report also includes the following statements for the Water System Operating Fund: balance sheet; statement of changes in retained earnings; statement of operations; statement of revenue—estimated and actual; schedule of operating expenses; statement of expenditures and encumbrances compared with appropriations; a schedule of expenditures by department, division, and object; and a statement of changes in fixed assets. The following statements for the Water System Capital Projects Fund are included: balance sheet, statement of changes in fund balances, and statement of appropriated fund balance by projects. For the Water Fund Revenue Certificate Interest and Redemption Fund a balance sheet and a statement of revenue, expenditures, and fund balance are presented, as well as a statement of revenue certificate debt and interest, a summary of water revenue certificates, a statement of combined debt requirements for each fiscal year through 1990–91, and separate statements of debt requirements for each issue of water revenue certificates.

In view of the information about these statements and schedules do you have the same conclusion as to the extent to which St. Petersburg follows the general recommendations for utility fund accounting as you did when you studied its Water Fund Combined Balance Sheet? Why or why not?

CITY OF ST. PETERSBURG, FLORIDA
WATER FUND
Combined Balance Sheet
September 30, 1971

Assets

Current Assets:		
Cash on hand and in banks	$ 34,359	
Due from other funds	8,475,000	
Accounts receivable, net	346,652	
Notes receivable	13,137	
Inventories	409,906	
Prepaid insurance	2,540	$ 9,281,594
Restricted Assets:		
Cash with paying agent		635,653
Projects in Progress:		
Expended to date		152,127
Fixed Assets		
Facilities and equipment	42,449,588	
Less allowance for depreciation	7,828,982	34,620,606
Total Assets		$44,689,980

Liabilities, Reserves, Retained Earnings, and Fund Balance

Current Liabilities:		
Vouchers and accounts payable	$ 72,283	
Retainage on contracts	20,538	
Customers deposits	20,485	
Escrow deposits	10,750	
Accrued salaries	13,192	$ 137,248
Current Liabilities (payable from restricted assets):		
Bonds and interest payable	199,060	
Debt payable before October 1, 1972	655,000	854,060
Other Liabilities:		
Debt payable after September 30, 1972		12,830,000
Reserves:		
Reserve for encumbrances	38,828	
Reserve for construction	1,423,831	1,462,659
Retained Earnings and Fund Balance:		
Equity in fixed assets	21,135,606	
Available, Operating Fund	2,780,768	
Unappropriated, Capital Projects Fund	3,550,689	
Fund balance, Interest and Redemption Fund	1,938,950	29,406,013
Total Liabilities, Reserves, Retained Earnings, and Fund Balance		$44,689,980

11–3. Statements F–1 through F–6 below present all the information to be found in the 1971 annual report of the City of Beloit, Wisconsin, about the Golf Course Operating Fund. They are reproduced without change. If you were a new member of the Beloit City Council how would you evaluate the operating policies and the financial management of the Fund, as evidenced in the statements below? What additional information would you request from the City Manager about the Golf Course and its operations?

F–1
City of Beloit, Wisconsin
Golf Course Operating Fund
December 31, 1971

Assets

Current Assets:		
Equity in Treasurer's Cash (F–3) (A–5)	$51,443.25	
Due from Other Funds	2,325.95	$ 53,769.20
Utility Plant in Service (F–4)		87,423.55
Total Assets		$141,192.75

F–1 (*Cont.*)

Liabilities, Contributions and Retained Earnings		
Current Liabilities:		
Accounts Payable	$ 385.48	
Due to Other Funds	15,757.82	
Advance Payments on Green Fees	622.50	$ 16,765.80
Municipal Contributions		77,999.06
Retained Earnings (F–2)		46,427.89
Total Liabilities, Contributions and Retained Earnings		$141,192.75

F–2
City of Beloit, Wisconsin
Golf Course Operating and Maintenance Fund
Analysis of Changes in Retained Earnings
January 1, 1971 to December 31, 1971

Retained Earnings, January 1, 1971		$ 46,515.86
Add:		
Net Income (F–5, F–6)	$15,749.03	
Correction of Prior Year Encumbrances	17.89	15,766.92
Total Balance and Additions		$ 62,282.78
Deduct:		
Net Income Transferred to General Fund	15,749.03	
Adjustment to Reserve	72.30	
Correction of Prior Year Encumbrances	33.56	15,854.89
Retained Earnings, December 31, 1971		$ 46,427.89

F–3
City of Beloit, Wisconsin
Golf Course Operating Fund
Statement of Source and Application of Cash Funds
January 1, 1971 to December 31, 1971

Cash Funds Were Provided By:		
Net Income (F–5, F–6)	$15,749.03	
Decrease Utility Plant in Service	2,039.81	
Decrease–Due from Other Funds	1,421.60	
Increase–Current Liabilities	15,892.90	
Decrease–Other Assets	69.25	$ 35,172.59
Cash Funds Were Applied To:		
Transfer of Net Income to General Fund	$15,749.03	
Adjustment of Reserve	72.30	
Prior Years Operations–Net	15.67	15,837.00
Increase in Cash Funds, 1-1-71 to 12-31-71		$ 19,335.59
Cash Balance, January 1, 1971		32,107.66
Cash Balance, December 31, 1971 (A–5), (F–1)		$ 51,443.25

F-4
City of Beloit, Wisconsin
Golf Course Operating Fund
Schedule of Fixed Assets and Depreciation
For the Year Ended December 31, 1971

	Assets			
	Balances 1-1-71	Additions	Deductions	Balances 12-31-71
Land	$ 25,400.00	$ 0	$ 0	$ 25,400.00
Buildings	23,048.18	0	00	23,048.18
Equipment	45,147.93	0	442.50	44,705.43
Other Facilities	20,000.00	0	0	20,000.00
Totals (F-1)	$113,596.11	$ 0	$442.50	$113,153.61

	Allowance for Depreciation				
	Balances 1-1-71	Depreciation Taken	Deductions	Balances 12-31-71	Net Asset Value
Land	$ 0	$ 1	$ 0	$ 0	$25,400.00
Buildings	18,774.60	190.00	0	18,964.60	4,083.58
Equipment	5,358.15	1,774.81	367.50	6,765.46	37,939.97
Other Facilities	0	0	0	0	20,000.00
Totals (F-1)	$24,132.75	$1,964.81	$367.50	$25,730.06	$87,423.55

F-5
City of Beloit, Wisconsin
Golf Course Operating Fund
Statement of Revenue and Expense—Actual and Budgeted
January 1, 1971 to December 31, 1971

	Budget	Actual	Excess[e] or Deficiency
Operating Revenue:			
Green Fees	$48,800.00	$59,086.18	$10,286.18[e]
Concessions	1,553.00	1,489.76	63.24
Total Operating Revenue	$50,353.00	$60,575.94	$10,222.94[e]
Operating Revenue Deductions Before Depreciation:			
Personal Services	$30,160.00	$28,278.09	$ 1,881.91
Contractual Services	8,778.00	10,076.68	1,298.68[e]
Materials and Supplies	7,730.00	6,803.33	926.67
Total Operating Revenue Deductions	$46,668.00	$45,158.10	$ 1,509.90
Net Operating Income Before Depreciation	$ 3,685.00	$15,417.84	$11,732.84[e]
Less: Depreciation	3,685.00	1,964.81	1,720.19
Net Operating Income	$ 0	$13,453.03	$13,453.03[e]
Add: Non-operating Income			
Interest Income	0	2,296.00	2,296.00[e]
Net Income to Retained Earnings (F-2)	$ 0	$15,749.03	$15,749.03[e]

F-6
City of Beloit, Wisconsin
Golf Course Operating Fund
Comparative Statement of Revenue and Expense
For the Years Indicated

	Year Ended December 31	
	1971	1970
Operating Revenue:		
Green Fees	$59,086.18	$53,608.35
Concessions	1,489.76	1,400.61
Total Operating Revenue	$60,575.94	$55,008.96
Operating Revenue Deductions Before Depreciation:		
Personal Services	$28,278.09	$30,676.92
Contractual Services	10,076.68	9,733.26
Materials and Supplies	6,803.33	10,130.51
Total Operating Revenue Deductions	$45,158.10	$50,540.69
Net Operating Income Before Depreciation	$15,417.84	$ 4,468.27
Less: Depreciation	1,964.81	2,419.26
Net Operating Income	$13,453.03	$ 2,049.01
Add: Non-operating Income		
Interest Income	2,296.00	2,008.06
Net Income to Retained Earnings (F-2)	$15,749.03	$ 4,057.07

11-4. The town board of Stinesville directed that $400,000 cash be transferred from the town's general fund as a permanent contribution to a newly created water fund. The cash represented the purchase price of the Ellet Water Company, plus an additional amount to serve as initial working capital for the new activity. At April 30, 197D, the effective date of purchase, the Ellet Company had the following after-closing trial balance:

	Debit	*Credit*
Land	$ 32,000	
Structures and improvements	507,000	
Allowance for depreciation—structures and improvements		$272,000
Equipment	156,000	
Allowance for depreciation—equipment		85,000
Cash	19,000	
Accounts receivable	44,000	
Estimated uncollectible receivables		16,000
Materials and supplies	18,000	
Vouchers payable		29,000
Accrued expenses		6,000
Capital stock		378,000
Retained earnings	10,000	
	$786,000	$786,000

The acquisition occurred as follows:

1. The municipal contribution was received on April 25, 197D.
2. As of April 30, 197D, the Stinesville water utility fund acquired the assets of the Ellet Water Company, excluding cash. Receivables were purchased at one-half of their face value. When the purchased assets were recorded the allowance for uncollectible receivables was increased to establish the new book value of receivables. The vendor's liabilities were assumed and a cash payment of $360,000 in full settlement was made.

Required:

a) Prepare in good form a balance sheet for the Town of Stinesville Water Utility Fund as of April 30, 197D. Assume that the format and account titles required by NARUC are used.

b) Comment on the financial structure of the Town of Stinesville Water Utility Fund with respect to the financial structure of a "typical" utility.

11–5. This problem continues the preceding problem. During the year ended April 30, 197E, the following transactions and events occurred in the Town of Stinesville Water Utility Fund:

1. On May 1, 197D, to finance needed plant improvements the Water Utility Fund borrowed $200,000 from a local bank on notes secured by a pledge of water utility revenues. The notes mature in five years and bear interest at the annual rate of 5%.
2. Accrued expenses at April 30, 197D, were paid in cash.
3. Billings to nonmunicipal customers for water usage during the year totaled $392,000.
4. Liabilities for the following were recorded during the year:

Materials and supplies	$ 37,900
Source of supply expenses	12,000
Pumping expenses	15,000
Water treatment expenses	21,000
Transmission and distribution expenses	64,000
Customer accounts expenses	98,000
Administrative and general expenses	73,000
Construction work in progress	203,000

5. Materials and supplies were used by the following departments in the following amounts: source of supply, $4,900; pumping, $3,000; treatment, $17,000; transmission and distribution, $18,000.
6. During fiscal 197E structures and improvements which had cost $81,000, with a book value now depreciated to $12,000, and equipment which had cost $37,000, with a book value now depreciated to $13,000, were sold for $15,000 cash.
7. $18,000 of old accounts receivable were written off.

8. During fiscal 197E the utility instituted a program of deposits, to reduce meter damage and customer defaults on water bills. Cash amounting to $6,400 was collected during the year.
9. Accounts receivable collections totaled $341,400 for the fiscal year.
10. $511,000 of accounts payable were paid in cash.
11. $120 was recorded as interest accumulated on customers' deposits. (Credit Miscellaneous Accruals.)
12. Depreciation expense for the year of $23,000 was recorded. Amortization of the plant acquisition adjustment in the amount of $1,000 was recorded.
13. Bills for materials and supplies, $7,000, were received and approved on April 30, 197E.
14. One year's interest on notes payable was paid.
15. Interest on long-term notes was charged to Construction Work in Progress.
16. The provision for uncollectible accounts was increased by an amount equal to one percent of the sales of water for the year.
17. Cash in the amount of $40,000 was transferred to Special Funds for eventual redemption of five-year notes. As required by the loan agreement, retained earnings in the amount of Special Funds was appropriated.
18. Nominal accounts for the year were closed.

Required:

a) Record the transactions for the year in general journal form.
b) Prepare a balance sheet as of April 30, 197E.
c) Prepare a statement of revenues, expenses, and retained earnings for the year ended April 30, 197E.

11–6. *a*) From your solution to Problems 11–4 and 11–5 prepare a Statement of Changes in Financial Position for the Town of Stinesville Water Utility Fund for the fiscal year ended April 30, 197E.

b) On the basis of your analysis of the financial statements prepared for Problems 11–4, 11–5, and 11–6, comment on any matters which should be brought to the attention of the management of the Town of Stinesville Water Utility Fund. What actions do you suggest that management should take?

11–7. From the following information about the Water Department of the City of X, prepare a worksheet showing the original trial balance, adjustments, and the extended profit and loss and balance sheet accounts. Also prepare in proper form fund balance sheet and operating statement for the year ended December 31, 1956, for the Water Department, using currently recommended account titles and statement format. (Encumbrances and Reserve for Encumbrances may be omitted from the balance sheet, but should be shown on the worksheet.)

Ledger Balances December 31, 1956

Cash–operating fund	$ 588,800
Cash–consumers' deposits	17,000
Prepayments	1,000
Accounts receivable:	
Consumer billing	65,000
Service	17,000
Sundry	700
Due from other funds	–
Supplies inventory	140,000
Encumbrances	145,000
Investments–consumers' deposits	50,000
Utility plant	6,000,000
Reserve for Encumbrances	145,000
Warrants payable	50,100
Due to other funds	–
Customers' advances for construction	–
Accounts payable–trade	47,000
Accounts payable–township	56,000
Water consumers' deposits	67,000
Revenue bonds payable	300,000
Accumulated depreciation	1,200,000
Surplus	4,500,000
Revenue	1,500,000
Expense:	
Production	340,000
Distribution	151,000
Office	90,000
Administrative and general	105,000
Cost of installations, repairs and parts	140,000
Interest on consumers' deposits	600
Interest on bonds	9,000
Allowances and adjustments	5,000

Note: Revenue bonds mature serially **$30,000** *each year.*

Examination of the records discloses the following data:

1. Included in error in accounts payable–trade:		
a) For reimbursement of metered postage (carried as a prepayment)		$ 500
b) Due to other City funds		18,500
2. Items included in book inventory that were not received until 1957		2,000
3. Computation of inventory items chargeable to distribution expense understated		1,000
4. Classified as accounts payable trade, should be accounts payable township		10,000
5. Unfilled orders not of record		1,000
6. 1957 expense purchases recorded as 1956 liabilities and charged to expense as follows:		
a) Production expense	$500	
b) Distribution expense	500	
c) Office expense	500	
d) Administrative and general expense	500	
7. Included in accounts receivable–service, but actually due from other funds		500
8. Credit balances included in accounts receivable–customers' advances for construction		1,000
9. Included in accounts receivable sundry but due from other City funds		50

10. Required adjustment to reduce unfilled orders and contracts (encumbrances) to proper estimates 2,600
11. Purchase order included in unfilled orders and contracts. This order a duplication of previously recorded expenditure 40,000
12. Unrecorded receivable from township for water consumed . 5,000

(AICPA, adapted)

11–8. Below are described some unrelated transactions of kinds experienced primarily by organizations engaged in providing conventional electric utility service. You are required to prepare entries in general journal form to record the transactions. Explanations are not required.

1. A customer who had failed to pay his electric bill of $14 the preceding month paid that bill and the current month's bill of $12.60 within the present month's discount period. The rate of penalty on delinquent bills was 6 percent.
2. The Transportation Expenses—Clearing account balance was distributed on the basis of the following information:

Cost charged to hauling poles for a new power line. . .	$150.00
Cost of transportation service performed for a private individual	17.50
Cost incurred in connection with dismantling a power line	269.00
Cost incurred in hauling material for a new building being erected by the utility's own working force . . .	188.00
Cost incurred in hauling coal for the utility's power plant	74.40
Balance of account before clearing	$698.90

3. Financial costs related to a building in process of construction were capitalized. The following were included:

   a) The appropriate amount of financial expense related to a $400,000 issue of 15-year term bonds, floated to finance the building. The bonds bore interest at 8 percent per year. The bonds were issued and construction of the building was begun and completed during the present year. The building was ready for use eight months after construction was started.

   b) $1,200 interest on the utility's own money was recorded as a cost of construction of the building.

4. Correction was made by appropriate debits and credits of an error in recording cost of a short stretch of line added to the transmission system during the year. The outlay of $3,780 had been debited to Accumulated Provision for Depreciation of Utility Plant.

5. During the year $29,760 cash was received from customers as advances in aid of construction. Also, during the year, $3,920 of customers' credit so established was applied against charges to customers for electric service received. (Record as separate transactions.)

11–9. The State Gas Company follows the practice of cycle billing in order to minimize peak work loads for its clerical employees. All customers are billed monthly on various dates, except in those cases when the meter readers are unable to enter the premises to obtain a reading.

The following information for the year ended September 30, 19x6, is presented by the company:

Cycle	*Billing Period*	*Customers Billed* *Number*	*Amount*	*Customers Not Billed*
1 . .	Aug. 7–Sept. 5, inclusive	2,760	$13,800.00	324
2 . .	Aug. 12–Sept. 10, inclusive	3,426	13,704.00	411
3 . .	Aug. 17–Sept. 15, inclusive	3,265	14,692.50	335
4 . .	Aug. 22–Sept. 20, inclusive	2,630	12,492.50	370
5 . .	Aug. 27–Sept. 25, inclusive	3,132	13,311.00	468

You are further advised that all customers have been billed for prior periods and that the company's experience shows that charges for those customers whose meters were not read average the same amount as the charges for the customers billed in their cycle. In addition, the company assumes that the customers' usage will be uniform from month to month.

From the above information, compute the unbilled revenues of the company as of September 30, 19x6, arising from cycles 1 and 3. (Do not compute revenues from cycles 2, 4, and 5.)

(AICPA, adapted)

11–10. The City of Larkspur provides electric energy for its citizens through an operating department. All transactions of the Electric Department are recorded in a self-sustaining fund supported by revenue from the sales of energy. Plant expansion is financed by the issuance of bonds which are repaid out of revenues.

All cash of the Electric Department is held by the city treasurer. Receipts from customers and others are deposited in the treasurer's account. Disbursements are made by drawing warrants on the treasurer.

The following is the post-closing trial balance of the department as of June 30, 19x4:

Cash on deposit with city treasurer	$ 2,250,000	
Due from customers	2,120,000	
Other current assets	130,000	
Construction in progress	500,000	
Land	5,000,000	
Electric plant	50,000,000*	
Accumulated depreciation–electric plant .		$10,000,000
Accounts payable and accrued liabilities . .		3,270,000
5 percent electric revenue bonds		20,000,000
Accumulated earnings		26,730,000
	$60,000,000	$60,000,000

***The plant is being depreciated on the basis of a 50-year composite life.**

During the year ended June 30, 19x5, the department had the following transactions:

1. Sales of electric energy, $10,700,000.
2. Purchases of fuel and operating supplies, $2,950,000.
3. Construction of miscellaneous system improvements (financed from operations), $750,000.
4. Fuel consumed, $2,790,000.
5. Miscellaneous plant additions and improvements placed in service, $1,000,000.
6. Wages and salaries paid, $4,280,000.
7. Sale on December 31, 19x4, of 20-year, 5 percent electric revenue bonds, with interest payable semiannually, $5,000,000.
8. Expenditures out of bond proceeds for construction of Larkspur Steam Plant Unit No. 1 and control house, $2,800,000.
9. Operating materials and supplies consumed, $150,000.
10. Payments received from customers, $10,500,000.
11. Expenditures out of bond proceeds for construction of Larkspur Steam Plant Unit No. 2, $2,200,000.
12. Warrants drawn on city treasurer in settlement of accounts payable, $3,045,000.
13. Larkspur Steam Plant placed in service on June 30, 19x5.

Required: A work sheet of the revenue fund of the Electric Department, showing:

a) The balance sheet amounts at June 30, 19x4.
b) The transactions for the year. (NOTE: Journal entries supporting your transactions are not required.)
c) The balance sheet amounts at June 30, 19x5.
d) The sources and applications of funds during the year.

(AICPA, adapted)

CONTINUOUS PROBLEMS

11–L. The city water utility is owned and operated by the City of Bingham. The water utility was originally constructed and operated by a private corporation but was sold to the city 30 years before the date of the balance sheet below, which was prepared at the end of the year prior to the year for which transactions are given.

CITY OF BINGHAM WATER UTILITY FUND
Balance Sheet as of June 30, 19py

Assets and Other Debits			
Utility Plant:			
Utility plant in service	$6,235,695		
Less: Accumulated provision for depreciation	1,247,139	$4,988,556	
Property held for future use		25,000	
Construction work in progress		94,700	
Utility plant acquisition adjustments	$ 265,000		
Less: Accumulated provision for amortization	159,000	106,000	
Total Utility Plant			$5,214,256
Current and Accrued Assets:			
Cash		83,340	
Due from other funds		7,000	
Customer accounts receivable	$ 77,720		
Less: Accumulated provision for uncollectible accounts	2,360	75,360	
Materials and supplies		47,073	
Total Current and Accrued Assets			212,773
Deferred Debits:			
Unamortized bond discount			32,600
Total Assets			$5,459,629
Liabilities and Other Credits			
Long-Term Debt:			
Revenue Bonds, 6%, J and J 1, mature in 20 years			$4,260,000
Current and Accrued Liabilities:			
Accounts payable		$ 39,210	
Customer deposits		27,638	
Matured interest		127,800	
Miscellaneous accruals		6,892	
Total Current and Accrued Liabilities			201,540
Contributions:			
Contributions from customers		$ 163,210	
City's contribution		425,000	588,210
Retained earnings			409,879
Total Liabilities and Other Credits			$5,459,629

You are required to:

a) Open a general journal for the Water Utility Fund and enter the following transactions as necessary. Use the account titles shown in Chapter 11.

1. Billings to nonmunicipal customers for water service for the year totaled $1,168,368. Billings to the City of Bingham for water service totaled $12,000.
2. Collections from customers totaled $1,175,568; from the city, $12,577.
3. Construction work authorized, including that to accommodate the extension of service to Irwinville (Problem 10–L), amounted to $234,000. As a part of this, a contract for $112,000 was signed with a private firm; the remainder of the work was to be done by water utility employees.
4. Materials and supplies in the amount of $260,800 were ordered. All of these were received during the period except $4,800 worth. The invoices otherwise agreed with the purchase orders and receiving reports and were approved for payment. A perpetual inventory system is used for all materials and supplies.
5. Payrolls totaling $289,765 for operations; $83,210 for maintenance; and $36,000 for construction were paid.
6. Materials and supplies issued during the period amounted to $120,000 for operations; $52,000 for maintenance; and $84,000 for construction.
7. All bond interest due during the year was paid. Debt discount was amortized on the straight-line basis.
8. Interest of $8,500 was charged to Construction Work in Progress.
9. A progress billing for $56,000 was received from the construction contractor and paid.
10. Assets under construction at the start of the year and some of those started during the year were completed and placed in service. The costs incurred on this construction totaled $206,350.
11. The water utility paid $178,342 to the general fund as a contribution in lieu of property taxes.
12. Collection efforts were discontinued on bills amounting to $1,965; the customers owing the bills had paid deposits to the water utility of $660, on which $12 of interest had been accrued as of balance sheet date (this utility leaves the accrued interest on deposits in "Miscellaneous Accruals"); the remainder due was written off.
13. Deposits amounting to $1,238 were applied to the final bills of customers discontinuing service; $36 of interest was accrued on these deposits. Additional deposits amounting to $1,460 were refunded by check to customers discontinuing service, as was $50 accrued interest on the deposits. Deposits totaling $3,427 were received from new customers.
14. Accounts payable at year end totaled $43,610.
15. Interest on deposits amounted to $628 (charge Operation Expense). Depreciation on utility plant was 2 percent of

the beginning balance (round charge to the nearest dollar). The Accumulated Provision for Uncollectible Accounts should equal $1,650. Make these and all other adjusting and closing entries necessary at year-end, including the entry for accrual of six months interest on bonds payable.

b) Prepare a balance sheet for the Water Utility Fund as of the end of the year.

c) Prepare a statement of income and expense for the Water Utility Fund for the year.

11–S. No enterprise fund is presented in this series of problems.

12

General Fixed Assets Group of Accounts

Only enterprise and intragovernmental service funds routinely account for property, plant, and equipment used in their operations. Trust funds which use fixed assets for the production of income, and special assessment funds which maintain their own fixed assets, also account for property, plant, and equipment. All other funds account only for assets which will be turned into cash during the regular operations of the fund. Thus property, plant, and equipment acquired by general, special revenue, and capital projects funds, and by special assessment funds which do not maintain their own fixed assets, are brought under accounting control by the creation of a "General Fixed Assets" group of accounts.

Accounting control of fixed tangible assets is generally deemed superior to that provided by a record system which is not formally integrated with the accounting information system. Records of individual assets of significant value or groups of assets of lesser unit value should include all information needed for planning an effective maintenance program, preparation of budget requests for replacements and additions, providing adequate insurance coverage, and fixing the responsibility for custody of the assets.

In accord with contemporary generally accepted accounting principles for profit-seeking businesses, general fixed assets are recorded at acquisition cost (or fair market value at time of receipt if assets are received by donation). If the cost of fixed assets was not recorded when the assets were acquired and is unknown when accounting control over the assets is established, it is acceptable to record them at estimated cost. The General Fixed Asset group is only an accounting entity, not a fiscal entity (therefore not a fund). It records no current assets and no liabilities of any kind. The offset to the fixed asset accounts is the set of equity accounts which indicate the sources from which the fixed assets were acquired. "Investment in General Fixed Assets from Capital Projects Funds—General Obligation Bonds," or "Investment in General Fixed Assets from General Fund Revenues," are examples of typical equity accounts of a General Fixed Assets account group. Balance sheets of this account group display to interested parties the total cost of each category of general fixed asset and the total amount contributed by each source used for the acquisition of these assets. Customarily a balance sheet is supplemented by a statement showing the description of and dollar amount of additions to and deductions from each fixed asset category during the year.

The cost of fixed assets used by funds which are expected to cover their full costs by sale of products or services is, of course, allocated to fiscal periods and to products or services by the "depreciation" mechanism, just as is done by profit-seeking businesses. *General* fixed assets are acquired for the production of general governmental services, however, not for the production of services that are sold. Therefore, the National Committee on Governmental Accounting's Principle No. 9 states that:

> Depreciation on general fixed assets should not be recorded in the general accounting records. Depreciation charges on such assets may be computed for unit cost purposes, provided such charges are recorded only in memorandum form and do not appear in the fund accounts.

The provision for the computation of depreciation for unit cost purposes is in recognition of the fact that general fixed assets may be used for activities financed by grants from other governmental units, and that depreciation may be an allowable expense under the terms of the grant. Additionally, unit costs stated on an accrual basis, including depreciation on general fixed assets, may be useful information to provide administrators and legislators concerned with the allocation of resources to programs, departments, and activities. To some extent a comparison of the accumulated depreciation on an asset with the cost of the asset may be relevant to the process of budgeting of outlays for replacement of capital assets. For these reasons, the American Institute of Certified Public Accountants sees no objection to recording depreciation in the General Fixed Assets group of accounts and reflecting the related allowance for depreciation in a statement of general fixed assets.[1]

General fixed assets may be thought of as those not used exclusively in the operations of any one fund nor belonging to any one fund. They include courthouses and city halls, public buildings generally, the land on which they are situated, highways, streets, sidewalks, equipment, and

[1] *Audits of State and Local Governmental Units*, 1974, p. 18.

other tangible assets with a life longer than one fiscal year that are not used by an enterprise, trust, intragovernmental service, or certain special assessment funds. Formerly, general fixed assets and general fixed liabilities were sometimes merged in a group under the heading of "capital fund" or "general property fund," but this practice is not currently recommended. A balance sheet for general fixed assets might appear as shown in Illustration 12–1.

Illustration 12–1

TOWN OF CLARENDON
Statement of General Fixed Assets
September 30, 19x5

Assets

Land		$ 89,000
Buildings		1,713,000
Improvements other than buildings		1,443,000
Equipment		511,000
Construction work in progress		186,000
Total General Fixed Assets		$3,942,000

*Investment in General Fixed Assets**

General fund revenues		$ 738,000
Special revenue fund revenues		539,000
Capital projects funds:		
General obligation bonds	$2,100,000	
Federal grants	102,000	
State grants	73,000	2,275,000
Special assessment funds:		
Assessment against property owners	$ 221,000	
City's share of cost	46,000	267,000
Private gifts		59,000
Unknown		64,000
Total Investment in General Fixed Assets		$3,942,000

*If sources of some fixed assets are not obtainable, this section may be divided into two subsections: "Investment in general fixed assets acquired after (a certain date)," and "Investment in general fixed assets acquired prior to (a certain date)." Details under the first subsection may be shown as above, with some such caption as "Sources unknown" under the latter. Another possibility for dealing with the latter group is to merely list them as "Unknown," as is done here.

General Fixed Assets

The asset accounts shown in Illustration 12–1 are those commonly found in municipal statements of general fixed assets. Additional or substitute accounts may be used as needed to present information relating to general fixed assets of a given municipality. As in commercial accounting, cost is the generally accepted basis of accounting for governmental fixed assets. Determination of what constitutes cost of a governmental fixed asset follows the criteria specified in intermediate financial accounting texts for the determination of cost of fixed assets of a profit-seeking entity. Similarly, the kinds of items which are reported in each fixed asset account are the same whether the reporting entity is a governmental body or a profit-seeking entity. Also, as is true in profit-seeking entities, the test of materiality is applied and items costing below an established minimum amount are not recorded in the asset accounts no matter how long their estimated useful lives, but are merely accounted for as expenditures of the acquiring fund. The following paragraphs are presented as a brief review of generally accepted principles of accounting for fixed assets.

Land

The cost of land acquired by a governmental unit through purchase should include not only the contract price but also such other related costs as taxes and other liens assumed, title search costs, legal fees, surveying, filling, grading, drainage, and other costs of preparation for the use intended. Governments are frequently subject to damage suits in connection with land acquisition, and the amounts of judgments levied are considered capital costs of the property acquired. Land acquired through forfeiture should be capitalized at the total amount of all taxes, liens, and other claims surrendered, plus all other costs incidental to acquiring ownership and perfecting title. Land acquired through donation should be recorded on the basis of appraised value at the date of acquisition; the cost of the appraisal itself should not be capitalized, however. Valuation of land obtained by donation is of importance chiefly for report, statistical, and other comparative purposes.

Buildings and Improvements Other Than Buildings

The nature of assets to be classified as Buildings is a matter of common knowledge; but if a definition is needed, perhaps they may be said to consist of those structures erected above ground for the purpose of sheltering persons or property. Improvements Other than Buildings consists of land attachments of a permanent nature, other than buildings, and includes, among other things, roads, bridges, tunnels, walks, walls, parking lots, etc.

The determination of the cost of buildings and improvements acquired by purchase is relatively simple, although some peripheral costs may be of doubtful classification between capital and revenue. The price paid for the assets constitutes most of the cost of purchased items; but legal and other costs, plus expenditures necessary to put the property into acceptable condition for its intended use, are proper additions. The same generalizations may be applied to acquisitions by construction under contract; that is, purchase or contract price, plus positively identified incidentals, should be capitalized. The determination of the cost of buildings and improvements obtained through construction by some agency of the governmental unit (often called "force account" construction) is attended by slightly more difficulty. In these cases, costs should include not only all the direct and indirect expenditures (including interest during the period of construction on debt incurred for purpose of financing construction) of the fund providing the construction but also materials and services furnished by other funds as well. The valuation of buildings and improvements acquired by donation should be established by appraisal. As in the case of land, one reason for setting a value on donated buildings and improvements is to aid in determining the total value of fixed property used by the government, and for reports and comparisons; however, more compelling reasons exist for setting a value on buildings and certain improvements: the need for obtaining proper insurance coverage and the need for being able to substantiate the insurance claim if loss should occur.

Some municipalities elect not to capitalize the cost of improvements such as roads, bridges, curbs and gutters, streets, sidewalks, drainage systems, and lighting systems because such assets are immovable, and generally of value only to the governmental unit. The American Institute of Certified Public Accountants does not feel that disclosure of the cost of such improvements is necessary for fair presentation of financial statements. If improvements are omitted from financial statements, the annual report should contain statistical data relative to them which would be of interest to residents, bondholders, and other readers of the annual report.

Equipment, or Machinery and Equipment

Machinery and equipment are most likely to be acquired by purchase, although construction by an intragovernmental service fund may be the source in some instances, in which case the same rules will apply as for buildings and improvements constructed by the governmental employees. The cost of machinery and equipment purchased should include the items conventional under commercial accounting practice: purchase price, transportation costs if not included in purchase price, installation cost, and other direct costs of readying for use. Cash discounts on governmental fixed assets purchased should be treated as a reduction of costs or as financial income. Donated equipment should be accounted for in the same manner, and for the same reasons, as donated buildings and improvements.

Construction Work in Progress

Construction Work in Progress, as an account classification of an enterprise fund, is discussed in Chapter 11. As a fixed asset classification in the General Fixed Assets Group it is needed to account for expenditures accumulated to balance sheet date on projects of capital projects funds, special assessment funds, or intragovernmental service funds for the purpose of acquiring or constructing general fixed assets. As described in the appropriate chapters, construction expenditures by those funds are ordinarily closed into Fund Balance at the end of each year, but the amounts are not capitalized in the funds doing the construction: the amounts are set up under the caption of Construction Work in Progress in the general fixed assets group of accounts.

Source Accounts or "Investment in General Fixed Assets"

Since the general fixed assets group is only a self-balancing set of accounts, not a fiscal entity, the self-balancing feature is achieved by the creation of a series of credit-balance accounts to record the sources from which general fixed assets were acquired. The Investment in General Fixed Assets accounts shown in Illustration 12–1 are those provided in *Governmental Accounting, Auditing, and Financial Reporting*, the recommendations of the National Committee on Governmental Accounting. If the accounts illustrated do not adequately describe the source of certain general fixed assets of a given municipality, other appropriately named accounts may be used.

Cost after Acquisition

Governmental accounting procedures should include clear-cut provisions for classifying costs incurred in connection with fixed assets after the original cost has been established. Expenditures closely associated with fixed assets will regularly occur in amounts of varying size, and responsible persons will be charged with deciding whether these are of a revenue nature or represent additions of permanent value.

In general, it may be said that any expenditure which definitely adds to a fixed asset or enhances the value of an integral part of it may be classified as a capital item. Thus, drainage of land, addition of a room to a building, and changes in equipment which increase its output or reduce its cost of operation are clearly recognizable as capital expenditures. Special difficulty arises in the case of large-scale expenditures which are partly replacements and partly additions or betterments. An example would be replacement of a composition-type roof with a roof of some more durable material. To the extent that the expenditure replaces the old roof, it should not be capitalized unless cost of the old roof is removed from the accounts; and to the extent that it provides a better roof, it should be capitalized. The distribution of the total cost in such a case is largely a matter for managerial determination. As suggested elsewhere, the need for exact discrimination between capital and revenue expenditures is not so pressing in government as in business, with an inclination toward the expenditure classification in all doubtful cases. Consistent with policy in recording original acquisition costs, some expenditures unquestionably representing increases in permanent values may, for convenience, be arbitrarily classified as of a revenue nature if the amount is less than some specified minimum or on the basis of any other criterion previously decided upon.

Expenditures that are partly replacements and partly additions or betterments occasion some accounting difficulty. The distribution of the expenditure having been decided upon, the estimated amount of addition or betterment might be added to the asset. Perhaps better results might be obtained by crediting the appropriate asset account for the cost of the replaced part, thus removing the amount, and then debiting the asset account for the total cost of the replacing item.

Reduction of Cost

Reductions in the cost of fixed assets may relate to the elimination of the total amount expended for a given item or items, or they may consist only of removing the cost applicable to a specific part. Thus, if an entire building is demolished, the total cost of the structure should be removed from the appropriate accounts; but if the separation applies only to a wing or some other definitely identifiable portion, the cost eliminated should be the amount estimated as applying thereto. Reductions in the recorded cost of fixed assets may be brought about by sale, retirement from use, destruction by fire or other casualty, replacement of a major part, theft or loss from some other cause, and possibly other changes. The cost of fixed assets held by a fund or the General Fixed Assets Group may sometimes be reduced by the transfer of a unit to another fund or to the General Fixed Assets Group.

Accounting for cost reductions consisting of entire units is a relatively simple matter if adequate records have been kept. Entries must be made in both controlling accounts and subsidiary ledger records to show the fact of the reduction. If a separate subsidiary ledger record is kept for the unit in question, that record should be removed from the ledger and stored in a file with other similar inactive records. If the reduction is only partial, the cost as shown by the subsidiary record must be modified to reflect the change, with a complete description of what brought about the change.

Since, under NCGA recommendations, depreciation is not formally recorded in the general ledger, the removal may be accomplished by crediting the ledger account recording its cost, and debiting the source account(s) which were credited when the asset was acquired. If a municipality follows the option allowed by the AICPA and records depreciation of general fixed assets, the accumulated depreciation account must also be debited to remove the amount related to the asset disposed of.

Governments sometimes trade fixed assets on new items. In the general fixed asset accounts the total cost of the old item should be removed and the total cost (not merely the cash payment) of the new one set up.

Illustrative Entries

Accession of an item by the general fixed assets group requires a debit to the appropriate general ledger asset account and a credit to an equity account indicating the source from which provided. Thus, if office equipment is purchased for the treasurer's office from general fund resources, the General Fixed Assets entry should be as follows:

Equipment	450	
Investment in General Fixed Assets—General Fund Revenues		450

Although purchased for the immediate use of one department, the equipment belongs to the general government and could, if desired, be transferred to other use. On the *general fund* books the foregoing transaction would appear as an appropriation expenditure, which would be recorded as follows, passing over reversal of the encumbrance:

Expenditures	450	
Vouchers Payable		450

In detailed accounts of the general fund the transaction would appear as a reduction of the amount appropriated for the treasurer's office.

General fixed assets purchased by a capital projects fund would be recorded in the same manner as if acquired from the general fund, the difference in entries being that the credit will show a capital projects fund as the source. It is conceivable that two or more funds might contribute to the total cost of a general fixed asset. This situation would interpose no special problem but would merely require that the credit clearly reveal the amount of cost contributed by each source.

General fixed assets constructed by a capital projects fund are accounted for in the general fixed assets group in the same manner as though purchased, if construction is initiated and completed in the same fiscal period. But if two or more periods are involved, additional steps are necessary. Assuming that capital expenditures of $250,000 (Federal grant) were made on an unfinished building project during a given year, the information would be taken up in General Fixed Assets by the following entry:

Construction Work in Progress	250,000	
Investment in General Fixed Assets—Capital Projects Fund—Federal Grant		250,000

It will be recalled from Chapter 6, on capital projects funds, that the correlative capital projects fund entry for the above would have been a closing of the Expenditures and Encumbrances accounts into Fund Balance. Following through from the foregoing entry, let it be assumed that the completion of construction in the next year entailed additional expenditures of $75,000 (provided by a Federal grant), which would have been accounted for by the capital projects fund in the normal manner. The additional expenditure would be recorded in the General Fixed Assets ledger as part of the cost of a completed project; and the previously suspended cost would be converted from its temporary account to the permanent one, as illustrated in the following compound entry:

Buildings	325,000	
Construction Work in Progress		250,000
Investment in Fixed Assets—Capital Projects Fund—Federal Grant		75,000

The contribution of the capital projects fund would now appear in the general fixed assets group as follows: Buildings, $325,000; Investment in General Fixed Assets—Capital Projects Fund—Federal Grant, $325,000.

Fixed assets acquired through a special assessment fund should be accounted for in the manner outlined for recording those provided through capital projects fund construction. Some technical difficulty may be experienced in exact apportionment of cost between property owners and the governmental unit. The amount expended is likely not to be the exact amount levied. In view of the fact that some authorities even question the propriety of capitalizing the property owners' contribution and that the whole group of accounts is more or less of a memorandum nature, it would seem that a careful approximation of the amount supplied by each party (property owners and governmental unit) would be acceptable.

Fixed assets contributed to the general group by a self-supporting fund bring a minor question. If the asset is of depreciable nature, at what figure should it be recorded in the accounts of the transferee—book value as shown by the transferor, or original cost? The answer seems to be book value, because that is the fairest measure of the contributor's sacrifice. In the event appraised value is greatly below unamortized cost, perhaps that value should be used. Assuming that a building that had cost $29,000, now $12,000 depreciated, is permanently surrendered to the general government, the following entry would be made in the *general fixed asset* accounts:

Buildings	17,000	
Investment in General Fixed Assets—Electric Utility Fund		17,000

The utility's accounting treatment of this transaction would be as shown below:

Accumulated Provision for Depreciation of Utility Plant	12,000	
Other Income Deductions	17,000	
Utility Plant in Service		29,000

Disposal of fixed assets involves no accounting problem if no cash or other extraneous assets are involved in the liquidation. The requirement is elimination of the asset and reduction of the equity account which records its source. Assuming that a building that cost $50,000, provided by a capital projects fund, is retired without revenue or expense to the governmental unit, the following entry in the *general fixed assets group* would suffice:

Investment in General Fixed Assets—Capital Projects Fund—Federal Grant	50,000	
Buildings		50,000

The subsidiary record or account for the building should receive appropriate notations about the transaction and thereafter be transferred to an inactive file.

Although cash is disbursed or received in connection with the disposal of general fixed assets, that fact would have no bearing on the entry to be made in that group of accounts. Cash disbursements in connection with the removal of an item from the general fixed assets group should appear among the transactions of the disbursing fund and classified according to the nature of the charge. Assuming that the general fund pays $300 for the demolition of the building, an entry in the following form should be made on the *general fund* books:

Expenditures	300	
Vouchers Payable (or Cash)		300

If cash arises from the disposal of a general fixed asset, some question may arise as to its disposition. Theoretically, it should be directed to the fund that provided the asset; but this may not always be possible. If the asset was provided by a capital projects fund, the contributing fund may have been liquidated before the sale occurs. Unless prescribed by law, disposition of the results of sale will be handled as directed by the trustees or other legislative body having jurisdiction over the asset and will be accounted for in the manner required by the accounting system of the recipient fund. Commonly, sales of general fixed assets are budgeted as Miscellaneous Revenue by the general fund. In such cases, when sales actually occur, the general fund debits Cash (or a receivable) for the selling price, and credits Revenues and the appropriate revenues ledger subsidiary account.

Detailed Property Accounts

Governmental organizations should keep both general and subsidiary records for fixed assets owned. General records consist primarily of general ledger accounts operated for control over groups of subsidiary records. Subsidiary records consist of the detailed records which are kept for individual items of fixed assets.

One or more of a number of purposes are served by the use of adequate fixed property records. The most important of these purposes are as follows:

1. As suggested elsewhere, fixed property records, properly kept, furnish information about the investment that taxpayers and others in the past have made for the benefit of future citizens and other users of government property, in contrast with expenditures for current purposes.
2. They provide a basis for adequate insurance coverage on insurable fixed assets. Although cost is not the major determinant of insurable value, it would be given consideration.
3. Properly kept records, providing for information on care and maintenance, assist in the budgeting of such costs and perhaps in singling out items on which current expenditures are abnormally high or possibly some that require minimum outlays for upkeep and maintenance.
4. They assist in fixing accountability for the custody of individual items and in determining who is responsible for seeing that care and maintenance requirements receive the attention to which they are entitled.
5. Since capital budgets are best developed on a long-term basis, reliable information about fixed assets now owned should be of material assistance in approximating future requirements.
6. Complete fixed assets records are indispensable for self-supporting funds as a basis for computing depreciation. For utility funds, they are absolutely essential in establishing the base that should be used in fixing charges for service or in judging the reasonableness of rate schedules already in effect.

The main classifications of fixed assets are shown in Illustration 12–1 and discussed in related paragraphs. The names of these classifications may be used as general ledger account titles; or more specific account titles may be used, with a code to designate the general classification to which the account belongs.

Subsidiary ledger accounts for fixed assets may be kept in whatever form is indicated by the data processing system in use. Whatever the form of the subsidiary record, it should provide for showing, among other things, a complete description of the asset, including the formal title and the serial number or other objective information for positive identification of the asset; complete data on increases and decreases of cost, including amounts, dates, and sources from which posted; and provision for memorandum entries related to depreciation, repairs, and maintenance. (See Illustrations 12–2 and 12–3.)

Illustration 12–2

TOWN OF DENTON

EQUIPMENT LEDGER*

Property Code No. E 413

Description Tractor

Manufacturer J.I. Case & Co.

Manufacturer's Serial No. 3796465	Model 4 NB
Date of Purchase June 20, 19X5	Reference V.R., 19X5, p. 34
Cost Total $ 6,746	Fund General
Invoice Price $ Same	Freight $ None
Installation $ None	Other $ 40.00, painting
Estimated Life (Years) 8	Estimated Salvage Value $ 500.00
Location City Garage	

DISPOSAL

Disposal Approved by	Reference
Reason	Date
How Disposed of (Sold, Scrapped, etc.)	
Age at Date of Disposal	Amount Realized

Date	Reference	Additions, Betterments, Major Repairs	Amount

*If used for a utility depreciable asset, this form should be modified to provide for entering periodic depreciation thereof and for adjustments of recorded depreciation, if any need to be made.

Classification of Subsidiary Accounts

An important advantage of keeping general fixed asset accounts in a flexible ledger is the ease of shifting items from one group to another. This is important because accountability and responsibility for general fixed assets may be indicated by a significant grouping of the accounts. Thus, ledger accounts for all property in the custody of a given department may be grouped together in the ledger. Within the departmental group, cards or accounts will be organized according to the standard groups of Land, Buildings, Improvements Other than Buildings, and Machinery and Equipment (or Equipment), or other general ledger titles. If subdivisions are recognized under the three main classes, such as different subclasses of Machinery and Equipment (or Equipment), subsidiary accounts may be so grouped.

In order to assure accurate records of accountability and responsibility for property, standard forms should be utilized for recording transfers. Such forms should provide for a complete description of the property transferred; the names of the transferor and the transferee; financial data, including cost and accumulated depreciation (for assets transferred from

Illustration 12–3

TOWN OF DENTON

LAND LEDGER

Property Code No. *L-34*

Location of Property *309 W. Third*
Legal Description *Huntington's Addition*
Dimensions *60' x 200'* Area *12,000 sq. ft.*
How Acquired *Donation* Fund *None*
Date Acquired *Aug. 6, 19X4* Reference *Journal, 19X4, p. 71*
Original Cost or Appraised Value $ *60,000* Use of Property *Recreation*
Appraised by *R. R. Mills & Co.*

Additional Costs

Amount	Reference	Description
$ 25	W.R., p. 91	Examination of title
190	W.R., p. 93	Clearing

Deed:

Kind *Quit claim* Date *Aug. 6, 19X4* Where Recorded *Deed Record 96, p. 7*
Abstract of Title (by Whom): *Monroe County Abstract Co.*
Date *July 21, 1959* Where Filed *Safe, Town Treasurer's Office*
Disposal Record:
Date of Disposal
Manner of Disposal
Amount Received $
Remarks *Donated by Alfred Huntington*

self-supporting funds); and blanks for the necessary authentication of the transfer. The transfer document should be prepared in at least three copies: one for the accounting office, one for the transferor department, and one for the transferee. The accounting department copy provides the basis for taking a subsidiary account from the section for one department and putting it in the section for the other department, thus effecting a change in the record of responsibility. The transferor's copy is his receipt to show he should no longer be charged. The transferee's copy serves as his inventory record. If desired, the transfer form may be used to record abandonment, retirement, or other permanent reduction in fixed assets; or, if preferred, a special form may be devised for this purpose.

Inventories of Fixed Assets

At least annually, all fixed property should be inventoried. This checks against losses not previously revealed and brings to light errors in records of accountability, that is, having one department charged with an item that is actually in the custody of another. Furthermore, a systematic physical inventory of fixed assets gives an opportunity for surveying their physical condition, with respect to their need for repairs, maintenance, or replacement. Property inventories need not be taken simultaneously in all departments but may be spread over a period of time, with due consideration for departmental or other transfers or changes during the period. As suggested elsewhere, government fixed assets, especially those that are movable, should be marked by a numerical or other form of code so that each item may be positively identified. The marking may be accomplished by the use of labels or tags, by the use of indelible ink, by stamping, or by other methods giving permanency. To save time in locating markings, rules should be established and observed concerning the exact points where they will be affixed on different types of equipment. Assets that cannot be located after diligent search should be written off in some prescribed manner, which should include approval by responsible persons.

Property inventories may follow the general plan pursued in checking mercantile and manufacturing inventories, with considerably less detail than in the latter types. Provisions should be made for accurate description of the items listed and for showing the departments or units charged for each group of assets. (See Illustration 12–4).

Illustration 12–4

TOWN OF DENTON

FIXED ASSET INVENTORY

Taken by *M. Kerr*

Sheet No. *1*
No. of Sheets *1*

Class of Property *Furniture*
Department *Treasurer's Office*
Date *December 29, 19X5*

Description	Manufacturer's No.	Serial No.	No. of Units	Unit Cost	Total
Tables, wooden	None	T 7-11	5	$120	$600
Desk, wooden	"	T 12	1	195	195
Chairs, wooden, office	"	T 1-6	6	35	210
Chairs, metal, swivel	"	T 13	1	90	90
Note: One wooden chair charged to this office could not be located.					

Statements of General Fixed Assets

For general fixed assets the basic exhibit is the statement of general fixed assets or, as it is sometimes captioned, the general fixed assets balance sheet. Its special contribution is to show the total cost of assets of the various groups in use by the general government and the sources from which they were derived. This statement is shown in Illustration 12–1.

Illustration 12–5

THE CITY OF SAN DIEGO
General Fixed Assets
Statement of General Fixed Assets
by Functions and Activities
June 30, 1973

Exhibit 31

	Total	*Land*	*Structures and Improvements*	*Equipment*
General Government				
Legislative	$ 128,776	$ –	$ –	$ 128,776
Executive	112,521	–	–	112,521
Finance	855,667	–	–	855,667
Law	77,173	–	–	77,173
Administrative offices	86,945	–	–	86,945
Planning and zoning	87,385	–	–	87,385
Personnel administration	93,376	–	–	93,376
Community development	442,325	–	–	442,325
Buildings and grounds	27,529,035	14,682,415	12,846,620	–
Total General Government	$ 29,413,203	$14,682,415	$12,846,620	$ 1,884,168
Public Safety				
Police department	$ 2,497,177	$ 78,574	$ 712,205	$ 1,706,398
Fire department	5,170,427	217,352	2,229,738	2,723,337
Inspection department	55,503	–	–	55,503
Total Public Safety	$ 7,723,107	$ 295,926	$ 2,941,943	$ 4,485,238
General Service Departments				
Public works shops and buildings	$ 4,623,037	$ 513,502	$ 1,474,600	$ 2,634,935
Streets and highways	539,619	120,387	216,629	202,603
Waste collection and disposal	207,989	119,638	28,580	59,771
Community concourse operations	360,128	–	–	360,128
Libraries	4,788,214	340,770	4,048,042	399,402
Parks and recreation	31,317,619	7,816,655	22,559,491	941,473
City employees' retirement system	3,777	–	–	3,777
Emergency service organization	26,916	–	–	26,916
Cemetery	85,155	1,685	57,913	25,557
Municipal airports	614,562	117,008	466,927	30,627
Zoo	17,354,155	– *	12,366,303	4,987,852
Public transportation	4,735,053	996,800	1,539,375	2,198,878
Total General Service Departments	$ 64,656,224	$10,026,445	$42,757,860	$11,871,919
Total General City Fixed Assets Allocated to Functions	$101,792,534	$25,004,786	$58,546,423	$18,241,325
Construction Work in Progress	2,110,356			
Total General City Fixed Assets	$103,902,890			

*Zoo land is included under Parks and Recreation with other Balboa Park land.

Illustration 12–6

THE CITY OF SAN DIEGO
General Fixed Assets
Statement of Changes in General Fixed Assets
by Functions and Activities
Year Ended June 30, 1973

Schedule 31-A

Function	*General Fixed Assets July 1, 1972*	*Additions**	*Deductions**	*General Fixed Assets June 30, 1973*
General Government				
Legislative	$ 111,705	$ 19,381	$ 2,310	$ 128,776
Executive	79,402	42,799	9,680	112,521
Finance	840,269	62,388	46,990	855,667
Law	69,450	10,352	2,629	77,173
Administrative offices	82,987	4,714	756	86,945
Planning and zoning	82,147	7,047	1,809	87,385
Personnel administration	66,365	30,930	3,919	93,376
Community development	555,482	84,137	197,294	442,325
Buildings and grounds	22,583,852	7,150,432	2,205,249	27,529,035
Total General Government	$24,471,659	$ 7,412,180	$2,470,636	$ 29,413,203
Public Safety				
Police department	$ 2,550,072	$ 498,855	$ 551,750	$ 2,497,177
Fire department	5,136,353	488,061	453,987	5,170,427
Inspection department	52,238	4,255	990	55,503
Total Public Safety	$ 7,738,663	$ 991,171	$1,006,727	$ 7,723,107
General Service Departments				
Public works shops and buildings	$ 2,900,293	$ 1,790,523	$ 67,779	$ 4,623,037
Streets and highways	570,094	12,616	43,091	539,619
Waste collection and disposal	205,651	3,523	1,185	207,989
Community concourse operations	330,200	53,485	23,557	360,128
Libraries	4,759,422	37,698	8,906	4,788,214
Parks and recreation	23,508,701	8,047,972	239,054	31,317,619
City employees' retirement system	3,720	57	–	3,777
Emergency service organization	33,891	–	6,975	26,916
Cemetery	91,803	3,402	10,050	85,155
Municipal airports	1,094,533	16,459	496,430	614,562
Zoo	13,215,826	4,213,111	74,782	17,354,155
Public transportation	3,749,878	985,175	–	4,735,053
Total General Service Departments	$50,464,012	$15,164,021	$ 971,809	$ 64,656,224
Total General City Fixed Assets Allocated to Functions	$82,674,334	$23,567,372	$4,449,172	$101,792,534
Construction Work in Progress				2,110,356
Total General City Fixed Assets				$103,902,890

*Includes transfers between departments.

Illustration 12–7

NAME OF GOVERNMENTAL UNIT
Statement of Changes in General Fixed Assets—by Sources
For the Fiscal Year Ended December 31, 19x2

	Total	*Land*	*Buildings*	*Improvements Other than Buildings*	*Equip-ment*	*Construction Work in Progress*
General Fixed Assets (Beginning of Year)	$5,299,600	$1,225,000	$2,361,000	$ 535,000	$375,600	$ 803,000
Add:						
Expenditures from capital project funds:						
General obligation bonds	1,038,650	–	440,000	67,550	37,100	494,000
Federal grants	–	–	–	–	–	–
State grants	–	–	–	–	–	–
County grants	625,000	–	–	–	–	625,000
Expenditures from general fund revenues	162,900	34,500	65,500	–	12,900	50,000
Expenditures from special revenue fund revenues	65,000	–	24,000	–	41,000	–
Expenditures from gifts	85,000	–	85,000	–	–	–
Expenditures from special assessments	631,300	–	–	484,200	–	147,100
Total Additions	2,607,850	34,500	614,500	551,750	91,000	1,316,100
Total Balances and Additions	7,907,450	1,259,500	2,975,500	1,086,750	466,600	2,119,100
Deduct:						
Fixed assets sold or traded	92,100	–	80,000	–	12,100	–
Loss by fire, flood, or calamity	32,000	–	30,000	–	2,000	–
Fixed assets worn out and written off	60,000	–	10,000	50,000	–	–
Capital projects fund projects of prior years completed	102,650	–	–	–	–	102,650
Special assessment projects of prior years completed	294,200	–	–	–	–	294,200
Total Deductions	580,950	–	120,000	50,000	14,100	396,850
General Fixed Assets (End of Year)	$7,326,500	$1,259,500	$2,855,500	$1,036,750	$452,500	$1,722,250

***Source: National Committee on Governmental Accounting, *Governmental Accounting, Auditing, and Financial Reporting*, p. 100.**

The purposes for which, and by whom, fixed assets were being used at a given date, ordinarily the end of a fiscal period, are set forth in a statement of general fixed assets classified by functions and activities. Illustration 12–5, which is taken from the annual report of the City of San Diego, California, is a good example of a statement of general fixed assets by functions and activities.

Another statement which should be of interest to taxpayers and citizens generally is one that shows changes in general fixed assets during a period of time (see Illustration 12–6). The value of this statement is that it not only accounts systematically for changes between one date and another, but also shows the extent to which responsible officials are investing for future requirements, in contrast to spending primarily for current requirements. In addition, the statement of changes serves as a reconcilement or transition between statements of general fixed assets for the ends of consecutive years. Illustration 12–6 is taken from the same annual report as is Illustration 12–5. Both statements are in formats suggested by the National Committee on Governmental Accounting.

A third statement which should be helpful to those who are attempting to understand the sources of changes in general fixed assets from the end of the preceding year to the end of the current year is shown in Illustration 12–7. The illustration is in the form suggested in *Governmental Accounting, Auditing, and Financial Reporting* by the National Committee on Governmental Accounting. The statement sets forth the sources of expenditures for additions to each asset category and the reasons for deductions from each asset category, during the year.

SELECTED REFERENCES

American Institute of Certified Public Accountants. *Audits of State and Local Governmental Units.* New York, 1974.

Derrick, Carl M. "Accounting Controls for Public Property," *Municipal Finance,* Vol. 35, no. 2 (November 1962), pp. 79–83.

Doyle, James J. Inventory Control of Public Property," *Public Property Management,* Special Bulletin 1957 F, pp. 5–8. Chicago: Municipal Finance Officers Association of the United States and Canada, November 15, 1957.

Monroe, W. M. "Fixed Asset Accounting," *Municipal Finance,* Vol. 39, no. 2 (November 1966), pp. 85–88.

National Committee on Governmental Accounting. *Governmental Accounting, Auditing, and Financial Reporting,* chap. 10. Chicago, 1968.

QUESTIONS

12–1. A governmental unit of considerable size has no organized record of any fixed property but proposes to establish one.

a) What would be the first major step in establishing a record of existing fixed assets?

b) What information is needed in addition to the location and condition of existing fixed assets in the governmental unit referred to in order to establish proper internal control over the unit's fixed assets?

12–2. To avoid unusually heavy expenditures in some fiscal periods, capital budgets ordinarily cover a period of several years, possibly 5 or 10. What is the significance of fixed asset records in connection with such a budget?

12–3. If a governmental unit acquires title to real estate by donation and records the property on the basis of present appraised value, the expenses of obtaining the appraisal may not be capitalized, but the costs of remodeling or rehabilitation may be added. Explain the difference.

12–4. One of the common objections to recording depreciation of general fixed assets is that the depreciation charge could not be fitted into the budget, since no cash or other asset is disbursed. What reasons are there for computing depreciation of general fixed assets?

12–5. "If depreciation of general fixed assets is computed, it should be recorded as a general fund expense." Discuss each proposition involved in this question. Cite authority to support the position you conclude is most in accord with generally accepted accounting principles.

12–6. Below are stated several transactions related to fixed property of a governmental unit. Which should be debited to asset accounts of the General Fixed Assets Group?

a) Contract price of land.
b) Contract price of new building.
c) Cost of demolishing and removing an old building from the site of the new.
d) Cost of land title abstract.
e) Six months' interest on money borrowed for purchase of a new building.
f) Mowing grass and weeds, and other care and maintenance activities for land.
g) Freight on equipment purchased.
h) Cost of assembling and testing a piece of complicated machinery.
i) Cost of securing an easement for right of way over an adjoining property.
j) Cost of a set of building plans which were not the ones followed in construction of the building.
k) Cost of renovating and reconditioning an old building purchased, before putting it into service.
l) An expenditure of $75.00 for land drainage.
m) A utility's share of the special assessment for a new street adjoining the utility property.

n) A share of the utility superintendent's salary, based upon actual time he spent in supervising construction of a new plant.

o) Unpaid taxes assumed by a government unit in acquisition of property from private sources.

p) Cost of periodic redecoration of the office of the mayor.

12–7. If one article of equipment is traded on another of the same kind and a trade-in allowance is received for the replaced article, which of the two methods listed below should be employed for changing the asset account?

a) Debit or credit the asset account, as required, for difference in cost of the two articles.

b) Remove the total cost of the replaced article, and add the total cost of the new one.

Since both methods would give the same final balance in the asset account, give a reason for your choice.

12–8. If cash is received upon disposal of a fixed asset, what difficulty may attend the effort to reimburse the fund or other source which supplied the fixed asset? Explain.

12–9. A certain municipal finance officer instructed his staff to analyze the Construction Work in Progress account at the end of each year to determine the amounts which should be debited to each general fixed asset account and the amount which should be credited to Construction Work in Progress. What records or documents should be created at that time to support the General Fixed Assets general ledger accounts?

12–10. A certain municipal finance officer instructed his staff

a) to ignore capital projects fund expenditures for items costing under $1,000 each when preparing entries to record the cost of general fixed assets. As a CPA auditing the statements of this municipality, would you take exception to this practice or not? Defend your position.

b) to ignore all special assessment fund expenditures for street paving, curbs, gutters, and sidewalks when preparing entries to record the cost of general fixed assets. As a CPA auditing the statements of this municipality, would you take exception to this practice or not? Defend your position.

EXERCISES AND PROBLEMS

12–1. Utilizing the municipal annual report obtained for Exercise 1–1, follow the instructions below:

a) Does the annual report contain a statement of fixed assets? If so, are only general fixed assets included, or are all fixed assets included no matter what fund, function, activity or department uses them? Does the statement specify the function or activity which uses the assets? What categories of fixed assets are shown in the statement? Are Improvements Other Than Buildings separately disclosed and described? Are fixed assets recorded at historical cost, estimated cost, appraised value, or a mixture of bases?

Is accumulated depreciation shown for depreciable assets? If not, is any reference made to memorandum computations of depreciation not incorporated in the statement? If no depreciation is disclosed, is any information given to enable the reader to judge the ages of the various depreciable assets? Is any information given in the letter of transmittal or other narrative material in the annual report which would enable the reader to relate the statement of existing fixed assets to any long-term plans or budgets for capital expenditures?

b) Does the statement of general fixed assets disclose the sources from which acquisition or construction of fixed assets were financed? If not, is the information disclosed elsewhere in the report? If so, are the sources for all fixed assets disclosed, or only those assets acquired since a certain date? Do the source accounts agree with those recommended by the National Committee on Governmental Accounting as discussed in Chapter 12? What three sources account for the major portion of fixed asset acquisitions? What percentage of the total cost, or other carrying value, of fixed assets is accounted for by each of the three major sources?

c) Does the report contain a statement of changes in general fixed assets? If so, does the statement disclose the sources from which fixed asset acquisitions and construction were financed? Does the statement disclose changes by function and activity, or merely by asset category?

d) Compare the general fixed asset information disclosed in the report with related information disclosed in statements of revenue funds, capital projects funds, special assessment funds, or elsewhere in the report. Does information about construction work in progress appear to be disclosed in the manner recommended by the NCGA? If not, is the information disclosed adequately, in your opinion? Is interest during construction on debt incurred to finance construction charged to construction work in progress? Is this true for just general obligation debt, or for both general obligation debt and special assessment debt?

Which fund, or funds, account for cash received, or receivables created, from sales of general fixed assets? Which fund, or funds, account for cash received, or receivables created, as a result of charging depreciation on general fixed assets as a cost of grants?

12–2. In addition to the statement of General Fixed Assets shown below, the only information about general fixed assets in the Kerrville, Texas, Annual Financial Report for the fiscal year ended May 31, 1972, are two items in the "General Fixed Assets" column of the Combined Balance Sheet: (1) an amount of $3,156,328 in the Assets and Other Debits section, described as "Fixed Assets (net)," and (2) an amount of $3,156,328 in the Liabilities section described as "General Fixed Assets—at cost."

Required:

a) To what extent does the information in the Kerrville annual report satisfy the information needs of (1) a new member of the City Council, (2) a resident interested in the financial management of assets of the city?

b) If you were a CPA auditing the city, should you give a clean opinion on the statements as they exist? If not, are there any changes which the client could make which would enable you to give a clean opinion? Is it likely that the statements as of May 31, 1972, could have been changed in accord with your specifications?

CITY OF KERRVILLE, TEXAS
Statement of General Fixed Assets
May 31, 1972

General fixed assets–at cost:		
Land	$ 143,330	
Buildings and structures	838,693	
Improvements other than buildings	1,734,363	
Automobiles and trucks	231,535	
Office furniture and equipment	19,144	
General furniture and equipment	189,263	$3,156,328
Investment in general fixed assets		
General Fixed Assets–at Cost		$3,156,328

12–3. Your examination of the accounts of your new client, the City of Delmas, as of June 30, 1971, revealed the following (Items 1, 2, 3, and 4 are intentionally omitted.):

5. On July 1, 1969, the City issued $400,000 in 30-year, 6% general obligation term bonds of the same date at par to finance the construction of a public health center. Construction was completed and the contractors fully paid a total of $397,500 in fiscal year 1970–71.

Required:

Prepare journal entries which should be made to establish a general fixed assets group of accounts for the City of Delmas and to record the events for the period given. (See, also, information in Problem 9–3 and Problem 10–3, if needed.) Also, prepare any necessary adjusting and closing entries as of June 30, 1971, the end of the fiscal year.

(AICPA, adapted)

12–4. Below are described a number of transactions, each of which had an effect on the general fixed assets group of accounts of a certain city. You are required to make an entry or entries for each transaction as it should have been recorded in the general fixed assets group of accounts. Explanations are not required.

1. During the year a capital projects fund completed a building project which had been initiated in the preceding year. The total cost of the project was $4,690,000, of which $2,580,000 had been spent or encumbered in the preceding year. Current year expenditures on the project, not encumbered in the prior year, were reported to have consisted of $1,500,000 from a federal grant, with the balance coming from proceeds of a general obligation bond issue.
2. All properties of the city library are accounted for as general fixed assets, and during the year the library purchased books at a total net cost of $25,000. The purchases were financed by money provided by a special revenue fund.
3. A manually operated typewriter was traded in on an electrically operated machine with a cash payment of $315. Price of the new machine to governmental bodies was $350. The manual machine had been purchased from general fund revenue for $145. Cash for the new machine was furnished by a special revenue fund.
4. A piece of heavy equipment was purchased by the street fund. Catalog price of the equipment was $6,000 with trade discounts of 10 and 5 percent. Terms of payment quoted by the manufacturer were 2/10, n/30. Payment for the equipment was made within the cash discount period.
5. A tract of land and a building located upon it were on the required right-of-way of an interstate highway and were sold to the state for $62,000 by the city. Cost of the building when erected was $49,800 and the estimated cost of the land was $13,000, both purchased from general fund revenue. It was estimated that one-third of the useful life of the building had expired at the time it was sold to the state.
6. A subdivision annexed by the city contained privately financed streets and sidewalks and a system of sewers. The best available information showed a cost of $120,000 for the sewer systems and $155,000 for the streets and sidewalks, of which $12,500 was estimated cost of the land. Both types of improvements were provided by the developers.
7. The cost of remodeling of the interior of the city hall was $21,650; $2,770 of this amount was classified as maintenance rather than improvement. In the remodeling process, walls, partitions, floors, etc. which were estimated to have cost $6,580 were removed and replaced. Cost of the total operation was provided by the general fund. The building had been built from proceeds of general obligation bonds sold by a capital projects fund.

12–5. Early in 1974, the Town of Lafayette, founded in 1901, embarked upon a program of establishing a coordinated and continuing record of its general fixed assets, with major responsibilities assigned to its accounting and legal departments. Specifically, the two departments were directed to produce an inventory of the town's general fixed assets at December 31, 1974, with a showing, insofar as possible, of the total amounts supplied by the various funds and other sources from which the fixed assets were obtained. Fortunately, a considerable portion of the general fixed assets had been acquired in rather recent years, after installation of a fairly complete accounting system. All available records for the prior period were scanned for expenditures of $100 or more, and these were listed and classified as to their capital or expense nature.

By December 31, 1974, the following summary of information about general fixed assets had been developed for 1901 to 1974 inclusive:

Objects of Expenditure or Gift	*Amount*	*Sources of Acquisition*	*Amount*
Land	$ 56,000	General fund	$2,770,000
Buildings	2,837,000	Special revenue funds	399,000
Improvements other than buildings	3,914,000	Capital projects funds	3,200,000
Equipment	1,623,000	Special assessment funds	130,000
Construction work in progress	106,000	Federal grants	1,200,000
		State grants	802,000
		Private gifts	73,000
Total	$8,536,000	Total	$8,574,000

Because of retirements, abandonments, destruction, and other forms of loss, properties supposed to have had the following total costs could not be located for inventory: buildings, $416,000; improvements other than buildings, $623,000; equipment, $311,000. However, assets of which no record was discovered were in possession of the city at the following appraised values as of December 31, 1974: land, $7,000; buildings, $60,000, equipment, $81,000.

The following amounts of the sources of acquisition listed above could not be associated with any general fixed asset included in the December 31, 1974, inventory: general fund, $821,000; special revenue funds, $76,000; capital projects funds, $513,000; state grants, $34,000; private gifts, $11,000. The special assessment fund investment could not be divided between property owners and town.

From the foregoing collection of information you are required to prepare in good form a statement of general fixed assets for the Town of Lafayette at December 31, 1974.

12–6. Following the close of the Town of Newton's fiscal year on April 30, 19x6, a member of the accounting staff was directed to assemble the necessary information and prepare a statement of changes in general fixed assets for the fiscal year ended on that date. From the town's annual financial report for fiscal 19x5, he ascertained that the following amounts of general fixed assets were owned at April 30, 19x5:

Land	$ 136,970
Buildings	1,761,520
Improvements other than buildings	2,095,740
Equipment	196,390
Construction work in progress	266,110

A summary of changes during fiscal year 19x6 contained the following information:

1. A building project underway at the end of fiscal 19x6 was being financed by a general obligation bond issue of $100,000 and a federal grant of $65,000, both accounted for through a capital projects fund. Of the federal authorization, $20,000 for planning and engineering had been received and spent and $42,000 of bond proceeds had been expended. Of the $42,000, purchase of land took $15,000.
2. Records of capital projects funds reported buildings completed during the year at a total cost of $209,720 and $51,880 spent on projects not completed at April 30, 19x6, all from general obligation bonds.
3. Special assessment funds added improvements other than buildings costing $137,100 during the year and reported total expenditures of $17,400 on a project not completed during the year.
4. The general fund spent $31,010 for acquisition of equipment and $9,850 for a parcel of land.
5. The street fund purchased equipment on which the cash outlay was $42,900, with allowances totaling $7,690 for equipment traded in. The equipment traded in had been purchased by the street fund at a total cost of $29,880.
6. Annexation added a portion of a sewer system and street improvements of which the estimated original cost was $198,400 and land to which an estimated cost of $13,940 was assigned.
7. Land having an appraised value of $75,000 was donated to the city, and additional land with an appraised value of $1,500 was received from the general fund, which had acquired it through tax foreclosure proceedings.
8. Of construction in progress at April 30, 19x5, $121,370 was reported as completed by a capital projects fund during fiscal 19x6, and $81,660 by special assessment funds.
9. Land acquired at an estimated cost of $1,200, on which a $7,000 building was located, was sold to the state highway department for a right-of-way at a price of $11,600.
10. An insurance settlement of $22,900 was received on a building which had cost $27,600 and a settlement of $17,600 was obtained on equipment of which the original cost was $21,360.
11. Construction activities during fiscal 19x6 required demolition of a building which had cost $31,460 and a bridge of which the estimated cost was $11,770. Equipment which had cost $19,300 could not be located and was presumed to have been stolen.

You are required to prepare a statement of changes in general fixed assets during the fiscal year ended April 30, 19x6. Show the sources of assets acquired and the causes of reductions. To conserve space, a "Total" column may be dispensed with. In the column headings,

"Improvements Other than Buildings" may be shortened to "Improvements."

12–7. A statement of general fixed assets of the Town of Murphysboro for 197D showed the following departmental balances for December 31:

Clerk–treasurer	$ 4,800
Fire department	463,170
Health department	12,050
Inspector of weights and measures	11,320
Mayor's office	16,090
Parks department	297,660
Police department	155,140
Public buildings (general government)	2,642,930
Street department	338,720
Town attorney	10,760

During 197E the following changes occurred:

1. The clerk-treasurer's office traded $980 of equipment on new equipment of $2,070 and purchased $1,230 additional.
2. The fire department acquired $362,950 of new equipment, partly by outright purchase and partly by trading $97,390 of old property.
3. The street department acquired new equipment for a cash outlay of $131,040 and a trade-in of old equipment on which an allowance of $15,030 was received. The equipment traded in had cost $68,730. Equipment which had cost $7,890 was scrapped.
4. The inspector of weights and measures succeeded in getting new equipment which cost $1,820. One piece of office equipment which had cost $170 was transferred from this office to that of the mayor.
5. The mayor's office acquired new equipment by purchase at a cost of $1,210. Old equipment which had cost $470 was traded on the new and one piece of equipment which had cost $150 could not be located at the time of annual inventory and was written off. $1,210 was the sum of allowance and cash outlay.
6. The parks department acquired $186,120 of new property by purchase, and property appraised at $21,040 by donation. Property which had cost $25,190 was worn out and retired. In addition, property which had cost $46,380 was stolen or destroyed by vandals.
7. $189,650 cash was spent on property for the police department. $21,830 was for major overhaul of various kinds of property, which did not add anything to its value, and $8,440 was for betterments to old equipment. The balance was for purchase of new property. Old property was traded on some of the new, and allowances totaling $9,610 were received. The property traded in had cost $41,620. Other property which had cost $4,630 was scrapped, with no residual value.

8. The total outlay (excluding transaction 9) on public buildings for the year was $766,190, of which $463,040 was for maintenance and upkeep; $86,470 was for remodeling the interior of one building. An architect estimated the cost of the part remodeled and removed at approximately $37,180. The remainder of the $766,190 was for additions. Structures which had cost $20,190 were demolished for various reasons.
9. For some years the town had been occupying a public building under a lease-purchase agreement. During the year the city exercised its option, paid the balance of the contract, and received title to the building, including the land on which it was situated. The total paid out under the contract was $178,200, of which, according to terms of the contract, $35,600 was rental and $17,300 was interest. All money was provided by the general fund.
10. Total outlay for health department equipment during the year was $19,010, of which $370 was for items costing less than the minimum amount to be capitalized. Health department equipment which had cost $2,330 was disposed of during the year, with no salvage value.
11. Two sets of law books costing a total of $950 and a typewriter costing $460 were the total additions to property in the town attorney's office during the year. Law books carried as property located in the office could not be accounted for and were written off in the total amount of $170.

You are required to prepare a statement of changes in the general fixed assets of the Town of Murphysboro during 197E, with the information classified by function and department. The main classification is by function, with departments listed under the function which each serves. Include columns for balance at December 31, 197D; 197E increases; 197E decreases; and balance, December 31, 197E.

12–8. At March 31, 19x5, the fixed property schedule of the Town of Benjamin was as follows:

General government:	
Land	$110,320
Buildings	507,100
Improvements other than buildings	163,490
Equipment	718,570
Fire protection:	
Land	21,430
Buildings	106,210
Equipment	301,850
Police protection:	
Equipment	122,480
Recreation:	
Land	618,770
Buildings	31,060
Improvements other than buildings	81,540
Equipment	59,000

Libraries:	
Land	76,390
Buildings	394,180
Improvements other than buildings	3,020
Equipment	294,670
Health and welfare:	
Land	115,930
Buildings	92,410
Improvements other than buildings	301,250
Machinery and equipment	14,980

Additional purchases during the year (all machinery or equipment) were as follows:

General government	$ 9,020
Fire department	20,730
Police department	11,650
Recreation department	16,760
Libraries	1,940
Health and welfare	9,010

A piece of equipment appraised at $5,710 was received from a Federal agency for general governmental use.

Reductions of machinery and equipment by sale during the year included $2,080 by the general government, $390 by the fire department, and $210 by health and welfare. Reductions by trade-in consisted of $470 by the police department and $680 by health and welfare.

Buildings sold during the year were $4,120 by the recreation fund and $12,860 by health and welfare.

Reductions from abandonment on account of obsolescence (all machinery and equipment) were $18,640 by the general government, $920 by the fire department, $430 by the police department, $270 by the recreation department, $120 by the library, and $1,310 by health and welfare. Improvements other than buildings abandoned consisted of $2,780 by the general government and $1,590 by health and welfare.

Prepare a statement for the year ended March 31, 19x6, showing the beginning balance of each class of fixed assets, the causes of change (purchases, received from other governmental units, sales, abandonment, trade-ins), and the amounts thereof, and the ending balance. Show totals for each function, considering fire protection and police protection as separate functions.

CONTINUOUS PROBLEMS

12–L. The Controller of the City of Bingham assigned you, and other top personnel on his staff, to audit the General Fixed Assets group of accounts—a task which had not been done in many years. The bookkeeper had been a marketing major in the university, but had never succeeded in getting his grade average high enough to allow him to graduate. He was able to show you the records he had been keeping, but was not able to give a very clear explanation as to why he kept them the way he did. The auditors found the following General Fixed Assets control account balances as of the audit cut-off date. (No source accounts had been kept.)

Land	$ 150,000	
Buildings	1,300,000	
Improvements other than buildings	5,520,000	
Equipment and miscellaneous	1,310,000	
Fund Balance		$8,280,000

You are required to:

a) Open a general journal for the General Fixed Assets group of accounts and make the entries necessary to state the accounts in accord with recommendations of the National Committee on Governmental Accounting. Additional information disclosed by your audit is presented below.

1. Analysis of the Land account disclosed that the balance was comprised of: (*a*) An amount of $25,000 entered in 1938 when the General Fixed Asset group was established; this amount was the estimated value of the City Hall site, the fire station sites, and city park land. The unimproved park land had been acquired as a gift from a citizen and was estimated in 1938 to be worth $2,000; the building sites had been acquired from the proceeds of general bond issues. (*b*) An amount of $40,000 entered in 1948 as the cost of two houses and lots. The houses were torn down and an addition to City Hall erected on one lot; the remainder was used as a parking lot for city-owned cars and for the private cars of city employees. This amount was financed under a grant from the federal government. (*c*) An amount of $60,000, dated 1954, which was financed by general obligation bonds issued for the purchase of land used as a public parking lot. The former property owners received $50,000; the mayor, who was a real estate dealer, $5,000 commission for arranging the transaction; and the mayor's brother, an attorney, $5,000 for handling the legal details. (*d*) An amount of $25,000 entered in 1963 as the cost of land purchased by the Water Utility from current operating funds; the land is being held by the Water Utility as the site of a projected new pumping station.
2. Analysis of the Buildings account disclosed that the balance was comprised of: (*a*) An amount of $650,000 entered in 1938 as the estimated value of City Hall and the fire stations, constructed from the proceeds of general bond issues. (*b*) Charges of $4,000 for demolishing the houses purchased in 1948, and

grading the land to the level of City Hall; $300,000 for the addition to City Hall; and $26,000 for paving the parking lot—all of which were financed from a grant by the federal government. (*c*) $100,000 for a golf club house in the park, constructed from part of the proceeds of a general bond issue. (*d*) $100,000 for a 240-acre estate to be used as a park. The mansion was worth $100,000 and the unimproved land $240,000, according to the real estate agent–mayor, and the park director estimated that the gardens, artificial lakes, and other improvements would cost $500,000 to duplicate. The entire purchase price was charged to Buildings; the amount had been paid over three years out of general fund appropriations for public works. Heirs of the individual who had sold the property to the city sued to set aside the sale, claiming the man must have been incompetent. It cost the city $120,000 to settle the claim out of court. This amount was paid from a general fund appropriation and charged to Buildings.

3. The following items had been entered in the Improvements Other than Buildings account: (*a*) Estimated cost of streets, curbs, and sidewalks as of July 1, 1938, $1,750,000. $750,000 had been financed from annual general fund appropriations during the years; the balance had been financed from various special assessment funds. (*b*) $200,000, the cost of constructing a municipal golf course on city park land, financed from a general obligation bond issue. (*c*) An aggregate of $3,570,000 spent for street paving and widening, curbs, sidewalks, bridges, and culverts. $1,785,000 of this was from the general fund appropriations, and the remainder from special assessment funds.
4. "Equipment and Miscellaneous" supporting data was in such an incomplete and obviously inaccurate state that the auditors secured permission to have an appraisal made. The cost of the appraisal was charged to a supplemental appropriation made under the General Government classification of the general fund. The appraisal cost $30,000; it was a thorough job and showed location, and condition, as well as appraised value of items classifiable as "Equipment and Miscellaneous." The proper balance of the account was found to be $2,416,000. The auditors could identify the sources of financing for only a portion of the equipment; therefore, it was decided to assume the sources to have contributed the following percentages of appraised value: general fund, 65 percent; special revenue funds, 15 percent; capital projects funds, 5 percent; special assessment funds, 5 percent; and grants from the Federal government, 10 percent.

b) None of the information presented in Problems 1–L through 11 L has been recorded by the General Fixed Assets bookkeeper. Record the applicable information in the General Fixed Assets general journal. (Expenditures of the City Hall Annex Construction Fund for Land and for Equipment are given in Problem 6–L; assume that the expenditures of that fund for Improvements Other Than Buildings amount to $80,260, and that the remainder of expenditures are proper charges to Buildings. Interest on City Hall annex bonds during the period of construction is not to be capitalized.)

c) Open a general ledger for the General Fixed Assets group of accounts and post your journal entries.

d) Prepare a Statement of General Fixed Assets as of year end.

12–S. As of December 31, 197A, the General Fixed Assets Group of the City of Smithville presented the following statement:

CITY OF SMITHVILLE
Statement of General Fixed Assets
December 31, 197A

General Fixed Assets	
Land	$ 618,000
Buildings	3,006,000
Improvements other than buildings	4,197,000
Equipment	928,000
Total General Fixed Assets	$8,749,000

Investment in General Fixed Assets from:	
Capital project funds:	
General obligation bonds	$4,000,000
Federal grants	1,236,000
State grants	431,000
General fund revenues	2,089,000
Special revenue fund revenues	364,000
Special assessments	629,000
Total Investment in General Fixed Assets	$8,749,000

1. Subsidiary records of the General Fixed Assets Group of accounts showed that the assets were assigned to functions and activities as shown below:

Function and Activity	*Total*	*Land*	*Buildings*	*Improvements*	*Equipment*
eneral Government	$1,922,000	$ 50,000	$1,504,000	$ 140,000	$228,000
ublic safety:					
Police	501,000	35,000	420,000	8,000	38,000
Fire	636,000	41,000	309,000	20,000	266,000
Building safety	38,000	3,000	22,000	5,000	8,000
ublic works	4,425,000	370,000	301,000	3,448,000	306,000
ealth and welfare	97,000	9,000	40,000	16,000	32,000
arks and recreation	1,130,000	110,000	410,000	560,000	50,000
Total	$8,749,000	$618,000	$3,006,000	$4,197,000	$928,000

2. Changes in general fixed assets resulting from general fund activities in 197B were as follows:

	Improvements		*Equipment*	
Function and Activity	*Cost of Additions*	*Cost of Assets Retired*	*Cost of Additions*	*Cost of Assets Retired*
General				
Government.			$ 40,000	$ 10,000
Public safety:				
Police			42,000	19,000
Fire.			36,000	24,000
Building				
safety			3,000	
Public works.	$30,000	$ 8,000	53,000	30,000
Health and welfare			16,000	8,000
Parks and recreation	24,000	6,000	18,000	10,000
Total.	$54,000	$14,000	$208,000	$101,000

3. Changes in general fixed assets occurred during 197B as a result of activities of the Street Improvement Fund (see Problem 6–S). Assume that $991,225 of the expenditures were financed from general obligation bonds, and the remainder from Federal grants.

Required:

a) Open a general journal for the general fixed assets group of accounts and record the changes resulting from activities of the General Fund and activities of the Street Improvement Fund.

b) Prepare a Statement of General Fixed Assets—by Function and Activity, as of December 31, 197B.

c) Prepare a Statement of Changes in General Fixed Assets—by Function and Activity for the year ended December 31, 197B.

13

General Long-Term Debt Group of Accounts

The management of state and local governmental debt requires good legal advice and good understanding of the principles of public finance, both backed by competently designed and operated financial management information systems. Accounting aspects of the financial management information system for each of the types of funds recommended for use by local governmental units are discussed in preceding chapters. The reader should recall that revenue funds, capital projects funds, debt service funds, intragovernmental service funds, and agency funds account for only short-term debt to be paid from fund assets. Enterprise funds and special assessment funds account for long-term debt serviced by the fund, as well as short-term debt to be paid from fund assets. Trust funds account for short-term debt arising from their operations, and for long-term debt related to assets in the fund principal.

General Long-Term Debt Group of Accounts

Debt instruments backed by the "full faith and credit" of a municipality are obligations of the municipality as a whole and not of the individual funds. In order to bring such debt under accounting control the general long-term debt group of accounts was created. General obligation bonds, time warrants, and notes having a maturity of more than one year from date of issuance are forms of debt accounted for by the general long-term debt group. Liability accounts have credit balances; in order for the General Long-Term Debt Group to be self-balancing it is necessary to create accounts which have debit balances even though no assets are assigned to the group (it is an account group, not a fund). The debit balance accounts which offset the long-term liabilities are of two categories: (1) amounts accumulated in debt service funds for repayment of general long-term debt, and (2) amounts which must be provided in future years for repayment of the general long-term debt. The sum of the two categories of debit balance accounts, therefore, equals the total amount of outstanding general long-term debt.

In Chapter 10 and Chapter 11 it is noted that bonds of special assessment funds and bonds of enterprise funds may be issued with covenants which give them the status of general obligation bonds although the intent is that the debt be serviced from the resources of the issuing fund. If the wording of the covenants or the bond ordinance is such that, in the opinion of competent legal counsel, the bonds are actually general obligation bonds, the National Committee on Governmental Accounting recommends that the bonds be shown as liabilities in both the issuing fund and in the Statement of General Long-Term Debt. If the wording of the covenants or the bond ordinance is such that the general liability is only a contingency, the NCGA recommends that the liability be disclosed in the body of the statement of the issuing fund, and that the contingent liability be disclosed by a footnote to the Statement of General Long-Term Debt. A suggested form of footnote is shown on page 260 of this text. The American Institute of Certified Public Accountants agrees with the NCGA recommendations for disclosure of liability and contingent liability on general obligation special assessment bonds, but is not in favor of "double reporting of the same liability" in the case of general obligation enterprise bonds. The AICPA position is that, if the bond ordinance makes it clear that enterprise bonds backed by the full faith and credit of the governmental unit are to be retired from enterprise fund resources, the bonds should show as liabilities of the enterprise fund only. The contingent liability of the general governmental unit for the bonds being serviced by enterprise funds is properly disclosed, the AICPA states, by footnote to the Statement of General Long-Term Debt. If the bond ordinance does not provide for service of the bond issue from enterprise fund resources, the AICPA states that the bond proceeds are in the nature of a contribution to the enterprise fund, and that the bond liability is to be accounted for by the General Long-Term Debt Group.

Illustrative Case

When general obligation long-term debt is issued it is necessary to debit Amount to be Provided for Payment of Term Bonds (or Serial Bonds or whatever phrase describes the debt issued) and credit Term Bonds Payable (Serial Bonds Payable, etc.) for the face value of debt issued. If the debt is issued at a premium and the premium transferred to a debt service fund, the amount of the premium should be debited to

Amount Available in Debt Service Fund for Payment of Term Bonds and credited to Amount to be Provided. . . . In Chapter 7 the illustrative entries show how the debt service funds of the Town of Alva account for the resources devoted to current interest payments and to retirement of serial bonds. In that chapter it is assumed that the town has an issue of regular 4% serial bonds amounting to $800,000 outstanding on December 31, 19y0; bonds of this issue in the amount of $50,000 are to mature on January 1, 19y1. The town also has outstanding a deferred 4% serial bond issue in the total amount of $2,000,000 as of December 31, 19y0; $200,000 worth of these bonds are to mature on January 1, 19y1. No assets are accumulated in the debt service fund for retirement of the regular serial bonds; cash in the exact amount needed for interest payments and principal payments during the year is transferred to the debt service fund from the general fund on January 1 of each year. As of December 31, 19y0, therefore, (under the modified accrual basis of accounting as explained in Chapter 7) the debt service fund has no assets, liabilities, or fund balance pertaining to the regular serial bonds.

For the deferred serial bonds the general fund budgets its contributions to the debt service fund in an amount equal to interest to be paid during the budget year, plus a level contribution of $80,000 a year. The debt service fund is responsible for investing the $80,000 contributions; interest earnings on the investments are added to the accumulated assets of the debt service fund to be used, when needed, for principal repayment. The December 31, 19y0, balance sheet of the debt service fund (Illustration 7–1) shows that the amount available in the debt service fund for principal repayment is $1,157,375; the fund also has $2,200 cash on deposit with a fiscal agent for use in paying matured interest coupons.

From the facts given in the two preceding paragraphs it can be seen that the Town of Alva Statement of General Long-Term Debt as of December 31, 19y0, would appear as shown in Illustration 13–1.

Entries in General Long-Term Debt accounts may be made on a current basis throughout the fiscal period as long-term debt is issued, as it is repaid, and as assets are added to debt service funds; or all the events of the period may be cumulated and appropriate entries made at period-end for the net effect of all events. In order to make the illustrative entries in this chapter correspond with the illustrative entries in Chapter 7, it is assumed that the town accountant elects to record in the general long-term debt group events as they occur.

On January 1, 19y1, the general fund transferred $161,000 cash to the debt service funds—$81,000 for the requirements of regular serial bonds and $80,000 for requirements of the deferred serial bonds. Of the $161,000, $50,000 is for redemption of regular serial bonds and $40,000 is to be invested for eventual redemption of deferred serial bonds; the

Illustration 13–1

TOWN OF ALVA
Statement of General Long-term Debt
December 31, 19y0

Amount Available and to be Provided for Payment of General Long-Term Debt		
Regular serial bonds:		
Amount to be provided		$ 800,000
Deferred serial bonds:		
Amount available in debt service fund	$1,157,375	
Amount to be provided	842,625	
Total Deferred Serial Bonds		2,000,000
Total Available and to Provided		$2,800,000
General Long-Term Debt Payable		
Regular serial bonds, 4% J and J1, final maturity 1/1/z6		$ 800,000
Deferred serial bonds, 4% J and J1, final maturity 1/1/z0		2,000,000
Total General Long-Term Debt Payable		$2,800,000

remainder of the $161,000 is for interest payments in 19y1. Under current recommendations of the NCGA only the increases in the assets held in the debt service funds for principal payment are accounted for by the general long-term debt group. Since these amounts are now available they are no longer "to be provided" and the entries below are appropriate:

		Debit	Credit
1a.	Amount Available in Debt Service Fund for Payment of Regular Serial Bonds	50,000	
	Amount to be Provided for Payment of Regular Serial Bonds		50,000
1b.	Amount Available in Debt Service Fund for Payment of Deferred Serial Bonds	40,000	
	Amount to be Provided for Payment of Deferred Serial Bonds		40,000

Also on January 1, 19y1, the liability for the bonds that matured on that date ($50,000 of regular serial bonds and $200,000 of deferred serial bonds) are recorded in the debt service funds; therefore the liability accounts of the general long-term debt group must be reduced correspondingly. At the time the bonds were recorded as liabilities of the debt service funds, the expenditure of assets of those funds was recognized. The entries below show the effect on the accounts of the general long-term debt group:

		Debit	Credit
2a.	Regular Serial Bonds Payable	50,000	
	Amount Available in Debt Service Fund for Payment of Regular Serial Bonds		50,000

2b.	Deferred Serial Bonds Payable	200,000	
	Amount Available in Debt Service Fund for Payment of Deferred Serial Bonds		200,000

During 19y1 there were no further transactions affecting the regular serial bonds; however, prior to July 1 the general fund transferred $40,000 to the debt service fund for investment and eventual use for redemption of deferred serial bonds. ($36,000 for interest was also transferred at the same time, but this is of no concern to the general long-term debt bookkeeper.) In the general long-term debt accounts the transfer is recorded as:

3.	Amount Available in Debt Service Fund for Payment of Deferred Serial Bonds	40,000	
	Amount to be Provided for Payment of Deferred Serial Bonds		40,000

Interest on investments is collected by the debt service fund as shown by entry no. 13 in Chapter 7. The corresponding entry in the general long-term debt group is:

4.	Amount Available in Debt Service Fund for Payment of Deferred Serial Bonds	24,250	
	Amount to be Provided for Payment of Deferred Serial Bonds		24,250

Accrued interest at year-end on debt service fund investments is recorded by that fund as shown by entry no. 16 of Chapter 7. The corresponding entry in the general long-term debt group is:

5.	Amount Available in Debt Service Fund for Payment of Deferred Serial Bonds	24,750	
	Amount to be Provided for Payment of Deferred Serial Bonds		24,750

If the town accountant had elected to have all events of 19y1 recorded in the general long-term debt group by a single combined entry (which would be, of course, the net result of entries 1a. through 5 above), the entry would be:

Regular Serial Bonds Payable	50,000	
Deferred Serial Bonds Payable	200,000	
Amount Available in Debt Service Fund for Payment of Deferred Serial Bonds		71,000
Amount to be Provided for Payment of Deferred Serial Bonds		129,000
Amount to be Provided for Payment of Regular Serial Bonds		50,000

The status of general long-term debt as of December 31, 19y1, is shown by Illustration 13–2.

Illustration 13–2

TOWN OF ALVA
Statement of General Long-Term Debt
December 31, 19y1

Amount Available and to be Provided for Payment of General Long-Term Debt		
Regular serial bonds:		
Amount to be Provided		$ 750,000
Deferred serial bonds:		
Amount available in debt service fund	$1,086,375	
Amount to be provided	713,625	
Total Deferred Serial Bonds		1,800,000
Total Available and to Be Provided		$2,550,000
General Long-Term Debt Payable		
Regular serial bonds, 4% J and J1, final maturity 1/1/z6		$ 750,000
Deferred serial bonds, 4% J and J1, final maturity 1/1/z0		1,800,000
Total General Long-Term Debt Payable		$2,550,000

Changes in Long-Term Debt

The reasons why the amounts of the items in Illustration 13–2 are not the same as the amounts of the same items in Illustration 13–1 are clear to those who have access to the underlying records (here illustrated in journal entry form), but readers of the annual report of the Town of Alva would not have access to the underlying records and should be furnished a statement summarizing the reasons for the changes during the year. In the illustrative case all changes in general long-term debt result from activities summarized in debt service fund statements; therefore adequate disclosure may be made by reference to those statements. If debt had been incurred during the year, however, the proceeds of the sale would have been recorded in a capital projects fund rather than in a debt service fund. In any given year it is common for debt issues to be authorized, previously authorized debt to be issued, and older issues to be retired. When a combination of events takes place, a statement of changes in long-term debt may be desirable. It is common practice for municipalities which report the details of changes in general long-term debt to include a combined statement the details of changes in special assessment fund debt, enterprise fund debt, and any other long-term debt. Illustration 13–3 is taken from the annual report of the City of Medford, Oregon. The schedule as shown in the Medford report

Illustration 13–3

CITY OF MEDFORD, OREGON
Schedule of Bonds and Bond Interest Payable
For the Fiscal Year Ended June 30, 1971

Description	*Interest Rates (%)*	*Date of Issue*	*Final Maturing Date*	*Bonds Outstanding 6/30/70*	*Bonds Matured*	*Bonds Retired*	*Bonds Outstanding 6/30/71*
General Obligation Bonds (Tax Supported):							
Arterial street bonds, series "B"	3	6/15/61	6/15/71	$ 12,000.00	$ 12,000.00	$ 12,000.00	$
Civic Center–City Hall bonds	3, 3.1, 3.2	4/1/65	4/1/85	1,725,000.00	115,000.00	115,000.00	1,610,000.00
Storm sewer bonds, series "C"	6, 5, 4.2	10/1/66	10/1/86	900,000.00	50,000.00	50,000.00	850,000.00
Arterial street bonds, series 1966	6, 5, 4.2	10/1/66	10/1/86	1,185,000.00	65,000.00	65,000.00	1,120,000.00
Total General Obligation Bonds (Tax Supported).				$3,822,000.00	$242,000.00	$242,000.00	$3,580,000.00
General Obligation Bonds (Revenue Supported):							
Sewage Disposal Purposes:							
Sewage treatment bonds	7.75, 7, 5.75, 5.9, 6, 6.1	11/1/69	11/1/94	$3,250,000.00	$	$	$3,250,000.00
Interceptor sewer bonds, series "A"	7, 6, 6.3, 6.5, 6.6, 6.7	3/1/70	3/1/90	500,000.00	15,000.00	15,000.00	485,000.00
Interceptor sewer bonds, series "B"	6.1	3/1/70	3/1/94	1,200,000.00	25,000.00	25,000.00	1,175,000.00
Total General Obligation Bonds (Revenue Supported) Sewage Disposal Purposes. . .				4,950,000 00	40,000.00	40,000.00	4,910,000.00
*Waterworks purposes:							
Water system enlargement bonds	2	7/1/50	7/1/80	1,560,000.00	115,000.00	115,000.00	1,445,000.00
Water system enlargement bonds, series "B" . .	6, 5.5, 4.2	10/1/66	10/1/86	2,540,000.00	70,000.00	70,000.00	2,470,000.00
Kenwood water district no. 1 bonds	3.25	4/1/54	4/1/74	12,000.00	3,000.00	3,000.00	9,000.00
Grandview water district no. 1 bonds	3.25	4/1/55	4/1/76	30,000.00	5,000.00	5,000.00	25,000.00
Total General Obligation Bonds (Revenue Supported) for Waterworks Purposes . . .				4,142,000.00	193,000.00	193,000.00	3,949,000.00
Total General Obligation Bonds (Revenue Supported)				$9,092,000.00	$233,000.00	$233,000.00	$8,859,000.00

*Reflected in the enterprise fund (water utility) operation.

included data for special assessment bonds and four additional columns detailing for all bond issues the matured interest payable at the beginning of the year, coupons matured, coupons redeemed, and matured interest payable at the end of the year; this material was deleted from the schedule in order to keep the illustration legible when reduced to fit the page.

Interest Payable in Future Years

Before 1968 the National Committee on Governmental Accounting recommended a "General Bonded Debt and Interest Group"; in 1968 the recommendation was changed to that discussed in the previous sections of this chapter. Some municipalities still use a general bonded debt and interest group. The essential difference, as the name of the group indicates, is that interest on long-term debt to date of maturity is computed and recorded in a credit-balance account called Interest Payable in Future Years. Offsetting the credit-balance account are two debit-balance accounts: Amount Available in Debt Service Funds for Payment of Interest, and Amount to be Provided for Payment of Interest.

The idea of trying to emphasize to readers of the financial statements the magnitude of the claim on municipal resources resulting from interest which will become payable in future years is appealing to fiscal conservatives, but disclosure of the total amount of future interest (not the present value of the interest) in a manner which makes it appear to be a present liability is not considered to be in accord with generally accepted principles of accounting. In order to disclose the future demands on resources resulting from the maturing of debt principal and the payment of interest, a schedule showing this information is often included in the annual report. One form this schedule may take is shown as Illustration 13–4.

Ratio of Bonded Debt to Assessed Valuation and Bonded Debt Per Capita

Another statement designed to set forth the extent and significance of bonded indebtedness is advocated by the National Committee on Governmental Accounting and is being employed by governmental units to an increasing extent. This is a statement showing the ratio of net general long-term debt to assessed valuation, and net long-term debt per capita. As indicated by the descriptive title, this statement correlates the long-term debt burden with the property to which it applies and with the source of payment, the citizenry. However, it may be pointed out that the latter comparison might carry greater significance if it were on a per taxpayer basis rather than a per capita basis. An example of the ratio statement is shown in Illustration 13–5.

Illustration 13–4

METROPOLITAN GOVERNMENT OF NASHVILLE AND DAVIDSON COUNTY
Annual Debt Service Funds Requirement–General Obligation Bonds
Urban Services District

Fiscal Year	*Principal*	*Interest*	*Total*
1972–73	$ 1,770,000.00	$ 1,439,498.75	$ 3,209,498.75
1973–74	1,814,000.00	1,371,996.25	3,185,996.25
1974–75	1,730,000.00	1,303,108.75	3,033,108.75
1975–76	1,762,000.00	1,235,428.75	2,997,428.75
1976–77	1,792,000.00	1,165,436.25	2,957,436.25
1977–78	2,076,000.00	1,097,526.25	3,173,526.25
1978–79	1,945,000.00	1,025,606.25	2,970,606.25
1979–80	2,020,000.00	955,423.75	2,975,423.75
1980–81	2,020,000.00	885,291.25	2,905,291.25
1981–82	1,955,000.00	815,915.00	2,770,915.00
1982–83	2,110,000.00	748,162.50	2,858,162.50
1983–84	2,115,000.00	675,970.00	2,790,970.00
1984–85	2,045,000.00	603,812.50	2,648,812.50
1985–86	2,045,000.00	533,325.00	2,578,325.00
1986–87	1,915,000.00	463,227.50	2,378,227.50
1987–88	1,790,000.00	396,182.50	2,186,182.50
1988–89	1,765,000.00	335,842.50	2,100,842.50
1989–90	1,550,000.00	279,842.50	1,829,842.50
1990–91	1,225,000.00	232,255.00	1,457,255.00
1991–92	1,180,000.00	192,992.50	1,372,992.50
1992–93	975,000.00	156,005.00	1,131,005.00
1993–94	910,000.00	122,142.50	1,032,142.50
1994–95	740,000.00	89,500.00	829,500.00
1995–96	690,000.00	64,287.50	754,287.50
1996–97	625,000.00	40,825.00	665,825.00
1997–98	580,000.00	25,675.00	605,675.00
1998–99	175,000.00	4,050.00	179,050.00
1999–00	50,000.00	225.00	50,225.00
2000–01	50,000.00	175.00	50,175.00
2001–02	50,000.00	125.00	50,125.00
2002–03	50,000.00	75.00	50,075.00
2003–04	50,000.00	25.00	50,025.00
Totals	$41,569,000.00	$16,259,953.75	$57,828,953.75

Debt Limitation

The debt statements already illustrated in this chapter are primarily useful for the information of administrators, legislative bodies, and others concerned with the impact of long-term debt upon the financial condition and activities of the governmental unit, particularly with reference to the resulting tax rates and taxes. Another matter of importance in relation to long-term indebtedness is legal limitation upon the amount of long-term indebtedness which may be outstanding at a given time, in proportion to the assessed value of property within the jurisdiction represented. This

Illustration 13–5

KANSAS CITY, MISSOURI
Ratio of Bonded Debt To Assessed Valuation and Bonded Debt per Capita
For Fiscal Years 1961–62 to 1970–71

Fiscal Year Ended April 30	*Population*	*Assessed Valuation*[2]	*Total General Obligation Bonded Debt*[3]	*Special Assessment and Utility General Obligation Bonded Debt*[4]	*Net General Obligation Bonded Debt Supported By Taxes*	*Ratio of Bonded Debt to Assessed Valuation*		*Per Capita Debt*	
						Total	*Net*	*Total*	*Net*
1962	480,000[1]	$ 963,529,076	$62,161,000	$11,706,000	$50,455,000	6.45%	5.24%	$129.50	$105.11
1963	482,000[1]	1,008,307,993	60,550,000	19,792,000	49,758,000	6.01	4.93	125.62	103.23
1964	484,000[1]	1,035,493,837	60,641,000	9,868,000	50,773,000	5.86	4.90	125.29	104.90
1965	486,000[1]	1,048,061,907	66,294,000	14,938,000	51,356,000	6.33	4.90	136.41	105.67
1966	488,000[1]	1,086,803,569	80,058,000	13,607,000	66,451,000	7.37	6.11	164.05	136.17
1967	490,000[1]	1,144,041,787	73,603,000	12,275,000	61,328,000	6.43	5.36	150.21	125.16
1968	492,000[1]	1,154,469,782	73,031,000	14,139,000	58,892,000	6.33	5.10	148.44	119.70
1969	494,000[1]	1,231,312,065	71,886,000	13,803,000	58,083,000	5.84	4.72	145.52	117.58
1970	495,405[1]	1,268,433,916	70,347,000	13,326,000	57,021,000	5.55	4.50	142.00	115.10
1971	507,409[1]	1,291,651,489	63,209,000	11,740,000	51,469,000	4.89	3.98	124.57	101.43
1972	507,409[1]	1,334,447,098	67,174,000	17,280,000	49,894,000	5.03%	3.74	132.39	98.97

[1] Population estimated. See Miscellaneous Statistics.

[2] Assessed valuation of taxable property within corporate limits of City for State and County purposes. See Statement of Legal Debt Margin.

[3] See Statement of Legal Debt Margin: General Obligation Bonds Payable.

[4] This debt includes amounts for water works improvements, principal and interest of which are paid from Water Department revenue; street and avenue improvements, and sanitary and storm sewer improvements, principal and interest of which are paid from special assessments against benefited property; and street improvements, principal and interest on which were paid from motor fuel tax revenues.

type of restriction is of importance as a protection of taxpayers against possible confiscatory tax rates. Even though tax-rate limitation laws may be in effect for a governmental unit, the limitation upon bonded indebtedness is usually needed because the prevailing practice is to exempt the claims of bondholders from the barrier of tax-rate restrictions. This is to say that, even though a law establishing maxima for tax rates is in the statutes, it will probably exclude debt service requirements from the restrictions of the law. This exclusion would be reiterated, in effect, in the bond indentures.

Before continuing a discussion of debt limitation, it seems well to clarify the meaning of the terms "debt limit" and "debt margin." Debt *limit* means the total amount of indebtedness of specified kinds which is allowed by law to be outstanding at any one time. The limitation is likely to be in terms of a stipulated percentage of the assessed valuation of property within the government's jurisdiction. It may relate to either a gross or a net valuation. The latter is logical, but probably not prevalent, because debt limitation exists as a device for protecting property owners from confiscatory taxation. For that reason, taxpaying property *only* should be used in regulating maximum indebtedness. In many governmental jurisdictions, there is much property which is legally excluded even from *assessment.* This includes property owned by governments, churches, charitable organizations, and some others depending upon state laws. *Exemptions*, which apply to property subject to assessment, are based on homestead or mortgage exemption laws, military service, economic status, and possibly some others. Both exclusions and exemptions reduce the amount of taxpaying property.

Debt *margin*, sometimes referred to as "borrowing power," is the difference between the amount of debt limit calculated as prescribed by law and the net amount of outstanding indebtedness subject to limitation. The net amount of outstanding indebtedness subject to limitation, unless otherwise specified by law, is the difference between total long-term indebtedness and a subtraction factor consisting of one or more of the following:

1. Special assessment fund bonds which are of the special-special assessment variety, unless these are specifically designated as full faith and credit liabilities.
2. Revenue bonds and revenue notes which are not secondarily secured by the full faith and credit of the issuing governmental unit.
3. Bonds issued by instrumentalities of the governmental unit, secured only by revenue and resources of the instrumentalities.
4. Amounts accumulated in debt service funds, or elsewhere, to apply on payment of indebtedness subject to the limitation.
5. Any other long-term indebtedness which, while normally subject

to debt limitations, is specifically exempt by statute or has been exempted by a favorable vote by taxpayers.

In practice, it is unwise to rely upon theoretical generalizations as to which debt is subject to limitation and which is not. For example, some governmental units require inclusion of bonds which have been authorized but not yet issued, presumably because this potential debt has, by authorization, passed beyond control through remonstrances and the ballot box. Debt limitations are established by state and local enact-

Illustration 13–6

KANSAS CITY, MISSOURI
Statement of Legal Debt Margin
As of April 30, 1972

		General Obligation Bonds		
		Ordinary Note A	*Additional Note B*	*Total*
Assessed valuation for state and county purposes for calendar year 1971:				
Platte County	$ 34,749,637			
Clay County	122,356,725			
Jackson County	1,181,341,136			$1,338,447,498
Constitutional debt limit		$133,844,750	$133,844,750	$ 267,689,500
General obligation bonds payable		$ 27,165,000	$ 40,009,000	$ 67,174,000*
Less: Cash and securities available for retirement of bonds		$ 249,115	$ 4,681,135	$ 4,930,250†
Total amount of bonds payable applicable to debt limit		$ 26,915,885	$ 35,327,865	$ 62,243,750
Margin above bonds payable		$106,928,865	$ 98,516,885	$ 205,445,750
General obligation bonds authorized but unissued		$ 8,977,000	$ 16,000,000	$ 24,977,000
Legal Debt Margin		$ 97,951,865	$ 82,516,885	$ 180,468,750

Note A–Section (b) and (c) of the State Constitution of 1945 permits any County or City, by a vote of two-thirds of the qualified electors thereof voting thereon, to incur an indebtedness for City or County purposes not to exceed 10% of the taxable tangible property therein as shown by the last completed assessment.

Note B–Section 26 (d) and (e) of the State Constitution of 1945 provides that any City may become indebted not exceeding in the aggregate an additional 10% . . . for the purpose of acquiring the right-of-way, constructing, extending, and improving streets and avenues and/or sanitary or storm sewer systems; and an additional 10% for purchasing or constructing waterworks, electric or other light plants . . . provided the total general obligation indebtedness of the City does not exceed 20% of the assessed valuation.

*This amount includes $17,369,000 General Obligation Bonds for improvements as follows: $119,000 for Water Works, $13,378,000 for Special Assessment Sanitary and Storm Sewers, $3,783,000 for Special Assessment Street and Avenue, and $89,000 for Street Improvements. The principal as well as interest maturities of Water Works Bonds have been, and will continue to be, financed from Water Department revenue. The principal as well as interest maturities of Special Assessment Bonds have been and will continue to be financed from Special Assessments against benefitting property. The principal as well as interest maturities of Street Improvement Bonds are financed from State collected gasoline taxes.

†This amount includes $457,847 General Debt and Interest Fund, $720,853 Street and Avenue Special Assessment and $3,751,550 Sewer Special Assessment Fund.

ments (constitutions, charters, laws, ordinances), and these are the only fully reliable sources of information.

Like the forms of most other statements in wide usage, the form of statements of debt limit and margin is variable. Some variations reflect differences of opinion as to the best form for setting forth the desired information, whereas some arise from differences in law. An example embodying the essentials of such a statement is shown in Illustration 13–6.

Overlapping Debt

Debt limitation laws ordinarily establish limits that may not be exceeded by each separate governmental unit affected by the laws. This means that the county government may incur indebtedness to the legal limit, a township within that county may do likewise, and a city within the township may become indebted to the legal limit, with no restriction because of debt already owed by larger territorial units in which it is located. As a result, a given parcel of real estate or object of personal property may be the basis of debt beyond the so-called "legal limit" and also may be subject at a given time to assessments for the payment of taxes to retire bonds issued by two or more governmental units. When this situation exists, it is described as "overlapping debt."

The extent to which debt may overlap depends upon the number of units represented within an area which are authorized to incur long-term indebtedness. These may include the state, county, township, city, school board, library board, hospital board, and probably others. To show the total amount of fixed debt against property located within a given jurisdiction, a statement of direct and overlapping debt may be prepared. A statement of this type begins with the direct debt, which is that owed by the governmental unit represented by the statement. To this direct debt are added amounts owing by other units and authorities which levy taxes against the same property on which the direct debt is based. A statement of direct and overlapping debt is shown in Illustration 13–7.

Combined Statement of Bonded Indebtedness and General Fixed Assets

An additional form of statement related to bonded indebtedness sometimes found in municipal reports is a combined statement of bonded indebtedness and general fixed assets. In such instances the difference between assets and debt is termed an "equity." This practice has no logical basis. Although large amounts of general fixed assets have been obtained through use of bond issues, the correlation ceases at that point. General bonded debt is not secured by general fixed assets, nor is it liquidated by revenue derived from their use. The combination of general fixed assets and general bonded debt in a single statement, therefore, is considered not in accord with generally accepted accounting principles.

Illustration 13–7

CITY OF TEMPE, ARIZONA
Statement of Direct and Overlapping Debt
June 30, 1972

	Net Outstanding Debt	*Percent to Tempe*[2]	*Tempe's Share of Debt*
Direct Debt:			
City of Tempe	$ 3,205,000[1]	100.0%	$ 3,205,000
City Improvement Districts	317,936	100.0	317,936
Overlapping Debt:			
Maricopa County	10,750,000	5.9	634,250
Maricopa Junior College	13,330,000	5.9	786,470
Tempe Union High School	6,110,000	86.8	5,303,480
Scottsdale High School	10,840,000	1.2	130,080
Mesa High School	11,285,000	2.3	259,555
Tempe Elementary No. 3	8,526,000	91.6	7,809,816
Scottsdale Elementary No. 48	7,602,000	1.2	91,224
Mesa Elementary No. 4	11,232,000	2.3	258,336
Kyrene Elementary No. 28	543,000	4.5	24,435
Total Direct and Overlapping Debt			$18,820,582

Note 1: Includes only those general obligation bonds supported through property taxes. Unredeemed matured bonds of $25,000 and July 1, 1972, maturities of $100,000 for which funds have been set aside have been excluded from gross outstanding debt of $3,330,000 at June 30, 1972.

Note 2: Debt allocation based on distribution of assessed valuation within overlapping tax districts as follows:

Taxing District	*Assessed Total*	*Valuation in Tempe*	*Percent in Tempe*
City of Tempe	$ 97,297,049	$97,297,049	100.0%
Maricopa County	1,644,191,013	97,297,049	5.9
Maricopa Junior College	1,644,191,013	97,297,049	5.9
Tempe Union High School	105,699,787	91,778,523	86.8
Scottsdale High School	215,567,817	2,540,151	1.2
Mesa High School	129,398,962	2,978,375	2.3
Tempe Elementary No. 3	99,921,809	91,515,722	91.6
Scottsdale Elementary No. 48	215,567,817	2,540,151	1.2
Mesa Elementary No. 4	129,398,962	2,978,375	2.3
Kyrene Elementary No. 28	5,777,978	262,801	4.5

SELECTED REFERENCES

AMERICAN INSTITUTE OF CERTIFIED PUBLIC ACCOUNTANTS. *Audits of State and Local Governmental Units.* New York, 1974.

NATIONAL COMMITTEE ON GOVERNMENTAL ACCOUNTING. *Governmental Accounting, Auditing, and Financial Reporting*, chap. 11. Chicago, 1968.

QUESTIONS

13–1. What provision in a bond indenture or bond ordinance is necessary for long-term debt to be classified as "general"? From the standpoint of an investor, which would you expect to offer greater safety: a municipal utility revenue bond or a general obligation bond? Why? Which would you expect to offer a higher yield? Why?

13–2. From the standpoint of a municipal finance officer, what are the factors which should be considered in determining whether a proposed bond issue for the construction of utility fixed assets should be a utility revenue bond or a general obligation bond?

13–3. If a bond ordinance provides for regular and recurring payments of interest and principal payments on a general obligation bond issue to be made from earnings of an enterprise fund, how should the bond liability be disclosed in the municipal annual report?

13–4. *a*) When long-term debt is issued at a premium or discount (some governmental units prohibit the latter), what is the effect on the statement of debt, that is, amount to be provided and amount of liability?

b) Would your answer be the same if the issue were at a premium which is required to be set aside for payment of interest or of principal?

13–5. In accounting for long-term debt and interest, some question may arise as to the proper time to transfer from the "to be provided" classification to the "available" classification. Since that is not a contractual situation, what practice or policy should be followed?

13–6. What are the reasons for reporting interest payable in future years? Why is this item not considered to be includible in the Statement of General Long-Term Debt?

13–7. In some governmental jurisdictions the calculation of debt margin must take into account the amount of bonds authorized but not issued. This reduces borrowing power at a given date. What do you think is the reason for including authorized but unissued bonds?

13–8. In some jurisdictions the statutory debt limit rate is low, but overlapping debt is not prohibited. From the standpoint of the property owner and taxpayer, how does that situation compare with a relatively high total limitation, such as 15 percent?

13–9. What is the relationship between a debt service fund and the general long-term debt group of accounts? What is the relationship between a capital projects fund and the general long-term debt group of accounts?

13–10. "Debt which is due the day after the date of the statement may properly be shown as *long-term* debt, yet bonds which have matured but which have not yet been paid should not be shown as long-term debt." Do you agree? Why or why not?

EXERCISES AND PROBLEMS

13–1. Utilizing the municipal annual report obtained for Exercise 1–1, follow the instructions below:

a) Does the report contain evidence that the municipality maintains a general long-term debt group of accounts? What evidence is there? If the municipality does not have a general long-term debt group, does the report specify that no such debt is outstanding, or does the report include a list of outstanding g. o. debt issues?

If the report contains a Statement of General Long-Term Debt, do the amounts shown in this statement as being available for payment of long-term debt agree with amounts shown in the statements of funds which perform the debt service function? If not, can you reconcile the differences?

How does the "amount available" for payment of each issue relate to the "amount to be provided" for payment of each issue? How does the total amount available relate to the total amount to be provided?

Refer to the special assessment funds balance sheets and to the enterprise funds balance sheets as well as to the Statement of General Long-Term Debt (or list of general debt outstanding): Are any special assessment bond issues or enterprise bond issues backed by the full faith and credit of the general governmental unit? If so, how are the primary liability and the contingent liability disclosed?

b) How are changes in long-term debt during the year disclosed? If there is a statement of changes, does the information in that statement agree with the statements presented for capital projects funds and debt service funds?

Are interest payments and principal payments due in future years disclosed? If so, does the report relate these future payments with resources to be made available under existing debt service laws and covenants?

c) Does the report contain information as to legal debt limit and legal debt margin? If so, is the information contained in the report explained in enough detail so that an intelligent reader (you) can understand how the limit is set, what debt is subject to it, what debt is not subject to it, and how much debt the municipality might legally issue in the year following the date of the report?

13–2. The following three statements relate to the general obligation bonded debt of Fayetteville, Arkansas; no other information is included in the annual report relative to general obligation debt or debt service.

Required:

a) To what extent does the information satisfy the information needs of (1) a potential purchaser of several of the outstanding bonds, and (2) a resident interested in the financial management of the city?

b) The CPA's short-form opinion accompanying the report in which the illustrated statements were included states that, with the excep-

CITY OF FAYETTEVILLE, ARKANSAS
1962 General Obligation Bond Fund
Statement of Cash Receipts and Disbursements
For the Year Ended December 31, 1970

Cash balance–January 1, 1970		$ 25,976
Add: Receipts		
Four mill tax levy	$133,844	
Collection of taxes due from other funds–prior year	35,289	
Collection of taxes due to other funds–current year	2,057	
Interest on investments	4,703	
Collection of interest due to other funds–current year	907	176,800
		$202,776
Less: Disbursements		
Bond principal	$ 89,000	
Interest and paying agents fees	29,582	
Purchase of investments	50,000	168,582
Cash balance–December 31, 1970		$ 34,194

CITY OF FAYETTEVILLE, ARKANSAS
1962 General Obligation Bond Fund
Balance Sheet
December 31, 1970

Assets and Funds to Be Provided

Cash in bank			$ 34,194
Investments			105,000
Total Assets			$ 139,194
Funds to be provided–January 1, 1970		$1,145,787	
Less: Revenues			
Four mill tax levy	$133,844		
Interest on investments	4,703		
Adjustment of interest and paying agents fees	73,495	212,042	
Funds to be provided–December 31, 1970*			933,745
			$1,072,939

Liabilities

Bonds payable in future years	$ 777,000
Interest and paying agents fees due in future years*	292,975
Due to other funds	2,964
	$1,072,939

*Interest and paying agents fees payable in future years were recomputed at the end of the year. Due to prepayment of bond principal in the current and prior years. The required funds to be provided for payment of interest and paying agents fees was reduced $73,495.

CITY OF FAYETTEVILLE, ARKANSAS
1962 General Obligation Bond Fund
Bonds Outstanding
December 31, 1970

Maturity	*Bond Numbers*	*Amount*
1972	176–208	$ 33,000
1973	209–241	33,000
1974	242–275	34,000
1975	276–309	34,000
1976	310–345	36,000
1977	346–381	36,000
1978	382–418	37,000
1979	419–457	39,000
1980	458–498	41,000
1981	499–541	43,000
1982	542–584	43,000
1983	585–629	45,000
1984	630–675	46,000
1985	676–724	49,000
1986	725–775	51,000
1987	776–827	52,000
1988	828–880	53,000
1989	881–935	55,000
1990	936–952	17,000
		$777,000

Note: Principal due: January 1
Paying agent: Worthen Bank and Trust Company
Little Rock, Arkansas
Interest rates:

Numbered	*Rate*
176–275	3.00%
276–381	3.25%
382–457	3.40%
458–952	3.50%

tion of accumulated balances of property, plant, and equipment, the financial statements are presented in conformity with "generally accepted principles of municipal accounting." Comment.

13–3. Your examination of the accounts of your new client, the City of Delmas, as of June 30, 1971, revealed the following (Items 1 through 5 intentionally omitted.):

6. For the health center bonds the City sets aside General Fund revenues sufficient to cover interest (payable semiannually on July

1 and January 1 of each year) and $5,060 to provide for the retirement of bond principal, the latter transfer being made at the end of each fiscal year and invested at the beginning of the next. Your investigation reveals that such investments earned $304 during fiscal year 1970–71, the exact amount budgeted. This $304 was received in cash and will be invested at the beginning of the next year.

Required:

a) From the information above (and the information in Problems 9–3, 10–3, and 12–3, if needed) prepare in general journal form entries to establish a general long-term debt group of accounts for the City of Delmas, and to record the effect on these accounts of all events which occurred through June 30, 1971.

(AICPA, adapted)

13–4. Below are stated a number of unrelated transactions which indirectly affect a general long-term debt group of accounts.
Required: For each prepare in general journal form the necessary entry in the general long-term debt group. Explanations may be omitted.

1. A special tax levy of $50,000, designated to provide cash for retirement of serial bonds which had been issued some years previously, was recorded by a debt service fund. An estimate of $1,000 for uncollectible taxes was recorded simultaneously.
2. A $500,000 issue of serial bonds was sold for $512,500. The premium was transferred to a debt service fund where it was designated for payment on principal of the issue.
3. A summary of debt service funds operations during the year showed additions of $120,300 for liquidation of principal of serial bonds and $18,990 to be applied on interest. The effect of these increases had not been recorded in the general long-term debt group.
4. $250,000 par value of general obligation serial bonds were issued in partial refunding of a $300,000 par value issue of term bonds. The difference was settled with $42,500 which had been accumulated in prior years in a debt service fund, and the balance by a general fund disbursement from cash which had not been segregated.

13–5. You have just accepted accounting responsibility for the City of Rockford. As of the end of the preceding fiscal year your predecessor had prepared the following trial balance:

CITY OF ROCKFORD
General Long-Term Debt and Interest Group
Trial Balance, December 31, 19x5

	Debit	*Credit*
Amount available in debt service funds for payment of term bonds	$ 263,100	
Amount to be provided for payment of term bonds	806,900	
Amount to be provided for payment of notes	75,000	
Amount provided for payment of interest.	54,200	
Amount to be provided for payment of interest.	191,800	
4½% term bonds payable (19y6)		$ 500,000
3½% sinking fund bonds payable (19y3). . . .		320,000
4% refunding bonds payable (term, 19x9)		250,000
Deficit funding notes payable, 5%		75,000
Interest payable in future years		246,000
	$1,391,000	$1,391,000

Required:

a) As of January 1, 19x6, prepare in general journal form an entry to convert the General Long-Term Debt and Interest Group to a General Long-Term Debt Group to conform with the current recommendations of the National Committee on Governmental Accounting. (All of the bonds and notes listed on the trial balance are found to be general obligation in character and not yet matured.)

b) Prepare in general journal form an entry for each of the following events which occurred in 19x6 to record the effects upon the accounts of the General Long-term Debt Group.

1. $500,000 par value 4½ percent term bonds, scheduled to mature on February 1, 19y6, were retired as of February 1, 19x6, after interest due on this date had been paid by the general fund. The retirement was accomplished with a cash payment of $200,000 from a debt service fund and the issue of $300,000 of 4 percent term refunding bonds to mature on February 1, 19z1, interest payable August 1 and February 1.
2. A $150,000 issue of five-year notes payable was sold on March 1. The rate of interest was 5 percent, payable March 1 and September 1.
3. $100,000 par value of term bonds were sold at 102, and the premium was transferred to a debt service fund and designated for use in paying interest on the bonds. The date of issue was May 1, with retirement on May 1, 19z6. The rate of interest was 5 percent per year, payable November 1 and May 1.

4. The city annexed territory which included a village with $80,000 par value of 5 percent serial bonds still outstanding. Assumption of the debt occurred on September 15; $10,000 of the issue was scheduled to mature January 1, 19x7, with $10,000 additional maturing each six months thereafter. The village had no accumulation of money for payment of principal or interest. Interest dates are January 1 and July 1.
5. $300,000 par value of serial bonds were issued on October 1; $60,000 par value of the issue was scheduled to mature each year beginning October 1, 19x7. Interest at 4 percent per year on the issue is payable semiannually on April 1 and October 1.
6. Records of the city treasurer showed gross additions of $137,200 to debt service funds during 19x6, of which $100,000 was for principal of term bonds and the remainder for interest. This total included the amount listed in transaction 3.

c) Prepare a Statement of General Long-Term Debt as of December 31, 19x6.

13–6. In his initial engagement with the Town of Jamestown, an auditor chose to prepare a statement of changes in general bonded debt and notes payable for the year ended December 31, 197B. There was no organized record of such indebtedness at the beginning of the year. The following information was discovered:

1. At the end of 197B, $50,000 was still outstanding on an issue of 3 percent serial bonds which mature at the rate of $25,000 per year. The payment during the year had been made.
2. The general fund having carried a deficit for the past few years, it was decided to fund the deficit with an issue of four-year notes totaling $120,000, to be retired at the rate of $30,000 per year. The deficit funding notes were to be paid through the medium of a debt service fund. They were issued on July 1, 197B.
3. At the end of 197B, $100,000 par value of general obligation special assessment bonds were outstanding, from an original amount of $300,000. Annual maturities of $25,000 had been paid on schedule.
4. Upon maturity of $400,000 of sinking fund bonds scheduled to mature in 197A, only $100,000 of assets was available for their retirement. Interest on the issue having been paid regularly, it was possible to refund the unpaid balance without difficulty, for which purpose an issue of 4¾ percent serial bonds was floated. The refunding issue matured at the rate of $30,000 per year. The first payment was made in 197B.
5. As of December 31, 197A, the city had outstanding $200,000 of 4 percent serial bonds which had been issued to finance a revenue-producing recreation facility. During 197B bonds in the amount of $50,000 were paid. Although primarily revenue in source of payment, the bonds were full faith and credit instruments.

6. During 197B, a $300,000 issue of 4½ percent term bonds matured, with little provision having been made for their payment. The bonds were closely held, and arrangements were made with holders of all but $25,000 to accept 4½ percent refunding serial bonds. Cash was paid to creditors who declined to accept refunding bonds.

You are required to analyze the above information and prepare a statement of changes in general bonded debt and notes payable for Jamestown for 197B. It is to be assumed that all provisions for payment have been complied with.

13–7. At April 30, 19x6, all property inside the limits of Oakland City was situated within five governmental units, each authorized to incur long-term debt. At that date, net long-term debt of the five was as follows:

Fairfield County	$ 496,200
Blue River Township	62,800
Oakland City–civil city	5,988,700
Oakland City–school district	3,009,500
Oakland City–general hospital	299,100

The last three have common territorial limits.

Assessed values of property at the same date were: county, $280,400,000; township, $154,220,000; city, $98,140,000. You are required to do the following things:

a) Prepare a statement of direct and overlapping debt for Oakland City.

b) Compute the actual ratio (in percent carried to tenths) of total debt applicable to Oakland City property to assessed value of property within the city limits.

c) Compute the share of the city's direct and overlapping debt which pertained to the Reliable Manufacturing Company, having an assessed valuation of $4,907,000 at April 30, 19x6.

13–8. In preparation for an ambitious program of public improvements, the city council and administration, City of Jackson, took steps to formalize the records of the municipality's debt position. An accountant employed to investigate and to organize his findings produced the following listing of outstanding long-term indebtedness as of December 31 of the current year.

Municipal auditorium bonds, $4,000,000.
Electric plant bonds, $250,000.
Refunding bonds, $300,000.
Special assessment bonds, $500,000.
Street improvement bonds, $250,000.
Water utility bonds, $3,000,000.
Golf course clubhouse bonds, $150,000.

Other information obtained by the accountant included the following items:

1. Assessed valuation of real and taxable personal property in the city totaled $100,000,000.
2. The rate of debt limitation applicable to the City of Jackson was 8 percent of total real and taxable personal property valuation.
3. No general liability existed in connection with the special assessment bonds.
4. Electric plant, water utility, and golf clubhouse bonds were of the revenue variety. No general public liability attached to the first and last, but the second carried a full faith and credit contingency provision and by law was subject to debt limitation.
5. The amount of assets segregated for debt retirement at December 31, of the current year was $1,300,000.
6. None of the above items would be reduced within less than six months.

You are required to prepare a statement of legal debt margin for the city of Jackson, as of December 31, of the current year.

CONTINUOUS PROBLEMS

13–L. At the end of the current year, the City of Bingham has the following bond issues outstanding in addition to those mentioned in Problems 1–L through 12–L:

Description of Issue (All bonds are dated July 1 of the year of issue.)	*No. of Years to Final Maturity*	*Face Amount Outstanding*	*Amt. Provided for Retirement of Issue*
5% General obligation, 10-year serial	1	$200,000	$100,000
4½% General obligation, 20-year serial	4	200,000	50,000
4½% Special Assessment, 20-year serial	5	100,000	None
4% General obligation, 20-year term.	10	600,000	260,380
3½% General obligation, 25-year serial	15	500,000	None
3¼% General obligation, 20-year term.	15	500,000	None

You are required to:

a) Open a general journal for the general long-term debt group of accounts.

1. Enter the above information in the general journal in conformance with National Committee on Governmental Accounting recommendations. The 4½% special assessment bonds are not backed by the full faith and credit of the City of Bingham.
2. Enter pertinent transactions from Problems 1–L through 11–L. You need not refer to 12–L.

b) In order to provide for the retirement of bond issues with early maturities or high interest rates, the City of Bingham plans on an issue of 20-year 4% general obligation bonds. Before determining the amount of the issue, the controller asks you to compute the legal general obligation debt margin of the city. The general obligation debt limit of a municipality in this state is 3% of the assessed value of property located within a governmental unit's geographical boundaries. The assessed value as of the most recent date of assessment is $160,000,000.

c) Prepare a statement of general long-term debt as of the end of the year.

13–S. As of December 31, 197A, the General Long-Term Debt Group of accounts of the City of Smithville presented the following statement:

CITY OF SMITHVILLE
Statement of General Long-Term Debt
December 31, 197A

Amount Available and To Be Provided for the Payment of General Long-Term Debt	
Term Bonds:	
Amount available in debt service funds	$1,330,000
Amount to be provided	670,000
Total Available and to Be Provided	$2,000,000
General Long-Term Debt Payable	
Term bonds payable:	
2⅝%, due 1/1/7E	$ 600,000
2¾%, due 1/1/7F	400,000
3¼%, due 1/1/8A	1,000,000
Total General Long-Term Debt Payable	$2,000,000

a) Record in general journal form the effect of the following on the accounts of the General Long-Term Debt Group:

1. During 197B the Term Bond Debt Service Fund raised through its own tax levies sufficient revenues to pay the interest on all general obligation term bonds. Earnings on investments of the Term Bonds Debt Service Fund, and revenues from taxes levied by that fund, increased the Fund Balance to $1,430,000 as of December 31, 197B. No term bonds were issued or repaid in 197B.
2. Problems 6–S and 7–S provide information about the issuance

of general obligation serial bonds during 197B and about the activities of the Serial Bond Debt Service Fund during 197B. (It will be necessary to create accounts since all existing accounts relate to term bonds, as shown in the December 31, 197A, Statement of General Long-Term Debt.)

b) Prepare a Statement of General Long-Term Debt as of December 31, 197B.

c) If the assessed valuation of property within the City of Smithville is $60,000,000, and the legal general obligation debt limit is 8 percent of assessed valuation, what is the legal debt *margin* of the City as of December 31, 197B?

d) Prepare a schedule showing the amount of interest and principal payments on outstanding general long-term debt for each year until all debt outstanding on December 31, 197B, matures.

14

Summary of Funds and Groups; Interfund Transactions; Financial Reports; Evaluation of Presently Recommended Governmental Accounting

Chapters 3 through 13 present extended discussions of the nature of funds and groups which the National Committee on Governmental Accounting recommends for use by all governmental units except national governments and their agencies. The reasons why each fund or group is recommended, and the essential characteristics of accounting for typical transactions of the funds or groups, are discussed in those chapters. In the first section of this chapter the objective is to summarize the nature, purposes, and accounting characteristics of each fund and group. In the second section of this chapter interfund transactions are reviewed. The third section of this chapter presents a discussion of governmental financial reports, and the concluding section presents an evaluation of the system of accounting presently recommended by the National Committee on Governmental Accounting for use by state and local governmental units.

SUMMARY OF THE NATURE AND ACCOUNTING CHARACTERISTICS OF FUNDS AND ACCOUNT GROUPS

A fund is an independent fiscal and accounting entity with a self-balancing set of accounts recording assets and resources, and related liabilities, reserves, and equities, which are segregated for the purpose of carrying on specific activities or attaining certain objectives in accordance with legal restrictions or agreements. The National Committee on Governmental Accounting recommends eight categories of funds, and two account groups, for use by state and local governmental units: general funds, special revenue funds, capital projects funds, debt service funds, trust and agency funds, intragovernmental service funds, special assessment funds, and enterprise funds, the general fixed assets group, and the general long-term debt group.

Revenue Funds

General Fund is the name given to the entity which accounts for all the assets and resources used for financing the general administration of the governmental unit and the traditional services provided to its residents. Operating funds and current funds are names sometimes given to funds that function as a general fund.

The typical governmental unit now engages in many activities which are financed by revenues designated by law for a particular purpose. In order to demonstrate compliance with such laws it is recommended that a *Special Revenue Fund* be used to account for the receipt and use of each such restricted category of revenue.

Both general funds and special revenue funds are known as Revenue Funds. In terms of accounting characteristics both types of revenue funds are alike. Revenue funds record in their accounts the effect of the budget when it becomes a legal document. Estimated Revenues, a control account for all sources of revenues available to the fund and which are to be utilized during the budget period, is debited for the total amount of revenues expected to be realized during the budget period. Appropriations, a control account for all categories of expenditures authorized in the legally approved budget, is credited. Fund Balance, the account which serves the function of a capital account in the accounts of a profit-seeking entity, is debited or credited for the difference between Estimated Revenues and Appropriations.

Accounting for revenue funds differs from accounting for profit-seeking entities in more respects than just the obvious one of formally recording the budget in the accounts. Two principal sources of difference are:

1. Expenditures of a revenue fund are made for the purposes specified in the appropriations budget, and are not made in the hope of generating revenues as is true of profit-seeking entities; therefore, income determination which is the principal focus of accounting for profit-seeking entities is of no concern at all in accounting for revenue funds.

2. The sources and amounts of revenues of a revenue fund relate to a budget for a particular time period, generally one year, so a revenue fund can be said to have a year-to-year life, rather than an indefinite life as is true of a profit-seeking entity. Thus the going-concern assumption which is basic to accounting for profit-seeking entities is not entirely applicable to accounting for revenue funds.

Legally approved appropriations are authorizations to incur liabilities for specified purposes in specified amounts during a specified time period. Penalties provided by law may be imposed upon governmental administrators who expend governmental resources in a manner in any way contrary to that authorized in appropriation ordinances or statutes. For that reason it is recommended that Encumbrances, a control account supported by the Appropriations Expenditures subsidiary ledger, be debited, and Reserve for Encumbrances, a contingent liability account, be credited when purchase orders, contracts, or other commitment documents are issued. When goods or services have been received, a liability is incurred and an appropriation is deemed to have been expended (under accrual accounting theory); thus if the appropriation has previously been encumbered, it is necessary to reverse the encumbrance entry at the time the Expenditure account is debited and the liability account is credited.

Revenues of a revenue fund are to be recognized on the *modified accrual* basis. That is, those items of revenue for which a valid receivable can be recorded in advance of their due date, such as property taxes, are recorded on the accrual basis; all other items of revenue are recorded on the cash basis. Revenues and Expenditures are nominal proprietary accounts and are closed to Fund Balance at the end of a fiscal period. Estimated Revenues, Appropriations, and Encumbrances, all referred to as *budgetary* accounts, are also closed to Fund Balance at the end of a fiscal period. Therefore, when budgetary and nominal accounts have been closed, the real proprietary accounts remain open and their balances should be reported in a fund balance sheet. The real proprietary accounts of a revenue fund consist of accounts for liquid assets which are available for fund operations, current liabilities which are to be paid from fund assets, and Fund Balance. If inventories of materials and supplies are owned by a revenue fund they should be included as an asset, but a Reserve for Inventory of Supplies should be created by charge against Fund Balance in the amount of the inventory. Reserve for Inventory of Supplies, and Reserve for Encumbrances, are disclosed on a revenue fund balance sheet in a section between the liabilities and the Fund Balance. Fund Balance, therefore, represents the net amount of liquid assets available for appropriation and expenditure for legally approved purposes.

Capital Projects Funds

The receipt and disbursement of all moneys from the sale of general obligation bonds issued for the construction or acquisition of capital facilities, along with the receipt and disbursement of all moneys from other sources such as grants from other governmental units, transfers from other funds, or gifts from citizens for the construction or acquisition of capital facilities, are accounted for by capital projects funds.

A capital projects fund exists because certain resources are dedicated to a given purpose; all activities of the fund have the objective of accomplishing that purpose. Therefore, it is not considered necessary for budgetary accounts other than Encumbrances to be used. Encumbrances, and Reserve for Encumbrances, are considered desirable because of the large number of commitment documents which are issued for a typical governmental capital project. The encumbrance entry is reversed and Expenditures of a capital projects fund are recognized when goods and services are received and the corresponding liability is recorded. Revenues of a capital projects fund are recognized on a *full accrual* basis, under the recommendations of the NCGA. The life of a capital projects fund is the length of time from legal approval of the project until completion of the project and formal acceptance of the capital assets by the governmental unit. The life of a capital projects fund generally does not coincide with a fiscal period; therefore, nominal accounts and encumbrances are ordinarily closed at year-end to facilitate preparation of annual statements. Neither the fixed assets nor any long-term liabilities resulting from the project are accounted for by a capital projects fund. Only assets which will be converted into cash and disbursed for the project are to be accounted for by a fund of this category. Similarly, only liabilities which are to be paid out of fund assets are accounted for by capital projects funds. Fund Balance of a capital projects fund represents the excess of current assets over the sum of current liabilities and contingent liabilities (Reserve for Encumbrances) or, therefore, the amount available for expenditure for the approved purposes of the fund.

Debt Service Funds

General obligation long-term debt issued and the interest thereon must be serviced primarily from revenue raised in years subsequent to the issue. Laws of superior jurisdictions, and bond indentures, commonly require local governmental units to establish funds to account for debt service revenue.

It is recommended that serial bond debt service funds record Estimated Revenues and Appropriations. Term bond debt service funds also use budgetary accounts but the titles Required Additions and Required Earnings are used instead of Estimated Revenues, as explained in Chapter 7. Encumbrance accounting is ordinarily not needed for debt service funds because the only appropriations for these funds are for the payment of interest and the payment of matured bonds payable.

Although a major portion of the revenues of a debt service fund arise from taxes levied year-by-year, a portion of the revenues arise from interest on investments. Since the fund must stay in existence until all general long-term debt is repaid, in most cases the fund may be said to have an unlimited life.

The modified accrual basis of accounting is recommended for use by debt service funds. As defined by the NCGA, this term has the same meaning for the revenues both of debt service and of revenue funds, but whereas the expenditures of a revenue fund are to be accounted for on the full accrual basis, the expenditures of a debt service fund for interest and matured bonds are to be accounted for on the cash basis. The AICPA accepts this treatment as being in accord with generally accepted accounting principles.

As is true of revenue funds and capital project funds, a regular serial bond debt service fund accounts for only current assets and current liabilities (matured interest and matured principal payments), and the Fund Balance represents the excess of current assets available for fund purposes. A term bond debt service fund or a deferred serial bond debt service fund ordinarily is expected to accumulate assets over the life of the bonds; it is prudent for the assets to be held in the form of high quality investments which are readily marketable or which will mature by the time cash is needed. The debt to be retired by the debt service fund is recorded by the general long-term debt group, not the debt service fund (until maturity).

Trust and Agency Funds

Trust and agency funds are used to account for assets held by a municipality in fiduciary capacity. A governmental unit which collects taxes for other units would have need for an agency fund, for example. Employees' retirement funds are a very common form of trust fund.

Agency Funds. An agency relationship may be accounted for satisfactorily within the accounting structure of a general fund, or other fund, if the amounts collected pursuant to the agency are small in relation to total fund assets, and if the amounts are remitted to the owner without an appreciable lapse of time. If the amounts collected are relatively large, however, or if they are held for an appreciable time, or if the law requires it; an agency fund should be established. A very simple set of proprietary accounts ordinarily suffices for an agency fund because all fund assets are held as agent, and are entirely offset by a liability to the owner. At year-end if all assets have been collected and have been remitted to the owner, the agency fund would have no balances to report in the annual statement.

Trust Funds. Trust funds differ from agency funds in that a trust fund generally holds assets and manages them for the beneficiaries over a substantial period of time. As discussed in Chapter 8, trust fund accounting problems often relate to the distinction between trust principal and trust income, and to the distinction between expendability and nonexpendability. The life of a trust fund is the duration of the trust. Full accrual accounting is recommended for trust funds operated for the production of income (although the "general rule of law" still seems to be that cash basis accounting will have to be used unless the donor specifies that the accrual basis will be used). If the generation of net income is the objective of a trust fund, it seems obvious that accounting principles derived for profit-seeking entities are applicable. Thus fixed assets which were given by the donor as a part of the trust principal, or which have been acquired in pursuit of the trust objectives, and long-term debt related to trust assets, are accounted for by the trust fund, as well as current assets and current liabilities of the trust.

Budgetary accounts are not used by trust funds operated as businesses, but are recommended for use by public employee retirement trust funds, expendable trust funds similar in character to general funds, and Federal general revenue sharing trust funds.

Intragovernmental Service Funds

If governmental resources are segregated for the purpose of providing services to several departments or funds of the same governmental unit, the resources are accounted for by an Intragovernmental Service Fund. Funds in this category may be operated at many different levels of relationship to legislative supervision; in this summary it is assumed that the financial objective of the fund is to recover the full cost of operations and to earn enough net income to allow for replacement of inventories and facilities in periods of rising prices. Accordingly, although budgets should be prepared for managerial use, it is not necessary to record the budget in the accounting system. Full accrual accounting should be used for revenues and for costs and expenses (these terms are used rather than "expenditures" because the latter refers to appropriation accounting). The life of an intragovernmental service fund is indefinite, so the going concern assumption may be applied to accounting decisions. Current assets and fixed assets used in intragovernmental service fund operations should be accounted for by the intragovernmental service fund. Long-term debt to be repaid from earnings of the fund should also be accounted for by the intragovernmental service fund, as should all other liabilities to be paid from fund assets. Since net income is retained in the fund, a Retained Earnings Account is needed as well as accounts which disclose the amount and source of the permanent capital of the fund.

Enterprise Funds

In contrast with intragovernmental service funds, resources that are utilized by a municipality to provide services on a user-charge basis to the general public are accounted for by an enterprise fund. Municipally-owned utilities are common examples of activities accounted for by enterprise funds. Almost any form of business engaged in by individuals, partnerships, and corporations may also be owned and operated by a governmental unit, however, and would be accounted for by an enterprise fund. Utilities or other enterprises which would be regulated if they were investor-owned should use the charts of accounts and accounting and statistical definitions required of investor-owned enterprises in the same industry. Other municipally-owned enterprises should use charts of accounts and definitions established by trade associations for the appropriate industry. In general, principles of accounting established for profit-seeking entities apply. Differences between regulatory accounting and accounting for nonregulated industries are discussed in Chapter 11.

The life of an enterprise is assumed to be indefinite. Full accrual accounting is used. All assets used in fund operations, and all debt to be serviced from fund earnings, are included in enterprise fund accounts. A Retained Earnings account, as well as accounts which disclose the amount and source of the permanent capital of the fund, are utilized.

Special Assessment Funds

Special assessment funds are designed to account for the construction or purchase of public improvements (such as streets, sidewalks, or sewer systems) financed wholly or in part by special levies against property owners who are deemed benefited by the improvements to an extent materially greater than the general body of taxpayers. The purpose of special assessment funds is quite similar to the purpose of capital projects funds; therefore Encumbrance and Expenditure accounts relating to construction activities of both categories are also similar. Significant differences arise, however, because of the means of financing the acquisition of the capital assets. Because assessments against property owners may be sizeable it is common to allow the property owners to pay their assessments in installments over several years. In order to make payments as required by construction contractors, therefore, a special assessment fund may need to borrow money on an intermediate-term or long-term basis. Special assessment debt to be serviced wholly or partly from assessments and interest on the assessments is to be recorded as a liability of the special assessment fund. (If the debt has secondary backing from the "full faith and credit" of a governmental unit, the debt also should be disclosed as a footnote to the statement of general long-term debt of that governmental unit). Fixed assets constructed or acquired from resources of a special assessment fund ordinarily become general fixed assets of a governmental unit and, consequently, are *not* accounted for by a special assessment fund. Current assets and current liabilities are accounted for by funds in this category.

As is true of other categories of funds not required by law to operate under a budget in the sense that revenue funds and debt service funds are, the operations of a special assessment fund should be budgeted, but the budget need not be recorded in the accounts.

The life of a special assessment fund is the longer of two events: the length of time required to construct or acquire the assets for which the fund was created, or the length of time required to repay all money borrowed by the special assessment fund.

General Fixed Assets

Only enterprise and trust funds routinely account for property, plant, and equipment used in their operations, as do intragovernmental service funds that are expected to cover all indirect costs as well as all direct costs. All other funds account only for assets which will be turned into cash during the regular operations of the fund. Thus property, plant, and equipment acquired by general, special revenue, and capital projects funds, and by special assessment funds, are brought under accounting control by the creation of a general fixed assets group of accounts. No other assets are recorded in the general fixed assets group. No liabilities at all are recorded in the accounts of this group. The credit-balance accounts which offset the fixed asset accounts to create a self-balancing group show the source of the investment in general fixed assets.

Depreciation on general fixed assets is not recorded by any fund or group, if recommendations of the NCGA are followed. The AICPA, however, allows for depreciation to be recorded by the general fixed assets group, and accumulated depreciation accounts to be deducted from related assets in the Statement of General Fixed Assets.

General Long-Term Debt

Debt instruments which are backed by the "full faith and credit" of a municipality are obligations of the municipality as a whole and not of the individual funds. The general long-term debt group was created to account for such debt. No other debt and no assets are recorded in the group. The amount of long-term (and intermediate-term) debt is offset by accounts entitled "Amount Available in Debt Service Funds for Payment of_____Bonds (or Notes)" and "Amount to be Provided for Payment of_____Bonds (or Notes)".

SUMMARY OF INTERFUND TRANSACTIONS

Transactions, or events, which affect the accounts of more than one fund or account group of a single governmental unit, have been noted in the discussions and illustrative entries of preceding chapters. A brief review of interfund transactions and events at this point should aid the reader in reinforcing his understanding of the relationships that exist among the funds and groups.

Each fund is (1) a fiscal entity, (2) an accounting entity, and, in a sense, (3) a legal entity. Each account group is only an accounting entity, not a fiscal entity nor, in any sense, a legal entity. Events and transactions which must be recognized in more than one accounting entity of a single governmental unit may be classified in the following manner:

1. Interfund loans and advances.
2. Transfers which are revenues of the transferee and expenditures of the transferor.
3. Transfers which reimburse the transferee for expenditures made by the transferee on behalf of the transferor.
4. Recurring periodic transfers made primarily for the purpose of shifting resources from one fund to another.
5. Nonrecurring transfers made in compliance with special statutes or ordinances which do not qualify as revenues or expenditures to the receiving or disbursing funds.
6. Acquisition of general fixed assets.
7. Creation of general long-term debt, or repayment of principal of general long-term debt.

Examples of each of the seven classes of interfund events or transactions, and entries which record them in each affected fund or group, are illustrated in following paragraphs.

Interfund Loans and Advances

The terms "loans" and "advances" are used to indicate amounts which are temporarily transferred from one fund to another, but which will have to be repaid in due time.

Since each fund is, in a sense, a legal entity, the interfund receivables and payables resulting from loans and advances must be disclosed in a combined balance sheet. They may not be eliminated, as would be proper in the preparation of consolidated statements for parent and subsidiary profit-seeking corporations.

Interfund loans and advances are discussed and illustrated in Chapters 9 and 11. The Supplies Fund of the Town of Merrill received a $100,000 long-term advance from the Water Utility Fund of the town. (The Supplies Fund also received a contribution from the General Fund, which is reviewed below under the Nonrecurring Transfers caption). The effect of the advance on each fund is

Supplies Fund

Cash	100,000	
Advance from Water Utility Fund		100,000

Water Utility Fund

Long-Term Advance to Supplies Fund	100,000	
Cash		100,000

Partial repayment of the advance was made at year-end:

Supplies Fund

	Debit	Credit
Advance from Water Utility Fund	5,000	
Cash		5,000

Water Utility Fund

	Debit	Credit
Cash	5,000	
Long-Term Advance to Supplies Fund		5,000

Transfers to Be Shown as Revenues of the Transferee and Expenditures of the Transferor

One of the most common examples of the type of interfund transaction which properly results in the recognition of revenue by one fund and the recording of an expenditure by another fund is the provision to the general fund of fire hydrants and water for fire protection by a municipally owned water utility; illustrative entries are given in Chapters 3 and 11 for this type of interfund transaction. The effect upon the general ledger accounts of the Town of Merrill's General Fund and Water Utility Fund for fire protection service provided by the utility is:

General Fund

	Debit	Credit
Expenditures	30,000	
Due to Water Utility Fund		30,000

Water Utility Fund

	Debit	Credit
Due from General Fund	30,000	
Sales of Water		30,000

The Water Utility Fund of the Town of Merrill received services from General Fund departments, as is also common. The entries to record the resulting expenditures and revenues, as given in Chapters 3 and 11 are:

General Fund

	Debit	Credit
Due from Water Utility Fund	25,000	
Revenues		25,000

Water Utility Fund

	Debit	Credit
Contribution in Lieu of Taxes	25,000	
Due to General Fund		25,000

The net effect of the transactions between the two funds of the Town of Merrill is that the General Fund owes the Water Utility Fund $5,000. It is considered proper for the balance sheet of each fund to show this net amount as a receivable or payable but, again, the interfund item must be disclosed in a combined balance sheet for all funds.

Transfers in the Nature of Reimbursements of Expenditures

If one fund performs services for another fund on an incidental, rather than recurring, basis administrators and accountants may consider it to be more reasonable for the fund receiving the services to reimburse the fund rendering the services for their cost (or estimated cost). The same situation might occur if materials or supplies were transferred from one fund to another on an incidental basis. No transfers of this nature are included in illustrative entries of preceding chapters. If the city engineers' office, a General Fund Department, performed services of an incidental nature for the Street Fund, assumed to be a special revenue fund in this example, the following entries would reflect the transfer (assuming that $2,600 is assumed to reflect fairly the expenditure the city engineers' office incurred for the benefit of the Street Fund):

General Fund

Cash	2,600	
Expenditures		2.600

Street Fund

Expenditures	2,600	
Cash		2,600

Recurring Periodic Shifts of Resources

An example of a transfer of resources which would occur at regular periodic intervals, but which would not result in a true revenue or a true expenditure to the fund raising the "revenue" appears in Chapter 7: Revenue to be used for debt service activities of the Town of Alva is raised by the General Fund and transferred to the Regular Serial Bond Debt Service Fund and to the Deferred Serial Bond Debt Service Fund. Entries in the General Fund for transfers were not discussed or illustrated in the chapters dealing with revenue funds in order to limit the number of new situations the reader was exposed to at that point. The following entries would appear to disclose appropriately the shift of resources from the General Fund to the Regular Serial Bond Debt Service Fund:

General Fund

Transfers to Regular Serial Bond Debt Service Fund	81,000	
Cash		81,000

Regular Serial Bond Debt Service Fund

Cash	81,000	
Revenues		81,000

The transfer illustrated above also has an effect upon the General Long-Term Debt group of accounts of the Town of Alva, as illustrated in Chapter 13. For the sake of comparison, entry 1b from Chapter 13 is reproduced below (recall that the long-term debt group records only that portion of the transfer which is to be used for repayment of principal):

General Long-Term Debt Group

	Debit	Credit
Amount Available in Debt Service Fund for Payment of Regular Serial Bonds	50,000	
Amount to be Provided for Payment of Regular Serial Bonds		50,000

Another example of a regularly recurring transfer of resources which does not meet the definition of revenue or expenditure for the transferring fund is given in *Audits of State and Local Governmental Units* by the AICPA. The case cited therein is the collection of revenue by a state general fund for transfer to the state school aid fund, a special revenue fund. The AICPA points out that the total transfers received and total transfers disbursed should be included as separate items in each fund's statement of revenues and expenditures or equivalent financial statement.[1]

Nonrecurring Transfers Made in Compliance with Special Statutes . . . . .

In Chapter 9, the first entry in the illustrative case of the Town of Merrill Supplies Fund reflects the transfer of inventory and cash from the General Fund of that town as a contribution of working capital which is not expected to be repaid. This transfer would have to have been authorized by appropriate legal action, and therefore is an example of a nonrecurring transfer made in compliance with special statutes or ordinances which does not result in revenues or expenditures to the receiving or disbursing fund. The transfer is stated to have taken place in the year following the year for which illustrative entries are shown for the Town of Merrill General Fund, so the entries in that fund are not shown in Chapter 3. The entries to be made by both funds at the time of the transfer are:

General Fund

	Debit	Credit
Fund Balance	25,000	
Reserve for Inventory of Supplies	12,300	
Cash		25,000
Inventory of Supplies		12,300

Supplies Fund

	Debit	Credit
Cash	25,000	
Inventory of Supplies	12,300	
Contribution from General Fund		37,300

[1] *Audits of State and Local Governmental Units*, p. 11.

An example similar to the one discussed above is the contribution of capital by a general fund to a utility fund. The return of part or all of such contributions would also be a transfer of the nature comprehended in this category. A further example would be the transfer of residual equity balances of discontinued funds to general or debt service funds, normally required by statute.

Acquisition of General Fixed Assets

Preceding discussions of the general fixed assets group of accounts have emphasized that the group was created to place under accounting control assets acquired through expenditures of general funds, special revenue funds, capital projects funds, and special assessment funds, none of which account for fixed assets. Chapter 12 illustrates several sets of entries in funds financing the acquisition of general fixed assets and corresponding entries in the general fixed assets group of accounts. For review purposes one set of entries involving the purchase of office equipment by a general fund is shown below:

General Fund

Expenditures	450	
Vouchers Payable		450

General Fixed Assets Group

Equipment	450	
Investment in General Fixed Assets—General Fund Revenues		450

Creation or Repayment of General Long-Term Debt

One event which must be recorded in both a fund and in the general long-term debt group of accounts is the issuance of general obligation bonds so that the proceeds may be used for the acquisition of capital facilities. In the Town of Alva case presented in Chapter 7, the town has outstanding a serial bond issue in the amount of $2,000,000, as of December 31, 19y0. At the time the bonds were sold, assuming they were sold at par for the acquisition of capital facilities, the following entries were necessary:

Capital Projects Fund

Cash	2,000,000	
Revenues		2,000,000

General Long-Term Debt Group

Amount to be Provided for Payment of Deferred Serial Bonds	2,000,000	
Deferred Serial Bonds Payable		2,000,000

Similarly, when the first $200,000 of bonds matures, the liability is transferred from the General Long-Term Debt Group to the Deferred Serial Bond Debt Service Fund for payment:

Deferred Serial Bond Debt Service Fund

Expenditures	200,000	
Bonds Payable		200,000

General Long-Term Debt Group

Deferred Serial Bonds Payable	200,000	
Amount Available in Debt Service Fund for Payment of Deferred Serial Bonds		200,000

GOVERNMENTAL FINANCIAL REPORTS

Public financial reporting is defined by the National Committee on Governmental Accounting as "the total process of communicating any facts, events, and judgments concerning the financial condition and operations of a governmental jurisdiction."[2] The NCGA definition includes oral reports as well as written; informal reports as well as formal; and popular reports as well as technical. Reports for internal use as well as reports for all categories of external uses are included. The author of this text believes that reports of any nature can be made intelligently only by a person who has a thorough understanding of the assumptions and conventions on which the information reported (and the data underlying that information) are based. For that reason the primary focus of Chapters 3 through 13 is upon the nature of the funds and account groups recommended for use by state and local governmental units and the bases on which statements and schedules for these funds and groups are prepared. In the following paragraphs the discussion in preceding chapters is briefly summarized and placed in perspective.

Need for Periodic Reports

Persons concerned with the day-to-day operations and activities accounted for by governmental funds and groups should be familiar with much of the data processed by the accounting information system because it results from the events and transactions with which they are involved. It is easy for these persons to become overconfident of the intuitive "feel" they develop from their daily involvement. Past events were not always as remembered, and the relative significance of events changes over time. Similarly, administrators at succeedingly higher levels in the organization may feel that participation in decision-making, and observation of the apparent results of past decisions, obviate the necessity for periodic analysis of accounting and statistical reports prepared objectively and with neutrality. Financial reports should be prepared and distributed at intervals throughout a fiscal period as well as at period end.

[2] *Governmental Accounting, Auditing, and Financial Reporting,* p. 104.

Interim Financial Reports

Administrators of a governmental unit have greatest need for interim financial reports, although members of the legislative branch of the governmental unit (particularly those on its finance committee) should also find them of considerable use. Other users of interim reports are news media and residents who are particularly concerned with aspects of the financial management of the unit.

A complete interim financial report should include at least the following statements and schedules:

1. Statement of Actual and Estimated Revenue (for each revenue fund and debt service fund)
2. Statement of Actual and Estimated Expenditures (for each revenue fund and debt service fund)
3. Comparative Statement of Revenue and Expense (for each enterprise and intragovernmental service fund)
4. Combined Statement of Cash Receipts, Disbursements, and Balances—All Funds.
5. Forecast of Cash Positions—All Funds.[3]

Statements and schedules in addition to those listed above are needed by governmental units with varied and complex activities. A statement of investments held, and their market values, is an example of an additional statement that is of wide utility.

Schedules of past due receivables from taxes, special assessments, and utility customers may also be needed at intervals.

Complete interim reports should be prepared and distributed at regular intervals throughout a fiscal period, generally monthly, although small governmentul units which have little financial activity may find a bimonthly or quarterly period satisfactory. Partial interim reports dealing with only those items of considerable current importance should be prepared and distributed as frequently as their information would be of value. For example: reports of market values of investments and of purchases and sales may be needed by a relatively small number of users on a daily basis during certain critical periods.

Annual Financial Reports

Governmental annual financial reports are needed by the same individuals and groups who should receive interim reports. They are also often required to be distributed to agencies of higher governmental jurisdictions, and to major creditors. Other users include: financial underwriters,

[3] Ibid., p. 104

municipal bond rating agencies; municipal bond analysts; libraries; other municipalities; associations of governmental administrators, accountants, and finance officers; and college professors and students.

The three major sections of a complete annual report include the introductory material, the financial statements and schedules, and the statistical tables. Introductory material includes such obvious, but sometimes forgotten, items as title page and contents page, the letter of transmittal, and the opinion of the independent auditor.

The "letter of transmittal" may be literally that—a letter from the chief finance officer addressed to the chief executive and governing body of the governmental unit—or it may be a narrative over the signature of the chief executive. In either event the letter or narrative material should cite legal and policy requirements for the report and discuss briefly the important aspects of the financial condition and financial operations of the governmental unit as a whole and of the unit's funds and groups. Significant changes since the prior annual report and changes expected during the coming year should be brought to the attention of the reader of the report.

Laws relating to the audit of governmental units vary markedly from state to state. In some, all state agencies and all governmental units created pursuant to the state law are required to be audited by an audit agency of the state government. In others, local governmental units have the choice of being audited by the state agency or by independent certified public accountants, but are required to be audited by the state agency if they fail to secure audits by independent certified public accountants after a specified time.

As noted in Chapter 8, audits of Federal general revenue sharing trust funds of state and local governmental units, must be made in accord with *Standards for Audit of Governmental Organizations, Programs, Activities & Functions* issued by the Comptroller General of The United States.[4] The same standards should be used in the audit of the receipt and disbursement of other Federal grants and of activities financed wholly or partially by such grants. Certified public accountants are also bound by the provisions of the AICPA's *Audits of States and Local Governmental Units.*

Financial Section. The financial section should contain sufficient information to disclose fully and present fairly the financial position and results of financial operations during the fiscal year. Generally, both combined statements and schedules, and statements and schedules for each fund category and each account group are needed. The National Committee on Governmental Accounting recommends that a minimum of four com-

[4] Washington, DC: United States Government Printing Office, 1972.

Illustration 14–1

NAME OF GOVERNMENTAL UNIT
Combined Balance Sheet—All Funds
December 31, 19x2

	General Fund	Special Revenue Funds	Debt Service Funds	Capital Projects Funds	Enterprise Fund	Intra-governmental Service Fund	Trust and Agency Funds	Special Assessment Funds	General Fixed Assets	General Long-Term Debt
Assets and Other Debits										
Cash	$258,000	$101,385	$ 43,834	$ 431,600	$ 257,036	$ 29,700	$ 216,701	$232,185	–	–
Cash with fiscal agents	–	–	102,000	–	–	–	–	–	–	–
Investments (net)	65,000	37,200	160,990	–	–	–	1,239,260	–	–	–
Interest receivable on investments	50	25	1,557	–	–	–	2,666	–	–	–
Interest receivable—special assessments	–	–	–	–	–	–	–	350	–	–
Accounts receivable (net)	8,300	3,300	–	100	21,980	–	–	–	–	–
Unbilled accounts receivable	–	–	–	–	7,150	–	–	–	–	–
Notes receivable (net)	–	–	–	–	2,350	–	–	–	–	–
Loans receivable	–	–	–	–	–	–	35,000	–	–	–
Taxes receivable—delinquent (net)	40,500	2,500	2,843	–	–	–	–	–	–	–
Interest and penalties receivable on taxes (net)	3,000	–	227	–	–	–	–	–	–	–
Tax liens receivable (net)	14,800	–	759	–	–	–	–	–	–	–
Taxes receivable for other units	–	–	–	–	–	–	580,000	–	–	–
Special assessments receivable	–	–	–	–	–	–	–	644,100	–	–
Special assessment liens receivable	–	–	–	–	–	–	–	1,935	–	–
Advances to other funds	65,000	–	–	–	–	–	–	–	–	–
Due from other funds	2,000	–	–	15,000	2,000	12,000	11,189	–	–	–
Due from other governments	30,000	75,260	–	625,000	–	–	–	–	–	–
Inventories	7,200	5,190	–	–	23,030	40,000	–	–	–	–
Prepaid expenses	–	–	–	–	1,200	–	–	–	–	–
Restricted assets—Enterprise Fund:										
Cash	–	–	–	–	113,559	–	–	–	–	–
Investments (net)	–	–	–	–	176,800	–	–	–	–	–
Interest receivable on investments	–	–	–	–	650	–	–	–	–	–
Land	–	–	–	–	211,100	20,000	–	–	1,259,500	–
Buildings (net)	–	–	–	–	356,982	55,500	–	–	2,855,500	–
Improvement other than buildings	–	–	–	–	3,538,957	12,000	–	–	1,036,750	–
Machinery and equipment	–	–	–	–	1,640,007	15,600	–	–	452,500	–
Construction work in progress	–	–	–	–	22,713	–	–	–	1,722,250	–
Amount available for retirement of term bonds	–	–	–	–	–	–	–	–	–	198,205
Amount to be provided for retirement of term bonds	–	–	–	–	–	–	–	–	–	201,795
Amount available for retirement of serial bonds	–	–	–	–	–	–	–	–	–	14,005
Amount to be provided for retirement of serial bonds	–	–	–	–	–	–	–	–	–	2,385,995

Liabilities										
Vouchers payable	$107,861	$ 33,850	$ –	$ 29,000	$ 131,071	$ 15,000	$ –	$ 20,600	$ –	$ –
Accounts payable	10,400	–	–	–	–	–	–	–	–	–
Contracts payable	57,600	18,300	–	69,000	26,107	–	–	50,000	–	–
Judgments payable	–	2,000	–	19,600	–	–	–	11,200	–	–
Due to other funds	24,189	2,000	–	4,000	–	–	–	–	–	–
Due to fiscal agent	–	–	–	–	139	–	–	–	–	–
Taxes collected in advance	15,000	–	–	–	–	–	–	–	–	–
Customer deposits	–	–	–	–	63,000	–	–	–	–	–
Accrued liabilities	–	–	–	–	49,175	–	4,700	10,700	–	–
Advance from general fund	–	–	–	–	–	65,000	–	–	–	–
Advance from municipality–general obligation bonds	–	–	–	–	700,000	–	–	–	–	–
Matured bonds payable	–	–	100,000	–	–	–	–	–	–	–
Matured interest payable	–	–	2,000	–	–	–	–	–	–	–
General obligation bonds payable–term	–	–	–	–	–	–	–	–	–	400,000
General obligation bonds payable–serial	–	–	–	–	–	–	–	–	–	2,400,000
Revenue bonds payable	–	–	–	–	1,846,000	–	–	–	–	–
Special assessment bonds payable	–	–	–	–	–	–	–	555,000	–	–
Total Liabilities	$215,050	$ 56,150	$102,000	$ 121,600	$2,815,492	$ 80,000	$ 4,700	$647,500	$	$2,800,000
Reserves and Fund Balances/Retained Earnings										
Reserve for encumbrances	38,000	52,355	–	943,500	–	–	–	185,000	–	–
Reserve for inventory of supplies	7,200	5,190	–	–	–	–	–	–	–	–
Reserve for advance to central garage fund	65,000	–	–	–	–	–	–	–	–	–
Reserve for revenue bond debt service	–	–	–	–	5,000	–	–	–	–	–
Reserve for revenue bond retirement	–	–	–	–	109,822	–	–	–	–	–
Reserve for revenue bond contingency	–	–	–	–	14,333	–	–	–	–	–
Reserves–employees retirement system	–	–	–	–	–	–	1,426,201	–	–	–
Contribution from customers	–	–	–	–	72,000	–	–	–	–	–
Contribution from subdividers	–	–	–	–	870,666	–	–	–	–	–
Contribution from municipality	–	–	–	–	450,000	–	–	–	–	–
Contribution from general fund	–	–	–	–	–	95,000	–	–	–	–
Investment in general fixed assets	–	–	–	–	–	–	–	–	7,326,500	–
Fund balance	169,100	111,165	210,210	6,600	–	–	653,915	46,070	–	–
Retained earnings	–	–	–	–	2,038,201	9,800	–	–	–	–
Total Liabilities, Reserves, and Fund Balances/Retained Earnings	$494,350	$224,860	$312,210	$1,071,700	$6,375,514	$184,800	$2,084,816	$878,570	$7,326,500	$2,800,000

Source: National Committee on Governmental Accounting, *Governmental Accounting, Auditing, and Financial Reporting*, pp. 108–109.

bined statements and three combined schedules be presented in each governmental annual financial report:

1. Combined Balance Sheet—All Funds
2. Combined Statement of Revenue—Estimated and Actual—General and Special Revenue Funds
3. Combined Statement of General Governmental Expenditures Compared With Authorizations—General And Special Revenue Funds
4. Combined Statement of Cash Receipts and Disbursements—All Funds
5. Combined Schedule of Delinquent Taxes Receivable by Funds
6. Combined Schedule of Bonds Payable by Funds
7. Combined Schedule of Investments by Funds

Illustrations 14–1, 14–2, 14–3, and 14–4 are reproduced from *Governmental Accounting, Auditing and Financial Reporting* to illustrate forms

Illustration 14–2

NAME OF GOVERNMENTAL UNIT
Combined Statement of Revenue–Estimated and Actual
General and Special Revenue Funds
For the Fiscal Year Ended December 31, 19x2

Source (Fund)	*Estimated Revenues*	*Actual Revenues*	*Actual Over (Under) Estimated*
Taxes:			
(General)	$ 882,500	$ 881,300	$ (1,200)
(Special revenue)	189,500	189,300	(200)
Total Taxes	1,072,000	1,070,600	(1,400)
Licenses and permits:			
(General)	125,500	103,000	(22,500)
Intergovernmental revenue:			
(General)	200,000	186,500	(13,500)
(Special revenue)	837,600	831,100	(6,500)
Total Intergovernmental Revenue	1,037,600	1,017,600	(20,000)
Charges for services:			
(General)	90,000	91,000	1,000
(Special revenue)	78,000	79,100	1,100
Total Charges for Services	168,000	170,100	2,100
Fines and forfeits:			
(General)	32,500	33,200	700
Miscellaneous revenue:			
(General)	19,500	19,500	–
(Special revenue)	81,475	71,625	(9,850)
Total Miscellaneous Revenue	100,975	91,125	(9,850)
Total Revenue	$2,536,575	$2,485,625	$(50,950)

Source: National Committee on Governmental Accounting, *Governmental Accounting, Auditing, and Financial Reporting*, p. 11.

NAME OF GOVERNMENTAL UNIT

Combined Statement of General Governmental Expenditures and Encumbrances Compared with Authorizations
General and Special Revenue Funds
For the Fiscal Year Ended December 31, 19x2

Function (Fund)	*Reserve for Encumbrances 19x1*	*Expenditures 19x1*	*Credit (Charge) to Fund Balance*	*19x2 Appropriations (Revised)*	*19x2 Expenditures*	*Encumbrances December 31, 19x2*	*19x2 Unencumbered Balance*
General government:							
(General)	$ 2,100	$ 1,500	$ 600	$ 129,000	$ 120,305	$ 4,200	$ 4,495
(Parking meter) (note 1)	400	100	300	25,000	24,900	100	–
Total General Government	2,500	1,600	900	154,000	145,205	4,300	4,495
Public safety:							
(General)	5,500	5,600	(100)	277,300	252,795	6,550	17,955
(Parking meter) (note 2)	800	300	500	56,000	55,600	400	–
(Motor vehicle license) (note 3)	1,900	1,400	500	208,500	198,000	10,000	500
(Juvenile rehabilitation) (note 4)	2,400	2,200	200	205,000	197,500	5,500	2,000
Total Public Safety	10,600	9,500	1,100	746,800	703,895	22,450	20,455
Highways and streets:							
(General)	10,000	9,400	600	94,500	86,000	5,500	3,000
(State gasoline tax) (note 5)	2,000	1,000	1,000	436,000	416,000	16,500	3,500
Total Highways and Streets	12,000	10,400	1,600	530,500	502,000	22,000	6,500
Sanitation (general)	9,500	9,350	150	50,000	46,900	3,000	100
Health (general)	3,600	3,650	(50)	47,750	40,850	4,600	2,300
Welfare (general)	800	800	–	51,000	46,000	2,100	2,900
Culture–recreation:							
(General)	2,000	2,000	–	59,000	53,400	3,850	1,750
(Parks)	5,050	5,050	–	272,000	251,400	14,000	6,600
Total Recreation	7,050	7,050	–	331,000	304,800	17,850	8,350
Education (general)	4,000	3,900	100	591,450	555,250	8,200	28,000
Total–General and Special Revenue Funds	$50,050	$46,250	$3,800	$2,502,500	$2,344,900	$84,500	$73,100

Note 1. Portion of expenditures from Parking Meter Fund allocated to operating expenses of the traffic court (General Government–Judicial).
Note 2. Remainder of expenditures from Parking Meter Fund allocated to operating expenses of Police Department (Public Safety).
Note 3. Entire proceeds of Motor Vehicle License Fund allocated to operating expenses of Police Department (Public Safety).
Note 4. Entire proceeds of Juvenile Rehabilitation Fund allocated to operation of juvenile rehabilitation centers (Public Safety–Corrections).
Note 5. Entire proceeds of State Gasoline Tax Fund allocated to street maintenance (Highways).

Source: National Committee on Governmental Accounting, ***Governmental Accounting, Auditing, and Financial Reporting,*** **p. 112.**

Illustration 14–4

NAME OF GOVERNMENTAL UNIT
Combined Statement of Cash Receipts and Disbursements—All Funds
For the Fiscal Year Ended December 31, 19x2

Fund	*Balance 1-1-x2*	*Receipts*	*Disburse-ments*	*Balance 12-31-x*
General fund	$ 184,600	$1,317,500	$1,243,600	$ 258,5
Special revenue funds:				
Parks	29,525	258,500	248,500	39,5
State gasoline tax	14,710	422,500	414,750	22,4
Motor vehicle license	1,320	201,000	196,900	5,4
Parking meter	16,060	79,700	79,500	16,2
Juvenile rehabilitation	8,320	207,600	198,200	17,7
Debt service funds:				
1970 Civic Center	–	2,500	–	2,5
1941 school building	25,219	8,230	7,145	26,3
1966 parks and playgrounds	760	23,725	20,210	4,2
1960 street, bridge, and drainage	4,305	92,250	85,800	10,7
Capital projects funds:				
Municipal auditorium	260,000	1,250	246,000	15,2
Barton Heights Recreation Center	–	414,500	414,500	–
Storm sewer system	33,000	–	25,000	8,0
City-County Civic Center	–	1,381,250	1,069,000	312,2
Congress Avenue bridge	66,100	100,000	70,000	96,1
Enterprise funds:				
Water and sewer fund	137,760	1,420,986	1,301,710	257,0
Intragovernmental service funds:				
Central garage fund	50,000	96,000	116,300	29,7
Trust and agency funds:				
Employees' retirement	56,050	214,216	194,095	76,1
Endowment revenues	900	2,150	2,370	6
Performance deposits	20,750	5,200	5,000	20,9
Endowment principal	3,140	42,460	43,150	2,4
Revolving loan principal	5,450	20,000	15,000	10,4
School district tax	25,800	800,000	725,000	100,8
Hospital medical services	7,600	42,800	45,200	5,2
Special assessment funds:				
Improvement District No. 77	201,640	50,900	202,200	50,3
Improvement District No. 79	105,900	7,900	26,050	87,7
Improvement District No. 80	–	203,095	109,000	94,0
Total–All Funds	$1,258,909	$7,416,212	$7,104,180	$1,570,9

Balances Classified by Depository:	
Change and petty cash funds	11,5
Bank A	1,085,7
Bank B	257,0
Bank C	216,7
Total Balances 12-31-x2	$1,570,9

Source: National Committee on Governmental Accounting, *Governmental Accounting, Auditi* *and Financial Reporting*, p. 11.

of the four combined statements which are recommended by the National Committee on Governmental Accounting. Since the funds and groups are separate entities note that in all cases the statements are truly *combined*, not consolidated. For the same reason total columns are not used in combined statements of separate fund categories and account groups.

Statements and schedules which should be presented in governmental annual reports to disclose the position and operations of the individual fund categories and account groups are illustrated in Chapter 3 through 13. Note that combined statements of all funds *within a single category*—for example, all debt service funds—may properly include a column in which the total of similar items for all funds within the category is shown. Illustrations 7–4, 7–5, and 7–6 are good examples of combined statements for fund categories. The total column of the statement of all funds within a given category is carried to the column for that category in the combined statement of all funds and groups.

Statistical Section. In addition to the output of the accounting information system presented in the financial section of the governmental annual report a considerable amount of statistical data is needed by the reader who is more than casually interested in the activities of the governmental unit. Seventeen tabulations considered essential to adequate and full understanding of financial affairs by the National Committee on Governmental Accounting are:

1. General Governmental Expenditures by Function—Last Ten Fiscal Years.
2. General Revenues by Source—Last Ten Fiscal Years.
3. Tax Revenues by Source—Last Ten Fiscal Years.
4. Property Tax Levies and Collections—Last Ten Years.
5. Assessed and Actual Value of Taxable Property—Last Ten Fiscal Years.
6. Property Tax Rates and Tax Levies—All Overlapping Governments—Last Ten Fiscal Years.
7. Special Assessment Collections—Last Ten Fiscal Years.
8. Ratio of Net General Bonded Debt to Assessed Value and Net Bonded Per Capita—Last Ten Fiscal Years.
9. Computation of Direct and Overlapping Debt.
10. Computation of Legal Debt Margin.
11. Ratio of Annual Debt Service Expenditures for General Bonded Debt to Total General Expenditures.
12. Schedule of Revenue Bond Coverage—Last Ten Fiscal Years.
13. Debt Service Requirements to Maturity—General Obligation Bonds (plus similar statements for revenue and special assessment bonds).
14. Summary of Debt Service Charges to Maturity.
15. Schedule of Insurance in Force.

16. Salaries and Surety Bonds of Principal Officials.
17. Miscellaneous Statistical Data.

EVALUATION OF PRESENTLY RECOMMENDED MUNICIPAL ACCOUNTING[5]

Municipalities which follow the recommendations of the National Committee on Governmental Accounting utilize, as required, eight types of funds and two additional self-balancing groups of accounts. In the first section of this chapter the nature of each fund or group is reviewed. Interfund transactions and relationships are discussed in the second section of this chapter, and present recommendations concerning annual reports of local governmental units are presented in the preceding section. Some evaluation of the present recommendations of the National Committee on Governmental Accounting is implicit in the discussions in Chapters 3 through 13. It is the purpose of this section to make explicit this author's evaluation of the manner in which the parts of the system and the system as a whole meet the needs of administrators, legislators, creditors, taxpayers, and the general public.

Municipal Administrators—Legal Needs

With respect to the legal needs of municipal administrators the currently recommended municipal accounting information system admirably does what it was designed to do: the budgetary accounts of general, special revenue, debt service, and certain other funds provide a convenient reminder that the budget is a legal document which specifies how revenue will be raised, effectively places a ceiling on the amount of revenue that may be raised from each source, itemizes the purposes for which obligations may be incurred, and specifies the amounts which may be obligated for those purposes. The fund structure itself provides similar control in the case of construction projects financed by grants, general obligation bond issues, or special assessments, by requiring the establishment of separate capital projects or special assessment funds for each legally authorized project. In the event the law authorizes a fund to operate on a self-financing basis without annual legislative budgetary review, the recommended information system dispenses with budgetary accounts and in other respects also is similar to systems used by investor-owned enterprises carrying on the same activities.

For those activities of a municipality which are subject to budgetary

[5] This section is based on Leon E. Hay, *Municipal Accounting in the 1970's; MFOA Special Bulletin, 1971B*. Chicago: Municipal Finance Officers Association, 1971.

control, the currently recommended municipal accounting information system focuses the attention of administrators on liquid assets and current liabilities. Fixed assets used in the general operations of the municipality, or long-term debt which is backed by the full faith and credit of the municipality, are recorded in accounting entities separate from those used to account for day-to-day operations of the municipality. Although the municipal system appears somewhat awkward in comparison with the unified systems used by business entities, it provides adequate accounting control over all assets and liabilities.

Legal Needs of Municipal Legislators, Taxpayers, and Creditors

The currently recommended general fund system was designed to, and does, meet the needs of the members of the legislative branch of a municipal government for periodic reports which demonstrate that the budget approved by the legislative branch is, in fact, being adhered to. The system also provides for reports of assets available to meet current and future liabilities for the general operations of the municipality.

Taxpayers and long-term creditors of a municipality and authorities of jurisdictions superior to the municipality are also expected to be interested in being assured that the elected and appointed members of the municipal government are conducting the affairs of the municipality in accord with legal requirements. Legal requirements were presumably established to minimize the occurrence of undetected dishonesty on the part of governmental officials concerned with the levy and collection of taxes and other forms of revenue, and the purchase of and payment for goods and services. Any accounting system must be supplemented by appropriate and effective internal control procedures and subjected to audit by competent and impartial auditors in order for readers of reports prepared from the accounts to have confidence that the reports fairly present the information they purport to present. Thus in this discussion it is assumed that adequate internal control will be provided and that municipal reports and accounts will be examined by qualified independent auditors. (Chapter 21 deals with the subject of auditing in some detail.)

What then, are the needs not met by the currently recommended general fund accounting information system?

Planning and Controlling Resource Allocations

The most imperative information need in contemporary municipalities is for data which will enable legislators and administrators to allocate the scarce resources of the municipality among competing demands for municipal services in some manner which approximates the optimal. Recognition of this need is rather recent. Until the last two decades the great majority of municipalities in the United States, or anywhere else, were routinely involved in the provision of services to the public on a rather modest scale. Salaries of municipal employees tended to be low and the annual budget could be supported in most instances without excessive complaint from local taxpayers. In 1902, the earliest year for which figures are available, local governmental expenditures amounted to less than $1 billion; state and Federal expenditures brought *total* governmental expenditures to only a little over $1.5 billion. Seventy years later local governmental expenditures were on the order of $120 billion, and state and Federal expenditures brought the total to well over $400 billion. While the rate of growth of governmental expenditures should slow down in the decade to come, it seems certain that governmental bodies at all levels will experience increasingly greater difficulty in allocating their available resources among competing demands.

The Process of Resource Allocation

In well-managed businesses the process of allocating scarce resources among alternative uses in a systematic and rational manner has for most of the twentieth century been accomplished by means of preparation of a comprehensive budget including estimated financial statements. Within the last two decades the resource allocation process has been refined by the use of mathematical models and computer simulations to disclose the effects of alternative plans and policies acceptable to management. In spite of the fact that businesses are generally characterized by the phrase "profit-seeking," it is easy to find many instances in which the choice among alternative plans of resource allocation is made on the basis of subjective evaluations of qualitative factors, rather than objective measurement of profit or other quantitative factors. Thus although governmental budgeting has been defined in a recent authoritative publication as "a plan of proposed expenditures together with the proposed means of financing them,"[6] it is not surprising that there has been some experimenting in municipalities with the business concept of a budget as a means of aiding administrators and legislators to make a rational choice among alternatives.

Terms used for business budgeting concepts adapted to the governmental setting include: performance budgeting, program budgeting, and planning-programming-budgeting system (shortened to PPBS). In all these (discussed in Chapter 2) the proposed input of resources is matched with the expected output of services. Not all definitions agree, but for present purposes we may regard program budgeting as a budgeting format which discloses the full cost of a function without regard to the number of organizational units that might be involved in performing

[6] National Committee on Governmental Accounting, *Governmental Accounting, Auditing, and Financial Reporting,* p. 5.

the various aspects of the function, whereas a performance budget format relates the input and output of each unit individually. A planning-programming-budgeting system represents an extension of the program budgeting concept to include (1) identification of the fundamental objectives of the municipality, (2) explicit consideration of future-year implications, and (3) systematic analysis of alternative ways of meeting the governmental objectives. Systematic analysis, sometimes called "systems analysis," "cost/benefit analysis," or "cost/effectiveness analysis," may, of course, be used separately from PPBS. The terms are not synonymous but are closely enough related to be so treated here. Quantitative techniques such as model building and simulation studies may be utilized as aids in evaluating alternative allocations of governmental resources just as they may for evaluating business alternatives. However sophisticated or however simple the methods used to develop information to aid in the resource allocation process, any method can produce useful output only if the data input are sufficiently reliable. Input data into any of these methods may be classified as either *cost* data or *benefit* data.

Measurement of Costs in Business Accounting

Measurement of costs has been of some concern to accountants for at least five hundred years in the Western world. For the last fifty years measurement of "actual" costs has received concentrated, systematic attention, as have standard costs and expected costs. Not all the problems in these areas—or even the definition of cost, itself—have been solved to the satisfaction of accountants (and certainly the solutions reached by accountants have not always been satisfactory to nonaccountants), but the problems are rather well-defined and a number of practitioners and academicians are working toward solutions. Any comprehensive treatment of the nature, recognition, and measurement of costs for use in business decision-making seems to require approximately 800 pages in contemporary accounting texts. For present purposes it suffices to observe that the following are currently accepted as truisms. (1) There is no *one* true cost of anything; what may appropriately be considered as the "cost" of an item, activity, program, department, or any other unit, for any given decision, is not usually the "cost" for any other given decision. (2) There are two strata of cost that often need to be distinguished: the direct costs of an activity (department, item, program, etc.), i.e., a cost incurred because of some identifiable action by or for the activity; and the indirect or overhead costs of the activity, i.e., costs incurred to make the activity possible, but not incurred directly by the activity. (3) The accrual concept of cost is generally more useful than the cash concept of cost—cost should be recognized when service is received, not when cash is disbursed.

Measurement of Benefits in Business Accounting

It is probable that costs as computed by accountants have always been matched in the minds of decision-makers with the related benefits. Historical costs of a profit-seeking enterprise are matched with the revenues resulting from those costs in the traditional Income Statement; revenues, of course, are considered to be a measure of benefits in a profit-seeking entity. Similarly, expected operating costs are matched with expected revenues from operations—formally, if written budgets are prepared; mentally, or on scratch paper, if planning is not formalized. Capital budgeting techniques, also more highly developed in the profit-seeking sector, provide for an explicit matching of probable costs and probable revenues resulting from each proposal. The nature, recognition, and measurement of revenues is as difficult a subject as the nature, recognition, and measurement of costs, but the complexities are not of concern here. For present purposes it is adequate to emphasize that the accrual accounting concept that revenue should be recognized when service is rendered is generally more useful than the cash basis concept of recognizing revenue when cash is received.

Measurement in Governmental Accounting

In governmental and other non-profit entities operational budgeting and capital budgeting techniques have not been able to provide a satisfactory matching of costs and benefits (except in the case of enterprise funds and those trust and intragovernmental service funds operated in a manner similar to private businesses). Neither does the recommended municipal accounting information system provide this matching of historical costs and benefits resulting from costs. The reasons are more complex than those which first come to mind. Obviously, benefits are not measured by the presence, absence, increase, or decrease of revenue; therefore, we know we have the question of measurement of benefits. There is also the question of translating accounting data designed to measure the expenditure of appropriations into data which measure the cost of services rendered.

Structure of Accounts

The accounting information system presently recommended for use by state and local governmental units provides for complete correlation of budgetary and proprietary accounts. Expenditures and encumbrances must relate to specific appropriations in order to be legally proper; therefore, the system must provide for each appropriation a means of matching routinely (1) the amount approved in the original appropriations budget, (2) any subsequent change in the legally approved amount, (3) outstanding encumbrances against that appropriation, and (4) expenditures of the appropriation. Thus if the appropriation budget is structured in the traditional "line-item" manner, showing salaries, travel, contractual services, supplies, and other expenses, and capital outlays for each office on the organization chart, the expenditure accounting system must be structured in exactly the same manner. Under these conditions the accounting system provides information about the costs of programs only in the relatively uncommon cases in which an office engages in only one program. It is possible to synthesize program expenditures by analysis of line-item expenditures, but any such analysis involves assumptions about the bases for allocation which are difficult to justify. The analysis itself often is awkward and time-consuming. These problems of analysis can be avoided if the municipal appropriations budget is structured on the program basis rather than the traditional basis. If program budgets are used, the accounting system will routinely match program encumbrances and program expenditures with program appropriations.

Although the use of program budgeting accounting will routinely provide program expenditures, it will not necessarily provide program costs.

Translating Expenditures into Costs

Expenditures for Materials or Supplies. An expenditure occurs when a liability authorized by an appropriation is created. Since a liability is created when personal or contractual services are received, expenditures for services fit the accrual definition of cost. However, when materials or supplies are received an appropriation is expended, but there is no "cost" until the materials or supplies are used. If the inventory of materials or supplies at the end of a period is approximately the same as at the beginning of a period, expenditures for these items during the period may be a reasonably close approximation of cost during the period. Although reasonably level inventories in total may be common, there is no assurance that the usage of supplies for each program during a period corresponds to expenditures for supplies for each program during that period. If the supply cost of a given program is small in relation to total costs of that program, again expenditure accounting may provide a reasonable approximation of cost. If inventories fluctuate widely, or if some programs are heavy users of expensive supplies while other programs are light users of inexpensive supplies, the presently recommended municipal accounting system (which provides for the use of inventory accounts) must be supplemented by a system to provide for routine reporting of supply usage by programs.

Depreciation. As is true in the case of the purchase of materials and supplies, an appropriation is expended when a capital asset is acquired or constructed. By definition, a capital asset has a service life expected to extend over more than one fiscal period. The process of allocating the cost of a capital asset to the periods during which the asset is used is called *depreciation* accounting. The system of accounting presently recommended by the NCGA does not allow for the recording of depreciation of general fixed assets (although the system specifically provides for recording of depreciation by enterprise funds and other business-like activities). The presently recommended system further complicates the determination of depreciation expense by programs in that it requires general fixed assets to be accounted for by the general fixed assets group, not by the fund entity which accounts for the operations of the department or activity using the long-lived assets in the provision of services (nor even the fund entity which expended an appropriation in order to acquire the asset).

Recommended records of the general fixed-assets group provide enough information (cost of each asset, its estimated useful life, its location or the department to which it is assigned) to enable depreciation to be computed in a system divorced from the currently recommended accounting system. It would be relatively simple for a governmental unit to use a cost accounting system separate from the closed double-entry system created to give information needed to meet legal constraints; the cost system may, therefore, selectively focus on only those programs or activities for which depreciation would be a significant element of cost.

It is fairly apparent that the assignment of depreciation expense as a program or activity cost is not difficult if the asset being depreciated is used for only one program or activity. If an asset benefits more than one program or activity (such as a building occupied by several departments), an equitable and clerically feasible basis for allocation of the total depreciation expense must be found. Presently recommended records of the general fixed asset group would not necessarily provide the appropriate information, but it would not be difficult to supplement existing records by statistical studies and Bayesian estimates of knowledgeable personnel. Thus, although the currently recommended governmental accounting information system is designed to focus upon legal constraints, it can and should be supplemented to provide depreciation expense chargeable to each program or activity in all instances in which depreciation is a significant element of cost. (The designers of accounting systems for agencies of the Federal government of the United States have provided for routine recording of depreciation expense and other program expenses as well as the recording of appropriation expenditures, as explained in Chapter 16.)

Other Common Costs. In addition to depreciation of assets used by several departments or used for several activities, there are other items which may be called "common costs." Salaries, and other expenses, of the general municipal administration, and the cost of operating motor pools, cafeterias, and other central services are classical examples. The cost accounting subsystem proposed above should be used to accumulate all such common costs and to allocate them to the program benefited in order to provide "full cost" information for those decisions in which its use is relevant.

Measurement of Costs Ex Ante

Underlying the discussion in the above section on translating expenditures into costs is the assumption that cost is being measured *ex post*. The observations in that section would hold true in developing program costs *ex ante*, but only in the rather near future for which costs will result from activities which may be planned with a reasonable degree of certainty. The costs of proposed programs, however, must often be projected for many years in the future (as much as 100 years in the case of natural resources programs). Capital budgeting techniques widely advocated for use by both profit-seeking businesses and governmental bodies—and actually used to some extent by both—provide for discounting future costs to their value at the time the decision to accept or reject the project is to be made. Economists argue among themselves as to the correct discount rate to use in these computations. The answer is probably easier in the case of municipal projects than projects proposed for the Federal government; at least there appears to be some agreement that the rate paid on tax-exempt municipal bonds would be appropriate. This conclusion is an oversimplification however, because it is logical to allow for opportunity costs and political and social costs as well as accounting costs, i.e.: (1) If available general obligation bonding power is used to finance one given proposed project, no general obligation bonding power would be available for present alternative projects or for future alternative projects until the growth of assessed valuation and the retirement of debt allowed new bond issues; therefore, other financing sources, probably bearing higher rates, would have to be used. So, should all projects be discounted at the higher rates? (2) If the proposed construction of new freeways would split neighborhoods, isolating people from accustomed schools, churches, or shopping centers, as well as cause the condemnation of homes and the forced relocation of numerous residents (who also need to be thought of as voters), what *are* the costs which should be charged to the project? Even if the cost factors can be identified, with what degree of certainty can they be measured?

Measurement of Benefits

In contrast to the problem of measurement of costs of municipal programs, which can be solved *ex post* at least by a reorientation of traditional municipal accounting and the supplementation of it by additional statistical data, traditional governmental accounting offers little help in the solution of the problem of measurement of benefits. Nor does traditional business accounting offer much help. Determination of the existence or absence of a benefit of a municipal program is a subjective matter rather than the objective one faced by businesses which can define a benefit as revenue. Both direct benefits and spillover benefits may be claimed by proponents of a proposed program. Some benefits, of both categories, may be measurable in monetary units, some may be quantifiable but not in monetary terms; some may be expressed in terms of increased cultural or recreational opportunities or other values of doubtful quantifiability. Further, each of the above categories can be subdivided on the basis of the expected timing of the occurrence of benefits (the range is from immediately upon approval of the project to possibly 100 years in the future); on the basis of the degree of certainty of the occurrence of the benefits (ranging from reasonably certain to highly conjectural); and on the basis of dependence of the occurrence of the benefits on events external to the program under consideration (the range is from independent to highly dependent; the occurrence of the external events themselves may be of varying probabilities). Nonetheless, in spite of all the difficulties, rational allocation of resources requires the best available information as to benefits expected to result from a proposed program to be matched with the best available information as to costs of the same program. Before a purported benefit can be identified as true benefit, the objectives of the municipality and the objectives of the proposed program must be identified. Relative to this, Hinrichs points out:

> . . . the student of government decision making must not always assume that obscure and obfuscated objectives are totally lacking in function. Many times objectives are uncertain, changing, conflicting; this may not be the time for total inaction but instead a time of discovering and discussing objectives in the very process of moving in a general direction. Objectives often are a result of a feed-back process in getting the job underway and in working toward broader goals.[7]

Equally pragmatic, and equally relevant to the present discussion is a comment by Hatry on the problem of expressing benefits in monetary terms:

> Realistically most governmental problems involve major objectives of a nondollar nature. Not only is it very difficult for analysts to assign dollar "values" to such nondollar objectives, but it is also questionable whether it would be desirable even if it could be done. Thus, questions of the value of such effects as reducing death rates, reducing illness incidences and severities, improving housing conditions, and increasing recreational opportunities should not become simply a problem of estimating the dollar values of these things.

[7] Harley M. Hinrichs and Graeme M. Taylor. *Program Budgeting and Benefit-Cost Analysis*. Pacific Palisades, CA: Goodyear Publishing Co., Inc., 1969, p. 13.

> The analysts should rather concentrate upon the estimation and presentation, for each alternative, of full information as the actual dollar effects and the effects upon the nonmonetary criteria. *This is the primary function of program analysis.*[8] (emphasis added)

If the anticipated benefits from a program cannot be stated in quantitative terms, they must be stated verbally. In order to be of value in the management process the statement must be explicit and in operational terms, not "God and Motherhood" generalities.

Relation of Long Term Benefit/Cost Analysis to Planning

The statement of anticipated benefits from a proposed program should follow from a statement of objectives for the program. The statement of program objectives should be expanded into a plan of action to achieve the objectives, which in turn serves as a basis for planning costs of the program. Unless this course is followed, administrators and legislators will not be able to allocate resources of the governmental unit wisely, nor will administrators be able to manage resources committed to approved programs. Legislators and the public have a right to expect this integration of long-range analysis and fiscal period planning, so that they may evaluate the actions of the administrators in following the plan as well as the success of the programs in achieving the stated objectives.

Conclusion

The presently recommended governmental accounting system was designed to and does meet the needs of administrators for information to keep the municipal government operating within the legal constraints imposed by the legislative body and creditors of the governmental units and laws of superior jurisdictions. The system was also designed to and does enable administrators to demonstrate to legislators, creditors, and to the public through financial reports that legal constraints have been adhered to. Additionally, the presently recommended system focuses the attention of administrators, legislators, creditors, and the public upon the liquid assets available to meet current liabilities and available for appropriation for routine governmental services. Appropriate accounting is also provided by the recommended system for governmental enterprises and other activities which are outside the category of routine services.

Although the presently recommended municipal accounting system meets the historically important information needs of the administrators, legislators, creditors, and taxpayers, these groups now and in the foreseeable future are faced with information needs beyond the capabilities of the present system. The rate of growth in urban population and the rate of growth in the demands of that population for governmentally

[8] Ibid., p. 101

provided services together create an imperative need for rational allocation of governmental resources among competing uses. At the municipal level the scarcity of available resources with respect to alternative uses is particularly noticeable. Thus the presently recommended municipal information system must be modified to provide information for rational resource allocation.

Modification of the accounting system alone will solve few problems. Governmental administrators and legislators must accept and practice the essential elements of the planning-programming-budgeting system: (1) they must identify and state explicitly the fundamental objectives of the municipality; (2) they must critically examine both cost and benefit data for each ongoing and proposed municipal program in the light of fundamental objectives (the data must disclose both direct and spillover effects and specify future year implications); and (3) they must systematically analyze alternative ways to reach municipal objectives. In order to facilitate these needed improvements in governmental resource allocation, the governmental accounting, as explained in Chapters 3 through 13, must be structured to furnish program expenditure information and to provide for the routine reporting of program benefits measurable in dollars. Additionally, the presently recommended system must be supplemented or modified so that program expenditure information is routinely translated into accrual based cost information; management accounting techniques developed for profit-seeking businesses may be applied in the governmental field to achieve this. Neither contemporary accounting for profit-seeking businesses, nor contemporary governmental accounting, offer much help in the measurement of benefits of governmental programs either *ex post* or *ex ante*; improvement in both areas is urgently needed.

SELECTED REFERENCES

American Institute of Certified Public Accountants. *Audits of State and Local Governmental Units*, New York, 1974.

Clark, Joseph F. *Classification of Accounts and Financial Reporting, MFOA Special Bulletin 1968E*. Chicago: Municipal Finance Officers Association, 1968.

Comptroller General of the United States *Standards for Audit of Government Organizations, Programs, Activities & Functions*, Washington: United States General Accounting Office, 1972.

Hay, Leon E. *Municipal Accounting in the 1970's, MFOA Special Bulletin 1971B*. Chicago: Municipal Finance Officers Association, 1971.

Hinrichs, Harley H. and Taylor, Graeme M. *Program Budgeting and Benefit-Cost Analysis*. Pacific Palisades, Calif.: Goodyear Publishing Co., 1969.

National Committee on Governmental Accounting. *Governmental Ac-*

counting, Auditing and Financial Reporting. Chicago, Municipal Finance Officers Association, 1968.

QUESTIONS

14–1. The new mayor of the city in which you live asks you to explain to him why the preceding administration did not have just one set of accounts for the city. Keeping several sets of accounts sounds a little dishonest to him, or, at least, a make-work project for accountants. What is your answer to him?

14–2. What is the minimum number of funds a municipality could keep if it were attempting to adhere to generally accepted accounting principles? Explain.

14–3. "Revenue funds should be used to account for the collection of all sources of revenue. Disbursement funds should be used to account for cash disbursements for all purposes." Explain why you agree or disagree with this quotation.

14–4. *a*) State the principal reasons for the use of several funds in the accounts of governmental units.

b) List five kinds of funds frequently found in the accounting system of a municipality, and discuss briefly the content of each. (AICPA)

14–5. A municipal chief executive contends that since he is titular head of all municipal activities, he has authority to transfer assets from one fund to another on a temporary basis, because "it is all in the family". What is the merit, if any, of the mayor's contention?

14–6. "Since each fund and group is a separate entity it is contrary to generally accepted accounting principles to record a single event or transaction in more than one fund or group." Do you agree? Why, or why not? If you disagree give at least three examples of events or transactions which should be recorded in more than one fund or group.

14–7. Under what conditions may interfund receivables and payables properly be offset against each other? Under what conditions would it be improper to offset interfund receivables and payables?

14–8. A municipally-owned enterprise which receives services from departments accounted for by the general fund makes an annual "contribution in lieu of taxes" to the general fund. The enterprise fund accountant feels that these annual amounts should be debited to "Contributions from Municipality," since the enterprise is really returning to the general fund in installments that fund's original capital contribution to the enterprise.

a) How should the original contribution by the general fund to the enterprise fund have been accounted for by the general fund? Why?

b) How should the annual contributions by the enterprise fund to the general fund be accounted for by the general fund? Why?

c) How should the annual contributions be accounted for by the enterprise fund? Why?

14–9. A single balance sheet in which like items of all funds are consolidated into single figures has the valuable attribute of being very compact. Why, then, is the consolidated balance sheet for all funds not used more extensively?

14–10. Combined balance sheets in columnar form are common in published financial statements of units of government. What do you think of the value or practicability of combined columnar statements of revenue and expenditures?

14–11. Write the numbers 1 through 8 on a sheet of paper. Beside each number write the letter corresponding with the best answer to each question.

1. When used in fund accounting, the term "fund" usually refers to

   a) A sum of money designated for a special purpose.
   b) A liability to other governmental units.
   c) The equity of a municipality in its own assets.
   d) A fiscal and accounting entity having a set of self-balancing accounts.

2. Depreciation on the fixed assets of a municipality should be recorded as an expense in the

   a) Enterprise (utility) fund.
   b) General fund.
   c) Special assessment fund.
   d) Special revenue fund.

3. In municipal accounting the accrual basis is recommended for

   a) Only agency, debt service (sinking), enterprise (utility), general and special revenue funds.
   b) Only capital projects (bond), enterprise (utility), intragovernmental service (working capital), special assessment and trust (endowment) funds.
   c) Only enterprise (utility), general and intragovernmental service (working capital) funds.
   d) None of the funds.

4. Fixed and current assets are not accounted for in the same fund, with the exception of the

   a) General fund.
   b) Intragovernmental service (working capital) fund.
   c) Special assessment fund.
   d) Special revenue fund.

5. The balance sheet in the financial report of a municipality may be prepared

a) On a consolidated basis after eliminating the effects of interfund transactions.
b) On a combined basis showing the assets and equities of each fund with a total column indicating the aggregate balance for each identical account in all of the funds.
c) On a combined basis showing the assets and equities of each fund, but without a total column indicating the aggregate balance for each identical account in all of the funds.
d) For each fund on a separate page but never presenting all funds together on the same page.

6. The presence of an Expenditures Chargeable to Reserve for Encumbrances account in a city's general fund trial balance indicates that the ordinance governing the lapsing of appropriations provides that encumbrances outstanding at the end of the fiscal year

   a) Lapse.
   b) Lapse, but outstanding purchase orders are honored out of a special contingency fund.
   c) Lapse, but a new appropriation is made to cover them in a subsequent year.
   d) Do not lapse.

7. The budget which relates input of resources to output of services is the

   a) Line-item budget.
   b) Object-of-expenditure budget.
   c) Performance budget.
   d) Resource budget.

8. The activities of a street improvement project which is being financed by requiring each owner of property facing the street to pay a proportionate share of the total cost should be accounted for in the

   a) Capital projects (bond) fund.
   b) General fund.
   c) Special assessment fund.
   d) Special revenue fund.

(AICPA, Theory)

14–12. Write the numbers 1 through 18 on a sheet of paper. Beside each number write the letter corresponding with the best answer to each question.

1. The operations of a public library receiving the majority of its support from property taxes levied for that purpose should be accounted for in

   a) The general fund.
   b) A special revenue fund.
   c) An enterprise fund.
   d) An intragovernmental service fund.
   e) None of the above.

2. The liability for general obligation bonds issued for the benefit of a municipal electric company and serviced by its earnings should be recorded in

   a) An enterprise fund.
   b) The general fund.
   c) An enterprise fund and the general long-term debt group.
   d) An enterprise fund and disclosed in a footnote in the statement of general long-term debt.
   e) None of the above.

3. The liability for special assessment bonds which carry a secondary pledge of a municipality's general credit should be recorded in

   a) An enterprise fund.
   b) A special revenue fund and general long-term debt group.
   c) A special assessment fund and the general long-term debt group.
   d) A special assessment fund and disclosed in a footnote in the statement of general long-term debt.
   e) None of the above.

4. The proceeds of a federal grant made to assist in financing the future construction of an adult training center should be recorded in

   a) The general fund.
   b) A special revenue fund.
   c) A capital projects fund.
   d) A special assessment fund.
   e) None of the above.

5. The receipts from a special tax levy to retire and pay interest on general obligation bonds issued to finance the construction of a new city hall should be recorded in a

   a) Debt service fund.
   b) Capital projects fund.
   c) Revolving interest fund.
   d) Special revenue fund.
   e) None of the above.

6. The operations of a municipal swimming pool receiving the majority of its support from charges to users should be accounted for in

   a) A special revenue fund.
   b) The general fund.
   c) An intragovernmental service fund.
   d) An enterprise fund.
   e) None of the above.

7. The fixed assets of a central purchasing and stores department organized to serve all municipal departments should be recorded in

a) An enterprise fund and the general fixed assets group.
b) An enterprise fund.
c) The general fixed assets group.
d) The general fund.
e) None of the above.

8. The monthly remittance to an insurance company of the lump sum of hospital-surgical insurance premiums collected as payroll deductions from employees should be recorded in

   a) The general fund.
   b) An agency fund.
   c) A special revenue fund.
   d) An intragovernmental service fund.
   e) None of the above.

9. Several years ago a city provided for the establishment of a sinking fund to retire an issue of general obligation bonds. This year the city made a $50,000 contribution to the sinking fund from general revenues and realized $15,000 in revenue from securities in the sinking fund. The bonds due this year were retired. These transactions require accounting recognition in

   a) The general fund.
   b) A debt service fund and the general long-term debt group of accounts.
   c) A debt service fund, the general fund and the general long-term debt group of accounts.
   d) A capital projects fund, a debt service fund, the general fund and the general long-term debt group of accounts.
   e) None of the above.

10. A city realized large capital gains and losses on securities in its library endowment fund. In the absence of specific instructions from the donor or state statutory requirements, the general rule of law holds that these amounts should be charged or credited to

    a) General fund income.
    b) General fund principal.
    c) Trust fund income.
    d) Trust fund principal.
    e) None of the above.

11. The activities of a central motor pool which provides and services vehicles for the use of municipal employees on official business should be accounted for in

    a) An agency fund.
    b) The general fund.
    c) An intragovernmental service fund.
    d) A special revenue fund.
    e) None of the above.

12. A transaction in which a municipal electric utility paid $150,000

out of its earnings for new equipment requires accounting recognition in

a) An enterprise fund.
b) The general fund.
c) The general fund and the general fixed assets group of accounts.
d) An enterprise fund and the general fixed assets group of accounts.
e) None of the above.

13. In order to provide for the retirement of general obligation bonds, a city invests a portion of its general revenue receipts in marketable securities. This investment activity should be accounted for in

a) A trust fund.
b) The enterprise fund.
c) A special assessment fund.
d) A special revenue fund.
e) None of the above.

14. The activities of a municipal employee retirement plan which is financed by equal employer and employee contributions should be accounted for in

a) An agency fund.
b) An intragovernmental service fund.
c) A special assessment fund.
d) A trust fund.
e) None of the above.

15. A city collects property taxes for the benefit of the local sanitary, park and school districts and periodically remits collections to these units. This activity should be accounted for in

a) An agency fund.
b) The general fund.
c) An intragovernmental service fund.
d) A special assessment fund.
e) None of the above.

16. A transaction in which a municipal electric utility issues bonds (to be repaid from its own operations) requires accounting recognition in

a) The general fund.
b) A debt service fund.
c) Enterprise and debt service funds.
d) An enterprise fund, a debt service fund and the general long-term debt group of accounts.
e) None of the above.

17. A transaction in which a municipality issued general obligation serial bonds to finance the construction of a fire station requires accounting recognition in the

a) General fund.
b) Capital projects and general funds.
c) Capital projects fund and the general long-term debt group of accounts.
d) General fund and the general long-term debt group of accounts.
e) None of the above.

18. Expenditures of $200,000 were made during the year on the fire station in item 17. This transaction requires accounting recognition in the

a) General fund.
b) Capital projects fund and the general fixed assets group of accounts.
c) Capital projects fund and the general long-term debt group of accounts.
d) General fund and the general fixed assets group of accounts.
e) None of the above.

(AICPA)

EXERCISES AND PROBLEMS

14–1. Utilizing the municipal annual report obtained for Exercise 1–1, and your answers to the questions asked in Exercise 1–1, and the corresponding exercises in Chapters 2 through 13, comment on the following:

a) Does the report contain all introductory material recommended by the National Committee on Governmental Accounting (see Chapter 14)? Is the introductory material presented in such a manner that it communicates significant information effectively—do you understand what they are telling you and why they are telling it to you? On the basis of your study of the entire report list any additional information you feel should have been included in the introductory section and explain why you feel it should have been included. On the basis of your study of the entire report, do you think the introductory material presents the information fairly? Comment on any information in the introductory section that you feel is superfluous, and explain.

b) 1. Do the All Funds combined statements and schedules in the financial section present the information recommended by the National Committee on Governmental Accounting (see Chapter 14)? Is a Total column provided in the All Funds statements and schedules? Are the All Funds statements and schedules cross-referenced to each other? Are they cross-referenced to the statements and schedules of individual funds and account groups?

2. Review your answers to the questions asked in Exercises 3–1, 4–1, and 5–1 in the light of your study of subsequent chapters of the text and your analysis of all portions of the annual report. If you feel that your earlier answers were not entirely correct, change them in accord with your present understanding of generally accepted accounting principles and proper disclosure of the financial position and financial operations of a governmental unit.

Review your answers to Exercise 6–1, and all subsequent exercises in this series, in the light of knowledge you have gained since you prepared the answers. If any of your earlier answers should be changed, change them.

c) Are statistical tables presented in the annual report in accord with the recommendations of the National Committee on Governmental Accounting (see Chapter 14)? Make note of any data omitted. Make note of any additional data presented. If recommended data have been omitted, to what extent does each omission impair your ability to understand the report? To what extent does each additional table, chart, graph, or other statistical presentation add to your understanding of the governmental unit, its problems, its financial position, past and probable future changes in its financial position, financial operations, or past and probable future changes in financial operations?

d) Does the report include a copy of an MFOA Certificate of Achievement in Financial Reporting, or refer to the fact that the municipality has received one? (The certificate was formerly called a "Certificate of Conformance" and was awarded permanently; the Certificate of Achievement is to be awarded for a two-year period.) If the report has been awarded a certificate, does your review indicate it was merited? If the report has not been awarded a certificate does your review indicate that the report should be eligible for one?

e) Specify the most important information needs which a municipal annual report should fulfill for each of the following:

1. Municipal administrators
2. Members of the city council
3. Interested residents
4. Creditors or potential creditors

In what ways does the municipal annual report you have analyzed meet the information needs you have specified for each of the four groups, assuming that members of each of the groups make an effort to understand municipal reports equivalent to the effort you have made. In what way does the report fail to meet the information needs of each of the four groups?

14–2. The Combined Balance Sheet—All Funds taken from an annual report of the City of Tempe, Arizona, is shown on pages 428–29.

a) If you were a resident interested in a general overview of the financial condition of the city, to what extent would you find the illustrated statement useful?

b) If you were a CPA expressing an opinion on the financial statements of the City of Tempe, would you be able to give an unqualified opinion insofar as you can tell from the combined balance sheet?

14–3. The first list below consists of the types of funds recommended for use by a municipality. The second list contains a number of transactions that occurred in one municipality. List the transaction numbers on a sheet of paper and indicate opposite the number of the transaction the letter(s) corresponding with the fund(s) and/or group(s) (if any) in which each transaction would customarily be recorded. All transactions are to be strictly construed.

a) General fund
b) Special revenue fund
c) Special assessment fund
d) Capital projects fund
e) Intragovernmental service fund
f) Debt service fund
g) Trust fund
h) Agency fund
i) Enterprise fund
j) General fixed assets group
k) General long-term debt group

Transactions:

1. City motor vehicle license fees, to be used for street expenditures, were collected.
2. An issue of bonds, the proceeds of which were to be used for the erection of a new city hall, was sold.
3. Real estate and personal property taxes, which had not been assessed or levied for any specific purpose, were collected.
4. Salaries of personnel in the office of the mayor were paid.
5. An issue of bonds, to be used to pay for the improvement of streets in the residential district, was authorized. The debt is to be serviced by assessments on property benefited.
6. Sums of money were received from employees by payroll deductions, to be used for the purchase of United States government bonds for those employees individually.
7. A sum of money was appropriated, to be advanced from moneys on hand, to finance the establishment of a city garage for servicing city-owned transportation equipment.
8. A contribution was received from a private source. The use of the income earned on the investment of this sum of money was specifically designated by the donor.
9. Materials, to be used for the repair of the streets, were purchased.
10. Interest was paid on city hall building bonds after construction was completed.
11. Payment was made to the contractor for progress made in the erection of a new city hall.

CITY OF TEMPE, ARIZONA
Combined Balance Sheet
All Funds
June 30, 1972

	General Fund (Exhibits B)	Special Revenue Funds (Exhibits C)	Debt Service Funds (Exhibits D)	Capital Projects Funds (Exhibits E)	Enterprise Funds (Exhibits F)	Trust and Agency Funds (Exhibits G)	Special Assessment Funds (Exhibits H)	General Fixed Assets (Exhibits I)	General Long-term Debt (Exhibits J)
Assets and Other Debits									
Cash (Exhibit A–3)	$ (97,189)	$ 30,665	$ 34	$ 154	$ 9,131	$22,518	$ 5,170		
Cash with fiscal agents			190,642						
Investments, at cost (Exhibit A–6)		2,684,700		1,172,951	2,116,348	54,637	118,000		
Deposits				121,978					
Due from other funds	4,097,703	2,700,957	2,418	246,944	237,416	55	63,301		
Accounts receivable	30,961	228,351		23,550	145,325				
Accrued interest receivable					16,883				
Delinquent property taxes receivable (Note 3)	30,155								
Supply inventories, at average cost	94,885								
Prepaid expenses	551								
Restricted assets–water and sewer enterprise									
Cash					76				
Cash with fiscal agents					440,965				
Investments at cost (Exhibit A–6)					452,152				
Due from other funds					165,949				
Special assessments receivable							248,998		
Land					43,366			$ 3,482,557	
Buildings (net)					2,343,974			5,192,978	
Improvements other than buildings (net)					11,069,663			1,764,160	
Machinery and equipment (net)					240,954			2,376,466	
Streets								3,926,403	
Construction work in progress					738,141			1,375,548	
Amount available for retirement of serial bonds									$ 100,000
Amount to be provided for retirement of serial bonds									6,490,000
Amount to be provided for retirement of purchase contracts									5,878,857
Total Assets and Other Debits	$4,157,066	$5,644,673	$193,094	$1,565,577	$18,020,343	$77,210	$435,469	$18,118,112	$12,468,857

Liabilities									
Accounts payable	$ 159,536	$ 30,837		$ 877,569	$ 57,173				
Trust liabilities and deposits	127,546				41,124				
Due to other funds	2,418,333	4,317,657		775,166			$ 3,585		
Advance from municipality–GO bonds					3,285,000				
Matured bonds payable (Exhibit A–5)			$ 25,000		55,000				
Matured interest payable			5,334		160,965		108		
General obligation bonds payable (Exhibit A–5)									$ 6,590,000
Revenue bonds payable (Exhibit A–5)					6,800,000				
Special assessment bonds payable (Exhibit A–5)							317,936		
Purchase contracts					3,873				5,878,857
Total Liabilities	2,705,415	4,348,494	30,334	1,652,735	10,403,135		321,629		12,468,857
Reserves and Fund Balances/Retained Earnings									
Reserve for encumbrances	96,519	33,422							
Reserve for supply inventories	94,885								
Reserve for accounts receivable	30,961	228,351							
Reserve for delinquent property taxes receivable	30,155								
Reserve for July 1, 1972, maturities (Exhibit D–1)			160,392						
Reserve for future interest (Exhibit H–1)							49,566		
Reserve for deferred assessment (Exhibit H–1)							3,812		
Reserve for revenue bond debt service					126,833				
Reserve for revenue bond retirement					491,345				
Contributions and retained earnings prior to 7-1-67					3,210,164				
Contributions after 7-1-67:									
Contributions from customers					89,936				
Contributions from Federal government					516,150				
Contributions from other cities					169,587				
Investment in general fixed assets								$18,118,112	
Fund balance	1,199,131	1,034,406	2,368	(87,158)		$77,210	60,462		
Retained earnings after 7-1-67					3,013,194				
Total Liabilities, Reserves, and Fund Balances/Retained Earnings	$4,157,066	$5,644,673	$193,094	$1,565,577	$18,020,343	$77,210	$435,469	$18,118,112	$12,468,857

12. Proceeds received from the sale of a revenue bond issue were used for the purchase of the privately owned water utility in the city.
13. Property taxes, which were designated to be set aside for the eventual retirement of the city hall building bonds, were collected.
14. The city garage was reimbursed for sevices on the equipment of the fire and police departments.
15. Various amounts were paid by property owners for the benefits they received from the street improvement project.
16. Interest was paid on city hall building bonds before construction was completed.
17. Interest was paid on bonds issued for the purchase of the water utility.
18. The water hydrant rental was paid.
19. Interest was paid on bonds issued for payment of the improvement of streets in the residential district.
20. Interest was received on the investment of moneys set aside for the retirement of city hall building bonds.

(Indiana State Board of Accounts, adapted)

14–4. Record in general journal form each of the following transactions in all the groups and funds affected. Indicate clearly the fund or group to which each entry pertains.

1. During the year expenditures of a capital projects fund totaled $2,360,000 on a building project not completed at the end of the year, and that amount was closed to Fund Balance at the end of the year. Of the expenditures, $1,004,000 was financed from proceeds of a general bond issue in the preceding year, and the balance came from a Federal grant received in the current year.
2. Valuable books and documents appraised at $14,300 were received by the public library, from an individual. The library does not maintain its own accounting record of books, pictures, equipment, etc.
3. An issue of $300,000 general obligation bonds was authorized for a capital projects fund during the year and was sold at par. A building was purchased from the proceeds during the year at a total cost of $298,000 and the $2,000 balance in the capital projects fund was transferred to the debt service fund to be applied to retirement of the bonds. In the capital projects fund you may omit the encumbrance entries.
4. A building which had been acquired at a cost of $7,500 and equipment of which the total cost was $12,000 were disposed of during the year. Both had been purchased by special revenue funds. $50 cash was paid by the general fund for demolition and removal of the building, and it received $350 from disposal of the equipment.

5. An addition to the city hall, to be used partly by the water fund, was erected at a total cost of $127,000, financed equally by the water fund* and the general fund.
6. A special assessment fund sewer project was completed at a total cost of $730,000, of which $290,000 had been fully recorded in the preceding year. Of the amount spent in the current year $300,000 was from a Federal grant, $120,000 was supplied by property owners, and the balance was the city's share of the cost. (Record closing out of the special assessment fund expenditures for the year and make necessary entries in the general fixed assets group. Omit other special assessment fund entries.)
7. A special assessment fund which had taken title to a parcel of land for nonpayment of assessments transferred the land to the city government. Charges against the property when it had been taken by the city consisted of $4,300 delinquent assessments, $100 costs in connection with the foreclosure and sale, and $20 interest receivable at the time the lien was foreclosed. At the date of transfer the land was appraised at $11,500.
8. The municipal electric fund donated* to the city general government one-third of a parcel of land for which the utility had paid $30,000. At the date of acquisition by condemnation, the land was estimated to have a present value of $24,000. Since the land was nondepreciable, none of the premium paid for it had been amortized.

14–5. Below are stated a number of transactions, some of which are related and some not. Each transaction except the first affects the accounts of more than one fund or group. You are required to make all necessary entries for the transactions. Group all entries for each transaction, and show the fund or group to which each entry relates. Explanations may be omitted.

1. $1,400,000 par value of 4 percent, 20-year general obligation bonds were authorized for construction of a municipal administration building.
2. An intragovernmental service fund paid preliminary costs of $25,000 for the benefit of the administration building capital projects fund, which is to reimburse the service fund as soon as possible.
3. The bonds were sold at 98.
4. The debt to the intragovernmental service fund was paid.
5. During the first year, capital projects fund expenditures, in addition to the amount paid by the intragovernmental service fund, totaled $815,000, and total expenditures were closed at the end of the year. (Only the closing entry is required for this transaction.)

* Other Income Deductions is the title prescribed by leading utility regulatory commissions to record donations made by a utility.

6. Also during the first year the general fund transferred revenues in the amount of $75,000 to a debt service fund. The payment had been budgeted by the general fund but was not encumbered.
7. During the second year, with additional expenditures of $526,000, for which the entry may be omitted, the project was completed. All accounts of the capital projects fund were closed, and the balance of cash was transferred to the debt service fund mentioned in (6).
8. The debt service fund retired $100,000 par value of serial bonds.

14–6. The City Hall Construction Fund was established on July 1, 19x2, to account for the construction of a new city hall financed by the sale of bonds. The building was to be constructed on a site owned by the city.

The building construction was to be financed by the issuance of 10-year $2,000,000 general obligation bonds bearing interest at 4%. Through prior arrangements $1,000,000 of these bonds were sold on July 1, 19x2. The remaining bonds are to be sold on July 1, 19x3.

The only funds in which transactions pertaining to the new city hall were recorded were the City Hall Construction Fund and the General Fund. The Construction Fund's trial balance follows:

CITY OF LARNACA
City Hall Construction Fund
June 30, 19x3

	Debit	*Credit*
Cash	$ 893,000	
Appropriation expenditures	140,500	
Encumbrances	715,500	
Accounts payable		$ 11,000
Reserve for encumbrances		723,000
Appropriations		1,015,000
	$1,749,000	$1,749,000

An analysis of the Appropriation Expenditures account follows:

	Debit
1. A progress billing invoice from General Construction Company (with which the city contracted for the construction of the new city hall for $750,000—other contracts will be let for heating, air conditioning, etc.) showing 10% of the work completed	$ 75,000
2. A charge from the General Fund for work done in clearing the building site	11,000
3. Payments to suppliers for building materials and supplies purchased	14,500
4. Payment of interest on bonds outstanding	40,000
	$140,500

An analysis of the Reserve for Encumbrances account follows:

	Debit (Credit)
1. To record contract with General Construction Company .	$(750,000)
2. Purchase orders placed for materials and supplies	(55,000)
3. Receipt of materials and supplies and payment therefor. .	14,500
4. Payment of General Construction Company invoice less 10% retention.	67,500
	$(723,000)

An analysis of the Appropriations account follows:

	Debit (Credit)
1. Face value of bonds sold.	$(1,000,000)
2. Premium realized on sale of bonds	(15,000)
	$(1,015,000)

Required:

a) Prepare a worksheet for the City Hall Construction Fund at June 30, 19x3 showing

1. Preliminary trial balance.
2. Adjustments. (Formal journal entries are not required.)
3. Adjusted trial balance.

b) Prepare the formal adjusting journal entries for the following funds and groups of accounts. (Closing entries are not required.)

1. General Fixed Assets Group.
2. General Fund.
3. General Long-Term Debt Group.

(AICPA, adapted)

14–7. You were engaged as auditor of the City of Druid as of July 1, 19x2. You found the following accounts, among others, in the General Fund for the fiscal year ending June 30, 19x2:

Special Cash

Date	*Reference*	*Dr.*	*Cr.*	*Balance*
8/ 1/x1.	CR 58	301,000		301,000
9/ 1/x1.	CR 60	80,000		381,000
12/ 1/x1.	CD 41		185,000	196,000
2/ 1/x2.	CD 45		4,500	191,500
6/ 1/x2.	CR 64	50,500		242,000
6/30/x2.	CD 65		167,000	75,000

Bonds Payable

Date	*Reference*	*Dr.*	*Cr.*	*Balance*
8/ 1/x1.	CR 58		300,000	300,000
6/ 1/x2.	CR 64		50,000	350,000

Construction in Progress–Main Street Sewer

Date	*Reference*	*Dr.*	*Cr.*	*Balance*
12/ 1/x1.	CD 41	185,000		185,000
6/30/x2.	CD 65	167,000		352,000

Interest Expense

Date	*Reference*	*Dr.*	*Cr.*	*Balance*
2/ 1/x2.	CD 45	4,500		4,500
6/ 1/x2.	CR 64		500	4,000

Assessment Income

Date	*Reference*	*Dr.*	*Cr.*	*Balance*
9/ 1/x1.	CR 60		80,000	80,000

Premium on Bonds

Date	*Reference*	*Dr.*	*Cr.*	*Balance*
8/ 1/x1.	CR 58		1,000	1,000

The accounts resulted from the project described below:

The city council authorized the Main Street Sewer Project and a ten-year bond issue of $350,000 to permit deferral of assessment payments. According to the terms of the authorization the property owners were to be assessed 80 percent of the estimated cost of construction and the balance was made available by the city during October 19x1. On September 1, 19x1, the first of five equal annual assessment installments was collected from the property owners. The deferred assessments were to bear interest at 5⅝% from September 1, 19x1. The project was expected to be completed by October 31, 19x2.

Required:

a) Prepare entries in general journal form to record all special assessment fund transactions in accord with current recommendations for special assessment fund accounting. Prepare closing entries as of June 30, 19x2.

b) Prepare entries in general journal form that should be made in all funds and groups other than the Special Assessment Fund to record properly the results of the transactions of the Main Street Sewer Project.

(AICPA, adapted)

14–8. The accounts of the City of Daltonville were kept by an inexperienced bookkeeper during the year ended December 31, 19x5. The following trial balance of the General Fund was available when you began your examination:

CITY OF DALTONVILLE
General Fund Trial Balance
December 31, 19x5

Cash	$ 75,600	
Taxes receivable–current year	29,000	
Estimated losses–current year taxes receivable		$ 9,000
Taxes receivable–prior year	4,000	
Estimated losses–prior year taxes receivable		5,100
Appropriations		174,000
Estimated revenues	180,000	
Building addition constructed	25,000	
Serial bonds paid	8,000	
Expenditures	140,000	
Special assessment bonds payable		50,000
Revenues		177,000
Accounts payable		13,000
Fund balance		33,500
	$461,600	$461,600

Your examination disclosed the following:

1. The estimate of losses of $9,000 for current year taxes receivable was found to be a reasonable estimate.
2. The Building Addition Constructed account balance is the cost of an addition to the municipal building. The addition was constructed during 19x5 and payment was made from the General Fund as authorized.
3. The Serial Bonds Paid account reports the annual retirement of general obligation bonds issued to finance the construction of the municipal building. Interest payments of $3,800 for this bond issue are included in Expenditures.
4. A physical count of the current operating supplies at December 31, 19x5, revealed an inventory of $6,500. The decision was made to record the inventory in the accounts; expenditures are to be recorded on the basis of usage rather than purchases.
5. Operating supplies ordered in 19x4 and chargeable to 19x4 appropriations were received, recorded, and consumed in January 19x5. The outstanding purchase orders for these supplies, which were not recorded in the accounts at year end, amounted to $4,400. The vendors' invoices for these supplies totaled $4,700. Appropriations lapse one year after the end of the fiscal year for which they are made.
6. Outstanding purchase orders at December 31, 19x5, for operating supplies totaled $5,300. These purchase orders were not recorded on the books.
7. The special assessment bonds were sold in December 19x5 to finance a street paving project. No contracts have been signed for this project and no expenditures have been made.
8. The balance in the Revenues account includes credits for $10,000 for a note issued to a bank to obtain cash in anticipation of

tax collections to pay current expenses and for $900 for the sale of scrap iron from the City's water plant. The note was still outstanding at year end. The operations of the water plant are accounted for by a separate fund.

Required:

a) Prepare the formal adjusting and closing journal entries for the General Fund.

b) The foregoing information disclosed by your examination was recorded only in the General Fund even though other funds or groups of accounts were involved. Prepare the formal adjusting journal entries for any other funds or groups of accounts involved.

(AICPA, adapted)

14–9. You were engaged to examine the financial statements of the City of Homer for the year ended June 30, 1969, and found that the bookkeeper had recorded all transactions in the General Fund. You were furnished the General Fund Trial Balance, which appears below:

CITY OF HOMER
General Fund Trial Balance
June 30, 1969

Debits	
Cash	$ 125,180
Cash for construction	174,000
Taxes receivable–current	8,000
Assessments receivable–deferred	300,000
Inventory of materials and supplies	38,000
Improvements authorized	15,000
Estimated revenues	4,135,000
Interest expense	18,000
Encumbrances	360,000
Appropriation expenditures	4,310,000
Total Debits	$9,483,180

Credits	
Allowance for uncollectible current taxes	$ 7,000
Vouchers payable	62,090
Interest payable	18,000
Liability under street improvement project	10,000
Bonds payable	300,000
Premium on bonds	3,000
Reserve for inventory	36,000
Reserve for encumbrances	360,000
Appropriations	4,450,000
Interest revenue	21,000
Fund balance	106,090
Revenues	4,110,000
Total Credits	$9,483,180

Your audit disclosed the following:

1. Years ago the City Council authorized the recording of inventories, and a physical inventory taken on June 30, 1969 showed that materials and supplies with a cost of $37,750 were on hand at that date. The inventory is recorded on a perpetual basis.
2. Current taxes are now considered delinquent and it is estimated that $5,500 of such taxes will be uncollectible.
3. Discounts of $32,000 were taken on property taxes. An appropriation is not required for discounts, but an allowance for them was not made at the time the tax levy was recorded. Discounts taken were charged to Appropriation Expenditures.
4. On June 25, 1969, the State Revenue Department informed the city that its share of a state-collected, locally-shared tax would be $75,000.
5. New equipment for the Police Department was acquired at a cost of $90,000 and was properly recorded in the General Fund.
6. During the year 100 acres of land was donated to the city for use as an industrial park. The land had a value of $250,000. No recording has been made.
7. The City Council authorized the paving and widening of certain streets at an estimated cost of $365,000, which included an estimated $5,000 cost for planning and engineering to be paid from the General Fund. The remaining $360,000 was to be financed by a $10,000 contribution from the city and $350,000 by assessments against property owners payable in seven equal annual installments. A $15,000 appropriation was made for the city's share at the time the annual budget was recorded, and the toal $365,000 was also recorded as an appropriation. The following information is also relevant to the street improvement project:

   a) Property owners paid their annual installment plus a $21,000 interest charge in full.
   b) Special assessment bonds of $300,000 were authorized and sold at a premium of $3,000. An $18,000 liability for interest was properly recorded. The city does not amortize bond premium or discount.
   c) The city's $15,000 share was recorded as an expenditure during the year. The $5,000 for planning and engineering fees were paid. Construction began July 5, 1968, and the contractor has been paid $200,000 under the contract for construction which calls for performance of the work at a total cost of $360,000. This $360,000 makes up the balance in the Reserve for Encumbrances.
   d) The Cash for Construction account was used for all receipts and disbursements relative to the project. It is made up of the proceeds of the bond issue and collection of assessment installments and interest minus payments to the contractor.

Required:

Prepare a worksheet to adjust the account balances at June 30, 1969, and to distribute them to the appropriate funds or groups of accounts. It is recommended that the worksheet be in the order of the General Fund Trial Balance and have the following column headings:

1. Balance per books.
2. Adjustments—debit.
3. Adjustments—credit.
4. General Fund.
5. Special Assessment Fund.
6. General Fixed Assets.

Number all adjusting entries. Formal journal entries or financial statements are not required. Supporting computations should be in good form.

(AICPA)

14–10. At the start of your examination of the accounts of the City of Waterford, you discovered that the bookkeeper failed to keep the accounts by funds. The following trial balance of the General Fund for the year ended December 31, 197A was available.

CITY OF WATERFORD
General Fund Trial Balance
December 31, 197A

	Debit	*Credit*
Cash	$ 207,500	
Taxes receivable–current	148,500	
Estimated uncollectible current taxes		$ 6,000
Expenditures	760,000	
Revenues		992,500
Land	190,000	
Construction work in progress (River Bridge)	130,000	
Bonds payable (River Bridge)		200,000
Contracts payable (River Bridge)		25,000
Contracts payable (River Bridge)–retained percentage		5,000
Vouchers payable		7,500
Fund balance		200,000
Total	$1,436,000	$1,436,000

Your examination disclosed the following:

1. The budget for the year 197A, not recorded on the books, estimated revenues and expenditures as follows: revenues $815,000; expenditures $775,000.

2. Outstanding purchase orders at December 31, 197A, for operating expenses not recorded on the books totaled $2,500.
3. Included in the Revenues account is a credit of $190,000 representing the value of land donated by the state as a grant-in-aid for construction of the River Bridge.
4. During the year $300,000 worth of general obligation bonds payable were authorized for the River Bridge project; $100,000 of these are still unissued, the remainder having been sold at par.
5. Examination of the subledger containing the details of the Expenditures account revealed the following items included therein:

Current operating expenses	$472,000
Additions to structures and improvements	210,000
Equipment purchases	10,000
General obligation bonds paid	50,000
Interest paid on general obligation bonds	18,000

Required:

Prepare a worksheet showing the given General Fund trial balance, entries to correct the general fund accounts and to establish additional funds or groups as recommended by the NCGA. The following column headings are recommended:

General Fund Trial Balance—Debit	General Fund—Debit
General Fund Trial Balance—Credit	General Fund—Credit
Adjustments—Debit	Capital Projects Fund
Adjustments—Credit	General Fixed Assets
	General Long-Term Debt

Number all adjusting and transaction entries. Formal journal entries are not required.

(AICPA, adapted)

14–11. The City of Happy Hollow has engaged you to examine its financial statements for the year ended December 31, 1971. The City was incorporated as a municipality and began operations on January 1, 1971. You find that a budget was approved by the City Council and was recorded, but that all transactions have been recorded on the cash basis. The bookkeeper has provided the following Operating Fund trial balance.

	Debits	*Credits*
Cash	$238,900	
Expenditures	72,500	
Estimated revenues	114,100	
Appropriations		$102,000
Revenues		108,400
Bonds payable		200,000
Premium on bonds payable		3,000
Fund balance		12,100
Totals	$425,500	$425,500

Additional information is given below:

1. Examination of the appropriation-expenditure ledger revealed the following information:

	Budgeted	*Actual*
Personal services	$ 45,000	$38,500
Supplies	19,000	11,000
Equipment.	38,000	23,000
Totals	$102,000	$72,500

2. Supplies and equipment in the amounts of $4,000 and 10,000, respectively, had been received, but the vouchers had not been paid at December 31.
3. At December 31, outstanding purchase orders for supplies and equipment not yet received were $1,200 and $3,800, respectively.
4. The inventory of supplies on December 31, was $1,700 by physical count. The decision was made to record the inventory of supplies. A city ordinance requires that expenditures are to be based on purchases, not on the basis of usage.
5. Examination of the revenue subsidiary ledger revealed the following information:

	Budgeted	*Actual*
Property taxes.	$102,600	$ 96,000
Licenses	7,400	7,900
Fines	4,100	4,500
Totals	$114,100	$108,400

It was estimated that 5 percent of the property taxes would not be collected. Accordingly, property taxes were levied in an amount so that collections would yield the budgeted amount of $102,600.

6. On November 1, 1971, Happy Hollow issued 8% General Obligation Term Bonds with $200,000 face value for a premium of $3,000. Interest is payable each May 1 and November 1 until the maturity date of November 1, 1985. The city council ordered that the cash from the bond premium be set aside and restricted for the eventual retirement of the debt principal. The bonds were issued to finance the construction of a city hall, but no contracts had been let as of December 31.

Required:

a) Prepare a worksheet showing the trial balance as given, adjustments, and distributions to the proper funds or groups of accounts in conformity with generally accepted accounting principles applicable to governmental entities. (Formal adjusting entries are not required.)

b) Identity the financial statements that should be prepared for the General Fund. (You are not required to prepare these statements.)

c) Draft formal closing entries for the General Fund.

(AICPA)

14–12. The Cobleskill City Council passed a resolution requiring a yearly cash budget by fund for the City beginning with its fiscal year ending September 30, 1973. The City's financial director has prepared a list of expected cash receipts and disbursements, but he is having difficulty subdividing them by fund. The list follows:

Cash receipts		
Taxes:		
General property	$ 685,000	
School	421,000	
Franchise	223,000	
		1,329,000
Licenses and permits:		
Business licenses	41,000	
Automobile inspection permits	24,000	
Building permits	18,000	
		83,000
Intergovernmental revenue:		
Sales tax	1,012,000	
Federal grants	128,000	
State motor vehicle tax	83,500	
State gasoline tax	52,000	
State alcoholic beverage licenses	16,000	
		1,291,500
Charges for services:		
Sanitation fees	$ 121,000	
Sewer connection fees	71,000	
Library revenues	13,000	
Park revenues	2,500	
		207,500
Bond issues:		
Civic center	347,000	
General obligation	200,000	
Sewer	153,000	
Library	120,000	
		820,000
Other:		
Proceeds from the sale of investments	312,000	
Sewer assessments	50,000	
Rental revenue	48,000	
Interest revenue	15,000	
		425,000
		$4,156,000

Cash disbursements

General government	$ 671,000
Public safety	516,000
Schools	458,000
Sanitation	131,000
Library	28,000
Rental property	17,500
Parks	17,000
	1,838,500
Debt service:	
General obligation bonds	618,000
Street construction bonds	327,000
School bonds	119,000
Sewage disposal plant bonds	37,200
	1,101,200
Investments	358,000
State portion of sales tax	860,200
Capital expenditures:	
Sewer construction (assessed area)	114,100
Civic center construction	73,000
Library construction	36,000
	223,100
	$4,381,000

The financial director provides you with the following additional information:

1. A bond issue was authorized in 1972 for the construction of a civic center. The debt is to be paid from future civic center revenues and general property taxes.
2. A bond issue was authorized in 1972 for additions to the library. The debt is to be paid from general property taxes.
3. General obligation bonds are paid from general property taxes collected by the general fund.
4. Ten percent (10%) of the total annual school taxes represents an individually voted tax for payment of bonds the proceeds of which were used for school construction.
5. In 1970, a wealthy citizen donated rental property to the City. Net income from the property is to be used to assist in operating the library. The net cash increase attributable to the property is transferred to the library on September 30 of each year.
6. All sales taxes are collected by the City; the state receives 85% of these taxes. The state's portion is remitted at the end of each month.
7. Payment of the street construction bonds is to be made from assessments previously collected from the respective property owners. The proceeds from the assessments were invested and the principal of $312,000 will earn $15,000 interest during the coming year.
8. In 1972, a special assessment in the amount of $203,000 was made on certain property owners for sewer construction. During

fiscal 1973, $50,000 of this assessment is expected to be collected. The remainder of the sewer cost is to be paid from a $153,000 bond issue to be sold in fiscal 1973. Future special-assessment collections will be used to pay principal and interest on the bonds.

9. All sewer and sanitation services are provided by a separate enterprise fund.
10. The federal grant is for fiscal 1973 school operations.
11. The proceeds remaining at the end of the year from the sale of civic center and library bonds are to be invested.

Required:

Prepare a budget of cash receipts and disbursements by fund for the year ending September 30, 1973. All interfund transfers of cash are to be included.

(AICPA)

CONTINUOUS PROBLEMS

14–L *a*) Assemble all statements and schedules prepared for your solutions to Problems 1–L through 13–L.

b) From your solutions to Problems 1–L through 13–L prepare a combined balance sheet for all funds and account groups of the City of Bingham. (Do not include 10–L; Irwinville is not a part of the City of Bingham.)

c) On the basis of the financial information that you prepared for 14–L *a*) and *b*), prepare a letter of transmittal covering as many of the points suggested in Chapter 14 as possible.

d) Would you expect a certified public accountant to express an unqualified opinion on the financial statements of the City of Bingham. Why or why not?

14–S *a*) Assemble all statements and schedules prepared for your solutions to Problems 1–S through 13–S.

b) Briefly itemize the points you feel the city's Finance Director should be sure to cover in his letter of transmittal to accompany the financial report of the City of Smithville (you may limit your comments to items relating to the statements and schedules prepared for "S" problems).

c) Would you expect a certified public accountant to express an unqualified opinion on the financial statements of the City of Smithville? Why or why not?

15

Cash Procedures and Accounting

Because of its high state of liquidity and ease of transfer, cash occupies a preeminent position in the attention of accountants and auditors. Its usefulness to the rightful owners and its attractiveness to others cause it to be widely sought by means usually fair but sometimes foul. Furthermore, possibilities for honest mistakes are numerous in the receipt, custody, and disbursement of cash. Administrators, accountants, and auditors must be constantly alert in their endeavors that only fair or legal methods be used and that loss through error be reduced to a minimum. These observations are no less true of governmental cash than of that belonging to private individuals or enterprises. In fact, the greater separation in government of the ones who pay and the ones who spend, and the need for protection of those by whom government is financed, may constitute an even greater obligation for safeguarding public cash. Although parts of the following discussion may incidentally be applicable to cash in general, special reference is intended to cash of governments.

Requirements for Adequate Cash Accounting

Some elements of desirable cash procedure pertain strictly to cash in one or another of its forms. Other elements may relate not only to cash but also to other financial aspects of the governmental unit concerned. As one example, some cash accounting procedures are closely related to accounting for revenue and expenditures, others to the reduction of noncash assets. It may be said that, in general, adequate cash accounting procedures must include the following:

1. Provision for determining, in so far as is reasonably possible, that the goverment receives all the cash to which it is legally entitled.

2. Accurate and complete accounting for cash that is received, with some forecasting of cash to be received during a future period.
3. Adequate protection of cash between the time of receipt and the time of disbursement.
4. Accurate and complete accounting for cash disbursed, sometimes supplemented by a schedule of anticipated expenditures during a future period.

An indispensable element of good cash procedure, whatever other safeguards may exist, is a carefully planned and diligently applied system of internal control of the kind discussed in earlier chapters. In addition to the main scheme of internal control, there are numerous other techniques—such as the bonding of all employees handling cash and regular annual audits—which serve to prevent or reveal irregularities; but detailed discussion of these precautions is not appropriate here.

Determining Whether All Cash That Ought to Be Received Is Received

One situation permitting a definite, clear-cut comparison between cash that should be received and cash actually received is found in the case of certain governmental revenue that is accounted for on the accrual basis. If one or more units or departments of government are charged with ascertaining and billing a given kind of revenue, whereas another department accounts for collection, the arrangement represents a very desirable form of control over cash. The best illustration of a situation such as the one described above is the prevailing practice and plan of handling the assessment, billing, and collection of property taxes. In one state, for example, assessing and billing are functions of the assessors' and auditors' offices, and collection rests with the treasurer. Because of direct and indirect checks upon taxes reported as unpaid, the possibilities for the diversion of cash collected from taxpayers, without disclosure, is reduced to a minimum. Unfortunately, this control device cannot overcome defects in the assessment procedure which may undervalue property or entirely omit it from the basic inventory. However, this latter deficiency is more of a revenue than a cash problem.

Other forms of governmental revenue activity which lend themselves to the use of an accrual or semiaccrual basis are utility services, some kinds of licenses and permits, revenue from the use of money and property, and revenue from other agencies. Utility services are furnished on a contractual basis; and with the proper use of service, billing, and collection forms, a close degree of correlation between the amount due and the amount received is possible. Many kinds of licenses and permits are granted for privileges to operate at specified locations or within given areas, and failure to obtain a license or permit is readily ascertainable. Assuring that fees arising from licenses and permits will be accounted for is largely a matter of using prenumbered authorization forms, for which strict accounting must be made. Money and property are of such tangible nature that accrual of income for their use and receipt of cash from that source are readily ascertainable through record keeping and the exercise of reasonable care. Also subject to exact verification are receipts from the sale of bonds, from the issuance of notes, and from special assessment levies.

Some forms of revenue do not lend themselves to the use of accrual accounting; but once having reached the realization stage, accurate accounting for the cash to be received is largely a matter of well-organized and well-administered procedures. Thus, it is not possible to determine accurately the amounts of income or gross receipts taxes which each taxpayer should pay; but once the taxpayer has acknowledged his liability by filing a return, or his employer has filed an informational return, there can be close correlation between amounts of cash that should be received and amounts actually finding their way into the treasury. On the municipal level, there is no practicable way of accruing revenue from parking meters; but once the money has been placed in the meter, determination of whether it gets into the bank account is a matter of establishing recognized safeguards around its movement from meter to bank account, that is, at least one check or control at every stage.

The nature of some kinds of revenue or receipts and the manner of collecting them almost defy conclusive accounting for the proceeds. Not only do they not lend themselves to accrual accounting; but for some it is difficult to determine whether they have been collected and, if so, in what amount. In this category are fines, forfeitures, and penalties, some kinds of fees, refunds on disbursements, collection of receivables previously written off, and miscellaneous transactions not formally recorded until cash is received.

In summary, to assure that cash collected will be fully accounted for:

1. The accrual basis of accounting should be used wherever possible, in order to establish liability of some employee or department to account formally for realization into cash of the asset recorded by the accrual.
2. Wherever possible, prenumbered forms should be used as a sort of receipt to be issued to the payer; every one of the numbered forms should be strictly accounted for; and payers should be encouraged to demand a formal, written receipt.
3. A system of internal control or check should be developed with the smallest possible number of weaknesses under the prevailing conditions and circumstances.

A possible flow chart for cash receipts is shown in Illustration 15–1.

Illustration 15–1

Flow Chart of Receipts Transactions*

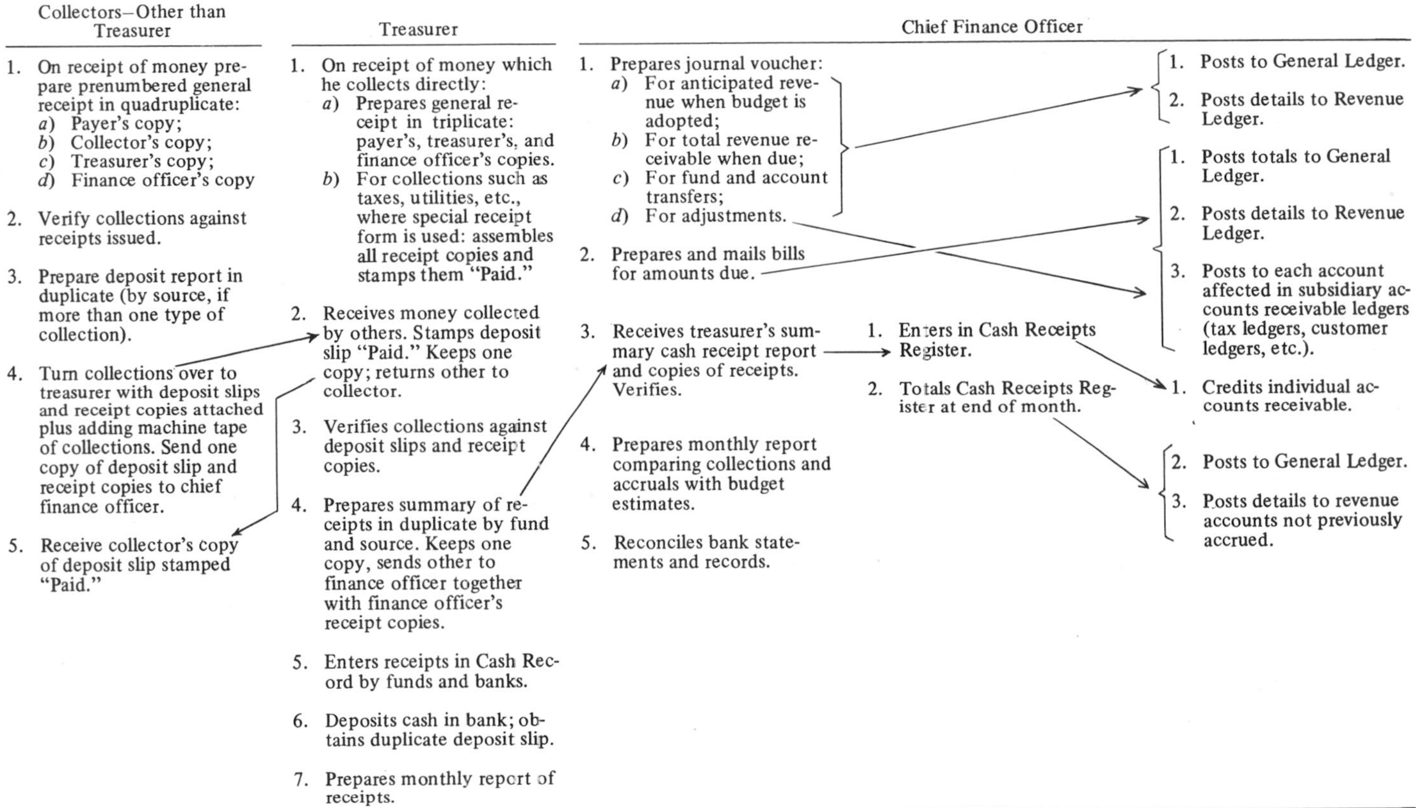

Collectors—Other than Treasurer

1. On receipt of money prepare prenumbered general receipt in quadruplicate:
   a) Payer's copy;
   b) Collector's copy;
   c) Treasurer's copy;
   d) Finance officer's copy
2. Verify collections against receipts issued.
3. Prepare deposit report in duplicate (by source, if more than one type of collection).
4. Turn collections over to treasurer with deposit slips and receipt copies attached plus adding machine tape of collections. Send one copy of deposit slip and receipt copies to chief finance officer.
5. Receive collector's copy of deposit slip stamped "Paid."

Treasurer

1. On receipt of money which he collects directly:
   a) Prepares general receipt in triplicate: payer's, treasurer's, and finance officer's copies.
   b) For collections such as taxes, utilities, etc., where special receipt form is used: assembles all receipt copies and stamps them "Paid."
2. Receives money collected by others. Stamps deposit slip "Paid." Keeps one copy; returns other to collector.
3. Verifies collections against deposit slips and receipt copies.
4. Prepares summary of receipts in duplicate by fund and source. Keeps one copy, sends other to finance officer together with finance officer's receipt copies.
5. Enters receipts in Cash Record by funds and banks.
6. Deposits cash in bank; obtains duplicate deposit slip.
7. Prepares monthly report of receipts.

Chief Finance Officer

1. Prepares journal voucher:
   a) For anticipated revenue when budget is adopted;
   b) For total revenue receivable when due;
   c) For fund and account transfers;
   d) For adjustments.
2. Prepares and mails bills for amounts due.
3. Receives treasurer's summary cash receipt report and copies of receipts. Verifies.
4. Prepares monthly report comparing collections and accruals with budget estimates.
5. Reconciles bank statements and records.

1. Enters in Cash Receipts Register.
2. Totals Cash Receipts Register at end of month.

1. Posts to General Ledger.
2. Posts details to Revenue Ledger.

1. Posts totals to General Ledger.
2. Posts details to Revenue Ledger.
3. Posts to each account affected in subsidiary accounts receivable ledgers (tax ledgers, customer ledgers, etc.).

1. Credits individual accounts receivable.

2. Posts to General Ledger.
3. Posts details to revenue accounts not previously accrued.

*Municipal Finance Officers Association of the United States and Canada, *Simplified Municipal Accounting* (Chicago, 1950), p. 92.

After receipt of cash has been made a matter of record, the next step is proper and complete reporting. Since a governmental unit may operate several funds, it is important to determine with certainty and to report the one to which each receipt belongs. Ownership of most cash is ascertainable without difficulty, but some collections may be of such miscellaneous nature that the classification should be settled by someone with recognized authority to decide doubtful cases. Within each fund, it is imperative to indicate the exact credit to be recorded for the cash received. These credits may be to receivables, to revenue accounts for income not previously accrued, to liability accounts, to asset accounts for investments or properties sold, to expenditures accounts for refunds, and to others. Reporting of collections should be done in some prescribed form with supporting documents arranged in a predetermined manner, the entire arrangement devised to accomplish accurate and speedy recording of the transactions represented. Cash receipts should be delivered or deposited in total, without reductions for disbursements; but this admonition is sometimes ignored for convenience.

Classification by Fund

Techniques and rules for recording cash received by a governmental unit are primarily responsibilities of the accounting department. It is charged with assuring that receipts are distributed to the various funds or activities to which they pertain. In simpler terms, this means that the accounting department must see that each fund or activity gets the cash to which it is rightfully entitled. Concerning the other side of the transaction, the sources from which cash is received must be recorded with accuracy. If it came from individuals or others to whom some charge had been made on a prior occasion, its recording must provide for properly crediting the accounts of those who had previously been charged. If no formal charge had been made, the credit will indicate the revenue or other source from which the collection originated, in order that statements and other financial reports may be prepared.

Media for the recording of cash receipts by the accounting department will normally consist of duplicate copies of receipts, stubs of licenses, etc., issued, but sometimes will consist only of classified summaries of departmental collections. These media may originate in departments, in special cashiers' offices, or in the main office of the treasury itself. Preferably, media and records for cash collections submitted to the accounting department should include not only copies or portions of the underlying document for each transaction but also a formal summarization showing sources and ownership of cash collected. These evidences may be accompanied by one or more copies of a bank deposit slip if the collection was deposited directly by the collecting agency, or by the collectors themselves.

Going a step further in control, some procedures may require formal permission by the controller before the collections may be presented to the treasurer. This permission may be in the form of a document known as a *deposit warrant*, *pay-in warrant*, or order, which is basically a formal acknowledgment that the collections and records thereof are accepted and an authorization to the treasury to receive them. One large city requires mulitple copies of a "treasury deposit slip" to be presented with departmental collections. If the collections and report are in order, two copies are authenticated to indicate acceptance of the departmental report and approval for transfer of the collection to the treasury.

Two kinds of postings will be made from the media accumulated in the recording and handling of cash receipts. These are postings to detailed accounts and postings to summary or control accounts. Postings to accounts with customers and other debtors, existing in the form of receivables, may possibly be made from registers or other summaries of cash received; but the better practice seems to be to make postings of this sort from copies of receipts, from stubs, or from other basic evidence of the transaction, with postings to the receivables control being made from a summary of all collections on receivables. Ledgers of customers' accounts and ledgers of revenues and expenditures may be kept in central computer files, in departmental offices (as for utilities), or in the general office of accounts. Postings to revenue subsidiary ledger accounts may be made from totals of groups or batches of media representing collections of each kind of revenue. Postings to the Revenues controlling account will be made in the form of some total figure, such as the amount of all revenue collected during the day or possibly month, depending upon the form of original-entry record used.

Custody and Protection of Cash

As mentioned previously, one device used to protect against loss is the bonding of all employees entrusted with handling cash. To make this safeguard protective to the fullest extent, daily or other frequent checks must be made upon cash in the custody of the individuals bonded. A common practice contributing to this end is the preparation of daily or other periodic cash statements accounting for beginning balances, increases, decreases, and ending balances. Wherever possible, increase and decrease totals should be properly substantiated by documentary evidence—for example, copies of paid *warrants for disbursements*. A disbursement warrant is essentially a formal certification of the validity of a debt, with authorization or direction to a financial agent to pay the debt. A warrant, therefore, advances a claim one step beyond a voucher in the payment process.

Under some circumstances, variations may exist between cash as shown by the accounting department and cash according to the treasurer's records. Certain transactions may have been recorded by one and not by the other. Accounting for warrants payable is a common source of difference between the two sets of records. Let it be assumed that the accounting department credits Cash to record warrants drawn upon the treasury, whereas the treasurer credits Cash only when a check is issued or when the warrant is countersigned and issued, if the warrant serves as a bill of exchange after signature by the treasurer. At a given time, warrants issued by the accounting department but not yet covered by payments in the treasurer's office would cause the records of cash in the two offices to differ. On the other hand, the accounting department may treat warrants as liability instruments and not credit Cash (and debit Warrants Payable) until evidence of disbursement has been received from the treasurer's office. In this event, warrant payments which have not yet been taken up on the controller's books would cause variance between the two Cash accounts. Thus, in governmental accounting, cash reconciliations must recognize not only deposits in transit, outstanding checks, and other similar causes of difference found in reconciling individual and commercial bank accounts, but also another set of differences in the form of variances between accounting and treasury records. To be complete, governmental cash reconciliations must be extended to incorporate both sets of variations.

The selection of depositories of public funds must be made with extreme care to provide a maximum of safety. Some states, if not all, have enacted statutes more or less regulating deposits of public funds. In some states, public funds are given priority of settlement over private deposits in the liquidation of banks. In others, certain standards of safety are prescribed, such as classification as a national bank or protection by the Federal Deposit Insurance Corporation, or both. However, the maximum direct insurance provided by FDIC protection is only $20,000 except for some very special types of trust funds in the custody of the governmental unit.[1] Another common form of protection is the requirement that the depository of public funds must give security in excess of the amount of deposits of public funds which it holds. At least one state requires banks to enter into a formal contract with the governmental unit to cover their extra liability as public depositories.

Corollary to the protection of cash is the question of investing temporary excess funds in readily marketable securities. Any supplementary revenue which may be earned by a governmental unit reduces by that much burden on taxpayers; but it should be borne in mind that safety is of paramount importance in handling public money, which limits the investment field to items of gilt-edge quality.

How many bank accounts should a governmental unit maintain?

[1] In February 1974, the United States House of Representatives voted to extend 100 percent insurance to time deposits of state and local governments. Senate hearings on this bill were scheduled for March 19–21, 1974.

Should it have a separate bank account (not necessarily in separate banks) for each fund, bearing in mind that some states and municipalities may have a multiplicity of funds? To this question there is no one answer which will satisfactorily cover all situations. One argument favoring numerous bank accounts is that it is thus simpler to correlate the cash of each fund with the bank balance which belongs to it than if cash of several funds is mingled in one account. A second argument favoring separate bank accounts for each fund is that unauthorized interfund borrowing through fund overdrafts is made more difficult. If cash of two or more funds is deposited in one bank account, the cash of one fund may be overdrawn without showing as a bank overdraft, because of being covered by cash belonging to the other fund. Favoring a limited number of bank accounts are the arguments that fewer bank reconciliations are necessary at the end of each month and that consolidation of fund cash into a small number of accounts gives more substantial balances and minimizes overdrafts and service charges which might result from numerous small balances.

In determining the number of bank accounts to be used, convenience and details of the situation must be weighed carefully before making a decision. If only a few funds exist, a separate bank account for each one may be desirable and feasible. If the governmental unit has many funds, some consolidation would probably be advisable or even necessary—perhaps a separate bank account for each type of fund, such as general, trust, etc. Different colors of checks can be used to distinguish between disbursements applicable to the several funds participating in the joint account. The exact measure of consolidation or separation to be practiced should be the one which, based on experience, gives maximum accuracy with a minimum of time and effort.

Large municipalities and states have the problem of accounting for cash that is collected in regional, district, or departmental offices and which cannot well be delivered to the main treasury for acknowledgment and deposit. A sound and convenient method for handling such collections is to require them to be deposited daily to the credit of the governmental unit to which they belong. This reduces the danger of loss and also makes the collection promptly available for use by the fund to which it belongs. Multiple copies of receipted tickets should be obtained for these deposits, enough to provide at least one each for the depositing agent, the controller, and the treasurer of the governmental unit represented. Best results are obtained if the controller's and treasurer's copies are mailed to them by the depository.

Cash Records

As suggested elsewhere, the form of records used to account for cash in the control of a governmental finance officer is subject to numerous variations; however, at least two requirements are fundamental:

1. The finance officer's (treasurer's) records must show exactly the amount of cash in his custody. This must include both bank balances and undeposited receipts.
2. The finance officer's records must show the ownership of all the cash in his custody, that is, the amount belonging to each fund.

Charges to his cash accounts and credits to his equity accounts will derive largely from collections turned over for the credit of the funds. Credits to his cash accounts and charges to equity accounts will derive principally from disbursement documents, probably either a warrant for payment presented by the controller, countersigned by the treasurer, and issued to the creditor, or a check based upon a warrant presented by the controller. Another type of change may be an interfund transfer based upon a transfer warrant and not requiring a disbursement document; however, some governmental units require that even interfund settlements be accomplished by a disbursement warrant or check. Although records of the treasurer's office are likely to be more or less simple in form, they must provide for the ultimate in accuracy and be of such nature as to facilitate frequent proving and reporting of funds on hand.

Two kinds of situations may arise to complicate record keeping for the treasury. One of these is the receipt of uncollectible checks and counterfeit money, and the other is shortages and overages. To provide a measure of protection against uncollectible checks, some governmental units require a notation on each check to show the number of the receipt or other document issued for the check. This facilitates correlating the check with the transaction and allows it to be charged back, sometimes with an additional penalty charge, if it was for payment of a receivable, or allows cancellation of the license, permit, or other privilege represented. To minimize the danger of loss from accepting counterfeit money, special memoranda, usually involving identification of the payer, may be required on all currency exceeding a given denomination. Cashiers or other collecting agents may be held chargeable for counterfeits accepted. To reduce disruption of regular procedures on account of uncollectible checks, some governmental units operate a special cash revolving fund from which to finance uncollectible checks. Exact details of this plan may vary, but one common characteristic is that restitution is made directly to the revolving fund when the delayed item is collected.

Cash shortages and overages are unavoidable in handling large amounts of cash. Practices in accounting for these conditions vary extensively in the field of governmental accounting. Every reasonable effort should be made to determine the cause of each shortage and to correct it. If the effort is unsuccessful, the responsible cashier may be charged with the amount of the shortage; or it may be classified and accounted for as an additional disbursement. Shortages of large amounts which arise from misappropriation or other gross irregularities should be recovered from the cashier's bondsman. Causes of overages, likewise, should be carefully investigated and corrections made, if possible. Unadjusted overages should be credited to a revenue or other balance account. Some governmental units operate a Cash Short or Over account for recording shortages and overages for which adjustments or corrections have not been possible. One thoroughly reprehensible practice in handling cash overages and shortages is to make no record of them but to operate an unofficial fund into which overages are placed and from which shortages are made up. On the contrary, every individual overage and shortage should be made a matter of record, for administrative use. Employees experiencing a high frequency of shortages and overages should be relieved of cashier duties.

Accounting for Disbursements

Although custody of governmental cash is primarily a responsibility of the finance officer, general accounting for disbursements, as well as for collections, is principally a duty of the chief accountant. In addition to making sure that all disbursements are properly classified as to the account or accounts to be charged, he must also be on guard that only legal, authorized purposes shall be served; that all laws, rules, and regulations governing the form, manner, and method of disbursing have been complied with; and that the amount and timing of payments are correct. Use of a well-developed voucher system is one of the best ways of making sure that a claim for payment receives regular, methodical scrutiny before final approval. Having been approved for payment, and a full record of the liability and related accounting facts having been made, the liability is passed to the finance officer in the form of a warrant or order for payment. Unlike the related voucher, the payment warrant will ordinarily cover only a few points, although an extra copy of the voucher might be utilized as a warrant. Among those points are the name of the fund to which the payment is to be charged; the amount ordered to be paid; identification of the claim, preferably by number, to which the warrant pertains; and authentication by the accounting officer. Payment warrants are of two general types. If the document is to be exclusively an order to pay, the actual disbursement will require the writing of a check, identification of which should be recorded on the warrant, and vice versa. Another form of warrant, previously referred to, is initially an order to pay; but by the insertion of a depository's name and the signature of the finance officer, it becomes a bill of exchange, to be accounted for as a Cash (or bank) credit.

If prescribed accounting procedures entail some delay between the issuance and payment of warrants, they may require accounting recognition as very current liabilities during the interval. Vouchers Payable would be debited and Warrants Payable credited by the accounting department to record this advancement of the claim toward payment. Upon receipt of official advice that payment has been made, Warrants Payable would be debited. If payment of the warrant follows promptly upon presentation to the finance department, it may be the practice to classify the issuance as a disbursement, with a debit to the liability account and a credit to Cash. Because of these variances in practice, a warrant is sometimes merely a form of liability and at other times a cash disbursement medium.

Cash Statements

Some cash statements serve the primary purpose of internal control, whereas others are chiefly instruments for general administration and guidance. In the former category are daily cash statements and periodic reconciliations, to mention the more common ones. In the latter are periodic statements setting forth receipts and disbursements by source and purpose and by funds, or in some less detailed form; detailed statements along other lines for individual funds or groups of funds; statements for a year to date, with projection into the future to forecast the probability of having to borrow; and others.

Treasurer's Daily Cash Statement

Statements of this type may serve two purposes:

1. They provide a constant check upon the treasurer's records as a means of detecting irregularities and normal errors.
2. They provide daily information on the amount of money unrestricted and available for use.

If some collections and disbursements are handled outside the main offices, the validity of the treasurer's daily statements requires immediate reporting of these extramural transactions in order that they may be incorporated in the summary report without undue delay to its preparation and issuance. In so far as possible, the treasurer's daily report (see Illustration 15–2) should be supported by documentary evidence of changes included therein.

At the end of each month, daily cash reports may be recapitulated in a monthly cash report of the same form. Daily cash reports aid the treasurer in detecting irregularities that may have occurred in his department, either in handling or in reporting cash; and they are useful also to the controller as a means of constant check on the treasurer's activity. Both daily and monthly reports may be expanded to show transfers in and transfers out, or any other form of information that may contribute to more effective control. Whether subsidiary to the daily cash report

Illustration 15–2

COUNTY OF RANDOLPH
All Funds
Treasurer's Daily Report
December 18, 19x9

Explanation	*General Fund*	*Library Fund*	*Trust Funds*	*Special Assessment Funds*	*Total*
Balance, preceding day	$15,000	$9,000	$82,000	$13,000	$119,000
Receipts for today	4,200	160		4,100	8,460
Total.	$19,200	$9,160	$82,000	$17,100	$127,460
Disbursements for today	14,300	6,280		600	21,180
Closing balance, today	$ 4,900	$2,880	$82,000	$16,500	$106,280

shown in Illustration 15–2 or in addition to it, the treasurer may be required to submit a daily list of disbursements, either in the form of warrants countersigned and issued or in the form of warrants paid by check.

Other Cash Reports

Also at the end of each month, the treasurer may be called upon to submit, in addition to the summary described above, an analysis of cash balances, including both bank deposits and actual cash, subdivided by funds—that is, a simple cash balance sheet for each fund.

For inclusion in the published annual report, it may be desirable to provide a somewhat more elaborate statement including the following:

1. A summary of cash transactions by funds for the year, with an indication of fund equities in the closing balances.
2. A statement showing the composition of the total ending balance.
3. The treasurer's certification.

A good example of such a statement is shown in Illustration 15–3.

It is desirable that summaries of bank balances be supplemented by information to indicate that these balances are fully protected in the event that the depository should experience financial difficulty. The information may be given in various forms. An example of one possible form is shown in Illustration 15–4.

The last one of the treasurer's statements to be mentioned here is a bank reconciliation, in which the treasurer accounts for differences between ending bank balances per his records and ending bank balances per bank statements. This statement has the usual purposes of bank reconciliations: first, to explain normal differences between the two sets of figures; and, second, to bring to light possible variances requiring investigation and possibly other action, such as corrections or adjustments.

Illustration 15–3

CITY OF MIDDLETOWN
Treasury Department

To the City Auditor:

General statement of accountability of the City Treasurer of the city of Middletown for funds of the said city for the year ended December 31, 1974.

Fund	*Balance at January 1, 1974*	*Receipts for Period*	*Total for Period*	*Disbursements for Period*	*Balance at December 31, 1974*
General	$ 911,678.92	$ 6,270,021.11	$ 7,181,700.03	$ 6,341,189.09	$ 840,510.94
Improvement	385,373.69	7,181,546.35	7,566,920.04	5,113,228.10	2,453,691.94
School	218,552.07	2,863,286.94	3,081,839.01	2,944,106.91	137,732.10
Pension	4,896.28	54,139.27	59,035.55	54,019.32	5,016.23
Sinking	817,753.98	792,903.89	1,610,657.87	683,868.90	926,788.97
Water	897,187.91	870,094.86	1,767,282.77	992,343.86	774,938.91
Lillian May Cocke	592.60	8.88	601.48		601.48
Federal airport	50,839.30	31,471.03	82,310.33	58,042.97	24,267.36
1955 annex fund	1,102,818.09	437,192.71	1,540,010.80	1,079,760.11	460,250.69
Total	$4,389,692.84	$18,500,665.04	$22,890,357.88	$17,266,559.26	$5,623,798.62

CERTIFICATE

I hereby certify that the foregoing is a true statement of my accountability to the city of Middletown for the funds of the various accounts thereof for the year ending December 31, 1974; that said foregoing statement is correct; and that to cover the amount of accountability to the said city of Middletown at December 31, 1974, as stated in the foregoing statement, I hold the following:

Cash in hand	$ 11,773.81
Cash in the First National Exchange Bank	2,157,323.25
Cash in the Colonial-American National Bank	395,893.23
Cash in the Mountain Trust Bank	529,594.58
Cash in the Bank of Virginia	380,000.00
Cash in the Liberty Trust Branch–Colonial-American National Bank	50,000.00
Roanoke city bonds	58,000.00
U.S. government bonds, water fund	541,100.00
U.S. Treasury bonds, improvement fund	1,500,000.00
Coupons paid held for warrant	113.75
	$5,623,798.62

H. E. WAHL, City Treasurer

Dated January 13, 1975

Illustration 15–4

VILLAGE OF CLAREMORE
Bank Balances, Insurance, and Collateral
As of February 28, 1975

Explanation	*Balance in Account*	*Date Designated*	*Insurance FDIC*	*Collateral*	
				Amount	*Description*
First National Bank, Two Harbors	$16,910.88	4-4-70	$15,000	$39,400	U.S. bonds
Commercial State Bank, Two Harbors	29,621.03	7-1-71	15,000	50,000	U.S. bonds

Cash reconciliations should also be prepared by the controller. Prior to preparation of his own reconciliations, the controller should be provided with a copy of the treasurer's reconciliation and with reports of bank balances obtained directly from the depositories themselves. A standard certificate form may be furnished the banks for supplying this information, or copies of bank statements in the conventional form may be utilized. Reconciliations by the controller will likely be somewhat more complex than those prepared by the treasurer because the former must bring into agreement not two balances but three: his own, the treasurer's, and the bank's.

Because of the irregularity of cash receipts and the relatively uniform rate of expenditure, proper financial management of governmental funds dictates systematic forecasting of cash positions. This practice will indicate in advance the probable needs for temporary financing, or it may suggest the possibility of deferring expenditures and thus avoiding the borrowing of funds. One plan of cash forecasting involves a detailed estimate of receipts by funds, followed by a summary taking into account beginning balances and expenditures as well as estimated receipts. An acceptable form for estimating receipts is suggested by Illustration 15–5.

Illustration 15–5

TOWN OF NASHVILLE
General Fund
Statement of Actual and Estimated Receipts for
Year to Date, This Month, and Next Month
August 31, 1975

	Year to Date			*This Month*		*Next Month*
Class of Revenue	*Budget Estimate*	*Actual*	*Difference*	*Estimated*	*Actual*	*Estimated*
1. Taxes	$46,000	$49,000	$3,000	$ 500	$ 700	$1,300
2. Licenses and permits	2,500	2,100	400*	350	475	950
3. Other classes	17,900	21,300	3,400	2,100	3,050	3,400
Total General Fund	$66,400	$72,400	$6,000	$2,950	$4,225	$5,650

*Deficiency

If normal receipts are expected to be insufficient to cover requirements to a given date, the result will be a negative balance, which will be approximately the amount of financing required from outside the fund. The necessity for a loan may be indicated also by expanding the statement by including the title "Loans Required," which will permit showing formally the amount of borrowing expected to be necessary. Information for preparation of the two statements shown in Illustrations 15–5 and 15–6 will be obtained from pertinent records accumulated for the current

Illustration 15–6

TOWN OF AVONDALE
All Funds
Forecast of Cash Position for
May, 1975

Item	*General Fund*	*Sewer Fund*	*Other Funds*	*Total*
Cash at beginning of month	$ 18,700	$179,600	$113,200	$311,500
Estimated receipts (see schedule)	99,200	4,200	287,900	391,300
Total.	$117,900	$183,800	$401,100	$702,800
Estimated expenditures	21,400	137,000	274,800	433,200
Estimated balance at end of month. . .	$ 96,500	$ 46,800	$126,300	$269,600

year to date, from records of actual receipts for comparable segments of the prior year or years, and from other sources which may reflect probable changes from past experience. To illustrate, amounts to be received from other agencies frequently will be announced a considerable time before the actual payment is made. Such information may foretell a very definite change up or down. Likewise, cash to be received from property tax levies will tend to vary directly with the amounts levied, so changes in amounts of levies should be evaluated in forming estimates of future receipts from that source.

Cash reports on an annual basis for which controllers are responsible include summaries of estimated receipts and disbursements classified by funds and sources; an annual, detailed statement of receipts and disbursements for each fund (or group of funds of a given type); and an annual combined statement of receipts and disbursements for all funds. Estimates of total receipts and disbursements for a fiscal period are essentially a part of the process of budget making and are referred to in Chapter 2, on that subject. They are prepared along the same lines as cash forecasts for shorter periods (see Illustration 15–6). The annual statement of cash receipts and disbursements for each fund is typically a part of the reporting procedure for individual funds. However, the combined statement of receipts and disbursements for all funds may be regarded primarily as a cash reporting device which assists in rounding out the complete record of the cash that has been available, what has been done with it, and what is left, for correlation with the treasurer's report on his own stewardship of cash.

In preparing the combined statement of cash receipts and disbursements for all funds, the most convenient source of information should be utilized. It is quite likely that statements of cash receipts and disbursements by funds will be found most satisfactory for this purpose, because the combined report will be substantially a condensation of information contained in the individual fund statements. The form of the combined statement may be modified to suit individual preferences and special conditions or requirements but in general will probably follow the pattern of Illustration 15–7.

Illustration 15–7

CITY OF LA CROSSE
Summary of Cash Receipts and Disbursements
For the Year 1974

Fund	*Beginning Balance*	*Receipts*	*Transfers In*	*Transfers Out*	*Disbursements*	*Ending Balance*
eneral fund	$ 20,000	$ 500,000		$ 41,000	$ 452,000	$ 27,000
reet fund	2,000	231,000	$ 18,000		239,000	12,000
rust funds	12,000	62,000	39,000	7,000	87,000	19,000
ther funds	240,000	872,000	53,000	62,000	761,000	342,000
ll Funds	$274,000	$1,665,000	$110,000	$110,000	$1,539,000	$400,000

Conclusion

The cash procedures described in this chapter represent a few of the many possibilities for cash accounting. Some would be entirely unsuited to use by small units of government, and no attempt should be made to follow them. Others might be adaptable with modifications. Bearing in mind the elusive nature of cash, governmental administrators should adopt the best procedures possible, under prevailing conditions, to make sure that the governmental unit receives all cash to which it is entitled; that cash is fully safeguarded while in the government's possession; and that it is spent for only legal, authorized purposes. These precepts are important for the benefit of citizens and for the protection of public officials as well.

SELECTED REFERENCES

American Institute of Certified Public Accountants. *Audits of State and Local Governmental Units.* New York, 1974.

Betts, Bert A. "Treasury and Cash Management," *Municipal Finance,* Vol. 38, no. 1 (August 1965), pp. 57–60.

Horn, Frederick E. "Managing Cash," *Journal of Accountancy,* Vol. 117, no. 4 (April 1964), pp. 56–62.

Kaufman, Stuart F. "Internal Control Principles Applied to Banks," *Journal of Accountancy,* Vol. 117, no. 4 (April 1964), pp. 49–55.

Klose, Ralph A., and Ferguson, Don E. *Cash Handling Manual.* Wichita, Kans.: City of Wichita Finance Director, November 1960.

Maddison, Lawrence B. "Nongovernmental Methods of Internal Control," *Municipal Finance,* Vol. 25, no. 2 (November 1952), pp. 83–86.

MUNICIPAL FINANCE OFFICERS ASSOCIATION OF THE UNITED STATES AND CANADA. *Finance Department Organization*, Special Bulletin 1958 H. Chicago, 1958.

QUESTIONS

15–1. A public improvement project was accomplished by a combination of using the municipality's own working force and contracting with a private contractor. Before completion of a project a quantity of materials was salvaged and sold for cash. Suggest internal control procedures which would encourage municipal employees to deposit the cash to the city's account rather than their own.

15–2. Many medium-sized and almost all large cities have computerized their accounting systems fully. What impact upon cash control would you expect this to have had? Why?

15–3. Satisfactory accounting for cash from court fines and penalties is a continuing problem for governmental units which have those sources of revenue. Suggest a practicable system which would give acceptable control.

15–4. Some large governmental units permit managers of branch collecting offices to make deposits in the managers' own names. State three difficulties or complications which might arise from that practice.

15–5. Sometimes a governmental unit with a limited amount of cash will endeavor to "window-dress" its liabilities at the end of a fiscal period by writing and recording checks in payment of the liabilities, but will hold the checks until a later date, thus avoiding a bank overdraft. Would you consider such checks as outstanding in preparing a bank reconciliation? If you were an outside auditor charged with preparing correct financial statements for the governmental unit, what would you do about the situation described?

15–6. A common procedure for collecting parking meter receipts includes the following operations:

a) Collections are made by an unattended policeman equipped with a sizable container.

b) The meter is opened, the coin receptacle removed, and its contents poured into the policeman's container.

c) The container is taken to police headquarters for emptying, sorting, and counting.

Comment on the acceptability of the internal control.

15–7. Bank service charges are customarily deducted from each depositor's account. If state law requires a municipality to prepare a warrant for each expenditure, how can the city treasurer adhere to the law and conform with banking practice?

15–8. A governmental unit has recently abandoned the practice of requiring public officers and employees who handle cash, or are responsible for handling it, to be bonded. Enumerate reasons in favor of the action of this governmental unit; enumerate reasons why the bonding practice should have been retained.

15–9. *a*) State in a general way what disposition should be made of the Cash Short and Over account in financial statements of a governmental unit.

b) Is the disposition of the Cash Short and Over account any more difficult for a governmental unit than for a commercial enterprise?

15–10. The cash procedures system of the municipality provided for signing of cash disbursement warrants by its chief accounting officer, with countersigning by the treasurer before issue. Accustomed to being absent from his office a great deal, the treasurer followed the practice of signing his name to a number of blank warrant forms, so that his absence would not delay payment of creditors. Comment on this practice.

15–11. In the process of preparing a prenumbered warrant to be issued by the treasurer's office as a disbursement instrument, an error was made, and a substitute warrant was prepared. What disposition should have been made of the first document?

15–12. Some governmental accounting systems require a pay-in warrant or other authorization before cash receipts are formally accepted from a collection agency or office. What is the purpose of that requirement?

EXERCISES AND PROBLEMS

15–1. An auditor examined the records (single-entry) of a county treasurer as of March 31, and determined the facts stated below:

The sum of all cash ledger balances up to and including last settlement (reconciliation) between the auditor and treasurer was $272,480. The Depository (or treasurer's) Record showed a March 31 balance of $386,303.

Collections made and receipted by the treasurer subsequent to his last settlement with the auditor (not in cash ledger balances) were as follows: general taxes, $108,500; ditch assessments, $580; bank and savings and loan taxes, $4,975; advertising costs for tax sale, $6.00; and dog tax, $5.00. The treasurer had collected $154 from sale of hunting licenses but had failed to make a record of the collection.

Demand fees totaling $10 which belonged to the county sheriff had not yet been removed from cash. Cash not yet receipted but on hand in the office at the close of business on March 31 amounted to $407.

Examination of receipts and cash transaction memoranda revealed that a $57.50 collection had been receipted to the auditor as $37.50, while a $29 collection had been receipted as $19.

Outstanding warrants at March 31 totaled $1,550 and a deposit of $8,851 was in transit. The bank statement showed a balance of $379,002 at March 31.

From the foregoing information, you are required to prepare a reconciliation between the sum of all cash ledger balances and the depository record balance, and another between the bank statement and the depository record balance. Do not reconcile to actual cash balances in either case.

(Indiana State Board of Accounts, adapted)

15–2. Two sets of cash records are kept for the Johnson County Home, one by the county treasurer and one by the home superintendent.

The cash balance on the treasurer's books at January 1, 19x1, was $2,350. The superintendent's books showed $1,250. The difference was due to a payment received from a state agency on December 31, 19x0, and recorded by the treasurer on that date but not recorded by the superintendent until the next year.

On the superintendent's record, 19x1 receipts totals were $87,800, and total disbursements were $84,110. Among the receipts were $65 from sale of toys made by the children and $85 from sale of agricultural products, neither of which had been reported to the county treasurer by the end of the year. The sum of $750 cash contributed to the home by an anonymous donor was first reported to the county treasurer in January, 19x2. Disbursements not of record on the treasurer's books until 19x2 were $395 paid by the superintendent for Christmas presents and $130 for a Christmas party. Another cause of difference was a $100 underfooting of disbursements by the superintendent.

At the end of December the treasurer had paid a utility bill of $30 and a grocery bill of $580, neither of which was reported to the superintendent until the next month. The treasurer showed a December receipt of $1,320 for the home from a state agency, but this was not entered in the superintendent's records until the following month. As of December 31, 19x1, the treasurer's books showed a balance of $5,175.

a) Prepare a reconciliation of the balance per the treasurer's books and the balance per the superintendent's books as of December 31, 19x1.

b) Determine the correct cash balance as of December 31, 19x1, and prepare any correcting or adjusting entries the treasurer would need to make as of December 31, 19x1.

15–3. The balance sheet of Monroe City's general fund as of December 31, 19x4, and a summary of the fund's cash account for 19x5 are shown below:

Assets		*Liabilities, Reserves, Fund Balance*	
Cash	$1,300	Accounts payable	$ 800
Taxes Receivable	3,500	Reserve for Encumbrances	1,100
		Fund Balance	2,900
	$4,800		$4,800

Cash

Jan. 1 Balance	$ 1,300	Accounts payable	$ 800
Prior years' taxes	3,200	Prior year's orders and	
Current year's taxes	76,000	contracts	1,200
Other current revenues	6,000	Current year's orders and	
Sale of old equipment	600	contracts	80,000
Temporary loans	20,000	Stores purchased*	3,000
		Petty cash†	500
		Temporary loans	18,000

***Central storeroom established during year to be accounted for by the general fund. Issues to departments whose expenses are met from this fund amounted to $1,600; the balance is the inventory December 31, 19x5.**

†Petty cash fund established during the year, for use for general operations of the city.

Note: The only taxes considered collectible at the end of 19x5 are current ones amounting to $7,000. Unfilled orders and contracts at 12/31/x5 amount to $900.

Required:

Prepare in good form a general fund balance sheet for Monroe City as of December 31, 19x5.

15–4. Heltonville's accounting system provides for the controller to approve all vouchers that are to be paid and to enter them in a voucher register. When time for payment of the debt arrives, the controller issues a warrant or order to pay, sends the voucher and related warrant to the treasurer, and changes the liability to Warrants Payable. Upon receipt of payment advices from the treasurer, the controller records payment. The controller also records receipts of cash.

Show in general journal form, without explanations, the entries which should have been made on the controller's books for the following transactions which occurred during November:

1. Approval of voucher no. 2120 for personal services, $35,000.
2. Warrant no. 2701 issued for voucher no. 2120.
3. Payment advice received for warrant no. 2701.
4. Collection of current taxes previously accrued, $7,080.
5. Approval of voucher no. 2121 for contractual services for October, $1,180. The transaction had been encumbered for $1,100.
6. Approval of voucher no. 2122 for purchase of office machines, $781. The purchase had been encumbered for $775.
7. Warrant no. 2702 issued for voucher no. 2118, approved in October, for $3,605.
8. Parking meter receipts, $2,434.
9. Payment advice received for warrant no. 2702.
10. Approval of voucher no. 2123 for purchase of uniforms for Police Department, $640. This transaction had been encumbered for $650.
11. Warrant no. 2703 issued for voucher no. 2122.
12. Collection of delinquent taxes previously accrued, $726.
13. Payment advice received for warrant no. 2703.

14. Warrant no. 2704 issued for voucher no. 2119, approved in October, for $5,120.
15. Payment advice received for warrant no. 2704.
16. Parking meter receipts, $1,327.
17. Approval of voucher no. 2124 for a previously recorded judgment of $3,225.
18. Collection of property taxes not due until next year, $104.

15–5. Below is given a collection of information about cash balances, receipts, and disbursements of certain funds of the Town of Milroy:

On March 18, cash balances of the funds were as follows:

General fund	$ 93,600
Capital projects fund	283,851
Stores and service fund	21,780
Special assessment fund no. 86	53,312

Cash receipts on March 19 were as follows:

General fund:	
Taxes	$ 9,576
Parking meter receipts	217
License fees	12
Revenue from other agencies	5,207
Capital projects fund:	
Sale of bonds	48,000
Refund by supplies vendor	10
Stores and service fund:	
Payment of amount due from general fund	529
Special assessment fund No. 86:	
Current assessments	6,885
Delinquent assessments	420
City's share of cost	10,200
Interest on assessments	456

Cash payments on March 19 were as follows:

General fund:	
Payments for personal services	$ 2,850
Payment for commodities bought on account	1,650
Payment of bond interest	2,400
Payment of amount due to stores and service fund	529
Remittance of withholding tax	876
Capital projects fund:	
Payroll	10,200
Contracts payable	110,000
Accounts payable	9,861
Cash purchase of construction supplies	162
Stores and service fund:	
Heat, light, and power	219
Payment for supplies bought on account	4,660
Cash purchase of supplies which are accounted for on a perpetual inventory basis	240

You are required to do the following things (use one cash account):

a) For each fund, prepare a compound entry for March 19 cash receipts.

b) For each fund, prepare a compound entry for March 19 cash disbursements.

c) Prepare a treasurer's daily cash report for all funds.

15–6. All disbursements of the City of Bedford are made on warrants issued by the controller and countersigned by the treasurer. The controller records all disbursements as credits to Cash at the time the warrants are issued. Since the warrants become bills of exchange upon being countersigned, the treasurer records cash disbursements as such at the time he countersigns the warrants. On May 31, the controller's books showed the following balances:

General fund	$112,600
Intragovernmental service fund	10,200
Capital projects fund	94,300
Debt service fund	12,000

The balances according to the treasurer's books were as follows:

Explanation	*First National Bank*	*Lawrence National Bank*	*State Trust Company*
General fund	$115,260		
Intragovernmental service fund		$10,322	
Capital projects fund			$98,327
Debt service fund			12,000

A separate bank account is kept for each fund. The bank statements showed the following balances on May 31:

First National Bank	$117,131
Lawrence National Bank	10,859
State Trust Company (capital projects fund)	106,165
State Trust Company (debt service fund)	12,136

The treasurer reports that the following countersigned warrants have not been returned by the bank:

General fund:	
No. 1702	$ 937
1712	489
1714	1,825
1717	715
1718	220
Intragovernmental service fund:	
No. 2431	42
2440	125
2442	283
2443	94
Capital projects fund:	
No. 3674	3,500
3680	740
3684	1,285
3686	375
3687	2,460
Debt service fund:	
No. 4128	820
4131	392
4133	540
4134	260

The following warrants have been issued by the controller but have not been countersigned by the treasurer:

General fund:	
No. 1720	$2,200
1721	300
1722	160
Intragovernmental service fund:	
No. 2444	75
2445	47
Capital projects fund:	
No. 3688	1,450
3689	870
3690	1,707

The following deposits, made on May 31, did not appear on the bank statements:

General fund	$3,200
Capital projects fund	1,500
Debt service fund	2,000

Certain items on the bank statement had not been recorded on the books, as follows:

Interest credited by the bank:	
General fund	$903
Capital projects fund	978
Debt service fund	124
Exchange charges by the bank:	
General fund	18
Intragovernmental service fund	7

You are required to do the following things:

a) Prepare a schedule of outstanding warrants and one of warrants issued by the controller but not countersigned by the treasurer. Totals from these schedules are to be used for requirements (*b*) and (*c*).

b) Prepare a reconciliation in which the bank balance for each fund is reconciled to the treasurer's balance for each fund, which, in turn, is reconciled to the controller's balance for each fund.

c) Prepare a three-part reconciliation in which the balance per bank statement for each fund is reconciled to the actual cash balance, the balance per treasurer's books is reconciled to the actual cash balance, and the balance per controller's books is reconciled to the actual cash balance.

15–7. The City of Sycamore operates on an accrual basis with respect to both revenues and expenditures. It maintains two bank accounts at the First National Bank, one for the general fund and one for the enterprise fund. You are asked to prepare from the following data (*a*) a statement reconciling the balances per the bank with the balances of cash for each fund per the controller's books on December 31, before any correcting entries are made; and (*b*) the journal entries necessary to correct the controller's records, assuming books had been closed.

1. Balance per bank statement: general fund, $50,000; enterprise fund, $28,000.
2. The bank made service charges of $50. Of this amount, $20 was chargeable to the general fund and the remainder to the enterprise fund. These charges have not been recorded by the city.
3. The following checks were outstanding:

General fund:	
G114	$ 115
G115	200
G116	300
G117	150
Enterprise fund:	
U901	50
U902	5
U903	65
U904	1,000

4. Check G108 was for $100 but was recorded in error on the controller's books as $110 because the voucher payable was for that amount.
5. On December 30, the treasurer wrote check G112 for $53 in payment of a voucher chargeable against the enterprise fund. The controller caught this error and corrected it on his books, but the check had already been cashed. To date, no action has been taken on this matter.
6. Checks G116 and G117 were written on December 31. Check G116 was mailed on that day, whereas check G117 was not mailed until January 5. Both were recorded by the controller as December disbursements.
7. Owing to an oversight, general fund money received on December 31, ($250 from taxes receivable, $50 from fines, and check U904 described below), was not recorded until its deposit on January 5. The total deposit on that day—which included also January receipts—was $2,000; and the entire amount was recorded as a January receipt on the controller's books.
8. Check U904 is a payment in lieu of taxes made to the general fund and turned over to that fund on December 31, but not put through for collection by the general fund until January 5. [See item (7) above.]
9. Enterprise accounts receivable in the amount of $300 were collected on December 31, and reflected on the records, but were not deposited until January 2.

(Municipal Finance, adapted)

15–8. The General Medical Institute is a nonprofit corporation without capital stock which accounts for its activities in a single fund. Its comparative financial statements follow:

GENERAL MEDICAL INSTITUTE
Comparative Statement of Revenues and Expenses
For the Years Ended October 31, 19x8 and 19x9

	19x9	*19x8*	*Increase (Decrease)*
Revenue from services rendered:			
Services to patients	$360,000	$304,000	$ 56,000
Less free services	36,000	38,000	(2,000)
Net revenue from services rendered	$324,000	$266,000	$ 58,000
Operating expenses:			
Department expenses:			
Medical services	$ 32,700	$ 29,300	$ 3,400
Medicine and supplies	14,600	10,500	4,100
Nursing services	89,900	76,200	13,700
Therapy services	34,300	31,300	3,000
Dietary	40,700	37,100	3,600
Housekeeping and maintenance	37,300	29,500	7,800
Administration and other	33,700	23,400	10,300
General expenses:			
Rental of leased premises (net)	–	3,100	(3,100)
Depreciation–building and equipment	9,900	8,300	1,600
Provision for uncollectible accounts	5,400	3,500	1,900
Interest expense	6,500	–	6,500
Loss on sale of equipment	2,000	–	2,000
Other	16,200	6,500	9,700
Total expenses	$323,200	$258,700	$ 64,500
Excess of revenues from services rendered over expenses of patient care	$ 800	$ 7,300	$ (6,500)
Other income (expenses):			
Research	$ (13,300)	$ (13,200)	$ (100)
Gain on sale of investments	18,600	3,500	15,100
Investment income	16,500	13,300	3,200
Contributions	10,300	14,800	(4,500)
Grant from government designated for expansion	335,000	–	335,000
Miscellaneous	2,700	1,500	1,200
Total other income	$369,800	$ 19,900	$349,900
Excess of Revenues over Expenses	$370,600	$ 27,200	$343,400

GENERAL MEDICAL INSTITUTE
Comparative Balance Sheets
October 31, 19x8 and 19x9

Assets	*19x9*	*19x8*	*Increase (Decrease)*
Cash	$ 28,600	$ 18,500	$ 10,100
Accounts receivable–patients (net)	75,500	55,500	20,000
Investments (cost)	413,100	463,100	(50,000)
Prepaid expenses	2,200	1,600	600
Land, building, equipment (net)	327,200	333,700	(6,500)
Construction in progress	793,800	–	793,800
Total Assets	$1,640,400	$872,400	$768,000
Liabilities and Fund Balance			
Liabilities:			
Accounts payable–construction	$ 110,800	–	$110,800
Less: Receivables from government agencies	80,000	–	80,000
Accounts payable–construction (net)	$ 30,800	–	$ 30,800
Accounts payable–current operations	11,800	$ 10,200	1,600
Mortgage payable	365,000	–	365,000
Total Liabilities	$ 407,600	$ 10,200	$397,400
Fund balance:			
Balance, January 1	$ 862,200	$835,000	$ 27,200
Excess of revenues over expenses for year	370,600	27,200	343,400
Balance, December 31	$1,232,800	$862,200	$370,600
Total Liabilities and Fund Balance	$1,640,400	$872,400	$768,000

The audit working papers contain the following additional information:

1. Accounts Receivable—Patients are stated at the net of the Allowance for Bad Debts account, which amounted to $10,000 at October 31, 19x8 and $14,600 at October 31, 19x9. During the year bad debts totaling $800 were written off.
2. The research activities are net of research grants aggregating $10,000. Included as a research expense is depreciation of $6,600 on special research equipment.
3. During 19x9 the construction of a new building was begun. The estimated cost of the building and equipment is $1,000,000. The expansion is being financed as follows:

Grant from government	$ 335,000
Mortgage (repayment to begin upon completion of building)	500,000
Special features installed at the request of government agencies and to be paid for by the agencies	80,000
Institute's available funds	85,000
Total	$1,000,000

4. New therapy equipment costing $15,000 was purchased in 19x9 and replaced therapy equipment with a book value of $5,000 which was sold for $3,000.
5. To obtain additional cash working capital, investments with a cost of $50,000 were sold during July.

Prepare a statement accounting for the increase in cash for the year ended October 31, 19x9, to be included in the annual report of the General Medical Institute. The statement should set forth information concerning cash applied to or provided by:

a) Operations.
b) Research activities.
c) Acquisitions of assets.
d) Other sources of funds.

(AICPA, adapted)

16

Federal Government Accounting

Although an accounting structure has been provided for the Federal government of the United States of America by statutes since 1789, the development of the structure lagged far behind the growth in complexity of governmental operations. Occasional efforts of varying effectiveness were made during the first 160 years of the existence of the Federal government to improve the usefulness of its accounting, budgeting, and financial reporting systems, but it was not until after the close of World War II that efforts appear to have been sustained over a significant period of time. The professional accounting consultants to the first and second Hoover Commissions generally are given credit for giving direction to the effort. The views of these consultants as to the nature of accounting appropriate for governmental use were evidently colored by the recommendations of the National Committee on Governmental Accounting—the recommendations elaborated on in Chapters 3–14 of this text—and were strongly influenced by the use in private business of accrual accounting as an aid to financial management. For these reasons, this chapter is focused on the aspects of Federal accounting which differ from the municipal accounting concepts explained in previous chapters.

Accounting and Auditing Policies of the Congress

The creation of the legal framework of the Federal government is the prerogative of the Congress. The accounting and auditing policies of the Congress, therefore, are of fundamental importance to an understanding of Federal accounting. The major policies are expressed in Public Law 784 of the 81st Congress:

Sec. 111. It is the policy of the Congress in enacting this part that—

(*a*) The accounting of the Government provide full disclosure of the results of financial operations, adequate information needed in the management of operations and the formulation and execution of the Budget, and effective control over income, expenditures, funds, property, and other assets.

(*b*) Full consideration be given to the needs and responsibilities of both the legislative and executive branches in the establishment of accounting and reporting systems and requirements.

(*c*) The maintenance of accounting systems and the producing of financial reports with respect to the operations of executive agencies, including central facilities for bringing together and disclosing information on the results of the financial operations of the Government as a whole, be the responsibility of the executive branch.

(*d*) The auditing for the Government, conducted by the Comptroller General of the United States as an agent of the Congress, be directed at determining the extent to which accounting and related financial reporting fulfill the purposes specified, financial transactions have been consummated in accordance with laws, regulations or other legal requirements and adequate internal financial control over operations is exercised, and afford an effective basis for the settlement of accounts of accountable officers.

(*e*) Emphasis be placed on effecting orderly improvements resulting in simplified and more effective accounting, financial reporting, budgeting, and auditing requirements and procedures and on the elimination of those which involve duplication or which do not serve a purpose commensurate with the cost involved.

(*f*) The Comptroller General of the United States, the Secretary of the Treasury, and the Director of the Bureau of the Budget conduct a continuous program for the improvement of accounting and financial reporting in the Government.

The Comptroller General, the Secretary of the Treasury, and the Director of the office often known as the Bureau of the Budget initiated a program for the improvement of accounting and financial reporting in 1947, even before the Congress officially expressed its desire that the three officials do so. Consistent with developments in thought concerning the role of accounting in business management, the program was rapidly broadened in scope until it is now known as the "Joint Financial Management Improvement Program." Since 1966 the Chairman of the Civil Service Commission has participated in this program in recognition of the critical problems of recruiting, classifying, and training people engaged in accounting and other financial management work. In 1970 the Bureau of the Budget was redesignated as the Office of Management and Budget and its functions changed accordingly. In Mid-1973 a number of the financial management functions were transferred from the Office of Management and Budget to the General Services Administration, and the Administrator of General Services was added as a principal in the Joint Financial Management Improvement Program.

A joint program involving the Comptroller General, the Secretary of the Treasury, the Director of the Office of Management and Budget, and the Administrator of General Services, is necessary because the Congress has divided responsibility for accounting and for financial management in the Federal government among not only these four individuals but also the heads of the multitude of civilian and military agencies in the executive branch of the government. The nature of the principal responsibilities, and their interrelationships, is explained in brief in the following sections.

Comptroller General. The Comptroller General of the United States is the head of the General Accounting Office, an agency of the legislative branch of the government. He is appointed by the President with the advice and consent of the Senate for a term of office of 15 years. Under current law the Comptroller General is responsible for prescribing the principles, standards, and related requirements to be observed by each executive agency in the development of its accounting system. The principles, standards, and requirements prescribed by the Comptroller General must be consistent with the policies of the Congress quoted in the preceding section and should be reasonably related to generally accepted principles of accounting as espoused by the profession.

The General Accounting Office has the statutory duty of cooperating with executive agencies in the development of their accounting systems, and cooperating with the Treasury Department in the development of the system of central accounting and reporting. The agency accounting system and the Treasury centralized accounts are to be approved by the Comptroller General when deemed by him to be adequate and in conformity with the principles, standards, and related requirements prescribed by him. The Comptroller General also has the responsibility under sections 201 and 202 (a) of the Legislative Reorganization Act of 1970 to cooperate with the Secretary of the Treasury, Director of the Office of Management and Budget, and Administrator of General Services in developing, establishing and maintaining (1) a standardized information and data processing system for budgetary and fiscal data, and (2) standard classifications of programs, activities, receipts, and expenditures of Federal agencies.

Just as the appropriational authority of municipalities and state governments rests in their legislative bodies, the appropriational authority of the Federal government rests in the Congress. The Congress is, therefore, interested in determining that financial and budgetary reports from executive, judicial, and legislative agencies are reliable; that agency financial management is intelligent, efficient, and economical; and that legal requirements have been met by the agencies. Under the assumption that the reports of an independent audit agency would aid in satisfying these interests of the Congress, the General Accounting Office was created as the audit agency of the Congress itself. The standards of auditing followed by the GAO are discussed in Chapter 21 of this text. In addition to reporting to the Congress the results of its audits, the General Accounting Office is directed by law to review agency accounting systems and make such reports thereon to the Congress as the Comptroller General deems necessary.

Secretary of the Treasury. The Secretary of the Treasury is the head of the Department of the Treasury, a part of the executive branch of the Federal government. The Secretary of the Treasury is a member of the Cabinet of the President, appointed by the President with the advice and consent of the Senate to serve an indefinite term of office. The Department of the Treasury was created in 1789 to receive, keep, and disburse monies of the United States, and to account for them. From the beginning, the word "receive" was construed as "collect," and the Internal Revenue Service, Bureau of Customs, and other agencies active in the enforcement of the collection of revenues due the Federal government are parts of the Treasury Department, as are the Bureau of the Mint, Bureau of Engraving and Printing, Bureau of Public Debt, Office of Treasurer of the United States, and the Bureau of Accounts. The latter two are of most concern in this chapter.

The Secretary of the Treasury is responsible for the preparation of "such reports for the information of the President, the Congress, and the public as will present the results of the financial operations of the Government" (Sec. 114, PL 784, 81st Congress). An additional responsibility of the Secretary of the Treasury is the maintenance of a system of central accounts to provide a basis for consolidation of the accounts of the various executive agencies with those of the Treasury Department.

Statutes provide that the reports of the Secretary of the Treasury shall include financial data needed by the Office of Management and Budget, and that the Treasury Department's system of central accounting and reporting shall be consistent with the principles, standards, and related requirements established by the Comptroller General. Instructions and requirements relating to central accounting, central financial reporting, and various other fiscal matters have been codified by the Treasury Department in the *Treasury Fiscal Requirements Manual* for guidance of departments and agencies.

Director of the Office of Management and Budget. The Director of the Office of Management and Budget is appointed by the President without Senate confirmation because he is a member of the President's staff, not a Cabinet officer. Accordingly, the Office of Management and Budget is a part of the Executive Office of the President. As the direct representative of the President with the authority to control the size and nature of appropriations requested of each Congress, it is obvious that the Director of the Office of Management and Budget is an extremely powerful figure in the Federal government.

The Congress requires the following with respect to the Budget (Sec. 102, PL 784, 81st Congress):

> Sec. 102. (a) Section 201 of such Act [the Budget and Accounting Act of 1921] is amended to read as follows:
>
> "Sec. 201. The President shall transmit to Congress during the first fifteen days of each regular session, the Budget, which shall set forth his Budget message, summary data and text, and supporting detail. The budget shall set forth in such form and detail as the President may determine—
>
> "(a) functions and activities of the Government;
>
> "(b) any other desirable classifications of data;
>
> "(c) a reconciliation of the summary data on expenditures with proposed appropriations;
>
> "(d) estimated expenditures and proposed appropriations necessary in his judgement for the support of the Government for the ensuing fiscal year, except that estimated expenditures and proposed appropriations for such year for the legislative branch of the Government and the Supreme Court of the United States shall be transmitted to the President on or before October 15 of each year, and shall be included by him in the Budget without revision;
>
> "(e) estimated receipts of the Government during the ensuing fiscal year, under (1) laws existing at the time the Budget is transmitted and also (2) under the revenue proposals, if any, contained in the Budget;
>
> "(f) actual appropriations, expenditures, and receipts of the Government during the last completed fiscal year;
>
> "(g) estimated expenditures and receipts, and actual or proposed appropriations of the Government during the fiscal year in progress;
>
> "(h) balanced statements of (1) the condition of the Treasury at the end of the last completed fiscal year, (2) the estimated condition of the Treasury at the end of the fiscal year in progress, and (3) the estimated condition of the Treasury at the end of the ensuing fiscal year if the financial proposals contained in the Budget are adopted;
>
> "(i) all essential facts regarding the bonded and other indebtedness of the Government; and
>
> "(j) such other financial statements and data as in his opinion are necessary or desirable in order to make known in all practicable detail the financial condition of the Government."

It should be noted that the congressional requirements for the budget, listed above, have a number of accounting implications in addition to the explicit historical comparisons which necessitate cooperation among the Office of Management and Budget, Treasury Department, and General Accounting Office. Implicit in the requirements for projections of revenues and receipts is the mandate that the Office of Management and Budget coordinate closely with the Council of Economic Advisers in the use of macroeconomic (the study of the economic system in its aggregate) and macroaccounting (accounting for the economy in the aggregate) forecasts. Macroaccounting is beyond the scope of this text, yet the subject is of great, and increasing, importance in the financial management of the Federal government; and the reader who desires an understanding of Federal financial policies and their integration with political, social, and economic policies should be knowledgeable in the macroeconomic and macroaccounting areas.

The Office of Management and Budget is not only concerned with preparation and submission of the budget; it is also directed by the Congress "to evaluate and develop improved plans for the organization, coordination, and management of the executive branch of the Government with a view to efficient and economical service" (Sec. 104, PL 784, 81st Congress). One important device utilized by the Office of Management and Budget in its effort to improve management of executive agencies, and to relate this effort to justifications for appropriations requested of the Congress, has been the adoption of the business concept of relating budgeted expenditures to planned activities in a meaningful manner. This concept was once known in the Federal government as the Planning-Programming-Budgeting System, usually shortened to PPBS. The ability to present a provable relationship lies in the development of agency cost accounting as well as agency appropriation accounting.

Administrator of General Services. The Administrator of General Services, appointed by the President by and with the advice and consent of the Senate, directs the programs of the General Services Administration.

The General Services Administration was established by the Congress in 1949 as an independent agency in the executive branch of the Federal Government to provide an economical and efficient system for the management of its property and records, including such activities as construction and operation of buildings, procurement and distribution of supplies, disposal of surplus property, traffic and communications management, stockpiling of strategic and critical materials, and creation, preservation, and disposal of records. In 1973 the President, in order to consolidate similar functions, reassigned to the General Services Administration a number of functions formerly performed by the Office of Management and Budget. Financial management functions of the GSA are now centralized within its Office of Federal Management Policy; five major elements of this office are the Office of Management Systems and Special Projects, the Office of Procurement Management, the Office of Property Management, the Office of Automated Data Processing Management, and the Office of Financial Management. Responsibility for issuing Circulars to set forth policies and procedures which must be followed by agencies of the Federal Government in the management, accounting, reporting, and audit of activities now under the jurisdiction of the Office of Federal Management Policy was also transferred from the OMB to the GSA. The effect of these circulars on state and local governmental agencies, nonprofit entities, and certified public accountants is brought out in Chapters 20 and 21 of this text.

Accounting Principles in the Federal Government

The accounting principles and standards prescribed by the Comptroller General of the United States are summarized in the General Accounting Office *Manual for Guidance of Federal Agencies*. The manual emphasizes that the Treasury Department and the Office of Management and Budget participated in the development of the statement of accounting principles and standards; it also emphasizes that the responsibility for establishing and maintaining adequate systems of accounting and control is placed by statute upon the head of each executive agency.

Financial management responsibilities for Federal departments and agencies include the administration of funds and the utilization of property and personnel for authorized programs, activities, or purposes, in an effective, efficient, and economical manner. Accordingly, Federal governmental accounting systems are designed to emphasize the following three aspects of management accountability:

1. Fiscal accountability, which includes fiscal integrity, disclosure, and compliance with applicable laws and regulations.
2. Managerial accountability, which is concerned with the efficient and economical use of personnel and other resources.
3. Program accountability, which is designed to assess whether programs are achieving their intended objectives and whether the best program options have been selected to achieve these objectives from the standpoint of total cost and outputs.

The General Accounting Office manual stresses the role of accounting in agency management and the need for appropriate data on the cost of carrying out operations. The necessity for the accounting system to promote compliance with the law is, of course, also emphasized.

Fund accounting, in a broad sense, is required in the Federal government to evidence agency compliance with requirements of existing legislation. One of the most important acts which causes Federal agencies to adhere to fund accounting concepts is the "Antideficiency Act" (Section

3679 of the Revised Statutes). The principal purposes of this act are to prevent the incurring of obligations or the making of expenditures or disbursements which would create deficiencies in appropriations and funds, to fix responsibility within an agency for excess obligations and expenditures, and to assist in bringing about the most effective and economical use of appropriations and funds. (Title 2, Subsection 10.1, GAO manual.)

Two general types of funds are found in Federal government accounting: (1) those used to account for resources derived from the general taxing and revenue powers or from business operations of the government, and (2) those used to account for resources held and managed by the government in the capacity of custodian or trustee. OMB Circular A–34 provides the following elaboration of the two general types:

1. Funds derived from general taxing and revenue powers and from business operations.
   - A. General fund
   - B. Special funds
   - C. Public enterprise funds
   - D. Intragovernmental funds
   - E. Foreign currency funds
2. Funds held by the government in the capacity of custodian or trustee.
   - A. Trust funds
   - B. Deposit funds

General fund. The general fund is credited with all receipts which are not earmarked by law, and charged with payments out of appropriations of "any money in the Treasury not otherwise appropriated" and out of general borrowings.

Strictly speaking there is only one general fund in the entire Federal government. The Bureau of Accounts of the Treasury Department accounts for the centralized cash balances (the cash is under the control of the Treasurer of the United States; cash accounts subsidiary to those of the Bureau of Accounts are maintained by the Treasurer), the appropriations control accounts, and unappropriated balances. On the books of an agency each appropriation is treated as a fund with its own self-balancing group of accounts; these agency "funds" are subdivisions of *the* general fund. The interrelationships of agency and Treasury accounts are illustrated in a subsequent section of this chapter.

Special funds. Receipt and expenditure accounts established to account for receipts of the government which are earmarked by law for a specific purpose, but which are not generated from a cycle of operations for which there is continuing authority to reuse such receipts (as is true for revolving funds), are classified as "special fund accounts" in

Federal usage. The term and its definition are very close to that of the classification "special revenue funds" used in municipal accounting.

Public enterprise funds. A public enterprise fund is defined in OMB Circular A–34 as a revolving fund credited with collections, primarily from outside of the Government, that are earmarked to finance a continuing cycle of business-type operations, in which the Government is the owner of the enterprise.

Intragovernmental funds. Intragovernmental funds are of two types:

> *Revolving.* A revolving fund is credited with collections, primarily from other agencies and accounts, that are earmarked by law to carry out a cycle of intragovernmental business-type operations, in which the Government is the owner of the activity. This type of fund is quite similar to the type of municipal fund discussed in the chapter on intragovernmental service funds.
>
> *Management (including working funds).* These are funds in which there are merged moneys derived from two or more appropriations, in order to carry out a common purpose or project, but not involving a cycle of operations. Management funds include consolidated working funds which are set up to receive (and subsequently disburse) advance payments, pursuant to law, from other agencies or bureaus.

Foreign currency funds. A foreign currency fund is established to account for foreign currency acquired without payment of United States dollars and which may be expended without charge to dollar appropriations.

Trust funds. Trust funds are established to account for receipts which are held in trust for use in carrying out specific purposes and programs in accordance with agreement or statute. In distinction to revolving funds and special funds, the assets of trust funds are frequently held over a period of time and may be invested in order to produce revenue. For example, the assets of the Federal Old Age and Survivors Insurance Trust Fund is invested in United States bonds.

The corpus of some trust funds is used in business-type operations. In such a case the fund is called a "trust revolving fund." In general the discussion of trust funds in Chapter 8 is applicable in principle to Federal trust funds.

Deposit funds. Combined receipt and expenditure accounts established to account for receipts held in suspense temporarily and later refunded or paid to some other fund, or receipts held by the government as a banker or agent for others and paid out at the discretion of the owner, are classified within the Federal government as "deposit fund accounts." They are similar in nature to the "agency funds" established for municipalities.

Definition of Terms

Certain terms are used in the Federal government in place of those used in municipal accounting, or in slightly different senses. For example:[1]

Accrued expenditures. Charges to the expenditure account during a given period that reflect liabilities incurred, and the need to pay for: (*a*) services performed by employees, contractors, vendors, carriers, grantees, lessors, and other payees; (*b*) goods and other tangible property received; and (*c*) amounts becoming owed under programs for which no current service or performance is required (such as annuities, insurance claims, other benefit payments, and some cash grants; but excluding the repayment of debt, which is considered neither an obligation nor an expenditure). Expenditures accrue regardless of when cash payments are made; whether invoices have been rendered; or in some cases, whether goods or other tangible property have been physically delivered. For purposes of reports under this Circular, accrued expenditures will be reported net of income earned and recoveries. See section 23 for further exposition of the concept and its application to particular types of transactions.

Allocation. Transfers of obligational authority from one agency or bureau to another agency or bureau which are set aside in "transfer appropriation accounts" to carry out the purposes of the parent appropriation or fund.

Allotment. Authority delegated by the head or other authorized employee of an agency to agency employees to incur obligations within a specified amount pursuant to an apportionment or reapportionment of an appropriation or other statutory provision.

Apportionment. A distribution made by OMB of amounts available for obligation in an appropriation or fund account into amounts available for specified time periods, activities, functions, projects, objects, or combinations thereof. The amounts so apportioned limit the obligations that may be incurred.

Obligations incurred. Amounts of orders placed, contracts awarded, services received, and similar transactions during a given period which will require payments during the same or a future period. Such amounts will include disbursements to pay obligations not preceded by the recording of obligations and will reflect adjustments for differences between obligations previously recorded and actual disbursements for those obligations. See section 22 for a more detailed explanation of the concept of obligations, and section 25 for application to specific types of transactions.

Reserves. Portions of appropriations, funds, or contract authority set aside by OMB for (*a*) contingencies; (*b*) savings which are made possible by or through changes in requirements, greater efficiency of operations, or other developments subsequent to the date on which the authority was made available; and (*c*) subsequent apportionment.

[1] All definitions in this section are taken from Office of Management and Budget Circular A-34, Part II, Sec. 21.1. Part III of this OMB Circular is to be reissued by the GSA as a Federal Management Circular, but the quoted definitions will remain a part of OMB Circular A-34.

Federal Account Structure

The account structure appropriate to the funds used in Federal government accounting has been established by the Comptroller General as:

Accounts for assets
Accounts for liabilities
Accounts for investment of the U.S. government
Accounts for investment of others (if applicable)
Accounts for revenues and costs

The first four of the categories are balance sheet accounts, as is true in any branch of accounting; nominal accounts are grouped in the fifth category. The following sections of this chapter illustrate the essential features of the basic account structure of the Federal government.

Federal Agency Balance Sheet Accounts

The balance sheet of a hypothetical nonbusiness-type Federal agency as of the first day of the current fiscal year is shown in Illustration 16–1. Consistent with instructional material used within the Federal government, the current fiscal year is denoted 19CY; the immediately prior fiscal year, 19PY; and the fiscal year immediately following the current one, 19BY, for "Budget Year." The fiscal year in the United States government is the 12-month period from July 1 through the following June 30.

Illustration 16–1

FEDERAL AGENCY
Balance Sheet
July 1, 19CY

Assets			*Liabilities and Investment of the U.S. Government*	
Current Assets:			Current Liabilities:	
Fund balances with U.S. Treasury–19PY		$ 675,000	Accounts payable	$ 275,000
Inventories		610,000		
Total Current Assets		$1,285,000	Total Current Liabilities	$ 275,000
Fixed Assets:			Unliquidated obligations–19PY	400,000
Equipment	$3,000,000			
Less: Accumulated depreciation	600,000		Investment of the U.S. government	3,010,000
Total Fixed Assets		2,400,000		
Total Assets		$3,685,000	Total Liabilities and Investment of U.S. government	$3,685,000

Some significant differences between Illustration 16–1 and balance sheets of municipalities are obvious at first glance. First, although this Federal agency is not a business-type operation, fixed assets as well as current assets are accounted for in a single self-balancing group of accounts. Not only are fixed assets included, but depreciation is charged—a situation not approved of for municipalities by the National Committee on Governmental Accounting. Within the Federal government, however, the Comptroller General has consistently taken the position that the principles of accrual accounting are applicable in nonbusiness-type agencies as well as business-type agencies. Since the concept of depreciation is fundamental to accrual accounting, the Comptroller General has said (GAO manual, Title 2, Subsection 12.5h):

> Procedures shall be adopted by each agency to account for depreciation (or amortization of cost) of capital assets whenever need arises for a periodic determination of the cost of all resources consumed in performing services. This information is needed when:
>
> (1) The financial results of operations in terms of costs of performance in relation to revenues earned, if any, are to be fully disclosed in financial reports.
> (2) Amounts to be collected in reimbursement for services performed are to be determined on the basis of the full cost of performance pursuant to legal requirements or administrative policy.
> (3) Investment in fixed property assets used is substantial and there is a need to assemble total costs to assist management and other officials in making cost comparisons, evaluating performance, and devising future plans.
> (4) Total cost of property constructed by an agency is needed to determine the amount to be capitalized.

A second significant difference between Federal government balance sheets and municipal balance sheets lies in the equity section. The "Fund Balance" account of a municipal general fund represents the net liquid assets available for appropriation and expenditure. The "Investment of the U.S. Government" account of a Federal agency represents the net assets of the agency acquired from prior appropriations. It is true that the net assets of the Federal agency are available for use by the agency, but they are not necessarily liquid.

A third difference between Illustration 16–1 and a municipal general fund balance sheet is related to the difference in equity accounts. The agency in Illustration 16–1 has inventories which amount to approximately one-sixth of total assets. In a municipality such sizable inventories would ordinarily be accounted for in a separate fund; at a minimum, a Reserve for Inventories would be created by a charge to Fund Balance equal in amount to the inventory carrying value. No such segregation was made in the Investment of the U.S. Government account of the Federal agency, because the objective of the Federal agency accounting system is an accrual accounting portrayal, not a liquidity accounting portrayal.

A final difference, other than purely terminological ones, which may be noted between the balance sheet of the Federal agency and that of a municipality is the use of the current asset account title "Fund Balances with U.S. Treasury" instead of the more familiar title, "Cash." A Federal agency, typically, does not have a bank account, as a municipality or a privately owned business would; rather, it has a claim against the United States Treasury. The relationships among agency accounts and Treasury accounts are illustrated below.

Illustrative Transactions and Entries

1. If the agency whose July 1, 19CY balance sheet is presented in Illustration 16–1 receives from the Congress a one-year appropriation for $2,500,000 the Treasury Bureau of Accounts would prepare a formal notice to the agency after the appropriation act has been signed by the President and the following entries would be made:

Agency accounts:

Fund Balances with U.S. Treasury—19CY.............	2,500,000	
Unapportioned Appropriation—19CY.........		2,500,000

Bureau of Accounts:

Fund Balances with U.S. Treasury—19CY (agency).....	2,500,000	
Undisbursed Appropriations and Funds (agency)		2,500,000

Treasurer of the United States:

No entry necessary

2. When the Office of Management and Budget approves the quarterly apportionments, the agency would be notified. Assuming that, in the case illustrated, the OMB approved apportionments of $600,000 for each quarter and reserved $100,000 (see definition of *reserve* on page 480), the agency would record the apportionments:

Agency accounts:

Unapportioned Appropriation—19CY..................	2,400,000	
Unallotted Apportionments—19CY...........		2,400,000

3. If, upon notification of the apportionments, the agency head allotted the entire first-quarter apportionment, the event would be recorded in the agency accounts only, in the following manner:

Agency accounts:

Unallotted Apportionments—19CY.......................	600,000	
Unobligated Allotments—19CY..................		600,000

All three entries—for the annual appropriation, the apportionments by the OMB, and for the first-quarter allotment—would be made as of July 1, the first day of the current fiscal year, although in some years the appropriation bill may not have been actually enacted by that date. The substance of the three entries is that agency managers have new obligational authority totaling $600,000 for the operations of the first quarter, and so must manage the activities of the agency accordingly, even though the Congress did appropriate $2,500,000 for the year.

4. Operations of the agency during the first quarter are accounted for in the following entries:

a) Goods were ordered in the amount of $82,000, utilities and other fixed expenses for July were estimated as $10,000, payroll and fringe benefits for July were estimated as $108,000. Obligations were recorded for all commitments.

Agency accounts:

Unobligated Allotments—19CY	200,000	
Unliquidated Obligations—19CY		200,000

b) Accounts payable as of July 1 are paid by checks drawn on the Treasurer of the United States. Checks drawn are reported to the Bureau of Accounts, which then records the expenditures and credits "Checks Outstanding." The Treasurer enters the check when it is paid, and reports to the Bureau of Accounts checks paid, so that Checks Outstanding may be debited and Cash—Treasurer of the U.S. credited. The entries shown below give the net effect on the books of the Bureau of Accounts.

Agency accounts:

Accounts Payable	275,000	
Fund Balances with U.S. Treasury—19PY		275,000

Bureau of Accounts:

Expenditures—General and Special Funds—19PY	275,000	
Cash—Treasurer of the U.S.		275,000

Treasurer of the United States:

Checks Paid	275,000	
Cash in Bank		275,000

c) Goods and equipment ordered in 19PY, and shown as Unliquidated Obligations—19PY in Illustration 16–1, are received in 19CY and the liability is recorded. Note that two entries are required in the agency accounts: an entry to record the liquidation of the obligations and consequent expenditure of the prior year appropriation, and an entry to record assets acquired and liabilities incurred. The assumed analysis of the $400,000 unliquidated obligations is shown in the entry illustrated below:

Agency accounts:

Unliquidated Obligations—19PY	400,000	
Expended Appropriation—19PY		400,000
Inventories	150,000	
Equipment	250,000	
Accounts Payable		400,000

d) Payrolls for the first four weeks of the month were vouchered for payment in the amount of $59,000 for Department 1 of the agency, and $40,000 for Department 2. Utilities and fixed expenses in the amount of $10,000 were also vouchered for payment; $4,000 of this applied to activities of Department 1 and $6,000 to Department 2. Because the agency needs to relate costs to activities for managerial purposes, as well as to meet the requirements of the Office of Management and Budget and the Comptroller General, the agency is departmentalized according to activities performed. Costs are accumulated departmentally at the time they become certain in amount, rather than at the time they are estimated.

Agency accounts:

Unliquidated Obligations—19CY	109,000	
Expended Appropriation—19CY		109,000
Department 1	63,000	
Department 2	46,000	
Accounts Payable		109,000

e) Materials used in the activities of Departments 1 and 2 amounted to $120,000 and $85,000, respectively.

Agency accounts:

Department 1	120,000	
Department 2	85,000	
Inventories		205,000

f) Accounts payable in the amount of $460,000 were paid; $400,000 of this related to goods and equipment ordered in 19PY and received in 19CY (see transaction *c*), therefore it is chargeable against 19PY Fund Balances with U.S. Treasury; the remaining $60,000 of payments relate to the payroll for the first two weeks of the month ($50,000) and utilities and fixed expenses, $10,000.

Agency accounts:

Accounts Payable	460,000	
Fund Balances with U.S. Treasury—19PY		400,000
Fund Balances with U.S. Treasury—19CY		60,000

Bureau of Accounts:

Expenditures—General and Special Funds—19PY	400,000	
Expenditures—General and Special Funds—19CY	60,000	
Cash—Treasurer of the U.S.		460,000

Treasurer of the United States (when checks are presented):

Checks Paid	460,000	
Cash in Bank		460,000

g) In order to prepare accrual based financial statements for the month, the following items were taken into account: (1) Gross payroll for the last three days of the month, $5,000 for Department 1, and $4,000 for Department 2. (2) Invoices or receiving reports for goods received, but for which vouchers have not yet been prepared, $35,000; distributable to Department 1, $6,000; Department 2, $6,000; and Inventory, $23,000. (3) Depreciation of equipment, $25,000; $16,000 chargeable to Department 1, and $9,000 chargeable to Department 2. Because the obligations for the items in parts (1) and (2) have become certain in amount and the relevant departmental cost accounts or inventory account can be charged, the amounts should be shown in financial statements as Accounts Payable, not as Unliquidated Obligations. It is customary to record the entry for the liquidation of the obligation and expenditure of the appropriation at this time even though no voucher is as yet prepared. Inasmuch as depreciation [part(3)] is not an expense chargeable against the appropriation, the accrual of depreciation expense does not affect any of the appropriation, apportionment, allotment, or obligation accounts, but is recorded as in commercial accounting, by a debit to the departmental expense accounts and a credit to the Accumulated Depreciation account.

Agency accounts:

Department 1	27,000	
Department 2	19,000	
Inventory	23,000	
Accounts Payable		44,000
Accumulated Depreciation—Equipment		25,000
Unliquidated Obligations—19CY	44,000	
Expended Appropriation—19CY		44,000

h) In addition to the adjusting entries, illustrated above, closing entries should be made to facilitate the preparation of accrual based financial statements. (For monthly statements the following entries ordinarily are made only in worksheet form). The only accounts of the hypothetical Federal agency which should be closed are the two Expended Appropriation accounts, which represent additions to the equity account, Investment of the U.S. Government; and the departmental cost accounts, which represent decreases in the equity account.

Agency accounts:

Expended Appropriation—19PY	400,000	
Expended Appropriation—19CY	153,000	
Investment of the U.S. Government		553,000
Investment of the U.S. Government	360,000	
Department 1		210,000
Department 2		150,000

Month-End Financial Statements

After all the entries illustrated above have been made, the Federal agency balance sheet for July 31, 19CY shown in Illustration 16–2 can be prepared.

Illustration 16–2

FEDERAL AGENCY
Balance Sheet
July 31, 19CY

Assets

Current Assets:		
Fund balances with U.S. Treasury–19CY	$2,440,000	
Inventories	578,000	
Total Current Assets		$3,018,000
Fixed Assets:		
Equipment	$3,250,000	
Less: Accumulated depreciation	625,000	
Total Fixed Assets		2,625,000
Total Assets		$5,643,000

Liabilities, Appropriations, and Investment of the U.S. Government

Current Liabilities:		
Accounts payable	$ 93,000	
Total Current Liabilities		$ 93,000
Appropriation accounts–19CY:		
Unapportioned appropriation	$ 100,000	
Unallotted apportionments	1,800,000	
Unobligated allotments	400,000	
Unliquidated obligations	47,000	
Total Unexpended Appropriations–19CY		2,347,000
Investment of the U.S. Government		3,203,000
Total Liabilities, Appropriations, and Investment of the U.S. Government		$5,643,000

In Illustration 16–1 it was assumed that all of the 19PY appropriation had been apportioned, allotted, and obligated; this assumption was made at that point in order to focus the attention of the reader upon major differences between balance sheets for Federal agencies and those for municipalities. The assumption was realistic, however, because the agency's authority to obligate a one-year appropriation expires at the end of the year for which the appropriation was made. Fund Balances with the U.S. Treasury pertaining to a one-year appropriation remain available for payment of liabilities and obligations incurred under that appropriation for a limited period of time; unneeded balances should be returned to the general fund control promptly without waiting for expiration of the time-limit.

All accounts relating to the unexpended appropriation for the Federal agency for 19CY are net worth accounts, and are, for that reason, grouped in Illustration 16–2. The appropriations for 19PY and 19CY expended in July, 19CY, are also net worth, or equity, in character, but differ from the unexpended appropriation in that the expenditure of appropriations has resulted in the acquisition of net assets for the use of the Federal agency. The expended appropriation accounts were, therefore, closed to the Investment of the U.S. Government account and are a part of that balance in Illustration 16–2. It is customary to prepare a statement detailing the changes in the Investment of the U.S. Government account for the period; one form of this statement is shown as Illustration 16–3.

Illustration 16–3

FEDERAL AGENCY
Statement of Changes in the Investment of the United States Government
for July, 19CY

Investment of the U.S. Government, July 1, 19CY		$3,010,000
Add: Expended appropriation–19PY	$400,000	
Expended appropriation–19CY	153,000	553,000
Total		$3,563,000
Less: Cost of activities performed in July		360,000
Investment of the U.S. Government, July 31, 19CY		$3,203,000

In the example given, the Federal agency received no fees, rents, interest, or other revenues; consequently, no statement of operations need be prepared. In order that agency operating management, and others interested in the efficient operation of the agency, can be informed of the costs of agency activities performed in July, a Statement of Costs of Activities Performed, shown as Illustration 16–4, is prepared. It is assumed in this example that Department 1 performs one activity and that Department 2 performs another, so that detailing the costs by departments shows the costs of performing activities.

The costs of activities performed are reported in Illustration 16–4 on the accrual basis, and therefore represent the *consumption* during the period of goods and services in the performance of agency activities. Financial management of the agency is concerned also with reporting in the same manner as agency budgets were prepared, so that operating results may be compared with planned results. If the budget of the agency is prepared on the obligation basis, reports should show amounts authorized, total obligations incurred (subdivided between expenditures and unliquidated obligations) and the unobligated balance of each authorization. Expenditure data should be in terms of accrual accounting. That is, an expenditure should be recognized when goods are received *by* an agency or services are performed *for* the agency. In the continuing example of the Federal agency, and in general, the accrued expenditure

Illustration 16–4

FEDERAL AGENCY
Statement of Costs of Activities Performed
for July, 19CY

Department 1:		
Salaries and wages	$ 64,000	
Materials used	126,000	
Utilities and other expenses	4,000	
Depreciation	16,000	
Total Department 1 activity costs for July, 19CY		$210,000
Department 2:		
Salaries and wages	$ 44,000	
Materials used	91,000	
Utilities and other expenses	6,000	
Depreciation	9,000	
Total Department 2 activity costs for July, 19CY		150,000
Total Federal Agency Activity Costs for July, 19CY		$360,000

total is the same as the total expended appropriation figures by years. This relationship emphasizes that an expenditure is deemed to take place at the time goods or services are received, regardless of whether cash is disbursed.

Accrued expenditures are related to obligations through the change in the balance of unliquidated obligations. For example, in the Federal agency during July, goods and services ordered (obligations incurred) amounted to $200,000; goods and services ordered before July and not yet received on July 1 (unliquidated obligations, July 1) totaled $400,000. Thus, a total of $600,000 worth of goods and services had been ordered. At the end of July, $47,000 worth were still on order (unliquidated obligations, July 31). Therefore, $553,000 worth of goods and services were received in July (accrued expenditures). The relationship of accrued expenditures to costs of activities performed by the Federal agency in July is shown in Illustration 16–5.

Illustration 16–5

Accrued expenditures for July	$553,000
Less: Expenditures for equipment	250,000
Expenditures for salaries, materials and other expenses	$303,000
Add: Inventories, July 1	610,000
Goods and services available for use	$913,000
Less: Inventories, July 31	578,000
Goods and services used in July, exclusive of depreciation	$335,000
Add: Costs not chargeable to appropriation–depreciation	25,000
Cost of Activities Performed (Illustration 16–4)	$360,000

Control of Obligations

The journal entries illustrated earlier in this chapter are based on the assumption that the agency *prevalidates* its obligations. Prevalidation implies that each proposed obligation be compared with the balance of Unobligated Allotments to determine that the balance is sufficient to allow the release of the proposed obligation. Thus, under a system of prevalidation it is necessary to record in an obligation control register each obligation document before it is released by the agency. A separate register should be kept for each appropriation. The register may be used as a book of original entry; the total dollar amount of obligations recorded during a period is the amount to be debited to Unobligated Allotments and credited to Unliquidated Obligations. It is reasonable, also, to record in the obligation control register the liquidation of each obligation, so that a listing of the obligations issued but not yet liquidated, as shown by the register, will agree in total with the balance of the Unliquidated Obligations account. Thus the reguister, and the documents supporting it, serve as a subsidiary ledger. Illustration 16–6 shows one form of obligation control register which may be used.

Illustration 16–6

FEDERAL AGENCY
Obligation Control Register
Appropriation 19CY

Liquidation		*Obligation*			*Debit Unobligated Allotments Credit Unliquidated Obligations*	*Unobligated Allotment Balance*
Date	*Ref.*	*Date*	*Ref.*	*Explanation*		
		July 1	AA–1	1st Qr. Allotment		$600,000
		July 2	PO6601	Purchases–XYZ Co.	$ 48,000	552,000
		July 2	PO6602	Purchases–ABE Co.	34,000	518,000
July 23	Vo. 663	July 2	FE	Utilities and Fixed Exp.	10,000	508,000
July 17	Vo. 608	July 2	WP–1	Payroll and P/R Taxes–July	108,000	400,000

Since invoices received are not always exactly equal in amount to the related obligations documents it is necessary, in the system described, to record in the register adjustments to bring the estimated expenses into accord with the actual. If any obligation documents are canceled, the cancellation should also be recorded in the register to enable routine correction of the accounts.

Prevalidation of obligations, and the use of the obligation control register as a book of original entry, are suggested by the Comptroller General as helpful procedures, but are not required. In fact, in accord with the emphasis upon accounting as an aid to agency financial management, the Comptroller General, through the General Accounting Office, encourages agencies to simplify accounting systems to the maximum extent practicable, consistent with good control and the reporting requirements of the Treasury and the Office of Management and Budget. One agency makes no use at all of the Unliquidated Obligations account during an accounting period; all obligation documents are recorded as credits to Accounts Payable. Whenever it is necessary to prepare financial statements, the documents which comprise the subsidiary ledger of Accounts Payable are sorted into those for undelivered orders (Unliquidated Obligations) and those properly classifiable as Accounts Payable, and an adjusting journal entry is prepared so that the agency's financial statements are on the same basis as those of other agencies.

Statements of the Treasurer of the United States

The Treasurer of the United States acts as a banker for the Federal government, as is illustrated by the Federal agency example discussed in preceding pages. The Treasurer issues a *Daily Statement of the U.S. Treasury* which reports total monetary assets and liabilities in the Treasurer's account, the deposits in and withdrawals from the account, and the effect of the day's operations on the public debt. A more detailed statement showing receipts and disbursements is published monthly, as is a detailed statement of public debt outstanding. The Treasurer also issues an annual *Summary of Fiscal Operations*, a *Statement of United States Dollar Funds* held by or for his account, a statement of foreign currencies held abroad for his account, and such other reports as are necessary to reflect his stewardship. Illustration of the Treasurer's statements is not necessary to the purposes of this chapter.

Statements of the Treasury Bureau of Accounts

The central accounts maintained by the Bureau of Accounts of the Department of the Treasury represent consolidated accounts only with respect to cash assets and liabilities, and cash operations. The system reflects expenditures and appropriation balances on a checks-issued basis, obtained from monthly statements of disbursing officers and/or the agencies for which they disburse. Receipts are reported to the Bureau of Accounts monthly by disbursing and collecting officers on the basis of collections or deposits. The consolidated information is reported monthly and annually by the Bureau of Accounts. The annual report is available from the Government Printing Office under the title, *Combined Statement of Receipts, Outlays, and Balances of the United States Government*. The format of one of the principal exhibits in the annual report is shown in Illustration 16–7.

Statement of Budget Appropriations, Outlays, and Balances

Only the segment of the Treasury statement reporting data concerning the Legislative branch is reproduced in Illustration 16–7; the actual statement reports similar data for all executive agencies, and the judicial branches of the Federal government.

Illustration 16–7
Summary of Budget Appropriations, Outlays, and Balances, Fiscal Year 19CY
(in thousands of dollars)

Organization	*Balances Beginning of Fiscal Year*	*Appropriations and Other Obligational Authority*	*Transfers, Borrowings, and Investments (Net)*	*Outlays (Net)*	*Balances Withdrawn and Other Transactions*	*Balances End of Fiscal Year*
Legislative Branch						
Fund resources:						
Undisbursed funds	115,664	591,687	–29	501,742	14,676	190,904
Proprietary receipts from the public	–	14,131	–	–14,131	–	–
Intrabudgetary receipts . .	–	–304	–	–304	–	–
Unfunded contract authority	7,876	–285	–	–	–	7,591
Investments in public debt securities	282	–	29	–	–	311
Accounts receivable	71,186	–	–	–	–24,663	95,849
Unfilled customer orders .	16,341	–	–	–	–4,501	20,842
Fund equities:						
Unobligated balance	–85,419	–	–	–	54,483	–139,902
Accounts payable.	–53,205	–	–	–	21,262	–74,467
Undelivered orders	–55,637	–	–	–	17,043	–72,680
Total Legislative Branch	17,090	576,967	–	487,307	78,300	28,450

If all appropriations were available for obligation during a single fiscal year, as was true of the Federal agency example discussed in previous sections of this chapter, the balance in the final column of Illustration 16–7 would be zero. Appropriations made to finance the ordinary operations of an agency are customarily one-year appropriations; but in recognition of the fact that not all programs or activities fit a fiscal-year pattern, the Congress also makes multiple-year appropriations, no-year appropriations, and, on occasion, permanent appropriations. *Multiple-year appropriations* are available for incurring obligations for a definite period in excess of one fiscal year. *No-year appropriations* are available for incurring obligations for an indefinite period of time. *Permanent appropriations* may provide that revenues from particular sources may be applied without further congressional action to specific purposes, or may provide that a fixed amount be expended annually for a continuing purpose without additional congressional action. The impact of prior years' permanent appropriations on budget authority is substantial. For example, benefit payments under the Social Security trust funds are estimated in excess of $65 billion for fiscal year 1974.

Comparison of Accounting for Local Governmental Revenue Funds and Accounting for Federal Agencies (journal entries)

Item	Local Governmental Revenue Funds Legal Track Only	Federal Agency Legal Track	Federal Agency Management Track

1. Passage of appropriations (and for municipality revenue) ordinances	Estimated Revenues
	    Appropriations
	    Fund Balance
		Fund Balance with U.S. Treasury
		    Unapportioned Appropriation	

2. Revenues accrued	Taxes Receivable Revenues	No equivalent for taxes. User charges, if any, recognized as billed	
3. Apportionment by OMB	No equivalent	Unapportioned Appropriation Unallotted Apportionment	
4. Allotment by agency head	No equivalent*	Unallotted Apportionment Unobligated Allotment	

5. Goods or services ordered	Encumbrances
	    Reserve for Encumbrances
		Unobligated Allotment
		    Unliquidated Obligations	

6. Goods or services received	Reserve for Encumbrances
	    Encumbrances
	Expenditures
	    Accounts Payable
		Unliquidated Obligations
		    Expended Appropriation
			Expense or asset account
			    Accounts Payable

7. Liability paid (Expenditure recorded in (6) in both municipality and Federal agency)	Accounts Payable
	    Cash
		No entry	Accounts Payable
			    Fund Balance With U.S. Treasury

8. Supplies used	No entry	No entry	Cost account Inventory

9. Physical inventory	Inventory
	    Expenditures
	Fund Balance
	    Reserve for Inventory
		No entry	Entry for (6) assumes perpetual inventory; would need entry for (9) if physical inventory and book inventory differed

10. Depreciation computed	No entry	Not an expenditure of appropriations; will never require a check to be drawn on U.S. Treasury	Cost account Accumulated Depreciation

11. Closing entries	Appropriations
	Revenues
	    Estimated Revenues
	    Encumbrances
	    Expenditures
	    Fund Balance
		Expended Appropriations
		    Investment of U.S. Government
			Investment of U.S. Government
			    Cost accounts

*As discussed in Chapter 2, some local governmental units utilize allotment accounting. In such cases the credit in entry no. 1 would be to "Unallotted Appropriations," and an entry no. 4 would be necessary to record the debit to that account and the credit to "Allotments."

Summary—Federal Governmental Accounting

Federal government accounting in the United States is the statutory responsibility of the Comptroller General, the Secretary of the Treasury, the Director of the Office of Management and Budget, and the head of each agency in the executive branch. Federal agency accounting is directed at providing information for intelligent financial management of agency activities and programs to the end they may be operated with efficiency and economy, as well as providing evidence of adherence to legal requirements. At the agency level each appropriation is treated as a fund, although, from the overall point of view, it is a subdivision of the one general fund which exists for the entire government. Fund accounting used by Federal agencies bears more resemblance to accrual accounting used by businesses than it does to general fund accounting used by municipalities: fixed assets, as well as current assets, are accounted for in each appropriation fund; depreciation on fixed assets is charged as a cost of operations, even though it is not chargeable against appropriation apportionments.

At the overall level, the Bureau of Accounts of the Department of the Treasury consolidates only cash asset and liability and cash operations accounts, on an historical basis. Agency accrual accounting information is used by the Office of Management and Budget as an aid to the President in planning and controlling the activities and programs of the executive agencies.

Comparison of Federal Governmental Accounting and Local Governmental Revenue Fund Accounting

Illustration 16–8 presents a comparison of local governmental revenue fund accounting and accounting for Federal agencies in the form of journal entries needed to record typical transactions. As emphasized by the headings of the illustration, and by the discussions in earlier chapters, accounting for local governmental revenue funds is presently focussed on legal compliance. The focus of Federal agency accounting, in contrast, is broadened to include information needed for the management of agency resources as well as for compliance with legal requirements.

SELECTED REFERENCES

Borth, Daniel. "Accounting in the Federal Government: Progress and Retrogression," *Federal Accountant,* Vol. 13, no. 4 (June 1964), pp. 24–37.

Enke, Ernest. "The Accrual Concept in Federal Accounting," *The Federal Accountant,* Vol. 22, no. 1 (March 1973), pp. 4–9.

Gustafson, George A. "Critical Issues in Governmental Accounting," *The Federal Accountant,* Vol. 22, no. 1 (March 1973), pp. 10–23.

Pujol, Maurice P. "Congressional Control of Expenditures," *Federal Accountant,* Vol. 13, No. 1 (September 1963), pp. 39–57.

WEITZEL, FRANK H. "Comptrollership Trends in the Federal Government," *Federal Accountant*, Vol. 13, No. 4 (June 1964), pp. 4–23.

Publications of U.S. Government Agencies

EXECUTIVE OFFICE OF THE PRESIDENT, OFFICE OF MANAGEMENT AND BUDGET. *The Bureau of The Budget*, June, 1962.

———. *Circular A-34, Instructions Relating to Budget Execution.* Part II, "Terminology and Concepts" is especially useful.

COMPTROLLER GENERAL OF THE UNITED STATES. *Annual Report.*

GENERAL ACCOUNTING OFFICE. *Manual for Guidance of Federal Agencies.*

———. *Illustrative Accounting Procedures for Federal Agencies: Application of the Accrual Basis of Accounting . . .* , 1962; *Accounting for Accrued Expenditures*, 1969.

———. *Frequently Asked Questions About Accrual Accounting in the Federal Government*, 1970.

———. *Accounting Principles and Standards for Federal Agencies*, 1972.

JOINT FINANCIAL MANAGEMENT IMPROVEMENT PROGRAM. *Annual Progress Report.* Issued yearly since 1949.

REPORT OF THE PRESIDENT'S COMMISSION ON BUDGET CONCEPTS. October, 1967.

TREASURY DEPARTMENT COMBINED STATEMENT OF RECEIPTS, OUTLAYS, AND BALANCES OF THE UNITED STATES. Issued Annually.

QUESTIONS

16–1. What reasons, other than historical accident, might exist for the division of responsibility for Federal financial management among the Comptroller General, the Director of the Office of Management and Budget, the Secretary of the Treasury, the Administrator of General Services, and the heads of executive agencies?

16–2. Describe concisely the role each of the following plays in Federal financial management:

a) Director of the Office of Management and Budget.
b) The Administrator of General Services.
c) Secretary of the Treasury.
d) Comptroller General.
e) Chairman of the Civil Service Commission.
f) Head of an executive agency.

16–3. What is the significance of Public Law 784 of the 81st Congress?

16–4. Compare the degree of adherence to the basic concepts of accrual accounting assumed in the principles prescribed by the Comptroller General with that degree of adherence assumed in the recommendations of the National Committee on Governmental Accounting.

16–5. Compare and contrast, from the standpoint of usefulness for financial management, the general structure of accounting recommended for local governmental units by the National Committee on Governmental

Accounting and that prescribed for Federal agencies by the Comptroller General. Your answer must include a concise statement of the essential NCGA recommendations and a concise statement of the essential features of Federal agency accounting.

16–6. What is the significance in Federal financial management of the central accounts maintained by the Bureau of Accounts of the Department of the Treasury?

16–7. What is the significance in Federal financial management of the concept of *obligations?*

16–8. What is the significance in Federal financial management of the concept of *cost?*

16–9. Compare and contrast the nature of the Investment of the U.S. Government account with that of the Fund Balance account used by municipalities.

16–10. Distinguish between the terms *allotment*, *allocation*, *apportionment*, and *reserve*, as used in the Federal government.

EXERCISES AND PROBLEMS

16–1. The following tabulation, based on actual figures for a recent year for a Federal agency whose costs are about 90 percent for employee salaries and benefits, illustrates the relationships between cash disbursements and accrued expenditures.

			Difference	
Month	*Cash Disburse-ments*	*Accrued Expendi-tures*	*Amount*	*Percent of Accrued Expendi-tures*
		(000 omitted)		
January	$ 4,465	$ 5,173	$ 708	13.7
February	4,548	4,559	11	.2
March	6,514	4,802	-1,712	-35.6
April	4,808	4,914	106	2.2
May	4,505	5,045	540	10.7
June	4,659	5,345	686	12.8
July	4,804	5,522	718	13.0
August	7,467	5,500	-1,967	-35.8
September	5,297	5,739	442	7.7
October	5,276	6,050	774	12.8
November	5,436	5,332	-104	-2.0
December	5,168	6,011	843	14.0
Total for year	$62,947	$63,992	$1,045	1.6

Required:

Since the difference between accrued expenditures and cash disbursements for this year is only 1.6 percent, is there any reason why the agency should spend additional funds to install and maintain an accrual accounting system? Explain your answer.

16–2. The appropriation request of the Soil Conservation Service of the United States Department of Agriculture for a recent year is shown below. For each element of the request designated by a letter, match one of the descriptive sentences indicated by a number.

Appropriation Request for Conservation Operations
(000 omitted)

a) Total operating costs	$132,000	
b) Deduct costs not requiring outlays of funds (depreciation, office space occupied without charge, and increase in accrued annual leave)	–5,615	
Total funded operating costs	126,385	
Add proposed capital outlay (for equipment, etc.)	2,000	
c) Total funded program costs	128,385	
Add increase in stores and unpaid undelivered orders.	50	
d) Total obligations. .	128,435	
e) Add unpaid obligations at start of year	7,540	
e) Deduct unpaid obligations tions at end of year . .	–6,003	
f) Outlays	$129,972	

1. This is the amount of proposed appropriation for this program which the Congress is requested to make.
2. Estimated amount of cash disbursements for the year.
3. This amount represents the estimated total costs of this program that will require the expenditure of funds.
4. These are adjustments to the estimated obligations to be incurred for the year to arrive at the estimated cash disbursements for the year.
5. This amount represents the estimated cost of resources to be consumed in carrying out this program.
6. This amount represents the portion of the estimated cost of operations not requiring a current expenditure of funds.

16–3. *a*) From the information tabulated on page 498, determine the June 30, 19CY Balance for the organizations shown.

b) Which of the two agencies probably receives the larger no-year (or multiple-year) appropriation? Why?

c) Which of the two agencies probably has the larger construction program? Why?

Appropriations, Outlays, and Balances, Fiscal Year 19CY
(in millions of dollars)

Title	*Balances beginning of fiscal year*	*Appropriations and other obligational authority*	*Transfers, borrowings, and investments (net)*	*Outlays (net)*	*Balances withdrawn and other transactions*	*Balance[s] end o[f] fiscal year*
Department of XYZ	309	9,691	–	8,212	48	
Department of LMN	1,015	6,085	–100	6,000	–	

16–4. One amount is missing in the following trial balance of a certain agency of the Federal government, and the debits are not distinguished from the credits.

Required:

a) Compute the missing amount.
b) Prepare in good form a balance sheet for the agency as of year end.

Accounts Payable	$ 300,000
Accounts Receivable	50,000
Accumulated Depreciation–Plant and Equipment	2,300,000
Expended Appropriations	2,600,000
Fund Balances with U.S. Treasury	1,200,000
Inventories	900,000
Investment of the U.S. Government	?
Operating Costs	2,500,000
Plant and Equipment	8,400,000
Unliquidated Obligations	900,000

16–5. The Illdiana Valley Commission was authorized by the Congress to start operations on July 1 of a certain year.

a) Record the following transactions in general journal form, as they should appear in the accounts of the Illdiana Valley Commission. Use expense accounts named to describe the nature of each expense.

1. The Illdiana Valley Commission received official notice that the one-year appropriation passed by the Congress and signed by the President amounted to $6,000,000 for operating expenses.
2. The Office of Management and Budget notified the Commission of the following schedule of apportionments: first quarter, $2,000,000; second quarter; $1,500,000; third quarter, $1,250,000; and fourth quarter, $1,250,000.

3. The Illdiana Valley Commissioner allotted $1,000,000 for the first month's operations.
4. Obligations were recorded for salaries and fringe benefits, $370,000; furniture and equipment, $300,000; supplies, $250,000; rent and utilites, $50,000.
5. Payroll for the first two weeks in the amount of $150,000 was paid.
6. Invoices approved for payment totaled $390,000; of the total, $200,000 was for furniture and equipment, $150,000 for supplies, and $40,000 for rent.
7. Liability was recorded for the payroll for the second two weeks, $160,000; and for the FICA taxes for the four weeks, $31,000.
8. Invoices totaling $380,000 were paid.
9. Accruals recorded at month-end were: salaries $29,000, and utilities $10,000. Supplies costing $40,000 were used during the month. No depreciation is to be charged by this agency.
10. Necessary closing entries were prepared.

b) Show in general journal form any entries that would be made for the above transactions by (1) the Bureau of Accounts of the Treasury, and (2) the Treasurer of the United States.

c) Prepare a balance sheet for the Illdiana Valley Commission as of July 31.

d) Prepare a statement of costs of activities performed in July.

16–6. The trial balance as of May 31, 19CY, of the Atomic Authority, an agency of the executive branch of the Federal government, is shown below:

	Debit	*Credit*
Fund balances with U.S. Treasury	$ 1,635,772	
Inventories	942,000	
Plant and equipment	7,651,633	
Accumulated depreciation–plant and equipment		$ 2,332,628
Construction work in progress	581,818	
Accounts payable		328,123
Advances from other federal agencies		43,518
Unapportioned appropriations–19CY		100,000
Unallotted apportionments–19CY		150.000
Unobligated allotments–19CY		650,000
Unliquidated obligations–19CY		364,131
Expended appropriations–19CY		2,630,724
Investment of the U.S. government, July 1, 19CY		6,600,637
Production costs	1,502,496	
Development costs	507,343	
Research costs	286,866	
Small program costs	91,833	
	$13,199,861	$13,199,861

Required:

a) Prepare a balance sheet for the Atomic Authority, as of May 31, 19CY.
b) Prepare a statement of changes in Investment of the U.S. government, for the period July 1–May 31, 19CY.
c) If the amount of depreciation included in 19CY costs is $242,000 and no equipment was purchased, compute (1) total activity costs for the 11 months ended May 31, (2) total accrued expenditures for that period. The July 1, 19CY, inventory amounted to $457,814.

16–7. The balance sheet of the Throttlebottom Commemorative Commission, of the United States Department of Culture, is given below:

THROTTLEBOTTOM COMMEMORATIVE COMMISSION
Balance Sheet, June 30, 19PY

Assets			*Liabilities and Investment of the United States Government*	
Current Assets:			Current Liabilities:	
Fund balances with U.S. Treasury–19PY		$1,350,000	Accounts payable	$ 750,
Accounts receivable. .		50,000		
Inventories.		315,000		
Total Current Assets		$1,715,000	Total Current Liabilities	$ 750,
			Unliquidated obligations–19PY	600,
Fixed Assets:				
Equipment.	$600,000		Investment of the U.S. government. .	905,
Less: Accumulated depreciation	60,000	540,000		
Total Assets. . .		$2,255,000	Total Liabilities and Investment of the U.S. Government	$2,255,

a) Record the June 30, 19PY, balances in T accounts.
b) Record directly in T accounts the following transactions:

1. A one-year appropriation for $10,000,000 is authorized by the Congress and the bill is signed by the President.
2. The Office of Management and Budget apportions $6,000,000 to the agency and reserves $4,000,000.
3. The agency head allots $5,000,000 to his subordinates.
4. Obligation documents totaling $5,000,000 are recorded.
5. Goods and services were received and liabilities recorded for: payroll, $3,000,000; equipment, $400,000; and materials added to inventory, $600,000. The equipment and $200,000 worth of the materials had been ordered in the prior year; the remainder of the materials and the payroll relate to obligations of the current year.
6. Materials issued during the period were: sold at cost plus 20 percent on open account, $100,000 (cost); and used in

operations, $500,000. (Credit Income for total sales; close the account to Investment of the U.S. Government at year-end.)

7. Collections on accounts receivable amounted to $80,000; this amount was returned to the U.S. Treasury (debt Funds Returned to U.S. Treasury, an account to be closed to Investment of the U.S. Government at year-end).
8. Liabilities paid totaled $4,350,000.
9. Depreciation is recorded at the rates of 10 percent on the beginning balance and 5 percent on the additions during the year.
10. Accruals as of June 30, 19CY, are recorded for: payroll, $300,000; materials added to inventory, $60,000.

c) Prepare a trial balance as of June 30, 19CY
d) Prepare closing entries as of June 30, 19CY
e) Prepare a balance sheet as of June 30, 19CY
f) Prepare a Statement of Operations for 19CY—show "Income" as a deduction from total costs.

16–8. The following trial balances were prepared for a Federal agency at the end of its first month of existence by a new accountant whose only prior experience had been as a bookkeeper in the accounting department of a large city.

INTERSTATE SPORTS COMMISSION
Trial Balance
July 31, 19–

	Debit	*Credit*
General Fund		
Accounts Payable		$1,043,000
Allotments		1,600,000
Due from U.S. Treasury	$3,140,000	
Encumbrances	50,000	
Estimated Revenues	3,500,000	
Expenditures	1,203,000	
Fund Balance	100,000	
Inventory of Supplies	100,000	
Reserve for Encumbrances		50,000
Reserve for Inventory		100,000
Revenues		3,400,000
Unalloted Appropriations		1,900,000
	$8,093,000	$8,093,000
General Fixed Assets Group		
Buildings	$ 720,000	
Equipment	180,000	
Improvements Other Than Buildings	45,000	
Investment in General Fixed Assets–General Fund Revenues		$1,000,000
Land	55,000	
	$1,000,000	$1,000,000

Early in the second month of the agency's existence (before any transactions of the second month have been posted) you are sent to the agency to see how the new accountant is getting along. After looking over the trial balances you ask to see the underlying accounts. (These are reproduced below. Related debits and credits are indicated by the same number. Explanations appear with the debit member of each entry.)

General Fund Accounts

Accounts Payable

Checks requested from U.S. Treasury	(7)	260,000	(5)	1,150,000
			(6)	153,000

Allotments

			(3)	1,600,000

Due from U.S. Treasury

OMB Apportionment	(2)	3,400,000	(7)	260,000

Encumbrances

Option to purchase land, building, and equipment—$1,000,000; supplies ordered 200,000	(4)	1,200,000	(5)	1,150,000

Estimated Revenues

Congressional appropriation	(1)	3,500,000		

Expenditures

Title taken to Land, etc., $1,000,000; supplies received, $150,000	(5)	1,150,000	(8)	100,000
Salaries and wages	(6)	153,000		

Fund Balance

To set up Reserve for Inventory	(8)	100,000		

Inventory of Supplies

Month-end physical inventory	(8)	100,000		

Reserve for Encumbrances

See explanation in Expenditures account	(5)	1,150,000	(4)	1,200,000

Reserve for Inventory

			(8)	100,000

Revenues

			(2)	3,400,000

Unallotted Appropriations

Allotment for July	(3)	1,600,000	(1)	3,500,000

General Fixed Assets Group

Buildings

See General Fund entry (5); expected life 30 years	(5)	720,000		

Equipment

See GF entry (5); expected life 10 years	(5)	180,000		

Improvements Other Than Buildings

See GF entry (5); expected life 15 years	(5)	45,000		

Investment in General Fixed Assets—General Fund Revenues

			(5)	1,000,000

Land			
See GF entry (5)	(5)	55,000	

Required:

a) Prepare entries in general journal form to state the accounts of the Interstate Sports Commission correctly as of July 31, 19___.

b) Prepare a trial balance for the Interstate Sports Commission as of July 31, 19___.

17

Public School Accounting

According to the most recent Census of Governments, one out of every five local governmental units in the United States is a public school district. Public school *districts* are independent governmental units. Public school *system* is a broader term which includes "dependent schools"—that is, school systems administered by agencies of county or city governments. In 25 states responsibility for public schools rests solely with independent school districts; in 5 more all school systems which provide education through grade 12 are independent, but at least one institution in each of these 5 states is operated by a city or county government. Washington, D.C., and 4 states have only dependent public schools; the remaining 16 states have some independent districts and some dependent systems. The term "Local Education Agency" is a broad term sometimes used to include school district, public school, intermediate education agency, and school system.

The number of public school districts in the United States declined drastically in the last three decades as the result of an active and effective program of school district consolidation and reorganization. The Census of Governments reports that in 1941–42 there were 108,579 public school districts; in 1951–52, 67,355; in 1956–57, 50,454; in 1961–62, 34,678; in 1966–67, 21,782; and in 1971–72, 15,780. (The number of dependent school systems decreased somewhat during that time period also, but mostly because of Census Bureau reclassifications.) If the curve of public school expenditures were plotted for the 1941–1972 period, the rate of increase in expenditures would be at least equal to the rate of decrease in numbers of school districts. Between 1950 and 1972 public elementary and secondary school expenditures grew from $5.8 billion to $47.6 billion.

Public school accounting is closely related to accounting for general governmental units discussed in the preceding chapters of this text. It is also related to accounting for colleges and universities, the subject of Chapter 18. Because public schools are of such fundamental importance socially and politically, as well as financially, to all citizens and taxpayers in this country, this chapter is devoted to a brief treatment of public school accounting. Public school budgeting is not covered in this chapter in any detail because the reader is assumed to be familiar with the material in Chapter 2 of this text. That discussion is entirely applicable in principle to independent school district budgeting; the only portion of Chapter 2 which does not apply to budgeting for dependent school systems is that portion dealing with the computation of local tax revenues, since revenues are raised for dependent systems by the governmental unit which operates the schools.

The Literature of Public School Accounting

Because of the large scale on which states participate in financing local schools, it is not surprising that they exercise extensive control, through printed instructions and statutory law, over the financial recording and reporting practices of the units receiving their support. In one state all school financial activities, except those related to extracurricular affairs, are required to be accounted for and reported on state-prescribed forms. Between this and complete local autonomy there are doubtless many different combinations and degrees of state and local control and supervision of accounting and reporting. In addition to state and locally generated instructions about public school accounting, there exists a considerable body of material about public school accounting in textbooks and scholarly publications in the professional field of education. Federal aid to education is bringing increasing participation of the Federal government in molding school accounting and reporting procedures.

The most authoritative publications in the field of public school accounting are those in the State Educational Records and Reports Series developed and compiled in the United States Office of Education, National Center for Educational Statistics. The most recent and most comprehensive of the handbooks in this series is *Handbook II, Revised; Financial Accounting Classifications and Standard Terminology for Local and State School Systems.*[1] Also in this series is *Handbook II-B: Principles of Public School Accounting.*[2] Two other useful books in the field are: *Public School Fund Accounting Principles and Procedures,*[3] and *Uniform*

---

[1] U.S. Department of Health, Education, and Welfare, Office of Education, State Educational Records and Reports Series: Handbook II, Revised (Washington, D.C.: U.S. Government Printing Office, 1973.)

[2] U.S. Department of Health, Education, and Welfare, Office of Education, State Educational Records and Reports Series: Handbook II-B (Washington, D.C.: U.S. Government Printing Office, 1967).

[3] Sam B. Tidwell (New York: Harper & Bros. 1965).

System of Accounts for School Districts, Double-Entry Basis.[4] Although there exists a sizable volume of material on public school accounting, the remainder of this chapter reflects extensive reliance upon the references named above.

The discussion in the remainder of this chapter relates to the general processes of accounting and reporting, with little attention to details. This policy is followed because most of the related particulars have been covered in earlier chapters and do not merit repetition at this stage. Answers to questions about a given type of school system fund should be sought by reference to the appropriate preceding chapter relating to funds of local governmental units.

OUTLINE OF PUBLIC SCHOOL ACCOUNTING

Purposes of Public School Accounting

Depending upon the degree of elaboration, the purposes of public school accounting may be few or many. For present requirements they will be described in three general statements, each of which might be amplified into a number of subordinate purposes. The three are:

1. To assist in the administration of public school resources, to the end of producing maximum private and public benefit from the services offered.
2. To assist in compliance with all laws and regulations pertaining to the use of money and other assets received from local, state, and Federal sources.
3. To provide school officials with adequate information for full and accurate reporting of their stewardship of the public school system, to (*a*) the public, (*b*) students of education, and (*c*) governmental agencies.

Originally the sole responsibility of local communities, public schools have now evolved into a joint project of state and local government, with growing participation by the Federal government. This tripartite arrangement magnifies the importance of the second purpose stated above, but the first is paramount.

Fund Structures

Kinds of Funds Used. Because of the diversity of conditions under which the thousands of public school systems operate and the variety of state and local laws and regulations affecting them, the fund structures in use represent a wide range of combinations. As for other kinds of governmental units, this is a situation strongly influenced, but not predominantly so, by the size of the school organization.

[4] State of New York Department of Audit and Control, Division of Municipal Affairs (Albany, 1965).

Seven types of funds are recommended by the USOE for public school management and control purposes:

General Fund
Special Revenue Fund
Capital Projects Fund
Debt Service Fund
Food Service Fund
Pupil Activity Fund
Trust and Agency Funds

Other funds such as endowment funds and "permanent school funds" also may be needed by local education agencies. In addition to the recommended funds, it is also recommended that school units employ two groups of accounts which do not qualify as funds. These are the general fixed assets and the long-term debt groups.

General and Special Revenue Funds. General funds and special revenue funds as recommended by the USOE for use by local education agencies are similar in all essential respects to funds of the same name recommended by the National Committee on Governmental Accounting for use by governmental units, as discussed in Chapters 3, 4, and 5 of this text. Under the laws of the various states, however, use of the general fund, by whatever name it is designated, may be either broadly inclusive or somewhat restricted. In one state it provides for administration, instruction, health, guidance, transportation, housekeeping (maintenance and operation of plant), and some other less conspicuous services. In other states some of these responsibilities are delegated to special revenue funds. In some states statutory restrictions upon the use of revenue from certain sources are combined with the requirement of a special revenue fund to account for receipt and use of the revenue. A similar requirement is common for Federally provided revenue.

Capital Projects Fund. In recent years capital improvements for school systems have assumed such magnitude that the use of special funds to account for their financing has become a practical necessity. Due to widespread and almost exclusive use of bonds for financing public improvements in earlier years, the related funds were called bond funds; but present-day financing of local school capital improvements is shared in so heavily by the state and Federal governments that a capital projects, or capital improvements, caption seems more descriptive. School capital projects funds, therefore, are identical to capital projects funds discussed in Chapter 6 of this text.

Debt Service Fund. In the event that a school system chooses or is required to accumulate assets for payment of principal and interest on long-term debt, a special fund is needed to account for receipt and disbursement of the assets. This type of fund, formerly referred to in most cases as a sinking fund, has recently been given the more descriptive name of debt service fund. Its major function is to facilitate budgeting and accounting for required revenues and expenditures for debt service purposes, just as is true of governmental debt service funds explained in Chapter 7 of this text.

Food Service Fund. General and special revenue funds, capital projects funds, and debt service funds recommended for use by schools are familiar to the reader who has studied preceding chapters. Food service funds, however, have no counterparts in general governmental units. The food service operations of a school system—"the preparation and serving of regular and incidental meals, lunches, or snacks in connection with school activities, and the delivery of food"[5]—are generally financed, wholly or partially, by charges for the food served. The food service operation often is not subject to the same laws governing the instructional activities of the schools. Accordingly, it is recommended that food service operations be accounted for in a separate food service fund.

Pupil Activity Fund. School-sponsored pupil activities and interscholastic activities are customarily supported in whole or in part by income from pupils participating in the activities, gate receipts, and other fund raising activities. Direct or indirect support may also be provided by use of revenue sources of the general or special revenue funds. Revenues raised by or for pupil activities, and related expenditures, should be accounted for in a pupil activity fund.

Trust and Agency Funds. School systems frequently find themselves serving in the capacity of trustee or agent for the custody and administration of assets of which they do not have outright ownership. For example, many school organizations are trustees for numerous award funds; and as employers all act as agents of state and Federal agencies for withholdings, sometimes in sizable amounts, from the pay of faculty, administration, and maintenance employees. Much of the material presented in Chapter 8 of this text, therefore, relates to school trust and agency fund accounting.

Endowment Funds and Permanent School Funds. Although not generally found at the local education agency level, endowment funds or permanent school funds are sometimes required. School endowment funds are closely related to the first form of trust fund explained in Chapter 8 of this text; endowment fund accounting *per se* is discussed in Chapter 18, College and University Accounting, because endowment funds are more often encountered in higher educational institutions than in primary and secondary schools. Permanent school funds are needed in some jurisdictions to account for money, securities, or land set aside to earn income to be expended for public school purposes. Permanent school fund assets "have been derived in most cases from the sale of State land set aside

[5] *Handbook II, Revised,* p. 127.

by Federal and/or State government, rents and royalties, and from surplus revenue returned to the State by the Federal Government."[6] Permanent school funds, therefore, are more generally found at the State level than at the local level.

Account Groups. Well-managed school systems should make use of two other accounting and reporting devices that are similar to funds but, as explained in earlier chapters, do not technically qualify as such. Although they may be found under various names, they are actually the general fixed assets and long-term debt groups. General fixed assets are those used for instructional and general administrative purposes. Accounting procedures for other fixed assets used by school systems are similar to those required for the enterprise or trust funds maintained by the general government. Chapters 12 and 13 describe general fixed asset accounting and general long-term debt accounting, respectively.

Classification of Revenues

"Revenue" is defined in *Handbook II, Revised* as "additions to assets which do not increase any liability, do not represent the recovery of an expenditure, do not represent the cancellation of certain liabilities without a corresponding increase in other liabilities or a decrease in assets, and do not represent contributions of fund capital in Food Service and Pupil Activity funds."[7] As is true for governmental units, school revenues should be classified by fund and source.

The source classification presented by the USOE publication is:

1000 Revenue from Local Sources
- 1100 Taxes
- 1200 Revenue from local governmental units other than local education agencies
- 1300 Tuition
- 1400 Transportation fees
- 1500 Earnings on investments
- 1600 Food services
- 1700 Pupil activities
- 1900 Other revenue from local sources

2000 Revenue from Intermediate Sources
- 2100 Grants-in-aid
- 2200 Revenue in lieu of taxes
- 2300 Revenue for/on behalf of the local education agency

3000 Revenue from State Sources
- 3100 Grants-in-aid
- 3200 Revenue in lieu of taxes
- 3300 Revenue for/on behalf of the local education agency

4000 Revenue from Federal Sources
- 4100 Grants-in-aid
- 4200 Revenue in lieu of taxes
- 4300 Revenue for/on behalf of the local education agency

[6] Ibid., p. 134.

[7] Ibid., p. 12.

An additional level of detail provided in the USOE revenue source classification system is not illustrated above. The nature of the detail is readily apparent; for example, revenue account 1100, Taxes, comprehends account 1110, Ad Valorem Taxes levied by Local Education Agency; 1120, Ad Valorem Taxes Levied by Another Governmental Unit; 1130, Sales and Use Taxes; 1140, Income Taxes; 1180, Other Taxes; and 1190, Penalties and Interest on Taxes.

"Intermediate" sources of revenue are administrative units or political subdivisions between the local education agency and the State. "Grants-in-aid" from intermediate, State, or Federal governments are contributions from general revenue sources of those governments, or, if related to specific revenue sources of those units, are distributed on a flat grant or equalization basis. "Revenue in lieu of taxes," analogous to payment from an enterprise fund to a general fund discussed in Chapter 11, are payments made out of general revenues of intermediate, State, or Federal governments to a local education agency because the higher governmental units own property located within the geographical boundaries of the local unit which is not subject to taxation. "Revenue for/on behalf of the local education agency" includes all payments made by intermediate, State, or Federal governments for the benefit of the local system; payments to pension funds, or a contribution of fixed assets, are examples.

Classification of Expenditures

The expenditure classification system recommended by the United States Office of Education is intended to promote the effective utilization of resources by linking financial transactions with resource items concerning curriculum, school staff, facilities, and with types of pupils. Using the chart of accounts in this manner "provides an opportunity to establish cost centers representing areas of educational effort and to account for the costs of such entities or *programs*."[8] Thus, the USOE recommendations are designed to facilitate program budgeting, and the planning-programming-budgeting-evaluating system approach to planning and controlling resource utilization.

An expenditure, as in accounting for general governmental units, may be defined as a decrease in fund assets, or an increase in fund liabilities, which results in a decrease in fund balance. In the USOE system the purposes and objects for which expenditures are made are categorized into types. These types are called *dimensions*, such as (1) Fund, (2) Object, (3) Function, (4) Operational Unit, (5) Program, (6) Source of Funds, (7) Fiscal Year, (8) Instructional Organization, (9) Assignment, (10) Term and (11) Special Cost Center. Fiscal year and fund dimensional classifications are self-explanatory. Examples of an object classifica-

[8] Ibid., p. 60.

tion are: Salaries, Employee Benefits, Purchased Services, Supplies and Materials, Capital Outlay, and Transfers.

Functional classes of school expenditures are: Instruction, Supporting Services, Community Services, Nonprogramed Charges, and Debt Services. Instructional Organization classes are: Elementary School, Middle/Junior High School, High School, Adult/Continuing Education School, Junior College, and Other. In practice the functional classification is often the same as the major program classifications; subclassifications in the program dimension would relate to specified programs and operational units.

The USOE chart of expenditure accounts system also provides for coding by operational unit (school building, warehouses, bus garages, administration building, etc.), source of funds (local, intermediate, State, Federal, other), term (fall term—day, fall term—night, etc.), job classification activity (official/administrative, professional-educational, technical, clerical, crafts and trades, etc.), and any special cost centers which may appear to be useful in a given school system.

ILLUSTRATIVE ENTRIES

General fund. To demonstrate approved accounting methods for some of the typical financial transactions of a school system general fund, a beginning trial balance, a series of transactions and entries, and an ending trial balance are illustrated in the next few pages. Infrequent or unusual transactions are omitted because of the wide variety of such transactions in all states and, therefore, the limited applicability to any one state.

Transactions and entries for the year, both in summary form, were as follows:

The annual budget for fiscal 19x4 was recorded, with $993,000 estimated revenues and $1,017,000 appropriations.

		Debit	Credit
1.	Estimated Revenues	993,000	
	Fund Balance	24,000	
	Appropriations		1,017,000

(Subsidiary ledger accounts would be shown for Estimated Revenues and Appropriations.)

19x3 taxes payable in 19x4 were levied in the amount of $489,000, of which $55,000 was designated for other funds. Estimated uncollectible taxes were $39,000 and the balance was revenue.

		Debit	Credit
2.	Taxes Receivable	489,000	
	Due to Other Funds		55,000
	Estimated Uncollectible Taxes		39,000
	Revenues		395,000

An encumbrance was recorded for the total amount of contracted salaries for the year. (This transaction is optional but it may assist in keeping expenditures for personal services within the amount budgeted for that purpose.)

3. Encumbrances	791,000	
Reserve for Encumbrances		791,000

The amounts recorded as receivables during the year were as shown below:

4. Due from Other Funds	11,600	
Due from State Government	499,600	
Due from Federal Government	87,600	
Accounts Receivable	7,900	
Revenues		606,700

Commitment documents (purchase orders, contracts, etc.) issued during 19x4 for normal expenditures other than contractual salaries included $28,010 for personal services; $119,630 for equipment; $29,760 for transfers of students to other school systems; $30,580 for utilities and other contractual services; and $11,030 for various other expenses.

5. Encumbrances	219,010	
Reserve for Encumbrances		219,010

Cash collections for the year included $9,660 from other funds; $456,690 from taxes; $7,400 from accounts receivable; $493,650 from state aid; $86,390 from the Federal government; and $1,510 from interest on temporary investments.

6. Cash	1,055,300	
Due from Other Funds		9,660
Taxes Receivable		456,690
Accounts Receivable		7,400
Due from State Government		493,650
Due from Federal Government		86,390
Revenues		1,510

$24,300 of overdue taxes receivable were classified as uncollectible during the year and written off in compliance with applicable laws.

7. Estimated Uncollectible Taxes	24,300	
Taxes Receivable		24,300

All temporary investments were sold for a net amount of $40,950, which included gain and a small amount of accrued interest.

8. Cash	40,950	
Investments		40,650
Revenues		300

Except for those already reported in previous transactions, expenditures for the year totaled $1,013,280. Of that amount, $51,830 was credited to the state teachers' retirement system and the remainder was vouchered. These expenditures included reimbursements of the petty cash fund. Encumbrances related to these same expenditures totaled $1,006,910, the remaining expenditures being for miscellaneous unencumbered costs. Of the expenditures total, $10,000 was for land, $151,000 for buildings, and $37,000 for equipment, all for general purposes.

		Debit	Credit
9.	Reserve for Encumbrances	1,006,910	
	Expenditures	1,013,280	
	Encumbrances		1,006,910
	Vouchers Payable		961,450
	Due to State Teachers' Retirement System		51,830

Cash was paid to the state teachers' retirement system in the amount of $49,040.

		Debit	Credit
10.	Due to State Teachers' Retirement System	49,040	
	Cash		49,040

(Vouchering of this payment is omitted for the purpose of conserving space. If permitted by law, this withholding might be administered with other withholdings such as those for FICA payments, Federal income taxes, etc., in one or more agency funds.)

Payments on vouchers payable totaled $972,320.

		Debit	Credit
11.	Vouchers Payable	972,320	
	Cash		972,320

Cash in the amount of $50,000 was paid to other funds.

		Debit	Credit
12.	Due to Other Funds	50,000	
	Cash		50,000

Some of the transactions conducted by the imaginary Trenton Consolidated Schools general fund would, in actual practice, affect another fund for which an entry would be required. The discussion of interfund transactions in Chapter 14 is also applicable to the present case.

If the foregoing entries were posted to a ledger with the beginning balances as shown in December 31, 19x3, after-closing trial balance (Illustration 17–1) the result would be the December 31, 19x4, trial balance shown in Illustration 17–2.

Balance sheets, statements of revenue, statements of expenditures, statements of cash receipts and disbursements, and statements of changes in fund balance are the most common kinds of general financial reports

Illustration 17–1

TRENTON CONSOLIDATED SCHOOLS
General Fund
After Closing Trial Balance, December 31, 19x3

	Debit	Credit
Cash	$ 37,530	
Petty cash	200	
Taxes receivable*	56,700	
Estimated uncollectible taxes		$ 15,070
Accounts receivable	600	
Due from other funds	3,215	
Due from state government	19,775	
Investments	40,650	
Vouchers payable		19,265
Due to state teachers' retirement system**		13,890
Fund balance		110,445
	$158,670	$158,670

*Note that only one account is used to control both current and delinquent taxes.
**Represents amounts withheld from teachers' pay or to be contributed by school system.

used for school system general funds. Statements of changes in financial position are useful for supplementing and explaining the revenue and expenditures statements. Since a general fund balance sheet at the end of a period shows only the residue of an annual financial program, it carries less importance than the same kind of a statement of a business

Illustration 17–2

TRENTON CONSOLIDATED SCHOOLS
General Fund
Trial Balance, December 31, 19x4

	Debit	Credit
Cash	$ 62,420	
Petty cash	200	
Taxes receivable	64,710	
Estimated uncollectible taxes		$ 29,770
Accounts receivable	1,100	
Due from other funds	5,155	
Due from state government	25,725	
Due from Federal government	1,210	
Vouchers payable		8,395
Due to other funds		5,000
Due to state teachers' retirement system		16,680
Reserve for encumbrances		3,100
Estimated revenues	993,000	
Fund balance		86,445
Appropriations		1,017,000
Encumbrances	3,100	
Expenditures	1,013,280	
Revenues		1,003,510
	$2,169,900	$2,169,900

enterprise. Much of what the commercial enterprise has to work with during the ensuing year is shown in its balance sheet, but the right to receive both private and public support is not reflected in a school system general fund statement of financial condition at the end of a given year, because the support is not available until the following year.

Balance Sheet. A balance sheet is more informative if it compares conditions at the ends of two consecutive periods. A portion of such a statement for the ends of 19x3 and 19x4 is shown below (Illustration 17–3.)

Illustration 17–3

TRENTON CONSOLIDATED SCHOOLS
General Fund
Comparative Balance Sheet
December 31, 19x4 and 19x3

Assets		*19x4*		*19x3*
Cash		$ 62,420		$ 37,530
Petty cash		200		200
Taxes receivable	$64,710		$56,700	
Less: Estimated uncollectible taxes	29,770		15,070	
Taxes receivable, net		34,940		41,630
Accounts receivable		1,100		600
Due from other funds		5,155		3,215
Due from state government		25,725		19,775
Due from Federal government		1,210		–
Investments		–		40,650
Total Assets		$130,750		$143,600

Liabilities, Reserves, and Fund Balance	19x4	19x3
Vouchers payable	$ 8,395	$ 19,265
Due to other funds	5,000	–
Due to state teachers' retirement system	16,680	13,890
Total Liabilities	$ 30,075	$ 33,155
Reserve for encumbrances	3,100	–
Fund balance	97,575	110,445
Total Liabilities, Reserves, and Fund Balance	$130,750	$143,600

Statement of Changes in Fund Balance. Statements of changes in fund balance of a revenue fund are found in a number of forms, some simple and some more complicated as well as possibly more informative. A simple form of such a statement (Illustration 17–4) will show why the fund balance of Trenton Consolidated Schools general fund declined from $110,445 to $97,575 during 19x4.

Although of some importance as part of a complete statement of responsibility, it is doubtful that the statement of changes in fund balance has any more than nominal value for administrative purposes. Ordinarily

Illustration 17–4

TRENTON CONSOLIDATED SCHOOLS
General Fund
Statement of Changes in Fund Balance for 19x4

Fund balance, December 31, 19x3			$110,445
Add:			
Excess of appropriations over expenditures and outstanding encumbrance, December 31, 19x4:			
Appropriations	$1,017,000		
Expenditures and encumbrances	1,016,380	$ 620	
Excess of actual over estimated revenues:			
Actual revenues	$1,003,510		
Estimated revenues	993,000	10,510	
Total Additions			11,130
Total Beginning Balance and Additions			$121,575
Deduct:			
Excess of appropriations over estimated revenues:			
Appropriations	$1,017,000		
Estimated revenues	993,000		
Total Deductions			24,000
Fund Balance, December 31, 19x4			$ 97,575

it would have little meaning to a school administrator or trustee not possessing a special knowledge of accounting.

Statement of Cash Receipts and Disbursements. Statements of cash receipts and disbursements for school system general funds should follow the general pattern of such statements for revenue funds, but with account or item titles appropriate to sources of school system receipts and purposes of disbursements. In general these should conform rather closely to revenue source titles and expenditure account titles. Statements of this sort are not of major importance, but when prepared on a "this month and year to date and same month last year and year to date" basis (Illustration 17–5) they assist in controlling cash flow and in construction of cash budgets for subsequent years.

Revenue Statements. Revenue statements of a school system may take any one of a number of forms: estimated for year and actual, year to date; given month and year to date, consecutive years; and year to date, consecutive years, with changes in amounts and percentages—to mention a few. A partial illustration of the last form of statement is shown below, using sources and classes from a published manual

If revenues are recorded on a strictly cash basis, considerable similarity will exist between revenues and cash receipts for a given period. Any use of the accrual basis introduces a degree of variation between cash receipts from a given class of revenue and actual earnings from the same

Illustration 17–5

Comparative Statement of Cash Receipts and Disbursements
February and Fiscal Year to Date, 19x4 and 19x3

	19x4		19x3	
Items (or other heading)	*February*	*Year to Date*	*February*	*Year to Date*
Balance at Beginning	$470,000	$490,000	$455,000	$476,000
Receipts:				
Taxes—current year	$ 30,000	$ 58,000	$ 27,000	$ 53,000

(This form is continued through both the receipts and disbursements sections and concludes with a showing of cash balances at the ends of the periods covered by the statement.)

class. In Illustration 17–6 the large amount of real property taxes shown for the first two months indicates use of the accrual basis. Revenue statements are valuable both for current management of revenue and for planning revenue budgets for future periods.

Illustration 17–6

Comparative Statement of Revenues
January 1 to February 28, 19x4 and 19x3

			Increase-(Decrease)	
Sources and Classes	*19x4*	*19x3*	*Amount*	*Percent*
Real property taxes:				
Real property taxes	$1,966,070	$1,733,180	$232,890	13.4
Nonproperty taxes:				
Taxes on consumer utility bills	$ 46,300	$ 43,220	$ 3,080	7.1
Admissions and dues tax	17,590	18,610	(1,020)	(5.5)

Expenditures Statements. Statements of expenditures are definitely the one most important kind of report in the statement repertory of school administrators. Responsible for complying with many laws and regulations affecting expenditure of educational funds, and striving for most effective use of money dedicated to the benefit of the school population, school officials require different kinds of expenditure statements in discharging their duties. School expenditure statements may relate to time periods, to educational programs, to locations (schools), to activities (transportation, instruction, etc.), comparison of estimated and actual, and other matters of interest to school board members.

It is not advisable to illustrate, in this chapter, more than one of the types mentioned, for which purpose the time period type will be employed (Illustration 17–7). However, with the great amount of financial information that most school systems are required to record, it is possible for a competent and imaginative accountant to devise numerous kinds

Illustration 17–7

Comparative Statement of Expenditures by Function
Amount Expended Year to Date Compared with Amount Budgeted
January 1 to February 28, 19x4 and 19x3

	19x4		*19x3*		*% Expended*	
Function	*Annual Budget*	*Expended to Date*	*Annual Budget*	*Expended to Date*	*19x4*	*19x3*
Instruction						
Regular programs	$1,970,000	$237,000	$1,769,000	$208,100	12.0	11.8
Special programs	604,320	76,310	589,060	61,060	12.6	10.4
Adult programs	96,950	1,650	83,120	1,170	1.7	1.4
Total instruction	$2,671,270	$314,960	$2,441,180	$270,330	11.8	11.1
Supporting Services						
Support service–pupils	$ 683,190	$ 98,450	$ 501,870	$ 74,990	14.4	14.9
Support services–instructional staff	18,030	106,380	61,250	60,040	90.1	98.0

of reports which will assist school administrators in the critical appraisal and control of expenditures. For this purpose it is certain that reports showing the progress of expenditures programs *during* the periods to which they relate are the most useful.

There are a few general observations which seem appropriate to school system revenue fund statements and, to some extent, to statements of nonrevenue funds:

1. They should be clear and concise, preferably confined to a single page.
2. They should be presented promptly after the date or period to which they apply; oral or written explanations may give a clearer understanding of formal statements.
3. Details of items in the main statements should be reported in separate schedules, if information about details is considered useful.
4. The comparative form of most financial statements is superior to the single date or period form because it helps to disclose trends of progress or retrogression.
5. Few, if any, financial statements are self-explanatory, but must be interpreted by the user or some other person competent to do so, if maximum benefit is to be derived from them.

Other Kinds of Funds

A one-chapter presentation of public school accounting does not permit a complete explanation of all funds and account groups used by school systems. The general nature and operations of the majority of school funds and account groups is similar to that explained in chapters concerned with accounting for local governmental units. Some operations which relate especially to local education agencies are discussed in following paragraphs.

Special Revenue Funds. The pupil transportation function may be performed by the local education agency, by investor-owned carriers, by municipally-owned bus lines, by parents, or by any combination thereof. If the function is performed by the school system the busses may be owned, operated, and maintained by individuals or organizations under contract with the school system; the system may own and maintain the busses and employ the drivers; or, again, combinations are found. If the local system owns and operates and maintains part or all of the busses and supports the function entirely from local general revenue sources the function should be accounted for by the general fund. Generally, however, other governmental units provide part of the support for the function with revenues which may be used only for that function; in such cases the pupil transportation function should be accounted for by a special revenue fund.

A significant difference between the recommendations of the National Committee on Governmental Accounting and the recommendations of the USOE *Handbook II, Revised* pertaining to special revenue fund accounting is that the latter illustrates a special revenue fund balance sheet in which fixed assets used in the fund's operations are included. In order to compute transportation costs in a meaningful manner it is suggested that a memorandum charge be computed for depreciation of buildings, equipment, and improvements other than buildings devoted to the transportation function. It is probable that the USOE recommends memorandum recording of depreciation rather than formal recording in the accounts because the assets devoted to the transportation function are ordinarily acquired from the expenditure of appropriations of tax revenues or of borrowed moneys which will be repaid from tax revenues. As suggested by the use of the terms "tax revenues" and "appropriations," to the extent that special revenue operations are financed in this manner, budgetary accounts are required.

Food Service Funds and Pupil Activity Funds. Illustrations of food service fund and pupil activity fund balance sheets contained in *Handbook II, Revised* show that fixed assets used by those funds are accounted for by those funds. The handbook is not clear as to whether depreciation on such fixed assets should be recorded formally in the accounts or merely recorded by memorandum. It is probable, however, that present thinking is that revenues from user charges are not expected to finance acquisition of any significant portion of future fixed assets of these funds; therefore memorandum recording of depreciation is appropriate. Unless required by law, budgetary accounts need not be used by food service funds or pupil activity funds. Prudent financial management dictates, however, that operations of each kind of function and activity be budgeted so that it is subject to control by the administrators and board of trustees responsible for the over-all operation of the local education agency.

MEASURING THE EFFECTIVENESS OF EXPENDITURES FOR PUBLIC SCHOOLS

In discussing and illustrating the operations of the kinds of funds used by public school systems and the statement forms adapted to financial reporting, attention has been confined to quantitative performances. Honest use of accounting and reporting procedures heretofore discussed can and does enable school administrators to ascertain the cost of programs if they have been defined for a given school system; the average cost of transportation for one mile or for any given period of time; to measure the per-pupil average cost of instruction in one course for one semester or any other length of time; and to determine the outlay per cost unit for the many other activities included in the school program. Among school systems using comparable accounting and reporting techniques, numerous comparisons of statistics may be made to demonstrate the apparent superiority of one school system over another or others. Unfortunately there is no positive correlation between what is spent and what is accomplished in the way of improving the pupils' minds and characters, which presumably is still the main purpose of the public school program. Subjective accomplishment does not necessarily vary in proportion to objective performance. A higher unit cost does not guarantee a superior quality of pupil attainment, even though it may create a more favorable learning environment than exists in lower cost systems. An imposing school plant, a large array of administrators, advisors, counselors, etc., and a faculty roster replete with high academic degrees may possibly mean better education, but not invariably so. Positively reliable comparisons of bona fide educational cost performance of a school system would, if they were possible, need to take cognizance of such variables as the natural ability of pupils; their home environment; the superior instructional ability of some teachers, irrespective of their formal academic achievements, and therefore not accurately reflected by the amount spent for instructional salaries. The occasional reports of pupils having reached the upper levels of a public school system without having learned to read tend to raise questions about what is really being accomplished with the public school dollar. With the employment of professional public relationists to "interpret" the schools to the public, the task of sound and dependable appraisal has become even more difficult.

In short, in the absence of a single criterion, such as amount of net income or net loss, for evaluating accomplishment and in the presence of many intangible influences, some helpful and some detrimental to educational attainment, conventional techniques for evaluating financial information are not sufficient. Only by the application of well-informed, impartial judgement, preferably grounded in a good understanding of the fundamental educational process, can the conventional financial reports and statistics of public school operations lead to decisions which will generate maximum benefit to pupils and public. Structuring budgeting, accounting, and reporting in accord with the PPBS principles discussed in Chapter 2 will materially aid cost/benefit analysis of public school expenditures and proposed expenditures.

SELECTED REFERENCES

American Institute of Certified Public Accountants. *Managing Public School Dollars.* New York: AICPA, 1972.

Association of School Business Officials of the United States and Canada. *50th Annual Volume of Proceedings, Addresses, and Research Papers,* pp. 280–82. Chicago, 1965, and succeeding annual volumes.

Davis, Clifford M. *A Manual of Accounting Principles and Procedures for Student Activity Funds.* Association of School Business Officials of the United States and Canada. Chicago, 1957.

Hirsch, Werner Z. and Marcus, Morton J. *Program Budgeting for Primary and Secondary Public Education,* Institute of Government and Public Affairs, University of California at Los Angeles, 1970.

Lindman, Eric L. *Approaches to Program Accounting for Public Schools,* CSEIP Occasional Report No. 34, University of California at Los Angeles, 1968.

Nash, Agnes B. *Accounting for Federally Aided Projects.* Special Bulletin 1967 B. Municipal Finance Officers Association of the United States and Canada. Chicago, 1967.

State of Illinois. *Illinois Financial Accounting Manual for Local School Systems,* Circular Series A, Number 164. Office of the Superintendent of Public Instruction, Division of Finance and Statistics. Springfield, 1965.

State of New York, Department of Audit and Control, Division of Municipal Affairs. *Uniform System of Accounts for School Districts, Double-Entry Basis.* Albany, 1965.

Tidwell, Sam B. *Public School Fund Accounting Principles and Procedures.* New York: Harper & Bros., 1965.

U.S. Department of Health, Education, and Welfare, Office of Education. *Financial Accounting: Classifications and Standard Terminology for Local and State School Systems.* State Educational Records and Reports Series: Handbook II, Revised. Washington, D.C.: U.S. Government Printing Office, 1973. (DHEW Publication No: OE73–11800)

———. *Principles of Public School Accounting*. State Educational Records and Reports Series: Handbook II-B. Washington, D.C.: U.S. Government Printing Office, 1967.

QUESTIONS

17–1. What accounting significance is there to the distinction between the terms "school system" and "school district"?

17–2. If you were asked to assist the new business manager of your local public schools to learn more about public school accounting than is contained in Chapter 17 of this text, to what sources would you direct him?

17–3. What do you consider to be the major benefit of the revenue and expenditure classifications of accounts developed under the direction of the U.S. Office of Education?

17–4. Auditors of a very large school system's financial records discovered three trust funds, each of which had been established more than half a century previously, for awarding medals for outstanding academic-related accomplishments. For the last 30 years the only entries in these three funds had been for receipt of interest on investments. Total assets of the funds (no liabilities) exceeded $10,000. What, if anything, do you think the auditors should have done about the situation?

17–5. Because the debt margin of most school systems has tended to be very low during the last quarter century, there has been widespread use of holding corporations to obtain school real estate. When the facilities so acquired are "paid out" and title passes to the school corporations, what should be stated as the source of the investment in fixed assets representing the newly acquired facilities?

17–6. Compare and contrast the kinds of funds recommended for use by a public school district with those recommended for use by general governmental units.

17–7. If the pupil transportation function is accounted for by a special revenue fund in accord with current USOE recommendations, how would that special fund balance sheet differ from the balance sheet of a general governmental special revenue fund?

17–8. A certain public school district's general fund showed estimated revenues of $986,000 for the year, and $978,700 revenues realized during the first six months of the year. During the second half year $45,000 was borrowed. What could account for the need to borrow money with more than 99 percent of the year's revenue realized during the first half of the year?

17–9. The subject of budgeting is not treated in detail in Chapter 17. To what extent do you feel that the information in Chapter 2 is applicable to public school districts? Why?

EXERCISES AND PROBLEMS

17–1. The annual report of a midwestern school system, which has not yet adopted the expenditure classifications recommended in *Handbook II, Revised,* gives the following comparison of per-student costs for the 19x4–x5 school year:

Activity	*This System*	*National Average*
Administration	$ 11.02	$ 15.40
Instruction.	345.94	311.15
Coordinate activities	14.86	30.45
Operation of plant and equipment	38.76	38.25
Maintenance of plant and equipment. . .	12.94	12.50
Fixed charges	10.12	15.00
Auxiliary services	3.11	.10
Capital outlay	69.60	9.30
Indebtedness.	52.49	40.55

a) From the foregoing information, prepare a comparison of unit costs in the following form, using the national average as the base figure:

			This System–Over (Under)	
Activity	*This System*	*National Average*	*Amount*	*Percent*
Administration . .	$11.02	$15.40	$(4.38)	(28.4)

b) Ignoring the probability of variations due to unusual circumstances, which of the foregoing averages appear to be favorable to the midwestern school system? Which ones appear to be unfavorable? What unusual circumstance or circumstances might account for the great disparity of average capital outlay? Are any two of the unusual averages related?

17–2. Below are listed several items, with amounts, which might appear in the statement used for calculating the amount of property tax required for a certain year by the general fund of a school district which operates on a strict cash basis. Items are listed in approximately alphabetical order.

Balance of cash, June 30, 197A.	$ 120,000
Current operating expenditures during 197B	1,420,000
Debt service requirements during 197B	230,000
Estimated expenditures during first six months of 197C. . . .	980,000
Payments for transfers of students to other school districts, 197B	32,000

Payment of current operating expenses, last six months of 197A.	661,000
Probable receipts from state government, last six months of 197A.	92,000
Probable amounts to be received for transfers from other school districts: balance of 197A, $18,000; during 197B, $49,000	67,000
Probable amount to be received from state and federal governments during 197B	617,000
Receipts expected from county distribution of property taxes, second half of 197A	579,000
Revenues expected to be received from miscellaneous sources during 197B.	24,000
Budgeted payment of cash to transportation fund, last half of 197A	17,000
Working balance permitted at end of 197B: 30% of estimated expenditures during first half of next year	

You are required to do the following things:

a) Compute the amount of working balance which will be on hand at December 31, 197A if estimates given above are realized.
b) State the amount of working balance to be provided for the beginning of 197C if the maximum legal amount is to be on hand.
c) Compute the total cash which must be provided for 197B expenditures if all estimated requirements, including working balance, are allowed.
d) Compute the amount of nontax cash receipts expected for 197B if all estimates for the year are realized.
e) Compute in simple form the amount of money which will be required from property taxes in 197B to satisfy all requirements to the end of that year.

17–3. A combined balance sheet included in the annual report of a large public school system is illustrated on the following pages. Comment on the statement with respect to the apparent adherence of the school system to the accounting and reporting principles discussed in Chapter 17.

17–4. A number of transactions in the illustration of school system general fund accounting, beginning with the trial balance of Trenton Consolidated Schools general fund at December 31, 19x3, (Illustration 17–1) affected another fund or group of accounts. You are required to do the following things (Assume that the Trenton school system has the kinds of funds and groups named as appropriate for public school accounting.):

Refer to the transactions and entries leading up to the December 31, 19x4, trial balance (Illustration 17–2) and for each transaction that affects another fund or group of accounts make the entry required for the other fund or group of accounts. If the name of the other fund (or funds) is not apparent from the transaction, record it as

XYZ SCHOOL SYSTEM
Balance Sheet
June 30, 1973

Assets	*Total*	*Current Fund*	*School Lunch Fund*	*School Construction Fund*	*Ware-house Fund*	*Employee Benefit Plan Trust Fund*	*Independent Activity Funds In Schools*	*General Fixed Assets*
Cash	$ 12,534,295	$ 7,865,789	$	$ 3,392,356	$	$ 322,348	$ 953,802	$
Accounts receivable:								
County	18,034,419			18,034,419				
State	4,194,266	2,230,103	150,720	1,813,443				
Federal government	2,906,678	2,906,678						
Other	335,721	199,231	305			100,000	36,185	
Due from other funds	2,257,058	2,141,849				115,209		
Inventories and prepaid expenses	895,007	40,700	72,718		668,509		113,080	
Construction in progress (Schedule 7)	87,391,836							87,391,836
Undistributed construction cost	4,192,748			4,192,748				
Investment securities—at cost	3,859,354					3,859,354		
Land, buildings, and additions—at estimated replacement value for projects completed before June 30, 1959 ($74,168,344) and at actual cost for projects completed thereafter ($112,808,028)	186,976,372							186,976,372
Furniture and equipment—at cost or estimated value where cost is not known (excluding $3,935,474 carried as construction in progress)	22,531,708							22,531,708
Total Assets	$346,109,462	$15,384,350	$223,743	$27,432,966	$668,509	$4,396,911	$1,103,067	$296,899,916

Liabilities								
Accounts payable and other liabilities	$ 4,951,963	$ 395,704	$	$ 4,193,461	$	$ 103,728	$ 259,070	$
Taxes and other amounts withheld from employees	1,673,259	1,673,259						
Accrued salaries and wages	4,936,578	4,936,578						
Due to other funds	2,257,058	615,209	489,345	983,995	168,509			
Tuition and other revenue collected in advance	227,476	112,267				115,209		
Federal funds (Public Law 874) reserved for fiscal year 1974	5,675,874	5,675,874						
Reserve for encumbrances–outstanding purchase orders	581,563	581,563						
Unexpended balances of restricted purpose grants (Schedule 17)	7,667	7,667						
Total Liabilities	20,311,438	13,998,121	489,345	5,177,456	168,509	218,937	259,070	
Fund balances (Exhibit B)	325,798,024	1,386,229	(265,602)	22,255,510	500,000	4,177,974	843,997	296,899,916
Total Liabilities and Fund Balances	$346,109,462	$15,384,350	$223,743	$27,432,966	$668,509	$4,396,911	$1,103,067	$296,899,916

an "other fund" or "other funds" transaction, as for transaction 2 of that series:

Other Funds:		
Due from General Fund	55,000	
Revenues		55,000

17–5. After six months of its 19x5 fiscal year, Brookville School Corporation general fund had the following trial balance:

BROOKVILLE SCHOOL CORPORATION
General Fund
Trial Balance, June 30, 19x5

	Debit	*Credit*
Cash	$ 60,630	
Taxes receivable	285,700	
Estimated uncollectible taxes		$ 45,700
Accounts receivable	3,500	
Due from other funds	78,320	
Due from state government	318,470	
Investments	15,650	
Vouchers payable		30,255
Due to other funds		67,120
Reserve for encumbrances		425,000
Fund balance		64,695
Estimated revenues	986,000	
Appropriations		1,030,000
Revenues		991,700
Encumbrances	425,000	
Expenditures	481,200	
	$2,654,470	$2,654,470

During the second half of 19x5 the following transactions occurred:

1. Encumbrance documents totaling $99,010 were issued to vendors, contractors, and others.
2. Three contracts in the total amount of $10,130 were issued.
3. All investments were sold for $15,890, which included $210 accumulated interest and $30 gain.
4. Routine cash collections for the second half of the year included $46,050 from other funds, $194,000 from current year's taxes, $2,690 from overdue taxes, $2,400 from accounts receivable, and $293,650 from state aid already recorded as a receivable.
5. Equipment estimated to cost $10,970 was ordered for a special educational program.
6. During the last half-year $25,100 of overdue taxes were classified as uncollectible and written off.
7. Routine expenditures during the second half of 19x5 totaled $532,080, of which $510,250 was vouchered and $21,830 credited to the agency fund for state teachers' retirement contributions. These expenditures had been encumbered at $529,210.

8. $75,520 cash was paid to other funds for liabilities previously recorded.
9. $533,220 of vouchers payable were paid.
10. Budgetary and nominal accounts for the year were closed.

You are required to do the first or both of the following parts:

a) Journalize the Brookville School Corporation's general fund transactions for the second half of 19x5. Explanations may be omitted.

b) Record the June 30 balances in T accounts, post the journal entries for the second half of the year, and prepare a balance sheet as of year-end.

17–6. In 19x6 the Town of Sumter school system officials decided to seek a Federal grant for partial financing of a vocational education project in the community. Preliminary investigation and planning having been completed, an application for financial assistance was presented to the appropriate Federal agency for a grant of $126,000. The balance of the estimated total project cost of $180,000 was to be supplied by a $36,000 grant of state aid and $18,000 from the school system general fund. In 19x7 the project, No. 33, was approved by the state and Federal governments, and a special revenue fund was established. The following transactions occurred during 19x7:

1. The project budget based upon the assumption of 100 percent collection and use of the available funds was recorded.
2. The amount to be received from the school system general fund was recorded.
3. $5,000 for use in paying initial costs was received from the general fund.
4. Purchase orders, contracts, and other commitments were incurred at a total estimated cost of $47,500.
5. Unencumbered costs were vouchered in the amount of $4,500.
6. Federal and state agencies were billed for $27,000 and $9,000 respectively.
7. Goods and service orders which had been encumbered at $28,900 were received. Vouchers payable were recorded for them in a total amount of $29,600.
8. Additional billings to Federal and state agencies were made in the amount of $63,000 and $17,000 respectively.
9. Additional commitments were recorded for $18,000 worth of supplies and for estimated salaries and contractual services of $103,200 for the balance of the project life.
10. Settlement was received in full for all amounts billed to the state and Federal governments, and the balance of its contribution was received from the school system general fund.
11. In preparation for a special report, $31,200 was paid on vouchers payable.
12. Expenditures were vouchered in the amount of $71,100. They had been encumbered for $69,200.

13. Payments on vouchers payable since the last previous report of payment totaled $69,700.
14. A proposed expenditure of $10,000 for advisory services, which had already been encumbered, was disapproved by the grantor Federal agency.
15. $30,500 and $8,000 were billed to the Federal and state agencies, respectively.
16. Performance was received on $54,300 additional encumbrances, the actual cost being $1,100 less than the estimated amount.
17. Amounts due from state and Federal agencies were received.
18. Before all money available to the project had been used, enrollment declined to such a level that a decision was made to discontinue operations, other than payment of necessary debts, this to be followed by normal dissolution operations for the project. Of total contracts for services and commodities outstanding, $1,700 were canceled; delivery was taken or had previously been taken on the balance at a total cost of $5,000. Vouchers were prepared accordingly.
19. All unpaid vouchers were liquidated.

You are required to do the following things:

a) Journalize and post the foregoing transactions, or post directly from transactions to ledger accounts.

b) Using the percentage apportionment of total cost provided for in the contract, determine each participant's share of actual costs.

c) Calculate each participant's total payments to the fund and determine for each participant the amount owing by it or to it.

17–7. You were engaged to examine the financial statements of the Mayfair School District for the year ended June 30, 19x7, and were furnished the General Fund trial balance which appears on page 531.

Your examination disclosed the following information:

1. The recorded estimate of losses for the current year taxes receivable was considered to be sufficient.
2. The local government unit gave the school district twenty acres of land to be used for a new grade school and a community playground. The unrecorded estimated value of the land donated was $50,000. In addition a state grant of $300,000 was received and the full amount was used in payment of contracts pertaining to the construction of the grade school. Purchases of classroom and playground equipment costing $22,000 were paid from general funds.
3. Five years ago a 4% 10-year sinking fund bond issue in the amount of $1,000,000 for constructing school buildings was made and is outstanding. Interest on the issue is payable at maturity. Budgetary requirements of an annual contribution of $90,000 and accumulated

MAYFAIR SCHOOL DISTRICT
General Fund Trial Balance
June 30, 19x7

	Debit	Credit
Cash	$ 47,250	
Taxes receivable—current year	31,800	
Estimated losses—current year taxes		$ 1,800
Temporary investments	11,300	
Inventory of supplies	11,450	
Buildings	1,300,000	
Estimated revenues	1,007,000	
Appropriations—operating expenses		850,000
Appropriations—other expenditures		150,000
State grant revenue		300,000
Bonds payable		1,000,000
Vouchers payable		10,200
Due to machine shop fund		950
Operating expenses:		
Administration	24,950	
Instruction	601,800	
Other	221,450	
Debt service from current funds (principal and interest)	130,000	
Capital outlays (equipment)	22,000	
Revenues from tax levy, licenses, and fines		1,008,200
Fund balance		87,850
Totals	$3,409,000	$3,409,000

earnings to date aggregating $15,000 were accounted for in separate Debt Service Fund accounts.

4. Outstanding purchase orders for operating expenses not recorded in the accounts at year end were as follows:

Administration	$1,000
Instruction	1,200
Other	600
Total	$2,800

5. The school district operated a central machine shop. Billings amounting to $950 were properly recorded in the accounts of the General Fund but not in the Machine Shop Fund.

Required:

a) Prepare the formal adjusting and closing entries for the General Fund.

b) The foregoing information disclosed by your examination was recorded only in the General Fund. Prepare the formal adjusting journal entries for the (1) General Fixed Asset Group, (2) Long-Term Debt Group, and (3) Machine Shop Fund.

(AICPA, adapted)

17–8. The Board of Education of the Victoria School District is developing a budget for the school year ending June 30, 19y0. The budgeted expenditures follow:

VICTORIA SCHOOL DISTRICT
Budgeted Expenditures
For the Year Ending June 30, 19y0

Current operating expenditures:			
Instruction:			
General	$1,401,600		
Vocational training.	112,000	$1,513,600	
Pupil service:			
Bus transportation	$ 36,300		
School lunches	51,700	88,000	
Attendance and health service.		14,000	
Administration		46,000	
Operation and maintenance of plant		208,000	
Pensions, insurance, etc.		154,000	
Total current operating expenditures			$2,023,600
Other expenditures:			
Capital outlays from revenues.		$ 75,000	
Debt service (annual installment and interest on long-term debt)		150,000	
Total other expenditures			225,000
Total Budgeted Expenditures			$2,248,600

The following data are available:

1. The estimated average daily school enrollment of the school district is 5,000 pupils, including 200 pupils enrolled in a vocational training program.
2. Estimated revenues include equalizing grants-in-aid from the state of $150 per pupil. The grants were established by state law under a plan intended to encourage raising the level of education.
3. The Federal government matches 60 percent of state grants-in-aid for pupils enrolled in a vocational training program. In addition the Federal government contributes toward the cost of bus transportation and school lunches a maximum of $12 per pupil based on total enrollment within the school district but not to exceed 6⅔ percent of the state per-pupil equalization grants-in-aid.
4. Interest on temporary investment of school tax receipts and rents of school facilities are expected to be $75,000 and are earmarked for special equipment acquisitions listed as Capital Outlays from Revenues in the budgeted expenditures. Cost of the special equipment acquisitions will be limited to the amount derived from these miscellaneous receipts.
5. The remaining funds needed to finance the budgeted expenditures of the school district are to be raised from local taxation. An allowance of 9 percent of the local tax levy is necessary for possible tax abatements and losses. The assessed valuation of the property located within the school district is $80,000,000.

Required:

a) Prepare a schedule computing the estimated total funds to be obtained from local taxation for the ensuing school year ending June 30, 19y0, for the Victoria School District.

b) Prepare a schedule computing the estimated current operating cost per regular pupil and per vocational pupil to be met by local tax funds. Assume that costs other than instructional costs are assignable on a per capita basis to regular and vocational students.

c) Without prejudice to your solution to part (*a*), assume that the estimated total tax levy for the ensuing school year ending June 30, 19y0 is $1,092,000. Prepare a schedule computing the estimated tax rate per $100 of assessed valuation of the property within the Victoria School District.

(AICPA, adapted)

17–9. The following budget was proposed for 19x9 for the Mohawk Valley School District general fund:

Fund balance, January 1, 19x9	$128,000
Revenues:	
Taxes	112,000
Investment income	4,000
Total	$244,000
Expenditures:	
Operating	$120,000
County treasurer's fees	1,120
Bond interest	50,000
Fund balance, December 31, 19x9	72,880
Total	$244,000

A general obligation bond issue of the school district was approved in 19x8. The proceeds are to be used for a new school. There are no other outstanding bond issues. Information about the bond issue follows:

Face	$1,000,000
Interest rate	5%
Bonds dated	January 1, 19x9
Coupons mature	January 1 and July 1, beginning July 1, 19x9

Bonds mature serially at $100,000 per year starting January 1, 19y1.

The school district uses a separate bank account for each fund. The general fund trial balance at December 31, 19x8 follows:

	Debit	*Credit*
Cash	$ 28,000	
Temporary investments–U.S. 4% bonds, interest payable May 1 and November 1	100,000	
Fund balance		$128,000
	$128,000	$128,000

The County Treasurer will collect the taxes and charge a standard fee of 1 percent on all collections. The transactions for 19x9 were as follows:

January 1—The proposed budget was adopted, and the taxes were levied.

February 28—Tax receipts from County Treasurer, $49,500, were deposited.

April 1—Bond issue was sold at 101 plus accrued interest. The premium and interest sold were transferred to the general fund to be used for payment of bond interest.

April 2—The school district disbursed $47,000 for new school site.

April 3—A contract for $950,000 for the new school was approved.

May 1—Interest was received on temporary investments.

July 1—Interest was paid on bonds.

August 31—Tax receipts from County Treasurer, $59,400 were deposited.

November 1—Payment on new school construction contract, $200,000, was made.

December 31—Operating expenses paid during year were $115,000.

Required:

Prepare the formal journal entries to record the foregoing 19x9 transactions in the following funds or groups of accounts, as explained in this chapter.

a) General Fund.
b) Capital Projects Fund.
c) General Fixed Assets Group.
d) General Long-term Debt Group.

Each journal entry should be dated the same as its related transaction as given above. Make the journal entries for each fund and group of accounts in a group by themselves. Explanations may be very brief, but should be precise. (Because certain transactions related to payment of interest are plainly specified in the problem as pertaining to the general fund, a debt service fund cannot be used for the solution.)

(AICPA, adapted)

18

College and University Accounting

In the preceding chapter the nature of fund accounting recommended for use by public schools is discussed and contrasted with that recommended for use by state and local governmental units of a general nature. In this chapter and the following one the discussions are related to two types of institutions that make extensive use of fund principles: colleges and universities, and hospitals. Many institutions in each category receive a significant portion of their financing from governmental sources. Other types of not-for-profit institutions such as religious, welfare, health, and fraternal organizations, labor unions, and clubs, also commonly use fund accounting; because of the similarities accounting for such entities is not discussed specifically in this text, but may be deduced from the discussions in these and preceding chapters.

Present-day accounting for institutions of higher learning is patterned rather closely upon the recommendations of a small number of organizations and individuals having special interests in accounting for such institutions. In this chapter an attempt will be made to present a summarization of their current views and recommendations. Much greater detail may be obtained by consulting the excellent references listed in the bibliography at the end of this chapter.

Comparison with Municipal Accounting

Colleges and universities may be likened to a municipality with its separate organization and with its financial affairs reflected by the use of a number of funds or types of funds. However, educational institutions generally select administrative employees principally on a merit basis, rather than by election or political appointment. Selection on a merit basis should contribute to better trained personnel, and should provide for continuity of administration in contrast with units of general government whose administrators are elected or appointed at regular intervals.

Colleges and universities also have an advantage over municipalities in that, even in those benefiting from extensive governmental financing, the measure of regulation by law is far less than for municipalities. Flexibility and adaptability to local circumstances are greatly enhanced by this advantage.

Although colleges and universities use fund accounting, the combination of funds and the emphasis on funds differ from those discussed in previous chapters. Revenue funds and trust funds predominate in the accounting structure of educational institutions. Agency funds are ordinarily required for some responsibilities of the institutions; and for their auxiliary enterprises, enterprise or intragovernmental service funds are used.

The basic authoritative publication in the college and university accounting field is *College and University Business Administration,* published by the American Council on Education. The ACE publication identifies and defines funds recommended for use by colleges and universities as follows:

> *Current funds*—funds available for current operations, including those for restricted as well as unrestricted purposes.
>
> *Loan funds*—funds which are loanable to students, faculty, and staff.
>
> *Endowment and similar funds*—funds whose principal is non-expendable as of the date of reporting and is invested, or is available for investment, for the purpose of producing income.
>
> *Annuity and life income funds*—funds acquired by an institution subject to annuity contracts, living trust agreements, or gifts and bequests reserving life income to one or more beneficiaries.
>
> *Plant funds*—funds to be used for the construction, rehabilitation, and acquisition of physical properties for institutional purposes; funds already expended for plant properties; funds set aside for the renewal and replacement thereof; and funds accumulated for the retirement of indebtedness thereon.
>
> *Agency funds*—funds in the custody of the institution but not belonging to it.[1]

Because of the great diversity of educational institutions—diversity in operations, size, wealth, and financial structure—no one chart of accounts will exactly fit all, or even a large percentage, of them. Individual differences must be taken into account; and a chart to fit the institution should be formulated rather than endeavoring to mold the institution's financial structure and operations to any given chart of accounts. Balance sheet accounts needed by a typical larger college or university are shown

[1] American Council on Education. *College and University Business Administration, Revised Edition.* Washington, D.C.: Author, 1968, pp. 143–48.

in Illustration 18–1. Typical current funds revenues and expenditure accounts are shown in Illustration 18–2. Many of the accounts shown in both illustrations are control accounts and must be supported by subsidiary ledgers in which are recorded detail needed for management of the institution and compliance with statutes; regulations; terms of grants, gifts, and endowments; and board and administrative directives. Most transactions of educational institutions are recorded in the conventional manner for similar transactions of governmental funds. Some peculiarities in terminology and in accounting for each of the funds recommended for use by colleges and universities exist, however; the more important of these are discussed and illustrated in following sections of this chapter.

Current Funds

Assets and liabilities available for current operations are accounted for by the "Current Funds group," in American Council on Education terminology. The word "group" is associated with the word "fund" in a manner which seems strange to the reader who is familiar with fund accounting for state and local governmental units. The confusion may be clarified by reference to the practice discussed in Chapter 11 of keeping several subfunds within the Enterprise Fund of a municipality. Colleges and universities have two kinds of current funds: restricted and unrestricted. Assets which are available for all purposes of the institution at the discretion of the governing board are *unrestricted.* Assets which are available for current operating purposes subject to limitations placed on them by persons or organizations outside the institution are *restricted.* For administrative purposes the assets of the two kinds of current funds may be properly commingled, but the fund balances of each kind must be accounted for separately. For financial reporting purposes the current funds group is subdivided into unrestricted current funds and restricted current funds. Illustration 18–1 shows that assets of each category, and related liabilities and fund balances, are reported separately. Revenues, expenditures, and transfers of current funds also must be classified as being related to restricted or unrestricted funds as shown by Illustration 18–2. Combined balance sheets of individual funds may be presented in a vertical format as shown by Illustration 18–1, or in a columnar format. A Statement of Changes in Fund Balances which should accompany the balance sheet would normally be in the same vertical or columnar format as the balance sheet. Illustration 18–3 shows a columnar form of Statement of Changes in Fund Balances.

Unrestricted Current Funds

All colleges and universities—and all other organizations—should prepare budgets whether or not required by law; properly prepared budgets are essential to good management. Colleges and universities which are

Illustration 18–1

HYPOTHETICAL UNIVERSITY
Balance Sheet, June 30, 19–

Assets

Current funds:		
Unrestricted:		
Cash	$ 289,400	
Investments, at cost (approximate market $685,000)	686,400	
Accounts receivable, less allowance for doubtful accounts of $5,900	280,400	
Notes receivable, less allowance for doubtful notes of $1,000	86,500	
Inventories, at cost	146,900	
Prepaid expenses and deferred charges	114,900	$ 1,604,500
Restricted:		
Cash	$ 187,600	
Investments, at cost (approximate market $110,000)	107,000	
Accounts receivable–principally agencies of the U.S. Government	472,700	767,300
Total Current Funds		$ 2,371,800
Loan funds:		
Cash	$ 19,900	
Investments, at cost (approximate market $20,000)	19,700	
Notes receivable, less allowance for doubtful notes of $7,700	386,700	
Total Loan Funds		$ 426,300
Endowment and similar funds:		
Cash	$ 7,900	
Investments, at cost (approximate market $1,910,000)	1,466,000	
(Funds held in trust by others, approximate market value of $78,300, earnings thereon to benefit the University)		
Total Endowment and Similar Funds		$ 1,473,900
Annuity and life income funds:		
Cash	$ 4,500	
Investments, at cost (approximate market $285,000)	223,900	
Total Annuity and Life Income Funds		$ 228,400

Liabilities and Fund Balances

Current funds:		
Unrestricted:		
Temporary notes payable to banks	$ 200,000	
Accounts payable and accrued expenses	200,000	
Provision for encumbrances	86,000	
Deposits	112,000	
Deferred revenues	102,100	
Fund balances (Form 4)	904,400	$ 1,604,500
Restricted:		
Accounts payable and accrued expenses	$ 170,200	
Provision for endowment income stabilization	12,000	
Fund balances (Form 5)	585,100	767,300
Total Current Funds		$ 2,371,800
Loan funds:		
Fund balances (Form 6)	$ 426,300	
Total Loan Funds		$ 426,300
Endowment and similar funds:		
Mortgages payable on real estate		$ 27,500
Fund balances (Form 7):		
Endowment funds	$ 980,000	
Term endowment funds	340,000	
Quasi-endowment funds	102,000	
Net adjusted gains and losses	24,400	1,446,400
Total Endowment and Similar Funds		$ 1,473,900
Annuity and life income funds:		
Undistributed income	$ 400	
Fund balances (Form 8)	228,000	
Total Annuity and Life Income Funds		$ 228,400

Assets			
Plant funds:			
Unexpended plant funds:			
Cash	$ 270,900		
Investments, at cost (approximate market $740,000)	736,200		
Appropriations receivable	300,000		
Accounts receivable	348,100	$ 1,655,200	
Funds for renewals and replacements:			
Cash	$ 109,500		
Investments, at cost (approximate market $180,000)	177,700	287,200	
Funds for retirement of indebtedness:			
Cash	$ 57,000		
Investments, at cost (approximate market $260,000)	254,800	311,800	
Investment in plant, at cost:			
Land	$ 1,025,000		
Buildings	19,755,200		
Improvements other than buildings	922,400		
Equipment	6,631,800		
Construction in progress	1,934,800	30,269,200	
Total Plant Funds			$32,523,400
Agency funds:			
Cash		$ 87,300	
Investments, at cost (approximate market $70,000)		68,900	
Total Agency Funds			$ 156,200

Liabilities and Fund Balances			
Plant funds:			
Unexpended plant funds:			
Accounts payable		$ 178,800	
Advances from U.S. Government		260,000	
Temporary notes payable to banks		350,000	
Bonds payable		400,000	
Fund balances (Form 9)		466,400	
		$ 1,655,200	
Funds for renewals and replacements:			
Fund balances (Form 10)		287,200	
Funds for retirement of indebtedness:			
Fund balances (Form 11)		311,800	
Investment in plant:			
Notes payable	$ 310,000		
Bonds payable	3,974,800		
Net investment in plant (Form 12) (Fund Bal.)	25,984,400	30,269,200	
Total Plant Funds			$32,523,400
Agency funds:			
Fund balances (Form 13)		$ 156,200	
Total Agency Funds			$ 156,200

Note: Details of the ending fund balances may be shown in the statements of changes in fund balances, as illustrated in these forms, or in the balance sheet.

Source: American Council on Education. ***College and University Business Administration*****, *Revised Edition*, pp. 238–39.**

Illustration 18–2

HYPOTHETICAL UNIVERSITY
Statement of Current Funds Revenues, Expenditures, and Transfers
for the Year Ended June 30, 19–

	Total	*Unrestricted*	*Restricte*
Revenues (Form 15):			
Educational and general:			
Student tuition and fees	$ 964,100	$ 964,100	
Governmental appropriations	2,688,000	2,326,400	$ 361,60
Endowment income (including $6,500 received from funds held in trust by others)	39,000	12,000	27,00
Gifts	472,700	441,400	31,30
Sponsored research:			
Governmental	1,008,000		1,008,00
Nongovernmental	200,000		200,00
Other separately budgeted research	61,000	61,000	
Other sponsored programs:			
Governmental	27,000		27,00
Nongovernmental	10,000		10,00
Recovery of indirect costs–sponsored programs	30,000	30,000	
Sales and services of educational departments	43,200	43,200	
Organized activities relating to educational departments	59,500	59,500	
Other sources	28,000	24,900	3,10
Total Educational and General	$5,630,500	$3,962,500	$1,668,00
Student aid	81,200		81,20
Auxiliary enterprises	1,153,500	1,153,500	
Total Revenues	$6,865,200	$5,116,000	$1,749,20
Expenditures (Form 16):			
Educational and general:			
Instruction and departmental research	$2,282,600	$1,899,500	$ 383,10
Organized activities relating to educational departments	79,700	79,700	
Sponsored research	1,208,000		1,208,00
Other separately budgeted research	61,000	61,000	
Other sponsored programs	37,000		37,00
Extension and public service	27,500	6,400	21,10
Libraries	124,700	105,900	18,80
Student services	181,800	181,800	
Operation and maintenance of physical plant	417,200	417,200	
General administration	167,600	167,600	
Staff benefits	368,100	368,100	
General institutional expenses	224,100	224,100	
Total Educational and General	$5,179,300	$3,511,300	$1,668,000
Student aid	194,400	113,200	81,200
Auxiliary enterprises (including debt service of $205,800)	1,130,900	1,130,900	
Total Expenditures	$6,504,600	$4,755,400	$1,749,200
Transfers:			
To:			
Loan funds for supplements to U.S. Government grants (Form 6)	$ 4,000	$ 4,000	
Quasi-endowment funds (Form 7)	100,000	100,000	
Plant funds for:			
Additions (Form 9)	150,000	150,000	
Renewals and replacements (Form 10)	43,500	43,500	
Retirement of indebtedness (Form 11)	17,500	17,500	
Total Transfers	$ 315,000	$ 315,000	
Excess of Revenues over Expenditures and Transfers	$ 45,600	$ 45,600	$ —

Source: American Council on Education. *College and University Business Administration, Revised Edition*, pp. 242–43.

Illustration 18–3

HYPOTHETICAL UNIVERSITY
Statement of Changes in Fund Balances
for the Year Ended June 30, 19–

	Current Funds					Plant Funds		
	Unre-stricted	Restricted	Loan Funds	Endowment and Similar Funds	Annuity and Life Income Funds	Unexpended	Net investment in plant	Agency Funds
Balances, July 1, 19–	$837,800	$ 355,164	$383,180	$1,313,700	$223,300	$969,200	$25,178,900	$119,500
Excess of revenues over expenditures and transfers	45,600							
Governmental appropriations		380,000				600,000		
Endowment income		47,136	140					
Gifts and grants		198,900	36,400	33,000	10,000	75,000	20,000	
Sponsored research		1,351,500						
Other sponsored programs		52,000						
Other sources		3,100				10,000		36,700
Interest and investment income			4,200		11,700	27,000		
Income added to principal				3,000				
Accrued interest on sale of bonds						3,000		
Transfers from (to) other funds		(30,000)	4,000	103,000	(3,000)	416,800		
Additions to physical properties from:								
Current funds							80,000	
Unexpended plant funds						(651,400)	651,400	
Gains or (losses) on sales of securities				14,700	(1,000)	500		
Expenditures		(1,749,200)				(187,200)		
Refunds to grantors		(23,500)						
Expiration of term endowment	21,000			(21,000)				
Uncollectible notes charged off			(1,160)					
Death and teachers' cancellations			(460)					
Payments to beneficiaries and annuitants					(13,000)			
Bonds retired						(112,500)	112,500	
Note payments						(15,000)	15,000	
Interest paid						(70,000)		
Disposals of physical properties							(73,400)	
Balances, June 30, 19–	$904,400*	$ 585,100	$426,300	$1,446,400	$228,000	$1,065,400	$25,984,400	$156,200

*The Governing Board has allocated $125,000 of this balance for specific operating purposes.
Source: American Council on Education. *College and University Business Administration, Revised Edition*, pp. 242–43.

privately supported need not record their budgets in their fund accounts, but colleges and universities which receive governmental appropriations for operating and capital needs ordinarily are required to treat approved budgets as legal documents. For the latter group, therefore, much of the discussion in Chapter 2, and in the other chapters dealing with general governmental funds, is applicable in principle. The account titles suggested by the American Council on Education differ from those recommended for general governmental use, as shown by the entry below; the only essential difference in the entry to record the budget, however, is that the difference between budgeted revenues and budgeted expenditures is not carried directly to Fund Balance but to an intermediate account, for which the title Unallocated Revenues is suggested.

Unrealized Revenues	25,000,000	
Estimated Expenditures		24,800,000
Unallocated Revenues		200,000

Revisions in budgeted revenues and budgeted expenditures during a budget period would be recorded by appropriate debits or credits to the accounts shown in the entry above. At year-end the balances of the three accounts will still be equal in total, and they may therefore be closed by an entry that is the reverse of the one illustrated. Thus, Unrestricted Current Fund Balance at all times represents net assets of that category, rather than being a mixture of budgetary and proprietary amounts as is true of a governmental general fund Fund Balance account.

Colleges and universities which use budgetary accounting should also record encumbrances, for reasons discussed in earlier chapters. All colleges and universities, whether they use budgetary accounting or not, should recognize revenues and expenditures of unrestricted current funds on the accrual basis to the extent practicable for an entity which is not concerned with the determination of net income. Because college fiscal years and academic years rarely coincide, it is common for tuition and fees collected near the end of a fiscal year to relate in large portion to services to be rendered by the institution during the ensuing fiscal year. Accordingly, the portion of revenues received in advance, from all sources available for unrestricted current use, is recognized as Deferred Revenues, a balance sheet account.[2] Typical unrestricted current funds revenue and expenditure accounts are shown in Illustration 18–2.

Restricted Current Funds

Restricted current funds are expendable for those operating purposes specified by donors. "Donors," in this sense, includes individuals, partner-

[2] The AICPA audit guide, *Audits of Colleges and Universities*, p. 7, states that "revenues and expenditures of an academic term such as a summer session, which is conducted over a fiscal year-end, should be reported totally within the fiscal year in which the program is predominantly conducted."

ships, profit-seeking corporations, not-for-profit corporations, and governmental agencies. The assets may be received directly by the restricted current funds or they may be transferred to restricted current funds as income from endowment funds. In some instances appropriations of general governmental units for college operations are restricted as to the purposes for which they may be expended. In such event, the legal budget related to the restricted appropriation should be recorded in the accounts of restricted current funds. Budgets relating to receipts from donors, and the disbursement of those receipts, ordinarily need not be formally recorded in the accounts, although since the amount from each grant or gift is limited in amount as well as restricted in purpose it may be appropriate to use encumbrance accounts. In any event, expenditures of restricted current funds should be recognized on the accrual basis. It is also recommended that revenues of restricted current funds be recognized on the accrual basis; however, in practice it is probable that the modified accrual criterion of "material and available" is used because there is often great difficulty in determining the date on which a grant from a governmental agency gives rise to *available* revenues. Typical restricted current funds balance sheet and revenue and expenditure accounts are shown in Illustrations 18–1 and 18–2.

Loan Funds

Assets which are loanable to students, faculty, and staff of an educational institution are provided by gifts, by grants, by income from endowment funds, by transfers from other funds, and, in some cases, from loans made to the institution for that purpose. The intent is that the loan fund be operated on a revolving basis: repayments of loans, and interest received on the loans, are deposited in the loan fund and are then available for lending to other eligible persons. Interest earned on loans, and interest earned on temporary investment of loan fund cash, are expected to offset wholly or partially the cost of administration of the loan fund and the loss from uncollectible loans. In accord with the conventions of accrual accounting the estimated loss from uncollectible loans, and uncollectible interest on loans, should be considered as an expense of each period. The related allowance account should be deducted from Notes Receivable on the balance sheet. Since some assets are given to the institution under very specific restrictions as to who may receive loans, and other assets may be used in accord with policies set by the governing board of the institution, loan fund accounts and reports must be in detail sufficient to demonstrate that the donor's restrictions and board policies are being adhered to. Loan funds balance sheet accounts are shown in Illustration 18–1. Additions to and deductions from loan fund balances are reported in a statement of changes in Loan Fund balances, rather than a statement of revenues and expenditures.

Endowment and Similar Funds

Funds "whose principal is nonexpendable as of the date of reporting and is invested, or is available for investment, for the purpose of producing income" are classified as "endowment and similar funds."[3] Endowment funds, the ACE defines as funds which donors have stipulated, as a condition of the gift, that the principal is to be maintained inviolate and in perpetuity, with only the income from the investments available to be expended.[4] "And similar" in the fund title refers to term endowment funds and quasi-endowment funds. *Term endowment funds* are defined in the same manner as endowment funds, with the exception that the conditions of the gift provide that the assets are released from inviolability to permit all or a part of them to be expended upon the happening of a particular event or the passage of a stated period of time. *Quasi-endowment funds* are sometimes called "funds functioning as endowments"; they are funds established by the governing board of the institution to account for assets which are to be retained and invested.

Accounts and reports of endowment and similar funds should disclose separately each subgroup within the category, as is done in Illustration 18–1. Reports should disclose funds in this category for which the income is unrestricted in use and those for which the income is restricted in specific uses, if the distinction exists in a given situation.

Problems encountered in accounting for endowment and similar funds of educational institutions are much like those discussed in Chapter 8 of this text in relation to nonexpendable trust funds of a governmental unit. Specific problems of accounting for endowment funds are discussed in some detail in Chapter 19 in relation to hospital endowment funds; the discussion in that chapter applies also to college and university endowment funds. Accounting for investments of endowment and other funds is discussed in detail in Appendix 3. Statements and schedules illustrated in Chapters 8 and 19, and in Appendix 3, are appropriate for use in reporting the condition and results of operations of endowment and similar funds of educational institutions.

Annuity and Life Income Funds

"Annuity and life income funds are funds acquired by an institution subject to agreements requiring payments to one or more designated beneficiaries during the life of those individuals."[5] If the agreement requires the institution to pay a specified amount, the fund is an *annuity* fund. If the agreement requires only that the institution pay the income

[3] Ibid., p. 144.

[4] Ibid., p. 145.

[5] Clarence Scheps and E. E. Davidson. *Accounting for Colleges and Universities, Revised Edition,* Baton Rouge: Louisiana State University Press, 1970, p. 231.

earned by the assets of the fund, it is a *life income* fund. It should be obvious that agreements under which an educational institution accepts either life income or annuity funds should be carefully drawn by competent lawyers in consultation with competent accountants and investment managers in order to protect the interests of the receiving institution as well as of the donor. The definition of "income" is one of the matters needing most careful attention. From the accounting point of view, income should be defined in accrual terms, so that the principal of the gift will not be eroded by failure to deduct appropriate depreciation and amortization charges. It is also in the interest of the institution that an equitable allocation of indirect administrative expenses be permitted as well as a deduction for direct expenses of administering each annuity and life income fund. From this brief discussion it is apparent that accounting problems of annuity and life income funds tend to be similar to those of endowment funds.

A balance sheet for annuity and life income funds is shown as a part of Illustration 18–1. In addition to the accounts shown in that statement, accounts must be maintained in sufficient detail to enable determination of net income for each of the funds in the category, and to demonstrate compliance with all provisions of the agreement under which the institution accepted the funds. If operations of annuity and life income funds involve businesses or firms, it is appropriate that income statements be prepared. If operations of these funds are less complex, a statement of changes in fund balances, supported by appropriate schedules, may provide adequate disclosure.

Plant Funds

A plant fund of a college or university differs from the general fixed assets group of a governmental unit in that it accounts for current assets set aside to be used for the construction, rehabilitation, and acquisition of capital assets, as well as the fixed assets themselves, and assets set aside for the retirement of indebtedness on fixed assets. As shown in Illustration 18–1, a plant fund also accounts for debt related to fixed assets; separate Fund Balance accounts are kept to show the net equity in current assets held for plant fund purposes, the net equity in assets held for retirement of indebtedness, and the net invested in plant.

A number of transactions affecting plant funds also affect other funds, and are illustrated in the *Illustrative Transactions* section of this chapter.

Agency Funds

As is true of general governmental units and public schools, colleges and universities often act as agents of others for the collection, custodianship, and disbursement of assets. Activities of this nature are properly accounted for by *agency funds*. Inasmuch as assets are commonly held in a college agency fund for longer periods of time than is true of general governmental agency funds, there are usually asset and equity balances to be shown in a year-end balance sheet (see Illustration 18–1). With that exception, the discussion of agency funds of governmental units (Chapter 8) is generally applicable to college and university agency funds.

ILLUSTRATIVE TRANSACTIONS

One of the simplest ways–even if not the easiest–of acquiring plant property is through gift. Assuming a gift of plant land and buildings appraised at $5,000 and $25,000, respectively, the following entry would be made in the plant fund accounts:

Investment in plant:

1.	Land	5,000	
	Buildings	25,000	
	Net Investment in Plant		30,000

If the gift were in the form of cash, to be used at a later date for the purchase of land and buildings, the following trio of entries would record the transactions:

Unexpended plant funds:

2a.	Cash	30,000	
	Unexpended Plant Funds Balance		30,000

The use of the contribution to record the purchase of land and buildings is illustrated as follows:

Unexpended plant funds:

2b.	Unexpended Plant Funds Balance	30,000	
	Cash		30,000

Investment in plant:

2c. (Same as entry no. 1.)

If the cash gift were designated for a certain purpose, some instituitions might record its receipt in a Reserve for Purchases of Land (or other property) account, in preference to the Unexpended Plant Funds Balance account. A similar credit could be used to record the accumulation of receipts from other sources, to be spent subsequently for plant additions.

Accounting for transfers of unrestricted current fund cash to Unexpended Plant Funds for eventual property acquisition is recorded by the following entries:

Unrestricted current funds:

3a.	Transfers to Unexpended Plant Funds	80,000	
	Cash		80,000

In practice the foregoing entry probably would have been routed through the Vouchers Payable account.

Unexpended plant funds:

3b. Cash	80,000	
Unexpended Plant Funds Balance		80,000

The purchase of the property would require entries in the Unexpended Plant Funds and the Investment in Plant Funds accounts. The structure of these two entries is obvious from the previous examples.

The purchase of permanent equipment from unrestricted current funds cash need not be recorded in the Unexpended Plant Funds account if a single current funds disbursement is involved. The disbursements should be recorded as an expenditure of the current fund; the acquisition must, of course, be recorded in the Investment in Plant fund.

Unrestricted current funds:

4a. Expenditures	2,000	
Cash		2,000

Investment in plant:

4b. Equipment	2,000	
Net Investment in Plant		2,000

A third common method of increasing the property of educational institutions is through bond issues. Accounting for property acquisitions by this means departs materially from the procedure for similar operations by governmental units generally. Proceeds from the sale of bonds and the liability for the bonds are recorded as follows:

Unexpended plant funds:

5. Cash	5,000,000	
Bonds Payable		5,000,000

Had the bonds brought less than the amount required for acquiring the property, the deficiency might be covered by other unexpended plant funds cash, or by a transfer from current funds. Purchase or construction of the property requires a transfer of the liability from the "Unexpended" to the "Invested" subfund:

Unexpended plant funds:

6a. Bonds Payable	5,000,000	
Cash		5,000,000

Investment in plant funds:

6b. Property (itemized)	5,000,000	
Bonds Payable		5,000,000

Accounting for the retirement of the bonds assumed to have been issued in the above examples does not conform to the standard practice prevalent in general governmental accounting. Assuming serial-type bonds, the accumulation of money for their retirement might be recorded as follows:

Unrestricted current funds:

7a.	Transfers to Funds for Retirement of Indebtedness......	50,000	
	Cash..................................		50,000

Funds for retirement of indebtedness:

7b.	Cash..	50,000	
	Retirement of Indebtedness Fund Balance......		50,000

Retiring $100,000 par value of the bonds would be recorded by the following simultaneous entries:

Funds for retirement of indebtedness:

8a.	Retirement of Indebtedness Funds Balance.............	100,000	
	Cash..................................		100,000

Investment in plant funds:

8b.	Bonds Payable..................................	100,000	
	Net Investment in Plant....................		100,000

All the preceding examples have assumed the acquisition of property in finished form. Conversion from cash to property may have to be accounted for through the intermediate or construction stage. This being the case, payments applicable to the final cost of the property, assumed to be a dormitory, may be recorded as follows:

Unexpended plant funds:

9.	Construction in Progress............................	40,000	
	Cash..................................		40,000

Completion of the project would require two entries, as shown below:

Unexpended plant funds:

10a.	Unexpended Plant Funds Balance....................	750,000	
	Construction in Progress..................		750,000

Investment in plant funds:

10b.	Buildings..	750,000	
	Net Investment in Plant..................		750,000

It would appear that no serious violation of sound theory would result from the inclusion of the construction account in the "investment in plant funds" group. Under this plan, intersection transfers of accountability would be based upon applications of cash to the construction project, rather than upon completion.

Although educational institutions rely heavily upon gifts and grants to finance property replacements as well as additions, some follow the policy of advance provision for replacements through the medium of an accumulation reserve ordinarily financed by the current fund. A separate subfund of the Plant Funds is utilized to record assets set aside for renewals and replacements, as shown by the following entries.

Unrestricted current funds:

11a.	Transfers to Funds for Renewals and Replacements....	60,000	
	Cash....................................		60,000

Funds for Renewals and Replacements:

11b.	Cash..	60,000	
	Renewals and Replacements Fund Balance....		60,000

If amounts of money are large, or if some time is to elapse before the cash held for plant renewals and replacements will be used, prudent financial management dictates that it be invested in marketable securities of high quality. The same is true of cash transferred to Unexpended Plant Funds and Funds for Retirement of Indebtedness. In each case, earnings on investments should be added to the particular subfund to which the investments belong.

Depreciation of Fixed Assets

Colleges and universities may have three general classes of fixed assets: educational plant, auxiliary enterprise properties, and real estate held as an investment by endowment funds.

Educational plant. With regard to educational plant—buildings and equipment used primarily for instruction and research, for administrative purposes, and for service operations such as power plants, shops, and storage facilities—the weight of authority prohibits depreciation expense from being recognized in unrestricted current funds accounts. Justification for the prohibition stems from the thought that college students should not be expected to pay fees which are set to recover depreciation of educational plant inasmuch as the plant was acquired from gifts or governmental appropriations (and presumably will be replaced from similar sources).

Depreciation on educational plant used in the performance of activities supported by grants or contracts is ordinarily considered to be an allowable cost, just as is true of governmental general fixed assets used in activities supported by grants. Under these conditions depreciation computations are generally made in sufficient detail to support claims for reimbursement from grantors or contractors. In spite of the long-time importance of grants and contracts as a means of support, the American Council on Education's most recent recommendations are firmly against any accounting recognition of depreciation on educational plant. The American Institute of Certified Public Accountants agrees that depreciation expense on physical plant should not be recorded in unrestricted current funds; however, the AICPA does state that it is permissible for an accumulated depreciation allowance to be reported in the Investment in Plant balance sheet, and the provision for depreciation to be reported in the statement of changes in the balance of the investment in plant fund.[6]

If from reimbursements under grants or contracts, or other sources, an institution generates current funds revenues which may be set aside for eventual renewal or replacement of educational plant, a transfer should be made as illustrated by entries 11a and 11b above.

Auxiliary enterprise plant. The foregoing generalizations hold for plant used by auxiliary enterprises, although the enterprises are intended to be self-supporting and generally accepted accounting principles would logically apply. The logic, however, does not seem to be as apparent to the American Council on Education as it does to this author. Under ACE recommendations auxiliary enterprise current funds, and auxiliary enterprise plant is accounted for in the plant funds. In lieu of depreciation accounting for auxiliary enterprise plant, the ACE allows "Provisions for Renewals and Replacements" to be reported under that caption in the schedules of current expenditures of the enterprises. (These schedules support the Statement of Current Funds Revenues, Expenditures, and Transfers, as shown in Illustration 18–2.) Cash or other liquid assets in an amount equal to the provision should be transferred to Funds for Renewals and Replacements.

Endowment funds plant; annuity and life income funds plant. In contrast to the recommendations with regard to educational plant and auxiliary enterprises plant, the ACE does recommend that depreciation on plant held as investment of endowment funds be recognized in the accounts of the endowment funds. Similarly, depreciation in property held under annuity and life income agreements should be recognized as an element in the determination of the net income of those funds. Although the propriety of this recommendation is clear to accountants, there are some states in which the legal presumption is that the income beneficiary is entitled to net income computed on the cash basis, rather than the accrual basis. For that reason, educational institutions commonly attempt to have donors specify in the agreement under which the institution accepts the property that accrual basis accounting will be followed.

Conclusion

The limits of a single chapter permit little more than mention of the salient features of accounting for educational institutions. The effect of this restriction is aggravated by variations in the size of educational institutions, variations in the nature and sources of revenue, and diversity

[6] American Institute of Certified Public Accountants. *Audits of Colleges and Universities,* New York, 1973, p. 15.

of activities carried on by individual institutions. As suggested earlier in this chapter, some measure of the limitation may be overcome by reference to the excellent publications listed in the following bibliography. However, many individual situations and problems in college and university accounting can be interpreted only in the light of sound accounting theory and the intentions of the responsible officials. They are not explained in any book or other publication.

SELECTED REFERENCES

American Council of Education. *College and University Business Administration, Rev. ed. Washington: Author*, 1968.

American Institute of Certified Public Accountants. *Audits of Colleges and Universities.* New York, 1973.

Badger, Henry Glenn. *Junior College Accounting Manual.* Washington, D.C.: American Association of Junior Colleges and American Council on Education, 1945.

Bastable, C. W. "*Collegiate Accounting Needs Re-Evaluation,*" *Journal of Accountancy*, Vol. 136, No. 6 (December 1973), pp. 51–57.

Cary, William L. and Bright, Craig B. *The Law and the Lore of Endowment Funds.* New York: Ford Foundation Educational Endowment Series, 1969.

Englander, Louis. *Accounting Principles and Procedures of Philanthropic Institutions.* New York: New York Community Trust, 1957.

Feyerharm, Robert W. "Budgetary Accounting Procedures and Accounting Forms for Small Colleges and Universities," *Accounting Review*, Vol. XXX, No. 1 (January, 1955), pp. 80–85.

Scheps, Clarence and Davidson, E. E. *Accounting for Colleges and Universities, Rev. Ed.* Baton Rouge: Louisiana State University Press, 1970.

QUESTIONS

18–1. The classroom buildings of a state university were constructed from funds appropriated by the state legislature. Dormitories and athletic plant were constructed from funds derived from the sale of revenue bonds and from gifts from alumni and friends. In what fund groups should the various classes of buildings be accounted for? Give reasons for your answers.

18–2. Many educational institutions today provide numerous large-scale nonacademic services, e.g., intercollegiate athletics, food service, and housing, for the benefit of the student body. Does this cause any difficulty in accounting for and measuring the cost of strictly educational services?

18–3. What risk may attend the acceptance of an endowment subject to payment of a fixed-amount annuity to the donor?

18–4. Educational institutions as employers are required to make one or more forms of compensation withholdings on account of each of their employees. These deductions may be accounted for by use of an agency fund. Can you think of any alternative to the agency fund method?

18–5. Cash control and accounting constitute special problems for colleges and universities. Why is this true?

18–6. A university journalism department objected to having the financial activities of the university press fully controlled by a well-developed accounting system. The reason given was that such an arrangement would interfere with the conduct of the printing establishment. What is your opinion of the validity of the argument?

18–7. Is there any basic difference between the Deferred Revenue from Student Fees account in a college balance sheet and the Deferred Interest Income account often found in commercial enterprise balance sheets? Explain.

18–8. Explain fully how the plant fund accounts of a college or university differ from the general fixed assets group of accounts of municipality.

18–9. Educational institutions (also hospitals) often receive pledges or subscriptions of amounts for financing some project of the institution. Although practice varies, amounts pledged or subscribed frequently are not formally recorded in the accounts until collected, that is, they are accounted for on the cash basis. What do you consider to be the probable reason for that policy?

18–10. A small college reports that it has no formal accounting manual but depends upon the experience and memory of its chief accounting officer, an employee of many years. What is your appraisal of this situation?

EXERCISES AND PROBLEMS

18–1. The condition of the current funds of X University at the end of the 19x5–x6 fiscal year is shown on page 553. Transactions affecting these funds during the year 19x6–x7 are given below. You are required to prepare journal entries for the transactions given and to prepare a current funds balance sheet as of June 30, 19x7.

1. Fees charged to the students during the year amounted to \$1,800,000, of which \$1,750,000 was collected in cash. The Allowance for Doubtful Accounts was increased by \$2,000.
2. Collections of accounts receivable at the beginning of the year totaled \$15,000. Accounts amounting to \$900 were written off as uncollectible.
3. At June 30, 19x7, the amount of deferred revenue from student fees was \$117,600.
4. Temporary investments in the amount of \$8,000 held at the beginning of the year were sold for \$8,200. Restricted current funds

X UNIVERSITY
Balance Sheet
June 30, 19x6

Assets

Current funds:		
A. Unrestricted:		
Cash		$ 37,000
Accounts receivable–student fees	$19,000	
Less: Allowance for doubtful accounts	1,000	18,000
Due from restricted funds		6,000
State appropriation receivable		64,000
Supplies inventory, at cost		11,000
Total Unrestricted Current Funds		$136,000
B. Restricted:		
Cash	$ 1,000	
Investments, at cost	23,000	
Total Restricted Current Funds		24,000
Total Current Funds		$160,000

Liabilities, Reserves, and Balances

Current funds:		
A. Unrestricted:		
Vouchers Payable		$ 3,000
Deferred revenues		31,000
Reserve for supplies inventory		11,000
Fund balances		91,000
Total Unrestricted Current Funds		$136,000
B. Restricted:		
Due to unrestricted funds	$ 6,000	
Fund balances	18,000	
Total Restricted Current Funds		24,000
Total Current Funds		$160,000

cash spent for authorized purposes amounted to $2,200; an additional $6,000 was transferred to unrestricted funds in payment of the liability existing on June 30, 19x6.

5. During the year, purchases, salaries and wages, utility bills, and other expenses totaling $1,600,000 were vouchered. Unpaid vouchers at the end of the year amounted to $39,000.
6. Supplies inventory at the end of the year amounted to $20,000, according to physical count.
7. During the year the state appropriation of $64,000 was received. A further appropriation for current general purposes of $70,000 was made by the state, but had not been paid to the University by year-end.
8. Unrestricted fund cash in the amount of $130,000 was used to purchase and retire bonds payable of the plant funds.
9. Income received from investments of restricted current funds amounted to $950; an additional $150 interest was accrued at year end.

18–2. The balance sheet of X University as of June 30, 19x6, indicated the following with respect to the loan funds:

Loan Funds:			
Cash		$ 7,000	
Investments		13,000	
Notes Receivable	$29,600		
Accrued Interest Receivable.	330		
	$29,930		
Less Allowance for Doubtful Notes and Interest	600	29,330	
Total Loan Funds			$49,330
Loan Funds:			
Loan fund balances.			$49,330
Total Loan Funds			$49,330

You are required to prepare loan funds journal entries from the following transactions which occurred in the year 19x6–x7; you are also required to prepare a loan funds balance sheet as of June 30, 19x7.

1. A bequest of $10,000 in securities was received by X University. The decedent specified that both principal and interest were to be used for student loans.
2. Loans made to students during the year totaled $20,000; all loans were secured by notes; repayments on these loans during the year amounted to $4,040 ($4,000 principal and $40 interest).
3. One loan of $200 and accrued interest of $24 (as of balance sheet date) was written off as uncollectible.
4. Notes receivable of prior years in the amount of $8,000 were collected during the year. Interest collected on notes receivable in cash during the year amounted to $930, including the balance accrued at June 30, 19x6, less write-off.
5. Dividends and interest on loan fund investments collected in cash during the year amounted to $420. Accrued interest receivable at the end of the year amounted to $370. The Allowance for Doubtful Notes and Interest was increased to $750.

18–3. The balance sheet of X University as of June 30, 19x6, indicated the following with respect to endowment and similar funds:*

Endowment and similar funds:	
Cash	$ 3,000
Cash–pool.	9,000
Securities, at cost.	120,000
Securities–pool, at cost	551,000
Real estate	170,000
Funds held by trustee	87,000
Total Endowment and Similar Funds	$940,000

* Accounting for pooled investments is discussed in Chapter 19 and in Appendix 3; this problem does not involve detailed knowledge of that material and may be solved by use of account titles given in the problem.

Endowment and similar funds:		
Vouchers payable		$ 8,000
Due to plant funds		4,000
Reserve for realized gains and losses on pooled investments		15,000
Reserve for replacement of real estate		71,000
Endowment funds balances:		
Unrestricted	$650,000	
Restricted	130,000	780,000
Quasi-endowment funds		62,000
Total Endowment and Similar Funds		$940,000

You are required to prepare journal entries to record the following transactions which relate to the fiscal year 19x6–x7; you are also required to prepare a balance sheet as of June 30, 19x7.

1. Funds held by the trustee in the amount of $17,000 were transferred by the trustee to the Endowment Fund Cash account.
2. Vouchers payable on June 30, 19x6, were paid.
3. Income amounting to $15,000 was received from pooled investments; and income amounting to $3,000 was received from securities of unpooled, unrestricted endowment funds. Premium on pool securities to be amortized in 19x6–x7 was determined to be $2,100.
4. Securities of unrestricted endowment funds carried at $25,000 were revalued to market, $26,812, and transferred to the pool.
5. Pool securities carried at $53,000 were sold for $52,000 and the proceeds reinvested in other securities for the account of the pool.
6. Gross cash income of real estate was $20,000. Expenses attributable to the real estate in the amount of $14,900 were vouchered during the year. Vouchers payable at year end amounted to $3,800.
7. The Reserve for Replacement of Real Estate was increased by $3,300.
8. The amount due plant funds on June 30, 19x6, was transferred from pool cash during the year. Net income of the pool for 19x6–x7 was to be transferred to plant funds in 19x7–x8. Net income from the real estate was to be transferred to the unrestricted current funds in 19x7–x8, as was income from unrestricted, unpooled investments.

18–4. The balance sheet of X University as of June 30, 19x6, indicated the following with respect to annuity and life income funds. From the transactions below, prepare journal entries and a balance sheet as of June 30, 19x7.

Annuity and life income funds:		
Cash	$ 4,000	
Investments	41,000	
Total Annuity and Life Income Funds		$45,000
Annuity and life income funds:		
Fund balances:		
For unrestricted use	$28,000	
For student loans	17,000	
Total Annuity and Life Income Funds		$45,000

1. On August 1, 19x6, a tract of land with fair market value of $50,000 was received under an agreement that X University would pay the donor $2,500 each year on the anniversary date of the agreement as long as the donor lived. No restrictions were placed on the use of the principal of the fund or any income in excess of $2,500 per year.
2. Cash income received by annuity and life income funds during the year totaled $2,850, of which $2,600 was disbursed to annuitants and $250 was transferred to unrestricted current funds.
3. During the year one annuitant died; her contribution, $7,000, was transferred in the form of securities to the loan funds.

18–5. The balance sheet of X University as of June 30, 19x6, indicated the following with respect to plant funds. From the transactions given below, prepare journal entries and a plant funds balance sheet as of the end of the year.

Plant funds:		
A. Unexpended:		
Cash		$ 20,000
Investments		61,000
Due from other funds		4,000
Total Unexpended Plant Funds		$ 85,000
B. Investment in plant:		
Land	$ 112,000	
Buildings	3,260,000	
Equipment	983,000	
Construction in progress	212,000	
Total Investment in Plant		4,567,000
Total Plant Funds		$4,652,000

Plant funds:		
A. Unexpended:		
Vouchers payable	$ 82,000	
Unexpended plant fund balance	3,000	
Total Unexpended Plant Funds.		$ 85,000
B. Investment in plant:		
Bonds payable	$ 260,000	
Investment in plant:		
From operations	3,075,000	
From gifts	408,000	
From governmental appropriations	824,000	
Total Investment in Plant		4,567,000
Total Plant Funds		$4,652,000

1. Unrestricted current fund cash in the amount of $130,000 was used to purchase and retire bonds payable of the plant funds of that face value.
2. The amount due from other funds at the beginning of the year was received. Notice was received at year-end that the amount of $12,900 would be transferred from the endowment funds to the plant funds in the following year.
3. A grant of $800,000 was made to X University by the X Founda-

tion, to be used for buildings and equipment. The grant was to be paid to the university in equal installments over an eight-year period; the sum for the current year was received in cash.

4. Invoices and payrolls amounting to $30,000 for the work in progress were vouchered. Vouchers in the amount of $102,000 were paid during the year.
5. The work in progress, an addition to the School of Business building, was considered to be completed. It was determined that 80 percent of the total cost was to be charged to Buildings and 20 percent to Equipment. The total cost had been financed from gifts.
6. A firm of architects engaged to prepare plans for a new dormitory submitted an invoice for $8,500 for services performed by them this year. (You may credit Accrued Expenses Payable.)

18–6. From the following trial balance of the accounts of Watson College and the additional information given, prepare a balance sheet in the proper institutional form:

June 30, 19x1

	Debit	*Credit*
Cash	$ 43,500	
Deposit accounts		$ 2,500
Income from endowment investments		85,500
Income from college operations		100,000
College operating expenses	195,000	
Interest accrued on securities purchased	500	
Inventories:		
School supplies	5,000	
General	3,000	
Investments:		
Bonds	875,500	
Mortgages	270,000	
Stocks	990,000	
Real estate	100,000	
Mortgages payable, secured by college plant		250,000
College plant:		
Land	95,000	
Buildings	1,000,000	
Ground improvements	50,000	
Equipment	160,000	
Profit on sale of endowment fund investments		4,000
Prepaid college expenses	2,000	
Accounts receivable:		
Students	3,000	
Miscellaneous	1,000	
Notes receivable	20,000	
Notes payable		2,000
Accounts payable		3,000
Allowance for doubtful accounts receivable		500
Allowance for depreciation of buildings held as endowment fund investment		5,500
Reserve for contingencies		5,000
Excess of assets over liabilities		3,355,500
	$3,813,500	$3,813,500

1. An analysis of the Cash account shows that the cash should be divided as follows:

Current funds:	
Imprest cash	$ 1,000
On deposit	35,000
Loan funds	2,000
Endowment funds	4,000
Funds subject to annuity agreements	1,500
	$43,500

2. Investments were all made from endowment funds, with the exception of $25,500 in bonds, purchased from funds subject to annuity agreements. The income and principal of the latter funds are to be used to make certain definite payments during the life of the annuitants. The excess of annuity payments over income has been charged to the principal of the fund.
3. Notes receivable represent loans made to students from funds that are restricted to that purpose.
4. Memorandum records show that $11,500 of endowment funds are loaned temporarily to the current fund.
5. These records also show that $50,000 of endowment funds are invested in the college plant, in full accord with the endowment terms.
6. The income from $895,000 of endowment principal is restricted.
7. It was decided that the allowance for depreciation of real estate carried among the investments be funded.

(AICPA, adapted)

18–7. Zenith Junior College had always kept its accounts on a so-called "commercial" basis and not in the form ordinarily used by educational institutions. The balance sheet of June 30, 19x4, and the related statements of income and expenses for the year ended on that date were made up as follows:

Balance Sheet
June 30, 19x4

Assets

Current assets:		
Cash	$ 6,000	
Tuition fees receivable	8,000	
Inventory of supplies	2,000	$ 16,000
Endowment fund investments:		
Rented real estate—at cost	$ 75,000	
Less: Allowance for depreciation	15,000	
	$ 60,000	
Mortgages, 6 per cent—at cost	140,000	
$210,000 of 5 per cent public utility bonds—at cost (market value $202,000)	220,000	420,000
Plant and equipment—at cost		$ 830,000
		$1,266,000

Liabilities

Current liabilities:		
Bank loans	$ 15,000	
Accounts payable	9,000	$ 24,000
First-mortgage bonds, 5 percent, maturing at the rate of $15,000 semiannually on June 30 and December 31 of each year		300,000
Endowment fund principal		540,000
Capital:		
Balance at July 1, 19x3	$395,000	
Excess of income over expenses for the year ended June 30, 19x4, per annexed statement	7,000	402,000
		$1,266,000

Statement of Income and Expenses
For the Year Ended June 30, 19x4

Income:		
Tuition		$230,000
Endowment income:		
Rentals	$ 8,100	
Mortgage interest	8,400	
Bond interest	10,500	27,000
Income from auxiliary enterprises		65,000
Unrestricted donations		33,000
Miscellaneous		4,000
Total income		$359,000
Expenses:		
Instruction and research	$185,000	
Expenses of auxiliary enterprises	80,000	
Administration	34,000	
Operation and maintenance	35,375	
Depreciation of rented real estate	1,500	
Bond interest	16,125	352,000
Excess of Income over Expenses		$ 7,000

The above statements were criticized as misleading, and the college authorities desire that they be prepared in a form more generally used for educational institutions.

An examination of the books and records brought out the following additional information:

The original college property was completed ten years ago at a cost of $750,000. It was financed by a 5 percent bond issue of $600,000 and by $150,000 appropriated from unrestricted gifts received at the time of organization of the college. Additions costing $80,000 have since been made from current funds, of which $10,000 was spent in the year ended June 30, 19x4.

The endowment funds are restricted in respect of principal to their investment in marketable securities and other income-producing properties or to outlays for college buildings and equipment. Income from the investments can be used for any purpose. The endowment fund assets are less than the endowment fund principal because investments had been sold from time to time when cash was needed to pay maturing bonds and meet expenses.

Rentals and mortgage interest had been received regularly at the end of every month or quarter; and also the June 30, 19x4, coupon of the public utility bonds had been collected on that date, so that no revenues other than the $8,000 of tuition fees remained outstanding.

The trustees adopted a policy of charging depreciation on income-producing properties so as to provide a reserve for their ultimate replacement. The amount of this depreciation is to be funded.

The "capital" of June 30, 19x4, is made up as follows:

Unrestricted gifts at organization	$300,000
Excess of income over expenses	102,000
	$402,000

Required:

a) Set forth in what respects the statements as prepared are unsatisfactory.

b) Show, in the form of properly explained journal entries, how the above balance sheet should be adjusted.

c) Prepare a balance sheet in the form that is customary for educational institutions; also, prepare a statement of income and expenses.

(AICPA, adapted)

18–8. The bookkeeper for the Jacob Vocational School resigned on March 1, 1968, after he prepared the following general ledger trial balance and analysis of cash as of February 29, 1968:

JACOB VOCATIONAL SCHOOL
General Ledger Trial Balance
February 29, 1968

Debits

Cash for general current operations	$258,000
Cash for restricted current uses	30,900
Stock donated by D. E. Marcy	11,000
Bonds donated by E. T. Pearce	150,000
Building	33,000
Land	22,000
General current operating expenses	38,000
Faculty recruitment expenses	4,100
Total	$547,000

Credits

Mortgage payable on fixed assets	$ 30,000
Income from gifts for general operations	210,000
Income from gifts for restricted uses	196,000
Student fees	31,000
Unappropriated surplus	80,000
Total	$547,000

Analysis of Cash
For the Six Months Ended February 29, 1968

Cash for general current operations:			
Balance, September 1, 1967		$ 80,000	
Add: Student fees	$ 31,000		
Gift of W. L. Jacob	210,000	241,000	
		321,000	
Deduct: General current operation expenses	38,000		
Payment on land and building	25,000	63,000	$258,000
Cash for restricted uses:			
Gift of W. L. Jacob for faculty recruitment		35,000	
Less faculty recruitment expenses		4,100	30,900
Checking account balance, February 29, 1968			$288,900

You were engaged to determine the proper account balances for the school as of August 31, 1968, the close of the school's fiscal year. Your examination disclosed the following information:

1. D. E. Marcy donated 100 shares of Trans, Inc. stock in September 1967 with a market value of $110 per share at the date of donation. The terms of the gift provide that the stock and any income thereon are to be retained intact. At any date designated by the board of directors the assets are to be liquidated and the proceeds used to assist the school's director in acquiring a personal residence. The school will not retain any financial interest in the residence.
2. E. T. Pearce donated 6 percent bonds in September 1967 with par and market values of $150,000 at the date of donation. Annual payments of $3,500 are to be made to the donor during his lifetime. Earnings in excess of these payments are to be used for current operations in the following fiscal year. Upon the donor's death the fund is to be used to construct a school cafeteria.
3. No transactions have been recorded on the school's books since February 29, 1968. An employee of the school prepared the following analysis of the checking account for the period from March 1 through August 31, 1968:

Balance, March 1, 1968			$288,900
Deduct: General current operating expenses	$14,000		
Purchase of equipment	47,000	$61,000	
Less student fees		8,000	
Net expenses		53,000	
Payment for director's residence	11,200		
Less sale of 100 shares of Trans, Inc. stock	10,600	600	53,600
Total			235,300
Add: Interest on 6% bonds		9,000	
Less payments to E. T. Pearce		3,500	5,500
Balance, August 31, 1968			$240,800

Required:

Prepare a worksheet presenting the trial balance at February 29, 1968, adjusting entries, transaction entries from March 1 through August 31, 1968, and distributions to the proper funds or groups of accounts. The following column headings are recommended for your worksheet:

1. Trial Balance, February 29, 1968.
2. Adjustments and Transactions—Debit.
3. Adjustments and Transactions—Credit.
4. General Current Fund.
5. Restricted Current Funds.
6. Plant Funds—Invested in Plant.
7. E. T. Pearce Annuity Fund.

Number all adjusting and transaction entries. Formal journal entries and statements are not required. Supporting computations should be in good form.

(AICPA)

19

Hospital Accounting

In years gone by, many hospitals were operated with little regard for the precepts of good financial management: philanthropists could be relied upon to cover operating deficits and provide new buildings and equipment. Over the last three decades, the increasing difficulty of raising money to cover deficits and building programs has forced the majority of hospitals to adopt a businesslike approach to the management of their financial resources. This change of attitude has forced a commensurate improvement in the quality of hospital accounting. A second important factor which forced an improvement in hospital accounting in the years since World War II is the rapid growth in popularity of third-party payment plans, such as Blue Cross and Medicare. Third-party payments are the source of well over half of the revenue of many hospitals. Third-party payors in many jurisdictions have required hospitals to utilize uniform accounting and statistical definitions and reports. The impact of Federal controls over hospital pricing is forcing those hospitals which had heretofore resisted change to adopt good financial management techniques.

Leadership in the improvement of hospital accounting has been taken by the American Hospital Association and the Hospital Financial Management Association. The former has provided accounting manuals for the use of its member hospitals and others. Although the systems published by the association have not been exactly fitted to hospitals of all classes, they have embodied general principles which, with adaptations and modifications, can be used by a majority of hospitals staffed with competent accounting personnel. The use of a uniform reporting system contributes to the efficiency of management because it permits dependable comparison of financial and operating statistics with those of other hospitals functioning under similar conditions.

GENERAL OUTLINE OF HOSPITAL ACCOUNTING

Accounting for hospitals bears considerable similarity to accounting for colleges and universities, particularly in respect to funds used. Accounting for governmentally operated hospitals bears some similarity to accounting for local governmental units in that publicly supported hospitals may be required to operate budgetary accounts and to incorporate these in their accounting and reporting systems. Public support of hospitals may take the form of direct contributions or of payments on behalf of patients eligible for service at public expense, or both. In well-developed accounting systems for hospitals, major attention is given to provisions for measuring costs of services rendered.

The chart of accounts published by the American Hospital Association recommends the following funds:

Operating Fund	Plant Fund
Specific Purpose Fund	Construction Fund
Endowment Fund	Other Funds (Agency Funds, etc.)

Explanation of Groups of Accounts

Operating fund accounts are used to account for the routine activities of the hospital. Balance sheet accounts of this section record the current assets and current liabilities related to performance of the hospital's service, with an equity or balancing account. The nominal accounts record in detail the earnings from services rendered by the hospital, and in even greater detail the costs of performing the services. In one respect, hospital accounting is materially at variance with the practice of municipalities and of educational institutions: depreciation of hospital fixed assets is regarded as an operating expense and formally recorded in operating fund accounts.

The *specific purpose* fund classification is employed by hospitals to record the principal and income of assets which may be used only for purposes specified by the donors (usually in the area of research and education). This fund is not used to record cash, securities, etc., designated for hospital plant assets, and funds whose principal must be kept intact.

Asset accounts of the *endowment fund* are of the kinds conventional for endowment funds in general: permanent investments, cash, and interfund receivables. If endowment fund assets include real estate, some of it may have been received subject to a mortgage. Mortgages assumed should appear as endowment fund liabilities until paid.

The *plant fund* consists mostly of fixed assets employed in housing hospital activities and rendering service, bonds and mortgages payable incurred in connection with the acquisition of properties, and plant fund capital accounts. Accumulated depreciation accounts, used for the normal purposes of such accounts, are included with related fixed asset accounts.

An account for plant assets under construction may be found in the plant fund if the institution has made expenditures for uncompleted plant; however, the AHA manual suggests the use of *construction fund* for this purpose if significant sums of money are involved.

Hospitals may acquire assets for improvements and replacements. If so, they are incorporated in the Plant Fund section of the institution's ledger and balance sheet. They are described as "assets restricted for improvement, replacement, and expansion of plant." Cash, investments (including land held for future hospital use), and pledges receivable are examples of assets which may be held in the plant fund until used for the purchase or construction of fixed assets. If depreciation is "funded," i.e., if cash or securities in the amount of depreciation charges are set aside, such amounts are recorded in this account group.

Hospitals sometimes act as agent for doctors and nurses in collecting for services which the latter, as individuals, have furnished through the medium of the hospital. Although not included as a part of the standard chart of accounts, it is recommended by the American Hospital Association that assets and liabilities related to claims by doctors and nurses against patients be recorded in a separate *agency fund*, an example of the *other funds* category provided by the AHA.

Chart of Accounts for Hospitals

The chart of accounts illustrated below is the one published by the American Hospital Association. As with other institutions and enterprises, no one chart of accounts will fit every organization. Adaptations must be made, taking into account the size of the institution, the volume and nature of services rendered, the financial structure, and the availability of competent accounting personnel. The volume and nature of services rendered are especially important in determining the selection of nominal accounts, which in the following chart are represented by control account titles. The chart of accounts recommended by the American Hospital Association is designed to permit contraction or expansion to meet the requirements of the individual hospital while retaining a basic uniformity in the manner of recording and reporting financial information.

The AHA chart of accounts provides for the use of a numerical code with five digits. The three digits to the left of the decimal point indicate control accounts. They conform to the following pattern.[1]

[1] American Hospital Association, (Chicago, 1966), p. 26.

Assets: 110–196

110–114	Operating Fund
120–122	Specific Purpose Fund
130–132	Endowment Fund
140–146	Plant Fund
150–155	Construction Fund
160–196	Other Funds

Liabilities: 217–298

217	Operating Fund
227	Specific Purpose Fund
237–238	Endowment Fund
247–248	Plant Fund
257–258	Construction Fund
267–298	Other Funds

Capital Accounts: 219–299

219	Operating Fund
229	Specific Purpose Fund
239	Endowment Fund
249	Plant Fund
259	Construction Fund
269–299	Other Funds

Revenue Accounts: 310–599

310–389	Nursing Service Revenue
402–499	Other Professional Service Revenue
500–529	Deductions from Revenue
530–599	Other Revenue

Expense Accounts: 600–999

600–699	Nursing Services
700–799	Other Professional Services
800–899	General Services
900–949	Fiscal Services
950–979	Administrative Services
980–999	Unassigned

It is evident from the list above that the first digit, at the left, has the following use:

1	Asset
2	Equity
3	Nursing Service Revenue
4	Other Professional Service Revenue
5	Deductions from Revenues; Other Revenue
6	Nursing Service Expense
7	Other Professional Services Expense
8	General Services Expense
9	Fiscal and Administrative Expense

For balance sheet accounts, the second digit indicates the fund group:

1 Operating Fund
2 Specific Purpose Fund
3 Endowment Fund
4 Plant Fund
5 Construction Fund
6–9 Other Funds

The third digit of a balance sheet account number shows the account classification:

0 Cash
1 Investments
2 Receivables
3 Inventory
4 Prepaid Expenses
5 Land, Buildings, and Equipment
6 Accumulated Depreciation
7 Current Liabilities
8 Noncurrent Liabilities
9 Fund Balance

The AHA does not prescribe the use of the two digits to the right of the decimal point in the case of balance sheet accounts, but illustrates their possible use. For example, account number 112 indicates an asset (1– –); of the operating fund (–1–); specifically, receivables (– –2). If a zero is used as a fourth digit to indicate inpatients, and a 1 is used as the fifth digit to indicate that the patients have been discharged from the hospital, the full account number would be 112.01.

In order to promote effective financial management of hospital resources, the AHA chart for revenue and expense accounts is based upon the concepts of responsibility accounting. Accordingly, the second and third digits of the account numbers are used to indicate the organizational unit of the hospital which is responsible for the revenue or expense. Thus, since 30 indicates a pediatric nursing unit, the account number for revenue from the pediatric nursing unit would be 330, and the account for expense of the same unit would be 630. In the case of revenue accounts the fourth and fifth digits, the AHA suggests, might be used to indicate the type of patient, type of service, financial status, or type of accommodation. The fourth and fifth digits of an expense account number would be used to denote the nature of the expense.

Since the AHA chart of accounts was prepared principally for use by nongovernmental hospitals, the omission of budgetary accounts is to be expected. However, the structure can be adapted to use by public hospitals. If a normal budget recorded in the accounts is not required, no material change in the chart is necessary. Should either the law or the policy of the hospital require the incorporation of budgetary transactions in the ledger, it may be accomplished by extension of the operating fund balance sheet section, although some of the budgetary accounts are not actually of the usual balance sheet classification. Specifically, there can be added, after balance sheet assets in the ledger, accounts for estimated revenues, encumbrances, and appropriation expenditures. After the operating fund liability accounts in the ledger may be added accounts for reserve for encumbrances, and appropriations. The location of budgetary accounts in the positions suggested for them is not entirely consistent with their classifications but is probably more convenient than any other which might be found. An alternative to this inconsistency is to carry budgetary accounts as an independent unit, using the main or proprietary ledger for administration and control purposes, and operating the budgetary unit on an independent basis to comply with legal requirements.

The bulk of entries for hospital transactions are of a more or less routine nature and need not be explained and illustrated here. Some special practices and situations characteristic of hospital accounting, however, are discussed below.

Operating Fund Transactions

Accounting for amounts due from patients presents somewhat more difficulty than accounting for receivables of a business firm. Hospitals must keep detailed records of patients which include exact information about the time of admission and discharge, and an account, with supporting evidence wherever possible, of all chargeable services received by the patient during his stay, in addition to complete medical records for each patient. A few of the patients will pay their entire account; large numbers will pay a portion and a third party will pay the remainder. Each third-party payor has a different set of rules governing the manner in which it is to be billed and the amounts it will pay for various services. Accordingly, it is desirable for a hospital to keep a number of subsidiary ledgers of accounts receivable, such as "Patients In House," "Private Pay Patients Discharged," "Blue Cross Patients," "Medicare Patients," "Commercial Insurance Patients," and "Welfare Patients." No distinction between notes and open accounts is made in the ledger, although subsidiary records may be kept to show the analysis, if desired.

A typical entry for recording a charge to patients' receivables would be as follows:

	Debit	Credit
112 Inpatient Receivables—In House	500	
343 Revenue from Daily Patient Services—Psychiatric		500

It is important to note that although a patient may be entitled to service at a reduced rate, he should be charged at the standard price for the services he receives. Adjustments to the net price are considered as deductions from revenues, rather than as expenses. Deductions from revenue arise because of charity service, courtesy discounts to employees or others, or adjustments resulting from contracts with third-party payors. For example, assuming a total reduction of $35 because of contractual agreement, the following entry would be made:

510 Contractual Adjustments	35	
112 Inpatient Receivables—Blue Cross		35

According to long-standing hospital custom, the provision for bad debts is also classified as a revenue deduction, rather than as an operating expense.

Specific Purpose Fund Transactions

A specific purpose fund is used to account for assets received from an outside source, to finance a specific project; thus it is comparable with an unrestricted trust fund, as discussed in Chapter 8.

As income is earned on specific purpose fund assets, it is to be recorded as an increase in the specific purpose fund balance. The fund exists, however, to support particular activities of the hospital; in recognition of this fact, the Fund Balance is to be debited and Due to Operating Fund credited, to indicate that cash in the amount of the income is to be transferred from the specific purpose fund to the operating fund. The corresponding entry in the operating fund accounts is a debit to Due from Specific Purpose Fund and a credit to Income Transfers from Specific Purpose Fund.

It is possible that disbursements of specific purpose fund cash may be made for operating fund assets or expenses (or even for plant fund assets, if consistent with the terms of the donor of the specific purpose fund assets). Assuming $250 of specific purpose fund cash was disbursed for nursing education expenses, the following entries would be made:

Specific Purpose Fund:

229 Specific Purpose Fund Balance	250	
120 Specific Purpose Fund Cash		250

Operating Fund:

691 Diploma School of Nursing	250	
572 Income Transfers from Specific Purpose Fund		250

It is also true that disbursements may be made from operating fund cash for purposes which are ultimately to be covered by specific purpose fund income transfers. In such cases, the following entries should be made, assuming the same amounts and expenses as in the preceding example:

Operating Fund:

Account	Debit	Credit
691 Diploma School of Nursing	250	
110 Operating Fund Cash		250
(To record the disbursements.)		
112.90 Due from Specific Purpose Fund	250	
572 Income Transfers from Specific Purpose Fund		250
(To record the receivable from the specific purpose fund.)		
110 Operating Fund Cash	250	
112.90 Due from Specific Purpose Fund		250
(To record receipt of reimbursement from specific purpose fund.)		

Specific Purpose Fund:

Account	Debit	Credit
229 Specific Purpose Fund Balance	250	
227.90 Due to Operating Fund		250
(To record disbursement by operating fund to be reimbursed.)		
227.90 Due to Operating Fund	250	
120 Specific Purpose Fund Cash		250
(To record payment of liability to operating fund.)		

Separate subaccounts should be maintained for the balance of each individual specific purpose fund.

Endowment Fund Transactions

The hospital endowment fund is used to account for donated assets, the principal of which must be retained intact. The income from hospital endowment fund assets is expendable as the donor directed—either for general operating purposes, or for named items or projects. Thus the hospital endowment fund is a trust fund, as discussed in Chapter 8. The discussion in that chapter concerning the problems involved in distinguishing between principal and income are relevant, also, to hospital endowment funds.

In order to be able to show that the terms of each endowment have been complied with, it is desirable to keep records for each separate endowment. Ordinarily such records may be in memorandum form, or may be kept as subsidiary accounts controlled by the balance sheet accounts provided for the Endowment Fund by the American Hospital Association manual. Asset accounts provided are cash, investments, and receivables. Donated securities and real estate are to be recorded in the endowment fund at fair market value at date of acquisition; investments purchased by the fund are to be recorded at cost. Separate accounts are provided for current liabilities and long-term liabilities; the latter consist mainly of mortgages outstanding against endowment fund real estate. The Endowment Fund Balance account is to be subdivided into two accounts: Endowment Fund Principal—Income Unrestricted, and Endowment Fund Principal—Income Restricted.

In order to simplify portfolio management, obtain a greater degree of investment diversification for individual endowments, and reduce brokerage, taxes, and bookkeeping expense, it is desirable to *pool* the individual endowments for investment purposes. When investments are pooled, or merged, earnings, and gains and losses on sales, are allocated on the basis of the relative contributions of each fund to the pool. To insure an equitable division of earnings, gains, and losses, it is customary to revalue the assets of *each* endowment to their fair market value as of the time an endowment is brought into the pool or removed from the pool.

The following entries illustrate recommended practices for accounting for investments of hospital endowment funds, both pooled and nonpooled. (Some transactions illustrated could affect one or more other funds in addition to those assumed in the examples.) Accounting for investments is reviewed in greater detail in Appendix 3.

Forty thousand dollars, par value, of National Power Company 9 percent bonds are purchased at 102½ and accrued interest of $450:

Endowment Fund:

Investments	41,000	
Cash in Bank—Unrestricted		41,000

Operating Fund (or other fund designated to receive the income from this investment):

Income Transfers from Endowment Fund	450	
Operating Fund Cash		450

Semiannual interest of $900 is collected on the investment, and $25 of the premium is amortized:

Endowment Fund:

Cash In Bank—Unrestricted	25	
Investments		25

Operating Fund:

Operating Fund Cash	875	
Income Transfers from Endowment Fund		875

From the above entries, it will be noted that amoritzation of premium on investments is a funded transaction; that is, to replace the amount of premium amortized in the principal fund, the operating fund supplies an equal amount of cash, thus relieving the endowment fund of a principal reduction which would result from a mere book entry.

Twenty thousand dollars, par value, of city of Y serial 8's are purchased at 98 and accrued interest of $280:

Endowment Fund:

Investments	19,600	
Cash in Bank—Unrestricted		19,600

Operating Fund:

Income Transfers from Endowment Fund	280	
Operating Fund Cash		280

Ten thousand dollars, par value, of bonds, on which there was a balance of unamortized premium of $1,100 at the last interest date, are sold for 107 and accrued interest of $160. Premium amortization accumulated since the last interest date is $65:

Endowment Fund:

Cash in Bank—Unrestricted	10,765	
Endowment Fund Principal—Income Unrestricted	335	
Investments		11,100

Operating fund:

Operating Fund Cash	95	
Income Transfers from Endowment Fund		95

The loss charged to the Endowment Fund Principal—Income Unrestricted account is:

Par value of investment		$10,000
Unamortized premium—last interest date	$1,100	
Less: Amortization since last interest date	65	1,035
Book value of investment at date of sale		$11,035
Selling Price		10,700
Loss on sale		$ 335

Accounting for Pooled Investments

The first accounting operation in the conversion of investment from a nonpool to a pool basis is the valuation of each fund's contribution to the pool as of the formation date. This is ordinarily accomplished by ascertaining the market value of securities or other assets to be transferred by each fund and, in effect, "selling" them to the pool at the new valuation. Differences between book value and market value are treated as gains or losses of the individual funds and credited or debited to their respective balances. Accounting for the creation of a pool, and its operations, is illustrated in the following example:

Memorial Hospital has two small endowments which are to be pooled for investment purposes. At the date the pool is to be created, the endowment given by Mr. Smith consists of securities recorded by the hospital at fair market value at date of acquisition, $5,920; accrued interest on those securities, $90; and interest received in cash and not yet transferred to the operating fund, $90. The endowment from Mrs. Jones was received, originally, in cash in the amount of $7,000. Securities costing $6,760 were purchased from this cash, leaving $240 uninvested principal cash. The hospital plant fund, rather than the operating fund, is the income beneficiary of the Jones endowment. At the date the pool is to be created, there is $140 accrued interest; all interest received in cash has been transferred to the plant fund.

From the data above it is apparent that the subsidiary records of the hospital endowment fund show the balance of the unrestricted Smith endowment to be $5,920, the amount due the operating fund to be $180, the balance of the restricted Jones endowment to be $7,000, and the amount due the plant fund $140, as of the date the pool is to be created.

On the date the pool is created the market value of the investments of each endowment should be determined. Assuming that the market value of the Smith investments is $5,800, and the market value of the Jones investments is $6,960, the following entry should be made to restate the two endowments to fair market value as of the time they are pooled:

	Debit	Credit
Endowment Fund Principal—Income Unrestricted	120	
Investments	80	
Endowment Fund Principal—Income Restricted		200

The above entry in the Investments control accounts shows the net effect of the increase in the carrying value of the Jones endowment investments and the decrease in the carrying value of the Smith endowment investments; the appropriate facts would be recorded in the proper subsidiary accounts. Assuming for the sake of simplicity that the Memorial Hospital has no other endowments, the balance sheet of the Endowment Fund immediately prior to pooling would be:

MEMORIAL HOSPITAL
Endowment Fund Balance Sheet
As of Date Pool Is to Be Created

Assets		*Liabilities and Capital*	
Cash in bank–unrestricted	$ 90	Due to operating fund	$ 180
Cash in bank–restricted	240	Due to plant fund	140
Investments	12,760	Total Liabilities	$ 320
Accrued interest	230	Fund principal–income unrestricted	$ 5,800
		Fund principal–income restricted	7,200
Total Assets	$13,320	Total Liabilities and Capital	$13,320

Inasmuch as the $240 cash relating to the Jones endowment is a part of the principal, it is proper to transfer it to the pool at the same time the Jones endowment investments are transferred. The entry for the creation of the pool, therefore, is:

	Debit	Credit
Cash—Pool	240	
Investments—Pool	12,760	
Cash in Bank—Restricted		240
Investments		12,760

There is, of course, no point in transferring to the pool the $90 cash income received on the Smith endowment, the accrued interest on both endowments, and the related liabilities. When income is received in cash after creation of the pool, however, it is necessary to determine how much of the cash is a collection of the accruals (remembering that the Smith endowment income is unrestricted and the Jones endowment income is restricted), and how much cash represents income of the pool, to be distributed later. For example, assuming that $295 cash is received from the investments now pooled, the following entry should be made:

Cash—Pool	65	
Cash in Bank—Unrestricted	90	
Cash in Bank—Restricted	140	
Undistributed Earnings of Pooled Investments		65
Accrued Interest Receivable		230

Any subsequent receipt of cash income from pooled investments would be debited to Cash—Pool and credited to Undistributed Earnings of Pooled Investments. Earnings of pooled investments are distributed to the proper recipients on the basis of the relative contributions of the various member funds of the pool.

When the liabilities to the operating fund and plant fund are paid, the endowment fund would make the following entry:

Due to Operating Fund	180	
Due to Plant Fund	140	
Cash in Bank—Unrestricted		180
Cash in Bank—Restricted		140

The cooperative nature of investment pooling is well demonstrated by the procedure employed in accounting for gains and losses on pooled investments. No attempt is made to identify gains or losses on individual investments with the particular funds which contributed the investments; but all such transactions are summarized in one account, the Reserve for Realized Gains and Losses on Pooled Investments. To illustrate the mechanics of this plan, let it be assumed that pooled investments carried on the books at $2,900 are sold for $2,770 cash. The proceeds, plus $200 cash put into the pool from the Jones endowment, are reinvested. If both transactions are journalized, the entries would be:

Cash—Pool	2,770	
Reserve for Realized Gains and Losses on Pooled Investments	130	
Investments—Pool		2,900
Investments—Pool	2,970	
Cash—Pool		2,970

Had a gain resulted from the sale of pooled investments, a credit to the reserve would have been required. Periodically, the net realized gain or loss, the balance of the reserve account, is distributed to the pooled endowments on the basis of their relative contributions. If the Memorial Hospital had only the transactions illustrated above, the $130 loss would be distributed 58/130 to the Smith endowment principal, and

72/130 to the Jones endowment principal (because the contributions were $5,800 and $7,200, respectively). The following entry would result:

Endowment Fund Principal—Income Unrestricted	58	
Endowment Fund Principal—Income Restricted	72	
Reserve for Realized Gains and Losses on Pooled Investments		130

Comparable in effect to a corporate stock dividend, the above entry would make no relative change in the equities of the individual endowments, nor would their relative shares in pool income be increased. The elimination of a debit balance in the reserve likewise would only proportionally reduce the balances of individual funds; it would have no influence on income-sharing ratios. Therefore, the entry to distribute the balance of the Undistributed Earnings account, assuming that accrued interest in the amount of $260 had been recorded at year-end as a debit to Accrued Interest and credit to the Undistributed Earnings account, is:

Undistributed Earnings of Pooled Investments	325	
Due to Operating Fund		145
Due to Plant Fund		180

The balance sheet of the Endowment Fund after the illustrated entries have been posted appears below.

MEMORIAL HOSPITAL
Endowment Fund Balance Sheet
As of (Year End)

Assets		*Liabilities and Capital*	
Cash–pool	$ 105	Due to operating fund	$ 145
Investments–pool	12,830	Due to plant fund	180
Accrued interest	260	Total Liabilities	$ 325
		Principal–income unrestricted	5,742
		Principal–income restricted	7,128
Total Assets	$13,195	Total Liabilities and Capital	$13,195

Plant Fund Transactions

Hospital plant funds, accounted for in accord with American Hospital Association recommendations, record: long-lived assets, such as land, buildings, fixed equipment, major movable equipment, and minor equipment; accumulated depreciation; current assets held for expansion, replacement, or improvement of long-lived assets; long-term debt incurred in connection with the acquisition of plant fund assets; current liabilities such as accrued interest payable on the long-term debt; and the fund balance accounts. Fund balance accounts provided are: Fund Balance Invested in Plant; Fund Balance Reserved for Plant Replacement, Improvement, and Expansion—Donor Restricted; Fund Balance Reserved for

Plant Replacement, Improvement, and Expansion—Restricted by Board Action; and Unrealized Appreciation of Plant Assets.

The reader will note from the above accounts that plant fund accounting recommended by the American Hospital Association differs from accounting procedures recommended for general fixed assets by the National Committee on Governmental Accounting in that depreciation is to be recorded. A further variation from fund accounting theory, and a variation from generally accepted principles of financial accounting for profit-seeking businesses, is indicated by the final account title listed above: Unrealized Appreciation of Plant Assets. The AHA manual provides that plant fund assets are to be recorded at cost, if purchased, or at fair market value if received as a gift; however, the manual promotes the suggestion that hospitals periodically engage "qualified" appraisal firms to determine the "current replacement cost" of the plant assets. The appraisal figure is to be recorded in the plant fund asset accounts and in the Unrealized Appreciation equity account. Subsequent provisions for depreciation are to be computed on the basis of the recorded "current replacement cost." The American Institute of Certified Public Accountant's *Hospital Audit Guide* points out that carrying property at replacement cost and basing depreciation on replacement cost are *not* in accord with generally accepted accounting principles.

Purchase of plant assets. When plant fund cash is disbursed for long-lived assets, the following entries are made (assume that fixed equipment costing $750 is purchased):

Plant Fund (only fund affected):

Fixed Equipment	750	
Plant Fund Cash		750
Fund Balance Reserved for Plant Improvement and Expansion	750	
Fund Balance Invested in Plant		750

Some hospitals do not transfer cash to the plant fund, but purchase fixed assets directly from operating fund cash. In such a case the purchase of additional fixed equipment in the amount of $750 would be recorded by entries in both funds:

Operating Fund:

Operating Fund Balance	750	
Operating Fund Cash		750

Plant Fund:

Fixed Equipment	750	
Fund Balance Invested in Plant		750

Depreciation. Entries to amortize fixed asset costs are recorded both in the plant fund and in the operating fund. For example, assuming that depreciation of buildings is $1,000, the following entries should be made:

Operating Fund:

	Debit	Credit
Provision for Depreciation	1,000	
Due to Plant Fund		1,000

Plant Fund:

	Debit	Credit
Fund Balance—Invested in Plant	1,000	
Accumulated Depreciation of Buildings		1,000
Due From Operating Fund	1,000	
Fund Balance Reserved for Plant Improvement and Expansion		1,000

To assure the availability of money for improvement, replacement, and expansion of plant, it is a desirable practice for hospitals to transfer cash from the operating fund to the plant fund in amounts at least equal to periodic depreciation charges. Entries to record the transfer of cash in an amount equal to the depreciation charge are:

Operating Fund:

	Debit	Credit
Due to Plant Fund	1,000	
Operating Fund Cash		1,000

Plant Fund:

	Debit	Credit
Plant Fund Cash	1,000	
Due from Operating Fund		1,000

Sale or other disposal of plant assets. The removal of hospital fixed assets from the accounts, whether because of replacement, retirement, destruction, or any other reason, involves the following entries, as recommended by AHA (assume major movable equipment costing $1,000, with $900 accumulated depreciation, is sold for cash for $150):

Plant Fund:

	Debit	Credit
Plant Fund Cash	150	
Accumulated Depreciation of Major Movable Equipment	900	
Major Movable Equipment		1,000
Gain on Disposal of Plant Assets		50
Fund Balance Invested in Plant	150	
Fund Balance Reserved for Plant Improvement and Expansion		150

Operating Fund:

	Debit	Credit
Operating Fund Balance	50	
Gain on Disposal of Assets		50

At the end of the accounting period the Gain on Disposal of Plant Assets account balance should be closed to Fund Balance Invested in Plant; the net effect of the plant fund entries, therefore, is that the unamortized cost of the asset disposed of is charged to the Fund Balance Invested in Plant account. The Gain on Disposal of Assets account balance is closed at the end of the accounting period to Operating Fund Balance, so there is no net effect at all on the operating fund accounts. The apparent reason for the cumbersome procedure recommended by the AHA is that the authors of the AHA manual felt the gain on sale of assets should appear in the income statement, which is to be prepared from revenue and expense accounts, all of which are considered to relate to the operating fund. Inasmuch as the entire proceeds of the sale of assets is retained by the plant fund to be used for plant improvement, replacement, or expansion, the AHA recommendations result in an income statement which shows the receipt of revenue which is not available for operations and is not related to the activities of the operating fund.

Budgets for Hospitals[2]

Hospitals, though service institutions, must have an inflow of funds equal to their outflow of funds. Since this is the case, prudent management will attempt to forecast the outlays for a definite period and forecast the income for the same period. Equating anticipated income and outgo means that *future operations must be planned.* "Planning future operations" is a phrase which defines budgeting as it is thought of today in successful businesses. Budgeting is not merely planning financial affairs, but developing an integrated plan for all phases of the operations of the organization. If this is done properly, each department knows the objectives of the organization and has determined to what extent and in what manner the department will contribute to them. The predetermination of the role each department is to play in achieving the hospital objectives enables management to measure the success each department has in attaining its objectives. Frequent measurement helps keep each department on the proper path. Thus budgeting is of considerable usefulness to management.

Some hospitals use comprehensive budgets for managerial purposes but do not incorporate the budgetary provision in the accounts. Other hospitals do record their budgets in the ledger by including the necessary accounts after the general fund balance sheet accounts, even though some of them are not balance sheet items. This arrangement is discussed in the section of this chapter pertaining to the chart of accounts. If permitted by law or other pertinent regulations, budgetary accounts may be carried in a separate group, which, although considered a part of the ledger, avoids mingling them with the proprietary accounts which are more useful to hospital management.

It is possible to generalize that although every hospital should have an annual budget, it is important that the budget be administered intelli-

[2] For a more complete treatment of this subject see Leon E. Hay, *Budgeting and Cost Analysis for Hospital Management.* (2d ed.; Bloomington, Ind.: Pressler Publications, 1963), chaps. 8–11, 14.

gently. For a hospital, or for any other enterprise, good financial management requires that outlays be evaluated in terms of results achieved. Insistence upon rigid adherence to a budget not related to actual work load (as is the case in some governmental agencies) tends to make the budget useless as a management tool. Thus, unless budgetary accounts are required by law, they may well be dispensed with.

Financial Statements of Hospitals

Important individual statements of hospitals include balance sheets for each fund, statements of changes in fund balances, income and expense statements, and a great number of statistical statements. Statements of the last kind are important in hospital accounting because of their value in helping to analyze the financial results of the many kinds of services performed. Not all hospitals use the same statistical statements, nor do they attach equal significance to given statements; these are factors upon which experience and judgment have a strong bearing. Statements of the first three kinds named above—balance sheets, statements of changes in fund balances, and operating statements—will be illustrated with a single example for each group, although, in practice, deviations from the forms illustrated are commonplace.

The typical balance sheet of a hospital is a composite of fund balance sheets. Owing to certain interrelationships which exist among hospital funds and which have been discussed elsewhere, the statement is more closely integrated than the combined balance sheets of municipalities. Illustration 19–1 shows a balance sheet in the form presented in the AHA manual. It will be noted that intrafund classification of assets and liabilities into current, deferred, and fixed is absent. This segregation is provided substantially by the fund basis of grouping. Because of its incidental nature, the agency fund is omitted from Illustration 19–1. The American Institute of Certified Public Accountants' *Hospital Audit Guide* recommends some modifications to the AHA presentation; the AICPA recommended format is shown in Illustration 19–4.

Statements of changes in fund balances explain why a fund's balance at one date is different from its balance at another date. Statements of this kind may be prepared for all the hospital's funds; one schedule, for the operating fund, is shown here (Illustration 19–2), in the AHA format. A comparable statement in the AICPA format is shown as Illustration 19–5.

On account of the extensive classification of the operating accounts of hospitals, their statements of income and expense may be prepared in a variety of forms, the one chosen depending upon the preference of the hospital management. Illustration 19–3 shows a form which is consistent with the AHA recommended balance sheet and statement of changes in fund balance shown in Illustrations 19–1 and 19–2. Illustration

19–6 shows a Statement of Revenues and Expense suggested in the AICPA *Hospital Audit Guide* in lieu of the AHA format of income statement.

Modifications Preferred by AICPA

Financial statements in formats suggested by the AHA are shown in Illustrations 19–1, 19–2, and 19–3. Comparable statements in formats

Illustration 19–1

PORTLAND GENERAL HOSPITAL
Balance Sheet–Assets
December 31, 19x5

Operating Fund			
Cash			$ 16,000
Temporary investments			17,000
Accounts and notes receivable		$ 44,000	
Less: Allowances for uncollectible notes and accounts		5,000	39,000
Accrued interest receivable			600
Due from plant fund			2,000
Supplies inventory			38,000
Total Operating Fund Assets			$112,600
Specific Purpose Fund			
Cash			$ 1,000
Investments			18,000
Accrued interest receivable			300
Total Specific Purpose Fund Assets			$ 19,300
Endowment Fund			
Cash			$ 3,000
Due from temporary funds			10,000
Investments (book value):			
Stock		$100,000	
Real estate		60,000	
Mortgages receivable		115,000	275,000
Total Endowment Fund Assets			$288,000
Plant Fund			
Cash		$ 7,000	
Investments		51,000	
Due from operating fund		12,000	70,000
Land		$ 30,000	
Buildings	$820,000		
Less: Accumulated depreciation	160,000	660,000	
Fixed equipment	$152,000		
Less: Accumulated depreciation	29,000	123,000	
Major movable equipment	$ 71,000		
Less: Accumulated depreciation	30,000	41,000	
Minor movable equipment (nondepreciable)		18,000	
Net land, buildings, and equipment			872,000
Total Plant Fund Assets			$942,000

Illustration 19–1 (*Continued*)

PORTLAND GENERAL HOSPITAL
Balance Sheet—Liabilities and Capital
December 31, 19x5

Operating Fund

Vouchers payable		$ 8,000
Salaries, wages, and fees payable		7,000
Withholding taxes payable		1,500
Due to plant fund		12,000
Total Liabilities		$ 28,500
Operating Fund Balance		84,100
Total Operating Fund Equities		$112,600

Specific Purpose Fund

Due to endowment fund		$ 10,000
Specific purpose fund balance		9,300
Total Specific Purpose Fund Equities		$ 19,300

Endowment Fund

Mortgages payable		$ 30,000
Endowment fund principal:		
Income unrestricted	$180,000	
Income restricted	78,0000	258,000
Total Endowment Fund Equities		$288,000

Plant Fund

Vouchers payable	$ 4,000	
Due to operating fund	2,000	
Bonds payable	85,000	
Total Liabilities		$ 91,000
Plant fund balance:		
Invested in plant	$787,000	
Reserved for plant replacement and expansion	64,000	
Total plant fund balance		851,000
Total Plant Fund Equities		$942,000

preferred by the AICPA are shown in Illustrations 19–4, 19–5, and 19–6. A primary difference is that the AICPA committee charged with the preparation of the *Hospital Audit Guide* was greatly impressed with the distinction between *donor-restricted funds* and *board-designated funds*. The former are of the nature discussed at length in Chapter 8 in regard to trust funds of general governmental units, and discussed in earlier sections of this chapter in relation to specific purpose funds, endowment funds, and assets donated to the hospital for plant replacement and expansion purposes. Board-designated funds are assets which the governing body of the hospital has set aside for certain purposes—such as "funded" depreciation—but which may be made available for any other purposes, the AICPA stresses, upon further board action. Accordingly the

Illustration 19–2

PORTLAND GENERAL HOSPITAL
Statement of Changes in Operating Fund Balance
For the Year 19x5

Balance, December 31, 19x4	$71,320
Add: Net income for year	15,180
	$86,500
Deduct: Transfer to endowment fund	2,400
Balance, December 31, 19x5	$84,100

AICPA recommends that only donor-restricted funds be shown as Restricted in the financial statements, and that board-designated funds be shown together with the Current Funds in the Unrestricted section of financial statements.

Gifts not restricted by the donor, and unrestricted income from endowment funds, should be shown as "Nonoperating Revenue" in a Statement of Revenues and Expenses, or in a combination income and fund balance statement, the AICPA recommends. As Illustration 19–6

Illustration 19–3

PORTLAND GENERAL HOSPITAL
Income Statement For the Year 19x5

Patient service revenues:		
Nursing service revenues	$773,750	
Other professional service revenues	653,000	
Gross patient service revenues		$1,426,750
Deductions from patient service revenues:		
Charity service	$ 38,250	
Contractual adjustments	35,000	
Provision for bad debts	17,000	
Total deductions from patient service revenues		90,250
Net patient service revenues		$1,336,500
Other revenues:		
Contributions and grants	$ 7,600	
Income from operating fund investments	478	
Income transferred from specific purpose funds	1,022	
Total other revenues		9,100
Total revenues		$1,345,600
Expenses:		
Nursing service expenses	$570,000	
Other professional service expenses	335,000	
General service expenses	271,000	
Fiscal service expenses	48,420	
Administrative service expenses	106,000	
Total expenses		1,330,420
Net Income for the Year		$ 15,180

AICPA SAMPLE HOSPITAL
BALANCE SHEET
December 31, 19–
With Comparative Figures for 19–

Unrestricted Funds

Assets	*Current Year*	*Prior Year*
Current:		
Cash	$ 133,000	$ 33,000
Receivables (Note 3)	1,382,000	1,269,000
Less estimated uncollectibles and allowances	(160,000)	(105,000)
	1,222,000	1,164,000
Due from restricted funds	215,000	–
Inventories (if material, state basis)	176,000	183,000
Prepaid expenses	68,000	73,000
Total current assets	1,814,000	1,453,000
Other:		
Cash (Note 2)	143,000	40,000
Investments (Notes 1 and 2)	1,427,000	1,740,000
Property, plant, and equipment (Notes 4 and 5)	11,028,000	10,375,000
Less accumulated depreciation	(3,885,000)	(3,600,000)
Net property, plant, and equipment	7,143,000	6,775,000
Total (Note 2)	$10,527,000	$10,008,000

Liabilities and Fund Balances	*Current Year*	*Prior Year*
Current:		
Notes payable to banks	$ 227,000	$ 300,000
Current installments of long-term debt (Note 5)	90,000	90,000
Accounts payable	450,000	463,000
Accrued expenses	150,000	147,000
Advances from third-party payors	300,000	200,000
Deferred revenue	10,000	10,000
Total current liabilities	1,227,000	1,210,000
Deferred revenue–third-party reimbursement (Note 4)	200,000	90,000
Long-term debt (Note 5):		
Housing bonds	500,000	520,000
Mortgage note	1,200,000	1,270,000
Total long-term debt	1,700,000	1,790,000
Fund balance*	7,400,000	6,918,000
Total	$10,527,000	$10,008,000

Restricted Funds

Assets	*Current Year*	*Prior Year*
Specific purpose funds:		
Cash	$ 1,260	$ 1,000
Investments (Note 1)	200,000	70,000
Grants receivable	90,000	–
Total specific purpose funds	$ 291,260	$ 71,000
Plant replacement and expansion funds:		
Cash	$ 10,000	$ 450,000
Investments (Note 1)	800,000	290,000
Pledges receivable, net of estimated uncollectible	20,000	360,000
Total plant replacement and expansion funds	$ 830,000	$ 1,100,000
Endowment funds:		
Cash	$ 50,000	$ 33,000
Investments (Note 1)	6,100,000	3,942,000
Total endowment funds	$ 6,150,000	$ 3,975,000

Liabilities and Fund Balances	*Current Year*	*Prior Year*
Specific purpose funds:		
Due to unrestricted funds	$ 215,000	$ –
Fund balances:		
Research grants	15,000	30,000
Other	61,260	41,000
	76,260	71,000
Total specific purpose funds	$ 291,260	$ 71,000
Plant replacement and expansion funds:		
Fund balances:		
Restricted by third-party payors	$ 380,000	$ 150,000
Other	450,000	950,000
Total plant replacement and expansion funds	$ 830,000	$ 1,100,000
Endowment funds:		
Fund balances:		
Permanent endowment	$ 4,850,000	$ 2,675,000
Term endowment	1,300,000	1,300,000
Total endowment funds	$ 6,150,000	$ 3,975,000

See accompanying Notes to Financial Statements.

*Composition of the fund balance may be shown here, on the Statement of Changes in Fund Balances, or in a footnote.

Source: AICPA, *Hospital Audit Guide*, pp. 40–41.

shows, the effect of this recommendation is to reverse the position of the "Other Revenues" and "Expenses" sections of the AHA recommended income statement (Illustration 19–3).

The fact that Illustrations 19–4, 19–5, and 19–6 are in comparative form, whereas Illustrations 19–1, 19–2, and 19–3 are not, is not a difference between the recommendations of the AHA and AICPA; either, both, or neither set of illustrations could be in comparative format depending on the availability of data and the preference of the persons preparing the statements.

Illustration 19–5

AICPA SAMPLE HOSPITAL
STATEMENT OF CHANGES IN FUND BALANCES
Year Ended December 31, 19–
With Comparative Figures for 19–

	Current Year	*Prior Year*
Unrestricted Funds		
Balance at beginning of year	$6,918,000	$6,242,000
Excess of revenues over expenses	84,000	114,000
Transferred from plant replacement and expansion funds to finance property, plant, and equipment expenditures	628,000	762,000
Transferred to plant replacement and expansion funds to reflect third-party payor revenue restricted to property, plant, and equipment replacement	(230,000)	(200,000)
Balance at end of year	$7,400,000*	$6,918,000
Restricted Funds		
Specific purpose funds:		
Balance at beginning of year	$ 71,000	$ 50,000
Restricted gifts and bequests	35,000	20,000
Research grants	35,000	45,000
Income from investments	35,260	39,000
Gain on sale of investments	8,000	–
Transferred to:		
Other operating revenue	(100,000)	(80,000)
Allowances and uncollectible accounts	(8,000)	(3,000)
Balance at end of year	$ 76,260	$ 71,000
Plant replacement and expansion funds:		
Balance at beginning of year	$1,100,000	$1,494,000
Restricted gifts and bequests	113,000	150,000
Income from investments	15,000	18,000
Transferred to unrestricted funds (described above)	(628,000)	(762,000)
Transferred from unrestricted funds (described above)	230,000	200,000
Balance at end of year	$ 830,000	$1,100,000
Endowment funds:		
Balance at beginning of year	$3,975,000	$2,875,000
Restricted gifts and bequests	2,000,000	1,000,000
Net gain on sale of investments	175,000	100,000
Balance at end of year	$6,150,000	$3,975,000

See accompanying Notes to Financial Statements.

*Composition of the balance may be shown here, on the balance sheet, or in a footnote.
Source: AICPA, *Hospital Audit Guide*, p. 43.

Illustration 19-6

AICPA SAMPLE HOSPITAL
STATEMENT OF REVENUES AND EXPENSES
Year Ended December 31, 19–
With Comparative Figures for 19–

	Current Year	*Prior Year*
Patient service revenue	$8,500,000	$8,000,000
Allowances and uncollectible accounts (after deduction of related gifts, grants, subsidies, and other income–$55,000 and $40,000) (Notes 3 and 4)	(1,777,000)	(1,700,000)
Net patient service revenue	6,723,000	6,300,000
Other operating revenue (including $100,000 and $80,000 from specific purpose funds)	184,000	173,000
Total operating revenue	6,907,000	6,473,000
Operating expenses:		
Nursing services	2,200,000	2,000,000
Other professional services	1,900,000	1,700,000
General services	2,100,000	2,000,000
Fiscal services	375,000	360,000
Administrative services (including interest expense of $50,000 and $40,000)	400,000	375,000
Provision for depreciation	300,000	250,000
Total operating expenses	7,275,000	6,685,000
Loss from operations	(368,000)	(212,000)
Nonoperating revenue:		
Unrestricted gifts and bequests	228,000	205,000
Unrestricted income from endowment funds	170,000	80,000
Income and gains from board-designated funds	54,000	41,000
Total nonoperating revenue	452,000	326,000
Excess of revenues over expenses	$ 84,000	$ 114,000

Source: AICPA, *Hospital Audit Guide*, p. 42.

Statistical and Cost Reports

In addition to the standard financial and operating reports, it is imperative that hospitals prepare numerous statistical analyses. This requirement derives from the variety of services rendered by hospitals and the range of economic status represented by the patients served. Many of the statistical analyses are related to unit costs; these predominate because hospital management, to be efficient, must know the relationship between revenue and costs of the various services furnished to patients. A discussion of cost accounting for hospitals is found in Chapter 20.

Although not an ingredient of the accounting system of hospitals, a standard glossary of terms and definitions is an absolute necessity. Clarity and uniformity of meaning are indispensable to the production of comparable financial and statistical data. "Contractual inpatient," "general inpatient," "full-pay visit," and the many other terms used in describing and measuring hospital activities must be defined with exactitude to obtain reliable reports. Hospital organizations have given much attention to the development of standard terms.

Conclusion

A single chapter on accounting for hospitals can touch upon only the most outstanding features. The probability of great variations in the operating and accounting procedures for individual hospitals must be kept in mind. Particularly influential in determining appropriate accounting procedures are the size of the unit and the sources of income. For further information the references cited below are recommended.

SELECTED REFERENCES

AMERICAN HOSPITAL ASSOCIATION. *Chart of Accounts for Hospitals.* Chicago, 1966.

AMERICAN INSTITUTE OF CERTIFIED PUBLIC ACCOUNTANTS. *Hospital Audit Guide.* New York, 1972.

HAY, LEON E. *Budgeting and Cost Analysis for Hospital Management.* 2nd ed. Bloomington, Ind.: Pressler Publications, 1963.

SEAWELL, L. VANN. *Introduction to Hospital Accounting.* Chicago: Hospital Financial Management Association, 1971.

———. *Hospital Accounting and Financial Management.* Chicago: Physicians' Record Co., 1964.

Periodicals

HOSPITALS. The journal of the American Hospital Association, Chicago, Illinois.

HOSPITAL FINANCIAL MANAGEMENT. The journal of the Hospital Financial Management Association, Chicago, Illinois. (Before October, 1968, the journal was titled *Hospital Accounting.* Before July, 1968, the organization was known as the American Association of Hospital Accountants.)

HOSPITAL MANAGEMENT. Clissold Publishing Co., Chicago, Illinois.

HOSPITAL PROGRESS. The journal of the Catholic Hospital Association, St. Louis, Missouri.

QUESTIONS

19–1. A nongovernmental hospital wishes to convert from the cash basis of accounting to an accrual system that will be practical to operate.

a) Name some sources of information available to the hospital accountant to help him develop the new system.
b) Outline the essential changes the hospital will have to make.

(Adapted from a Fellowship Examination of the Hospital Financial Management Association)

19–2. A certain hospital has recently had its plant and equipment appraised, as suggested in the American Hospital Association's *Chart of Accounts for Hospitals.* As recommended in that publication the controller has issued a plant fund balance sheet in which the assets are stated at appraisal value, less accumulated depreciation based on appraisal value. Would you expect the CPAs who audit this hospital to issue an unqualified opinion? Why or why not?

19–3. In hospital accounting the procedure followed in recording and assembling all charges to patients accounts is especially important. Why?

19–4. Hospital accounting manuals provide that service rendered to nonpaying or part-paying categories of recipients shall be billed at the regular price for a full-pay patient. What is the reason for this recommendation?

19–5. The AHA chart of accounts is discussed in this chapter. For what reason are numbers provided for each account title? What is the logic of the recommended numbering system?

19–6. Some hospital fixed assets, referred to as "minor equipment," are not depreciated. Additions and replacements are debited to the Minor Equipment account. At ends of fiscal periods the aggregate of such equipment is inventoried, and the equipment account balance is reduced to the inventory value.

a) Why is that method more suitable for the class of assets referred to than the conventional method?

b) Assuming that the Minor Equipment account has a balance of $21,000 at the end of the year, compared with an inventory valued at $15,700, make the necessary adjusting entry.

19–7. Underwriting of medical and hospital costs of an individual or family has become a widespread practice through the use of both private and governmental medical and hospital insurance and prepayment plans. Has the growth of third-party payment of hospital bills had any effect upon hospital accounting? Explain.

19–8. You have received an invoice from the Central Surgical Supply Company in the amount of $900, covering $500 of items chargeable to the operating fund laboratory supplies and $400 of items chargeable to the heart research fund (which is carried as one of the specific purpose funds on your books). This $400 includes $300 for major movable equipment and $100 for supplies. Payment to the vendor is to be made on one check only. Reimbursement to the operating fund is made in the subsequent month. Expendable supplies for the heart research fund are included in the hospital's operating expenses. Show the entries necessary to reflect these transactions on the books.

(Adapted from a Fellowship Examination of the Hospital Financial Management Association)

19–9. How do the accounting procedures found in the American Hospital Association manual differ from the principles of fund accounting as set forth by the National Committee on Governmental Accounting?

EXERCISES AND PROBLEMS

19–1. Memorial Hospital's fiscal year will end September 30, 1972. During the year the hospital has completed its most recent building program—the construction of a new wing opened on December 1, 1971.

The hospital's accounts contain an operating fund, a plant fund, and a building construction fund. The trial balance of the building construction fund at May 31, 1972, consisted of the following accounts and amounts:

	Debit	*Credit*
Cash in bank	$ 41,000	
Construction in progress	$5,000,000	
Payable to general contractor		$ 50,000
Bonds payable		$2,459,000
Bond interest paid	$ 128,000	
Investment income		$ 160,000
Fund balance		$2,500,000

An analysis of the construction file and other pertinent records revealed the following information:

The architect's report includes the following percentage breakdown of construction costs:

Description	*Percent of total construction cost*
Land improvements	1%
Building	39
Fixed equipment	40
Major movable equipment	20

A bond issue of $2,500,000, at 5.12 percent annual interest rate, was floated prior to completion of construction. The first annual principal payment on the bond issue in the amount of $41,000 was made on November 30, 1971. Further, the proceeds of the bond issue were invested by the building construction fund until needed for construction payments. An analysis of the interest earned account revealed the following:

Period held	*Income received*
12/1/70–11/30/71	$100,000
4/1/71– 1/31/72	$ 10,000
12/1/71– 5/31/72	$ 50,000

The hospital takes no depreciation in the year of acquisition.

Required:

Prepare journal entries as of May 31, 1972, to transfer the new wing to the plant fund and to close the building construction fund.

(FHFMA)

19–2. An analysis of the patient accounts function reveals that, under the current billing system, accounts are held for three days after discharge so that late charges and credits may be posted. The analysis also indicates that the unbilled accounts are broken down in the following manner:

Principal Payer	Awaiting Diagnosis	Benefits Missing	Ready To Bill	Other
	Number of Accounts Unbilled			
Medicare	40	83	285	24
Blue Cross	52	76	141	27
Welfare	36	82	115	28
Commercial Insurance	38	26	197	22
Self-Pay	–	–	53	27
	166	267	791	168
Number of Days (at 40 discharges per day)	4	7	21	4

Required:

a) Prepare a brief description of the situation for the administration.
b) Establish a list of priorities to handle the problem areas in the accounts receivable section.
c) Outline the corrective actions to be taken giving particular attention to (1) the number of accounts ready to bill and (2) the normal billing activities.
d) Explain the steps you feel should be taken to prevent a recurrence of this situation.

(FHFMA)

19–3. Having been appointed controller of Paragon Hospital, you find it necessary to make adjustments in the accounts for the year ended December 31, 19y1.

Fixed equipment and movable equipment have been carried in one account termed Equipment. On December 31, 19y0, the balance in the account was $694,250. Of this amount, $620,150 represents the cost of the fixed equipment and $74,100 the cost of the major movable equipment. Both assets were purchased March 15, 19y0. By using the composite method of depreciation for the year 19y0, depreciation of $69,425 was set up, and at the end of the year 19y1 , $72,837 was provided for depreciation.

It is now decided to adjust the accounts so as to provide depreciation reserves at the rate of 5 percent per annum for Fixed Equipment and 10 percent for Movable Equipment. It is also decided to separate the respective asset and reserve accounts on the books, and it is decided that only one half year's depreciation is to be claimed on assets in the year of acquisition.

During the year 19y1, the following additions were made to the assets:

Fixed equipment:	
March 15, 19y1	$38,750
October 1, 19y1	$75,125
Movable equipment:	
August 1, 19y1	$19,750
November 15, 19y1	$14,375

At December 31, 19y1 the balances shown on the books are as follows:

Equipment	$842,250
Allowance for depreciation	$142,262

Required:

Prepare a depreciation schedule for the two years and the necessary journal entries to be placed on the books, assuming the accounts have already been closed as of December 31.

(FHFMA, adapted)

19–4. The Whoville Hospital presents the following operating fund balance sheet as of September 30:

Assets			*Liabilities and Capital*	
Cash		$ 12,500	Accounts payable	$ 44,833
Inpatient receivables	$136,621		Salaries, wages, and fees payable	14,920
Less: Allowance for uncollectibles	15,222	121,399	Total Liabilities	$ 59,753
			Operating fund balance	142,291
Accrued interest receivable		5,000		
Inventory–supplies		63,145		
Total Assets		$202,044	Total Liabilities and Capital	$202,044

Required:

a) Record in general journal form the effect of the following transactions during October on the operating fund:

1. Summary of revenue journal:	
Nursing service revenues	$ 87,130 (gross)
Other professional service revenues	57,618 (gross)
Adjustments and allowances:	
Contracting agencies	2,180
Charity service	2,515
2. Summary of cash receipts journal:	
Grant from United Fund	8,000
Collections of receivables	122,278
Interest accrued September 30	5,000
3. Purchases journal:	
Administration	6,394
General service expenses	8,380
Nursing service expenses	16,240
Other professional services expenses	15,612
4. Payroll journal:	
Administration	$ 15,061
General service expenses	7,200
Nursing service expenses	34,030
Other professional service expenses	31,225
5. Summary of cash payments journal:	
Accounts payable for purchases	33,955
Accrued payroll	82,241
Transfer to plant fund–depreciation	11,000
6. Other information:	
October provision for uncollectible receivables	1,450
Accrued interest receivable, October 31	1,300

	September 30	October 31
Supplies inventory:		
Administration	$ 7,970	$ 7,340
General service expenses	8,734	8,968
Nursing service expenses	9,965	10,223
Other professional service expenses	36,476	35,990
Total	$63,145	$62,521

7. Nominal accounts were closed.

b) Prepare an operating fund balance sheet as of October 31.
c) Prepare an income statement for October.

19–5. The following transactions occurred in the specific purpose funds of the Jefferson Memorial Hospital:

1. Under the will of Samuel H. Smith, a bequest of $20,000 was received for the promotion of nursing education.
2. Pending the need of the money for the designated purpose, part of it was invested in $9,000 of par value City of Greenville 3 percent bonds, at 103 and accrued interest of $110.
3. An interest payment of $135 was received on the City of Greenville bonds.
4. The bonds were sold at 104 and accrued interest of $60.
5. The sum of $8,500 was transferred to the operating fund.
6. The income transfer from the Smith fund was used by the operating fund for the purpose designated.

Make journal entries for the above transactions.

19–6. The trustees of St. Mary's Hospital have decided to pool the investments of three of its endowment funds which, for present purposes, will be designated as A, B, and C. Accounting for investments of the three endowments had been conducted on the basis of cost. At the date of pooling, the composition of the three was as follows:

Assets	*A*	*B*	*C*
Cash	$ 1,000	$ 800	$ 1,120
Investments	58,000	29,360	87,000
Accrued interest	500	700	860
Total Assets	$59,500	$30,860	$88,980
Liabilities and Fund Principal			
Due to operating fund	$ 500	–	–
Due to plant fund	–	$ 700	$ 860
Fund principal–income unrestricted	59,000	–	–
Fund principal–income restricted	–	30,160	88,120
Total Liabilities and Fund Principal	$59,500	$30,860	$88,980

Preliminary to the pooling of the assets, it was decided to adjust investments to market value, and the following changes were agreed upon:

Endowment	*Book Value*	*Market*
A	$ 58,000	$ 59,000
B	29,360	29,200
C	87,000	88,880
	$174,360	$177,080

a) You are required to journalize the transactions stated below:

1. Entries were made to adjust the book value of investments to market value, as indicated above.
2. Except for $2,060, all cash was transferred to Cash—Pool.
3. Investments and accrued interest were transferred to Invest ments—Pool and Accrued Interest—Pool.
4. The amounts due the operating fund and the plant fund were paid from unpooled cash.
5. Interest received in cash on pool investments during the year totaled $3,850, including amounts accrued at the time of pooling.
6. Interest accrued on pool investments at the end of the year amounted to $2,240.
7. At the end of the year, it was decided to compute and record the liability to the beneficiaries of the three funds: operating fund for A, and plant fund for B and C, for earnings of the pool.

b) During the next year the following additional transactions occurred:

1. Amounts due the beneficiary funds were paid.
2. During the year, the D fund was given to the hospital and made a member of the pool, supplying cash of $900 and investments with a fair market value of $59,100. D's income is unrestricted. Assume that the market value of the pooled investments is the same as when the pool was created.
3. During the year, interest received in cash amounted to $5,640, including the amount accrued at the end of last year.
4. Pool investments carried at $20,600 were sold during the year at $23,400.
5. Interest accrued on investments at the end of the year totaled $2,900.
6. At the end of the year, it was decided to compute and record the liability to the beneficiaries of the individual en-

downments for earnings of the pool. Fund D was admitted to the distribution on the basis of one-half year in the pool.

c) At the end of three years, the Reserve for Realized Gains and Losses had reached the credit balance of $16,000, and it was decided to distribute the entire amount to the balances of the participating endowments, on the basis of their principal amounts at the beginning of the third year. Make the entry for that transaction.

19–7. Below is given the plant fund balance sheet of the Monroe County Hospital as of September 30, 19__.

MONROE COUNTY HOSPITAL
Plant Fund Balance Sheet
as of September 30, 19–

Assets

Cash		$ 16,557
Investments		200,000
Due from operating fund		577,389
Land		108,000
Buildings, at cost	$1,516,367	
Less: Accumulated depreciation	506,452	1,009,915
Fixed equipment, at cost	$ 330,217	
Less: Accumulated depreciation	173,607	156,610
Major movable equipment, at cost	$ 207,301	
Less: Accumulated depreciation	113,887	93,414
Minor equipment		24,114
Total Assets		$2,185,999

Equities

Fund Balance:	
Invested in plant	$1,392,053
Reserved for replacement and expansion	793,946
Total Equities	$2,185,999

a) Prepare, in general journal form, entries to record the effect on the plant fund of the following transactions:

1. On October 1, fixed equipment which cost $6,560, and for which accumulated depreciation totals $4,890, was traded for similar new equipment costing $9,840; the payment in cash amounted to $8,800. The payment was made from plant fund cash.
2. Depreciation charges for October amounted to $2,500 for the building, $2,750 for fixed equipment, and $3,800 for major movable equipment.

3. Cash in the amount of $20,000 was received from the operating fund to "fund" the October depreciation charges, the balance to be applied to the arrearage in funding depreciation charges of prior periods.
4. Cash in the amount of $50,000 was received from an anonymous donor to be used for the eventual erection of an addition to the nurses' dormitory.
5. Necessary closing entries were made.

b) Prepare a plant fund balance sheet as of October 31, 19___.

19–8. From the following trial balance and other information, prepare appropriate fund balance sheets and income statement for the year ending December 31, 19x3. All operating expenses should be charged to the Operating Expenses account.

COUNTY HOSPITAL
Trial Balance
December 31, 19x3

	Debit	*Credit*
Land	$ 100,000	
Buildings	500,000	
Furniture and equipment	150,000	
Cash–Operating Fund	50,000	
Accounts receivable–inpatients	49,500	
Accounts receivable–outpatients	500	
Inventory	35,000	
Investments	15,000	
Prepaid insurance	2,250	
Operating expenses	487,750	
Accounts payable		$ 9,000
Accumulated depreciation–buildings		60,000
Accumulated depreciation–furniture and equipment		22,500
Allowance for uncollectible accounts		8,500
Fund balance		700,000
Revenues from patient services		550,000
Other revenues		40,000
Totals	$1,390,000	$1,390,000

Other information:

a) Expense of estimated uncollectible accounts for the year has not been charged on the records—rate, 1½ percent of revenue from patient services.
b) Depreciation on buildings has not been charged—rate, 2½ percent per year.
c) Depreciation on furniture and equipment has not been charged—rate is 10½ percent per year. The hospital purchased new equipment on July 1, 19x3, which was entered on the records at a cost of $15,000. It has been the policy to apply the annual

depreciation rate on property and plant balances as of January 1 of each year, and to charge no depreciation on acquisitions during the year.

d) Unexpired insurance premiums as of December 31, 19x3, amounted to $2,000.

e) A Cash Change Fund of $300 was established July 5, 19x3. It had been charged on the records as an operating expense.

f) The hospital board, on December 31, 19x3, ordered accounts of inpatients totaling $4,225 written off as uncollectible. You will make this adjustment.

g) Interest of $450 on investments which were purchased from the Cash—Operating Fund was received December 31, 19x3, and has not been entered on records.

(Indiana State Board of Accounts, adapted)

19–9. Below is given a combined trial balance for the funds of the Bloomfield Hospital after closing on December 31, 19x5.

	Debit	*Credit*
Operating fund:		
Cash	$ 10,000	
Accounts receivable	30,000	
Allowance for uncollectible accounts		$ 8,600
Inventory of supplies	8,000	
Prepaid expenses	1,200	
Due from plant fund	2,000	
Accounts payable		11,000
Accrued expenses payable		1,600
Operating fund balance		30,000
Endowment fund:		
Cash	8,000	
Investments	146,000	
Endowment fund principal–income unrestricted		154,000
Plant fund:		
Cash	3,000	
Investments	69,400	
Land	108,000	
Buildings	1,105,000	
Accumulated depreciation on buildings		105,000
Fixed equipment	268,000	
Accumulated depreciation of fixed equipment		77,000
Major movable equipment	141,000	
Accumulated depreciation of major movable equipment		49,000
Minor equipment	83,000	
Mortgage bonds payable		64,000
Due to operating fund		2,000
Fund balance invested in plant		1,410,000
Fund balance reserved for plant improvement and expansion		70,400
	$1,982,600	$1,982,600

During 19x6 the following transactions, in summary form, occurred:

1. Gross earnings from services to patients, all charged to accounts receivable, were as follows:

Earnings from nursing services	$640,600
Earnings from other professional services	194,500

2. Deductions from gross earnings were as follows:

Charity Service	$ 9,000
Contractual adjustments	10,000
Provision for uncollectible receivables	18,000

3. Other revenue received or earned during the year included the following:

Income from endowment fund investments	$ 4,880
General contributions	32,600

4. Plant fund cash of $1,000 was invested in new fixed equipment.
5. One piece of major movable equipment, which cost $2,800 and currently had a book value of $200, was sold for $50.
6. Transactions vouchered during the year were as shown below:

Expenses accrued at end of last year	$ 1,600
Administrative service expenses	64,400
Fiscal service expense	$ 48,000
General service expense	165,000
Nursing service expense	402,600
Other professional service expense	94,720
Supplies	40,000

7. Operating fund cash in the amount of $4,000 was used to retire mortgage bonds payable with an equivalent face value; the operating fund will not be repaid.
8. The hospital received corporate stock with a current market value of $24,000, the income to be used for nursing education (credit Endowment Fund Principal—Income Restricted.)
9. Collections on accounts receivable during the year amounted to $794,200, and $3,100 of accounts receivable were written off.
10. Supplies issued during the year amounted to $32,000, which may be charged to Administrative Service expense.
11. The plant fund and the endowment fund paid the amounts due to the operating fund.
12. Cash payments on vouchers payable during the year amounted to $781,000; purchase discounts in the amount of $420 were taken.
13. Accrued expenses at December 31, 19x6 included fiscal service expense of $120 on plant fund bonds; administrative service expense, $870; and other professional service expense, $480. Prepaid expenses, consisting of other professional service expense, declined $400 during the year.

14. Accrued income on endowment fund investments was $540; and on plant fund investments, $180.
15. Depreciation of fixed assets was as follows:

Buildings	$31,500
Fixed equipment	26,800
Major movable equipment	20,000

16. The endowment fund transferred in cash to the operating fund the amount due.

You are required to do the following thing:

a) Record the 19x6 transactions.
b) Prepare a balance sheet for December 31, 19x6.
c) Prepare a statement of income and expenses for 19x6.
d) Prepare a statement of changes in the operating fund balance for 19x6.

19–10. The Smith Medical Foundation was established in 19x7 to finance research in the field of medical science. It leased building facilities from others from the date of its establishment to December, 19y4, at which time land and buildings adaptable to its operation were purchased.

Since it was desired to operate its plant property as a self-supporting entity, the foundation decided to account for its plant as a separate fund, by establishment of an operating fund and a plant fund. All cash is to be handled by the operating fund, with the plant fund being charged or credited with amounts applicable to it, until after the close of each year. At this time settlement will be made, if possible. The plant property is to be depreciated effective January 1, 19y5, at the rate of 5 percent per year. A depreciation "fund" is to be established.

The assets, debts, and capital accounts as of December 31 show the following:

SMITH MEDICAL FOUNDATION

	December 31	
Assets	*19y5*	*19y4*
Cash	$ 42,000	$ 36,000
Investments	217,000	67,000
Plant account	96,000	75,000
Unexpired insurance premiums	1,000	
Plant operations		1,000
Total Assets	$356,000	$179,000
Liabilities		
Accounts payable	$ 6,000	$ 4,000
Rents	3,000	
Balance	347,000	175,000
Total Liabilities	$356,000	$179,000

Upon analysis of the Plant account, you find the following:

Date	*Item*	*Debit*	*Credit*
9-30-y4	Cash donation for purchase of plant		$100,000
12-15-y4	Purchase of property	$175,000	
1-31-y5	Building improvements.	24,000	
3-31-y5	Building improvements.	15,000	
12-31-y5	Plant operation		18,000

Entries in the Plant Operation account consisted of:

Date	*Item*	*Debit*	*Credit*
12-31-y4	Coal, cleaning supplies, etc.	$ 1,000	
2-28-y5	Coal, cleaning supplies, etc.	4,000	
6-30-y5	Grading and seeding of grounds . . .	6,000	
7-31-y5	Cleaning supplies, etc.	1,200	
12-31-y5	Coal, cleaning supplies, etc.	4,000	
12-31-y5	Expired insurance premiums.	1,800	
12-31-y5	Plant account	18,000	
12-31-y5	To close the account		$36,000

Rents consisted of $3,000 per month received in 19y5 and rent for January 19y6, which was received on December 31, 19y5.

You obtain an appraisal of the land owned by the foundation, which gives a value of $75,000 at date of purchase.

a) You are to prepare journal entries setting up the plant fund and recording the transactions in the fund to December 31, 19y5.

b) You are to prepare a sectional balance sheet presenting the funds as of December 31, 19y5.

(AICPA, adapted)

19–11. The town of Mapleton built a hospital which was occupied March 1, 19x8. Monthly reports have been rendered for the first few months on a cash basis and have not shown separation of amounts by funds. You have been employed by the hospital as business manager, in December of the same year, and are to set up an accounting system on an accrual basis and to follow usual fund accounting practices. From the information presented below, prepare a statement showing the income and expense for the 10 months and a statement of financial position by funds.

1. The total contract price of the building was $1,200,000. This included fixed equipment of $350,000. The contractor was paid in the following manner:
   a) Cash of $600,000 which was contributed by the Federal government toward the hospital cost.
   b) Cash of $100,000 contributed by the county government toward the cost.
   c) Hospital bonds issued by the town in the amount of $500,000. These bonds are 5 percent bonds dated January 1, 19x8, due in 10 years, interest payable semiannually. They are

general obligation bonds of the town, but the town wishes to treat them in the hospital fund.

2. Equipment was initially obtained as follows (all was major equipment except minor equipment of $18,300):

   a) Purchased by the town for cash, $76,500.
   b) Purchased out of cash donations made by citizens for that purpose, $29,000.
   c) Donated equipment with an estimated value of $12,000.

3. The statement of cash receipts and disbursements, exclusive of items described above, for the 10 months was as follows:

Nursing service revenues	$226,570
Other professional service revenues	189,780
Miscellaneous income	1,030
Received from estate of James Jones, M.D.	25,000
Miscellaneous donations	20,410
Received from Beulah Williams	32,000
Donations from churches	3,700
Received from county for charity patients	1,840
Income from bonds	1,700
Total cash received	$502,030
Payroll and taxes paid thereon	$273,400
Supplies purchased	140,624
Major equipment purchased	47,250
Interest on bonds	12,500
Miscellaneous expenses	4,100
Total cash disbursed	$477,874
Balance of Cash, December 31, 19x8	$ 24,156

Investigation revealed the following additional information:

1. Inpatients' accounts on the books as of December 31, 19x8, amounted to $47,400. This amount is found to be divided between nursing and other professional services in the same proportion as cash already received. It is estimated that $4,360 of these accounts will never be collected.
2. Accrued unpaid wages at year-end amounted to $5,200, unpaid supply invoices amounted to $12,810, and accrued utilities amounted to $364. Prepaid insurance amounted to $720. Supplies on hand amounted to $13,800, at cost.
3. It has been decided to charge current income with depreciation on general hospital property at the following rates, based on the year-end balance of the asset accounts: building, 2 percent; fixed equipment, 5 percent; major equipment, 10 percent. Depreciation is to be computed for a full year. The reserve is to be funded.
4. The plant fund may borrow from the endowment fund.
5. The following facts were determined in respect to the donations:

   a) The donation from the estate of James Jones, M.D., received July 1, 19x8, was for the purchase of equipment.

b) The miscellaneous donations were made for general purposes of the operation of the hospital.

c) The Beulah Williams donation, received June 1, 19x8, consisted of cash and $40,000 face value of X Corporation 4¼ percent bonds, both to be treated in the endowment fund. Interest dates are June 1 and December 1. Income of this fund may be used for general operations of the hospital.

d) The donations from the churches are to be used for the purchase of equipment.

(FHFMA, adapted)

19–12. A newly elected board of directors of Central Hospital, a nonprofit corporation, decided that effective January 1, 1968:

a) The existing general ledger balances are to be properly adjusted and allocated to three separate funds (General Fund, John Central Endowment Fund and Plant Fund),

b) The totals of the John Central Endowment Fund and the Allowance for Accumulated Depreciation are to be fully invested in securities, and

c) All accounts are to be maintained in accordance with the principles of fund accounting. The board engaged you to determine the proper account balances for each of the funds.

The balances in the general ledger at January 1, 1968 were:

	Debit	*Credit*
Cash	$ 50,000	
Investment in U.S. Treasury bills	105,000	
Investment in common stock	417,000	
Interest receivable	4,000	
Accounts receivable	40,000	
Inventory	25,000	
Land	407,000	
Building	245,000	
Equipment	283,000	
Allowance for depreciation		$ 376,000
Accounts payable		70,000
Bank loan		150,000
John Central Endowment Fund		119,500
Surplus		860,500
Totals	$1,576,000	$1,576,000

The following additional information is available:

1. Under the terms of the will of John Central, founder of the hospital, "the principal of the bequest is to be fully invested in trust forevermore in mortgages secured by productive real estate in Central City and or in U.S. Government securities . . . and the income therefrom is to be used to defray current expenses."
2. The John Central Endowment Fund account balance consists of the following:

Cash received in 1871 by bequest from John Central.	$ 81,500
Net gains realized from 1926 through 1959 from sale of real estate acquired in mortgage foreclosures	23,500
Income received from 1960 through 1967 from 90-day U.S. Treasury bill investments	14,500
Balance per general ledger on January 1, 1968	$119,500

3. The Land account balance was composed of:

1890 appraisal of land at $10,000 and building at $5,000 received by donation at that time. (The building was demolished in 1910.).	$ 15,000
Appraisal increase based on insured value in land title policies issued in 1927	380,000
Landscaping costs for trees planted.	12,000
Balance per general ledger on January 1, 1968	$407,000

4. The Building account balance was composed of:

Cost of present hospital building completed in January 1927 when hospital commenced operations.	$300,000
Adjustment to record appraised value of building in 1937	(100,000)
Cost of elevator installed in hospital building in January 1953	45,000
Balance per general ledger on January 1, 1968	$245,000

The estimated useful lives of the hospital building and the elevator when new were 50 years and 20 years, respectively.

5. The hospital's equipment was inventoried on January 1, 1968. The cost of the inventory agreed with the Equipment account balance in the general ledger. The Allowance for Accumulated Depreciation account at January 1, 1968, included $158,250 applicable to equipment, and that amount was approved by the board of directors as being accurate. All depreciation is computed on a straight-line basis.
6. A bank loan was obtained to finance the cost of new operating room equipment purchased in 1964. Interest on the loan was paid to December 31, 1967.

Required:

Prepare a worksheet to present the adjustments necessary to restate the general ledger account balances properly and to distribute the adjusted balances to establish the required fund accounts. Formal journal entries are not required. Computations should be in good form and should be referenced to the worksheet adjustments which they support. In addition to trial balance columns, the following columnar headings are recommended for your worksheet:

Adjustments		*General Fund*		*John Central Endowment Fund*		*Plant Fund*	
Debit	*Credit*	*Debit*	*Credit*	*Debit*	*Credit*	*Debit*	*Credit*

(AICPA)

20

Cost Determination for Nonprofit Entities

Cost accounting, as discussed in standard college texts, is generally applicable to business operations of governmental units. It is less immediately obvious that cost accounting concepts are applicable to governmental activities of a nonbusiness nature, or to hospitals or universities or other nonprofit entities. Yet, almost without exception in the case of hospitals and universities, and in many instances in the case of governmental units, the explosive increase in demand for services, relative to the increase in resources, has forced the adoption of the techniques of good financial management, including cost accounting.

The use of cost as a measure of the input of resources into a program is discussed in Chapter 2 of this text, as are other uses of cost data in budgeting for improved financial management.

Cost accounting, in the sense of the routine collection of data concerning the costs of departments, programs, or products, through the mechanism of a double entry bookkeeping system, is not as frequently found in nonprofit entities as is cost *determination*, or the recasting of data derived from the fund accounts described in preceding chapters to obtain desired cost information. Cost determination procedures may be considered to be statistical, since they are done apart from the bookkeeping system and may be done at regular intervals or only on a special study basis.

Determination of Costs Applicable to Grants and Contracts

State and local governmental units and colleges and universities have found grants from the contracts with the Federal government an important source of financing. Allowable costs under grants and contracts ordinarily include indirect costs as well as direct costs. The computation of depreciation for the purpose of claiming it as an allowable cost under Federal contracts and grants is discussed in preceding chapters relating to accounting for governmental general fixed assets (Chapter 12) and accounting for college and university educational plant (Chapter 18). The United States Office of Management and Budget has issued guidelines for Federal agencies, state and local governmental units, and colleges and universities to set forth the "principles for determining costs applicable to grants and contracts." The following are specified as allowable, to the extent indicated, under the provisions of OMB Circular A–87[1]:

> 1. *Accounting.* The cost of establishing and maintaining accounting and other information systems required for the management of grant programs is allowable. . . .
>
> 2. *Advertising.* Advertising media includes newspapers, magazines, radio and television programs, direct mail, trade papers, and the like. The advertising costs allowable are those which are solely for:
>
> *a*) Recruitment of personnel required for the grant program.
>
> *b*) Solicitation of bids for the procurement of goods and services required.
>
> *c*) Disposal of scrap or surplus materials acquired in the performance of the grant agreement.
>
> *d*) Other purposes specifically provided for in the grant agreement.
>
> 3. *Advisory councils.* Costs incurred by State advisory councils or committees established pursuant to Federal requirements to carry out grant programs are allowable. . . .
>
> 4. *Audit service.* The cost of audits necessary for the administration and management of functions related to grant programs is allowable.
>
> 5. *Bonding.* Costs of premiums on bonds covering employees who handle grantee agency funds are allowable.
>
> 6. *Budgeting.* Costs incurred for the development, preparation, presentation, and execution of budgets are allowable. Costs for services of a central budget office are generally not allowable since these are costs of general government. However, where employees of the central budget office actively participate in the grantee agency's budget process, the cost of identifiable services is allowable.
>
> 7. *Building lease management.* The administrative cost for lease management which includes review of lease proposals, maintenance of a list of available property for lease, and related activities is allowable.
>
> 8. *Central stores.* The cost of maintaining and operating a central stores organization for supplies, equipment, and materials used either directly or indirectly for grant programs is allowable.

[1] Office of Management and Budget Circular A–87, Attachment B. OMB Bulletin 74–4 transferred to the General Services Administration the responsibility for reissuing Circular A–87 and a number of related OMB Circulars. As of February, 1974, the OMB Circulars are still in effect.

9. *Communications.* Communication costs incurred for telephone calls or service, telegraph, teletype service, wide area telephone service (WATS), centrex, telpak (tie lines), postage, messenger service and similar expenses are allowable.

10. *Compensation for personal services.*

a) *General.* Compensation for personal services includes all remuneration, paid currently or accrued, for services rendered during the period of performance under the grant agreement, including but not necessarily limited to wages, salaries, and supplementary compensation and benefits . . . .

b) *Payroll and distribution of time.* Amounts charged to grant programs for personal services, regardless of whether treated as direct or indirect costs, will be based on payrolls documented and approved in accordance with generally accepted practice of the State or local agency. . . .

11. *Depreciation and use allowances.*

a) Grantees may be compensated for the use of buildings, capital improvements, and equipment through use allowances or depreciation. Use allowances are the means of providing compensation in lieu of depreciation or other equivalent costs. . . .

b) The computation of depreciation or use allowance will be based on acquisition cost. Where actual cost records have not been maintained, a reasonable estimate of the original acquisition cost may be used in the computation. The computation will exclude the cost or any portion of the cost of buildings and equipment donated or borne directly or indirectly by the Federal Government through charges to Federal grant programs or otherwise, irrespective of where title was originally vested or where it presently resides. In addition, the computation will also exclude the cost of land. Depreciation or a use allowance on idle or excess facilities is not allowable, except when specifically authorized by the grantor Federal agency.

c) Where the depreciation method is followed, adequate property records must be maintained, and any generally accepted method of computing depreciation may be used. . . .

d) In lieu of depreciation, a use allowance for buildings and improvements may be computed at an annual rate not exceeding two percent of acquisition cost. The use allowance for equipment (excluding items properly capitalized as building cost) will be computed at an annual rate not exceeding six and two-thirds percent of acquisition cost of usable equipment.

e) No depreciation or use charge may be allowed on any assets that would be considered as fully depreciated, . . .

12. *Disbursing service.* The cost of disbursing grant program funds by the Treasurer or other designated officer is allowable. Disbursing services cover the processing of checks or warrants, from preparation to redemption, including the necessary records of accountability and reconciliation of such records with related cash accounts.

13. *Employee fringe benefits.* Costs identified under *a*) and *b*) below

are allowable to the extent that total compensation for employees is reasonable as defined in section B.10.

a) Employee benefits in the form of regular compensation paid to employees during periods of authorized absences from the job, such as for annual leave, sick leave, court leave, military leave, and the like, if they are: (1) provided pursuant to an approved leave system, and (2) the cost thereof is equitably allocated to all related activities, including grant programs.

b) Employee benefits in the form of employers' contribution or expenses for social security, employees' life and health insurance plans, unemployment insurance coverage, workmen's compensation insurance, pension plans, severance pay, and the like, provided such benefits are granted under approved plans and are distributed equitably to grant programs and to other activities.

14. *Employee morale, health and welfare costs.* The costs of health or first-aid clinics and/or infirmaries, recreational facilities, employees' counseling services, employee information publications, and any related expenses incurred in accordance with general State or local policy, are allowable. Income generated from any of these activities will be offset against expenses.

15. *Exhibits.* Costs of exhibits relating specifically to the grant programs are allowable.

16. *Legal expenses.* The cost of legal expenses required in the administration of grant programs is allowable. Legal services furnished by the chief legal officer of a State or local government or his staff solely for the purpose of discharging his general responsibilities as legal officer are unallowable. Legal expenses for the prosecution of claims against the Federal Government are unallowable.

17. *Maintenance and repair.* Costs incurred for necessary maintenance, repair, or upkeep of property which neither add to the permanent value of the property nor appreciably prolong its intended life, but keep it in an efficient operation condition, are allowable.

18. *Materials and supplies.* The cost of materials and supplies necessary to carry out the grant programs is allowable. Purchases made specifically for the grant program should be charged thereto at their actual prices after deducting all cash discounts, trade discounts, rebates, and allowances received by the grantee. Withdrawals for general stores or stockrooms should be charged at cost under any recognized method of pricing consistently applied. Incoming transportation charges are a proper part of material cost.

19. *Memberships, subscriptions and professional activities.*

a) *Memberships.* The cost of membership in civic, business, technical and professional organizations is allowable provided: (1) the benefit from the membership is related to the grant program, (2) the expenditure is for agency membership, (3) the cost of the membership is reasonably related to the value of the services or benefits received, and (4) the expenditure is not for membership in an organization which devotes a substantial part of its activities to influencing legislation.

b) *Reference material.* The cost of books, and subscriptions to civic, business, professional, and technical periodicals is allowable when related to the grant program.

c) *Meetings and conferences.* Costs are allowable when the primary purpose of the meeting is the dissemination of technical information relating to the grant program and they are consistent with regular practices followed for other activities of the grantee.

20. *Motor pools.* The costs of a service organization which provides automobiles to user grantee agencies at a mileage or fixed rate and/or provides vehicle maintenance, inspection and repair services are allowable.

21. *Payroll preparation.* The cost of preparing payrolls and maintaining necessary related wage records is allowable.

22. *Personnel administration.* Costs for the recruitment, examination, certification, classification, training, establishment of pay standards and related activities for grant programs, are allowable.

23. *Printing and reproduction.* Cost for printing and reproduction services necessary for grant administration, including but not limited to forms, reports, manuals, and informational literature, are allowable. Publication costs of reports or other media relating to grant program accomplishments or results are allowable when provided for in the grant agreement.

24. *Procurement service.* The cost of procurement service, including solicitation of bids, preparation and award of contracts, and all phases of contract administration in providing goods, facilities and services for grant programs, is allowable.

25. *Taxes.* In general, taxes or payments in lieu of taxes which the grantee agency is legally required to pay are allowable.

26. *Training and education.* The cost of in-service training, customarily provided for employee development which directly or indirectly benefits grant programs is allowable. Out-of-service training involving extended periods of time is allowable only when specifically authorized by the grantor agency.

27. *Transportation.* Costs incurred for freight, cartage, express, postage and other transportation costs relating either to goods purchased, delivered, or moved from one location to another are allowable.

28. *Travel.* Travel costs are allowable for expenses for transportation, lodging, subsistence, and related items incurred by employees who are in travel status on official business incident to a grant program. . . .

Costs Allowable with Approval of Grantor Agency. In addition to the costs listed above, the following items are specified in OMB Circular A–87 as being "Costs allowable with the approval of the grantor agency."

1. *Automatic data processing.* The cost of data processing services to grant programs is allowable. This cost may include rental of equipment or depreciation on grantee-owned equipment. The acquisition of equipment, whether by outright purchase, rental-purchase agreement

or other method of purchase, is allowable only upon specific prior approval of the grantor Federal agency as provided under the selected item for capital expenditures.

2. *Building space and related facilities.* The cost of space in privately or publicly owned buildings used for the benefit of the grant program is allowable subject to the conditions stated below. The total cost of space, whether in a privately or publicly owned building, may not exceed the rental cost of comparable space and facilities in a privately owned building in the same locality. The cost of space procured for grant program usage may not be charged to the program for periods of nonoccupancy, without authorization of the grantor Federal agency.

a) *Rental cost.* The rental cost of space in a privately owned building is allowable.

b) *Maintenance and operation.* The cost of utilities, insurance, security, janitorial services, elevator service, upkeep of grounds, normal repairs and alterations and the like, are allowable to the extent they are not otherwise included in rental or other charges for space.

c) *Rearrangements and alterations.* Cost incurred for rearrangement and alteration of facilities required specifically for the grant program or those that materially increased the value or useful life of the facilities (section C.3.) are allowable when specifically approved by the grantor agency.

d) *Depreciation and use allowances on publicly owned buildings.* These costs are allowable as provided in section B.11.

e) *Occupancy of space under rental-purchase or lease with option-to-purchase agreement.* The cost of space procured under such arrangements is allowable when specifically approved by the Federal grantor agency.

3. *Capital expenditures.* The cost of facilities, equipment, other capital assets, and repairs which materially increase the value or useful life of capital assets is allowable when such procurement is specifically approved by the Federal grantor agency. When assets acquired with Federal grant funds are *a*) sold, *b*) no longer available for use in a federally sponsored program, or *c*) used for purposes not authorized by the grantor agency, the Federal grantor agency's equity in the asset will be refunded in the same proportion as Federal participation in its cost. In case any assets are traded on new items, only the net cost of the newly acquired assets is allowable.

4. *Insurance and indemnification.*

a) Costs of insurance required, or approved and maintained pursuant to the grant agreement, is allowable.

b) Costs of other insurance in connection with the general conduct of activities is allowable subject to the following limitations:

1. Types and extent and cost of coverage will be in accordance with general State or local government policy and sound business practice.

2. Costs of insurance or of contributions to any reserve covering the risk of loss of, or damage to, Federal Government property is

unallowable except to the extent that the grantor agency has specifically required or approved such costs.

c) Contributions to a reserve for a self-insurance program approved by the Federal grantor agency are allowable to the extent that the type of coverage, extent of coverage, and the rates and premiums would have been allowed had insurance been purchased to cover the risks.

d) Actual losses which could have been covered by permissible insurance (through an approved self-insurance program or otherwise) are unallowable unless expressly provided for in the grant agreement. However, costs incurred because of losses not covered under nominal deductible insurance coverage provided in keeping with sound management practice, and minor losses not covered by insurance, such as spoilage, breakage and disappearance of small hand tools which occur in the ordinary course of operations, are allowable.

e) *Indemnification* includes securing the grantee against liabilities to third persons and other losses not compensated by insurance or otherwise. The Government is obligated to indemnify the grantee only to the extent expressly provided for in the grant agreement, except as provided in *d*) above.

5. *Management studies.* The cost of management studies to improve the effectiveness and efficiency of grant management for ongoing programs is allowable except that the cost of studies performed by agencies other than the grantee department or outside consultants is allowable only when authorized by the Federal grantor agency.

6. *Preagreement costs.* Costs incurred prior to the effective date of the grant or contract, whether or not they would have been allowable thereunder if incurred after such date, are allowable when specifically provided for in the grant agreement.

7. *Professional services.* Cost of professional services rendered by individuals or organizations not a part of the grantee department is allowable subject to such prior authorization as may be required by the Federal grantor agency.

8. *Proposal costs.* Costs of preparing proposals on potential Federal Government grant agreements are allowable when specifically provided for in the grant agreement.

Unallowable costs. The following items are specified in OMB Circular A–87 as items which are *not* allowable charges to Federal grants to or contracts with state and local governments:

1. *Bad debts.* Any losses arising from uncollectible accounts and other claims, and related costs, are unallowable.

2. *Contingencies.* Contributions to a contingency reserve or any similar provision for unforeseen events are unallowable.

3. *Contributions and donations.* Unallowable.

4. *Entertainment.* Costs of amusements, social activities, and incidental costs relating thereto, such as meals, beverages, lodgings, rentals, transportation, and gratuities, are unallowable.

5. *Fines and penalties.* Costs resulting from violations of, or failure

to comply with Federal, State and local laws and regulations are unallowable.

6. *Governor's expenses.* The salaries and expenses of the Office of the Governor of a State or the chief executive of a political subdivision are considered a cost of general State or local government and are unallowable.

7. *Interest and other financial costs.* Interest on borrowings (however represented), bond discounts, cost of financing and refinancing operations, and legal and professional fees paid in connection therewith, are unallowable except when authorized by Federal legislation.

8. *Legislative expenses.* Salaries and other expenses of the State legislature or similar local governmental bodies such as county supervisors, city councils, school boards, etc., whether incurred for purposes of legislation or executive direction, are unallowable.

9. *Underrecovery of costs under grant agreements.* Any excess of cost over the Federal contribution under one grant agreement is unallowable under other grant agreements.

Provisions applicable to educational institutions and hospitals. The provisions of OMB Circular A–87, quoted at length above, are applicable to state and local governments, except those with (1) publicly financed educational institutions subject to OMB Circular A–21,[2] and (2) publicly owned hospitals and other providers of medical care subject to requirements promulgated by sponsoring Federal agencies, largely those in the Department of Health, Education, and Welfare. Allowable costs for the latter two classes of nonprofit entity are reasonably similar to those quoted above, and are, therefore, not reproduced here.

Cost allocation plans. In addition to specification of the items of allowable cost, OMB Circulars provide that grantees must prepare a plan for allocation of costs to support the distribution of joint costs to grant programs. States and larger local governmental units are required to submit their cost allocation plans to the Department of Health, Education, and Welfare, which is responsible for "negotiation, approval, and audit" of cost allocation plans. Smaller local governmental units are currently authorized to retain their cost allocation plans for audit by a designated Federal agency. Some of the essential features of a cost allocation plan may best be illustrated here in the context of an example of hospital cost analysis.

Cost Analysis—A Hospital Example

Three terms are particularly important in the present discussion: direct cost, indirect cost, and full cost. A *direct cost* of a certain department is a cost incurred because of some definite action by or for the department (or program or project). Thus in a hospital the salary of the pharmacist

[2] See footnote 1 of this chapter. OMB Circular A–21 is still in effect as of February, 1974.

is a direct cost of the pharmacy department. A hospital pharmacy exists to serve the patients of the hospital, however, so from the viewpoint of an inpatient nursing station the pharmacist's salary is an *indirect* cost. Likewise, the direct costs of all departments which exist to facilitate the work of the nursing station are indirect costs from the viewpoint of the nursing station.

In order to determine the total cost, or *full cost,* of serving the patient, it is necessary to add the indirect costs to the direct costs. Although the process of cost allocation is illustrated here in relation to a hospital, it underlies all cost accounting and cost determination systems, and some adaptation of one of the three methods discussed below is used in every business and every nonprofit entity which attempts to determine costs (even if a "direct costing" system is used). A brief description of the three basic methods of distributing the costs of service departments is:[3]

METHOD 1. Costs of nonrevenue-producing departments are allocated to revenue-producing departments only.

METHOD 2. Costs of nonrevenue-producing departments are allocated in sequence to departments they serve, whether or not these produce revenue. Once the costs of a department have been allocated, the costing process for that department is closed, and it receives no further charges.

METHOD 3. Costs of nonrevenue-producing departments are allocated to *all* departments they serve. In a computerized system, using a process of successive iterations, the amounts of cost allocated to nonrevenue-producing departments may be reduced to insignificant amounts, which may then be closed to revenue-producing departments. In a noncomputerized system the number of iterations is generally reduced to two.

Although hospital administrators need to know the costs of services rendered in order to evaluate the rate structure, in order to measure the effectiveness of departmental supervisors, and in order to have a realistic basis for budgets, the primary reason why many hospitals have been concerned with cost determination is that a very large proportion of charges for services rendered to patients are paid by Blue Cross, insurance companies, Medicare, and governmental welfare agencies. Such contract purchasers generally require hospitals to report cost information periodically in a specified form. Method 3 is used in some jurisdictions because of the requirements of contract purchasers. Method 1 is not acceptable under Medicare regulations, and is not widely used at present.

The American Hospital Association recommends the use of Method

[3] For a more complete treatment of this subject see Leon E. Hay, *Budgeting and Cost Analysis for Hospital Management.* (2d ed.; Bloomington, Ind.: Pressler Publications, 1963) chaps. 1–7, 12.

2, as does the United Hospital Fund of New York. Method 2 is often called the "step-down" method because departmental costs are allocated in sequence. Under this method it is important that the departments be ranked so that the cost of the one which renders service to the greatest number of other departments, while receiving benefits from the least number of departments, is allocated first; and the cost of the one rendering service to the least number of other departments, while receiving benefits from the greatest number, is allocated last. Practical application of this theory often requires arbitrary decisions as to the sequence in which departmental costs are closed. A further probelm in cost allocation is the choice of bases. The American Hospital Association publication *Cost Finding and Rate Setting for Hospitals* lists possible allocation bases.[4] It suffices to say here that the base selected for the allocation of the expense of each department should meet two criteria:

1. It should result in a distribution which is fair to all departments concerned.
2. The application of the base should be clerically feasible.

An example of the application of the step-down method of allocating costs of nonrevenue-producing departments of the Frumerville Hospital is presented in Illustration 20–1. A glance at the worksheet shows that the method is aptly named, since the sequential closing of accounts gives the money columns the appearance of a series of steps. The worksheet technique here illustrated provides for the vertical distribution of general service department direct and allocated expenses. For example, the total direct expenses of the first department listed, Maintenance of Plant, are entered as negative figures (indicated by the parentheses enclosing the figures) on the first line in the second money column from the left. The amount of maintenance of plant expense allocated to each department served is entered on the appropriate line under the negative amount, i.e., $113,400 of the $252,000 maintenance of plant expense was allocated to the Operation of Plant department. Inasmuch as the additions to other departments total the amount distributed, the column total is zero. Likewise, the Operation of Plant expense is allocated to departments served. In this case the expense to be allocated is $468,000, the total of the direct expenses, $354,600, and the allocation of Maintenance of Plant expense, $113,400. Illustration 20–1 also shows that this method of cost analysis does not produce total cost figures for the nonrevenue-producing or "general service" departments. Many accountants feel that direct departmental costs are more useful for managerial purposes than total costs (which include indirect costs charged to the department on the basis of many assumptions). Total cost figures are necessary, however,

[4] American Hospital Association, *Cost Finding and Rate Setting for Hospitals* (Chicago, 1968).

Illustration 20–1

FRUMERVILLE HOSPITAL
Stepdown Method–Expense Distribution
Year Ended April 30, 19–

	Totals for Distribution	*Mainte-nance of Plant*	*Operation of Plant*	*House-keeping*	*Laundry and Linen*	*Cafeteria*	*Adminis-tration*	*Medical Supplies*	*Medical Records*	*Nursing Service*	*Dietary*	*Totals*
General Services												
1 Maintenance of plant	$ 252,000	(252,000)	–	–	–	–	–	–	–	–	–	–
2 Operation of plant	354,600	113,400	(468,000)	–	–	–	–	–	–	–	–	–
3 Housekeeping	357,000	2,520	2,340	(361,860)	–	–	–	–	–	–	–	–
4 Laundry and linen service	216,000	10,080	16,848	7,236	(250,164)	–	–	–	–	–	–	–
5 Cafeteria	23,640	756	14,508	7,236	1,251	(47,391)	–	–	–	–	–	–
6 Administration	844,800	7,560	28,548	25,332	249	6,918	(913,407)	–	–	–	–	–
7 Medical supplies	480,000	2,520	6,084	1,809	501	1,707	39,276	(531,897)	–	–	–	–
8 Medical records	132,000	2,520	4,680	10,857	–	1,137	25,575	–	(176,769)	–	–	–
9 Nursing service	1,800,000	1,764	7,020	2,532	6,504	20,709	466,752	–	–	(2,305,281)	–	–
10 Dietary	657,000	10,080	19,188	10,857	3,003	4,596	103,215	–	–	–	(807,939)	–
Special Services												
Operating rooms	482,460	25,200	28,548	3,618	41,778	3,459	77,640	79,785	–	–	–	$ 742,488
Delivery rooms	141,000	15,120	14,508	10,857	21,015	1,422	31,968	53,190	–	–	–	289,080
Radiology	300,000	10,080	14,508	14,475	3,003	1,707	29,276	–	–	–	–	383,049
Laboratory	381,000	7,560	16,848	14,475	3,003	3,459	77,640	–	–	–	–	503,985
Blood bank	219,000	2,016	3,744	5,427	249	570	12,789	–	–	–	–	243,795
Cost of medical supplies sold	–	–	–	–	–	–	–	265,947	–	–	–	265,947
Routine Services												
Medical and surgical	144,000	25,200	219,024	218,202	138,339	–	–	79,785	137,880	1,959,489	807,939	3,729,858
Nursery	13,500	3,024	23,868	7,236	18,762	–	–	26,595	8,838	345,792	–	447,615
Outpatient clinic	192,000	12,600	47,736	21,711	12,507	1,707	39,276	26,595	30,051	–	–	384,183
Totals	$6,990,000	0	0	0	0	0	0	0	0	0	0	$6,990,000

for negotiations with contract purchasers of hospital services. Hospitals must be reimbursed for the expenses of departments which serve other hospital departments as well as for the expenses of the departments which serve patients directly.

Reimbursement of hospitals by contract purchasers is frequently related to cost per patient day for inpatients and newborns. Illustration 20–2 shows the allocation of the costs of special professional service de-

Illustration 20–2

FRUMERVILLE HOSPITAL
Stepdown Method–Computation of Per Diem and Per Visit Costs
Year Ended April 30, 19–

	Total	*Inpatient*	*Nursery*	*Out-patient*
Routine Services				
Inpatient.	$3,729,858	$3,729,858	–	–
Nursery.	447,615	–	$447,615	–
Outpatient.	384,183	–	–	$384,183
Totals	$4,561,656	$3,729,858	$447,615	$384,183
Special Services				
Operating rooms	$ 742,488	$ 668,241	$ 2,226	$ 72,021
Delivery rooms	289,080	289,080	–	–
Radiology	383,049	255,495	3,063	124,491
Laboratory	503,985	387,564	7,560	108,861
Blood bank	243,795	241,845	1,950	–
Cost of medical supplies sold.	265,947	252,651	4,521	8,775
Totals	$2,428,344	$2,094,876	$ 19,320	$314,148
Totals	$6,990,000	$5,824,734	$466,935	$698,331
Patient days or visits		60,000	10,000	35,000
Routine service cost per day or visit		$62.16	$44.76	$10.98
Special service cost per day or visit		34.91	1.93	8.97
Total per day or visit cost		$97.07	$46.69	$19.95

partments of the Frumerville Hospital to the Inpatient (Medical and Surgical), Nursery, and Outpatient Clinic departments, and the calculation of per diem costs for the Inpatient and Nursery departments, and per visit cost for the Outpatient Department. Bases for such an allocation must be chosen in accord with the same criteria as govern the choice of bases for the allocation of nonrevenue-producing departments.

For managerial purposes—and in some cases, for reimbursement purposes—it is desirable to compute unit costs of services rendered by special service departments. In the Frumerville Hospital, to continue the same example, records indicate that 2,400,000 radiologic service units were rendered during the year (the Radiologic Section of the Connecticut

State Medical Society, in cooperation with the Connecticut Hospital Cost Commission, has issued a table of such units, reflecting the relative complexity and time consumption of various services). The total of direct and allocated costs of the Radiology department of Frumerville Hospital was $383,049 (see Illustration 20–1); therefore, the cost per radiologic service unit is $383,049 ÷ 2,400,000, or 15.96 cents.

Job Order Cost Accounting

In order to record the costs of programs or projects in a systematic manner, job order cost accounting may be used. In brief, the essential characteristic of a job order system is the routine identification of each element of the direct cost of a given project. If the system is operated manually or with a bookkeeping machine, a cost sheet (see Illustration 20–3) will be kept for each "job," or project. (Even if the system is computerized a similar concept is used.) Illustration 20–3 shows that the cost of materials requisitioned for the project and the cost of labor performed for the project are itemized on the cost sheet. The cost of any supplies purchased specifically for this project, or any other "overhead" item incurred for this project, would also be entered on the cost sheet; general overhead would be allocated to the job on the basis of a predetermined rate.

Process Cost Accounting

The construction activities, and many maintenance activities, of a nonprofit entity are best accounted for by a job order system. Some activities, such as the manufacture of crushed stone, asphalt, or concrete, are operated as continuous processes and are best accounted for by a process cost system. In contrast with a job order system which focuses on the accumulation of costs on a project basis, a process system focuses on the accumulation of costs on a time period basis. For example, the wages of workers assigned to the asphalt plant would be charged to an account for that activity; raw materials used in that activity and overhead allocable to that activity would be charged to the same account. The total costs incurred for the asphalt plant during a time period may be divided by the production of asphalt during that period to determine the average cost of the product for that period.

Cost Standards

Standard cost accounting systems are rarely found in governmental units or other nonprofit entities, but the use of cost standards apart from the books of account is rather common. Cost standards can be predetermined scientifically, as described in cost accounting texts for operations or activities which are performed repetitively. Cost estimates may be prepared for operations or activities which are performed less frequently.

Illustration 20–3

CITY OF X

JOB COST SHEET

Job.No. 69-33

Description of Job *Erect partitions in Public Health Office*

For *Public Health* Department

Account No. 363-009

Requisition No.

To Be Completed *Feb. 28, 19X5*

Completed

Reference *W/O 616*

Date	Explanation	Materials	Labor	Date	Explanation	Overhead	Other
2-19-X5	Req. 61-107	$187		2-28-X5	GJ6	$120	
2-19-X5	P/R		$40				
2-26-X5	P/R		80				
	Totals	$187	$120		Totals	$120	

SUMMARY

Item	Estimated	Actual
Direct labor	$185	$187
Materials	110	120
Overhead	110	120
Other (specify)		
Total	$405	$427

The standards, or estimates, are useful for planning purposes, and furnish a basis for control. Job order or process cost accounting systems yield historical costs for comparison with the standards or estimates; investigation of the variances between predetermined and historical costs enables management to take corrective action to improve the operations and to improve the planning process.

Clerical and Administrative Costs

A very large part of governmental expenditures are incurred for services of a general nature (such as the costs of the chief executive's office, costs of accounting and auditing, costs of boards and commissions, etc.) which are somewhat remote from the results any given subdivision is expected to accomplish. Furthermore, in smaller units of government, many offices or departments perform such a variety of services that separating their costs is practically impossible under their present schemes of organization. For determination of unit costs, departmentalization or some other form of specialization is necessary.

As is true for other applications of governmental cost accounting, ascertaining definitely the total outlay for services to be costed is of equal importance with measuring the activity. It is probable that, in costing clerical and administrative operations, chief emphasis should be upon direct costs, because of the difficulty of obtaining a satisfactory basis for overhead allocation. In fact, overhead relationships might be so uncertain that attempts to distribute them to special activities would produce misleading results. For example, some kinds of work, such as typing of documents, might be so uniform and routine that to charge supervisory costs to the department on a per capita employee basis would be entirely inequitable.

Although much remains to be done, with complete results probably never fully obtainable because of the general nature of administrative expenses, some progress has been made in establishing work units for office operations, of which the following are a few examples:

Office	Work Unit Basis
Public recorder	Number of documents or number of lines recorded.
Treasurer	Number of tax bills prepared.
	Number of tax bills collected.
	Number of bills, notices, and receipts mailed.
	Number of parking meters serviced.
	Amount of money collected.
	Number of licenses and permits issued.
	Number of checks or warrants written.
Accounting ...	Number of claims examined and approved.
	Number of tax bills computed and recorded.

Successful application of unit cost accounting in administrative departments, as is true for other classes of costs, depends upon the identification of expenses to be allocated and the definition of work units to be used. Further progress in the field appears to await greater separation of costs through departmentalization of outlays for administration and of work done.

Limitations on the Use of Unit Costs

It has been said that no unit costs are better than inaccurate ones, the reason being that unless they are reliable they may lead to unwarranted and erroneous conclusions on the part of administrators, taxpayers, and the public generally. Corollary to this, it may be said that crude unit costs, although both theoretically and technically correct, may be almost as misleading as inaccurate ones. No unit cost figure, especially in government, should be used as the basis for decisive action or opinions without careful evaluation in the light of all pertinent facts. Such influences as regional variations in personnel costs, differences in climate and other physiographic conditions, size of the organization represented, and density of population in the area served are some of the factors that must be recognized if they are present and given due weight in appraising differences in unit costs. The establishment of standard costs which take into account all local circumstances and conditions has been recommended as one method for obviating the effect of comparisons with figures that are not entirely analogous. Historical costs compiled by other governmental units may not be entirely acceptable as a standard of comparison. This is true because one or more factors which affect costs in one jurisdiction may be decidedly more or less influential, or even not present. Finally, the quality of service represented by the unit of product must never be lost sight of in reaching a judgment as to the reasonableness of unit costs. Even for such objective units as gallons of water and kilowatts of electricity, there are such intangible qualities as purity, taste, pressure, reliability, attention to complaints, and other service factors. For administrative government, on the other extreme, the possibilities for variance are far greater. At best, therefore, unit cost accounting in government and nonprofit entities is not an automatic process for turning out a standardized product, but only a means for helping to accomplish a desired end.

SELECTED REFERENCES

American Hospital Association. *Cost Finding and Rate Setting for Hospitals.* Chicago, 1968.

Clark, William H. An Area of Need for Cost-Revenue Studies," *Municipal Finance,* Vol. 36, no. 4 (May 1964), pp. 130–35.

Executive Office of the President, Office of Management and Budget. *Circular A-87 Principles for Determining Costs Applicable to Grants and Contracts with State and Local Governments.*

Fava, John L. "Work Measurement Standards," *Municipal Finance,* Vol. 34, no. 1 (August 1961), pp. 59–64.

Hay, Leon E. *Budgeting and Cost Analysis for Hospital Management.* 2d ed. Bloomington, Ind.: Pressler Publications, 1963.

MACE, RUTH L. "Cost-Revenue Research and the Finance Officer," *Municipal Finance* Vol. 36, no. 4 (May 1964), pp. 122–29.

MCCAFFERTY, BART. *Cost Accounting for Municipal Operations, Special Bulletin 1962E,* Municipal Finance Officers Association, 1962.

QUESTIONS

20–1. If governmental units, educational institutions, and hospitals exist in order to provide services needed by the public, or a segment of the public, and are not concerned with the generation of net income, why should they be interested in the determination of costs?

20–2. The finance officer of a small city has heard that certain items of cost may be allowable under Federal grants and contracts, even though they were not incurred specifically for the grant or contract. *a*) What name is generally given to this class of cost? *b*) To what source could the finance officer go to determine what costs are allowable under Federal grants and contracts?

20–3. In the 50 states of the United States of America, there are over 78,000 local governmental units—counties, townships, civil cities, school districts, drainage districts, fire protection districts, etc.—whose boundaries and functions often overlap. From the point of view of the cost of service rendered to the public, comment on this state of affairs. What other points of view should be considered besides the financial one?

20–4. Is it true that hospital cost analysis is important only for internal hospital management use? Why, or why not?

20–5. Why is departmentalization of personnel and operation essential to useful cost accounting?

20–6. Why are the "costs" found by *any* method of cost analysis subject to challenge?

20–7. In one state, there are numerous laws establishing mandatory minima for many costs of local government. This applies particularly to salaries of public officials and their deputies. What effect do such laws exert upon unit costs?

20–8. Identify each of the following as (1) a cost which is generally allocable to Federal grants and contracts, to the extent it reasonably applies, (2) a cost which is allocable with approval of the grantor agency, or (3) a cost which is *not* an allowable charge to Federal grants or contracts:

a) Advertising
b) Audit service
c) Automatic data processing
d) Bad debts
e) Budgeting
f) Capital expenditures
g) Contributions and donations
h) Depreciation
i) Employee fringe benefits
j) Interest and other financial costs

20–9. Below are listed a number of activities and work units in governmental cost determination. For each one, state one or more variable factors which might arise to cause variances in unit costs.

Street cleaning—linear mile.
Sweeping and collection of leaves—square yard.
Earth excavation—cubic yard.
Snow and ice removal—cubic yard.
Laying of mains—linear foot.
Servicing of parking meters—each.
School bus operation—pupil-day.
Billing of taxes—bill.
Solid waste collection—ton.
Recording documents—document.

20–10. What is the relationship between cost determination, as discussed in Chap. 20, and budget preparation, as discussed in Chap. 2 of this text?

EXERCISES AND PROBLEMS

20–1. The rate of pay of Russell Fowler, an employee of the Public Works Department of Middle City, is $160 for a 40-hour, five-day week. Employees of the municipality are subject to a state retirement plan. For 19x5 the city's contribution was 5 percent on the first $8,000 of the employee's compensation. In 19x5, there were 260 working days. However, employees of the department were allowed six paid holidays. Fowler received a two weeks' vacation, in addition to which he took the maximum amount of 15 days' sick leave allowed to each employee. On the days of the primary and general elections, employees were allowed to quit work two hours early to enable them to vote.

a) Assume that in 19x6 it is desired to charge the cost of Fowler's time on each project at the cost per hour of his service in 19x5. What cost per hour should be charged?

b) By what percentage does this exceed the nominal cost per hour of his service?

20–2. Jacksonburg Public Schools operate the school lunch fund as a special revenue fund, since it is not charged with the cost of building use, the cost of equipment use, or utility bills, but does prepare an operating statement for itemizing revenues and costs and determining the excess of cost over revenue, or the reverse. Trial balances of the fund at December 31, 19x5 and 19x6, were as follows:

Debits	*19x6*	*19x5*
Cash	$ 1,600	$ 1,385
State and federal aid receivable	150	290
Food inventory, beginning of year (cost)	2,000	3,150
Expenditures	206,300	210,910
	$210,050	$215,735
Credits		
Accounts payable	$ 500	$ 625
Fund balance	3,050	3,680
Revenues	206,500	211,430
	$210,050	$215,735

The inventory of food at cost at December 31, 19x6, was $2,570.

Revenues and expenditures for each of the two years were as follows:

Revenues	*19x6*	*19x5*
Sales of food	$151,080	$149,320
Food served to regular and student help	3,140	2,990
Food served to needy pupils	490	410
State and federal assistance	33,020	46,930
Contributions from local sources	18,770	11,780
	$206,500	$211,430
Expenditures		
Salaries of regular help	$120,355	$117,860
Cost of food served to regular and student help	3,115	3,010
Food supplied by federal government	25,660	28,010
Food purchases	48,140	44,350
Miscellaneous expenses	9,030	17,680
	$206,300	$210,910

You are required to prepare the following statement and answer the following questions, carrying percentages to the nearest tenth:

a) A comparative revenue and expense statement with a pair of columns headed "Increase–(Decrease)" with subheadings of "Amount" and "Percent."

b) What was the ratio of food cost to revenues for each of the two years?

c) The ratio of food cost to total revenue of Jacksonburg schools is comparable to the average of such ratio for commercial food service establishments in the geographical region where the schools are located. Do you consider this similarity of ratios commendable or reprehensible for the Jacksonburg school lunch program?

d) At what price or prices should food served without charge to employees and to needy children be recorded and subsequently reported in the statement of revenue and expenses?

e) Is it probable that the items of cost specifically stated to be not included (building use charge, equipment use charge, and utilities) would be material? Assuming that these three items would be material, how would you recommend that they be determined for inclusion in the cost computation? Is it probable that other items of indirect cost exist which might be material? If so, name several.

20–3. The administrator of General Hospital feels that laboratory revenue may be considerably less than total laboratory cost. At the present time, certain increases in rates of the General Hospital are under consideration. Based upon the expenses and statistics furnished, compute for the *laboratory only* the total cost. Use the step-down method.

GENERAL HOSPITAL
Schedule of Direct Expenses
For the Six Months Ended June 30, 19–

"Overhead" departments:		
Administration	$ 81,900	
Dietary	212,940	
Housekeeping	47,320	
Laundry	29,660	
Plant operation and maintenance	112,300	$484,120
"Revenue-producing" departments:		
Inpatient medical and nursing	$272,380	
Operating room	55,000	
X-ray	46,000	
Laboratory	45,000	
Outpatient direct expense	7,500	425,880
Total Expenses		$910,000

A summary of the statistical bases which will be needed in the apportionment of overhead expenses follows (all dietary expense is charged to inpatients):

Department	*No. Employees*	*No. Sq. Ft.*	*No. Lbs. Laundry*
Administration	12	3,000	3,000
Dietary	92	11,000	220,000
Housekeeping	38	500	9,000
Laundry	13	6,000	3,000
Plant operation and maintenance	18	5,000	2,500
Inpatient medical and nursing	103	50,500	1,198,000
Operating room	14	6,000	44,000
X-ray	2	1,500	2,000
Laboratory	12	2,000	2,000
Outpatient	3	1,000	6,000
Total	307	86,500	1,489,500

If revenue from the laboratory for this period was $52,000, what percentage of increase could be made in laboratory charges without charging for the service in excess of cost?

(FHFMA, adapted)

20–4. The Public Works department of the City of Hopewell has an agreement with the municipally owned electric utility whereby street lighting is charged to the department at the cost of generation, transmission, and distribution.

The total cost of generating, transmitting, and distributing electricity, exclusive of charges for the use of equipment, was $317,077 in a certain year. The Public Works department charges the utility for the use of municipal equipment, such charges being based on the actual cost of operation to the department. During the year, equipment units Nos. 3, 11, and 12 worked part of the time for the utility. Data regarding the number of hours operated and costs of operation are as follows:

Equipment Unit No.	*Cost of Operation*	*Total Miles (or Hours*) Operated*	*Miles (or Hours*) Operated for Utility*
3	$1,500	15,000	10,000
11	966	4,500*	3,000*
12	600	3,000*	2,800*

The utility generated a total of 66,382,000 kw.-hrs. (kilowatt hours), which were disposed as follows:

Used by utility itself:	
Station auxiliaries	3,925,000 kw.-hrs.
Other use by utility	565,000
Sales to Public Works department	1,567,000
Sales to other consumers	54,525,000
Lost and unaccounted for	5,800,000
Total	66,382,000 kw.-hrs.

Prepare a statement for the electric utility of the City of Hopewell, showing the cost of electricity furnished to the Public Works department for street lighting during the year ended December 31.

(*Municipal Finance*, adapted)

20–5. On the basis of the following data, prepare a statement for the City of Jonesboro for the year ended June 30, 19__, showing the total cost of refuse collection and the cost per ton or cubic yard, as the case may be (carry unit costs to mills).

Explanation	*Garbage*	*Rubbish*
By city forces:		
Salaries and wages	$384,000	$154,000
Materials and supplies	$ 26,000	$ 24,060
Equipment use	$200,560	$112,620
Tons collected	165,000	–
Cubic yards collected	–	248,000
Labor hours	90,000	61,500
By contract:		
Cost	$ 52,600	$ 16,400
Tons collected	18,000	
Cubic yards collected	–	26,000

Overhead for city force collection of garbage is $0.632 per labor hour; for rubbish, $0.616 per labor hour. Overhead for contract garbage collection, 7.6 percent of total cost (exclusive of overhead); for rubbish collection, 7.22 percent of total cost (exclusive of overhead).

(Indiana State Board of Accounts, adapted)

20–6. Troy Township Consolidated School is considering the purchase of school buses to replace the present system of contracting each year for the service by route and day. The present routing is considered to be best, and it is desirable that there be no increase or decrease in the number of buses. The following information is available regarding the present costs and routes:

Route Number	*Miles per Day*	*Contract Cost per Day*
1	100	$46.00
2	60	31.00
3	80	39.00
4	50	30.00
5	60	27.00

It is also the present practice to hire one of the school buses to transport teams to athletic events away from home and for certain other school purposes. By standing agreement with the bus contractors, they are paid $1 per mile for this service. Over the past three years, the service has cost the township an average of $1,500 per year for an average of 20 trips per year. There are 180 school days in the year.

It is estimated that the township would have the following costs if it owned and operated the school buses:

1. Cost of each school bus body, $12,000; cost of each chassis, $5,000; cost of having body placed on chassis, $200. It is estimated that each body would last 10 years and the chassis 5 years, with an estimated 10 percent of original cost as scrap value on each.
2. Gasoline would cost the township 30¢ per gallon, and it is estimated that the school buses would be able to average 10 miles per gallon of gasoline.
3. Drivers can be obtained on contract for $16 per day and per athletic trip, and they would be expected to take care of the minor servicing necessary on the buses they drive.
4. It is expected that the buses would be greased and the oil changed every 1,000 miles, the materials for which would cost the township $4 per change.
5. It is estimated that a pole-type shed to house and service the school buses would cost $19,000 and would have a life of 20 years.
6. Miscellaneous servicing equipment (small tools), with a 10-year life on the average, would cost $1,500.
7. Repairs, replacement of small parts and tires as necessary, and similar items, are estimated to cost $560 per year per bus.
8. Antifreeze and miscellaneous supplies and expenses are expected to total $650 per year for all buses.
9. Insurance premiums for a fleet-type policy on the buses is expected to cost $2,240 per year.

It will be assumed that the above items cover all the costs the township would incur in owning and operating the buses. You are required to do the following things:

a) Prepare a statement comparing the estimated costs with the present costs (to nearest whole cent) to determine whether or not it would be desirable for the township to own and operate the buses. Show all computations.

b) Assuming that all fixed costs would be reduced in proportion to the number of routes operated, on the basis of the above facts would it be economical for the township to continue the contracts on the present basis for any one or more of the routes?

(Indiana State Board of Accounts, adapted)

20–7. When the county council, county of Monroe, questioned the county treasurer about his requests for additional appropriations, he claimed that the large number of tax bills prepared and collected was responsible for the heavy expenses of his office. Since the duties of the treasurer's office are rather uniform and of limited range, it was decided to attempt a cost study in an effort to determine the veracity of the treasurer's contentions. As tax bills are numbered serially, it is possible to determine accurately the number prepared and collected. It was decided to divide the activities of the office into general administration, billing, and collecting. General administration consists of supervising the office and providing information to taxpayers, attorneys, and others. It would be measured on the basis of thousands of dollars of collections. Preparing bills and collecting would be measured on the basis of numbers of bills prepared and collected, respectively. The following information is available about the costs of the office:

1. The salary of the treasurer is $1,400 per month. His time is devoted to general administration, except that during approximately three months of each year he spends practically all his time on collections.
2. Two regular deputies each receive $900 per month. Their time is divided approximately four months to billing, four months to collections, and the remainder to general administration.
3. During the year the office spent $4,800 for extra help, of which two-thirds was chargeable to billing and one-third to collecting.
4. The office collected $90,000 of delinquent taxes, interest, and penalties during the year, of which the treasurer received 6 percent, to be credited equally to administration and collection.
5. Utility bills, stationery and stamps, repairs to office equipment, and retirement contributions, etc., totaled $13,140 for the year. This was distributed to administration, billing, and collection on the basis of personal services exclusive of fees charged to those operations, except that $4,500 spent for stamped envelopes was chargeable in total to collections.
6. The number of tax bills prepared during the year was 51,280, of which 740 were unpaid at the end of the year. The $90,000 of delinquent taxes collected during the year was on 625 bills.
7. Collection of current taxes during the year amounted to $3,000,000.

You are required to do the following things:

a) Prepare a schedule classifying the treasurer's office costs into the three classes mentioned.

b) Prepare a schedule to show the total cost for each class, number of units of service performed, and cost per unit (carry unit costs to mills).

20–8. The City of Kempton operates a Shop and Maintenance department as a part of the general fund. It is not the practice to make formal appropriations for this department because all of its costs are recovered from other departments. When work orders are issued by the various departments, the estimated cost of the projects is encumbered by the requisitioning department. Departments having work in process at the ends of fiscal periods provide a reservation of fund balance for the amount of the outstanding work orders, and this is covered by a new appropriation in the new period. At the end of the preceding year, outstanding departmental encumbrances for jobs to be done by the Shop and Maintenance department amounted to $7,680 and the following jobs were in process:

Job Order No.	*Cost to Date*	*Labor*	*Materials*	*Utilities*
871	$1,650	$ 860	$ 770	$20
875	790	120	660	10
876	1,220	430	750	40
877	830	190	630	10
Balance of Work in Process	$4,490	$1,600	$2,810	$80

During January of the current year, the following transactions, related to the Shop and Maintenance department, occurred:

1. The city council enacted a special appropriation to cover outstanding encumbrances for work to be done by the Shop and Maintenance department.
2. Work orders were issued against the Shop and Maintenance department for $45,610 of work to be done during the year. For these work orders the Shop and Maintenance department set up job orders numbered 878–883.
3. The Shop and Maintenance department requisitioned and received material from the Stores Inventory department as follows:

Job Order No.	*Amount*
875	$ 260
876	570
877	120
878	440
879	680
880	60
881	1,210
882	80
883	120

4. Departmental payroll for the Shop and Maintenance department for January amounted to $2,210; and, based on labor tickets, the following distribution was made:

Job Order No.	*Amount*
871	$ 60
875	180
876	220
877	350
878	405
879	640
880	85
881	270

Charges should be made directly to Work in Process.

5. Utility bills for the month had not been received at the end of the month, but charges to job orders for estimated utility bills were as follows:

Job Order No.	*Amount*
871	$ 5
875	10
876	10
877	15
878	15
879	30
880	5
881	50
882	5
883	10

6. During the month the following excess materials were returned to stores:

Job Order No.	*Amount*
879	$40
881	60

7. $20 worth of material issued for No. 878 and $10 for No. 876 were transferred to No. 882.
8. The following jobs were completed during January:

Job Order No.	*Estimated Cost*
871	$1,200
875	1,210
876	1,550
878	900

a) Make journal entries for the transactions stated or referred to above. Where charges or credits to jobs are concerned, state in your explanation the amount of charges or credits to each job.

b) For the jobs completed, make a cost summary to show details of cost for each one: total cost, estimated cost, and over- or underestimated cost.

20–9. You have been requested by the Hillcrest Blood Bank, a nonprofit organization, to assist in developing certain information from the bank's operations. You determine the following:

1. Blood is furnished to the blood bank by volunteers and when necessary by professional donors. During the year 2,568 pints of

blood were taken from volunteers and professional blood donors.

2. Volunteer donors who give blood to the bank can draw against their account when needed. An individual who requires a blood transfusion has the option of paying for the blood used at $25 per pint or replacing it at the blood bank. Hospitals purchase blood at $8 per pint.
3. The Hillcrest Blood Bank has a reciprocal arrangement with a number of other banks that permits a member who requires a transfusion in a different locality to draw blood from the local bank against his account in Hillcrest. The issuing blood bank charges a set fee of $14 per pint to the home blood bank.
4. If blood is issued to hospitals but is not used and is returned to the blood bank, there is a handling charge of $1 per pint. Only hospitals are permitted to return blood. During the year 402 pints were returned. The blood being returned must be in usable condition.
5. Blood can be stored for only 21 days and then must be discarded. During the year 343 pints were outdated. This is a normal rate of loss.
6. The blood bank sells serum and supplies at cost to doctors and laboratories. These items are used in processing blood and are sold at the same price that they are billed to the blood bank. No blood bank operating expenses are allocated to the cost of sales of these items.
7. Inventories of blood are valued at the sales price to hospitals. The sales price to hospitals was increased on July 1, 19x3. The inventories are as follows:

	Pints	*Sales Price*	*Total*
June 30, 19x3	80	$6	$480
June 30, 19x4	80	8	640

8. The following financial statements are available:

HILLCREST BLOOD BANK
Balance Sheet

Assets	*June 30, 19x3*	*June 30, 19x4*
Cash	$ 2,712	$ 2,093
U.S. Treasury Bonds	15,000	16,000
Accounts receivable–sales of blood:		
Hospitals.	1,302	1,448
Individuals.	425	550
Inventories:		
Blood.	480	640
Supplies and serum	250	315
Furniture and equipment, less depreciation.	4,400	4,050
Total Assets.	$24,569	$25,096
Liabilities and Fund Balance		
Accounts payable–supplies	$ 325	$ 275
Fund Balance	24,244	24,821
Total Liabilities and Fund Balance. .	$24,569	$25,096

HILLCREST BLOOD BANK
Statement of Cash Receipts and Disbursements
For the Year Ended June 30, 19x4

Balance, July 1, 19x3:			
Cash in bank			$ 2,712
U.S. Treasury Bonds			15,000
Total			$17,712
Receipts:			
From hospitals:			
Hillcrest Hospital	$7,702		
Good Samaritan Hospital	3,818	$11,520	
Individuals		6,675	
From other blood banks		602	
From sales of serum and supplies		2,260	
Interest on bonds		525	
Gifts and bequests		4,928	
Total receipts			26,510
Total to be accounted for			$44,222
Disbursements:			
Laboratory expense:			
Serum	$3,098		
Salaries	3,392		
Supplies	3,533		
Laundry and miscellaneous	277	$10,300	
Other expenses and disbursements:			
Salaries	$5,774		
Dues and subscriptions	204		
Rent and utilities	1,404		
Blood testing	2,378		
Payments to other blood banks for blood given to members away from home	854		
Payments to professional blood donors	2,410		
Other expenses	1,805		
Purchase of U.S. Treasury Bonds	1,000	15,829	
Total disbursements			26,129
Balance, June 30, 19x4			$18,093
Composed of:			
Cash in bank			$ 2,093
U.S. Treasury Bonds			16,000
Total			$18,093

Required:

a) Prepare a statement on the accrual basis of the total expense of taking and processing blood.

b) Prepare a schedule computing (1) the number of pints of blood sold, and (2) the number of pints withdrawn by members.

c) Prepare a schedule computing the expense per pint of taking and processing the blood that was used.

(AICPA, adapted)

20–10. Good Hope Hospital has completed its first year of operation as a qualified institutional provider under the health insurance (HI) program for the aged and wishes to receive maximum reimbursement for its allowable costs from the government. The Hospital has engaged you to assist in determining the amount of reimbursement due and has furnished the following financial, statistical, and other information:

1. The Hospital's charges and allowable costs for departmental inpatient services were:

Departments	*Charges for HI Program Beneficiaries*	*Total Charges*	*Total Allowable Costs*
Inpatient routine services (room, board, nursing)	$425,000	$1,275,000	$1,350,000
Inpatient ancillary service departments:			
X-ray	56,000	200,000	150,000
Operating room	57,000	190,000	220,000
Laboratory	59,000	236,000	96,000
Pharmacy	98,000	294,000	207,000
Other	10,000	80,000	88,000
Total ancillary	280,000	1,000,000	761,000
Totals	$705,000	$2,275,000	$2,111,000

2. For the first year the Reimbursement Settlement for Inpatient Services may be calculated at the option of the provider under either of the following apportionment methods:

   a) *The Departmental RCC* (*ratio of cost centers*) *Method* provides for listing on a departmental basis the ratios of beneficiary inpatient charges to total inpatient charges with each departmental beneficiary inpatient charge ratio applied to the allowable total cost of the respective department.

   b) *The Combination Method* (*with cost finding*) provides that the cost of routine services be apportioned on the basis of the average allowable cost per day for all inpatients applied to total inpatient days of beneficiaries. The residual part of the provider's total allowable cost attributable to ancillary (nonroutine) services is to be apportioned in the ratio of the beneficiaries' share of charges for ancillary services to the total charges for all patients for such services.

3. Statistical and other information:

   a) Total inpatient days for all patients 40,000

   b) Total inpatient days applicable to HI beneficiaries (1,200 aged patients whose average length of stay was 12.5 days) 15,000

   c) A fiscal intermediary acting on behalf of the government's medicare program negotiated a fixed "allowance rate" of $45 per inpatient day subject to retroactive adjustment as a reasonable cost basis for reimbursement of covered services to the hospital under the HI program. Interim payments based on an estimated 1,000 inpatient-days per month were received during the 12-month period subject to an adjustment for the provider's actual cost experience.

Required:

a) Prepare schedules computing the total allowable cost of inpatient services for which the provider should receive payment under the HI program and the remaining balance due for reimbursement under each of the following methods:
1. Departmental RCC method.
2. Combination method (with cost finding).

b) Under which method should Good Hope Hospital elect to be reimbursed for its first year under the HI program assuming the election can be changed for the following year with the approval of the fiscal intermediary? Why?

c) Good Hope Hospital wishes to compare its charges to HI program beneficiaries with published information on national averages for charges for hospital services.
Compute the following (show your computations):
1. The average total hospital charge for a HI inpatient.
2. The average charge per inpatient day for HI inpatients.

(AICPA)

21

Independent Verification of Reports of Financial and Operating Activities of Nonprofit Entities

Accounting and reporting principles developed by authoritative bodies for use by Federal, state and local governmental units, public schools, colleges and universities, and hospitals are presented and discussed in preceding chapters of this text. The relation of accounting and reporting to the operating activities of these entities is also discussed. Interim reports, annual reports, and certain special-purpose reports for each of the entities are illustrated. One of the special-purpose reports illustrated, the Report of Actual Use of Revenue Sharing Payment (Illustration 8–13), is typical of many others in that its purpose is to report to a superior level of government the activities of a subordinate governmental unit (or the activities of an educational institution, hospital, or other not-for-profit institution receiving a governmental grant or contract). The Comptroller General of the United States comments that the elaborate structure of interlocking relationships among all levels of government and between the executive and legislative branches of each has been accompanied by an increased demand for information about government programs:

> Public officials, legislators, and the general public want to know whether governmental funds are handled properly and in compliance with existing laws and whether governmental programs are being conducted efficiently, effectively, and economically. *They also want to have this information provided, or at least concurred in, by someone who is not an advocate of the program but is independent and objective.*[1] Emphasis added.

[1] Comptroller General of the United States. *Standards for Audit of Governmental Organizations, Programs, Activities & Functions.* Washington, D.C.: United States General Accounting Office, 1972. p. i.

Extended Concept of Governmental Auditing—Basic Premises

The Comptroller General expresses the view that the demand for independent verification of information has widened the scope of governmental auditing so that it is no longer a function concerned primarily with financial operations. "Instead, governmental auditing now is also concerned with whether governmental organizations are achieving the purposes for which programs are authorized and funds are made available, are doing so economically and efficiently, and are complying with applicable laws and regulations."[2] Extension of the audit objective beyond fair presentation of financial statements (and beyond compliance with applicable laws and regulations) to include a determination of whether an audited organization is achieving the purposes for which programs are authorized and whether it is doing so efficiently, effectively, and economically is a major step beyond auditing as it is presently viewed by the American Institute of Certified Public Accountants. The extended concept of auditing expressed by the Comptroller General is based on seven premises:

1. The term "audit" may be used to describe not only work done by accountants in examining financial reports but also work done in reviewing (a) compliance with applicable laws and regulations, (b) efficiency and economy of operations, and (c) effectiveness in achieving program results.
2. Public office carries with it the responsibility to apply resources in an efficient, economical, and effective manner to achieve the purposes for which the resources were furnished. This responsibility applies to all resources, whether entrusted to the public officials by their own constituency or by other levels of government.
3. A public official is accountable to those who provide the resources he uses to carry out governmental programs. He is accountable both to other levels of government for the resources such levels have provided and to the electorate, the ultimate source of all governmental funds. Consequently he should be providing appropriate reports to those to whom he is accountable. Unless legal restrictions or other valid reasons prevent him from doing so, the auditor should make the results of audits available to other levels of government that have supplied resources and to the electorate.
4. Auditing is an important part of the accountability process since it provides independent judgments of the credibility of public officials' statements about the manner in which they have carried out their responsibilities. Auditing also can help decisionmakers improve the efficiency, economy, and effectiveness of governmental operations by identifying where improvements are needed.

[2] Ibid., p. 3.

5. The interests of individual governments in many financially assisted programs often cannot be isolated because the resources applied have been commingled. Different levels of government share common interests in many programs. Therefore an audit should be designed to satisfy both the common and discrete accountability interests of each contributing government.
6. Cooperation by Federal, State, and local governments in auditing programs of common interest with a minimum of duplication is of mutual benefit to all concerned and is a practical method of auditing intergovernmental operations.
7. Auditors may rely upon the work of auditors at other levels of government if they satisfy themselves as to the other auditors' capabilities by appropriate tests of their work or by other acceptable methods.[3]

Few people would argue with the thoughts expressed in the premises numbered 2 through 7 above. Many professional accountants engaged in public practice, some internal auditors employed by profit-seeking organizations, and some accountants and auditors employed by governmental units of all levels or by other nonprofit entities are not yet prepared to accept the first premise. (The AICPA reaction to the first premise is discussed in this chapter under the heading *Audits of State and Local Governmental Units.*) The Comptroller General acknowledges that his extended view of the audit function is forward-looking and is not yet embodied in all audits presently being conducted. Further, he suggests that such an extensive scope may not always be desirable. "However, an audit that would include provision for the interests of all potential users of governmental audits would ordinarily include provision for auditing all the above elements of the accountability of the responsible officials."[4] In order to guide development of audits to cover the three elements specified by the Comptroller General (financial and compliance, economy and efficiency, and program results) representatives of the United States General Accounting Office prepared a statement of audit standards. Representatives of Federal executive departments and agencies administering the most important grant programs, audit representatives of state and local governments, and representatives of leading professional organizations were consulted by the GAO in the preparation of the statement. The statement, modeled after the AICPA statement of generally accepted auditing standards, is "intended for application to audits of all government organizations, programs, activities, and functions—whether they are performed by auditors employed by Federal, State, or local Governments; independent public accountants; or others qualified to perform parts of

[3] Ibid., pp. 3–4.

[4] Ibid., p. 2.

the audit work contemplated under these standards."[5] The audit standards are also intended to apply to both internal audits and audits of contractors, grantees, and other external organizations performed by or for a governmental entity. The audit standards relate to the scope and quality of audit effort and to the characteristics of the auditors' report.

The Office of Federal Management Policy of the General Services Administration has incorporated by reference the audit standards set forth in *Standards for Audit of Governmental Organizations, Programs, Activities & Functions* in Federal Management Circular FMC 73–2, "Audit of Federal Operations and Programs by Executive Branch Agencies." The provisions of the circular are applicable to all executive agencies, departments, and establishments whether performed by Federal auditors, auditors employed by other levels of government, or independent public accountants.

Extended Concept of Governmental Auditing—Standards

The *Standards for Audit of Governmental Organizations, Programs, Activities & Functions* presents a summarized statement of the standards. The standards are classified in three groups: General Standards, Examination and Evaluation Standards, and Reporting Standards. The similarity of these three groups, and of the standards within the groups, to the auditing standards considered binding upon certified public accountants will be obvious to many readers.[6]

The Auditing standards published by the Comptroller General are summarized as follows:

General Standards

1. The full scope of an audit of a governmental program, function, activity, or organization should encompass:
   a) An examination of financial transactions, accounts, and reports, including an evaluation of compliance with applicable laws and regulations.
   b) A review of efficiency and economy in the use of resources.
   c) A review to determine whether desired results are effectively achieved.

   In determining the scope for a particular audit, responsible officials should give consideration to the needs of the potential users of the results of that audit.
2. The auditors assigned to perform the audit must collectively possess adequate professional proficiency for the tasks required.

[5] Ibid., p. 1.

[6] Generally accepted auditing standards considered binding upon CPAs by vote of the members of the AICPA are currently published in the AICPA's *Statement on Auditing Standards, No. 1.* New York: American Institute of Certified Public Accountants, 1973.

3. In all matters relating to the audit work, the audit organization and the individual auditors shall maintain an independent attitude.
4. Due professional care is to be used in conducting the audit and in preparing related reports.

Examination and Evalution Standards

1. Work is to be adequately planned.
2. Assistants are to be properly supervised.
3. A review is to be made of compliance with legal and regulatory requirements.
4. An evaluation is to be made of the system of internal control to assess the extent it can be relied upon to ensure accurate information, to ensure compliance with laws and regulations, and to provide for efficient and effective operations.
5. Sufficient, competent, and relevant evidence is to be obtained to afford a reasonable basis for the auditor's opinions, judgments, conclusions, and recommendations.

Reporting Standards

1. Written audit reports are to be submitted to the appropriate officials of the organizations requiring or arranging for the audits. Copies of the reports should be sent to other officials who may be responsible for taking action on audit findings and recommendations and to others responsible or authorized to receive such reports. Copies should also be made available for public inspection.
2. Reports are to be issued on or before the dates specified by law, regulation, or other arrangement and, in any event, as promptly as possible so as to make the information available for timely use by management and by legislative officials.
3. Each report shall:
   a) Be as concise as possible but, at the same time, clear and complete enough to be understood by the users.
   b) Present factual matter accurately, completely, and fairly.
   c) Present findings and conclusions objectively and in language as clear and simple as the subject matter permits.
   d) Include only factual information, findings, and conclusions that are adequately supported by enough evidence in the auditor's working papers to demonstrate or prove, when called upon, the bases for the matters reported and their correctness and reasonableness. Detailed supporting information should be included in the report to the extent necessary to make a convincing presentation.
   e) Include, when possible, the auditor's recommendations for actions to effect improvements in problem areas noted in his audit and to otherwise make improvements in operations. Information on underlying causes of problems reported should be included to assist in implementing or devising corrective actions.

f) Place primary emphasis on improvement rather than on criticism of the past; critical comments should be presented in balanced perspective, recognizing any unusual difficulties or circumstances faced by the operating officials concerned.

g) Identify and explain issues and questions needing further study and consideration by the auditor or others.

h) Include recognition of noteworthy accomplishments, particularly when management improvements in one program or activity may be applicable elsewhere.

i) Include recognition of the views of responsible officials of the organization, program, function, or activity audited on the auditor's findings, conclusions, and recommendations. Except where the possibility of fraud or other compelling reason may require different treatment, the auditor's tentative findings and conclusions should be reviewed with such officials. When possible, without undue delay, their views should be obtained in writing and objectively considered and presented in preparing the final report.

j) Clearly explain the scope and objectives of the audit.

k) State whether any significant pertinent information has been omitted because it is deemed privileged or confidential. The nature of such information should be described, and the law or other basis under which it is withheld should be stated.

4. Each audit report containing financial reports shall:

a) Contain an expression of the auditor's opinion on whether the information contained in the financial reports is presented fairly. If the auditor cannot express an opinion, the reasons therefor should be stated in the audit report.

b) State whether the financial reports have been prepared in accordance with generally accepted or prescribed accounting principles applicable to the organization, program, function, or activity audited and on a consistent basis from one period to the next. Material changes in accounting policies and procedures and their effect on the financial reports are to be explained in the audit report.

c) Contain appropriate supplementary explanatory information about the contents of the financial reports as may be necessary for full and informative disclosure about the financial operations of the organization, program, function, or activity audited. Violations of legal or other regulatory requirements, including instances of noncompliance, shall be explained in the audit report.[7]

[7] Comptroller General of the United States, *op. cit.*, pp. 6–9. Correspondence between the GAO and the AICPA states that no significance is to be attached to the division in item 4 between "presened fairly" in 4*a* and "in accordance with" GAAP in 4*b*. The next revision of *Standards for Audit of Governmental Organization . . .* is to contain slightly revised wording (see *Journal of Accountancy*, January 1974, p. 39) to make this clear.

The statement of governmental auditing standards presented above is intentionally structured to permit separate performance of the financial and compliance, economy and efficiency, and program results audit objectives in the event concurrent audit of all three is not undertaken. The Comptroller General cautions that, "In memorandums of engagements between governments and independent public accountants or other audit organizations, the arrangements should specifically identify whether all, or specifically which, of the three elements of the audit are to be conducted."[8] Independent public accountants have had the need for specific, written memorandums of the scope of engagements forcefully pointed out to them by several recent well-known liability cases.

It is not appropriate in this text to give a full explanation of the implications of either the governmental auditing standards summarized above, or the AICPA's statement of auditing standards. It is appropriate, however, to point out that the AICPA reporting standards relate to the expression of an opinion by the independent auditor regarding the financial statements. The short-form report of the auditor customarily used contains the following "opinion" paragraph:

> In our opinion the aforementioned financial statements present fairly the financial position of X Company at December 31, 19_____, and the results of its operations and the changes in its financial position for the year then ended, in conformity with generally accepted accounting principles applied on a basis consistent with that of the preceding year.[9]

The governmental audit reporting standards summarized above, however, relate to what CPAs call long-form reports, or management letters. Note particularly Reporting Standard No. 3 which contains the prescriptions that the audit report should include, "when possible, the auditor's recommendations for actions to effect improvements in problem areas noted in his audit and to otherwise make improvements in operations." (paragraph *e*), and "place primary emphasis on improvement" (paragraph *f*), and "include recognition of the views of responsible officials of the organization, program, function, or activitiy audited on the auditor's findings" (paragraph *i*). A further marked difference between the nature of a CPA's short-form report and the nature of a governmental auditor's report is emphasized by paragraph *k* of Reporting Standard No. 3 which provides that the governmental auditor's report should "state whether any significant pertinent information has been omitted because it is deemed privileged or confidential."

Audits by Independent CPAs

Through the years the fact that the phrase "generally accepted accounting principles" did not appear to mean the same in the case of governmental entities and nonprofit entities as it did in the case of profit-

[8] Ibid., p. 3.

[9] *Statement on Auditing Standards, No. 1,* Par. 511.04.

seeking entities led to some disagreement within the accounting profession as to the propriety of CPAs using the standard short-form opinion with regard to the statements of governmental and nonprofit entities. The Auditing Standards Executive Committee of the American Institute of Certified Public Accountants has stated:

> If the statements are those of a not-for-profit organization, they may reflect accounting practices differing in some respects from those followed by enterprises organized for profit. In some cases generally accepted accounting principles applicable to not-for-profit organizations have not been clearly defined. In those areas where the independent auditor believes generally accepted accounting principles have been clearly defined, he may state his opinion as to the conformity of the financial statements either with *generally accepted accounting principles* or (less desirably) with *accounting practices* for not-for-profit organizations in the particular field, and in such circumstances he may refer to financial position and results of operations. In those areas where he believes generally accepted accounting principles have not been clearly defined, the provisions covering special reports as discussed under cash basis and modified accrual basis statements are applicable.[10]

In order to clarify the definition of "generally accepted accounting principles" in the cases of major categories of not-for-profit organizations the AICPA has issued four audit guides: *Audits of State and Local Governmental Units*, *Audits of Colleges and Universities*, *Hospital Audit Guide*, and *Audits of Voluntary Health and Welfare Organizations*. The modifications each of these guides makes in the pronouncements of other authoritative organizations with regard to financial reporting or accounting are cited at appropriate points in preceding chapters; the positions each takes on auditing are of interest here.

Audits of State and Local Governmental Units

The AICPA audit guide concerned with audits of state and local governmental units observes: "There is a similar objective in the audit of financial statements of a governmental unit or a commercial enterprise, namely, the expression of an opinion that the financial statements fairly present financial position and results of operations in conformity with generally accepted accounting principles."[11] The audit guide stresses, however, that a significant aspect of a governmental audit "is to ascertain whether, in obtaining and expending public funds, the unit has complied with the applicable statutes."[12] Budgetary accounting, the audit guide states, is one important area requiring accountability for financial compliance—auditors must be alert for unauthorized overexpenditures

[10] Ibid., ¶620.08.

[11] *Audits of State and Local Governmental Units*, p. 35.

[12] Ibid.

of appropriations. Other examples of financial compliance auditing given in the audit guide relate to a determination that the proceeds of special taxes are properly accounted for in special revenue funds, and a determination that the provisions of revenue bond indentures were followed by enterprise funds.

Audits of State and Local Governmental Units indicates that the AICPA does not accept the extended view of the scope of auditing presented in *Standards for Audit of Governmental Organizations, Programs, Activities & Functions* discussed in the preceding section of this chapter headed *Extended Concept of Governmental Auditing—Basic Premises.* The AICPA publication presents the following interpretations of what it terms "key provisions" of the standards issued by the Comptroller General (note that the first interpretation definitely rejects the first premise on which the extended view of the Comptroller General rests):

1. No auditor is expected to give an opinion on how efficient or economical an organization is or whether program results have been effectively achieved. In such cases, the auditor reports what he finds factually and makes a recommendation for improvements he deems appropriate.
2. Where a determination of compliance with federal or state laws or regulations is a part of the audit scope, the appropriate federal or state agency is responsible for providing a guide setting forth those laws or regulations with which compliance is to be determined.
3. Where technical determinations (engineering, actuarial, etc.) are to be made, the auditor should engage competent technical help either by direct employment or on a consulting basis.[13]

In amplification of item 2 above, the audit guide cautions that the independent auditor must be familiar with the general laws and local ordinances applicable to the governmental unit being examined. The guide emphasizes that work beyond that required for financial auditing should not be undertaken by an independent auditor unless it is provided for in the engagement memorandum.

Other items to be covered in the engagement memorandum, or agreement letter as it is sometimes called, include, besides the normal items to be covered in agreements with profit-seeking clients, specification of the funds, agencies, and operations to be examined, and specification of the supplemental schedules and statistical data, if any, to be covered by the opinion. The audit guide notes that in the audit of profit-seeking clients generally only one entity is under examination, whereas each separate fund of a governmental unit is, as discussed in detail in earlier chapters of this text, a separate fiscal and accounting entity. The necessity of covering in one examination and report a number of separate entities

[13] Ibid., p. 39.

poses problems in the design of an audit program. Factors to be considered by auditors in the preparation of programs are the subject of Chapter 5 of *Audits of State and Local Governmental Units.*

The relationship of the independent auditor's report to the annual published report of the governmental unit is the subject of Chapter 7 of *Audits of State and Local Governmental Units.* Chapter 14 of this text presents the NCGA recommendations concerning the content and presentation of published reports of governmental units. In brief, it is recommended that published reports consist of three sections: Introductory Section, including title page, contents, and letter of transmittal; Financial Section, including the independent auditor's opinion, combined financial statements and schedules, and financial statements and schedules of individual funds and account groups; and Statistical Section, including comparative financial data, schedules of legal debt margin, debt service requirements, etc. The audit guide emphasizes that the auditor's report should state explicitly what material included in the report he has examined, and his opinion, if any, on it.

In the opinion of the AICPA Committee which prepared the audit guide, the combined statements and schedules prescribed by the NCGA will not fairly present financial position and results of operations in conformity with generally accepted accounting principles. Therefore, separate financial statements of individual funds and account groups are needed.[14] The AICPA Committee also expressed the opinion that in the event that combined fund balance sheets were presented, use of a total column (prohibited under NCGA recommendations) should be optional as long as, if used, it is labeled "Memorandum Only." In regard to the auditor's short-form report, the AICPA audit guide specifies that the standard opinion language, "generally accepted accounting principles," is preferable to that specified by the NCGA, "generally accepted accounting principles applicable to governmental entities."

Audits of State and Local Governmental Units presents illustrations of ten possible forms of opinions. If the supplemental schedules are covered by the opinion, a three-paragraph short-form opinion, shown as Illustration 21–1, would be appropriate. Illustration 21–2 presents an appropriate report in the event that budgetary information is not reported.

Audits of Colleges and Universities

The principal point made in the audit guide relating to audits of Colleges and Universities and not discussed in Chapter 18 of this text is that the Statement of Current Funds Expenditures and Resources Utilized (sometimes used in place of a Statement of Current Funds Revenues, Expenditures, and Transfers) does not purport to present the results of operations or the net income for the period of the institution as a

[14] Ibid., p. 20.

Illustration 21–1

ALL FUNDS EXAMINED, UNQUALIFIED OPINION ON FINANCIAL STATEMENTS AND ON SUPPLEMENTAL SCHEDULES AND RELATED INFORMATION

Independent Auditors' Report

Honorable City Council,
City of X:

We have examined the financial statements of the various funds and account groups of the City of X for the year ended December 31, 19x2, listed in the foregoing table of contents. Our examination was made in accordance with generally accepted auditing standards, and accordingly included such tests of the accounting records and such other auditing procedures as we considered necessary in the circumstances.

In our opinion, the aforementioned financial statements present fairly the financial position of the various funds and account groups of the City of X at December 31, 19x2, and the results of operations of such funds and the changes in financial position of the Water Utility Fund for the year then ended, in conformity with generally accepted accounting principles applied on a basis consistent with that of the preceding year.

The accompanying supplemental schedules and related information presented on pages X to XX are not necessary for a fair presentation of the financial statements, but are presented as additional analytical data. This information has been subjected to the tests and other auditing procedures applied in the examination of the financial statements mentioned above and, in our opinion, is fairly stated in all material respects in relation to the financial statements taken as a whole.

(*s*) *Firm Name*

February 12, 19x3

Source: American Institute of Certified Public Accountants. *Audits of State and Local Governmental Units*, New York: AICPA, 1974, p. 12

whole, as would an income statement or a statement of revenues and expenses. Specifically, the statement of current funds expenses and resources utilized does not include a provision for depreciation, but does include charges for capital outlay, such as mandatory provisions for payment of principal of indebtedness, mandatory provisions for renewals and replacements of equipment, and expenditures from current funds for renewals and replacements of equipment. For these reasons the audit guide recommends the wording "results of operations" in the standard short-form opinion be replaced by "changes in fund balances and current funds expenditures and resources utilized."[15] Illustration 21–3 shows the resulting recommended short-form report on the audit of an educational institution in which no exceptions are expressed.

Hospital Audit Guide

In Chapter 19 of this text the principal differences between the recommendations of the American Hospital Association and the views of the

[15] *Audits of Colleges and Universities*, pp. 89–90.

Illustration 21–2

QUALIFICATION FOR FAILURE TO DISCLOSE INFORMATION REGARDING A BUDGET

Independent Auditors' Report

Honorable City Council,
City of X:

We have examined the balance sheet of the General Fund of the City of X as of December 31, 19x2, and the related statements of revenues and expenditures and changes in fund balance for the year then ended. Our examination was made in accordance with generally accepted auditing standards, and accordingly included such tests of the accounting records and such other auditing procedures as we considered necessary in the circumstances.

The accompanying statement of revenues and expenditures of the General Fund for the year 19x2 does not include a comparison with a formal budget, as required by generally accepted accounting principles, nor does the statement disclose, also as required by generally accepted accounting principles, that the City Council has failed to adopt a budget for such Fund, as required by law.

In our opinion, except for the omission of the information mentioned in the preceding paragraph, the aforementioned financial statements present fairly the financial position of the General Fund of the City of X at December 31, 19x2, and the results of its operations for the year then ended, in conformity with generally accepted accounting principles applied on a basis consistent with that of the preceding year.

(s) *Firm Name*

February 12, 19x3

Source: American Institute of Certified Public Accountants, *Audits of State and Local Governmental Units*, New York: AICPA, 1974, p. 123.

AICPA as to generally accepted accounting principles are discussed. The chapter in the AICPA *Hospital Audit Guide* which deals with independent auditors' reports relates to the necessity for qualification of the opinion in the event that investments are valued at market, or, presumably, fixed assets are shown at appraisal value and depreciation is based thereon.

Since it is customary for hospital annual reports to contain supplemental schedules, the auditor must either indicate in the opinion paragraph the responsibility he is taking for the schedules, or include a separate opinion on the schedules. In this respect independent auditors' opinions on hospital clients may require wording similar to that shown in Illustrations 21–1.

A further problem, peculiar to hospital audits, is the likelihood that under Medicare and other third-party payor programs the hospital and the third party may agree to a rate schedule for interim charges with the understanding that a retroactive adjustment may be made based upon allowable costs as contractually defined. The cost reports upon which the retroactive adjustments are based may not have been filed, or may

Illustration 21–3

RECOMMENDED FORM OF INDEPENDENT AUDITOR'S OPINION ON STATEMENTS OF AN EDUCATIONAL INSTITUTION

The Board of Trustees
Sample Educational Institution:

We have examined the balance sheet of Sample Educational Institution as of June 30, 19___, and the related statements of changes in fund balances and current funds revenues, expenditures, and other changes for the year then ended. Our examination was made in accordance with generally accepted auditing standards, and accordingly included such tests of the accounting records and such other auditing procedures as we considered necessary in the circumstances.

In our opinion, the aforementioned financial statements present fairly the financial position of Sample Educational Institution at June 30, 19___, and the changes in fund balances and the current funds revenues, expenditures and other changes for the year then ended, in conformity with generally accepted accounting principles applied on a basis consistent with that of the preceding year.

Source: American Institute of Certified Public Accountants. *Audits of Colleges and Universities.* New York: AICPA, 1973, p. 90.

not have been audited, as of the time the independent auditor is to express his opinion on the hospital financial statements, so that the amount of final settlement is uncertain and related receivables, or payables, shown in the statement are not properly determined. As explained in the *Hospital Audit Guide*, depending upon the circumstances and the auditor's judgment, it may be proper for the auditor to issue an "except for" opinion, a "subject to" opinion, an adverse opinion, or a disclaimer of opinion.

Audits of Voluntary Health and Welfare Organizations

Voluntary health and welfare organizations are those non-profit organizations which derive their revenue primarily from voluntary contributions, to be used either for general or specified purposes connected with health, welfare and the common good. It is recommended by authoritative groups such as the National Health Council and National Social Welfare Assembly that voluntary health and welfare organizations use fund accounting. Funds similar to those suggested for colleges and universities and for hospitals are considered appropriate for use by voluntary health and welfare organizations; therefore no separate chapter in this text is devoted to them. Auditing voluntary organizations tends to differ from auditing educational institutions and hospitals, however, because (1) the voluntary nature of contributions (and, often, the cash collection of contributions by large numbers of volunteer workers) creates internal control problems, (2) use of volunteer or semi-volunteer accounting and clerical personnel who are selected on the basis of availability rather than accounting competence or understanding of the fundamentals of internal control, and (3) the use of affiliates often without effective managerial control.

If the independent auditor, on the basis of his examination, may express an unqualified opinion the standard short-form report should be used. If the findings are such that a qualified opinion or an adverse opinion should be expressed, *Audits of Voluntary Health and Welfare Organizations* presents examples of appropriate wording.

SELECTED REFERENCES

AMERICAN INSTITUTE OF CERTIFIED PUBLIC ACCOUNTANTS. *Audits of Colleges and Universities.* New York, 1973.

———. *Audits of State and Local Governmental Units.* New York, 1974.

———. *Audits of Voluntary Health and Welfare Organizations.* New York, 1974.

———. *Hospital Audit Guide.* New York, 1972.

———. *Special Reports: Application of Statement on Auditing Procedure, No. 28.* New York, 1960.

———. *Statement on Auditing Standards, No. 1.* New York, 1973.

BARON, C. DAVID. "Obtaining Information for Government Program Evaluation," *The Federal Accountant.* Vol. 22, no. 2 (June 1973), pp. 33–39.

COMPTROLLER GENERAL OF THE UNITED STATES. *Standards for Audit of Governmental Organizations, Programs, Activities & Functions.* Washington, DC: General Accounting Office, 1972.

DITTENHOFER, M. A. "Audit Standards Applied to the Public Sector," *The Federal Accountant.* Vol. 20, no. 1 (March 1971), pp. 35–59.

KNIGHTON, LENNIS M. "Accounting for the Benefit of Public Programs," *The Federal Accountant.* Vol. 21, no. 1 (March 1972), pp. 4–19.

MORSE, ELLSWORTH H., JR. "The Auditor Takes On Program Evaluation," *The Federal Accountant.* Vol. 22, no. 2 (June 1973), pp. 4–13.

QUESTIONS

21–1. In the view of the Comptroller General of the United States, is governmental auditing primarily concerned with financial operations? Why or why not?

21–2. In what ways may the term "audit" be used, in the extended view, besides examination of financial operations?

21–3. What is the relationship of auditing to the accountability process?

21–4. Does *Standards for Audit of Governmental Organizations, Programs, Activities & Functions* apply to any audits except those made by General Accounting Office auditors? If so, to what others is it applicable?

21–5. Is it considered mandatory that governmental audits have all three objectives stated in General Standard No. 1 quoted in Chapter 21?

21–6. The standard short-form opinion used by certified public accountants sets forth that the financial statements are presented in conformity with "generally accepted accounting principles." How may an auditor determine if this phrase is applicable in the case of a given not-for-profit entity?

21–7. If you are a private accountant engaged to audit governmental accounts, what special interest should you have in the appropriation ordinance for the year in which your work is done?

21–8. If a large municipality regularly issues comprehensive reports of a popular nature, prepared by its own accounting and auditing staff, should this supplant audits and technical reports by independent auditors? Why?

21–9. Suppose that in auditing the accounts and transactions of a trust fund, you are confronted with a lack of conclusive evidence as to what the fund is supposed to do and can legally do. How would this affect the nature of your report, and what recommendation would you make?

21–10. Do the recommendations of the NCGA for financial reporting cause any difficulty in the wording of an independent auditor's short-form report? Explain.

12–11. What items particularly relevant to the audit of state and local governmental units should be covered explicitly in the written agreement between the independent auditor and the client unit?

21–12. What is the principal point made in *Audits of Colleges and Universities* with respect to the wording of the auditor's short-form report?

21–13. In what respect do Medicare and other third-party payor reimbursement agreements present a problem to the independent auditor?

21–14. What conditions sometimes encountered in the audit of voluntary health and welfare organizations may require an independent auditor to express a qualified opinion or an adverse opinion?

EXERCISES AND PROBLEMS

21–1. *a*) Outline an audit program to be followed in the audit of a large endowment fund held by a charitable institution. The assets consist principally of securities. This is your first audit of the fund.

b) Prepare an illustration of the principal working paper or papers you would use in the verification of the securities and the income from securities of the endowment fund. You need not use figures, provided the heading of each column is specific or provided you indicate what would be entered in each column.

(AICPA)

21–2. The short-form report of the independent auditor which appeared in the St. Petersburg, Florida, *Annual Financial Report* for the fiscal year ended September 30, 1971, is reproduced below. The report was issued before the publication of the AICPA's *Audits of State and Local Governmental Units.* If the report were to be issued now, should it be reworded in any respect or is it satisfactorily worded? Explain.

City Council
City of St. Petersburg

We have examined the balance sheets of the various funds of the CITY OF ST. PETERSBURG, FLORIDA as of September 30, 1971, and the related statements of financial operations for the year then ended. Our examination was made in accordance with generally accepted auditing standards and accordingly included such tests of the accounting records and such other auditing procedures as we considered necessary in the circumstances.

In our opinion, the above mentioned statements present fairly the financial position of the various funds and balanced account groups for the CITY OF ST. PETERSBURG, FLORIDA, at September 30, 1971, and the results of their operations for the year then ended, in conformity with generally accepted accounting principles applicable to governmental entities, applied on a basis consistent with that of the preceding year.

Certified Public Accountants

St. Petersburg, Florida
December 10, 1971

21–3. The "Report of Auditors" which appeared in the 1972–73 *Annual Report* of the City of Easton, Pa., is reproduced below in its entirety with the exception of a listing of "Revenue Receipts." No other information concerning the audit is presented in the *Annual Report.*

a) Comment on the "Report of Auditors" from the standpoint of the auditors' apparent adherence to AICPA standards.
b) Comment on the "Report of Auditors" from the standpoint of the auditors' apparent adherence to *Standards for Audit of Governmental Organizations, Programs, Activities & Functions.*
c) Comment on the "Report of Auditors" from the standpoint of an interested resident of Easton, Pa.

REPORT OF AUDITORS

Honorable Mayor and Members of Council
City of Easton
Pennsylvania

In accordance with your authorization, we have made an examination of the records of the City of Easton, County of Northampton, for the year ended December 31, 1972. The City budget for 1972 anticipated the revenues and expenditures of the Bureau of Water. We have included the Water Bureau's transactions in the Statements of

Budget Operations and Receipts and Disbursements for the year ended December 31, 1972, however, the Balance Sheet does not reflect the financial condition of the Bureau of Water as of December 31, 1972. The Balance Sheet, Operating Statement, and related supporting schedules of the Bureau of Water will be submitted in a separate report. The results of the audit of the City of Easton, County of Northampton, are herewith set forth.

SCOPE OF AUDIT

The cash was verified by count and reconciled.

All recorded receipts were traced to the depositories for the entire year.

Cancelled City vouchers were examined on a test basis for signature and endorsement and were checked for proper entry on the disbursement records of the Treasurer.

The balances on deposit were confirmed directly with the depositories.

A test of revenues and receipts was established and verified as to source and amount only insofar as the City Records permitted.

A test proof of the additions of the books of original entry was included as part of this examination.

Supplemental budget appropriations for the General Fund were checked for proper authorization.

Property tax records for the years 1956 through 1972 as maintained on the data processing tabulating equipment were reviewed, cash collections were reconciled with the cash receipts records of the City Treasurer's office and the general ledger records of the City. Uncollected Property Taxes for these years were established by tabulating the card records and reconciling the balances.

Cash collections for Per Capita taxes and Residence taxes for years 1964 and prior were verified with the cash receipts of the Treasurer's office.

The balances of all uncollected Residence Taxes and Per Capita Taxes for 1970, 1971 and 1972 were proved by tabulating tests and reconciled with the cash receipts records maintained in the Treasurer's office. During years 1965 through 1968 the City did not levy Residence or Per Capita Taxes.

Delinquent taxes and assessments are reported as reflected on the records and were not verified by communication with the taxpayers.

Our audit did not include an examination of the records of the Easton Area Earned Income Tax Office. A separate audit will be made of this office and a copy of the report will be furnished to the City.

The balances on the Assessment Receivable Ledger for both principal and interest were proved and reconciled with the various controlling accounts.

The audit did not and could not determine the character of services rendered for which payment had been made nor could it determine the quality, proper price or quantity of materials supplied for which claims had been passed.

Our examination of Payroll records included a check for approval by council, a test check for the accuracy of computations and a verification of payments made to hourly employees.

Confirmation of collateral pledged to secure deposits of the City of Easton.

Verification by correspondence of the investments held by the Easton National Bank and Trust Company for the City of Easton Employees Retirement Fund.

Our audit included an examination of employee surety bonds.

The Sinking Fund records were examined and the balances on deposit confirmed directly with the depositories.

GENERAL FUND COMMENTS

In our examination of vouchers and supporting documents, we found a number of vouchers without invoices and/or purchase orders. These invoices and purchase orders are filed in the Bureau of Water Department. We recommend that all the invoices and purchase orders be attached to the vouchers and maintained in one department.

During the course of our audit, we found that the Debit and Credit Memos supplied by the banks were not on file. These Debit and Credit Memos should be attached to the bank statements in order to support these transactions on the bank statements.

In order to properly control issuing licenses and permits, all licenses and permits issued should be consecutively numbered, and, a record maintained in the department issuing the license or permit, indicating the number, amount, and recipient of the license.

In examination of Payroll, we found various forms of time cards submitted to data processing for hourly employees. We recommend that a standard form made in duplicate, be used by all departments for hourly and overtime employees. As for any change in rates during the pay period covered, this should be signed by the department heads or by authorized personnel in the department. One copy should be filed in the department, and one copy forwarded to the data processing department and kept on file.

Section 51.40 of the State and Local Fiscal Assistance Act of 1972 provides that federal revenue sharing monies plus interest earned on such monies be appropriated or expended within 24 months of the date of the check. Although all entitlement checks are deposited in the same account, we recommend that a separate ledger be maintained on each entitlement check and disbursement of such money be applied to a designated entitlement period.

In our reconciliation of per capita and residence taxes, we noticed that 571 residents of the City of Easton, were exonerated of paying taxes. We were unable to locate such exonerations as being approved by council. We recommend in the future, that a detailed list of individuals be presented by the Treasurer's office to City Council for approval and such a list be made permanent part of the minutes of the City of Easton.

Information relative to the preparation of Assessment Liens Receivable was provided by the engineering department. Such assessments were for curbing and side walk improvements of Lafayette and Wood Streets. We recommend that an assessment receivable ledger be established for the recording of these assessments and that liens be properly filed to secure their collection.

For the years 1971, and 1972, we noticed that there was no activity in the Hacketts Park Improvement Fund. As of December 31, 1972, there was a cash balance of $8,951.61 uninvested. We recommend in the future that this balance be either invested or the account be closed out, and the balance thereof be transferred to the General Fund as Miscellaneous Revenue.

CASH ON DEPOSIT $117,596.07; ON HAND $1,575.00

This amount represents the cash on hand and on deposit as of December 31, 1972, in the General Fund. In addition, $56,362.19 is the balance of the first entitlement period of Federal Revenue Sharing Monies, and $18,862.37 is on deposit which was specifically reserved for resurfacing.

During 1971, the General Fund incurred the liability of a note in the amount of $100,000.00. In the year 1972, City Council authorized the transfer of this indebtedness to the five year Capital Improvement Fund. Our report reflects this transfer of the indebtedness.

PROPERTY AND RESIDENCE TAXES

During the course of this examination, it was noted that the total levy of property taxes increased from $1,034,959.12 in 1971 to $1,186,551.60 in 1972. This change was due mainly to an increase in the millage from 20.2 mills to 23.0 mills. The collection of current property taxes during the year increased from $966,217.57 in 1971, to $1,117,328.17 in 1972. The percentage of collection increased from 93.36% in 1971 to 94.17% in 1972.

The 1972 Budget anticipated current property taxes to be collected of $1,090,000.00. The actual cash collected from current property taxes against this anticipated figure amounted to $1,100,166.91. Residence and per capita taxes were enacted during 1969 in the amount of $10.00 in accordance with the third class city code. The 1972 Budget anticipated current residence and per capita taxes to be collected of $116,000.00. The actual cash collected from current residence and per capita taxes against this anticipated figure amounted to $108,900.03. Delinquent property, residence, and per capita taxes were anticipated at $66,000.00, whereas the amount collected was $67,770.51.

STATE AND LOCAL FISCAL ASSISTANCE ACT OF 1972

The first Federal Revenue Sharing check, covering the Entitlement period of January 1, 1972, to June 30, 1972, was received and deposited December 11, 1972.

On December 21, 1972, a check was drawn against the account made payable to the Estate of Anna McInerney in the amount of $178,899.81. This payment represents a purchase of land in Williams Township for the purpose of disposing solid waste. We have confirmed by correspondence with the City Solicitor that the aforementioned expenditure does indeed constitute a "Priority Expenditure" in accordance with Paragraph 51.31 of the Act.

PARKING METERS

The 1972 budget anticipated revenue from parking meters in the amount of $110,000.00. The amount realized amounted to $115,034.65, which is $5,034.65 more than anticipated.

The following is a comparison of parking meter revenues for the years 1966 through 1972.

Year	*Revenues*
1972	$115,034.65
1971	109,836.95
1970	63,282.05
1969	59,036.50
1968	66,441.60
1967	60,685.00
1966	70,580.75

SEWER REVENUE FUND COMMENTS

A statement of receipts and disbursements for the year ended December 31, 1972, is submitted in the report of the Department of Public Services. A more detailed report in accordance with the Lease agreement between the City and the City of Easton Authority will be presented in a separate audit report.

It has been determined by audit, that the General Fund has a liability to the Sewer Revenue Fund as of December 31, 1972, in the amount of $6,222.60, which is reflected on the General Fund Balance Sheet.

CAPITAL FUND COMMENTS

The capital fund is comprised of the following accounts:

Open Space Account
Hackett Park Improvement Fund
Sanitary Sewer Construction Fund
Five Year Capital Improvement Fund
Police Facilities Account

Details of these accounts are covered in the Financial Reports section.

HIGHWAY AID FUND

The details of this fund as shown on Exhibit D and Schedule D-1.

SINKING FUND COMMENTS

The cash balance as of December 31, 1972 is $442.74, of which $192.50 is reserved for the payment of matured interest coupons.

During the course of our audit, we found uncancelled coupons of the 1959 and 1962 bond issues which were redeemed by the bank and returned to the City of Easton. We recommend that at anytime a bank returns coupons uncancelled the City immediately cancel the coupons and notify the bank.

CITY DEBT

The funded debt of the City on December 31, 1972, was represented by $210,000.00 of general obligation bonds, $565,000.00 of water bonds and $410,000.00 improvement and equipment notes and $110,000.00 revenue and anticipation notes for a total of $1,295,000.00. During the year, $200,000.00 in Capital Improvement Notes, pledging the credit and taxing power of the City of Easton, was incurred.

21–4. The "Digest" appearing in the Comptroller General's Report to the Congress, "For Safer Motor Vehicles . . . ," appears on following pages. Comment on this report on the basis of its apparent adherence to governmental audit reporting standards published by the Comptroller General and summarized in Chapter 21.

DIGEST

WHY THE REVIEW WAS MADE

GAO reviewed enforcement activities of the National Highway Traffic Safety Administration to determine the extent to which the agency provided assurance to the public that motor vehicle and equipment manufacturers were meeting safety standards established pursuant to the National Traffic and Motor Vehicle Safety Act of 1966 (15 U.S.C. 1381).

In 1971 about 55,000 people died and 3.8 million people were injured as a result of about 16.4 million motor vehicle accidents in the United States. Property damage alone cost about $7.4 *billion.*

The goal of the Department of Transportation, of which the Safety Administration is an agency, is to reduce the highway fatality rate by one-third by 1980.

About 44 million new cars—38 million domestic and 6 million foreign—have been manufactured and marketed subject to Federal motor vehicle safety standards and regulations.

FINDINGS AND CONCLUSIONS

The Safety Administration's testing program—its major activity for determining compliance with Federal motor vehicle safety standards—has been funded at an average of $1.8 million a year over the past 3 years.

The testing program has provided little assurance to the American public that motor vehicles comply with the standards and thereby provide the safety benefits intended—protection against unreasonable risk of accidents, injury, or death.

The motor vehicle industry annually produces about 9 million vehicles, comprising 500 different makes and models. The Safety Administration has been testing about 55 vehicles each year for compliance with some of the safety standards. (See p. 8.)

Since the Safety Administration began testing, U.S. manufacturers have recalled millions of vehicles for various safety reasons. The Safety Administration's testing program has resulted in (1) four domestic vehicle recalls involving about 105,000 vehicles and (2) four recalls of vehicles produced by foreign manufacturers, involving 140,000 vehicles. Most of the domestic vehicles were recalled as a result of a single test. (See pp. 7 and 8.)

The Safety Administration can make a number of improvements to increase the testing program's effectiveness within the limits of available resources.

The Safety Administration selected vehicles and equipment for 1972 testing primarily on the basis of a sampling of manufacturers and equipment lines and consideration of prior test results or the lack of prior tests. The Safety Administration selected standard areas in which to test vehicles and equipment on the basis of its assessment of the "safety criticality" of the standards; this assessment included consideration of prior test experience and information from outside sources. (See pp. 10 and 11.)

Although the primary purpose in enforcing motor vehicle standards is to reduce injuries and deaths from traffic accidents, the Safety Administration has not systematically used traffic accident data and studies in selecting what to test for compliance.

The performance of vehicles and items of equipment in traffic accidents should be a major factor in selecting vehicle makes and models and equipment items for testing and in assigning testing priorities. (See pp. 12 to 14.) This would improve safety standards enforcement by focusing attention on indications of safety problems and on priority standard areas having a high potential for reducing traffic accidents, injuries, and deaths.

A total of 34 safety standards were effective on or before September 1, 1972. However, more than half of the funds obligated for compliance testing in the past 3 years was used for testing manufacturers' compliance with two tire safety standards. Less than a third was used for testing performance of a total vehicle to determine manufacturers' compliance with other safety standards, including those affecting the integrity of vehicles in crash situations. (See p. 18.)

GAO's review of accident data, information from tire studies, and the Safety Administration's test failure rates has indicated that the Safety Administration is emphasizing tire testing considerably more than is warranted. (See pp. 18 to 20.)

The Safety Administration's 1972 testing priorities were not fully in line with its prior test results and its classification of some standards as critical. Some realignment of testing priorities is indicated. (See pp. 21 to 23.)

Vehicle manufacturers are required to certify that their vehicles comply with the safety standards. More effective use of manufacturers' certification data to supplement and refine the Safety Administration's limited testing program could help the agency achieve its enforcement goals.

The Safety Administration should place major emphasis on systematically reviewing manufacturers' certification data for indications of (1) misinterpretation of the safety standards, (2) faulty test procedures or techniques, (3) inadequate testing, (4) failure to follow up on test failures, and (5) failure to assure continuing compliance with a standard.

The Safety Administration could then follow up on these indications. (See pp. 24 and 25.)

The agency needs to take more timely action to resolve test failure cases and particularly to have unsafe vehicle and equipment conditions corrected. Delays in resolving such cases could expose the public to unnecessary risks of accidents, injuries, and deaths. (See pp. 27 and 28.)

RECOMMENDATIONS

The Secretary of Transportation should require

—systematic use of accident data and studies as a key factor in selecting vehicles, equipment, and standard areas for compliance testing;

—evaluation of compliance testing priorities on the basis of accident data and studies and the results or prior compliance tests;

—expanded and systematic use of manufacturers' certification data to supplement and refine the Safety Administration's standards enforcement coverage; and

—timely action in resolving test failure cases, particularly in having unsafe vehicle and equipment conditions corrected.

AGENCY ACTIONS AND UNRESOLVED ISSUES

In commenting on a draft of this report, the Department stated essentially that it was doing as much and as well as could be expected with available resources. The Department said that

—it was using accident data as much as practicable and that it anticipated using it in the future;

—it reevaluated compliance-testing priorities annually;

—de-emphasizing tire testing would be retrogressive;

—it would continue to use manufacturers' certification data but such use involved manpower considerations and had limited surveillance usefulness; and

—although it could not fully control the time involved in having unsafe conditions identified through its enforcement program corrected, it had reduced the timelags.

The Department and automobile industry representatives cautioned that use of accident data should involve meaningful evaluation of its relationship to specific vehicle safety standards. Industry representatives said that valid judgments as to compliance of crash-involved vehicles with specific standards could not be reached by simply examining accident data.

The representatives agreed, however, that the results of accident investigations could indicate vehicle performance in relation to safety standards and could provide guidance in determining priorities for compliance checking and enforcement.

MATTERS FOR CONSIDERATION BY THE CONGRESS

This report shows that the Government can improve its efforts to insure that the purposes of the National Traffic and Motor Vehicle Safety Act of 1966 are being met through enforcement of Federal motor vehicle safety standards. It presents information to help the Congress assess the efforts being made to reduce motor vehicle accidents, injuries, and deaths and to bring the purposes stated in the law closer to achievement.

21–5. The town of Springfield had poor internal control over its cash transactions. The facts about its cash position at November 30 were as follows: The cash books showed a balance of $19,101.62, which included cash on hand. A credit of $300 on the bank's records did not appear on the books of the town. The balance per the bank statement was $15,750; and outstanding checks were no. 62 for $116.25, no. 183 for $150, no. 284 for $253.25, no. 8621 for $190.71, no. 8623 for $206.80, and no. 8632 for $145.28.

The treasurer removed all the cash on hand in excess of $3,794.41 and then prepared the following reconciliation:

Balance per books, November 30		$19,101.62
Add: Outstanding checks:		
No. 8621	$190.71	
No. 8623	206.80	
No. 8632	145.28	442.79
		$19,544.41
Deduct: Cash on hand		3,794.41
Balance per bank, November 30		$15,750.00
Deduct: Unrecorded credit		300.00
True cash, November 30		$15,450.00

a) How much did the treasurer remove, and how did he attempt to conceal his theft?

b) Taking only the information given, name two specific features of internal control which were apparently missing.

c) If the treasurer's October 31 reconciliation is known to be in order and you start your audit on December 5, for the year ended November 30, what specific auditing procedures would uncover the fraud?

(AICPA, adapted)

21–6. The City Hospital Board of Trustees is puzzled because the hospital has had a bad operating year for the year 19x8; but still, the hospital net working capital has increased over the previous year. The net loss for the year was $84,674. As the auditor, you are asked to explain the reason for such a situation to the board of trustees.

You are acquainted with the following facts and figures:

After the books were closed, office supplies worth $9,326, which had been previously charged to expense, were inventoried. This amount was added to the general fund balance as of December 31, 19x8.

During the year 19x8, assets costing $62,000, on which accumulated depreciation was $18,000, were sold for $30,000, and the difference charged to the operating loss.

	December 31	
Assets	*19x8*	*19x7*
Cash	$ 156,561	$ 189,284
Certificates of deposit	50,000	40,000
Accounts receivable	456,380	401,930
Interest receivable	300	600
Inventories	108,597	97,975
Deferred charges	8,399	11,485
Total Current Assets	$ 780,237	$ 741,274
Fixed assets	4,594,457	4,532,610
Allowance for depreciation	(969,719)	(790,654)
Investments	15,597	2,445
Total Assets	$4,420,572	$4,485,675
Liabilities and Equities		
Accounts payable	$ 181,122	$ 171,648
Accrued expenses	2,233	1,473
Total Current Liabilities	$ 183,355	$ 173,121
Reserve for pensions	90,000	89,989
General fund balance	4,147,217	4,222,565
Total Liabilities and Equities	$4,420,572	$4,485,675

Prepare an analysis suitable for presentation to the board.

(AICPA, adapted)

21–7. The clerk-treasurer of the City of Liberty is to resign on October 15, 197B, and you are assigned there on that date to audit the records and accounts as of that date. You verify the cash on hand and not deposited to be $2,362.

The previous audit, ended on December 31, 197A, showed the following condition of funds on that date:

General fund balance	$48,000	
Park fund balance	6,350	
Cemetery fund balance	1,500	
Street fund balance	150	
Police and firemen's pension fund balance	52,000	$108,000
Balance in banks, December 31	$54,570	
Outstanding checks, December 31	300	$ 54,270
Investments, pension fund, December 31		45,250
Cash on hand		8,480
		$108,000

Your audit reveals transactions entered on the records for the period as follows:

Cash received for the general fund: taxes, $85,000; licenses, $1,200; court fees, $600; miscellaneous, $200. Park fund: concessions and rents, $900. Cemetery fund: lots and service, $2,400. Street funds: gas tax, $17,500; refunds on driveway paving, $300. Pension fund: assessments, $450; interest, $1,100; investments cashed, $15,000.

Cash disbursements for the general fund: $101,000. Park fund, $8,000. Cemetery fund, $2,700. Street fund, $16,400. Pension fund, $22,000, including $15,000 for investments.

Your investigation reveals that cash was received by the clerk-treasurer and not entered or charged on the record, as follows: license fees, $650; concessions at park, $350; driveway paving by city, reimbursed by individuals, $90.

Also, it is revealed that $700 was disbursed from the park fund instead of the general fund, an error in posting. The clerk-treasurer overpaid his own salary from the general fund $150; and when his attention was called to this, he volunteered the information that he had also advanced himself $100 from the cash drawer in September, 197B.

A second check was issued to a street laborer for $80, correcting a check issued in the previous month. The original check was issued for $85 but was not canceled on the record or returned, but was cashed for the payee by the clerk-treasurer, as evidenced by the endorsement on the check.

The balance in banks at the close of business on October 15, 197B, was $35,526; pension fund investments, verified, were $40,000; and outstanding checks, verified, were $688.

Prepare a financial statement of all funds for the period, as shown by the records; and reconcile the total funds as of October 15, 197B, with bank, investments, and cash on hand.

Prepare an itemized statement of any discrepancies for which you will require the clerk-treasurer to make settlement; and outline how the settlement shall be made, so that each fund will show the proper and correct balance after adjustment and the total in all funds will agree with cash funds in the bank and investments on hand.

(Indiana State Board of Accounts, adapted)

21–8. You are auditing the accounts of a town clerk-treasurer. You find, in the ledger, accounts for a general fund, a street fund, and a bond fund. The original advertised budget for the street fund for the year you are examining consisted of the following three appropriations only:

Labor	$24,800
Materials	26,500
Equipment	18,000

In the appropriation and disbursement ledger accounts, you find the following record of transactions under the street fund:

LABOR ACCOUNT

Date		*Description*	*Warrant*	*Appropriation*	*Disbursements*	*Appropriation Balance*
Jan.	1	From advertised budget		$24,800		$24,800
	28	Street labor	115–142		$6,340	18,460
Feb.	23	Street labor	219–241		3,240	15,220
Mar.	8	Street labor	252–263		2,460	12,760
Apr.	15	Director of Internal Revenue, for withholding tax	294		1,204	11,556
June	10	Labor on municipal parking lots	371–388		7,320	4,236
July	15	Director of Internal Revenue, for withholding tax	424		732	3,504
Oct.	18	Street labor	510–523		3,200	304
Dec.	31	Director of Internal Revenue, for withholding tax	621		304	

MATERIALS ACCOUNT

Date		*Description*	*Warrant*	*Appropriation*	*Disbursements*	*Appropriation Balance*
Jan.	1	From advertised budget		$26,500		$26,500
	20	Asphalt mix for street	109		$10,400	16,100
Feb.	21	Repair of truck used on street	217		100	16,000
Mar.	12	Purchased used truck for street	268		3,600	12,400
Apr.	15	Auditor of State, gasoline tax distribution		4,920		17,320
May	12	Gas and oil for street trucks	301		2,490	14,830
June	6	Tile	367		4,000	10,830
July	14	Concrete for building fireplaces in park	422		800	10,030
Aug.	7	Street lights (utility bill)	451		2,280	7,750
Sept.	29	Refund received on tile purchased by warrant No. 367		100		7,850
Oct.	18	Labor on street	524–532		2,420	5,430
Nov.	2	Reimbursement for cutting weeds on private property		40		5,470
Dec.	11	To contractor for paving street	612		6,000	530
	31	Additional appropriations as advertised on this date		530		

EQUIPMENT ACCOUNT

Date		Description	Warrant	Appropriation	Disbursements	Appropriation Balance
Jan.	1	From advertised budget.		$18,000		$18,000
	9	Grading equipment			$16,000	2,000
Feb.	10	Fire hydrants for street curb.	189		1,500	500
	19	Shovels, picks, and tools	208		420	80

Without consideration of the dates or amounts paid in relation to the purpose or of the number of times any particular item occurs, what comments and questions would you have in examining the above accounts?

(Indiana State Board of Accounts, adapted)

Appendix 1

Governmental Accounting Terminology[1]

ABATEMENT. A complete or partial cancellation of a levy imposed by a governmental unit. Abatements usually apply to tax levies, special assessments, and service charges.

ACCOUNTABILITIES. Those resources for which a person or organization (including a governmental unit) must render an accounting, although he or it may not be personally liable for them. For example, a public official is responsible for the cash and other assets under his control and must account for them. Moreover, even if a trustee has disbursed all funds confided to his care and has relieved himself of liability, he is still obligated to account for them, and the items are, therefore, accountabilities.

ACCOUNT NUMBER. See CODING and SYMBOLIZATION.

ACCOUNTING PERIOD. A period at the end of which, and for which, financial statements are prepared. See also FISCAL PERIOD.

ACCOUNTING PROCEDURE. The arrangement of all processes which discover, record, and summarize financial information to produce financial statements and reports and to provide internal control (q.v.).[2]

ACCOUNTING SYSTEM. The total structure of records and procedures which discover, record, classify, and report information on the financial position and operations of a governmental unit or any of its fund, balanced account groups, and organizational components.

ACCOUNTS RECEIVABLE. Amounts owing on open account from private persons, firms, or corporations for goods and services furnished by a governmental unit (but not including amounts due from other funds of the same governmental unit).

---

[1] Most of the definitions in this list of terms are taken by permission from *Governmental Accounting, Auditing, and Financial Reporting* (Chicago, 1968), pp. 151–72, published by the National Committee on Governmental Accounting. A small number of definitions were supplied by the authors. They are indicated by an asterisk (*).

[2] The letters "q.v." signify "which see."

Note. Although taxes and assessments receivable are covered by this term, they should each be recorded and reported separately in *Taxes Receivable* and *Special Assessments Receivable* accounts. Similarly, amounts due from other funds or from other governmental units should be reported separately.

ACCRUAL BASIS. The basis of accounting under which revenues are recorded when earned and expenditures are recorded as soon as they result in liabilities for benefits received, notwithstanding that the receipt of the revenue or the payment of the expenditure may take place, in whole or in part, in another accounting period. See also ACCRUE and LEVY.

ACCRUE. To record revenues when earned and to record expenditures as soon as they result in liabilities for benefits received, notwithstanding that the receipt of the revenue or payment of the expenditure may take place, in whole or in part, in another accounting period. See also ACCRUAL BASIS, ACCRUED EXPENSES, and ACCRUED REVENUE.

ACCRUED EXPENSES. Expenses incurred during the current accounting period but which are not payable until a subsequent accounting period. See also ACCRUAL BASIS and ACCRUE.

ACCRUED INCOME. See ACCRUED REVENUE.

ACCRUED INTEREST ON INVESTMENTS PURCHASED. Interest accrued on investments between the last interest payment date and the date of purchase. The account is carried as an asset until the first interest payment date after date of purchase. At that time an entry is made debiting Cash and crediting the Accrued Interest on Investments Purchased account for the amount of interest purchased and an Interest Earnings account for the balance.

ACCRUED INTEREST PAYABLE. A liability account which represents the amount of interest accrued at the balance sheet date but which is not due until a later date.

ACCRUED REVENUE. Revenue earned during the current accounting period but which is not collected until a subsequent accounting period. See also ACCRUAL BASIS and ACCRUE.

ACCRUED TAXES PAYABLE. A liability for taxes which have accrued since the last payment date but which are not yet due. Normally, this liability will be found only in the enterprise fund of a governmental unit.

ACCRUED WAGES PAYABLE. A liability for wages earned by employees between the last payment date and the balance sheet date but which are not yet due.

ACCUMULATED DEPRECIATION. See ALLOWANCE FOR DEPRECIATION.

ACQUISITION ADJUSTMENT. Premium paid for a utility plant, over and above original cost less depreciation. Similar to goodwill in nonmonopolistic enterprises.*

ACTIVITY. A specific and distinguishable line of work performed by one or more organizational components of a governmental unit for the purpose of accomplishing a function for which the governmental unit is responsible. For example, "Food Inspection" is an activity performed in the discharge of the "Health" function. See also FUNCTION, SUBFUNCTION, and SUBACTIVITY.

ACTIVITY CLASSIFICATION. A grouping of expenditures on the basis of specific lines of work performed by organization units. For example, sewage treatment and disposal, garbage collection, garbage disposal, and street cleaning are activities performed in carrying out the function of sanitation, and the segregation of the expenditures made for each of these activities constitutes an activity classification.

ACTUARIAL BASIS. A basis used in computing the amount of contributions to be made periodically to a fund so that the total contributions plus the compounded earnings thereon will equal the required payments to be made out of the fund. The factors taken into account in arriving at the amount of these contributions include the length of time over which each contribution is to be held and the rate of return compounded on such contribution over its life. A trust fund for a public employee retirement system is an example of a fund set up on an actuarial basis.

AD VALOREM. In proportion to value. A basis for levy of taxes upon property.*

AGENCY FUND. A fund consisting of resources received and held by the governmental unit as an agent for others; for example, taxes collected and held by a municipality for a school district.

Note. Sometimes resources held by one fund of a governmental unit for other funds of the unit are handled through an agency fund. An example would be taxes held by an agency fund for redistribution among other funds. See also ALLOCATION.

ALLOCATE. To divide a lump-sum appropriation into parts which are designated for expenditure by specific organization units and/or for specific purposes, activities, or objects. See also ALLOCATION.

ALLOCATION. A part of a lump-sum appropriation which is designated for expenditure by specific organization units and/or for special purposes, activities, or objects. See also ALLOCATE.

ALLOT. To divide an appropriation into amounts which may be encumbered or expended during an allotment period. See also ALLOTMENT and ALLOTMENT PERIOD.

ALLOTMENT. A part of an appropriation which may be encumbered or expended during an allotment period. See also ALLOT and ALLOTMENT PERIOD.

ALLOTMENT PERIOD. A period of time less than one fiscal year in length during which an allotment is effective. Bimonthly and quarterly allotment periods are most common. See also ALLOT and ALLOTMENT.

ALLOTMENT LEDGER. A subsidiary ledger which contains an account for each allotment (q.v.) showing the amount allotted, expenditures, encumbrances, the net balance, and other related information. See also APPROPRIATION LEDGER.

ALLOWANCE FOR AMORTIZATION. The account in which are accumulated the amounts recorded as amortization of the intangible asset to which the allowance relates.*

ALLOWANCE FOR DEPRECIATION. The account in which are accumulated the amounts of cost of the related asset which have been charged to expense.

AMORTIZATION. (1) Gradual reduction, redemption, or liquidation of the balance of an account according to a specified schedule of times and amounts. (2) Provision for the extinguishment of a debt by means of a DEBT SERVICE FUND (q.v.).

ANNUITIES PAYABLE. A liability account which records the amount of annuities due and payable to retired employees in a public employee retirement system.

ANNUITY. A series of equal money payments made at equal intervals during a designated period of time. In governmental accounting the most frequent annuities are accumulations of debt service funds for term bonds and payments to retired employees under public employee retirement systems.

ANNUITY, AMOUNT OF. The total amount of money accumulated or paid during an annuity period from an annuity and compound interest at a designated rate.

ANNUITY PERIOD. The designated length of time during which an amount of annuity is accumulated or paid.

APPORTIONMENT. See ALLOTMENT.

APPRAISAL. (1) The act of appraising. See APPRAISE. (2) The estimated value resulting from such action.

APPRAISE. To make an estimate of value, particularly of the value of property.

Note. If the property is valued for purposes of taxation, the less inclusive term "assess" (q.v.) is substituted for the above term.

APPROPRIATION. An authorization granted by a legislative body to make expenditures and to incur obligations for specific purposes.

Note. An appropriation is usually limited in amount and as to the time when it may be expended. See, however, INDETERMINATE APPROPRIATION.

APPROPRIATION BILL, ORDINANCE, RESOLUTION, or ORDER. A bill, ordinance (q.v.), resolution (q.v.), or order (q.v.) by means of which appropriations are given legal effect. It is the method by which the expenditure side of the budget (q.v.) is enacted into law by the legislative body. In many governmental jurisdictions appropriations cannot be enacted into law by resolution but only by a bill, ordinance, or order.

APPROPRIATION EXPENDITURE. An expenditure chargeable to an appropriation.

Note. Since virtually all expenditures of governmental units are chargeable to appropriations, the term EXPENDITURES by itself is widely and properly used.

APPROPRIATION EXPENDITURE LEDGER. See APPROPRIATION LEDGER.

APPROPRIATION LEDGER. A subsidiary ledger containing an account for each appropriation. Each account usually shows the amount originally appropriated, transfers to or from the appropriation, amounts charged against the appropriation, the net balance, and other related information. If allotments are made and a separate ledger is maintained for them, each account in the appropriation ledger usually shows the amount appropriated, transfers to or from the appropriation, the amount allotted, and the unallotted balance. See also ALLOTMENT LEDGER.

ASSESS. To value property officially for the purpose of taxation.

Note. The term is also sometimes used to denote the levy of taxes, but such usage is not correct because it fails to distinguish between the valuation process and the tax levy process.

ASSESSED VALUATION. A valuation set upon real estate or other property by a government as a basis for levying taxes.

ASSESSMENT. (1) The process of making the official valuation of property for purposes of taxation. (2) The valuation placed upon property as a result of this process.

ASSESSMENT ROLL. In the case of real property, the official list containing the legal description of each parcel of property and its assessed valuation. The name and address of the last known owner are also usually shown.

In the case of personal property, the assessment roll is the official list containing the name and address of the owner, a description of the personal property, and its assessed value.

ASSETS. Property owned by a governmental unit which has a monetary value.

Note. Conventionally, debit balances subject to final disposition, such as deferred charges and prepaid expenses, are classified as assets at closing periods, even though the stated values may not represent the realizable values.

AUDIT. The examination of documents, records, reports, systems of internal control, accounting and financial procedures, and other evidence for one or more of the following purposes:

a) To ascertain whether the statements prepared from the accounts present fairly the financial position and the results of financial operations of the constituent funds and balanced account groups of the governmental unit in accordance with generally accepted accounting principles *applicable to governmental units* and on a basis consistent with that of the preceding year.

b) To determine the propriety, legality, and mathematical accuracy of a governmental unit's financial transactions.

c) To ascertain whether all financial transactions have been properly recorded.

d) To ascertain the stewardship of public officials who handle and are responsible for the financial resources of a governmental unit.

AUDIT PROGRAM. A detailed outline of work to be done and the procedure to be followed in any given audit.

AUDIT REPORT. The report prepared by an auditor covering the audit or investigation made by him. As a rule, the report should include: (*a*) a statement of the scope of the audit; (*b*) explanatory comments (if any) concerning exceptions by the auditor as to application of generally accepted auditing standards; (*c*) opinions; (*d*) explanatory comments (if any) concerning verification procedures; (*e*) financial statements and schedules; and (*f*) sometimes statistical tables, supplementary comments, and recommendations. The auditor's signature follows item (*c*) or (*d*).

AUDITED CLAIMS PAYABLE. Claims which have been processed and are eligible for payment.*

AUDITED VOUCHER. A voucher which has been examined and approved for payment.

AUDITOR'S OPINION. A statement signed by an auditor in which he states that he has examined the financial statements in accordance with generally accepted auditing standards (with exceptions, if any) and in which he expresses his opinion on the financial condition and results of operations of some or all of the constituent funds and balanced account groups of the governmental unit, as appropriate.

AUTHORITY. A governmental unit or public agency created to perform a single function or a restricted group of related activities. Usually such units are financed from service charges, fees, and tolls, but in some instances they also have taxing powers. An authority may be completely independent of other governmental units, or in some cases it may be partially dependent upon other governments for its creation, its financing, or the exercise of certain powers.

AUTHORITY BONDS. Bonds payable from the revenues of a specific authority (q.v.). Since such authorities usually have no revenue other than charges for services, their bonds are ordinarily revenue bonds (q.v.).

AUTOMATIC DATA PROCESSING (ADP). See ELECTRONIC DATA PROCESSING (EDP).

BALANCE SHEET. A statement which discloses the assets, liabilities, reserves, and equities of a fund or governmental unit at a specified date, properly classified to exhibit financial position of the fund or unit at that date.

Note. If a single balance sheet is prepared for several funds, it must be in columnar or sectional form so as to exhibit the accounts of each fund and balanced account group individually.

BETTERMENT. An addition made to, or change made in, a fixed asset which is expected to prolong its life or to increase its efficiency over and above that arising from maintenance (q.v.) and the cost of which is therefore added to the book value of the asset.

Note. The term is sometimes applied to sidewalks, sewers, and highways, but these should preferably be designated as "improvements" (q.v.).

BOND. A written promise to pay a specified sum of money, called the face value or principal amount, at a specified date or dates in the future, called the maturity date(s), together with periodic interest at a specified rate.

Note. The difference between a note and a bond is that the latter runs for a longer period of time and requires greater legal formality.

BOND ANTICIPATION NOTES. Short-term interest-bearing notes issued by a governmental unit in anticipation of bonds to be issued at a later date. The notes are retired from proceeds of the bond issue to which they are related. See also INTERIM BORROWING.

BOND DISCOUNT. The excess of the face value of a bond over the price for which it is acquired or sold.

Note. The price does not include accrued interest at the date of acquisition or sale.

BOND FUND. A fund formerly used to account for the proceeds of general obligation bond issues. Such proceeds are now accounted for in a CAPITAL PROJECTS FUND (q.v.).

BOND INDENTURE. The contract between a corporation issuing bonds and the trustees or other body representing prospective and actual holders of the bonds.*

BOND ORDINANCE OR RESOLUTION. An ordinance (q.v.) or resolution (q.v.) authorizing a bond issue.

BOND PREMIUM. The excess of the price at which a bond is acquired or sold over its face value.

Note. The price does not include accrued interest at the date of acquisition or sale.

BONDED DEBT. That portion of indebtedness represented by outstanding bonds. See GROSS BONDED DEBT and NET BONDED DEBT.

BONDED INDEBTEDNESS. See BONDED DEBT.

BONDS AUTHORIZED AND UNISSUED. Bonds which have been legally authorized but not issued and which can be issued and sold without further authorization.

Note. This term must not be confused with the term "margin of borrowing power" or "legal debt margin," either one of which represents the difference between the legal debt limit (q.v.) of a governmental unit and the debt outstanding against it.

BOOKS OF ORIGINAL ENTRY. The record in which the various transactions are formally recorded for the first time, such as the cash journal, check register, or general journal. Where mechanized bookkeeping methods are used, it may happen that one transaction is recorded simultaneously in several records, one of which may be regarded as the book of original entry.

Note. Memorandum books, check stubs, files of duplicate sales invoices, etc., whereon first or prior business notations may have been made, are not books of original entry in the accepted meaning of the term, unless they are also used as the media for direct posting to the ledgers.

BOOK VALUE. Value (q.v.) as shown by books of account.

Note. In the case of assets which are subject to reduction by valuation allowances, "book value" refers to cost or stated value less the appropriate allowance. Sometimes a distinction is made between "gross book value" and "net book value," the former designating value before deduction of related allowances and the latter after their deduction. In the absence of any modifier, however, the term "book value" is understood to be synonymous with "net book value."

BUDGET. A plan of financial operation embodying an estimate of proposed expenditures for a given period and the proposed means of financing them. Used without any modifier, the term usually indicates a financial plan for a single fiscal year.

Note. The term "budget" is used in two senses in practice. Sometimes it designates the financial plan presented to the appropriating body for adoption and sometimes the plan finally approved by that body. It is usually necessary to specify whether the budget under consideration is preliminary and tentative or whether it has been approved by the appropriating body. See also CURRENT BUDGET, CAPITAL BUDGET, CAPITAL PROGRAM, and LONG-TERM BUDGET.

BUDGET DOCUMENT. The instrument used by the budget-making authority to present a comprehensive financial program to the appropriating body. The budget document usually consists of three parts. The first part contains a message from the budget-making authority, together with a summary of the proposed expenditures and the means of financing them. The second consists of schedules supporting the summary. These schedules show in detail the information as to past years' actual revenues, expenditures, and other data used in making the estimates.

The third part is composed of drafts of the appropriation, revenue, and borrowing measures necessary to put the budget into effect.

BUDGET MESSAGE. A general discussion of the proposed budget as presented in writing by the budget-making authority to the legislative body. The budget message should contain an explanation of the principal budget items, an outline of the governmental unit's experience during the past period and its financial status at the time of the message, and recommendations regarding the financial policy for the coming period.

BUDGETARY ACCOUNTS. Those accounts which reflect budgetary operations and condition, such as estimated revenues, appropriations, and encumbrances, as distinguished from proprietary accounts. See also PROPRIETARY ACCOUNTS.

BUDGETARY CONTROL. The control or management of a governmental unit or enterprise in accordance with an approved budget for the purpose of keeping expenditures within the limitations of available appropriations and available revenues.

BUILDINGS. A fixed asset account which reflects the acquisition value of permanent structures used to house persons and property owned by a governmental unit. If buildings are purchased or constructed, this account includes the purchase or contract price of all permanent buildings and fixtures attached to and forming a permanent part of such buildings. If buildings are acquired by gift, the account reflects their appraised value at time of acquisition.

CALLABLE BOND. A type of bond which permits the issuer to pay the obligation before the stated maturity date by giving notice of redemption in a manner specified in the bond contract. Synonym: OPTIONAL BOND.

CAPITAL ASSETS. See FIXED ASSETS.

CAPITAL BUDGET. A plan of proposed capital outlays and the means of financing them for the current fiscal period. It is usually a part of the current budget. If a Capital Program is in operation, it will be the first year thereof. A Capital Program is sometimes referred to as a Capital Budget. See also CAPITAL PROGRAM.

CAPITAL EXPENDITURES. See CAPITAL OUTLAYS.

CAPITAL IMPROVEMENT PROGRAM. See CAPITAL PROGRAM.

CAPITAL OUTLAYS. Expenditures which result in the acquisition of or addition to fixed assets.

CAPITAL PROGRAM. A plan for capital expenditures to be incurred each year over a fixed period of years to meet capital needs arising from the long-term work program or otherwise. It sets forth each project or other contemplated expenditure in which the government is to have a part and specifies the full resources estimated to be available to finance the projected expenditures.

CAPITAL PROJECTS FUND. A fund created to account for all resources used for the acquisition of designated fixed assets by a governmental unit except those financed by special assessment and enterprise funds. See also BOND FUND.

CAPITAL RESOURCES. Resources of a fixed or permanent character, such as land and buildings, which cannot ordinarily be used to meet current expenditures.

CASH. Currency, coin, checks, postal and express money orders, and bankers' drafts on hand or on deposit with an official or agent designated as custodian of cash and bank deposits.

Note. All cash must be accounted for as a part of the fund to which it belongs. Any restrictions or limitations as to its availability must be indicated in the records and statements. It is not necessary, however, to have a separate bank account for each fund unless required by law.

CASH AUDIT. An audit of the cash transactions for a stated period for the purpose of determining that all cash received has been recorded, that all disbursements have been properly authorized and vouchered, and that the balance of cash is either on hand or on deposit. A cash audit can range from a complete inquiry into all cash transactions to one involving only some of them.

CASH BASIS. The basis of accounting under which revenues are recorded when received in cash and expenditures are recorded when paid.

CASH DISCOUNT. An allowance received or given if payment is completed within a stated period of time.

CERTIFIED PUBLIC ACCOUNTANT. An accountant to whom a state has granted a certificate showing that he has met prescribed educational, experience, and examination requirements designed to insure competence in the practice of public accounting. The accountant holding such a certificate is permitted to use the designation Certified Public Accountant, commonly abbreviated to CPA.

CHARACTER. A basis for distinguishing expenditures according to the periods they are presumed to benefit. See also CHARACTER CLASSIFICATION.

CHARACTER CLASSIFICATION. A grouping of expenditures on the basis of the time periods they are presumed to benefit. The three groupings are: (1) expenses, presumed to benefit the current fiscal period (but see note following EXPENSES); (2) provisions for retirement of debt, presumed to benefit prior fiscal periods primarily but also present and future periods; and (3) capital outlays, presumed to benefit the current and future fiscal periods. See also ACTIVITY, ACTIVITY CLASSIFICATION, FUNCTION, FUNCTIONAL CLASSIFICATION, OBJECT, OBJECT CLASSIFICATION, and EXPENSES.

CHARTERED ACCOUNTANT. A member of an Institute of Chartered Accountants in the British Empire. Admission to such institutes is dependent upon serving a period of apprenticeship and passing an entrance examination.

CHECK. A bill of exchange drawn on a bank and payable on demand; a written order on a bank to pay on demand a specified sum of money to a named person, to his order, or to bearer, out of money on deposit to the credit of the maker.

Note. A check differs from a warrant in that the latter is not necessarily payable on demand and may not be negotiable. It differs from a voucher in that the latter is not an order to pay.

CLEARING ACCOUNT. An account used to accumulate total charges or credits for the purpose of distributing them later among the accounts to which they are allocable or for the purpose of transferring the net differences to the proper account.

CODE. See CODING.

CODING. A system of numbering or otherwise designating accounts, entries, invoices, vouchers, etc., in such a manner that the symbol used reveals quickly certain required information. To illustrate the coding of accounts, the number "200" may be assigned to expenditures made by the Department of Finance and the letter "A" may be used to designate expenditures for personal services. Expenditures for personal services in the Department of Finance would then be designated, for posting and other purposes, by the code "200–A." Other examples are the numbering of monthly recurring journal entries so that the number indicates the month and the nature of the entry and the numbering of invoices or vouchers so that the number reveals the date of entry. See also SYMBOLIZATION.

COLLECTOR'S ROLL. See TAX ROLL.

COMBINATION BOND. A bond issued by a governmental unit which is payable from the revenues of a governmental enterprise but which is also backed by the full faith and credit of the governmental unit.

COMBINED BALANCE SHEET. A single balance sheet which displays the individual balance sheets of each class of funds and the balanced account groups of a governmental unit in separate, adjacent columns.

Note. There are no interfund eliminations or consolidations in a combined balance sheet for a governmental unit.

COMMITMENTS. See ENCUMBRANCES.

CONSCIENCE MONEY. Money received by governmental units in payment of previously undisclosed debts, usually based on embezzlement, tax evasion or theft.*

CONSTRUCTION WORK IN PROGRESS. The cost of construction work undertaken but not yet completed.

CONTINGENT FUND. Assets or other resources set aside to provide for unforeseen expenditures or for anticipated expenditures of uncertain amount.

Note. The term should not be used to describe a reserve for contingencies. The latter is set aside out of the fund balance of a fund but does not constitute a separate fund. Similarly, an appropriation for contingencies is not a contingent fund, since an appropriation is not a fund.

CONTINGENT LIABILITIES. Items which may become liabilities as a result of conditions undetermined at a given date, such as guarantees, pending law suits, judgments under appeal, unsettled disputed claims, unfilled purchase orders, and uncompleted contracts.

Note. All contingent liabilities should be shown on the face of the balance sheet or in a footnote thereto.

CONTINUING APPROPRIATION. An appropriation which, once established, is automatically renewed without further legislative action, period after period, until altered or revoked.

Note. The term should not be confused with INDETERMINATE APPROPRIATION (q.v.).

CONTINUOUS AUDIT. An audit in which the detailed work is performed either continuously or at short, regular intervals throughout the fiscal period. Such continuous work leads up to the completion of the audit upon the closing of the accounting records at the end of the fiscal period.

A continuous audit differs from a periodic audit, even though the detailed work may be performed on a monthly or other short-term basis, in that no report is made in the case of the former, except of irregularities detected and adjustments found to be necessary, until the end of a complete fiscal period. Moreover, the continuous audit differs from the periodic audit in that the certification of balance sheet and operating statement figures of the former may be deferred until the end of the fiscal period.

CONTROL ACCOUNT. An account in the general ledger in which are recorded the aggregate of debit and credit postings to a number of identical or related accounts called subsidiary accounts. For example, the Taxes Receivable account is a control account supported by the aggregate of individual balances in individual property taxpayers' accounts. See also GENERAL LEDGER and SUBSIDIARY ACCOUNT.

COST. The amount of money or money's worth exchanged for property or services.

Note. Costs may be incurred even before money is paid; that is, as soon as liability is incurred. Ultimately, however, money or money's worth must be given in exchange. Again, the cost of some property or service may, in turn, become a part of the cost of another property or service. For example, the cost of part or all of the materials purchased at a certain time will be reflected in the cost of articles made from such materials or in the cost of those services in the rendering of which the materials were used.

COST ACCOUNTING. That method of accounting which provides for the assembling and recording of all the elements of cost incurred to accomplish a purpose, to carry on an activity or operation, or to complete a unit of work or a specific job.

Cost Ledger. A subsidiary record wherein each project, job, production center, process, operation, product, or service is given a separate account to which all items entering into its cost are posted in the required detail. Such accounts should be so arranged and kept that the results shown in them may be reconciled with and verified by a control account or accounts in the general books.

Cost, Original. See Original Cost.

Cost Records. All ledgers, supporting records, schedules, reports, invoices, vouchers, and other records and documents reflecting the cost of projects, jobs, production centers, processes, operations, products, or services, or the cost of any of the component parts thereof.

Cost Unit. A term used in cost accounting to designate the unit of product or service whose cost is computed. These units are selected for the purpose of comparing the actual cost with a standard cost (q.v.) or with actual costs of units produced under different circumstances or at different places and times. See also Unit Cost and Work Unit.

Coupon Rate. The interest rate specified on interest coupons attached to a bond. The term is synonymous with nominal interest rate (q.v.).

Current. A term which, applied to budgeting and accounting, designates the operations of the present fiscal period as opposed to past or future periods.

Current Assets. Those assets which are available or can be made readily available to meet the cost of operations or to pay current liabilities. Some examples are cash, temporary investments, and taxes receivable which will be collected within about a year from the balance sheet date.

Current Budget. The annual budget prepared for and effective during the present fiscal year; or, in the case of some state governments, the budget for the present biennium.

Current Expenses. See Expenses.

Current Fund. See General Fund.

Current Funds. Funds the resources of which are expended for operating purposes during the current fiscal period. In its usual application in plural form, it refers to General, Special Revenue, Debt Service, and Enterprise Funds of a governmental unit. In the singular form, the current fund is synonymous with the general fund. See also General Fund.

Current Liabilities. Liabilities which are payable within a relatively short period of time, usually no longer than a year. See also Floating Debt.

Current Resources. Resources (q.v.) to which recourse can be had to meet current obligations and expenditures. Examples are current assets, estimated revenues of a particular period not yet realized, transfers from other funds authorized but not received, and in the case of certain funds, bonds authorized and unissued.

CURRENT REVENUE. Revenues of a governmental unit which are available to meet expenditures of the current fiscal year. See REVENUE.

CURRENT SPECIAL ASSESSMENTS. (1) Special assessments levied and becoming due during the current fiscal period, from the date special assessment rolls are approved by the proper authority to the date on which a penalty for nonpayment is attached. (2) Special assessments levied in a prior fiscal period but becoming due in the current fiscal period, from the time they become due to the date on which a penalty for nonpayment is attached.

CURRENT TAXES. (1) Taxes levied and becoming due during the current fiscal period, from the time the amount of the tax levy is first established to the date on which a penalty for nonpayment is attached. (2) Taxes levied in the preceding fiscal period but becoming due in the current fiscal period, from the time they become due until a penalty for nonpayment is attached.

CURRENT YEAR'S TAX LEVY. Taxes levied for the current fiscal period.

DATA PROCESSING. (1) The preparation and handling of information and data from source media through prescribed procedures to obtain such end results as classification, problem solution, summarization, and reports. (2) Preparation and handling of financial information wholly or partially by mechanical or electronic means. See also ELECTRONIC DATA PROCESSING (EDP).

DEBT. An obligation resulting from the borrowing of money or from the purchase of goods and services. Debts of governmental units include bonds, time warrants, notes, and floating debt. See also BOND, NOTES PAYABLE, TIME WARRANT, FLOATING DEBT, LONG-TERM DEBT, and GENERAL LONG-TERM DEBT.

DEBT LIMIT. The maximum amount of gross or net debt which is legally permitted.

DEBT SERVICE FUND. A fund established to finance and account for the payment of interest and principal on all general obligation debt, serial and term, other than that payable exclusively from special assessments and revenue debt issued for and serviced by a governmental enterprise. Formerly called a SINKING FUND.

DEBT SERVICE FUND REQUIREMENTS. The amounts of revenue which must be provided for a debt service fund so that all principal and interest payments can be made in full on schedule.

DEBT SERVICE REQUIREMENT. The amount of money required to pay the interest on outstanding debt, serial maturities of principal for serial bonds, and required contributions to a debt service fund for term bonds.

DEFERRED CHARGES. Expenditures which are not chargeable to the fiscal period in which made but are carried on the asset side of the balance sheet pending amortization or other disposition. An example is Discount on Bonds Issued.

Note. Deferred charges differ from prepaid expenses in that they usually extend over a long period of time (more than five years) and are not regularly recurring costs of operation. See also PREPAID EXPENSES.

DEFERRED CREDITS. Credit balances or items which will be spread over following accounting periods either as additions to revenue or as reductions of expenses. Examples are taxes collected in advance and premiums on bonds issued.

DEFERRED INCOME. See DEFERRED CREDITS.

DEFERRED SERIAL BONDS. Serial bonds (q.v.) in which the first installment does not fall due for two or more years from the date of issue.

DEFERRED SPECIAL ASSESSMENTS. Special assessments which have been levied but which are not yet due.

DEFICIENCY. A general term indicating the amount by which anything falls short of some requirement or expectation. The term should not be used without qualification.

DEFICIT. (1) The excess of the liabilities and reserves of a fund over its assets. (2) The excess of expenditures over revenues during an accounting period; or, in the case of Enterprise and Intragovernmental Service Funds, the excess of expense over income during an accounting period.

DELINQUENT SPECIAL ASSESSMENTS. Special assessments remaining unpaid on and after the date on which a penalty for nonpayment is attached.

DELINQUENT TAXES. Taxes remaining unpaid on and after the date on which a penalty for nonpayment is attached. Even though the penalty may be subsequently waived and a portion of the taxes may be abated or canceled, the unpaid balances continue to be delinquent taxes until abated, canceled, paid, or converted into tax liens.

Note. The term is sometimes limited to taxes levied for the fiscal period or periods preceding the current one, but such usage is not entirely correct. See also CURRENT TAXES, CURRENT YEAR'S TAX LEVY, and PRIOR YEARS' TAX LEVIES.

DEPOSIT. (1) Money placed with a banking or other institution or with a person either as a general deposit subject to check or as a special deposit made for some specified purpose. (2) Securities lodged with a banking or other institution or with a person for some particular purpose. (3) Sums deposited by customers for electric meters, water meters, etc.; and by contractors and others to accompany and guarantee their bids.

DEPOSIT WARRANT. A financial document prepared by a designated accounting or finance officer authorizing the treasurer of a governmental unit to accept for deposit sums of money collected by various departments and agencies of the governmental unit.

DEPRECIATION. (1) Expiration in the service life of fixed assets, other than wasting assets (q.v.), attributable to wear and tear, deterioration, action of the physical elements, inadequacy, and obsolescence. (2) The portion of the cost of a fixed asset, other than a wasting asset, which is charged as an expense during a particular period.

Note. In accounting for depreciation, the cost of a fixed asset, less any salvage value, is prorated over the estimated service life of such an asset, and each period is charged with a portion of such cost. Through this process, the entire cost of the asset is ultimately charged off as an expense.

DETAILED AUDIT. An audit in which an examination is made of the system of internal control and of the details of all transactions and books of account, including subsidiary records and supporting documents, as to legality, mathematical accuracy, complete accountability, and application of generally accepted accounting principles for governmental units.

DIRECT CHARGES. See DIRECT EXPENSES.

DIRECT DEBT. The debt which a governmental unit has incurred in its own name or assumed through the annexation of territory or consolidation with another governmental unit. See also OVERLAPPING DEBT.

DIRECT EXPENSES. Those expenses which can be charged directly as a part of the cost of a product or service, or of a department or operating unit, as distinguished from overhead and other indirect costs which must be prorated among several products or services, departments, or operating units.

DIRECT LABOR. The cost of labor directly expended in the production of specific goods or rendition of specific services.

DIRECT MATERIALS. The cost of materials which become an integral part of a specific manufactured product or which are consumed in the performance of a specific service.

DISBURSEMENTS. Payments in cash.

DOUBLE ENTRY. A system of bookkeeping which requires, for every entry made to the debit side of an account or accounts, an entry for a corresponding amount or amounts to the credit side of another account or accounts.

Note. Double entry bookkeeping involves the maintaining of a balance between assets on the one hand and liabilities, reserves, and fund equities on the other. To maintain this balance, it is necessary that entries for equal amounts be made in each group. Moreover, if a transaction affects only one group of accounts, such as assets, the amount or amounts debited to an account or accounts within the group must be offset by a credit to another account or accounts within the group for a corresponding amount or amounts. For example, a debit to Cash would be offset by a credit for a corresponding amount to Taxes Receivable or some other asset.

DUE TO FISCAL AGENT. Amounts due to fiscal agents, such as commercial banks, for servicing a governmental unit's maturing interest and principal payments on indebtedness.

EARNINGS. See INCOME and REVENUE.

EFFECTIVE INTEREST RATE. The rate of earning on a bond investment based on the actual price paid for the bond, the coupon rate, the maturity date, and the length of time between interest dates, in contrast with the nominal interest rate (q.v.).

ELECTRONIC DATA PROCESSING (EDP). Data processing by means of high-speed electronic equipment. See also DATA PROCESSING.

ENCUMBRANCES. Obligations in the form of purchase orders, contracts, or salary commitments which are chargeable to an appropriation and for which a part of the appropriation is reserved. They cease to be encumbrances when paid or when the actual liability is set up.

ENDOWMENT FUND. A fund whose principal must be maintained inviolate but whose income may be expended. An endowment fund is accounted for as a trust fund.

ENTERPRISE DEBT. Debt which is to be retired primarily from the earnings of publicly owned and operated enterprises. See also REVENUE BONDS.

ENTERPRISE FUND. A fund established to finance and account for the acquisition, operation, and maintenance of governmental facilities and services which are entirely or predominantly self-supporting by user charges. Examples of enterprise funds are those for water, gas, and electric utilities; swimming pools; airports; parking garages; and transit systems.

ENTRY. (1) The record of a financial transaction in its appropriate book of account. (2) The act of recording a transaction in the books of account.

EQUIPMENT. Tangible property of a more or less permanent nature (other than land, buildings, or improvements other than buildings) which is useful in carrying on operations. Examples are machinery, tools, trucks, cars, furniture, and furnishings.

ESTIMATED REVENUE. For revenue accounts kept on an accrual basis (q.v.), this term designates the amount of revenue estimated to accrue during a given period regardless of whether or not it is all to be collected during the period. For revenue accounts kept on a cash basis (q.v.) the term designates the amount of revenue estimated to be collected during a given period. Under the modified accrual basis (q.v.) recommended for some funds by the Committee, estimated revenues for many governmental revenues will include both cash and accrual basis revenues. See also REVENUE, REVENUE RECEIPTS, CASH BASIS, ACCRUAL BASIS, and MODIFIED ACCRUAL BASIS.

ESTIMATED REVENUE RECEIPTS. A term used synonymously with estimated revenue (q.v.) by some governmental units reporting their revenues on a cash basis. See also REVENUE and REVENUE RECEIPTS.

ESTIMATED UNCOLLECTIBLE ACCOUNTS RECEIVABLE (Credit). That portion of accounts receivable which it is estimated will never be collected. The account is deducted from the Accounts Receivable account on the balance sheet in order to arrive at the net amount of accounts receivable.

ESTIMATED UNCOLLECTIBLE CURRENT TAXES (Credit). A provision out of tax revenues for that portion of current taxes receivable which it is estimated will never be collected. The amount is shown on the balance sheet as a deduction from the Taxes Receivable—Current account in order to arrive at the net taxes receivable.

ESTIMATED UNCOLLECTIBLE DELINQUENT TAXES (Credit). That portion of delinquent taxes receivable which it is estimated will never be collected. The account is shown on the balance sheet as a deduction from the Taxes Receivable—Delinquent account to arrive at the net delinquent taxes receivable.

ESTIMATED UNCOLLECTIBLE INTEREST AND PENALTIES ON TAXES (Credit). That portion of interest and penalties receivable which it is estimated will never be collected. The account is shown as a deduction from the Interest and Penalties Receivable account on the balance sheet in order to arrive at the net interest and penalties receivable.

ESTIMATED UNCOLLECTIBLE TAX LIENS. That portion of tax liens receivable which it is estimated will never be collected. The account is shown as a deduction from the Tax Liens Receivable account on the balance sheet in order to arrive at the net amount of tax liens receivable.

EXHIBIT. (1) A balance sheet or other principal financial statement. (2) Any statement or other document that accompanies or is a part of a financial or audit report. See also SCHEDULES and STATEMENTS.

EXPENDABLE FUND. A fund whose resources, including both principal and earnings, may be expended. See also NONEXPENDABLE FUND.

EXPENDITURE DISBURSEMENTS. A term sometimes used by governmental units operating on a cash basis (q.v.) as a synonym for expenditures (q.v.). It is not recommended terminology.

EXPENDITURES. Where the accounts are kept on the accrual basis (q.v.) or the modified accrual basis (q.v.), this term designates the cost of goods delivered or services rendered, whether paid or unpaid, including expenses, provision for debt retirement not reported as a liability of the fund from which retired, and capital outlays. Where the accounts are kept on the cash basis (q.v.), the term designates only actual cash disbursements for these purposes.

Note. Encumbrances are not expenditures.

EXPENSES. Charges incurred, whether paid or unpaid, for operation, maintenance, interest, and other charges which are presumed to benefit the current fiscal period.

Note. Legal provisions sometimes make it necessary to treat as expenses some charges whose benefits extend over future periods. For example, purchases of materials and supplies which may be used over a period of more than one year and payments for insurance which is to be in force for a period longer than one year frequently must be charged in their entirety to the appropriation of the year in which they are incurred and classified as expenses of that year, even though their benefits extend also to other periods.

FACE VALUE. As applied to securities, this term designates the amount of liability stated in the security document.

FIDELITY BOND. A written promise to indemnify against losses from theft, defalcation, and misappropriation of public funds by government officers and employees. See also SURETY BOND.

FISCAL PERIOD. Any period at the end of which a governmental unit determines its financial position and the results of its operations.

FISCAL YEAR. A twelve-month period of time to which the annual budget applies and at the end of which a governmental unit determines its financial position and the results of its operations.

FIXED ASSETS. Assets of a long-term character which are intended to continue to be held or used, such as land, buildings, machinery, furniture, and other equipment.

Note. The term does not indicate the immobility of an asset, which is the distinctive character of "fixture" (q.v.).

FIXED CHARGES. Expenses (q.v.) the amount of which is more or less fixed. Examples are interest, insurance, and contributions to pension funds.

FIXED LIABILITIES. See BONDED DEBT.

FIXTURES. Attachments to buildings which are not intended to be removed and which cannot be removed without damage to the latter.

Note. Those fixtures with a useful life presumed to be as long as that of the building itself are considered a part of such a building; all others are classed as equipment.

FLOATING DEBT. Liabilities other than bonded debt and time warrants which are payable on demand or at an early date. Examples are accounts payable, notes, and bank loans. See also CURRENT LIABILITIES.

FORCE ACCOUNT METHOD. A method employed in the construction and/or maintenance of fixed assets whereby a governmental unit's own personnel are used instead of an outside contractor.

Note. This method also calls for the purchase of materials by the governmental unit and the possible use of its own equipment, but the distinguishing characteristic of the force account method is the use of the unit's own personnel.

FORFEITURE. The automatic loss of cash or other property as a punishment for not complying with legal provisions and as compensation for the resulting damages or losses.

Note. The term should not be confused with confiscation. The latter term designates the actual taking over of the forfeited property by the government. Even after property has been forfeited, it cannot be said to be confiscated until the governmental unit claims it.

FRANCHISE. A special privilege granted by a government permitting the continuing use of public property, such as city streets, and usually involving the elements of monopoly and regulation.

FULL FAITH AND CREDIT. A pledge of the general taxing power for the payment of debt obligations.

Note. Bonds carrying such pledges are usually referred to as general obligation bonds or full faith and credit bonds.

FUNCTION. A group of related activities aimed at accomplishing a major service or regulatory program for which a governmental unit is responsible. For example, public health is a function. See also SUBFUNCTION, ACTIVITY, CHARACTER, and OBJECT.

FUNCTIONAL CLASSIFICATION. A grouping of expenditures on the basis of the principal purposes for which they are made. Examples are public safety, public health, public welfare, etc. See also ACTIVITY, CHARACTER, and OBJECT CLASSIFICATION.

FUND. An independent fiscal and accounting entity with a self-balancing set of accounts recording cash and/or other resources together with all related liabilities, obligations, reserves, and equities which are segregated for the purpose of carrying on specific activities or attaining certain objectives in accordance with special regulations, restrictions, or limitations. See GENERAL FIXED ASSETS GROUP OF ACCOUNTS and GENERAL LONG-TERM DEBT AND INTEREST GROUP OF ACCOUNTS.

FUND ACCOUNTS. All accounts necessary to set forth the financial operations and financial position of a fund.

FUND BALANCE. The excess of the assets of a fund over its liabilities and reserves except in the case of funds subject to budgetary accounting where, prior to the end of a fiscal period, it represents the excess of the fund's assets and estimated revenues for the period over its liabilities, reserves, and appropriations for the period.

FUND BALANCE RECEIPTS. Receipts which increase the fund balance of a fund but which are not properly included in current revenues. Examples are taxes and accounts receivable which had previously been written off as uncollectible.

FUND BALANCE SHEET. A balance sheet for a single fund. See FUND and BALANCE SHEET.

FUNDED DEBT. Same as BONDED DEBT, which is the preferred term.

FUNDED DEFICIT. A deficit eliminated through the sale of bonds issued for that purpose. See also FUNDING BONDS.

FUND GROUP. A group of funds which are similar in purpose and character. For example, several special revenue funds constitute a fund group. See also RELATED FUNDS.

FUNDING. The conversion of floating debt or time warrants into bonded debt (q.v.).

FUNDING BONDS. Bonds issued to retire outstanding floating debt and to eliminate deficits.

FUND SURPLUS. See FUND BALANCE.

GENERAL AUDIT. An audit, made at the close of a normal accounting period, which covers all of the funds and balanced account groups of a governmental unit. Such audits may involve some detailed verifications, as determined by the professional judgment of the auditor, but usually they are based on appropriate tests and checks. See also SPECIAL AUDIT.

GENERAL FIXED ASSETS. Those fixed assets of a governmental unit which are not accounted for in an Enterprise, Trust, or Intragovernmental Service Fund.

GENERAL FIXED ASSETS GROUP OF ACCOUNTS. A self-balancing group of accounts set up to account for the general fixed assets of a governmental unit. See GENERAL FIXED ASSETS.

GENERAL FUND. A fund used to account for all transactions of a governmental unit which are not accounted for in another fund.

Note. The General Fund is used to account for the ordinary operations of a governmental unit which are financed from taxes and other general revenues.

GENERAL JOURNAL. A journal (q.v.) in which are entered all entries not recorded in special journals.

GENERAL LEDGER. A book, file, or other device which contains the accounts needed to reflect, in summary and in detail, the financial position and the results of financial operations of a governmental unit.

Note. In double entry bookkeeping (q.v.), the debits and credits in the general ledger are equal, and therefore the debit balances equal the credit balances. See also CONTROL ACCOUNT, SUBSIDIARY ACCOUNT, and SUBSIDIARY LEDGER.

GENERAL LONG-TERM DEBT. Long-term debt legally payable from general revenues and backed by the full faith and credit of a governmental unit. See LONG-TERM DEBT.

GENERAL LONG-TERM DEBT GROUP OF ACCOUNTS. A self-balancing group of accounts set up to account for the general long-term debt of a governmental unit. See GENERAL LONG-TERM DEBT.

GENERAL LONG-TERM DEBT AND INTEREST GROUP OF ACCOUNTS. Same as GENERAL LONG-TERM DEBT GROUP but with addition of information on related interest obligations.*

GENERAL OBLIGATION BONDS. Bonds for whose payment the full faith and credit of the issuing body are pledged. More commonly, but not necessarily, general obligation bonds are considered to be those payable from taxes and other general revenues. See also FULL FAITH AND CREDIT.

GENERAL OBLIGATION SPECIAL ASSESSMENT BONDS. See SPECIAL ASSESSMENT BONDS.

GENERAL REVENUE. The revenues (q.v.) of a governmental unit other than those derived from and retained in an enterprise.

Note. If a portion of the net income in an enterprise fund is contributed to another nonenterprise fund, such as the General Fund, the amounts transferred constitute general revenue of the governmental unit.

GOVERNMENTAL ACCOUNTING. The composite activity of analyzing, recording, summarizing, reporting, and interpreting the financial transactions of governmental units and agencies.

GOVERNMENTAL UNIT'S SHARE OF ASSESSMENT IMPROVEMENT COSTS. An account sometimes used in a Special Assessment Fund to designate the amount receivable from the governmental unit as its share of the cost of a special assessment improvement project. Usually shortened to GOVERNMENTAL UNIT'S SHARE OF COST.

GRANT. A contribution by one governmental unit to another unit. The contribution is usually made to aid in the support of a specified function (for example, education), but it is sometimes also for general purposes.

GRANTS-IN-AID. See GRANT.

GROSS BONDED DEBT. The total amount of direct debt of a governmental unit represented by outstanding bonds before deduction of any assets available and earmarked for their retirement. See also DIRECT DEBT.

GROSS REVENUE. See REVENUE.

IMPREST SYSTEM. A system for handling minor disbursements whereby a fixed amount of money, designated as petty cash, is set aside for this purpose. Disbursements are made from time to time as needed, a receipt or petty cash voucher being completed in each case. At certain intervals, or when the petty cash is completely expended, a report with substantiating petty cash vouchers is prepared and the petty cash fund is replenished for the amount of disbursements by a check drawn on the appropriate fund bank account. The total of petty cash on hand plus the amount of signed receipts or petty cash vouchers at any one time must equal the total amount of petty cash authorized. See also PETTY CASH.

IMPROVEMENTS. Buildings, other structures, and other attachments or annexations to land which are intended to remain so attached or annexed, such as sidewalks, trees, drives, tunnels, drains, and sewers.

Note. Sidewalks, curbing, sewers, and highways are sometimes referred to as "betterments," but the term "improvements" is to be preferred.

IMPROVEMENTS OTHER THAN BUILDINGS. A fixed asset account which reflects the acquisition value of permanent improvements, other than buildings, which add value to land. Examples of such improvements are fences, retaining walls, sidewalks, pavements, gutters, tunnels, and bridges. If the improvements are purchased or constructed, this account contains the purchase or contract price. If improvements are obtained by gift, it reflects the appraised value at time of acquisition.

INCOME. A term used in accounting for governmental enterprises to represent the excess of revenues earned over the expenses incurred in carrying on the enterprise's operations. It should not be used without an appropriate modifier, such as OPERATING, NONOPERATING, or NET. See also OPERATING INCOME, NONOPERATING INCOME, and NET INCOME.

Note. The term INCOME should not be used in lieu of REVENUE (q.v.) in nonenterprise funds.

INCOME BONDS. See REVENUE BONDS.

INDENTURE. See BOND INDENTURE.

INDETERMINATE APPROPRIATION. An appropriation which is not limited either to any definite period of time or to any definite amount, or to both time and amount.

Note. A distinction must be made between an indeterminate appropriation and a continuing appropriation. In the first place, whereas a continuing appropriation is indefinite only as to time, an indeterminate appropriation is indefinite as to both time and amount. In the second place, even indeterminate appropriations which are indefinite only as to time are to be distinguished from continuing appropriations in that such indeterminate appropriations may eventually lapse. For example, an appropriation to construct a building may be made to continue in effect until the building is constructed. Once the building is completed, however, the unexpended balance of the appropriation lapses. A continuing appropriation, on the other hand, may continue forever; it can only be abolished by specific action of the legislative body.

INDIRECT CHARGES. See OVERHEAD.

INDUSTRIAL AID BONDS. Bonds issued by governmental units, the proceeds of which are used to construct plant facilities for private industrial concerns. Lease payments made by the industrial concern to the governmental unit are used to service the bonds. Such bonds may be in the form of general obligation bonds (q.v.) or combination bonds (q.v.) or revenue bonds (q.v.).

INTEREST AND PENALTIES RECEIVABLE ON TAXES. The uncollected portion of interest and penalties receivable on taxes.

INTEREST RECEIVABLE ON INVESTMENTS. The amount of interest receivable on investments, exclusive of interest purchased. Interest purchased should be shown in a separate account.

INTEREST RECEIVABLE—SPECIAL ASSESSMENTS. The amount of interest receivable on unpaid installments of special assessments.

INTERFUND ACCOUNTS. Accounts in which transactions between funds are reflected. See INTERFUND TRANSFERS.

INTERFUND LOANS. Loans made by one fund to another.

INTERFUND TRANSFERS. Amounts transferred from one fund to another.

INTERGOVERNMENTAL REVENUE. Revenue received from other governments in the form of grants, shared revenues, or payments in lieu of taxes.

INTERIM BORROWING. (1) Short-term loans to be repaid from general revenues during the course of a fiscal year. (2) Short-term loans in anticipation of tax collections or bond issuance. See BOND ANTICIPATION NOTES and TAX ANTICIPATION NOTES.

INTERIM STATEMENT. A financial statement prepared before the end of the current fiscal year and covering only financial transactions during the current year to date. See also STATEMENT.

INTERNAL CONTROL. A plan of organization under which employees' duties are so arranged and records and procedures so designed as to make it possible to exercise effective accounting control over assets, liabilities, revenues, and expenditures. Under such a system, the work of employees is subdivided so that no single employee performs a complete cycle of operations. Thus, for example, an employee handling cash would not post the accounts receivable records. Moreover, under such a system, the procedures to be followed are definitely laid down and require proper authorizations by designated officials for all actions to be taken.

INTRAGOVERNMENTAL SERVICE FUND. A fund established to finance and account for services and commodities furnished by a designated department or agency to other departments and agencies within a single governmental unit. Amounts expended by the fund are restored thereto either from operating earnings or by transfers from other funds, so that the original fund capital is kept intact. Formerly called a Working Capital Fund.

INVENTORY. A detailed list showing quantities, descriptions, and values of property and frequently also units of measure and unit prices.

INVENTORY OF SUPPLIES. The cost value of supplies on hand.

INVESTIGATION. A special examination of books and records.

Note. The proper use of the word "investigation" in accountancy implies some particular object to be gained or particular result to be stated. It indicates something different from an audit and seldom requires qualification by the addition of "special" or any similar adjective.

INVESTMENT IN GENERAL FIXED ASSETS. An account in the general fixed assets group of accounts which represents the governmental unit's equity in general fixed assets (q.v.). The balance of this account is subdivided according to the source of funds which financed the asset acquisition, such as general fund revenues, special assessments, etc.

INVESTMENTS. Securities and real estate held for the production of income in the form of interest, dividends, rentals, or lease payments. The term does not include fixed assets used in governmental operations.

JOB ACCOUNT. An account pertaining either to an operation which occurs regularly (a "standing order") or to a specific piece of work (a "job order"), showing all charges for material and labor used and other expenses incurred, together with any allowances or other credits.

JOURNAL. Any book of original entry (q.v.). See also REGISTER.

JOURNAL VOUCHER. A voucher (q.v.) provided for the recording of certain transactions or information in place of or supplementary to the journals or registers. The journal voucher usually contains an entry or entries, explanations, references to documentary evidence supporting the entry or entries, and the signature or initials of one or more properly authorized officials. The collection of journal vouchers constitutes a journal.

JUDGMENT. An amount to be paid or collected by a governmental unit as the result of a court decision, including a condemnation award in payment for private property taken for public use.

JUDGMENT BONDS. Bonds issued to fund judgments (q.v.). See also FUNDING.

JUDGMENTS PAYABLE. Amounts due to be paid by a governmental unit as the result of court decisions, including condemnation awards in payment for private property taken for public use.

LAND. A fixed asset account which reflects the value of land owned by a governmental unit. If land is purchased, this account shows the purchase price and costs such as legal fees, filling and excavation costs, and the like, which are incurred to put the land in condition for its intended use. If land is acquired by gift, the account reflects its appraised value at time of acquisition.

LAPSE. (Verb) As applied to appropriations, this term denotes the automatic termination of an appropriation.

Note. Except for indeterminate appropriations (q.v.) and continuing appropriations (q.v.), an appropriation is made for a certain period of time. At the end of this period, any unexpended or unencumbered balance thereof lapses, unless otherwise provided by law.

LEASEHOLD. The right to the use of real estate by virtue of a lease, usually for a specified term of years, for which a consideration is paid.

LEDGER. A group of accounts in which are recorded the financial transactions of a governmental unit or other organization. A ledger is a summary of transactions according to the accounts affected.

LEGAL DEBT LIMIT. See DEBT LIMIT.

LEGAL INVESTMENTS. (1) Investments which savings banks, insurance companies, trustees, and other fiduciaries (individual or corporate) are permitted to make by the laws of the state in which they are domiciled, or under the jurisdiction of which they operate or serve. The investments which meet the conditions imposed by law constitute the legal investment list. (2) Investments which governmental units are permitted to make by law.

LEGAL OPINION. (1) The opinion of an official authorized to render it, such as an attorney general or city attorney, as to legality. (2) In the case of municipal bonds, the opinion of a specialized bond attorney as to the legality of a bond issue.

LEVY. (Verb) To impose taxes, special assessments, or service charges for the support of governmental activities. (Noun) The total amount of taxes, special assessments, or service charges imposed by a governmental unit.

LIABILITIES. Debt or other legal obligations arising out of transactions in the past which must be liquidated, renewed, or refunded at some future date.

Note. The term does not include encumbrances (q.v.).

LOAN FUND. A fund whose principal and/or interest is loaned to individuals in accordance with the legal requirements and agreements setting up the fund. Such a fund is accounted for as a trust fund. See also TRUST FUND.

LOANS RECEIVABLE. Amounts which have been loaned to persons or organizations, including notes taken as security for such loans. The account is usually found only in the Trust and Agency Funds balance sheet.

LOCAL IMPROVEMENT FUND. See SPECIAL ASSESSMENT FUND.

LOCAL IMPROVEMENT TAX. See SPECIAL ASSESSMENT.

LONG-TERM BUDGET. A budget prepared for a period longer than a fiscal year, or in the case of some state governments, a budget prepared for a period longer than a biennium. If the long-term budget is restricted to capital expenditures, it is called a CAPITAL PROGRAM (q.v.) or a CAPITAL IMPROVEMENT PROGRAM.

LONG-TERM DEBT. Debt with a maturity of more than one year after the date of issuance.

LUMP-SUM APPROPRIATION. An appropriation made for a stated purpose, or for a named department, without specifying further the amounts that may be spent for specific activities or for particular objects of expenditure. An example of such an appropriation would be one for the police department which does not specify the amounts to be spent for uniform patrol, traffic control, etc. or for salaries and wages, materials and supplies, travel, etc.

MACHINERY AND EQUIPMENT. See EQUIPMENT.

MATURED BONDS PAYABLE. Bonds which have reached or passed their maturity date but which remain unpaid.

MATURED INTEREST PAYABLE. Interest on bonds which has reached the maturity date but which remains unpaid.

MAINTENANCE. The upkeep of physical properties in condition for use or occupancy. Examples are the inspection of equipment to detect defects and the making of repairs.

MODIFIED ACCRUAL BASIS. A system under which some accruals, usually costs, are recorded but others, usually revenues, are not. The extent of modification varies in practice, depending upon the accountant's judgment.

MODIFIED CASH BASIS. Same as MODIFIED ACCRUAL BASIS.

MORTGAGE BONDS. Bonds secured by a mortgage against specified properties of a governmental unit, usually its public utilities or other enterprises. If primarily payable from enterprise revenues, they are also classed as revenue bonds. See also REVENUE BONDS.

MUNICIPAL. In its broadest sense, an adjective which denotes the state and all subordinate units of government. In a more restricted sense, an adjective which denotes a city or town as opposed to other units of local government.

MUNICIPAL BOND. A bond (q.v.) issued by a state or local governmental unit.

MUNICIPAL CORPORATION. A body politic and corporate established pursuant to state authorization for the purpose of providing governmental services and regulations for its inhabitants. A municipal corporation has defined boundaries and a population, and is usually organized with the consent of its residents. It usually has a seal and may sue and be sued.

Cities and towns are examples of municipal corporations. See also QUASI-MUNICIPAL CORPORATIONS.

MUNICIPAL IMPROVEMENT CERTIFICATES. Certificates issued in lieu of bonds for the financing of special improvements.

Note. As a rule, these certificates are placed in the contractor's hands for collection from the special assessment payers.

NET BONDED DEBT. Gross bonded debt (q.v.) less any cash or other assets available and earmarked for its retirement.

NET INCOME. A term used in accounting for governmental enterprises to designate the excess of total revenues (q.v.) over total expenses (q.v.) for an accounting period. See also INCOME, OPERATING REVENUE, OPERATING EXPENSES, NONOPERATING INCOME, and NONOPERATING EXPENSES.

NET PROFIT. See NET INCOME.

NET REVENUE. See NET INCOME.

NET REVENUE AVAILABLE FOR DEBT SERVICE. Gross operating revenues of an enterprise less operating and maintenance expenses but exclusive of depreciation and bond interest. "Net Revenue" as thus defined is used to compute "coverage" on revenue bond issues.

Note. Under the laws of some states and the provisions of some revenue bond indentures, net revenues used for computation of coverage are required to be on a cash basis rather than an accrual basis.

NOMINAL INTEREST RATE. The contractual interest rate shown on the face and in the body of a bond and representing the amount of interest to be paid, in contrast to the effective interest rate (q.v.). See also COUPON RATE.

NONEXPENDABLE FUND. A fund the principal and sometimes also the earnings of which may not be expended. See also ENDOWMENT FUND.

NONEXPENDITURE DISBURSEMENTS. Disbursements which are not chargeable as expenditures; for example, a disbursement made for the purpose of paying off an account payable previously recorded on the books.

NONOPERATING EXPENSES. Expenses (q.v.) incurred for nonoperating properties or in the performance of activities not directly related to supplying the basic service by a governmental enterprise. An example of a nonoperating expense is interest paid on outstanding revenue bonds. See also NONOPERATING PROPERTIES.

NONOPERATING INCOME. Income of governmental enterprises which is not derived from the basic operations of such enterprises. An example is interest on investments or on bank time deposits.

NONOPERATING PROPERTIES. Properties which are owned by a governmental enterprise but which are not used in the provision of basic services for which the enterprise exists.

NONREVENUE RECEIPTS. Collections other than revenue (q.v.), such as receipts from loans where the liability is recorded in the fund in which the proceeds are placed, and receipts on account of recoverable expenditures. See also REVENUE RECEIPTS.

NOTES PAYABLE. In general, an unconditional written promise signed by the maker to pay a certain sum in money on demand or at a fixed or determinable time either to the bearer or to the order of a person designated therein. See also TEMPORARY LOANS.

NOTES RECEIVABLE. A note payable held by a governmental unit.

OBJECT. As used in expenditure classification, this term applies to the article purchased or the service obtained (as distinguished from the results obtained from expenditures). Examples are personal services, contractual services, materials, and supplies. See also ACTIVITY, CHARACTER, FUNCTION, and OBJECT CLASSIFICATION.

OBJECT CLASSIFICATION. A grouping of expenditures on the basis of goods or services purchased; for example, personal services, materials, supplies, and equipment. See also FUNCTIONAL, ACTIVITY, and CHARACTER CLASSIFICATIONS.

OBJECTS OF EXPENDITURE. See OBJECT.

OBLIGATIONS. Amounts which a governmental unit may be required legally to meet out of its resources. They include not only actual liabilities, but also unliquidated encumbrances.

OBSOLESCENCE. The decrease in the value of fixed assets resulting from economic, social, technological, or legal changes.

OPERATING BUDGET. A budget which applies to all outlays other than capital outlays. See BUDGET.

OPERATING EXPENSES. (1) As used in the accounts of governmental enterprises, the term means those costs which are necessary to the maintenance of the enterprise, the rendering of services, the sale of merchandise, the production and disposition of commodities produced, and the collection of enterprise revenues. (2) The term is also sometimes used to describe expenses for general governmental purposes.

OPERATING INCOME. Income of a governmental enterprise which is derived from the sale of its goods and/or services. For example, income from the sale of water by a municipal water utility is operating income. See also OPERATING REVENUES.

OPERATING REVENUES. Revenues derived from the operation of governmental enterprises of a business character.

OPERATING STATEMENT. A statement summarizing the financial operations of a governmental unit for an accounting period as contrasted with a balance sheet (q.v.) which shows financial position at a given moment in time.

ORDER. A formal legislative enactment by the governing body of certain local governmental units which has the full force and effect of law. For example, county governing bodies in some states pass "orders" rather than laws or ordinances.

ORDINANCE. A formal legislative enactment by the council or governing body of a municipality. If it is not in conflict with any higher form of law, such as a state statute or constitutional provision, it has the full force and effect of law within the boundaries of the municipality to which it applies.

Note. The difference between an ordinance and a resolution (q.v.) is that the latter requires less legal formality and has a lower legal status. Ordinarily, the statutes or charter will specify or imply those legislative actions which must be by ordinance and those which may be by resolution. Revenue raising measures, such as the imposition of taxes, special assessments and service charges, universally require ordinances.

ORIGINAL COST. The total of assets given and/or liabilities assumed to acquire an asset. In utility accounting, the original cost to the first owner who dedicated the plant to service of the public.*

OUTLAYS. Synonymous with EXPENDITURES. See also CAPITAL OUTLAYS.

OVERDRAFT. (1) The amount by which checks, drafts, or other demands for payment on the treasury or on a bank exceed the amount of the credit against which they are drawn. (2) The amount by which requisitions, purchase orders, or audited vouchers exceed the appropriation or other credit to which they are chargeable.

OVERHEAD. Those elements of cost necessary in the production of an article or the performance of a service which are of such a nature that the amount applicable to the product or service cannot be determined accurately or readily. Usually they relate to those objects of expenditures which do not become an integral part of the finished product or service, such as rent, heat, light, supplies, management, supervision, etc.

OVERLAPPING DEBT. The proportionate share of the debts of local governmental units located wholly or in part within the limits of the reporting government which must be borne by property within each governmental unit.

Note. Except for special assessment debt, the amount of debt of each unit applicable to the reporting unit is arrived at by (1) determining what percentage of the total assessed value of the overlapping jurisdiction lies within the limits of the reporting unit, and (2) applying this percentage to the total debt of the overlapping jurisdiction. Special assessment debt is allocated on the basis of the ratio of assessments receivable in each jurisdiction which will be used wholly or in part to pay off the debt to total assessments receivable which will be used wholly or in part for this purpose.

PAY-AS-YOU-GO BASIS. A term used to describe the financial policy of a governmental unit which finances all of its capital outlays from current revenues rather than by borrowing. A governmental unit which pays for some improvements from current revenues and others by borrowing is said to be on a partial or modified pay-as-you-go basis.

PAY-IN WARRANT. See DEPOSIT WARRANT.

PENSION FUND. See RETIREMENT FUND.

PERFORMANCE BUDGET. A budget wherein expenditures are based primarily upon measurable performance of activities and work programs. A performance budget may also incorporate other bases of expenditure classification, such as character and object, but these are given a subordinate status to activity performance.

PERPETUAL INVENTORY. A system whereby the inventory of units of property at any date may be obtained directly from the records without resorting to an actual physical count. A record is provided for each item or group of items to be inventoried and is so divided as to provide a running record of goods ordered, received, and withdrawn, and the balance on hand, in units and frequently also in value.

PETTY CASH. A sum of money set aside for the purpose of making change or paying small obligations for which the issuance of a formal vouncher and check would be too expensive and time-consuming. Sometimes called a petty cash fund, with the term "fund" here being used in the commercial sense of earmarked liquid assets. See also IMPREST SYSTEM.

PETTY CASH VOUCHER. A voucher used to record individual disbursements of petty cash. See IMPREST SYSTEM.

POLL TAX. A head tax of a fixed amount, usually upon males and usually within a given range of ages.*

POSTAUDIT. An audit made after the transactions to be audited have taken place and have been recorded or have been approved for recording by designated officials if such approval is required. See also PREAUDIT.

POSTING. The act of transferring to an account in a ledger the data, either detailed or summarized, contained in a book or document of original entry.

PREAUDIT. An examination for the purpose of determining the propriety of proposed financial transactions and financial transactions which have already taken place but which have not yet been recorded; or, if such approval is required, before the approval of the financial transactions by designated officials for recording.

PREPAID EXPENSES. Expenses entered in the accounts for benefits not yet received. Prepaid expenses differ from deferred charges in that they are spread over a shorter period of time than deferred charges and are regularly recurring costs of operations. Examples of prepaid expenses are prepaid rent, prepaid interest, and premiums on unexpired insurance. An example of a deferred charge is unamortized discounts on bonds sold.

PREPAYMENT OF TAXES. The deposit of money with a governmental unit on condition that the amount deposited is to be applied against the tax liability of a designated taxpayer after the taxes have been levied and such liability has been established. See also TAXES COLLECTED IN ADVANCE.

PRIOR YEARS' TAX LEVIES. Taxes levied for fiscal periods preceding the current one.

PRIVATE TRUST FUND. A trust fund (q.v.) which will ordinarily revert to private individuals or will be used for private purposes; for example, a fund which consists of guarantee deposits.

PRO FORMA. For form's sake; an indication of form; an example. The term is used in conjunction with a noun to denote merely a sample form, document, statement, certificate, or presentation, the contents of which may be either wholly or partially hypothetical, actual facts, estimates, or proposals.

PROGRAM BUDGET. A budget wherein expenditures are based primarily on programs of work and secondarily on character and object. A program budget is a transitional type of budget between the traditional character and object budget, on the one hand, and the performance budget, on the other. See also PERFORMANCE BUDGET and TRADITIONAL BUDGET.

PROJECT. A plan of work, job, assignment, or task. Also used to refer to a job or task.

PROPRIETARY ACCOUNTS. Those accounts which show actual financial position and operations, such as actual assets, liabilities, reserves, fund balances, revenues, and expenditures, as distinguished from budgetary accounts (q.v.).

PUBLIC AUTHORITY. See AUTHORITY.

PUBLIC CORPORATION. See MUNICIPAL CORPORATION and QUASI-MUNICIPAL CORPORATION.

PUBLIC IMPROVEMENT FUND. See SPECIAL ASSESSMENT FUND.

PUBLIC TRUST FUND. A trust fund (q.v.) whose principal, earnings, or both, must be used for a public purpose; for example, a pension or retirement fund.

PURCHASE ORDER. A document which authorizes the delivery of specified merchandise or the rendering of certain services and the making of a charge for them.

QUASI-MUNICIPAL CORPORATION. An agency established by the state primarily for the purpose of helping the state to carry out its functions; for example, a county or school district.

Note. Some counties and other agencies ordinarily classified as quasi-municipal corporations have been granted the powers of municipal corporations by the state in which they are located. See also MUNICIPAL CORPORATIONS.

RATE BASE. The value of utility property used in computing an authorized rate of return as authorized by law or a regulatory commission.

REALIZE. To convert goods or services into cash or receivables. Also to exchange for property which is a current asset or can be converted immediately into a current asset. Sometimes applied to conversion of noncash assets into cash.*

REBATES. Abatements (q.v.) or refunds (q.v.).

RECEIPTS. This term, unless otherwise qualified, means cash received. See also REVENUE.

RECOVERABLE EXPENDITURE. An expenditure made for or on behalf of another governmental unit, fund, or department, or for a private individual, firm, or corporation, which will subsequently be recovered in cash or its equivalent.

REFUND. (Noun) An amount paid back or credit allowed because of an overcollection or on account of the return of an object sold. (Verb) To pay back or allow credit for an amount because of an overcollection or because of the return of an object sold. (Verb) To provide for the payment of a loan through cash or credit secured by a new loan.

REFUNDING BONDS. Bonds issued to retire bonds already outstanding. The refunding bonds may be sold for cash and outstanding bonds redeemed in cash, or the refunding bonds may be exchanged with holders of outstanding bonds.

REGISTER. A record for the consecutive entry of a certain class of events, documents, or transactions, with a proper notation of all the required particulars.

Note. The form of register for accounting purposes varies from a one-column to a multicolumnar sheet of special design whereon the entries are distributed, summarized, and aggregated for convenient posting to the accounts.

REGISTERED BOND. A bond the owner of which is registered with the issuing governmental unit, and which cannot be sold or exchanged without a change of registration. Such a bond may be registered as to principal and interest or as to principal only.

REGISTERED WARRANT. A warrant which is registered by the paying officer for future payment on account of present lack of funds and which is to be paid in the order of its registration. In some cases, such warrants are registered when issued; in others, when first presented to the paying officer by the holders. See also WARRANT.

REIMBURSEMENT. Cash or other assets received as a repayment of the cost of work or services performed or of other expenditures made for or on behalf of another governmental unit or department or for an individual, firm, or corporation.

RELATED FUNDS. Funds of a similar character which are brought together for administrative or reporting purposes; for example, Trust and Agency Funds.

REPLACEMENT COST. The cost as of a certain date of a property which can render similar service (but need not be of the same structural form) as the property to be replaced. See also REPRODUCTION COST.

REPRODUCTION COST. The cost as of a certain date of reproducing an exactly similar property new in the same place.

Note. Sometimes this term is designated as "reproduction cost new" to distinguish it from "depreciated reproduction cost," which is the reproduction cost of a given property less the estimated amount of accumulated depreciation applicable to it. In the absence of any modifier, however, the term "reproduction cost" is understood to be synonymous with "reproduction cost new." See also REPLACEMENT COST.

REQUISITION. A written demand or request, usually from one department to the purchasing officer or to another department, for specified articles or services.

RESERVE. An account which records a portion of the fund balance which must be segregated for some future use and which is, therefore, not available for further appropriation or expenditure. A Reserve for Inventories equal in amount to the Inventory of Supplies on the balance sheet of a General Fund is an example of such a reserve.

RESERVE FOR ADVANCE TO——FUND. A reserve which represents the segregation of a portion of a fund balance to indicate that assets equal to the amount of the reserve are tied up in a long-term loan to another fund and are, therefore, not available for appropriation.

RESERVE FOR DEPRECIATION. See ALLOWANCE FOR DEPRECIATION.

RESERVE FOR EMPLOYEES' CONTRIBUTIONS. A reserve in a trust fund for a public employee retirement system which represents the amount of accumulated contributions made by employee members plus interest earnings credited in accordance with applicable legal provisions.

RESERVE FOR EMPLOYER CONTRIBUTIONS. A reserve in a Trust Fund for a public employee retirement system which represents the amount of accumulated contributions paid by the governmental unit as employer plus interest earnings credited in accordance with applicable legal provisions.

RESERVE FOR EMPLOYER CONTRIBUTIONS—ACTUARIAL DEFICIENCY. A reserve in a Trust Fund for a public employee retirement system which represents the amount of the actuarial deficiency in contributions made by a governmental unit as employer.

RESERVE FOR ENCUMBRANCES. A reserve representing the segregation of a portion of a fund balance to provide for unliquidated encumbrances (q.v.). See also RESERVE.

RESERVE FOR INVENTORY OF SUPPLIES. A reserve which represents the segregation of a portion of fund balance to indicate that assets equal to the amount of the reserve are tied up in inventories and are, therefore, not available for appropriation.

RESERVE FOR MEMBERSHIP ANNUITIES. A reserve in a Trust Fund for a public employee retirement system which represents the amount set aside for payment of annuities to retired members. In a joint contributory system this reserve is established at the time of employee retirement by transfers from accumulations in the Reserve for Employees' Contributions and the Reserve for Employer Contributions accounts.

RESERVE FOR REVENUE BOND CONTINGENCY. A reserve in an Enterprise Fund which represents the segregation of a portion of retained earnings equal to current assets that are restricted for meeting various contingencies, as may be specified and defined in the revenue bond indenture.

RESERVE FOR REVENUE BOND DEBT SERVICE. A reserve in an Enterprise Fund which represents the segregation of a portion of retained earnings equal to current assets that are restricted to current servicing of revenue bonds in accordance with the terms of a bond indenture.

RESERVE FOR REVENUE BOND RETIREMENT. A reserve in an Enterprise Fund which represents the segregation of a portion of retained earnings equal to current assets that are restricted for future servicing of revenue bonds in accordance with the terms of a bond indenture.

RESERVE FOR UNCOLLECTED TAXES. A reserve representing the segregation of a portion of a fund balance equal to the amount of taxes receivable by a fund.

RESERVE FOR UNDISTRIBUTED INTEREST EARNINGS. An unallocated reserve in a Trust Fund for a public employee retirement system which represents interest earnings of the system that have not been distributed to other reserves such as the Reserve for Employees' Contributions and the Reserve for Employer Contributions.

RESERVE FOR VARIATIONS IN ACTUARIAL ASSUMPTIONS. An unallocated reserve in a Trust Fund for a public employee retirement system which reflects adjustments to reserves for retirement benefits in force resulting from variations in mortality, turnover, and interest experience.

RESOLUTION. A special or temporary order of a legislative body; an order of a legislative body requiring less legal formality than an ordinance or statute. See also ORDINANCE.

RESOURCES. The actual assets of a governmental unit, such as cash, taxes receivable, land, buildings, etc. plus contingent assets such as estimated revenues applying to the current fiscal year not accrued or collected, and bonds authorized and unissued. See CAPITAL RESOURCES and CURRENT RESOURCES.

RETAINED EARNINGS. The accumulated earnings of an Enterprise or Intragovernmental Service Fund which have been retained in the fund and which are not reserved for any specific purpose.

RETIREMENT ALLOWANCES. Amounts paid to government employees who have retired from active service or to their survivors. See ANNUITY.

RETIREMENT FUND. A fund out of which retirement annuities and/or other benefits are paid to authorized and designated public employees. A retirement fund is accounted for as a Trust Fund (q.v.).

REVENUE. For those revenues which are recorded on the accrual basis (q.v.), this term designates additions to assets which: (*a*) do not increase any liability; (*b*) do not represent the recovery of an expenditure; (*c*) do not represent the cancellation of certain liabilities without a corresponding increase in other liabilities or a decrease in assets; and (*d*) do not represent contributions of fund capital in Enterprise and Intragovernmental Service Funds. The same definition applies to those cases where revenues are recorded on the modified accrual or cash basis, except that additions would be partially or entirely to cash. See also ACCRUAL BASIS, MODIFIED ACCRUAL BASIS, CASH BASIS, NET REVENUE AVAILABLE FOR DEBT SERVICE, and RECEIPTS.

REVENUE BONDS. Bonds whose principal and interest are payable exclusively from earnings of a public enterprise. In addition to a pledge of revenues, such bonds sometimes contain a mortgage on the enterprise's property and are then known as mortgage revenue bonds.

REVENUE RECEIPTS. A term used synonymously with "revenue" (q.v.) by some governmental units which account for their revenues on a cash basis (q.v.). See also NONREVENUE RECEIPTS.

REVENUES COLLECTED IN ADVANCE. A liability account which represents revenues collected before they become due.

REVOLVING FUND. See INTRAGOVERNMENTAL SERVICE FUND.

SCHEDULES. (1) The explanatory or supplementary statements that accompany the balance sheet or other principal statements periodically prepared from the accounts. (2) The accountant's or auditor's principal work papers covering his examination of the books and accounts. (3) A written enumeration or detailed list in orderly form. See also EXHIBIT and STATEMENTS.

SCRIP. An evidence of indebtedness, usually in small denomination, secured or unsecured, interest-bearing or noninterest-bearing, stating that the governmental unit, under conditions set forth, will pay the face value of the certificate or accept it in payment of certain obligations.

SECURITIES. Bonds, notes, mortgages, or other forms of negotiable or nonnegotiable instruments. See also INVESTMENTS.

SELF-SUPPORTING OR SELF-LIQUIDATING DEBT. Debt obligations whose principal and interest are payable solely from the earnings of the enterprise for the construction or improvement of which they were originally issued. See also REVENUE BONDS.

SERIAL ANNUITY BONDS. Serial bonds in which the annual installments of bond principal are so arranged that the combined payments for principal and interest are approximately the same each year.

SERIAL BONDS. Bonds the principal of which is repaid in periodic installments over the life of the issue. See SERIAL ANNUITY BONDS and DEFERRED SERIAL BONDS.

SHARED REVENUE. Revenue which is levied by one governmental unit but shared, usually in proportion to the amount collected, with another unit of government or class of governments.

SHARED TAX. See SHARED REVENUE.

SHORT-TERM DEBT. Debt with a maturity of one year or less after the date of issuance. Short-term debt usually includes floating debt, bond anticipation notes, tax anticipation notes, and interim warrants.

SINKING FUND. See DEBT SERVICE FUND.

SINKING FUND BONDS. Bonds issued under an agreement which requires the governmental unit to set aside periodically out of its revenues a sum which, with compound earnings thereon, will be sufficient to redeem the bonds at their stated date of maturity. Sinking Fund bonds are usually also term bonds (q.v.).

SPECIAL ASSESSMENT. A compulsory levy made by a local government against certain properties to defray part or all of the cost of a specific improvement or service which is presumed to be of general benefit to the public and of special benefit to such properties.

Note. The term should not be used without a modifier (for example, "special assessments for street paving," or "special assessments for street sprinkling") unless the intention is to have it cover both improvements and services or unless the particular use is apparent from the context.

SPECIAL ASSESSMENT BONDS. Bonds payable from the proceeds of special assessments (q.v.). If the bonds are payable only from the collections of special assessments, they are known as "special-special assessment bonds." If, in addition to the assessments, the full faith and credit of the governmental unit are pledged, they are known as "general obligation special assessment bonds."

SPECIAL ASSESSMENT FUND. A fund set up to finance and account for the construction of improvements or provision of services which are to be paid for, wholly or in part, from special assessments levied against benefited property. See also SPECIAL ASSESSMENT and SPECIAL ASSESSMENT BONDS.

SPECIAL ASSESSMENT LIENS RECEIVABLE. Claims which a governmental unit has upon properties until special assessments (q.v.) levied against them have been paid. The term normally applies to those delinquent special assessments for the collection of which legal action has been taken through the filing of claims.

SPECIAL ASSESSMENT ROLL. The official list showing the amount of special assessments (q.v.) levied against each property presumed to be benefited by an improvement or service.

SPECIAL AUDIT. An audit which is limited to some particular phase of a governmental unit's activity, such as the examination of a Capital Projects Fund, or an audit which covers all of the governmental unit's activities for a shorter or longer period of time than the usual accounting period of one fiscal year. Such audits may involve some detailed verifications as determined by the professional judgment of the auditor, but usually they are based on appropriate tests and checks. See GENERAL AUDIT.

SPECIAL DISTRICT. An independent unit of local government organized to perform a single governmental function or a restricted number of related functions. Special districts usually have the power to incur debt and levy taxes; however, certain types of special districts are entirely dependent upon enterprise earnings and cannot impose taxes. Examples of special districts are water districts, drainage districts, flood control districts, hospital districts, fire protection districts, transit authorities, port authorities, and electric power authorities.

SPECIAL DISTRICT BONDS. Bonds issued by a special district. See SPECIAL DISTRICT.

SPECIAL FUND. Any fund which must be devoted to some special use in accordance with specific regulations and restrictions. Generally, the term applies to all funds other than the General Fund (q.v.).

SPECIAL REVENUE FUND. A fund used to account for revenues from specific taxes or other earmarked revenue sources which by law are designated to finance particular functions or activities of government. After the fund is established, it usually continues year after year until discontinued or revised by proper legislative authority. An example is a motor fuel tax fund used to finance highway and road construction.

SPECIAL-SPECIAL ASSESSMENT BONDS. See SPECIAL ASSESSMENT BONDS.

STANDARD COST. The predetermined cost of performing an operation or producing a product when labor, materials, and equipment are utilized efficiently under reasonable and normal conditions.

Note. Normal conditions exist when there is an absence of special or extraordinary factors affecting the quality or quantity of the work performed, or the time or method of performing it.

STATE-COLLECTED LOCALLY SHARED TAX. Tax collected by state, distributed in part to local governments.*

TAX NOTES. See TAX ANTICIPATION NOTES.

TAX RATE. The amount of tax stated in terms of a unit of the tax base; for example, 25 mills per dollar of assessed valuation of taxable property.

TAX RATE LIMIT. The maximum rate at which a governmental unit may levy a tax. The limit may apply to taxes raised for a particular purpose, or to taxes imposed for all purposes; and may apply to a single government, to a class of governments, or to all governmental units operating in a particular area. Overall tax rate limits usually restrict levies for all purposes and of all governments, state and local, having jurisdiction in a given area.

TAX ROLL. The official list showing the amount of taxes levied against each taxpayer or property. Frequently, the tax roll and the assessment roll (q.v.) are combined, but even in these cases the two can be distinguished.

TAX SALE CERTIFICATE. See TAX CERTIFICATE.

TAX SUPPLEMENT. A tax levied by a local unit of government which has the same base as a similar tax levied by a higher level of government, such as a state or province. The local tax supplement is frequently administered by the higher level of government along with its own tax. A locally imposed, state-administered sales tax is an example of a tax supplement.

TAX TITLE NOTES. Obligations secured by pledges of the governmental unit's interest in certain tax liens or tax titles.

TAXES. Compulsory charges levied by a governmental unit for the purpose of financing services performed for the common benefit.

Note. The term does not include specific charges made against particular persons or property for current or permanent benefits such as special assessments. Neither does the term include charges for services rendered only to those paying such charges as, for example, sewer service charges.

TAXES COLLECTED IN ADVANCE. A liability for taxes collected before the tax levy has been made or before the amount of taxpayer liability has been established.

TAXES LEVIED FOR OTHER GOVERNMENTAL UNITS. Taxes levied by the reporting governmental unit for other governmental units, which, when collected, are to be paid over to these units.

TAXES PAID IN ADVANCE. Same as TAXES COLLECTED IN ADVANCE. Also called PREPAID TAXES.

TAXES RECEIVABLE—CURRENT. The uncollected portion of taxes which a governmental unit has levied, which has become due but on which no penalty for nonpayment attaches.

TAXES RECEIVABLE—DELINQUENT. Taxes remaining unpaid on and after the date on which a penalty for nonpayment is attached. Even though the penalty may be subsequently waived and a portion of the taxes may be abated or canceled, the unpaid balances continue to be delinquent taxes until paid, abated, canceled, or converted into tax liens.

TEMPORARY LOANS. Short-term obligations representing amounts borrowed for short periods of time and usually evidenced by notes payable (q.v.) or warrants payable (q.v.). They may be unsecured, or secured by specific revenues to be collected. See also TAX ANTICIPATION NOTES.

TERM BONDS. Bonds the entire principal of which matures on one date. Also called sinking fund bonds (q.v.).

TERM BONDS PAYABLE. A liability account which records the face value of general obligation term bonds issued and outstanding.

TIME WARRANT. A negotiable obligation of a governmental unit having a term shorter than bonds, and frequently tendered to individuals and firms in exchange for contractual services, capital acquisitions, or equipment purchases.

TIME WARRANTS PAYABLE. The amount of time warrants outstanding and unpaid.

TRADITIONAL BUDGET. A term sometimes applied to the budget of a governmental unit wherein expenditures are based entirely or primarily on objects of expenditure. See also PROGRAM BUDGET and PERFORMANCE BUDGET.

TRANSFER VOUCHER. A voucher (q.v.) authorizing transfers of cash or other resources between funds.

TRIAL BALANCE. A list of the balances of the accounts in a ledger kept by double entry (q.v.), with the debit and credit balances shown in separate columns. If the totals of the debit and credit columns are equal or their net balance agrees with a control account, the ledger from which the figures are taken is said to be "in balance."

TRUST FUND. A fund consisting of resources received and held by the governmental unit as trustee, to be expended or invested in accordance with the conditions of the trust. See also ENDOWMENT FUND, PRIVATE TRUST FUND, and PUBLIC TRUST FUND.

TRUST AND AGENCY FUND. See AGENCY FUND and TRUST FUND.

UNALLOTTED BALANCE OF APPROPRIATION. An appropriation balance available for allotment (q.v.).

UNAMORTIZED DISCOUNTS ON BONDS SOLD. That portion of the excess of the face value of bonds over the amount received from their sale which remains to be written off periodically over the life of the bonds.

UNAMORTIZED DISCOUNTS ON INVESTMENTS (Credit). That portion of the excess of the face value of securities over the amount paid for them which has not yet been written off.

STATEMENTS. (1) Used in a general sense, statements are all of those formal written presentations which set forth financial information. (2) In technical accounting usage, statements are those presentations of financial data which show the financial position and the results of financial operations of a fund, a group of accounts, or an entire governmental unit for a particular accounting period. See also EXHIBIT and SCHEDULE.

STATUTE. A written law enacted by a duly organized and constituted legislative body. See also ORDINANCE, RESOLUTION, and ORDER.

STORES. Goods on hand in storerooms, subject to requisition and use.

STRAIGHT SERIAL BONDS. Serial bonds (q.v.) in which the annual installments of a bond principal are approximately equal.

SUBACTIVITY. A specific line of work performed in carrying out a governmental activity. For example, cleaning luminaires and replacing defective street lamps would be subactivities under the activity of street light maintenance.

SUBFUNCTION. A grouping of related activities within a particular governmental function. For example, "police" is a subfunction of the function "public safety."

SUBSIDIARY ACCOUNT. One of a group of related accounts which support in detail the debit and credit summaries recorded in a control account. An example is the individual property taxpayers' accounts for taxes receivable in the general ledger. See also CONTROL ACCOUNT and SUBSIDIARY LEDGER.

SUBSIDIARY LEDGER. A group of subsidiary accounts (q.v.) the sum of the balances of which is equal to the balance of the related control account. See also CONTROL ACCOUNT and SUBSIDIARY ACCOUNT.

SUBVENTION. A grant (q.v.).

SURETY BOND. A written promise to pay damages or to indemnify against losses caused by the party or parties named in the document, through nonperformance or through defalcation. An example is a surety bond given by a contractor or by an official handling cash or securities.

SURPLUS. See FUND BALANCE, RETAINED EARNINGS, and INVESTMENT IN GENERAL FIXED ASSETS.

SURPLUS RECEIPTS. A term sometimes applied to receipts which increase the balance of a fund but are not a part of its normal revenue; for example, collection of accounts previously written off. Sometimes used as an account title.*

SUSPENSE ACCOUNT. An account which carries charges or credits temporarily, pending the determination of the proper account or accounts to which they are to be posted. See also SUSPENSE FUND.

SUSPENSE FUND. A fund established to account separately for certain receipts pending the distribution or disposal thereof. See also AGENCY FUND.

SYMBOLIZATION. The assignment of letters, numbers, or other marks or characters to the ordinary titles of the ledger accounts. Each letter or number should have the same meaning wherever used and should be selected with great care so that it will indicate immediately and with certainty the title of the account, as well as its place in the classification. The use of proper symbols saves much time and space in making the book record and adds to its precision and accuracy. See also CODING.

SYNDICATE, UNDERWRITING. A group formed for the marketing of a given security issue too large for one member to handle expeditiously, after which the group is dissolved.*

TAX ANTICIPATION NOTES. Notes (sometimes called warrants) issued in anticipation of collection of taxes, usually retirable only from tax collections, and frequently only from the proceeds of the tax levy whose collection they anticipate.

TAX ANTICIPATION WARRANTS. See TAX ANTICIPATION NOTES.

TAX CERTIFICATE. A certificate issued by a governmental unit as evidence of the conditional transfer of title to tax-delinquent property from the original owner to the holder of the certificate. If the owner does not pay the amount of the tax arrearage and other charges required by law during the specified period of redemption, the holder can foreclose to obtain title. Also called "tax sale certificate" and "tax lien certificate" in some jurisdictions. See also TAX DEED.

TAX DEED. A written instrument by which title to property sold for taxes is transferred unconditionally to the purchaser. A tax deed is issued upon foreclosure of the tax lien (q.v.) obtained by the purchaser at the tax sale. The tax lien cannot be foreclosed until the expiration of the period during which the owner may redeem his property through paying the delinquent taxes and other charges. See also TAX CERTIFICATE.

TAX LEVY ORDINANCE. An ordinance (q.v.) by means of which taxes are levied.

TAX LIENS. Claims which governmental units have upon properties until taxes levied against them have been paid.

Note. The term is sometimes limited to those delinquent taxes for the collection of which legal action has been taken through the filing of liens.

TAX LIENS RECEIVABLE. Legal claims against property which have been exercised because of nonpayment of delinquent taxes, interest, and penalties. The account includes delinquent taxes, interest, and penalties receivable up to the date the lien becomes effective, and the cost of holding the sale.

UNAMORTIZED PREMIUMS ON BONDS SOLD. An account in an Enterprise Fund which represents that portion of the excess of bond proceeds over par value and which remains to be amortized over the remaining life of such bonds.

UNAMORTIZED PREMIUMS ON INVESTMENTS. That portion of the excess of the amount paid for securities over their face value which has not yet been amortized.

UNAPPROPRIATED BUDGET SURPLUS. Where the fund balance at the close of the preceding year is not included in the annual budget, this term designates that portion of the current fiscal year's estimated revenues which has not been appropriated. Where the fund balance of the preceding year is included, this term designates the estimated fund balance at the end of the current fiscal period.

UNAUDITED VOUCHERS. Claims which have been received but which have not yet gone through the total vouchering process.

UNBILLED ACCOUNTS RECEIVABLE. An account which designates the estimated amount of accounts receivable for services or commodities sold but not billed. For example, if a utility bills its customers bimonthly but prepares monthly financial statements, the amount of services rendered or commodities sold during the first month of the bimonthly period would be reflected in the balance sheet under this account title.

UNDERWRITING SYNDICATE. See SYNDICATE, UNDERWRITING.*

UNEARNED INCOME. See DEFERRED CREDITS.

UNENCUMBERED ALLOTMENT. That portion of an allotment not yet expended or encumbered.

UNENCUMBERED APPROPRIATION. That portion of an appropriation not yet expended or encumbered.

UNEXPENDED ALLOTMENT. That portion of an allotment which has not been expended.

UNEXPENDED APPROPRIATION. That portion of an appropriation which has not been expended.

UNIT COST. A term used in cost accounting to denote the cost of producing a unit of product or rendering a unit of service; for example, the cost of treating and purifying a thousand gallons of sewage.

UNIT TAX LEDGER. A ledger which records the assessed value and other data on taxable properties. Where the unit tax ledger system is used, there is an individual ledger card for each piece of taxable property; legal provisions permitting, this ledger functions in lieu of a tax roll.

UNLIQUIDATED ENCUMBRANCES. Encumbrances outstanding.

UNREALIZED REVENUE. See ACCRUED REVENUE.

UTILITY FUND. See ENTERPRISE FUND.

VALUE. As used in governmental accounting, this term designates (1) the act of describing anything in terms of money; or (2) the measure of a thing in terms of money. The term should not be used without further qualification. See also Book Value and Face Value.

Voucher. A written document which evidences the propriety of transactions and usually indicates the accounts in which they are to be recorded.

Voucher Check. A document combining a check and a brief description of the transaction covered by the check, the two parts separated by a perforated horizontal line, for separation of the two parts.*

Voucher System. A system which calls for the preparation of vouchers (q.v.) for transactions involving payments and for the recording of such vouchers in a special book of original entry (q.v.), known as a voucher register, in the order in which payment is approved.

Vouchers Payable. Liabilities for goods and services evidenced by vouchers which have been preaudited and approved for payment but which have not been paid.

Warrant. An order drawn by the legislative body or an officer of a governmental unit upon its treasurer, directing the latter to pay a specified amount to the person named or to the bearer. It may be payable upon demand, in which case it usually circulates the same as a bank check; or it may be payable only out of certain revenues when and if received, in which case it does not circulate as freely. See also Registered Warrant and Deposit Warrant.

Warrants Payable. The amount of warrants outstanding and unpaid.

Work in Process. The cost of partially completed products manufactured or processed, such as a partially completed printing job. Sometimes referred to as "work in progress." See also Construction Work in Progress.

Work in Progress. See Construction Work in Progress and Work in Process.

Work Order. A written order authorizing and directing the performance of a certain task and issued to the person who is to direct the work. Among the items of information shown on the order are the nature and location of the job, specifications of the work to be performed, and a job number which is referred to in reporting the amount of labor, materials, and equipment used.

Work Program. A plan of work proposed to be done during a particular period by an administrative agency in carrying out its assigned activities.

Work Unit. A fixed quantity which will consistently measure work effort expended in the performance of an activity or the production of a commodity.

Working Capital Fund. See Intragovernmental Service Fund.

Yield Rate. See Effective Interest Rate.

Appendix 2

Basic Principles Recommended by the National Committee on Governmental Accounting*

Legal Compliance and Financial Operations

1. A governmental accounting system must make it possible: (*a*) to show that all applicable legal provisions have been complied with; and (*b*) to determine fairly and with full disclosure the financial position and results of financial operations of the constituent funds and self-balancing account groups of the governmental unit.

Conflicts between Accounting Principles and Legal Provisions

2. If there is a conflict between legal provisions and generally accepted accounting principles applicable to governmental units, legal provisions must take precedence. Insofar as possible, however, the governmental accounting system should make possible the full disclosure and fair presentation of financial position and operating results in accordance with generally accepted principles of accounting applicable to governmental units.

The Budget and Budgetary Accounting

3. An annual budget should be adopted by every governmental unit, whether required by law or not, and the accounting system should provide budgetary control over general governmental revenues and expenditures.

---

* The principles presented here are quoted from National Committee on Governmental Accounting, *Governmental Accounting, Auditing and Financial Reporting* (Chicago: Municipal Finance Officers Association, 1968), pp. 3–14; a brief explanation of each principle is also presented on those pages.

Fund Accounting

4. Governmental accounting systems should be organized and operated on a fund basis. A fund is defined as an independent fiscal and accounting entity with a self-balancing set of accounts recording cash and/or other resources together with all related liabilities, obligations, reserves, and equities which are segregated for the purpose of carrying on specific activities or attaining certain objectives in accordance with special regulations, restrictions, or limitations.

Types of Funds

5. The following types of funds are recognized and should be used in accounting for governmental financial operations as indicated.

(1) The General Fund to account for all financial transactions not properly accounted for in another fund;

(2) Special Revenue Funds to account for the proceeds of specific revenue sources (other than special assessments) or to finance specified activities as required by law or administrative regulation;

(3) Debt Service Funds to account for the payment of interest and principal on long-term debt other than special assessment and revenue bonds;

(4) Capital Projects Funds to account for the receipt and disbursement of moneys used for the acquisition of capital facilities other than those financed by special assessment and enterprise funds;

(5) Enterprise Funds to account for the financing of services to the general public where all or most of the costs involved are paid in the form of charges by users of such services;

(6) Trust and Agency Funds to account for assets held by a governmental unit as trustee or agent for individuals, private organizations, and other governmental units;

(7) Intragovernmental Service Funds to account for the financing of special activities and services performed by a designated organization unit within a governmental jurisdiction for other organization units within the same governmental jurisdiction;

(8) Special Assessment Funds to account for special assessments levied to finance public improvements or services deemed to benefit the properties against which the assessments are levied.

Number of Funds

6. Every governmental unit should establish and maintain those funds required by law and sound financial administration. Since numerous funds make for inflexibility, undue complexity, and unnecessary expense in both the accounting system and the over-all financial administration, how-

ever, only the minimum number of funds consistent with legal and operating requirements should be established.

Fund Accounts

7. A complete self-balancing group of accounts should be established and maintained for each fund. This group should include all general ledger accounts and subsidiary records necessary to reflect compliance with legal provisions and to set forth the financial position and the results of financial operations of the fund. A clear distinction should be made between the accounts relating to current assets and liabilities and those relating to fixed assets and liabilities. With the exception of Intragovernmental Service Funds, Enterprise Funds, and certain Trust Funds, fixed assets should not be accounted for in the same fund with the current assets, but should be set up in a separate, self-balancing group of accounts called the General Fixed Asset Group of Accounts. Similarly, except in Special Assessment, Enterprise, and certain Trust Funds, long-term liabilities should not be carried with the current liabilities of any fund, but should be set up in a separate, self-balancing group of accounts known as the General Long-term Debt Group of Accounts.

Valuation of Fixed Assets

8. The fixed asset accounts should be maintained on the basis of original cost, or the estimated cost if the original cost is not available, or, in the case of gifts, the appraised value at the time received.

Depreciation

9. Depreciation on general fixed assets should not be recorded in the general accounting records. Depreciation charges on such assets may be computed for unit cost purposes, provided such charges are recorded only in memorandum form and do not appear in the fund accounts.

Basis of Accounting

10. The accrual basis of accounting is recommended for Enterprise, Trust, Capital Projects, Special Assessment, and Intragovernmental Service Funds. For the General, Special Revenue, and Debt Service Funds, the modified accrual basis of accounting is recommended. The modified accrual basis of accounting is defined as that method of accounting in which expenditures other than accrued interest on general long-term debt are recorded at the time liabilities are incurred and revenues are recorded when received in cash, except for material or available revenues which should be accrued to reflect properly the taxes levied and the revenues earned.

Classification of Accounts

11. Governmental revenues should be classified by fund and source. Expenditures should be classified by fund, function, organization unit, activity, character, and principal classes of objects in accordance with standard recognized classification.

Common Terminology and Classification

12. A common terminology and classification should be used consistently throughout the budget, the accounts, and the financial reports.

Financial Reporting

13. Financial statements and reports showing the current condition of budgetary and proprietary accounts should be prepared periodically to control financial operations. At the close of each fiscal year, a comprehensive annual financial report covering all funds and financial operations of the governmental unit should be prepared and published.

Appendix 3

Accounting for Investments

In governmental finance, investments consist of real estate, bonds and other forms of indebtedness, stock, patents, royalties, and possibly other assets. Governmental resources may be converted to these forms of investments for one or the other of the two following reasons:

1. To make profitable use of current revenue cash which would otherwise be idle until needed for financing regular activities of the fund. These are called short-term or temporary investments. Since they must be marketed at a rather definite time, in order to make cash promptly available when needed, they should be well seasoned and subject to practically no market fluctuation. Otherwise, their quick sale may result in a loss. Any kind of fund having temporary excess cash may wisely acquire short-term investments.
2. To produce income on a permanent basis. These are characterized as long-term or permanent investments. They should combine the factors of safety and maximum income. Proclivity to market fluctuations is not particularly objectionable in this class of investments. This is true because any items chosen for sale may be disposed of in a more deliberate manner than if the proceeds are required for current expenditure, and a sizable portion of bond investments may even be held to maturity.

Since short-term investments represent employment of cash not immediately needed for normal purposes, they may conceivably be acquired by any fund of the eight standard types. Long-term investments, on the contrary, are peculiar to trust funds, debt service funds, and enterprise funds, with the greatest amount held by those of the first-named type.

From an accounting standpoint the more difficult problems associated with fund investments are as follows:

1. Measuring and recording periodic income from investments.
2. Measuring and recording gain or loss on sale, or disposal in any other manner, of an investment.

In the next several paragraphs, these problems will be explored, first as they relate to permanent investments and afterwards as they affect temporary investments.

Permanent Investments

Permanent investments should be recorded at cost. This figure should include every outlay required to obtain clear title to the asset. Some of the more common elements of the cost of acquiring investments are purchase price, legal fees attendant upon the acquisition, and taxes and commissions to which the transaction is subject. The difference between par value of an investment and the cost of the investment determines the amount of premium or discount. Acquisition of property by donation is not uncommon for some kinds of trust funds. There being no purchase price to use as a base, at what figure should the gift be recorded? The preferred practice is to record the property at its value based upon competent appraisal or, in the absence of an appraisal, at $1.00. Since the major problems of accounting for investments arise in connection with securities—that is, stocks, bonds, mortgages, etc.—subsequent discussion will be confined to them.

To illustrate some of the procedures recommended for recording acquisition of securities, a few suggested entries are given below:

1. An endowment fund receives as a gift 500 shares of no-par-value stock of the Rex Manufacturing Company, currently quoted at $61.20 per share. The entry in the endowment fund would be as follows:

Investments	30,600	
Endowment Fund Balance		30,600

2. Noninterest-bearing United States treasury bills with a maturity value of $20,000 are bought as a short-term investment at a discount of 2⅜ percent.

Investments	19,525	
Cash		19,525

$20,000 × (100% − 2⅜%) = $20,000 × 97⅝%

3. Twenty-five bonds, par value $1,000 each, of Pacific City, were purchased at 96¼, with exchange fees and broker's commissions amounting to $105. The endowment fund entry would be as follows:

Investments	24,167.50	
Cash		24,167.50

The cost of the 25 bonds was calculated by multiplying $25,000 by 96¼ percent, which gave a product of $24,062.50, and then adding the $105 cost of acquisition. If, instead of being acquired at a net discount (amount below par value) of $832.50, the bonds had cost a total premium (amount above par value) of that figure, the Investments account would have been debited for $25,832.50.[1]

Except for perpetual bonds, which for practical purposes are nonexistent in the United States, all bonds, mortgages, notes, etc., (but not stock) have a maturity date, at which time holders of the bonds will receive the par value of their holdings. That is to say, as bonds approach the maturity date, whatever their values may have been or may now be, they approach par value. Thus, if the trust fund acquiring $25,000 par value of bonds for $24,167.50 holds them until maturity, it will gain $832.50. What is the proper distribution of this gain? Should it be recorded in the period in which the bonds were purchased or in the period in which they mature?

Had the discount been of small amount, either of the two periods, preferably the latter, could receive the credit without material distortion of results. However, if the amount is sizable, the preferred practice is to distribute it over the time the bonds are held. This method is preferred because it gives some part of the credit to each period and avoids distortion of income in any one period. The process of distributing total discount or premium over a number of periods is referred to as "amortization," although, as applied to discount, it is sometimes erroneously described as "accumulation," because reducing the discount builds up or accumulates the book value of the bond. If the bonds were acquired at a discount, the periodic amortization of discount is regarded as an addition to income for the period. It is not received in cash during the period but is represented by an increase in book value of the investment, subsequently to be realized in cash. Periodic amortization of premium is construed as a reduction of income, since it represents a decline in the investment's book value as compared with its purchase price. "Book" or "Carrying" value is cost plus discount amortized to date, or minus premium amortized to date.

The two most common methods of amortizing premium and discount are the straight-line and the scientific methods. The former consists of allocating to each period during which the investment is owned an equal amount of premium or discount. Thus, if the Pacific City bonds were purchased at a discount of $832.50, 10 periods before their maturity date, the straight-line method would credit $83.25 of the discount amortization to each of the 10 periods. Use of the scientific method, on the other hand, results in amortization at a regularly increasing amount, the first period receiving the smallest amount of credit, with the largest amount in the last period. Likewise, use of the straight-line method for amortizing

[1] An alternative method for recording cost of bonds is to record par value in one account, with premium and discount in separate accounts.

premium gives equal distribution of amounts. However, amortizing premium by the scientific method results in gradation of amounts, the first period being charged with the least, the last one with the most. The reason for the contrast in results from using the scientific method for discount and premium will be explained later.

Before embarking upon a detailed exposition of premium or discount amortization, a consideration of some general rules appears to be in order:

1. If investments having a designated maturity date are acquired as part of the original corpus of the trust, the general rule of law would not allow premium or discount amortization as adjustments of income. Gain or loss on disposal of such investments, by the same rule, is an adjustment of principal.
2. Circumstances may exist which minimize the importance of exact measurement of income in an accounting sense. Relatively small amounts of premium or discount on investments and absence of conflicting interests among beneficiaries are illustrations of such circumstances.
3. Because of probable changes in amounts of investments owned by long-term or large trusts, a *rate* of return is a more reliable *and* convenient criterion for judging efficiency of their management than is an *amount* of return. Use of the scientific method of amortization (as compared with straight-line) tends to produce a more uniform rate from period to period. This facilitates and fortifies comparisons.

Discussion of amortization in the next few pages will be predicated upon the assumption that it is a function of income determination. No elaboration of the opposite situation is necessary. Under the latter concept, premium and discount transactions are regarded as adjustments of principal and affect the accounts only at the time of acquisition and disposal of the related investments.

Explanation of Straight-Line Amortization

Amortization of discount on bond investments over the life of the bonds has a twofold effect, as follows:

1. It adds periodically to the value of the investment as shown by the books, that is, "book value" or "carrying value." Current market value at any given time may be materially different from the book value. Ordinarily, this is of no importance to the trust fund which owns the bond, since the investment is a long-term commitment of earning power.
2. The increase in book value allotted to each period is an addition to the income on the investment for that period. Thus, if the nominal rate of interest on Pacific City bonds is 4 percent per annum, payable seminannually, the nominal interest per period is 2 percent times $25,000, or $500. The nominal rate of interest is the rate named in the bond, which the issuing city covenants to pay on the par value of each bond. The effective interest on bonds acquired at a discount is the sum of the nominal interest plus the increase in the carrying value of the investment.

If bonds are acquired at a premium, their carrying value declines period by period. The effective interest on such bonds, therefore, is the remainder of nominal interest minus premium amortization.

From the foregoing statements, it is evident that the real earning on bonds bought at a discount or a premium is effective interest. Calculation of periodic effective income on a straight-line basis on $25,000 of par value bonds, nominal rate of interest 4 percent per annum, payable semiannually, may be illustrated as follows:

1. If purchased at a discount of $832.50, five years before maturity:

$$(\$25{,}000 \times 2\%) + \frac{\$832.50}{10} = \$583.25 \text{ periodical effective interest.}$$

2. If purchased at a premium of $832.50, five years before maturity:

$$(\$25{,}000 \times 2\%) - \frac{\$832.50}{10} = \$416.75 \text{ periodical effective interest.}$$

The process of discount amortization by the straight-line method may be represented by the schedule of amortization shown below:

Illustration 1

SCHEDULE OF DISCOUNT AMORTIZATION

Period	*Nominal Interest (2 Percent)*	*Effective Interest*	*Discount Amortization*	*Carrying Value of Investment at End of Period*
0	–	–	–	$24,167.50
1	$500	$583.25	$83.25	24,250.75
2	500	583.25	83.25	24,334.00
3	500	583.25	83.25	24,417.25
4	500	583.25	83.25	24,500.50
5	500	583.25	83.25	24,583.75
6	500	583.25	83.25	24,667.00
7	500	583.25	83.25	24,750.25
8	500	583.25	83.25	24,833.50
9	500	583.25	83.25	24,916.75
10	500	583.25	83.25	25,000.00

A schedule of premium amortization can be constructed on the pattern of the discount amortization table in Illustration 1. For the Discount Amortization column would be substituted one for Premium Amortization. Amounts in that column would be subtracted from, rather than added to, carrying value. Finally, carrying value at the end of Period 0 (same as beginning of Period 1) would be the sum of par value and premium.

Amortization schedules are not entirely necessary if the straight-line basis is used. Periodic amortization is easily determined by simple arithmetic, and effective interest is almost equally simple. The amounts and entries for nominal and effective interest are the same for each period.

Examination of the straight-line amortization table shown in Illustration 1 will reveal that, although the investment carrying value increased periodically, the *amount* of effective interest for each of the 10 periods remained stationary. This means that the effective *rate* of interest, obtained as the quotient of effective interest divided by carrying value of investment, declines each period, if discount is amortized equally by periods. Conversely, use of the straight-line method for amortizing premium would result in a periodically increasing effective rate of interest. Because of the importance of a regular rate of return in the management of investments, the straight-line basis for amortizing premium and discount is sometimes considered unacceptable. However, a very strong point in its favor is simplicity of operation.

Explanation of Scientific Amortization

The scientific method of amortization utilizes actuarial tables to develop a schedule in which effective interest and the amount of amortization are adjusted periodically to produce a fixed *rate* of effective interest. That is, the effective interest for each period, divided by the carrying value of the investment for that period, gives the same quotient, which is the rate of interest. How the scientific method operates will be demonstrated first as to bonds for which a premium was paid and then as to bonds acquired at a discount.

Referring to the Pacific City 4 percent bonds used as an example for straight-line amortization, let it be supposed that the safety factor of these bonds is such that they can command an effective rate of somewhat less than 2 percent semiannually. Further, let it be assumed that the governing body of a trust fund decides that a semi-annual yield of 1½ percent on these bonds is acceptable and accordingly decides to bid on $25,000 par value of them. What would be the bid price? It will depend upon the time the bonds have yet to run, which for present purposes will be assumed as three years.

What will the trust fund obtain if it becomes the successful bidder?

1. The right to receive $25,000 at the end of six periods.
2. The right to receive an interest payment of $500 at the end of each of the next six periods.

The series of interest payments is referred to as an "annuity," an annuity being defined as a series of equal payments, spaced at equal intervals of time. If each payment is made at the end of its respective period, the series is designated as an "ordinary annuity"; whereas if payments are made at the beginning of each period, the series becomes an "annuity due." Unless otherwise specified, "annuity" normally refers to the former.

Exact determination of the price that can be paid under the circumstances described, in order to obtain an effective or yield rate of 1½ percent, consists of the following steps:

1. Determining the actuarial worth today, at 1½ percent discount, of $25,000 for which the recipient will have to wait six periods.
2. Determining the actuarial worth today of an annuity of $500 at 1½ percent for six periods.

Both item 1 and item 2 require the use of mathematical tables giving various values of 1, or $1.00.

Reference to a table of present worths of 1 (Table A at the end of this Appendix) shows that the present worth of 1 for six periods at 1½ percent is 0.91454219. This means that if an investor considers his money to be worth a return of 1½ percent per period, he could afford to give slightly more than $0.91 for the right to receive $1.00 at the end of six periods. Multiplying 0.91454219 by $25,000 gives $22,863.55475 as the present worth of $25,000 discounted for six periods at 1½ percent.

A table of the present worths of an annuity of 1 (Table B) shows the present worth of an annuity of 1 at 1½ percent for six periods to be 5.6971872, which would produce a value of $2,848.5936 for an annuity of $500 under the same terms. Thus, it appears that for a return of 1½ percent semiannually on its investment, the trust fund management could bid the sum of $22,863.55475 and $2,848.5936, or $25,712.15, for the $25,000 of Pacific City bonds.

A schedule of effective interest and also of premium amortization on a scientific basis for the above investment would appear as shown in Illustration 2.

To demonstrate the structure of a schedule for amortizing discount by the scientific method, a table for that purpose is shown in Illustration 3. Without detailing the actuarial calculations involved, it will be assumed

Illustration 2

SCHEDULE OF PREMIUM AMORTIZATION
$25,000 Par Value 4 Percent Bonds, Interest Payable Semiannually
Acquired 3 Years before Maturity, to Yield 1½ Percent Semiannually

Period	*Nominal Interest (2 Percent)*	*Effective Interest (1½ Percent)*	*Premium Amortization*	*Carrying Value at End of Period*
0.	–	–	–	$25,712.15
1.	$500	$385.68	$114.32	25,597.83
2.	500	383.97	116.03	25,481.80
3.	500	382.23	117.77	25,364.03
4.	500	380.46	119.54	25,244.49
5.	500	378.67	121.33	25,123.16
6.	500	376.84*	123.16	25,000.00

*This figure was "forced" from $376.85, the correct effective interest on $25,123.16 at 1½ percent, in order to give the required difference for premium amortization. The need for "forcing" was brought about by dropping decimals.

Illustration 3

SCHEDULE OF DISCOUNT AMORTIZATION*
$25,000 Par Value 4 Percent Bonds, Interest Payable Semiannually
Acquired 3 Years before Maturity, to Yield 2½ Percent Semiannually

Period	*Nominal Interest (2 Percent)*	*Effective Interest (2½ Percent)*	*Discount Amortization*	*Carrying Value at End of Period*
0	–	–	–	$24,311.48
1	$500	$607.79	$107.79	24,419.27
2	500	610.48	110.48	24,529.75
3	500	613.24	113.24	24,642.99
4	500	616.07	116.07	24,759.06
5	500	618.98	118.98	24,878.04
6	500	621.96†	121.96	25,000.00

*This might be called a "schedule of carrying value accumulation."

†This figure was "forced" from $621.95, the correct effective interest on $24,878.04 at 2½ percent in order to give the required difference for discount amortization. The need for "forcing" was brought about by dropping decimals.

that a trust fund acquired the Pacific City 4 percent bonds on a 5 percent basis, that is, at a price to yield 2½ percent semiannually. In order to obtain a semiannual yield rate of 2½ percent on bonds paying a nominal rate of 2 percent on par value, the investment had to be bought at less than par. To obtain a yield rate of 2½ percent for six periods on $25,000 par value of bonds would necessitate their purchase for $24,311.48. The purchase price equals the present worth of $25,000 for six periods at 2½ percent, plus the present worth of an annuity of $500 under the same terms.

An alternative method for determining what purchase price will yield a given rate is as follows:

1. Determine the periodic interest at the nominal rate on the par value of the proposed purchase.
2. Determine the periodic interest at the desired effective or yield rate on the par value of the proposed purchase.
3. Find the difference between item 1 and item 2.
4. Find the present worth of an annuity of the amount of item 3 from time of purchase to maturity of the bonds, at the desired effective rate.
5. If the effective rate is higher, subtract the result in item 4 from the par value; if the nominal rate is higher, add the result of item 4 to the par value. The difference or sum will represent the cost which will yield the desired return.

Purchase Between Interest Periods

In buying bonds, it is not usually practicable to make the purchase on the first day of an interest period. The question arises as to the determination of carrying value when bonds are bought, say, two months after an interest date, with interest payable semiannually. To explain the method of ascertaining valuation between interest dates, it will be assumed that the purchase occurred in the sixth semiannual period before maturity. Valuation will be calculated for the beginning of the sixth and fifth interest periods. Valuation at the interim date will be ascertained by the process of interpolation, which in this instance would consist of taking one third of the change for the sixth period before maturity and applying that to the valuation at the beginning of the sixth period. Thus if the valuation at the beginning of the sixth period before maturity was $25,712.15 and premium amortization for that period was $114.32, interpolated valuation two months through the period would be $25,712.15 minus $\frac{\$114.32}{3}$, or $25,674.04. It will be observed that the above interpolation was calculated on the basis of arithmetical progression. This is consistent if the straight-line basis of amortization is employed, but does not conform strictly with the scientific basis, in which the amortization periodically increases.

Accounting for Income on Bonds—Straight Line Amortization

As stated previously, when discount on bond investments is amortized, periodic earnings on the investments consist of the nominal interest, received in cash, and the increase in value of the investment during the period. Referring to the schedule of straight-line amortization of discount (Illustration 1), it is seen that total earnings for the first period were $583.25, consisting of $500 cash plus an $83.25 increase in the carrying value of the investment. In general journal entry form, the first-period earnings would be recorded as follows:

Cash	500.00	
Investments	83.25	
Income on Bonds		583.25

By the nature of the straight-line method, the entry for each period's earnings would be the same.

Had the bonds been bought at a premium of $832.50, each period would have brought a reduction of $83.25 in the carrying value of the investment. The complete entry if premium amortization were involved would be as follows:

Cash	500	
Investments		83.25
Income on Bonds		416.75

This entry is based on the logic that in each $500 interest payment the trust fund is recovering $83.25 of the amount paid out as premium, leaving a net earning of $416.75. It will be observed that amortization of either premium or discount will bring the investment carrying value to par value at the end of the last interest period.

Accounting for Income on Bonds—Scientific Method

Unlike entries for income on bonds by the straight-line method, those based on the scientific method will not be the same in each period. If the bonds were acquired at a premium, for each period the premium amortization will be more and the amount of effective interest less than for the preceding period. If the bonds were acquired at a discount, both discount amortization and amount of effective interest will increase periodically.

The tabular summary of journal entries shown below portrays the change of amounts if the scientific method is used:

PERIODIC ENTRIES–BONDS ACQUIRED AT A PREMIUM

Accounts	*First Period*	*Second Period*	*Third Period*	*Fourth Period*
Cash, Dr	$500.00	$500.00	$500.00	$500.00
Investments, Cr.. . . .	114.32	116.03	117.77	119.54
Income on Bonds, Cr.	385.68	383.97	382.23	380.46

PERIODIC ENTRIES–BONDS ACQUIRED AT A DISCOUNT

Accounts	*First Period*	*Second Period*	*Third Period*	*Fourth Period*
Cash, Dr..	$500.00	$500.00	$500.00	$500.00
Investments, Dr. . . .	107.79	110.48	113.24	116.07
Income on Bonds, Cr.	607.79	610.48	613.24	616.07

Recording Discount and Premium Separately from Par Value

Thus far, discount and premium on bonds have been recorded in the same account with the par value of the bonds. That is, the purchase of $25,000 par value of bonds at a premium of $712.15 was recorded as a single debit, to Investments, of $25,712.15. The purchase of the securities at a discount of $688.52 was entered as a debit of $24,311.48. This practice is acceptable if the portfolio of investments includes only a few on which discount or premium must be amortized. However, as soon as bond investments reach any considerable proportions—say, at least 10 or 15—it becomes advantageous to record only par value in the Investments account, with supplementary accounts for premium and discount. To do so adds extra accounts to the ledger, but this is justified because it contributes to accuracy and to ease of discount and premium amortization. Operation of supplementary accounts for premium and discount may be illustrated by the following entries for the purchase of $25,000 par value of bonds, first at $25,712.15 and then at $24,311.48:

Investments	25,000.00	
Premium on Investments	712.15	
Cash		25,712.15
Investments	25,000.00	
Discount on Investments		688.52
Cash		24,311.48

It will be noted that the carrying value is determined by adding unamortized premium to par value or subtracting unamortized discount from par value.

Separation of unamortized premium or discount from par value alters the form of entries for amortization. Instead of direct credits and debits to the Investments account, changes will be made in the supplementary accounts, as illustrated below, with amounts based on tables heretofore used.

1. For collection of interest on bonds bought at a premium, the following entry will be made:

Cash	500.00	
Premium on Investments		114.32
Income on Bonds		385.68

2. For collection of interest on bonds bought at a discount, the entry will be as follows:

Cash	500.00	
Discount on Investments	107.79	
Income on Bonds		607.79

In so far as amortization is concerned, the two entries above have the same effect on the carrying value as if Investments had been credited for $114.32 in the first entry and debited for $107.79 in the second. As Premium on Investments is reduced by credits, it draws the carrying value nearer to par; as Discount on Investments is reduced by debits, it draws the carrying value nearer to par.

All the preceding discussion of amortization has related to bonds owned as long-term investments. What about amortization of discount or premium on stock investments, or on bonds held as short-term commitments? Discount or premium on stock cannot be systematically amortized by any method because stock has no maturity date and there is no time basis for distributing the premium or discount, nor does stock necessarily tend to approach par value with the passing of time. Concerning short-term bond investments, since their holding is only temporary, their market value may trend even further away from par value during the period of ownership; so reducing book value by writing off discount or premium might be contradictory to facts.

Adjusting Entries to Income on Investments

Correct financial statements for funds owning long-term investments require adjusting entries for income earned but not received. If the holding of investments is small, or if the amount of accrued income at ends of periods is not material in amount, adjusting entries are frequently dispensed with for reasons of economy of time and effort.

Income earned but not received, in the form of real estate rentals, may be recorded in the following routine form for such an adjustment, using an assumed amount:

Accrued Rental Income	320	
Rental Income		320

Dividends on stock investments are not earnings until the corporate board of directors has formally declared a dividend. This applies even though dividends on a certain stock have not been passed or omitted for many years. A trust fund closing its books on June 30 would violate accepted accounting practice to accrue one half of one year's dividends on stock of a corporation whose fiscal year coincides with the calendar year. However, if a dividend had been declared on June 20, payable to owners of record on July 10, the following entry, in an assumed amount, would be valid at June 30:

Dividends Receivable—Y Corporation Preferred Stock	400	
Dividend Income		400

Accrual of income on investments in bonds, mortgages, and notes is sound because interest on such indebtedness of a corporation is a fixed charge, not contingent upon approval by a board of directors. Calculating the amount of accrual on instruments of indebtedness such as those mentioned above is simple if they were acquired at par value. If acquired at a premium or discount that is being amortized, prorating of both nominal interest and amortization is necessary in the adjustment.

As an example of an adjusting entry for accrual of income on bonds purchased at a premium, figures will be taken from the table of premium amortization by the scientific method (Illustration 2). Let it be assumed that the interest dates on Pacific City bonds were May 1 and November 1,[2] and that Period 3 in the table began on May 1. If the fiscal period of the trust fund owning these bonds ended on June 30, the accrual of effective interest at June 30 would be $127.41, and amortization for

[2] Interest dates are sometimes indicated by the initial letters of the names of the months and the day date–for example, M and N 1.

the two months since May 1 would be $39.26. The adjusting entry for June 30 would be as follows:

Accrued Interest on Bond Investments	166.67	
Investments (or Premium on Investments)		39.26
Income on Bonds		127.41

An adjusting entry for accrued interest on bonds held at a discount may be framed on the basis of the above example.

The mission of some trust funds is to supply cash for more or less immediate purposes, such as tuition and other kinds of support or maintenance grants. Their primary interest is in periodical *spendable* income, which would exclude income accrued but not received and income based on amortization of discount. Amortization of discount adds to earnings only by adding to the carrying value of an investment (debit Unamortized Discount, credit Earnings). It is based upon an expected *future* receipt of cash, at maturity of the investment.

Then why *do* funds record amortization of premium which *reduces* the showing of cash income of the present period (debit Earnings, credit Unamortized Premium)? The reason is that premium on investments represents part of the investment cost. That part of a periodic interest receipt which is attributed to premium amortization (debit Cash, credit Unamortized Premium, and credit Earnings) is actually a recovery of part of the *earning power* cost and not a part of earnings.

Eliminating accruals of income and amortization of discount on investments is important where emphasis is on periodic cash income. Where emphasis is upon exact measurement of income over a long span of years the accrual basis yields more precise measurement of results.

Purchase of Accrued Interest on Investments

The purchase of bonds or other interest-bearing securities between interest dates will include the purchase of accrued interest. That is, the purchaser of an interest-bearing security between interest dates obtains certain earning power, plus an amount of income already earned. A purchase, midway between interest dates, of $25,000 par value of Pacific City 4's, interest payable semiannually, acquires $250 accrued interest, plus the bonds. If the total purchase price was $25,904.99, the investment, or earning power, cost $25,654.99; the outlay for accrued interest will be recovered at the next interest date. Entries for the purchase and for the collection of interest at the next interest date would be as follows:

Investments	25,000.00	
Premium on Investments	654.99	
Income on Bonds	250.00	
Cash		25,904.99
Cash	500.00	
Premium on Investments		57.16
Income on Bonds		442.84

Amounts in the above explanation and entries are based on purchase of the bonds midway in Period 1 as represented in the schedule of scientific amortization of premium (Illustration 2). Net income on bonds during the period of purchase was $442.84 less the $250 income purchased. This leaves a remainder of $192.84, which is one half the Period 1 effective interest as shown in the amortization schedule. When the accrued interest was purchased, a more accurate representation would have been a debit to Accrued Bond Interest or Accrued Interest Purchased. Had either account title been used, when collection occurred, a split would have been necessary to credit the special title debited for the $250. Debiting the income account when interest is purchased is technically inaccurate; but when total income for the period is recorded,

INCOME ON BONDS

Accrued interest purchased......	$250.00	Credit at next interest date......	$442.84

the adjustment for income purchased is automatic. The balance of the above account is $192.84, net income for the time the bonds were owned.

For reasons stated elsewhere, dividends on stock are not commonly accrued. However, owners of cumulative preferred stock sometimes calculate an accrual of dividend and add it to the price that buyers must pay to get the stock. In preparing statements of cash receipts and disbursements for trust and other funds which purchase accrued income, the outlay should be entitled Purchase of Accrued Interest on Investments or some similar name, regardless of the account debited for the acquisition.

Gain or Loss on Disposal of Investments

Investments may be disposed of by sale, through payment by the debtor at maturity of the debt, through liquidation of the debtor, and in a few other ways. Unless the transaction is consummated at exactly the book value of the investment at the time of disposal, there will be an accountable gain or loss. If a fund is nonexpendable as to both principal and income, obviously gain or loss, from whatever cause, is an adjustment of the fund balance. If the fund is expendable as to income but nonexpendable as to principal, accounting for gain or loss on disposal of investments will depend upon whether such transactions are governed by specific instructions established by the trustor, or by the so-called "general rule of law."[3] The individual or other authority establishing a trust has a legal right to specify whether such gains and losses are to be related to income or to principal. In the absence of such specific instructions, the general rule of law would operate and relate them to principal.

[3] As discussed in Chapter 8 (see footnote 4 of that chapter) there are signs that the rule is breaking down, particularly in respect to endowment funds of colleges and universities.

Every trust fund indenture should contain express provisions governing accounting for gains and losses on investments, as well as other kinds of debatable transactions. If such is not the case, fund trustees should make the necessary decisions, with due regard for all pertinent law, and incorporate them in their minutes.

Measurement of gain or loss on disposal of investments consists of finding the difference between (1) the net amount realized from the investment and (2) the book value of the investment at the date of disposal. If gross receipts from the sale of investments perchance include a charge for earnings accumulated since the interest or dividend date, the latter being very unusual, the amount thereof must be excluded from the selling price of the investment. Furthermore, brokerage or other fees incurred in consummating the sale must be deducted in finding the net selling price. In the discussion and examples to follow in this section, the decision as to whether gain or loss in each situation is chargeable to income or principal will be evaded by debiting Loss on Sale of Investments for all losses and crediting Gain on Sale of Investments for all gains. This will be done to conserve time and space. To illustrate accounting techniques for disposal of investments, it will be assumed, first, that the book value at the time of disposal is the same as the original cost and, then, that the original cost and the present book or carrying value are different.

The book value of investments at the time of disposal will be the same as the original cost under the following general conditions:

1. If the investment is corporate stock, because premium and discount on stock investments are not amortized.[4]
2. If the investments are bonds acquired at par value.
3. If the investments are bonds acquired at a premium or discount, and none has been amortized.
4. If the investment consists of assets subject to depreciation or amortization, but none has been recorded in any way.

Illustrative entries for the disposal of the above-named types of investments are as follows:

1. $5,000 par value of stock acquired for $5,125 was sold for $5,187.

	Debit	Credit
Cash	5,187	
Investments		5,125
Gain on Sale of Investments		62

2. $2,000 par value of bonds purchased at par were sold for $1,793 and accrued interest of $25.

	Debit	Credit
Cash	1,818	
Loss on Sale of Investments	207	
Investments		2,000
Bond Interest Income		25

[4] If there has been a stock dividend or stock split on stock since it was acquired the cost and book value *per share* will be lower.

3. $3,000 par value of bonds acquired at a premium of $25, of which none had been amortized, were sold for $3,060 and accrued interest of $40.

Cash	3,100	
Investments		3,025
Gain on Sale of Investments		35
Bond Interest Income		40

4. A building acquired for $27,000 and land that cost $1,000 were sold for $39,000. No depreciation had been recorded on the building.

Cash	39,000	
Buildings		27,000
Land		1,000
Gain on Sale of Investments		11,000

For at least two kinds of investments, the carrying value at the time of disposition will differ from the original cost. These are (1) depreciable fixed assets, ordinarily buildings, on which depreciation has been recorded, and (2) bonds bought for long-term investments, at either a premium or a discount, on which periodic amortization has been recorded. As to the bonds, if all the premium or discount has been written off, they will have been adjusted to par value. Accounting for proceeds at their maturity will be conducted as though they had been acquired at that figure. Disposal of a building for which an allowance for depreciation is carried, and disposal of bonds with a supplementary account for either premium or discount, will be alike in that book value of the investment is recorded in, and will have to be removed from, two accounts.

An additional complication arises when the disposal is made *during* a fiscal period, which is normal, since such transactions are not ordinarily timed to coincide with the beginning or ending of a fiscal period. This means that an adjustment must be made for depreciation or amortization since the last closing, in order to bring the book value up to date. The disposal of a building under such circumstances illustrates the principles involved. Let it be assumed that a building acquired as an investment at a cost of $18,000 had been depreciated in the amount of $8,100 to the end of the preceding fiscal period, at an annual rate of $900. If disposal is made for $10,000 net, three months after the last closing, the following entries should be made:

Depreciation—Buildings	225	
Allowance for Depreciation of Buildings		225
Cash	10,000	
Allowance for Depreciation of Buildings	8,325	
Investments		18,000
Gain on Sale of Investments		325

Correct accounting for disposal of bonds, the premium or discount on which is being amortized periodically, at a time between interest dates, requires that the carrying value be adjusted to the date of sale.

To illustrate the accounting entries involved, let the following assumptions be made about $25,000 par value of bonds:

Period Ending	*Nominal Interest (2 Percent)*	*Effective Interest (1½ Percent)*	*Amortization for Period*	*Carrying Value at End of Period*
December 31, 19x8	$500	$382.23	$117.77	$25,364.03
June 30, 19x9	500	380.46	119.54	25,244.49

Sale or other disposal of the bonds—say, on March 1, 19x9—would require that carrying value be brought one third of the way through the period ended on June 30, 19x9. Premium amortization for the two months since December 31, 19x8, is one third of $119.54, or $39.85, which would indicate a carrying value of $25,364.03 minus $39.85, or $25,324.18, for the investment at the interim date. The decrease in the carrying value may be recorded as follows:

Income on Bonds	39.85	
Premium on Investments		39.85

Assuming that the bonds were sold to net 100½ plus accrued interest, the transaction might be recorded by this entry:

Cash	25,291.67	
Loss on Sale of Investments	199.18	
Investments		25,000.00
Premium on Investments		324.18
Income on Bonds		166.67

The amount of loss appearing in this entry is the difference between the carrying value of the investment at March 1, 19x9, which is $25,324.18, and the net selling price of the bonds ($25,000 times 100½, or $25,125). The two entries shown above might be condensed into one, but such a lengthy explanation of the amounts would be required that two entries seem to be preferable to one.

For the purpose of saving time, as indicated in the beginning of this section, all gains on investments have been recorded as Gain on Sale of Investments; whereas all losses have been debited to Loss on Sale of Investments. In individual cases, it is necessary for the accountant to ascertain, in the light of all pertinent information, whether such gains and losses are in fact operating transactions affecting net income, or are adjustments of fund principal and therefore to be credited or debited to the Fund Balance account or other account recording the fund surplus.

Accounting for Pooled Investments

For a governmental unit owning a large volume of investments, with ownership distributed among a number of funds, pooling of investment custodianship and management offers an opportunity for increasing fund revenue. This is true (1) because management of a large volume of investments permits advantageous diversification, and (2) because it brings the possibility of greater flexibility in the investment program than if the investments of each individual fund were required to be managed separately. Pooling of investments consists of changing from individual fund ownership of specific investments to individual fund ownership of an undivided or undistributed interest or equity in a collection of investments. The exact plan of pool management and related accounting procedures are subject to many variations. The illustrations which follow represent only one possibility. Another plan of pool management is illustrated in Chapter 19.

Normally a first action in the pooling operation is an inventory of all the investments to be pooled by the participating member funds, as a measure of each fund's contribution to the pool. In addition to listing the investment items to be contributed by each fund, the inventory should show, as of the effective pooling date (1) the market value of the individual item (share of stock, bond, piece of real estate, etc.), (2) accrued interest on interest-bearing debts, (3) dividends declared but unpaid on stocks, and (4) any other rights or appendages of value which may be attached to property items (rents, royalties, etc.). Management of the pool may be either internal or in the hands of an independent fiscal agent.

The illustrations which follow are designed primarily to show the flow of financial information through a fund member of a pool, without discussion of the many possible variations. To simplify and shorten the examples, accounts for unamortized premium and unamortized discount will be omitted from the entries.

1. The inventory of investments to be pooled by the Kramer Memorial Fund of the city library showed the market value of investments to be pooled to be $387,000, compared with a book value of $361,000.

Investments	26,000	
Fund Balance		26,000

2. The investments were transferred to the pool:

Pool Investments	387,000	
Investments		387,000

On the books of the fund managing the pool the following entry would be appropriate:

Pool Investments	387,000	
Fund Balance (controlling account)		387,000

A subsidiary record would show the individual fund to be credited with the balance.

Had the memorial fund been recording differences between par value and cost for some or all of its investments, the Unamortized Premium and Unamortized Discount accounts would have been reclassified as pool items in the above entry, i.e., Unamortized Premium on Pool Investments, etc. The status of discount and premium amortization in the periodic statement of earnings has been discussed elsewhere.

The fund charged with management of pooled assets buys and sells as seems advisable in the light of market and other pertinent conditions and demands. Equilibrium of earnings over a number of periods on a given total of investments is a desirable feature for many trust funds. Equilibrium of investment is a semicontrollable factor in producing equilibrium of income. One device available for bringing this about is an account which has been called Reserve for Realized Gains and Losses on Pool Investments. When pool management disposes of an investment at a gain, the amount of gain is credited to the reserve account. This causes the holding back of cash which resulted from the gain and makes it available for investment. When investments are disposed of at a loss the amount of loss is debited to the reserve. An imaginary sale of pooled investments might yield the following entry:

Pool Cash	11,970	
Pool Investments		10,000
Unamortized Premium on Pool Investments		620
Reserve for Realized Gains and Losses		1,350

This transaction is not one to be recorded on the pool members' books. A similar entry would be made for a sale at a loss, except the balancing element would be the amount of the loss, debited to the reserve. Employment of a single reserve for recording all gains and losses on sales demonstrates the cooperative nature of investment pooling.

Reciept and distribution of income may be administered by the fund operating the investment pool or by a separate fund. Regardless of the fund managing income, the receipt thereof might be recorded as follows:

Pool Cash	3,000	
Undistributed Pool Income[5]		3,000

Income from pool investments is distributed to participants on the basis of their relative investments in the pool.

For the fund administering pool income a distribution would be recorded as follows:

Undistributed Pool Income	40,000	
Pool Cash		40,000

Obviously the distribution of income by members might have been recorded as a liability (debit Undistributed Pool Income, credit various Due to——accounts) prior to disbursement. Receipt of income from

[5] A more descriptive title for this account is Undistributed Income on Pool Investments.

pooled investments is recorded by the Kramer Memorial Fund in the same manner as any other receipt:

Cash	1,200	
Income on Investments (or Pool Investments)		1,200

Many details are involved in selecting the exact combination of procedures to be followed by a given institution or agency adopting the pooling method of accounting for some or all of its investments. Omitted from this discussion are other methods of measuring a participating fund's contribution to a pool, measurement of income by periods, accounting for gains and losses on disposal of investments, accounting for undistributed income, etc. Much of the variation in accounting procedure which exists is due to variations and conditions under which the pool is operated.

Subsidiary Records for Investments

Throughout the foregoing discussion of investment transactions, references have been made to general ledger accounts only. Obviously, from the amount of detailed information associated with investments, when the number of items exceeds 10 or 15, it becomes necessary to constitute the general ledger accounts as controlling accounts supported by a subsidiary account for each item. Furthermore, diversity of investments may call for two or more controlling accounts such as Stock, Bonds, Mortgages, Real Estate, Savings Accounts, and possibly others, each with its subsidiary ledger.

In accordance with rules stated elsewhere, ownership of large numbers of bonds makes it desirable to operate separate accounts for unamortized discount and unamortized premium. Use of the three controlling accounts for recording the bond carrying value does not require three separate subsidiary ledgers. In the one subsidiary ledger, one column (Par Value) supports the Bonds controlling account in the general ledger; the Unamortized Premium column in the subsidiary ledger supports the general ledger control of the same name; and finally, the Unamortized Discount column in the subsidiary record supports the Unamortized Discount control account in the general ledger.

Statements of Investments

For administration purposes, detailed statements of fund investments are indispensable. The form of such statements will vary, of course, from general summaries to well-classified schedules by items and funds. An example of the former is the statement of investments published by one institution in which a detailed listing of items by funds is given, with a columnar classification as to Certificates of Deposit, United States Treasury Bonds, Other Bonds, Capital Stock, Savings and Loan Shares, Real Estate, and others. No indication is given as to whether the figures shown are at original cost, amortized cost, or market value. (See below.)

Name of Fund and Item	*United States Government Bonds*	*Other Bonds*	*Savings and Loan Shares*	*Capital Stock*	*Etc.*
Memorial Fund:					
Treasury bonds	$14,000				
Standard Oil Company.				$1,620	
First Savings and Loan Company			$13,186		

Another statement of investment form provides for greater detail than the summary shown above. Examination of Illustration 4, presenting a partial statement modeled on a more elaborate form, reveals the superiority of the latter collection and arrangement of information.

One shortcoming of Illustration 4 is its limitation to use for bonds, mortgages, and notes. Because neither premium nor discount on stock is amortized, not even that form of investment can be satisfactorily included. Still less is the form suited to real estate, savings and loan shares, savings accounts, etc.

With some experience the imaginative and resourceful accountant can learn to prepare a schedule to fit whatever situation he feels should be analyzed for use by the management of the investments at hand. Some of the normal requirements would likely be:

1. Exact name and date or period of the schedule.
2. Exact description (name, number, date, etc.) of the items being scheduled.
3. Maturity or expiration date, if any.
4. Cost.
5. Par or maturity value.
6. Nominal rate of return.
7. Premium or discount if items are bonds.
8. Rate of depreciation or other form of amortization if items are subject to either of those processes.
9. Information totals which agree with controlling account balances, if any.
10. Any other information which, in brief form, would be of assistance in managing the investments.

Illustration 4

CITY OF X

Statement of Bond Investments—All Funds, June 30, 19x9

Description	Date Acquired	Bond or Certificate No.	Interest Rate	Maturity Date	Par Value	Unamortized Premium	Unamortized Discount	Total Book Value	Cost	Accrued Interest Purchased	Market Value
Trust and Agency Funds											
City Water 8's	19x1 and 19x3	Various	8%	June 30, 19y2	$ 46,300	$1,200	$400	$ 47,100	$ 48,920	$ 730	$ 47,430
General Gas Company first mortgage	19x5	922–927	7½%	July 31, 19y8	30,000	1,800		31,800	32,400	180	31,200
City of X sinking fund 5's	19x4	72–91	5%	March 31, 19y9	20,000	410		20,410	21,000		19,890
Total					$ 96,300	$3,410	$400	$ 99,310	$102,320	$ 910	$ 98,520
Representing the following:											
Employee retirement funds					$ 68,200	$2,800	$400	$ 70,600	$ 71,300	$ 405	$ 70,220
Guaranty deposit funds					7,100	160		7,260	7,400	280	7,115
Endowment funds					21,000	450		21,450	23,620	225	21,185
Total					$ 96,300	$3,410	$400	$ 99,310	$102,320	$ 910	$ 98,520
Enterprise Fund											
City of X sinking fund 3's	19x5	61–64	3%	March 31, 19y9	$ 4,000	$ 190	–	$ 4,190	$ 4,310	$ 70	$ 3,978
Western Power Company's 8½'s	19x1	189–191	8½%	June 30, 19z3	30,000	2,020		32,020	34,450	380	33,860
Total enterprise fund					$ 34,000	$2,210	–	$ 36,210	$ 38,760	$ 450	$ 37,838
Representing the following:											
Customers' deposits fund					$ 12,000	$ 640	–	$ 12,640	$ 13,720	$ 120	$ 13,200
Depreciation fund					22,000	1,570		23,570	25,040	330	24,638
Total					$ 34,000	$2,210	–	$ 36,210	$ 38,760	$ 450	$ 37,838
Total All Funds					$130,300	$5,620	$400	$135,520	$141,080	$1,360	$136,358

A. PRESENT WORTH OF 1 (AT COMPOUND INTEREST)

$$\frac{1}{(1+i)^n}$$

Periods	$\frac{1}{4}$%	$\frac{1}{2}$%	$\frac{3}{4}$%	1%	$1\frac{1}{4}$%	$1\frac{1}{2}$%
1.	0.9975 0623	0.9950 2488	0.9925 5583	0.9900 9901	0.9876 5432	0.9852 2167
2.	0.9950 1869	0.9900 7450	0.9851 6708	0.9802 9605	0.9754 6106	0.9706 6175
3.	0.9925 3734	0.9851 4876	0.9778 3333	0.9705 9015	0.9634 1833	0.9563 1699
4.	0.9900 6219	0.9802 4752	0.9705 5417	0.9609 8034	0.9515 2428	0.9421 8423
5.	0.9875 9321	0.9753 7067	0.9633 2920	0.9514 6569	0.9397 7706	0.9282 6033
6.	0.9851 3038	0.9705 1808	0.9561 5802	0.9420 4524	0.9281 7488	0.9145 4219
7.	0.9826 7370	0.9656 8963	0.9490 4022	0.9327 1805	0.9167 1593	0.9010 2679
8.	0.9802 2314	0.9608 8520	0.9419 7540	0.9234 8322	0.9053 9845	0.8877 1112
9.	0.9777 7869	0.9561 0468	0.9349 6318	0.9143 3982	0.8942 2069	0.8745 9224
10.	0.9753 4034	0.9513 4794	0.9280 0315	0.9052 8695	0.8831 8093	0.8616 6723
11.	0.9729 0807	0.9466 1489	0.9210 9494	0.8963 2372	0.8722 7746	0.8489 3323
12.	0.9704 8187	0.9419 0534	0.9142 3815	0.8874 4923	0.8615 0860	0.8363 8742
13.	0.9680 6171	0.9372 1924	0.9074 3241	0.8786 6260	0.8508 7269	0.8240 2702
14.	0.9656 4759	0.9325 5646	0.9006 7733	0.8699 6297	0.8403 6809	0.8118 4928
15.	0.9632 3949	0.9279 1688	0.8939 7254	0.8613 4947	0.8299 9318	0.7998 5150
16.	0.9608 3740	0.9233 0037	0.8873 1766	0.8528 2126	0.8197 4635	0.7880 3104
17.	0.9584 4130	0.9187 0684	0.8807 1231	0.8443 7749	0.8096 2602	0.7763 8526
18.	0.9560 5117	0.9141 3616	0.8741 5614	0.8360 1731	0.7996 3064	0.7649 1159
19.	0.9536 6700	0.9095 8822	0.8676 4878	0.8277 3992	0.7897 5866	0.7536 0747
20.	0.9512 8878	0.9050 6290	0.8611 8985	0.8195 4447	0.7800 0855	0.7424 7042
21.	0.9489 1649	0.9005 6010	0.8547 7901	0.8114 3017	0.7703 7881	0.7314 9795
22.	0.9465 5011	0.8960 7971	0.8484 1589	0.8033 9621	0.7608 6796	0.7206 8763
23.	0.9441 8964	0.8916 2160	0.8421 0014	0.7954 4179	0.7514 7453	0.7100 3708
24.	0.9418 3505	0.8871 8567	0.8358 3140	0.7875 6613	0.7421 9707	0.6995 4392
25.	0.9394 8634	0.8827 7181	0.8296 0933	0.7797 6844	0.7330 3414	0.6892 0583
26.	0.9371 4348	0.8783 7991	0.8234 3358	0.7720 4796	0.7239 8434	0.6790 2052
27.	0.9348 0646	0.8740 0986	0.8173 0380	0.7644 0392	0.7150 4626	0.6689 8574
28.	0.9324 7527	0.8696 6155	0.8112 1966	0.7568 3557	0.7062 1853	0.6590 9925
29.	0.9301 4990	0.8653 3488	0.8051 8080	0.7493 4215	0.6974 9978	0.6493 5887
30.	0.9278 3032	0.8610 2973	0.7991 8690	0.7419 2292	0.6888 8867	0.6397 6243
31.	0.9255 1653	0.8567 4600	0.7932 3762	0.7345 7715	0.6803 8387	0.6303 0781
32.	0.9232 0851	0.8524 8358	0.7873 3262	0.7273 0411	0.6719 8407	0.6209 9292
33.	0.9209 0624	0.8482 4237	0.7814 7158	0.7201 0307	0.6636 8797	0.6118 1568
34.	0.9186 0972	0.8440 2226	0.7756 5418	0.7129 7334	0.6554 9429	0.6027 7407
35.	0.9163 1892	0.8398 2314	0.7698 8008	0.7059 1420	0.6474 0177	0.5938 6608
36.	0.9140 3384	0.8356 4492	0.7641 4896	0.6989 2495	0.6394 0916	0.5850 8974
37.	0.9117 5445	0.8314 8748	0.7584 6051	0.6920 0490	0.6315 1522	0.5764 4309
38.	0.9094 8075	0.8273 5073	0.7528 1440	0.6851 5337	0.6237 1873	0.5679 2423
39.	0.9072 1272	0.8232 3455	0.7472 1032	0.6783 6967	0.6160 1850	0.5595 3126
40.	0.9049 5034	0.8191 3886	0.7416 4796	0.6716 5314	0.6084 1334	0.5512 6232

A. PRESENT WORTH OF 1 (AT COMPOUND INTEREST) (*Continued*)

$$\frac{1}{(1+i)^n}$$

Periods	2%	2½%	3%	4%	5%	6%
1.....	0.9803 9216	0.9756 0976	0.9708 7379	0.9615 3846	0.9523 8095	0.9433 9623
2.....	0.9611 6878	0.9518 1440	0.9425 9591	0.9245 5621	0.9070 2948	0.8899 9644
3.....	0.9423 2233	0.9285 9941	0.9151 4166	0.8889 9636	0.8638 3760	0.8396 1928
4.....	0.9238 4543	0.9059 5064	0.8884 8705	0.8548 0419	0.8227 0247	0.7920 9366
5.....	0.9057 3081	0.8838 5429	0.8626 0878	0.8219 2711	0.7835 2617	0.7472 5817
6.....	0.8879 7138	0.8622 9687	0.8374 8426	0.7903 1453	0.7462 1540	0.7049 6054
7.....	0.8705 6018	0.8412 6524	0.8130 9151	0.7599 1781	0.7106 8133	0.6650 5711
8.....	0.8534 9037	0.8207 4657	0.7894 0923	0.7306 9021	0.6768 3936	0.6274 1237
9.....	0.8367 5527	0.8007 2836	0.7664 1673	0.7025 8674	0.6446 0892	0.5918 9846
10.....	0.8203 4830	0.7811 9840	0.7440 9391	0.6755 6417	0.6139 1325	0.5583 9478
11.....	0.8042 6304	0.7621 4478	0.7224 2128	0.6495 8093	0.5846 7929	0.5267 8753
12.....	0.7884 9318	0.7435 5589	0.7013 7988	0.6245 9705	0.5568 3742	0.4969 6936
13.....	0.7730 3253	0.7254 2038	0.6809 5134	0.6005 7409	0.5303 2135	0.4688 3902
14.....	0.7578 7502	0.7077 2720	0.6611 1781	0.5774 7508	0.5050 6795	0.4423 0096
15.....	0.7430 1473	0.6904 6556	0.6418 6195	0.5552 6450	0.4810 1710	0.4172 6506
16.....	0.7284 4581	0.6736 2493	0.6231 6694	0.5339 0818	0.4581 1152	0.3936 4628
17.....	0.7141 6256	0.6571 9506	0.6050 1645	0.5133 7325	0.4362 9669	0.3713 6442
18.....	0.7001 5937	0.6411 6591	0.5873 9461	0.4936 2812	0.4155 2065	0.3503 4379
19.....	0.6864 3076	0.6255 2772	0.5702 8603	0.4746 4242	0.3957 3396	0.3305 1301
20.....	0.6729 7133	0.6102 7094	0.5536 7575	0.4563 8695	0.3768 8948	0.3118 0473
21.....	0.6597 7582	0.5953 8629	0.5375 4928	0.4388 3360	0.3589 4236	0.2941 5540
22.....	0.6468 3904	0.5808 6467	0.5218 9250	0.4219 5539	0.3418 4987	0.2775 0510
23.....	0.6341 5592	0.5666 9724	0.5066 9175	0.4057 2633	0.3255 7131	0.2617 9726
24.....	0.6217 2149	0.5528 7535	0.4919 3374	0.3901 2147	0.3100 6791	0.2469 7855
25.....	0.6095 3087	0.5393 9059	0.4776 0557	0.3751 1680	0.2953 0277	0.2329 9863
26.....	0.5975 7928	0.5262 3472	0.4636 9473	0.3606 8923	0.2812 4073	0.2198 1003
27.....	0.5858 6204	0.5133 9973	0.4501 8906	0.3468 1657	0.2678 4832	0.2073 6795
28.....	0.5743 7455	0.5008 7778	0.4370 7675	0.3334 7747	0.2550 9364	0.1956 3014
29.....	0.5631 1231	0.4886 6125	0.4243 4636	0.3206 5141	0.2429 4632	0.1845 5674
30.....	0.5520 7089	0.4767 4269	0.4119 8676	0.3083 1867	0.2313 7745	0.1741 1013
31.....	0.5412 4597	0.4651 1481	0.3999 8715	0.2964 6026	0.2203 5947	0.1642 5484
32.....	0.5306 3330	0.4537 7055	0.3883 3703	0.2850 5794	0.2098 6617	0.1549 5740
33.....	0.5202 2873	0.4427 0298	0.3770 2625	0.2740 9417	0.1998 7254	0.1461 8622
34.....	0.5100 2817	0.4319 0534	0.3660 4490	0.2635 5209	0.1903 5480	0.1379 1153
35.....	0.5000 2761	0.4213 7107	0.3553 8340	0.2534 1547	0.1812 9029	0.1301 0522
36.....	0.4902 2315	0.4110 9372	0.3450 3243	0.2436 6872	0.1726 5741	0.1227 4077
37.....	0.4806 1093	0.4010 6705	0.3349 8294	0.2342 9685	0.1644 3563	0.1157 9318
38.....	0.4711 8719	0.3912 8492	0.3252 2615	0.2252 8543	0.1566 0536	0.1092 3885
39.....	0.4619 4822	0.3817 4139	0.3157 5355	0.2166 2061	0.1491 4797	0.1030 5552
40.....	0.4528 9042	0.3724 3062	0.3065 5684	0.2082 8904	0.1420 4568	0.0972 2219

B. PRESENT WORTH OF AN ANNUITY (IF RENT IS 1)

$$\frac{1 - \frac{1}{(1+i)^n}}{i}$$

Periods	$\frac{1}{4}\%$	$\frac{1}{2}\%$	$\frac{3}{4}\%$	1%	$1\frac{1}{4}\%$	$1\frac{1}{2}\%$
1.	0.997 5062	0.995 0249	0.992 5558	0.990 0990	0.987 6543	0.985 2217
2.	1.992 5249	1.985 0994	1.977 7229	1.970 3951	1.963 1154	1.955 8834
3.	2.985 0623	2.970 2481	2.955 5562	2.940 9852	2.926 5337	2.912 2004
4.	3.975 1245	3.950 4957	3.926 1104	3.901 9656	3.878 0580	3.854 3847
5.	4.962 7177	4.925 8663	4.889 4396	4.853 4312	4.817 8350	4.782 6450
6.	5.947 8480	5.896 3844	5.845 5976	5.795 4765	5.746 0099	5.697 1872
7.	6.930 5217	6.862 0740	6.794 6379	6.728 1945	6.662 7258	6.598 2140
8.	7.910 7449	7.822 9592	7.736 6133	7.651 6778	7.568 1243	7.485 9251
9.	8.888 5236	8.779 0639	8.671 5764	8.566 0176	8.462 3450	8.360 5173
10.	9.863 8639	9.730 4119	9.599 5796	9.471 3045	9.345 5259	9.222 1846
11.	10.836 7720	10.677 0267	10.520 6745	10.367 6282	10.217 8034	10.071 1178
12.	11.807 2538	11.618 9321	11.434 9127	11.255 0775	11.079 3120	10.907 5052
13.	12.775 3156	12.556 1513	12.342 3451	12.133 7401	11.930 1847	11.731 5322
14.	13.740 9631	13.488 7078	13.243 0224	13.003 7030	12.770 5528	12.543 3815
15.	14.704 2026	14.416 6246	14.136 9950	13.865 0525	13.600 5459	13.343 2330
16.	15.665 0400	15.339 9250	15.024 3126	14.717 8738	14.420 2923	14.131 2641
17.	16.623 4813	16.258 6319	15.905 0249	15.562 2513	15.229 9183	14.907 6493
18.	17.579 5325	17.172 7680	16.779 1811	16.398 2686	16.029 5489	15.672 5609
19.	18.533 1995	18.082 3562	17.646 8298	17.226 0085	16.819 3076	16.426 1684
20.	19.484 4883	18.987 4192	18.508 0197	18.045 5530	17.599 3161	17.168 6388
21.	20.433 4048	19.887 9792	19.362 7987	18.856 9831	18.369 6950	17.900 1367
22.	21.379 9549	20.784 0590	20.211 2146	19.660 3793	19.130 5629	18.620 8244
23.	22.324 1445	21.675 6806	21.053 3147	20.455 8211	19.882 0374	19.330 8615
24.	23.265 9796	22.562 8662	21.889 1461	21.243 3873	20.624 2345	20.030 4054
25.	24.205 4659	23.445 6380	22.718 7555	22.023 1557	21.357 2686	20.719 6112
26.	25.142 6094	24.324 0179	23.542 1891	22.795 2037	22.081 2530	21.398 6317
27.	26.077 4159	25.198 0278	24.359 4929	23.559 6076	22.796 2992	22.067 6175
28.	27.009 8911	26.067 6894	25.170 7125	24.316 4432	23.502 5178	22.726 7167
29.	27.940 0410	26.933 0242	25.975 8933	25.065 7853	24.200 0176	23.376 0756
30.	28.867 8713	27.794 0540	26.775 0802	25.807 7082	24.888 9062	24.015 8380
31.	29.793 3879	28.650 8000	27.568 3178	26.542 2854	25.569 2901	24.646 1458
32.	30.716 5964	29.503 2836	28.355 6505	27.269 5895	26.241 2742	25.267 1387
33.	31.637 5026	30.351 5259	29.137 1220	27.989 6926	26.904 9622	25.878 9544
34.	32.556 1123	31.195 5482	29.912 7762	28.702 6659	27.560 4564	26.481 7285
35.	33.472 4313	32.035 3713	30.682 6563	29.408 5801	28.207 8582	27.075 5946
36.	34.386 4651	32.871 0162	31.446 8053	30.107 5050	28.847 2674	27.660 6843
37.	35.298 2196	33.702 5037	32.205 2658	30.799 5099	29.478 7826	28.237 1274
38.	36.207 7003	34.529 8544	32.958 0802	31.484 6633	30.102 5013	28.805 0516
39.	37.114 9130	35.353 0890	33.705 2905	32.163 0330	30.718 5198	29.364 5829
40.	38.019 8634	36.172 2279	34.446 9384	32.834 6861	31.326 9332	29.915 8452

B. PRESENT WORTH OF AN ANNUITY (IF RENT IS 1) (*Continued*)

$$\frac{1 - \frac{1}{(1+i)^n}}{i}$$

Periods	2%	2½%	3%	4%	5%	6%
1.....	0.980 3922	0.975 6098	0.970 8738	0.961 5385	0.952 3810	0.943 3962
2.....	1.941 5609	1.927 4242	1.913 4697	1.886 0947	1.859 4104	1.833 3927
3.....	2.883 8833	2.856 0236	2.828 6114	2.775 0910	2.723 2480	2.673 0120
4.....	3.807 7287	3.761 9742	3.717 0984	3.629 8952	3.545 9505	3.465 1056
5.....	4.713 4595	4.645 8285	4.579 7072	4.451 8223	4.329 4767	4.212 3638
6.....	5.601 4309	5.508 1254	5.417 1914	5.242 1369	5.075 6923	4.917 3243
7.....	6.471 9911	6.349 3906	6.230 2830	6.002 0547	5.786 3731	5.582 3814
8.....	7.325 4814	7.170 1372	7.019 6922	6.732 7449	6.463 2128	6.209 7938
9.....	8.162 2367	7.970 8655	7.786 1089	7.435 3316	7.107 8217	6.801 6923
10.....	8.982 5850	8.752 0639	8.530 2028	8.110 8958	7.721 7349	7.360 0871
11.....	9.786 8481	9.514 2087	9.252 6241	8.760 4767	8.306 4142	7.886 8746
12.....	10.575 3412	10.257 7646	9.954 0040	9.385 0738	8.863 2516	8.383 8439
13.....	11.348 3738	10.983 1850	10.634 9553	9.985 6479	9.393 5730	8.852 6830
14.....	12.106 2488	11.690 0122	11.296 0731	10.563 1229	9.898 6409	9.294 9839
15.....	12.849 2635	12.381 3777	11.937 9351	11.118 3874	10.379 6580	9.712 2490
16.....	13.577 7093	13.055 0027	12.561 1020	11.652 2956	10.837 7696	10.105 8953
17.....	14.291 8719	13.712 1977	13.166 1185	12.165 6689	11.274 0663	10.477 2597
18.....	14.992 0313	14.353 3636	13.753 5131	12.659 2970	11.689 5869	10.827 6035
19.....	15.678 4620	14.978 8913	14.323 7991	13.133 9394	12.085 3209	11.158 1165
20.....	16.351 4333	15.589 1623	14.877 4749	13.590 3263	12.462 2103	11.469 9212
21.....	17.011 2092	16.184 5486	15.415 0241	14.029 1600	12.821 1527	11.764 0766
22.....	17.658 0482	16.765 4132	15.936 9166	14.451 1153	13.163 0026	12.041 5817
23.....	18.292 2041	17.332 1105	16.443 6084	14.856 8417	13.488 5739	12.303 3790
24.....	18.913 9256	17.884 9858	16.935 5421	15.246 9631	13.798 6418	12.550 3575
25.....	19.523 4565	18.424 3764	17.413 1477	15.622 0799	14.093 9446	12.783 3562
26.....	20.121 0358	18.950 6111	17.876 8424	15.982 7692	14.375 1853	13.003 1662
27.....	20.706 8978	19.464 0109	18.327 0315	16.329 5858	14.643 0336	13.210 5341
28.....	21.281 2724	19.964 8887	18.764 1082	16.663 0632	14.898 1273	13.406 1643
29.....	21.844 3847	20.453 5499	19.188 4546	16.983 7146	15.141 0736	13.590 7210
30.....	22.396 4556	20.930 2926	19.600 4414	17.292 0333	15.372 4510	13.764 8312
31.....	22.937 7015	21.395 4074	20.000 4285	17.588 4936	15.592 8105	13.929 0860
32.....	23.468 3348	21.849 1780	20.388 7655	17.873 5515	15.802 6767	14.084 0434
33.....	23.988 5636	22.291 8809	20.765 7918	18.147 6457	16.002 5492	14.230 2296
34.....	24.498 5917	22.723 7863	21.131 8367	18.411 1978	16.192 9040	14.368 1411
35.....	24.998 6193	23.145 1573	21.487 2201	18.664 6132	16.374 1943	14.498 2464
36.....	25.488 8425	23.556 2511	21.832 2525	18.908 2820	16.546 8517	14.620 9871
37.....	25.969 4534	23.957 3181	22.167 2354	19.142 5788	16.711 2873	14.736 7803
38.....	26.440 6406	24.348 6030	22.492 4616	19.367 8642	16.867 8927	14.846 0192
39.....	26.902 5888	24.730 3444	22.808 2151	19.584 4848	17.017 0407	14.949 0747
40.....	27.355 4792	25.102 7751	23.114 7720	19.792 7739	17.159 0864	15.046 2969

C. AMOUNT OF 1 (AT COMPOUND INTEREST)

$$(1+i)^n$$

Periods	$\frac{1}{4}\%$	$\frac{1}{2}\%$	$\frac{3}{4}\%$	1%	$1\frac{1}{4}\%$	$1\frac{1}{2}\%$
1.	1.0025 0000	1.0050 0000	1.0075	1.01	1.0125	1.015
2.	1.0050 0625	1.0100 2500	1.0150 5625	1.0201	1.0251 5625	1.0302 25
3.	1.0075 1877	1.0150 7513	1.0226 6917	1.0303 01	1.0379 7070	1.0456 7838
4.	1.0100 3756	1.0201 5050	1.0303 3919	1.0406 0401	1.0509 4534	1.0613 6355
5.	1.0125 6266	1.0252 5125	1.0380 6673	1.0510 1005	1.0640 8215	1.0772 8400
6.	1.0150 9406	1.0303 7751	1.0458 5224	1.0615 2015	1.0773 8318	1.0934 4326
7.	1.0176 3180	1.0355 2940	1.0536 9613	1.0721 3535	1.0908 5047	1.1098 4491
8.	1.0201 7588	1.0407 0704	1.0615 9885	1.0828 5671	1.1044 8610	1.1264 9259
9.	1.0227 2632	1.0459 1058	1.0695 6084	1.0936 8527	1.1182 9218	1.1433 8998
10.	1.0252 8313	1.0511 4013	1.0775 8255	1.1046 2213	1.1322 7083	1.1605 4083
11.	1.0278 4634	1.0563 9583	1.0856 6441	1.1156 6835	1.1464 2422	1.1779 4894
12.	1.0304 1596	1.0616 7781	1.0938 0690	1.1268 2503	1.1607 5452	1.1956 1817
13.	1.0329 9200	1.0669 8620	1.1020 1045	1.1380 9328	1.1752 6395	1.2135 5244
14.	1.0355 7448	1.0723 2113	1.1102 7553	1.1494 7421	1.1899 5475	1.2317 5573
15.	1.0381 6341	1.0776 8274	1.1186 0259	1.1609 6896	1.2048 2918	1.2502 3207
16.	1.0407 5882	1.0830 7115	1.1269 9211	1.1725 7864	1.2198 8955	1.2689 8555
17.	1.0433 6072	1.0884 8651	1.1354 4455	1.1843 0443	1.2351 3817	1.2880 2033
18.	1.0459 6912	1.0939 2894	1.1439 6039	1.1961 4748	1.2505 7739	1.3073 4064
19.	1.0485 8404	1.0993 9858	1.1525 4009	1.2081 0895	1.2662 0961	1.3269 5075
20.	1.0512 0550	1.1048 9558	1.1611 8414	1.2201 9004	1.2820 3723	1.3468 5501
21.	1.0538 3352	1.1104 2006	1.1698 9302	1.2323 9194	1.2980 6270	1.3670 5783
22.	1.0564 6810	1.1159 7216	1.1786 6722	1.2447 1586	1.3142 8848	1.3875 6370
23.	1.0591 0927	1.1215 5202	1.1875 0723	1.2571 6302	1.3307 1709	1.4083 7715
24.	1.0617 5704	1.1271 5978	1.1964 1353	1.2697 3465	1.3473 5105	1.4295 0281
25.	1.0644 1144	1.1327 9558	1.2053 8663	1.2824 3200	1.3641 9294	1.4509 4535
26.	1.0670 7247	1.1384 5955	1.2144 2703	1.2952 5631	1.3812 4535	1.4727 0953
27.	1.0697 4015	1.1441 5185	1.2235 3523	1.3082 0888	1.3985 1092	1.4948 0018
28.	1.0724 1450	1.1498 7261	1.2327 1175	1.3212 9097	1.4159 9230	1.5172 2218
29.	1.0750 9553	1.1556 2197	1.2419 5709	1.3345 0388	1.4336 9221	1.5399 8051
30.	1.0777 8327	1.1614 0008	1.2512 7176	1.3478 4892	1.4516 1336	1.5630 8022
31.	1.0804 7773	1.1672 0708	1.2606 5630	1.3613 2740	1.4697 5853	1.5865 2642
32.	1.0831 7892	1.1730 4312	1.2701 1122	1.3749 4068	1.4881 3051	1.6103 2432
33.	1.0858 8687	1.1789 0833	1.2796 3706	1.3886 9009	1.5067 3214	1.6344 7918
34.	1.0886 0159	1.1848 0288	1.2892 3434	1.4025 7699	1.5255 6629	1.6589 9637
35.	1.0913 2309	1.1907 2689	1.2989 0359	1.4166 0276	1.5446 3587	1.6838 8132
36.	1.0940 5140	1.1966 8052	1.3086 4537	1.4307 6878	1.5639 4382	1.7091 3954
37.	1.0967 8653	1.2026 6393	1.3184 6021	1.4450 7647	1.5834 9312	1.7347 7663
38.	1.0995 2850	1.2086 7725	1.3283 4866	1.4595 2724	1.6032 8678	1.7607 9828
39.	1.1022 7732	1.2147 2063	1.3383 1128	1.4741 2251	1.6233 2787	1.7872 1025
40.	1.1050 3301	1.2207 9424	1.3483 4861	1.4888 6373	1.6436 1946	1.8140 1841

C. AMOUNT OF 1 (AT COMPOUND INTEREST) (*Continued*)

$$(1+i)^n$$

Periods	2%	2½%	3%	4%	5%	6%
1.....	1.02	1.025	1.03	1.04	1.05	1.06
2.....	1.0404	1.0506 25	1.0609	1.0816	1.1025	1.1236
3.....	1.0612 08	1.0768 9063	1.0927 27	1.1248 64	1.1576 25	1.1910 16
4.....	1.0824 3216	1.1038 1289	1.1255 0881	1.1698 5856	1.2155 0625	1.2624 7696
5.....	1.1040 8080	1.1314 0821	1.1592 7407	1.2166 5290	1.2762 8156	1.3382 2558
6.....	1.1261 6242	1.1596 9342	1.1940 5230	1.2653 1902	1.3400 9564	1.4185 1911
7.....	1.1486 8567	1.1886 8575	1.2298 7387	1.3159 3178	1.4071 0042	1.5036 3026
8.....	1.1716 5938	1.2184 0290	1.2667 7008	1.3685 6905	1.4774 5544	1.5938 4807
9.....	1.1950 9257	1.2488 6297	1.3047 7318	1.4233 1181	1.5513 2822	1.6894 7896
10.....	1.2189 9442	1.2800 8454	1.3439 1638	1.4802 4428	1.6288 9463	1.7908 4770
11.....	1.2433 7431	1.3120 8666	1.3842 3387	1.5394 5406	1.7103 3936	1.8982 9856
12.....	1.2682 4179	1.3448 8882	1.4257 6089	1.6010 3222	1.7958 5633	2.0121 9647
13.....	1.2936 0663	1.3785 1104	1.4685 3371	1.6650 7351	1.8856 4914	2.1329 2826
14.....	1.3194 7876	1.4129 7382	1.5125 8972	1.7316 7645	1.9799 3160	2.2609 0396
15.....	1.3458 6834	1.4482 9817	1.5579 6742	1.8009 4351	2.0789 2818	2.3965 5819
16.....	1.3727 8571	1.4845 0562	1.6047 0644	1.8729 8125	2.1828 7459	2.5403 5168
17.....	1.4002 4142	1.5216 1826	1.6528 4763	1.9479 0050	2.2920 1832	2.6927 7279
18.....	1.4282 4625	1.5596 5872	1.7024 3306	2.0258 1652	2.4066 1923	2.8543 3915
19.....	1.4568 1117	1.5986 5019	1.7535 0605	2.1068 4918	2.5269 5020	3.0255 9950
20.....	1.4859 4740	1.6386 1644	1.8061 1123	2.1911 2314	2.6532 9771	3.2071 3547
21.....	1.5156 6634	1.6795 8185	1.8602 9457	2.2787 6807	2.7859 6259	3.3995 6360
22.....	1.5459 7967	1.7215 7140	1.9161 0341	2.3699 1879	2.9252 6072	3.6035 3742
23.....	1.5768 9926	1.7646 1068	1.9735 8651	2.4647 1554	3.0715 2376	3.8197 4966
24.....	1.6084 3725	1.8087 2595	2.0327 9411	2.5633 0416	3.2250 9994	4.0489 3464
25.....	1.6406 0599	1.8539 4410	2.0937 7793	2.6658 3633	3.3863 5494	4.2918 7072
26.....	1.6734 1811	1.9002 9270	2.1565 9127	2.7724 6978	3.5556 7269	4.5493 8296
27.....	1.7068 8648	1.9478 0002	2.2212 8901	2.8833 6858	3.7334 5632	4.8223 4594
28.....	1.7410 2421	1.9964 9502	2.2879 2768	2.9987 0332	3.9201 2914	5.1116 8670
29.....	1.7758 4469	2.0464 0739	2.3565 6551	3.1186 5145	4.1161 3560	5.4183 8790
30.....	1.8113 6158	2.0975 6758	2.4272 6247	3.2433 9751	4.3219 4238	5.7434 9117
31.....	1.8475 8882	2.1500 0677	2.5000 8035	3.3731 3341	4.5380 3949	6.0881 0064
32.....	1.8845 4059	2.2037 5694	2.5750 8276	3.5080 5875	4.7649 4147	6.4533 8668
33.....	1.9222 3140	2.2588 5086	2.6523 3524	3.6483 8110	5.0031 8854	6.8405 8988
34.....	1.9606 7603	2.3153 2213	2.7319 0530	3.7943 1634	5.2533 4797	7.2510 2528
35.....	1.9998 8955	2.3732 0519	2.8138 6245	3.9460 8899	5.5160 1537	7.6860 8679
36.....	2.0398 8734	2.4325 3532	2.8982 7833	4.1039 3255	5.7918 1614	8.1472 5200
37.....	2.0806 8509	2.4933 4870	2.9852 2668	4.2680 8986	6.0814 0694	8.6360 8712
38.....	2.1222 9879	2.5556 8242	3.0747 8348	4.4388 1345	6.3854 7729	9.1542 5235
39.....	2.1647 4477	2.6195 7448	3.1670 2698	4.6163 6599	6.7047 5115	9.7035 0749
40.....	2.2080 3966	2.6850 6384	3.2620 3779	4.8010 2063	7.0399 8871	10.2857 1794

D. AMOUNT OF AN ANNUITY (IF RENT IS 1)

$$\frac{(1+i)^n - 1}{i}$$

Periods	$\frac{1}{4}\%$	$\frac{1}{2}\%$	$\frac{3}{4}\%$	1%	$1\frac{1}{4}\%$	$1\frac{1}{2}\%$
1.....	1.000 0000	1.000 0000	1.000 0000	1.000 0000	1.000 0000	1.000 0000
2.....	2.002 5000	2.005 0000	2.007 5000	2.010 0000	2.012 5000	2.015 0000
3.....	3.007 5063	3.015 0250	3.022 5563	3.030 1000	3.037 6562	3.045 2250
4.....	4.015 0250	4.030 1001	4.045 2254	4.060 4010	4.075 6270	4.090 9034
5.....	5.025 0626	5.050 2506	5.075 5646	5.101 0050	5.126 5723	5.152 2669
6.....	6.037 6252	6.075 5019	6.113 6314	6.152 0151	6.190 6544	6.229 5509
7.....	7.052 7193	7.105 8794	7.159 4836	7.213 5352	7.268 0376	7.322 9942
8.....	8.070 3511	8.141 4088	8.213 1797	8.285 6706	8.358 8881	8.432 8391
9.....	9.090 5270	9.182 1158	9.274 7786	9.368 5273	9.463 3742	9.559 3317
10.....	10.113 2533	10.228 0264	10.344 3394	10.462 2125	10.581 6664	10.702 7217
11.....	11.138 5364	11.279 1665	11.421 9219	11.566 8347	11.713 9372	11.863 2625
12.....	12.166 3828	12.335 5624	12.507 5864	12.682 5030	12.860 3614	13.041 2114
13.....	13.196 7987	13.397 2402	13.601 3933	13.809 3280	14.021 1159	14.236 8296
14.....	14.229 7907	14.464 2264	14.703 4037	14.947 4213	15.196 3799	15.450 3821
15.....	15.265 3652	15.536 5475	15.813 6792	16.096 8955	16.386 3346	16.682 1378
16.....	16.303 5286	16.614 2303	16.932 2818	17.257 8645	17.591 1638	17.932 3698
17.....	17.344 2874	17.697 3014	18.059 2739	18.430 4431	18.811 0534	19.201 3554
18.....	18.387 6482	18.785 7879	19.194 7185	19.614 7476	20.046 1915	20.489 3757
19.....	19.433 6173	19.879 7168	20.338 6789	20.810 8950	21.296 7689	21.796 7164
20.....	20.482 2013	20.979 1154	21.491 2190	22.019 0040	22.562 9785	23.123 6671
21.....	21.533 4068	22.084 0110	22.652 4031	23.239 1940	23.845 0158	24.470 5221
22.....	22.587 2403	23.194 4311	23.822 2961	24.471 5860	25.143 0785	25.837 5799
23.....	23.643 7084	24.310 4032	25.000 9634	25.716 3018	26.457 3670	27.225 1436
24.....	24.702 8177	25.431 9552	26.188 4706	26.973 4648	27.788 0840	28.633 5208
25.....	25.764 5748	26.559 1150	27.384 8841	28.243 1995	29.135 4351	30.063 0236
26.....	26.828 9862	27.691 9106	28.590 2708	29.525 6315	30.499 6280	31.513 9690
27.....	27.896 0587	28.830 3702	29.804 6978	30.820 8878	31.880 8734	32.986 6785
28.....	28.965 7988	29.974 5220	31.028 2330	32.129 0967	33.279 3843	34.481 4787
29.....	30.038 2133	31.124 3946	32.260 9448	33.450 3877	34.695 3766	35.998 7009
30.....	31.113 3088	32.280 0166	33.502 9018	34.784 8915	36.129 0688	37.538 6814
31.....	32.191 0921	33.441 4167	34.754 1736	36.132 7404	37.580 6822	39.101 7616
32.....	33.271 5698	34.608 6238	36.014 8299	37.494 0678	39.050 4407	40.688 2880
33.....	34.354 7488	35.781 6669	37.284 9411	38.869 0085	40.538 5712	42.298 6123
34.....	35.440 6356	36.960 5752	38.564 5782	40.257 6986	42.045 3033	43.933 0915
35.....	36.529 2372	38.145 3781	39.853 8125	41.660 2756	43.570 8696	45.592 0879
36.....	37.620 5603	39.336 1050	41.152 7161	43.076 8784	45.115 5055	47.275 9692
37.....	38.714 6117	40.532 7855	42.461 3615	44.507 6471	46.679 4493	48.985 1087
38.....	39.811 3982	41.735 4494	43.779 8217	45.952 7236	48.262 9424	50.719 8854
39.....	40.910 9267	42.944 1267	45.108 1704	47.412 2508	49.866 2292	52.480 6837
40.....	42.013 2041	44.158 8473	46.446 4816	48.886 3734	51.489 5571	54.267 8939

D. AMOUNT OF AN ANNUITY (IF RENT IS 1) (*Continued*)

$$\frac{(1+i)^n - 1}{i}$$

Periods	2%	2½%	3%	4%	5%	6%
1.....	1.000 0000	1.000 0000	1.000 0000	1.000 0000	1.000 0000	1.000 0000
2.....	2.020 0000	2.025 0000	2.030 0000	2.040 0000	2.050 0000	2.060 0000
3.....	3.060 4000	3.075 6250	3.090 9000	3.121 6000	3.152 5000	3.183 6000
4.....	4.121 6080	4.152 5156	4.183 6270	4.246 4640	4.310 1250	4.374 6160
5.....	5.204 0402	5.256 3285	5.309 1358	5.416 3226	5.525 6313	5.637 0930
6.....	6.308 1210	6.387 7367	6.468 4099	6.632 9755	6.801 9128	6.975 3185
7.....	7.434 2834	7.547 4302	7.662 4622	7.898 2945	8.142 0085	8.393 8377
8.....	8.582 9691	8.736 1159	8.892 3361	9.214 2263	9.549 1089	9.897 4679
9.....	9.754 6284	9.954 5188	10.159 1061	10.582 7953	11.026 5643	11.491 3160
10.....	10.949 7210	11.203 3818	11.463 8793	12.006 1071	12.577 8925	13.180 7949
11.....	12.168 7154	12.483 4663	12.807 7957	13.486 3514	14.206 7872	14.971 6426
12.....	13.412 0897	13.795 5530	14.192 0296	15.025 8055	15.917 1265	16.869 9412
13.....	14.680 3315	15.140 4418	15.617 7905	16.626 8377	17.712 9829	18.882 1377
14.....	15.973 9382	16.518 9528	17.086 3242	18.291 9112	19.598 6320	21.015 0659
15.....	17.293 4169	17.931 9267	18.598 9139	20.023 5876	21.578 5636	23.275 9699
16.....	18.639 2853	19.380 2248	20.156 8813	21.824 5311	23.657 4918	25.672 5281
17.....	20.012 0710	20.864 7305	21.761 5877	23.697 5124	25.840 3664	28.212 8798
18.....	21.412 3124	22.386 3487	23.414 4354	25.645 4129	28.132 3847	30.905 6526
19.....	22.840 5586	23.946 0074	25.116 8684	27.671 2294	30.539 0039	33.759 9917
20.....	24.297 3698	25.544 6576	26.870 3745	29.778 0786	33.065 9541	36.785 5912
21.....	25.783 3172	27.183 2741	28.676 4857	31.969 2017	35.719 2518	39.992 7267
22.....	27.298 9835	28.862 8559	30.536 7803	34.247 9698	38.505 2144	43.392 2903
23.....	28.844 9632	30.584 4273	32.452 8837	36.617 8886	41.430 4751	46.995 8277
24.....	30.421 8625	32.349 0380	34.426 4702	39.082 6041	44.501 9989	50.815 5774
25.....	32.030 2997	34.157 7639	36.459 2643	41.645 9083	47.727 0988	54.864 5120
26.....	33.670 9057	36.011 7080	38.553 0423	44.311 7446	51.113 4538	59.156 3827
27.....	35.344 3238	37.912 0007	40.709 6335	47.084 2144	54.669 1265	63.705 7657
28.....	37.051 2103	39.859 8008	42.930 9225	49.967 5830	58.402 5828	68.528 1116
29.....	38.792 2345	41.856 2958	45.218 8502	52.966 2863	62.322 7119	73.639 7983
30.....	40.568 0792	43.902 7032	47.575 4157	56.084 9378	66.438 8475	79.058 1862
31.....	42.379 4408	46.000 2707	50.002 6782	59.328 3353	70.760 7899	84.801 6774
32.....	44.227 0296	48.150 2775	52.502 7585	62.701 4687	75.298 8294	90.889 7780
33.....	46.111 5702	50.354 0345	55.077 8413	66.209 5274	80.063 7708	97.343 1647
34.....	48.033 8016	52.612 8853	57.730 1765	69.857 9085	85.066 9594	104.183 7546
35.....	49.994 4776	54.928 2074	60.462 0818	73.652 2249	90.320 3074	111.434 7799
36.....	51.994 3672	57.301 4126	63.275 9443	77.598 3139	95.836 3227	119.120 8667
37.....	54.034 2545	59.733 9479	66.174 2226	81.702 2464	101.628 1389	127.268 1187
38.....	56.114 9396	62.227 2966	69.159 4493	85.970 3363	107.709 5458	135.904 2058
39.....	58.237 2384	64.782 9791	72.234 2328	90.409 1497	114.095 0231	145.058 4581
40.....	60.401 9832	67.402 5535	75.401 2597	95.025 5157	120.799 7742	154.761 9656

Index

B

This book has been set in 10 and 9 point Janson, leaded 2 points. Chapter numbers are in 30 point Helvetica Medium and chapter titles are in 18 point Helvetica. The size of the type page is 27 by 45½ picas.